Ninth Edition

Today's Mathematics

PART 2: ACTIVITIES AND INSTRUCTIONAL IDEAS

James W. Heddens
Professor Emeritus, Kent State University

William R. Speer
Bowling Green State University

Merrill
an imprint of Prentice Hall
Upper Saddle River, New Jersey   Columbus, Ohio

Library of Congress Cataloging-in-Publication Data
Heddens, James W.
Today's mathematics / James W. Heddens, William R. Speer. — 9th ed.
p. cm.
Includes bibliographical references (p. -) and index.
Contents: pt. 1. Concepts and classroom methods—pt. 2. Activities and instructional ideas.
ISBN 0-13-493362-1 (set-IBM).—ISBN 0-13-659657-6 (set-MAC).—ISBN 0-13-589003-9 (pt. 1).—ISBN 0-13-589011-X (pt. 2)
1. Mathematics—Study and teaching (Elementary) I. Speer, William R. II. Title.
QA135.5.H42 1997
372.7—dc20 96-28398
CIP

Cover art: Melissa Taylor
Production Coordination: Elm Street Publishing Services, Inc.
Editor: Bradley J. Potthoff
Developmental Editor: Carol S. Sykes
Production Editor: Sheryl Glicker Langner
Production Manager: Deidra M. Schwartz
Cover Designer: Proof Positive/Farrowlyne & Assoc.
Director of Marketing: Kevin Flanagan
Advertising/Marketing Coordination: Julie Shough

This book was set in Helvetica Neue by Elm Street Publishing Services, Inc. and was printed and bound by Courier–Kendallville, Inc. The cover was printed by Phoenix Color Corp.

Printed in the United States of America
10 9 8 7 6 5 4 3 2 1

ISBN 0-13-493362-1

Prentice-Hall International (UK) Limited, *London*
Prentice-Hall of Australia Pty. Limited, *Sydney*
Prentice-Hall of Canada, Inc., *Toronto*
Prentice-Hall Hispanoamericana, S. A., *Mexico*
Prentice-Hall of India Private Limited, *New Delhi*
Prentice-Hall of Japan, Inc., *Tokyo*
Simon & Schuster Asia Pte. Ltd., *Singapore*
Editora Prentice-Hall do Brasil, Ltda., *Rio de Janeiro*

An Important Message for Students

Helping You Make the Most of the Resources in *Today's Mathematics*

The Activities and Instructional Ideas section of the ninth edition of *Today's Mathematics* is designed to aid you in your quest to understand more mathematics and to develop successful means of teaching mathematics. By presenting the material from the first section of the book in an activity format, you are able to examine the translation of theory into practice. Ideas that, for whatever reason, were not as clear as you might have hoped upon reading Part 1: Concepts and Classroom Methods are often unveiled when seen in the activity format. Also, the material in Part 2 can serve as a springboard for you to explore alternative ways of presenting, discussing, and assessing the material as you work with children.

Part 2 of the *Today's Mathematics* "package" provides a wealth of support material that teachers need to successfully deliver the vision of contemporary mathematics teaching and learning. Teachers quickly discover that even the best grade-level mathematics textbooks do not (in fact, *cannot*) present the mathematics to be learned in the myriad of ways required by the various learners in a classroom. Supplementary material is necessary, not only for individual teaching styles, but also to deal effectively with individual learning styles and individual levels of process and skill development.

Part 2 begins with three chapters that parallel the first three chapters of Learning Mathematics, Teaching Mathematics, and Assessing Mathematics of Part 1. In these chapters you will find invaluable reference material to help you implement the NCTM standards.

- The first chapter, Learning Mathematics, includes a summary of the content changes recommended in the *Curriculum and Evaluation Standards for School Mathematics.* All of the Curriculum Standards for grades K–4 and 5–8 are found here, along with a **current bibliography** for each standard. This bibliography should prove to be an excellent resource of supplementary ideas as you plan lessons for your students now and in the future. If you need to design a unit or set of lessons on a particular topic, these bibliographies will provide you with excellent starting points. Finally, to ensure that you comprehend the nature of the standards, an example of a complete curriculum standard has been reprinted in full. The chapter closes with a comprehensive bibliography with a focus on learning mathematics.
- The second chapter, Teaching Mathematics, includes a list of the Teaching Standards from the *Professional Standards for Teaching Mathematics,* with a **comprehensive bibliography** included to help you find supporting and clarifying articles and resources. An example of a complete teaching standard has been reprinted and is supported by a classroom vignette illustrating that standard "at work."
- The third chapter, Assessing Mathematics, draws from NCTM's *Assessment Standards for School Mathematics* and **fully lists the six assessment standards** that can be used to judge the quality of an assessment system and presents a **supporting bibliography.** A **complete example of an assessment standard** is included and supported with a **classroom vignette** describing how assessment might occur in practice.

For each of the content-oriented chapters (Chapters 4–16) in Part 1, Part 2 provides a similarly numbered chapter offering classroom-tested ideas for individual, small-group, and large-group use.

Each of these chapters begins with a **content overview** and a **sample lesson plan** illustrating the application of the content of the chapter for either the primary or intermediate grades. These can form a foundation from which to build your planning skills.

You will also find extensive **instructional and assessment ideas,** categorized along the grade-range lines of NCTM's *Curriculum and Evaluation Standards for School Mathematics,* that may be used either during actual instruction or as follow-up activities. These activities are easily transformed into seatwork, homework, motivations for new or extended lessons, learning center resources, or project-based activities. Many of these activities can be modified for either individual or cooperative group format and incorporate manipulatives, calculators, and computers where appropriate. The manipulatives used throughout this text are either commercial materials that are commonly found in elementary mathematics curricula or are of a "homemade" nature using materials readily available in the school or brought in from home.

Chapter 17 may prove to be a most valuable chapter for a beginning teacher. This chapter does not correspond to an equivalent chapter in Part 1. As the title indicates, this is an opportunity to "look back as you move forward" in pursuing your goal to become a teacher.

- Chapter 17 begins with an **overview of eight content strands commonly found in elementary mathematics curricula.** This is followed by a comprehensive discussion and a listing of **critical objectives** designed to make you feel more comfortable about how these strands unfold and interplay in grades K–8. As is so often the case in this text, the reading is supplemented by an **extensive bibliography** for those wishing to explore further.
- Another feature of Chapter 17 is the inclusion of a **checklist of mathematical concepts organized by concept clusters.** This checklist allows you the opportunity to identify a particular concept and explore that concept through its step-by-step development from its earliest foundations. Even though several concepts are intertwined in instruction, each often needs to be examined in isolation by the teacher to identify important prerequisite knowledge, skills, and experiences. The format of this checklist allows for this sort of in-depth analysis.
- Several **thematic mathematics activities** are included in Chapter 17. These are excellent resources for those teachers wishing to integrate mathematics with other disciplines. Even a cursory examination of the ideas presented in this section should give you the confidence to explore mathematics from a thematic base. What mathematics can we find at the zoo? At the grocery store? In health? In transportation? In geography? This is the place not only to find out but also to extend these ideas to other themes.
- Finally, Chapter 17 closes with a **vignette from the NCTM that is designed to show how the standards of curriculum, teaching, and assessment come together** in practice. Reading and reflecting on this vignette can help you envision the environment your own classroom should, and hopefully will, embody.

The appendices for Part 2 provide even more information to not only help you successfully complete this course, but also to aid you as you begin extended experiences in teaching children.

- **Appendices A and B** provide an overview of technology in the elementary grades by examining the role and applications of **calculator and computer use in K–8 mathematics.** Appendix B incorporates an overview of software types, applications, hypermedia, and telecommunications—including e-mail, the Internet, and the World Wide Web. It should be noted that additional activities can be found throughout the text, but these appendices provide the framework for incorporating technology in instruction.
- **Appendix C** provides a rich resource for teachers looking for **computer software that supports various mathematics concepts.** In this appendix, several software publishers are identified by name, address, and toll-free telephone numbers. This is followed by a listing of popular software and a coding of concepts that the software helps attain.
- **Appendix D** provides the name, address, and toll-free telephone numbers of the **suppliers of mathematics resource materials.** It would be to your advantage to add your name to the mailing lists of these companies to keep abreast of new developments, to become familiar with existing teaching and review materials, and to get ideas of materials that you can adapt and "manufacture" for your classroom use.

A SPECIAL APPLICATIONS PROGRAM FOR TEACHERS—*EXAM IN A CAN*

As teachers, you have the incredible task of managing your students' progress. But it doesn't end there. You must determine why students haven't mastered specific outcomes, the nature of their errors, reteach specific concepts, organize students into similar learning groups, and create custom worksheets for each student. The *Exam in a Can* math (and science) assessment software packages represent the kinds of assistance teachers need and deserve by focusing on important objectives through easy-to-use classroom assessment and record-keeping systems. **A fully operational version of this outstanding applications software tool has been bundled with this edition of *Today's Mathematics.***

Exam in a Can uses algorithms to generate fresh, objective-specific test, quiz, or worksheet items with virtually unlimited variations. The program saves teachers time by enabling them to quickly and easily print unlimited versions of individualized questions. *Exam in a Can* gives you unparalleled capabilities: textbook-quality illustrations, three dimensional graphs, and appropriate symbolic notation. Charts and graphs keyed to algorithms can vary to match the values used in individual test questions.

Exam in a Can—Today's Mathematics Version: It's as easy as . . .

1. CREATE a test or worksheet from the pre-written database of objectives. Selecting an objective more than once will generate different questions for that objective.
2. CHOOSE the exact iteration of the problems in either multiple choice or free response and preview them on the screen.
3. PRINT your test or worksheet and answer key complete with graphics, charts, diagrams, and perfect mathematics notation.

Exam in a Can provides a powerful authoring feature for users to add or edit questions. The *Exam in a Can* Editor gives content control to the teacher—*the teacher decides on the content*—the outcomes, the format (enhanced multiple choice, free response, and conceptual), and the level of difficulty. *Exam in a Can* can be designed to accompany specific textbooks or to meet school, district, or state testing requirements. The program's algorithm-based system also easily accommodates requirements for balanced representation of minorities and gender within test items. The *Exam in a Can* library contains thousands of model problems that can be adapted to your specific needs. *Exam in a Can* even facilitates the full scope of portfolio assessment.

Exam in a Can items are crafted to reflect the NCTM Standards and to work with the most popular textbooks and state mandated standards. The *Today's Mathematics* version of *Exam in a Can* presents problems and exercises dealing with number theory, decimals, fractions, integers, ratio, percent, proportion, measurement, perimeter, area, volume, geometry, patterns and functions, equations and inequalities, graphing, and probability and statistics.

Technology that helps teachers is part of the solution to doing better in the classroom. *Exam in a Can* is technology that makes dramatic sense. In short, *Exam in a Can* uses technology to do a critical part of a teacher's job in a better way . . . it saves teachers time and helps drive up test scores. Testing made easy, fast, and effective . . . so you can do a better job of what you do best: teach!

The completion of this text and this course is not a finish line, it is a starting line. The process of becoming a teacher is lifelong, and, consequently, professional development is a part of the job that cannot be ignored. As you set out on this journey, it is to your advantage to familiarize yourself with any and all resources that may help you become a master teacher. We sincerely believe that *Today's Mathematics* can be such a resource for you. We hope you feel the same.

James W. Heddens *William R. Speer*

Contents

Chapter 1

Learning Mathematics

Overview

It would be a mistake to assume that a person learns and develops mathematical concepts solely from contact with a classroom situation. Our mathematical successes and failures are influenced by many catalysts, each interacting in a complex manner which we may never fully understand. We do know, however, that the learning of mathematics begins long before any attempts of formal schooling and continues, except when blockaded by uncreative teaching and/or a lack of enlightening experiences, as a part of our life-long growth.

Chapter 1 in Part 1 of this text provides you with information to aid you in identifying the nature of mathematics and exploring a variety of theories that help to explain the manner in which children learn mathematical concepts. Topics center on the psychology of learning mathematics, learning theories in mathematics, and brief discussions of the works of selected contributors to these areas. Chapter 1 also introduces the first in a triumvirate of landmark publications from the National Council of Teachers of Mathematics, this one entitled *Curriculum and Evaluation Standards for School Mathematics* (1989). This publication presents a vision of what it means to be mathematically literate in today's world and sets forth standards to guide the revision of school mathematics to achieve this vision.

In the following pages you will find a wealth of resource information to support the theories discussed in Part 1 of this text. To assist you in digesting the nature of the changes proposed by the NCTM curriculum standards, a summary of content areas to receive increased or decreased attention leads off the chapter. This is followed by a list of each of the K-4 and 5-8 curriculum standards and accompanying bibliographies that can be used to find further information and classroom activities to implement the standards. Finally, the full text of a particular standard (Standard 10: Statistics at the 5-8 level) has been included in this chapter to provide the reader with the focus, discussion, elaboration, and exemplars found in the complete document.

SUMMARY OF CHANGES IN CONTENT AND EMPHASIS: K-4 MATHEMATICS*

Increased Attention	Decreased Attention
Number	**Number**
■ Number sense ■ Place-value concepts ■ Meaning of fractions and decimals ■ Estimation of quantities	■ Early attention to reading, writing, and ordering number symbolically
Operations and Computation	**Operations and Computation**
■ Meaning of operations ■ Operation sense ■ Mental computation ■ Estimation and the reasonableness of answers ■ Selection of an appropriate computational method ■ Use of calculators for complex computation ■ Thinking strategies for basic facts	■ Complex paper-and-pencil computations ■ Isolated treatment of paper-and-pencil computations ■ Addition and subtraction without renaming ■ Isolated treatment of division facts ■ Long division ■ Long division without remainders ■ Paper-and-pencil fraction computation ■ Use of rounding to estimate
Geometry and Measurement	**Geometry and Measurement**
■ Properties of geometric figures ■ Geometric relationships ■ Spatial sense ■ Process of measuring ■ Concepts related to units of measurement ■ Actual measuring ■ Estimation of measurements ■ Use of measurement and geometry ideas throughout the curriculum	■ Primary focus on naming geometric figures ■ Memorization of equivalencies between units of measurement
Probability and Statistics	
■ Collection and organization of data ■ Exploration of chance	
Patterns and Relationships	
■ Pattern recognition and description ■ Use of variables to express relationships	
Problem Solving	**Problem Solving**
■ Word problems with a variety of structures ■ Use of everyday problems ■ Applications ■ Study of patterns and relationships ■ Problem-solving strategies	■ Use of clue words to determine which operation to use
Instructional Practices	**Instructional Practices**
■ Use of manipulative materials ■ Cooperative work ■ Discussion of mathematics ■ Questioning ■ Justification of thinking ■ Writing about mathematics ■ Problem-solving approach to instruction ■ Content integration ■ Use of calculators and computers	■ Rote practice ■ Rote memorization of rules ■ One answer and one method ■ Use of worksheets ■ Written practice ■ Teaching by telling

SUMMARY OF CHANGES IN CONTENT AND EMPHASIS: 5-8 MATHEMATICS*

Increased Attention	Decreased Attention
Problem Solving	**Problem Solving**
■ Pursuing open-ended problems and extended problem-solving projects ■ Investigating and formulating questions from problem situations ■ Representing situations verbally, numerically, graphically, geometrically, or symbolically	■ Practicing routine, one-step problems ■ Practicing problems categorized by types (e.g., coin problems, age problems)
Communication	**Communication**
■ Discussing, writing, reading, and listening to mathematical ideas	■ Doing fill-in-the-blank worksheets ■ Answering questions that require only yes, no, or a number as responses
Reasoning	**Reasoning**
■ Reasoning in spatial contexts ■ Reasoning with proportions ■ Reasoning from graphs ■ Reasoning inductively and deductively	■ Relying on outside authority (teacher or an answer key)
Connections	**Connections**
■ Connecting mathematics to other subjects and to the world outside the classroom ■ Connecting topics within mathematics ■ Applying mathematics	■ Learning isolated topics ■ Developing skills out of context
Number/Operations/Computation	**Number/Operations/Computation**
■ Developing number sense ■ Developing operation sense ■ Creating algorithms and procedures ■ Using estimation both in solving problems and in checking the reasonableness of results ■ Exploring relations among representations of, and operations on, whole numbers, fractions, decimals, integers, and rational numbers ■ Developing an understanding of ratio, proportion, and percent	■ Memorizing rules and algorithms ■ Practicing tedious paper-and-pencil computations ■ Finding exact forms of answers ■ Memorizing procedures, such as cross-multiplication, without understanding ■ Practicing rounding numbers out of context
Patterns and Functions	**Patterns and Functions**
■ Identifying and using functional relationships ■ Developing and using tables, graphs, and rules to describe situations ■ Interpreting among different mathematical representations	■ Topics seldom in the current curriculum
Algebra	**Algebra**
■ Developing an understanding of variables, expressions, and equations ■ Using a variety of methods to solve linear equations and informally investigate inequalities and nonlinear equations	■ Manipulating symbols ■ Memorizing procedures and drilling on equation solving

continued

Increased Attention	Decreased Attention
Statistics	**Statistics**
■ Using statistical methods to describe, analyze, evaluate, and make decisions	■ Memorizing formulas
Probability	**Probability**
■ Creating experimental and theoretical models of situations involving probabilities	■ Memorizing formulas
Geometry	**Geometry**
■ Developing an understanding of geometric objects and relationships ■ Using geometry in solving problems	■ Memorizing geometric vocabulary ■ Memorizing facts and relationships
Measurement	**Measurement**
■ Estimating and using measurement to solve problems	■ Memorizing and manipulating formulas ■ Converting within and between measurement systems
Instructional Practices	**Instructional Practices**
■ Activity involving students individually and in groups in exploring, conjecturing, analyzing, and applying mathematics in both a mathematical and a real-world context ■ Using appropriate technology for computation and exploration ■ Using concrete materials ■ Being a facilitator of learning ■ Assessing learning as an integral part of instruction	■ Teaching computations out of context ■ Drilling on paper-and-pencil algorithms ■ Teaching topics in isolation ■ Stressing memorization ■ Being the dispenser of knowledge ■ Testing for the sole purpose of assigning grades

NCTM K-4 CURRICULUM STANDARDS AND RELATED READINGS*

Standard 1:

Mathematics as Problem Solving

In grades K-4, the study of mathematics should emphasize problem solving so that students can:

- use problem-solving approaches to investigate and understand mathematical content;
- formulate problems from everyday and mathematical situations;
- develop and apply strategies to solve a wide variety of problems;
- verify and interpret results with respect to the original problem;
- acquire confidence in using mathematics meaningfully.

Bledsoe, G. (1989). Hook your students on problem solving. *The Arithmetic Teacher, 37*(4).

Brady, R. R. (1991). A close look at student problem solving and the teaching of mathematics. *School Science and Mathematics, 91*(8).

*Reprinted with permission from the *Curriculum and Evaluation Standards for School Mathematics,* copyright 1989 by the National Council of Teachers of Mathematics.

Cemen, P. B. (1989). Developing a problem-solving lesson. *The Arithmetic Teacher, 37*(2).

Cobb, P., Yackel, E., Wood, T., Wheatley, G., and Merkel, G. (1988) Creating a problem-solving atmosphere. *The Arithmetic Teacher, 36*(1).

English, L. (1992). Problem solving with combinations. *The Arithmetic Teacher, 40*(2).

Fairbairn, D. M. (1993). Creating story problems. *The Arithmetic Teacher, 41*(3).

Farivar, S., and Webb, N. M. (1994). Helping and getting help—essential skills for effective group problem solving. *The Arithmetic Teacher, 41*(9).

Ford, M. I. (1990). The writing process: A strategy for problem solvers. *The Arithmetic Teacher, 38*(3).

Kersch, M. E., and McDonald, J. (1991). How do I solve thee? Let me count the ways! *The Arithmetic Teacher, 39*(2).

Kloosterman, P. (1992). Non-routine word problems: One part of a problem-solving program in the elementary school. *School Science and Mathematics, 92*(1).

Lampert, M. (1989). Arithmetic as problem solving. *The Arithmetic Teacher, 36*(7).

May, L. J. (1989). Making a drawing, making a list. *Teaching K-8, 19*(4).

Rosenbaum, L., Behounek, K. J., Brown, L., and Burcalow, J. V. (1989). Step into problem solving with cooperative learning. *The Arithmetic Teacher, 36*(7).

Rowan, T. E., (Ed.). (1990). The vision of problem solving in the standards. *The Arithmetic Teacher, 37*(9).

Schmalz, R. (1989). Classroom activities for problem solving. *The Arithmetic Teacher, 29*(1).

Szetela, W. (1987). The problem of evaluation in problem solving: Can we find solutions? *The Arithmetic Teacher, 35*(3).

Talton, C. F. (1988). Let's solve the problem before we find the answer. *The Arithmetic Teacher, 36*(1).

Standard 2:

Mathematics as Communication

In grades K-4, the study of mathematics should include numerous opportunities for communication so that students can:

- relate physical materials, pictures and diagrams to mathematical ideas;
- reflect on and clarify their thinking about mathematical ideas and situations;
- relate their everyday language to mathematical language and symbols;
- realize that representing, discussing, reading, writing, and listening to mathematics are a vital part of learning and using mathematics.

Bohning, G., and Radencich, M. C. (1989). Math action books for young readers. *The Arithmetic Teacher.*

Brown, N. (1993). Teacher to teacher: Writing mathematics. *The Arithmetic Teacher, 41*(1).

Carraher, T. N., Carraher, D. W., and Schliemann, A. (1987). Written and oral mathematics. *Journal for Research in Mathematics Education, 18.*

Ford, M. I. (1990). The writing process: A strategy for problem solvers. *The Arithmetic Teacher, 38*(3).

Gullatt, D. (1986). Help your students read mathematics. *The Arithmetic Teacher, 33*(9).

Hiebert, J. (1989). The struggle to link written symbols with understanding: An update. *The Arithmetic Teacher, 36*(7).

MacMath, R. (1987). Helping students tunnel their way to math and writing skills. *Learning.*

Matz, K., and Leier, C. (1992). Word problems and the language connection. *The Arithmetic Teacher, 39*(8).

Mumme, J., and Shepherd, N. (1990). Implementing the standards: Communication in mathematics. *The Arithmetic Teacher, 38*(1).

Richards, L. (1990). Measuring things in words: Language for learning mathematics. *Language Arts, 67.*

Sgroi, R. J. (1990). Communicating about spatial relationships. *The Arithmetic Teacher, 37*(6).

Shoecraft, P. (1989). 'Equals' means 'Is the same as.' *The Arithmetic Teacher, 36*(8).

Silverman, F., Winograd, K., and Strohauer, D. (1992). Student-generated story problems. *The Arithmetic Teacher, 39*(8).

Small, M. S. (1990). Do you speak math? *The Arithmetic Teacher, 37*(5).

Strand, S. (1990). Acting out numbers. *The Arithmetic Teacher, 37*(5).

Wilde, S. (1991). Learning to write about mathematics. *The Arithmetic Teacher, 38*(6).

Yancey, A. V., and Thompson, C. S. (1989). Children must learn to use diagrams. *The Arithmetic Teacher, 36*(7).

Standard 3:

Mathematics as Reasoning

In grades K-4, the study of mathematics should emphasize reasoning so that students can:

- draw logical conclusions about mathematics;
- use models, known facts, properties, and relationships to explain their thinking;
- justify their answers and solution processes;
- use patterns and relationships to analyze mathematical situations;
- believe that mathematics makes sense.

Davis, R. B. (1991). Research into practice: Giving pupils tools for thinking. *The Arithmetic Teacher, 38*(5).

Garofalo, J., and Mtetwa, D. K. (1990). Implementing the standards: Mathematics as reasoning. *The Arithmetic Teacher, 37*(5)

Hands-on, Inc. (1990). *Algebra: Kindergarten through grade nine.* Solvang, CA: Author.

Hands-on, Inc. (1989) *Logic: Kindergarten through grade nine.* Solvang, CA: Author.

Heddens, J. (1986). Bridging the gap between the concrete and the abstract. *The Arithmetic Teacher, 33*(6).

Holbrook, H., and Van de Walle, J. (1987). Patterns, thinking and problem-solving. *The Arithmetic Teacher, 34*(8).

Johnson, J. E. (1987). Do you think you might be wrong? Confirmation bias in problem solving. *The Arithmetic Teacher, 34*(9).

Kamii, C. (1987). Arithmetic: Children's thinking or their writing of correct answers? *The Arithmetic Teacher, 35*(3).

Krulik, S., and Rudnik, J. A. (1994). Reflect . . . for better problem solving and reasoning. *The Arithmetic Teacher, 41*(6).

Sanfiorenzo, N. R. (1991). Evaluating expressions: A problem-solving approach. *The Arithmetic Teacher, 38*(3).

Silver, E. A., and Smith, M. S. (1990). Research into practice: Teaching mathematics and thinking. *The Arithmetic Teacher, 37*(8).

Silverman, H. (Ed.). (1990). Ideas. Keeping in balance, maintaining the balance, shifting the balance, finding the balance. *The Arithmetic Teacher, 37*(7).

Stanic, G. (1990). Teaching mathematics and thinking. *The Arithmetic Teacher, 37*(8).

Thompson, P. W. (1994). Research into practice: Concrete materials and teaching for mathematical understanding. *The Arithmetic Teacher, 41*(9).

Trahanovsky-Orletsky, A. E. (1991). What's the problem? *Learning, 91.*

Wadlington, E., Bitner, J., Partridge, E., and Austin, S. (1992). Have a problem? Make the writing—mathematics connection. *The Arithmetic Teacher, 40*(4).

Standard 4:

Mathematical Connections

In grades K-4, the study of mathematics should include opportunities to make connections so that students can:

- link conceptual and procedural knowledge;
- relate various representations of concepts or procedures to one another;
- recognize relationships among different topics in mathematics;
- use mathematics in other curriculum areas;
- use mathematics in their daily lives.

Bell, K. (1988). Learn counting from storybooks. *The Reading Teacher, 41.*

Beougher, C. (1994). Making connections with teddy bears. *The Arithmetic Teacher, 41*(7)

Bohan, H., and Bohan, S. (1993). Extending the regular curriculum through creative problem solving. *The Arithmetic Teacher, 41*(2).

Brahier, D. J., Brahier, A. F., and Speer, W. R. IDEAS—elections. *The Arithmetic Teacher, 40*(3).

Cangelosi, J. S. (1988). Language activities that promote awareness of mathematics. *The Arithmetic Teacher, 36*(4).

Conaway, B., and Midkiff, R. B. (1994). Connecting literature, language, and fractions. *The Arithmetic Teacher, 41*(8).

Egsgard, J., Flewelling, G., Newell, C., and Warburton, W. (1988). *Making connections with mathematics.* Providence, RI: Janson Publications, Inc.

Fennell, F. (1982). The newspaper: A source for applications in mathematics. *The Arithmetic Teacher, 30*(2).

Flexer, R. J., and Topping, C. L. (1988). Mathematics on the home front. *The Arithmetic Teacher, 36*(2).

Fulkerson, P. (1992). Getting the most from a problem. *The Arithmetic Teacher, 40*(3).

Maddon, P. J. (1994). Teacher to teacher: Making story problems relevant. *The Arithmetic Teacher, 41*(9).

National Council of Teachers of Mathematics. (1992). *Curriculum and evaluation standards for school mathematics addenda series grades K-4: Making sense of data.* Reston, VA: Author.

Richards, L. (1990). Measuring things in words: Language for learning mathematics. *Language Arts, 67.*

Sherman, L. G. (1990). Making the math/science connection. *Instructor, 98*(7).

Stevenson, K. L. (1990). Teaching money with grids. *The Arithmetic Teacher, 37*(8).

Thiessen, D., and Matthias, M. (1992). *The wonderful world of mathematics: A critically annotated list of children's books in mathematics.* Reston, VA: National Council of Teachers of Mathematics.

Thompson, P. W. (1994). Research into practice: Concrete materials and teaching for mathematical understanding. *The Arithmetic Teacher, 41*(9).

Welchman-Tischler, (1992). *How to use children's literature to teach mathematics.* Reston, VA: National Council of Teachers of Mathematics.

Standard 5:

Estimation

In grades K-4, the curriculum should include estimation so students can:

- explore estimation strategies;
- recognize when an estimate is appropriate;
- determine the reasonableness of results;
- apply estimation in working with quantities, measurement, computation, and problem solving.

Harte, S. W., and Glover, M. (1993). Estimation is mathematical thinking. *The Arithmetic Teacher, 41*(2).

May, L. J. (1994). Benchmarks, estimation skills and the real world. *Teaching PreK-8, 24*(8).

May, L. J. (1989). Estimation: Another view. *Teaching PreK-8, 20*(1).

National Council of Teachers of Mathematics. (1993). *Curriculum and evaluation standards for school mathematics addenda series grades K-4: Number sense and operations.* Reston, VA: National Council of Teachers of Mathematics.

Parker, J., and Widmer, C. (1991). Teaching mathematics with technology: How big is a million? *The Arithmetic Teacher, 39*(1).

Reys, B. J., and Reys, R. E. (1990). Implementing the standards: Estimation-direction from the standards. *The Arithmetic Teacher, 37*(7).

Rubenstein, R. (1987). Estimation and mental computation. *The Arithmetic Teacher, 35*(1).

Singer, R. (1988). Estimation and counting in the block corner. *The Arithmetic Teacher, 35*(5).

Sowder, J. (1990). Mental computation and number sense. *The Arithmetic Teacher, 37*(7).

Trafton, P. R., and Zawojewski, J. (1987). Estimation and mental computation. *The Arithmetic Teacher, 34*(9).

Standard 6:

Number Sense and Numeration

In grades K-4, the mathematics curriculum should include whole number concepts and skills so that students can:

- construct number meanings through real-world experiences and the use of physical materials;
- understand our numeration system by relating counting, grouping, and place-value concepts;
- develop number sense;
- interpret the multiple uses of numbers encountered in the real world.

Bauch, J. P., and Hsu, H. J. (1988). Montessori: Right or wrong about number concepts? *The Arithmetic Teacher, 35*(6).

Crites, T., and Dougherty, B. (1989). Applying number sense to problem solving. *The Arithmetic Teacher, 36*(6).

Frank, A. R. (1989). Counting skills—A foundation for early mathematics. *The Arithmetic Teacher, 37*(1).

Gluck, D. H. (1991). Helping students understand place value. *The Arithmetic Teacher, 38*(7).

Greenes, C., Schulman, L., and Spungin, R. (1993). Developing sense about numbers. *The Arithmetic Teacher, 40*(5).

Hope, J. (1989). Promoting number sense in school. *The Arithmetic Teacher, 36*(6).

Meconi, L. J. (1992). Numbers, counting, and infinity in middle school mathematics. *School Science and Mathematics, 92*(7).

National Council of Teachers of Mathematics. (1993). *Curriculum and evaluation standards for school mathematics addenda series grades K–4: Number sense and operations*. Reston, VA: National Council of Teachers of Mathematics.

Ramondetta, J. (1994). Graph it! and make numbers make sense. *Learning, 22*(8).

Rathmell, E. E., and Leutzinger, L. P. (1991). Implementing the standards: Number representations and relationships. *The Arithmetic Teacher, 38*(7).

Sherman, H. J. (1992). Reinforcing place value. *The Arithmetic Teacher, 40*(3).

Slovin, H. (1992). Number of the day. *The Arithmetic Teacher, 39*(7).

Sowder, J. (1990). Mental computation and number sense. *The Arithmetic Teacher, 37*(7).

Sowder, J., and Schappelle, B. (1994). "Research into practice: Number sense-making. *The Arithmetic Teacher, 41*(7).

Thompson, C. S. (1989). Implementing the standards. Number sense and numeration in grades K-8. *The Arithmetic Teacher, 37*(1).

Thornton, C. A., and Tucker, S. C. (1989). Lesson planning: The key to developing number sense. *The Arithmetic Teacher, 36*(6).

Turkel, S., and Newman, C. M. (1988). What's your number? Developing number sense. *The Arithmetic Teacher, 35*(6).

Van de Walle, J. A. (1988). The early development of number relations. *The Arithmetic Teacher, 35*(6).

Whiten, D. J. (1989). Number sense and the importance of asking why. *The Arithmetic Teacher, 36*(6).

Standard 7:

Concepts of Whole Number Operations

In grades K-4, the mathematics curriculum should include concepts of addition, subtraction, multiplication, and division of whole numbers so that students can:

- develop meaning for the operations by modeling and discussing a rich variety of problem situations;
- relate the mathematical language and symbolism of operations to problem situations and informal language;
- recognize that a wide variety of problem structures can be represented by a single operation;
- develop operation sense.

Feinberg, M. M. (1990). Using patterns to practice basic facts. *The Arithmetic Teacher, 37*(8).

Fitzgerald, W. M., and Boyd, J. U. (1994). Teacher to teacher: A number line with character. *The Arithmetic Teacher, 41*(7).

Fuson, K. C. (1988). Subtracting by counting with one-handed finger patterns. *The Arithmetic Teacher, 35*(5).

Goldman, P. H. (1990). Teaching arithmetic averaging: An activity approach. *The Arithmetic Teacher, 37*(7).

Huinker, D. M. (1989). Multiplication and division word problems: Improving students' understanding. *The Arithmetic Teacher, 37*(2).

Kamii, C., Lewis, B. A., and Livingston, S. J. (1993). Primary arithmetic: Children inventing their own arithmetic. *The Arithmetic Teacher, 41*(4).

Mahlias, J. (1988). Do I add or subtract? *The Arithmetic Teacher, 36*(3).

Maier, E. A. (1987). Basic mathematical skills or school survival skills? *The Arithmetic Teacher, 35*(1).

McKillip, W. D., and Stanic, G. M. (1989). Developmental algorithms have a place in elementary school mathematics instruction. *The Arithmetic Teacher, 36*(5).

National Council of Teachers of Mathematics. (1993). *Curriculum and evaluation standards for school mathematics addenda series grades K-4: Number sense and operations.* Reston, VA: National Council of Teachers of Mathematics.

Ralston, A. (1987). Let them use calculators. *Technology Review, 90.*

Starkey, M. A. (1989). Calculating first graders. *The Arithmetic Teacher, 37*(2).

Thornton, C. A. (1989). Look ahead activities spark success in addition and subtraction. *The Arithmetic Teacher, 36*(8).

Tucker, B. F. (1989). Seeing addition: A diagnosis-remediation case study. *The Arithmetic Teacher, 36*(5).

Wearne, D., and Hiebert, J. H. (1994). Research into practice: Place value and addition and subtraction. *The Arithmetic Teacher, 41*(5).

Winson, B. (1992). Operations and number relations. *Instructor, 102*(3).

Standard 8:

Whole Number Computation

In grades K-4, the mathematics curriculum should develop whole number computation so that students can:

- model, explain, and develop reasonable proficiency with basic facts and algorithms;
- use a variety of mental computation and estimation techniques;
- use calculators in appropriate computational situations;
- select and use computation techniques appropriate to specific problems and determine whether the results are reasonable.

Bates, T. and Rousseau, L. (1986). Will the real division algorithm please stand up? *The Arithmetic Teacher, 33*(7).

Binswanger, R. (1988). Discovering division with logo. *The Arithmetic Teacher, 36*(4).

Broadbent, F. W. (1987). Lattice multiplication and division. *The Arithmetic Teacher, 34*(5).

Burns, M. (1991). Introducing division through problem-solving experiences. *The Arithmetic Teacher, 38*(8).

Carey, D. A. (1991). Number sentences: Linking addition and subtraction word problems and symbols. *Journal for Research in Mathematics Education, 22*(4).

Dubitsky, B. (1988). Making division meaningful with a spreadsheet. *The Arithmetic Teacher, 36*(3).

Englert, G. R., and Sinicrope, R. (1994). Making connections with two-digit multiplication. *The Arithmetic Teacher, 41*(8).

Goldman, P. H. (1990). Teaching arithmetic averaging: An activity approach. *The Arithmetic Teacher, 37*(7).

Graeber, A. O. (1993). Research into practice: Misconceptions about multiplication and division. *The Arithmetic Teacher, 40*(7).

Graeber, A. O., and Baker, K. M. (1992). Little into big is the way it always is. *The Arithmetic Teacher, 39*(8).

Huinker, D. M. (1989). Multiplication and division word problems: Improving students' understanding. *The Arithmetic Teacher, 37*(2).

Kamii, C., Lewis, B. A., and Livingston, S. J. (1993). Primary arithmetic: Children inventing their own arithmetic. *The Arithmetic Teacher, 41*(4).

Maier, E. A. (1987). Basic mathematical skills or school survival skills? *The Arithmetic Teacher, 35*(1).

Maletsky, E. (1987). Magic squares. In E. M. Maletsky (Ed.), *Teaching with student math notes.* Reston, VA: National Council of Teachers of Mathematics.

McKillip, W. D., and Stanic, G. M. (1989). Developmental algorithms have a place in elementary school mathematics instruction. *The Arithmetic Teacher, 36*(5).

National Council of Teachers of Mathematics. (1993). *Curriculum and evaluation standards for school mathematics addenda series grades K-4: Number sense and operations.* Reston, VA: National Council of Teachers of Mathematics.

Raltson, A. (1987). Let them use calculators. *Technology Review, 90.*

Stefanich, G. P., and Rokusek, T. (1992). An analysis of computational errors in the use of division algorithms by fourth-grade students. *School Science and Mathematics, 92*(4).

Thompson, F. (1991). Two-digit addition and subtraction: What works? *The Arithmetic Teacher, 38*(5).

Usnick, V. E. (1991). It's not drill AND practice, it's drill OR practice. *School Science and Mathematics, 91*(8).

Van de Walle, J. A. (1991). Implementing the standards: Redefining computation. *The Arithmetic Teacher, 38*(5).

Wiebe, J. H. (1989). Teaching mathematics with technology: Order of operations. *The Arithmetic Teacher, 37*(3).

Standard 9:

Geometry and Spatial Sense

In grades K-4, the mathematics curriculum should include two- and three-dimensional geometry so that students can:

- describe, model, draw, and classify shapes;
- investigate and predict the results of combining, subdividing, and changing shapes;
- develop spatial sense;
- relate geometric ideas to number and measurement ideas;
- recognize and appreciate geometry in their world.

Battista, M. T. (1988). A case for a logo-based elementary school geometry curriculum. *The Arithmetic Teacher, 36*(3).

Brahier, D. J., Hodapp, S., Martin, R., and Speer, W. R. (1992). Ideas—beginning a new school year. *The Arithmetic Teacher, 40*(1).

Bright, G. W., and Harvey, J. G. (1988). Learning and fun with geometry games. *The Arithmetic Teacher, 35*(8).

Buckner, P. G., and Woodward, E. (1987). Reflections and symmetry—a second-grade miniunit. *The Arithmetic Teacher, 35*(2).

Burger, W. F. (1988). An active approach to geometry. *The Arithmetic Teacher, 36*(3).

Claus, A. (1992). Exploring geometry. *The Arithmetic Teacher, 40*(1).

Del Grande, J. (1990). Spatial sense. *The Arithmetic Teacher, 37*(6).

Dunkels, A. (1990). Making and exploring tangrams. *The Arithmetic Teacher, 37*(6).

Hands-on, Inc. (1989). *Geometry: Kindergarten through grade nine.* Solvang, CA: Author.

Hersberger, J., and Talsma, G. (1991). Improving students' understanding of geometric definitions. *The Mathematics Teacher, 84*(7).

Izard, J. (1990). Developing spatial skills with three-dimensional puzzles. *The Arithmetic Teacher, 37*(6).

Jensen, R. J. (1988). Teaching mathematics with technology. Concept formation in geometry: A computer-aided, student-centered activity. *The Arithmetic Teacher, 35*(7).

Juraschek, W. (1990). Get in touch with shape. *The Arithmetic Teacher, 37*(8).

Larke, P. J. (1988). Geometric extravaganza: Spicing up geometry. *The Arithmetic Teacher, 36*(1).

Mansfield, H. (1985). Projective geometry in the elementary school. *The Arithmetic Teacher, 37*(7).

May, L. (1994). Shapes are everywhere. *Teaching PreK-8, 24*(6).

Morrow, L. J. (1991). Geometry through the standards. *The Arithmetic Teacher, 38*(8).

National Council of Teachers of Mathematics. (1993). *Curriculum and evaluation standards for school mathematics addenda series grades K-4: Geometry and spatial sense.* Reston, VA: National Council of Teachers of Mathematics.

Reynolds, J. A. (1985). Build a city. *The Arithmetic Teacher, 33*(1).
Rowan, T. E. (1990). The geometry standards in K-8 mathematics. *The Arithmetic Teacher, 37*(6).
Sgori, R. J. (1990). Communicating about spatial relationships. *The Arithmetic Teacher, 37*(6).
Wilson, P., and Adams, V. (1992). A dynamic way to teach angle and angle measure. *The Arithmetic Teacher, 39*(5).

Standard 10:

Measurement

In grades K-4, the mathematics curriculum should include measurement so that students can:

- understand the attributes of length, capacity, weight, area, volume, time, temperature, and angle;
- develop the process of measuring and concepts related to units of measurement;
- make and use estimates of measurement;
- make and use measurements in problem and everyday situations.

Andrade, G. S. (1992). Teaching students to tell time. *The Arithmetic Teacher, 39*(8).
Bass, H. (1993). Let's measure what's worth measuring. *Education Week, 13*(8).
Chancellor, D. (1992). Calendar mathematics: Time and time again. *The Arithmetic Teacher, 39*(5).
Coburn, T. G. (1987). Estimation and mental computation (teaching measurement estimation). *The Arithmetic Teacher, 34*(7).
Corwin, R. B., and Russell, S. J. (1990). *Measuring: From paces to feet. Used numbers: Real data in the classroom.* Palo Alto, CA: Dale Seymour Publications.
Fay, N., and Tsairides, C. (1989). Metric mall. *The Arithmetic Teacher, 37*(1).
Hands-on, Inc. (1991). *Measurement: Grades three through eight.* Solvang, CA: Author.
Harrison, W. R. (1987) What lies behind measurement? *The Arithmetic Teacher, 34*(7).
Hart, K. (1984). Which comes first—length, area, or volume? *The Arithmetic Teacher, 31*(9).
Hildreth, D. J. (1983). The use of strategies in estimating measurements. *The Arithmetic Teacher, 30*(5).
Kastner, B. (1989). Number sense: The role of measurement applications. *The Arithmetic Teacher, 36*(6).
Lindquist, M. M., and Rowan, T. E. (1989). Implementing the standards: The measurement standards. *The Arithmetic Teacher, 37*(2).
Markovits, Z., Hershkowitz, R., Taizi, N., and Bruckheimer, M. (1986). Estimeasure. *The Arithmetic Teacher, 34*(4).
May, L. (1994). Benchmarks, estimation skills and the real world. *Teaching PreK-8, 24*(8).
Mullen, G. S. (1985). How do you measure up? *The Arithmetic Teacher, 33*(2).
Neufeld, K. (1989). Body measurement. *The Arithmetic Teacher, 36*(9).
Nunes, T. (1993). Tools for thought: The measurement of length and area. *Learning and Instruction, 3.*
Parker, J., and Widmer, C. C. (1993). Patterns in measurement. *The Arithmetic Teacher, 40*(5).
Routledge, J. (1985). What's cooking? *The Arithmetic Teacher, 33*(2).
Sovchik, R., and Meconi, L. J. (1994). IDEAS: Measurement. *The Arithmetic Teacher, 41*(5).
Stevenson, C. L. (1990). Teaching money with grids. *The Arithmetic Teacher, 37*(8).
West, P. (1992). Pendulum is seen swinging 'back toward metrics'. *Education Week, 12*(8).

Standard 11:

Statistics and Probability

In grades K-4, the mathematics curriculum should include experiences with data analysis and probability so that students can:

- collect, organize, and describe data;
- construct, read, and interpret displays of data;
- formulate and solve problems that involve collecting and analyzing data;
- explore concepts of chance.

American Statistical Association. (1991). *Guidelines for the teaching of statistics in K-12 mathematics curriculum.* Landover, MD: Corporate Press.
Bright, G. W. (1989). Data bases in the teaching of elementary school mathematics. *The Arithmetic Teacher, 37*(1).
Bruni, J., and Silverman, H. (1986). Developing concepts in probability and statistics—and much more. *The Arithmetic Teacher, 33*(6).
Burns, M. (1988). Dice advice. *Instructor, 97*(5).
Burns, M. (1994). Probability games in a bag. *Instructor, 103*(9).
Chancellor, D. (1991). Calendar mathematics: Taking chances. *The Arithmetic Teacher, 39*(3)
Cook, M. (1993). Ideas: Combinations. *The Arithmetic Teacher, 41*(4).
Corwin, R. B., and Russell, S. J. (1990). Graphs that grow. *Instructor, 99*(8).
Dickinson, C. (1986). Gather, organize, display: Mathematics for the information society. *The Arithmetic Teacher, 34*(4).
Fennell, F. (1990). Implementing the standards: Probability. *The Arithmetic Teacher, 38*(4).
Friel, S. N., and Corwin, R. B. (1990). Implementing the standards: The statistics standards in K-8 mathematics. *The Arithmetic Teacher, 38*(2).
Hands-on, Inc. (1990). *Statistics, probability, and graphing: Kindergarten through grade nine.* Solvang, CA: Author.
Hitch, C., and Armstrong, G. (1994). Daily activities for data analysis. *The Arithmetic Teacher, 41*(5).
Korithoski, T. P., and Korithoski, P. A. (1993). Mean or meaningless. *The Arithmetic Teacher, 41*(4).
National Council of Teachers of Mathematics. (1992). *Curriculum and evaluation standards for school*

mathematics addenda series grades K-4: Making sense of data. Reston, VA: National Council of Teachers of Mathematics.

National Council of Teachers of Mathematics. (1981). *Teaching statistics and probability. (1981 Yearbook).* Reston, VA: Author.

Newman, C., and Turkel, S. (1985). The class survey: A problem solving activity. *The Arithmetic Teacher, 32*(9).

Ramondetta, J. (1994) Graph it! and make numbers make sense. *Learning, 22*(8).

Russell, S. J., and Corwin, R. B. (1990). Sorting: Groups and graphs. A unit of study for grades 2-3. From *Used numbers: Real data in the classroom.* Palo Alto, CA: Dale Seymour Publications.

Russell, S. J., and Corwin, R. B. (1989). Statistics: The shape of the data. A unit of study for grades 4-6. From *Used numbers: Real data in the classroom.* Palo Alto, CA: Dale Seymour Publications.

Shielack, J. F. (1990). Teaching mathematics with technology: A graphing tool for the primary grades. *The Arithmetic Teacher, 38*(2).

Shulte, A. P. (1987). Learning probability concepts in elementary school mathematics. *The Arithmetic Teacher, 34*(5).

Vissa, J. M. (1989). Probability and combinations for third graders. *The Arithmetic Teacher, 36*(4).

Vissa, J. M. (1987). Sampling treats from a school of fish (tagging goldfish crackers to teach estimation; proportions; central tendencies; structured sampling). *The Arithmetic Teacher, 34*(7).

Young, S. (1990). Ideas. *The Arithmetic Teacher, 38*(1).

Standard 12:

Fractions and Decimals

In grades K-4, the mathematics curriculum should include fractions and decimals so that students can:

- develop concepts of fractions, mixed numbers and decimals;
- develop number sense for fractions and decimals;
- use models to relate fractions to decimals and to find equivalent fractions;
- use models to explore operations on fractions and decimals;
- apply fractions and decimals in problem situations.

Carraher, T. N., and Schliemann, A. D. (1988). Research into practice, using money to teach about the decimal system. *The Arithmetic Teacher, 36*(4).

Cramer, K., and Bezuk, N. (1991). Multiplication of fractions: Teaching for understanding. *The Arithmetic Teacher, 39*(3).

Critchley, P. (1990). Expressing a fraction as a decimal. *Mathematics Teaching, 131.*

Edge, D. (1987). Fractions and panes. *The Arithmetic Teacher, 34*(8).

Esty, W. W. (1991). One point of view: The least common denominator. *The Arithmetic Teacher, 39*(4).

Hiebert, J. B. (1990). Decimal fractions. *The Arithmetic Teacher, 34.*

Klein, P. A. (1990). Remembering how to read decimals. *The Arithmetic Teacher, 37*(9).

Mack, N. K. (1990). Learning fractions with understanding: Building on informal knowledge. *Journal for Research in Mathematics Education, 21*(1).

Mick, H. W., and Sinicrope, R. (1989). Two meanings of fraction multiplication. *School Science and Mathematics, 89*(8).

Olson, M. (1991). Activities: A geometric look at greatest common divisor. *The Mathematics Teacher, 84*(7).

Olson, M. (1988). Fraction concepts and the conservation of area: Ideas for consideration. *School Science and Mathematics, 88*(3).

Ott, J. (1990). A unified approach to multiplying fractions. *The Arithmetic Teacher, 37*(7).

Post, T. (1989). Fractions and other rational numbers. *The Arithmetic Teacher, 37*(1).

Post, T., and Cramer, K. (1987). Children's strategies in ordering rational numbers. *The Arithmetic Teacher, 35*(2).

Pothier, Y., and Sawada, D. (1990). Partitioning: An approach to fractions. *The Arithmetic Teacher, 38*(4).

Rees, J. M. (1987). Two-sided pies: Help for improper fractions and mixed numbers. *The Arithmetic Teacher, 35*(4).

Ross, S. H. (1989). Parts, wholes, and place value: A developmental view. *The Arithmetic Teacher, 36*(6).

Sinicrope, R., and Mick, H. W. (1992). Multiplication of fractions through paper folding. *The Arithmetic Teacher, 40*(2).

Steffe, L. P., and Olive, J. (1991). The problem of fractions in the elementary school. *The Arithmetic Teacher, 38*(9).

Wiebe, J. H. (1985). Discovering fractions on a fraction table. *The Arithmetic Teacher, 33*(4).

Witherspoon, M. L. (1993). Fractions: In search of meaning. *The Arithmetic Teacher, 40*(8).

Woodward, E., and Gibbs, V. (1990). Finding least common multiples with a calculator. *School Science and Mathematics, 90*(6).

Standard 13:

Patterns and Relationships

In grades K-4, the mathematics curriculum should include the study of patterns and relationships so that students can:

- recognize, describe, extend, and create a wide variety of patterns;
- represent and describe mathematical relationships;
- explore the use of variables and open sentences to express relationships.

Bitter, G., and Edwards, N. (1989). Finding number patterns. *The Arithmetic Teacher, 37*(4).

Bright, G. W. (1988). Exploring patterns. *The Arithmetic Teacher, 36*(3).

Buckner, P. G., and Woodward, E. (1987). Reflections and symmetry—A second-grade miniunit. *The Arithmetic Teacher, 35*(2).

Evered, L. J. (1992). Folded fashions: Symmetry in clothing design. *The Arithmetic Teacher, 40*(4).

Feinberg, M. M. (1990). Using patterns to practice basic facts. *The Arithmetic Teacher, 37*(8).

Giganti, P. Jr., and Cittadino, M. J. (1990). The art of tessellation. *The Arithmetic Teacher, 37*(7).

Goldman, P. H. (1990). Teaching arithmetic averaging: An activity approach. *The Arithmetic Teacher, 37*(7).

Hands-on, Inc. (1990). *Patterns and functions: Kindergarten through grade nine.* Solvang, CA: Author.

Holbrook, H., and Van de Walle, J. (1987). Patterns, thinking, and problem solving. *The Arithmetic Teacher, 34*(8).

Litwiller, B. H., and Duncan, D. R. (1986). The extended subtraction table: A search for number patterns. *The Arithmetic Teacher, 33*(9).

National Council of Teachers of Mathematics. (1993). *Curriculum and evaluation standards for school mathematics addenda series grades K-4: Patterns.* Reston, VA: Author.

Newton, J. E. (1988). From pattern-block play to logo programming. *The Arithmetic Teacher, 35*(9).

Onslow, B. (1990). Pentominoes. *The Arithmetic Teacher, 37*(9).

Parker, J., and Widmer, C. C. (1993). Patterns in measurement. *The Arithmetic Teacher, 40*(5).

Tierney, C. (1985). Patterns in the multiplication tables. *The Arithmetic Teacher, 32*(7).

Van de Walle, J. A. (1988). The early development of number relations. *The Arithmetic Teacher, 35*(6).

Wiebe, J. H. (1985). Discovering fractions on a fraction table. *The Arithmetic Teacher, 33*(4).

NCTM 5-8 CURRICULUM STANDARDS AND RELATED READINGS*

Standard 1:

Mathematics as Problem Solving

In grades 5-8, the mathematics curriculum should include numerous and varied experiences with problem solving as a method of inquiry and application so that students can:

- use problem-solving approaches to investigate and understand mathematical content;
- formulate problems from situations within and outside mathematics;
- develop and apply a variety of strategies to solve problems, with emphasis on multi-step and nonroutine problems;
- verify and interpret results with respect to the original problem situation;
- generalize solutions and strategies to new problem situations;
- acquire confidence in using mathematics meaningfully.

Bohan, H., and Bohan, S. (1993). Extending the regular curriculum through creative problem solving. *The Arithmetic Teacher, 41*(2).

Brady, R. R. (1991). A close look at student problem solving and the teaching of mathematics. *School Science and Mathematics, 91*(8).

Cochener, D., and Cochener, D. (1993). How many miles per hour is that fan going? An experiment to implement problem solving in grades 5-8. *School Science and Mathematics, 93*(3).

Cox, S. (1988). The ultimate in problem solving. *The Arithmetic Teacher, 36*(2).

Day, R. P. (1986). A problem-solving component for junior high school mathematics. *The Arithmetic Teacher, 34*(2).

Fairbairn, D. M. (1993). Creating story problems. *The Arithmetic Teacher, 41*(3).

Farivar, S., and Webb, N. M. (1994). Helping and getting help—essential skills for effective group problem solving. *The Arithmetic Teacher, 41*(9).

Ford, M. I. (1990). The writing process: A strategy for problem solvers. *The Arithmetic Teacher, 38*(3).

Havel, P. (1985). Students categorize then solve problems. *The Arithmetic Teacher, 33*(3).

Kersch, M. E., and McDonald, J. (1991). How do I solve thee? Let me count the ways! *The Arithmetic Teacher, 39*(2).

Kloosterman, P. (1992). Non-routine word problems: One part of a problem-solving program in the elementary school. *School Science and Mathematics, 92*(1).

Krulik, S. (1987). Math and games. In E. M. Maletsky (Ed.), *Teaching with student math notes.* Reston, VA: National Council of Teachers of Mathematics.

Krulik, S., and Rudnik, J. A. (1984). *A sourcebook for teaching problem solving.* Newton, MA: Allyn and Bacon, Inc.

Rowan, T. E. (Ed.). (1990). The vision of problem solving in the standards. *The Arithmetic Teacher, 37*(9).

Shulte, A. (1987). Successful simulation. In E. M. Maletsky (Ed.), *Teaching with student math notes.* Reston, VA: National Council of Teachers of Mathematics.

Stonewater, J. (1988). Using developmental clues to teach problem solving. *School Science and Mathematics, 88*(4).

Szetela, W. (1987). The problem of evaluation in problem solving: Can we find solutions? *The Arithmetic Teacher, 35*(3).

Talton, C. F. (1988). Let's solve the problem before we find the answer. *The Arithmetic Teacher, 36*(1).

Standard 2:

Mathematics as Communication

In grades 5-8, the study of mathematics should include opportunities to communicate so that students can:

- model situations using oral, written, concrete, pictorial, graphical, and algebraic methods;
- reflect on and clarify their own thinking about mathematical ideas and situations;
- develop common understandings of mathematical ideas, including the role of definitions;
- use the skills of reading, listening, and viewing to interpret and evaluate mathematical ideas;
- discuss mathematical ideas and make conjectures and convincing arguments;
- appreciate the value of mathematical notation and its role in the development of mathematical ideas.

Brown, N. (1993). Teacher to teacher: Writing mathematics. *The Arithmetic Teacher, 41*(1).

Carraher, T. N., Carraher, D. W., and Schliemann, A. (1987). Written and oral mathematics. *Journal for Research in Mathematics Education, 18.*

Davison, D. M., and Pearce, D. L. (1988). Using writing activities to reinforce mathematics instruction. *The Arithmetic Teacher, 35*(8).

Davison, D. M., and Pearce, D. L. (1988). Writing activities in junior high mathematics texts. *School Science and Mathematics, 88*(8).

Easley, J., Taylor, H., and Taylor, J. (1990). Dialogue and conceptual splatter in mathematics classes. *The Arithmetic Teacher, 37*(7).

Farivar, S., and Webb, N. M. (1994). Helping and getting help—essential skills for effective group problem solving. *The Arithmetic Teacher, 41*(9).

Fennell, F., and Ammon, R. (1985). Writing techniques for problem solvers. *The Arithmetic Teacher, 33*(1).

Garbe, D. (1985). Mathematics vocabulary and the culturally different student. *The Arithmetic Teacher, 33*(2).

Gullatt, D. (1986). Help your students read mathematics. *The Arithmetic Teacher, 33*(9).

Hosmer, P. C. (1989). Students can write their own problems. *The Arithmetic Teacher, 36*(6).

Leidtke, W. (1988). One point of view: Let's talk about talking mathematics. *The Arithmetic Teacher, 35*(8).

Maletsky, E. (1987). Proof without words. In E. M. Maletsky (Ed.), *Teaching with student math notes.* Reston, VA: National Council of Teachers of Mathematics.

Miller, D., and England, D. A. (1989). Writing to learn algebra. *School Science and Mathematics, 89*(8).

Mumme, J., and Shepherd, N. (1990). Implementing the standards: Communication in mathematics. *The Arithmetic Teacher, 38*(1).

Rakow, S. J., and Gee, T. C. (1988). What reading techniques do mathematics teachers find valuable? *School Science and Mathematics, 88*(8).

Sgroi, R. J. (1990). Communicating about spatial relationships. *The Arithmetic Teacher, 37*(6). 1990.

Silverman, F., Winograd, K., and Strohauer, D. (1992). Student-generated story problems. *The Arithmetic Teacher, 39*(8).

Small, M. S. (1990). Do you speak math? *The Arithmetic Teacher, 37*(5).

Yancey, A. V., and Thompson, C. S. (1989). Children must learn to use diagrams. *The Arithmetic Teacher, 36*(7).

Standard 3:

Mathematics as Reasoning

In grades 5-8, reasoning shall permeate the mathematics curriculum so that students can:

- recognize and apply deductive and inductive reasoning;
- understand and apply reasoning processes, with special attention to spatial reasoning and reasoning with proportions and graphs;
- make and evaluate mathematical conjectures and arguments;
- validate their own thinking;
- appreciate the pervasive use and power of reasoning as a part of mathematics.

Buser, K., and Reimer, D. (1988). Developing cognitive strategies through problem solving. *Teaching Exceptional Children, 13*(4).

Davis, R. B. (1991). Research into practice: Giving pupils tools for thinking. *The Arithmetic Teacher, 38*(5).

Garofalo, J., and Mtetwa, D. K. (1990). Implementing the standards: Mathematics as reasoning. *The Arithmetic Teacher, 37*(5).

Hands-on, Inc. (1990). *Algebra: Kindergarten through grade nine.* Solvang, CA: Author.

Hands-on, Inc. (1989). *Logic: Kindergarten through grade nine.* Solvang, CA: Author.

Harnadek, A. (1990). Math mindbenders: Deductive reasoning in mathematics. *The Arithmetic Teacher, 37*(7).

Johnson, J. E. (1987). Do you think you might be wrong? Confirmation bias in problem solving. *The Arithmetic Teacher, 34*(9).

Kloosterman, P. (1992). Non-routine word problems: One part of a problem-solving program in the elementary school. *School Science and Mathematics, 92*(1).

Krulik, S., and Rudnik, J. A. (1994). Reflect . . . for better problem solving and reasoning. *The Arithmetic Teacher, 41*(6).

Schulte, A. (1987). Successful simulation. In E. M. Maletsky (Ed.), *Teaching with student math notes.* Reston, VA: National Council of Teachers of Mathematics.

Silver, E. A., and Smith, M. S. (1990). Research into practice: Teaching mathematics and thinking. *The Arithmetic Teacher, 37*(8).

Stanic, G. (1990). Teaching mathematics and thinking. *The Arithmetic Teacher, 37*(8).

Stewart, W. J. (1988). Stimulating intuitive thinking through problem solving. *The Clearing House, 62.*

Trahanovsky-Orletsky, A. E. (1991). What's the problem? *Learning, 91.*

Wadlington, E., Bitner, J., Partridge, E., and Austin, S. (1992). Have a problem? Make the writing—mathematics connection. *The Arithmetic Teacher, 40*(4).

Standard 4:

Mathematical Connections

In grades 5-8, the mathematics curriculum should include investigation of mathematical connections so that students can:

- see mathematics as an integrated whole;
- explore problems and describe results using graphical, numerical, physical, algebraic, and verbal mathematical models or representations;
- use a mathematical idea to further their understanding of other mathematical ideas;
- apply mathematical thinking and modeling to solve problems that arise in other disciplines, such as art, music, psychology, science, and business;
- value the role of mathematics in our culture and society.

Accavi, A. (1987). Using historical materials in the mathematics classroom. *The Arithmetic Teacher, 35*(4).

Anderson, A. (1994). Mathematics in context: Measurement, packaging, and caring for our environment. *School Science and Mathematics, 94*(3).

Bohan, H., and Bohan, S. (1993). Extending the regular curriculum through creative problem solving. *The Arithmetic Teacher, 41*(2).

Brahier, D. J., Brahier, A. F., and Speer, W. R. (1992). IDEAS—elections. *The Arithmetic Teacher, 40*(3).

Bright, G. W. (1988). Data bases in the teaching of elementary school mathematics. *The Arithmetic Teacher, 35*(5).

Cochener, D., and Cochener, D. (1993). How many miles per hour is that fan going? An experiment to implement problem solving in grades 5-8. *School Science and Mathematics, 93*(3).

Conaway, B., and Midkiff, R. B. (1994). Connecting literature, language, and fractions. *The Arithmetic Teacher, 41*(8).

Egsgard, J., Flewelling, G., Newell, C., and Warburton, W. (1988). Making connections with mathematics. Providence, RI: Janson Publications, Inc.

Fennell, F. (1982). The newspaper: A source for applications in mathematics. *The Arithmetic Teacher, 30*(2).

Flexer, R. J., and Topping, C. L. (1988). Mathematics on the home front. *The Arithmetic Teacher, 36*(2).

Fulkerson, P. (1992). Getting the most from a problem. *The Arithmetic Teacher, 40*(3).

Glatzer, D. J., and Glatzer, J. (1989). *Math connections* (Blackline masters, middle-school activities). Palo Alto, CA: Dale Seymour Publications.

Kersch, M. E., and McDonald, J. (1991). How do I solve thee? Let me count the ways! *The Arithmetic Teacher, 39*(2).

Konold, C. (1994). Teaching probability through modeling real problems. *The Mathematics Teacher, 87*(4).

Maddon, P. J. (1994). Teacher to teacher: Making story problems relevant. *The Arithmetic Teacher, 41*(9).

Martin, C. S., and Spence, C. (1988). Mathematics + social studies = learning connections. *The Arithmetic Teacher, 36*(4).

Newman, C. M., and Turkel, S. B. (1989). Integrating arithmetic and geometry with numbered points on a circle. *The Arithmetic Teacher, 36*(5).

Pagni, D. L. (1989). A television programming challenge: A cooperative group activity that uses mathematics. *The Arithmetic Teacher, 36*(5).

Pearce, D. L., and Davison, D. M. (1988). Teacher use of writing in the junior high mathematics classroom. *School Science and Mathematics, 88*(3).

Rees, R. D. (1990). Station break: A mathematics game using cooperative learning and role playing. *The Arithmetic Teacher, 37*(8).

Souviney, R., Britt, M., Gargiulo, S., and Huges, P. (1990). *Mathematical investigations. A series of situational lessons, book 1.* Palo Alto, CA: Dale Seymour Publications.

Terc, M. (1985). Coordinate geometry—art and mathematics. *The Arithmetic Teacher, 33*(2).

Standard 5:

Number and Number Relationships

In grades 5-8, the mathematics curriculum should include the continued development of number and number relationships so that students can:

- understand, represent, and use numbers in a variety of equivalent forms (integer, fraction, decimal, percent, exponential, and scientific notation) in real-world and mathematical problem situations;
- develop number sense for whole numbers, fractions, decimals, integers, and rational numbers;
- understand and apply ratios, proportions, and percents in a wide variety of situations;
- investigate relationships among fractions, decimals, and percents;
- represent numerical relationships in one- and two-dimensional graphs.

Bezuszka, S. (1987). Figurate numbers. In E. M. Maletsky (Ed.), *Teaching with student math notes.* Reston, VA: National Council of Teachers of Mathematics.

Coffield, P. (1987). Codes and counting. In E. M. Maletsky (Ed.), *Teaching with student math notes.* Reston, VA: National Council of Teachers of Mathematics.

Goldman, P. H. (1990). Teaching arithmetic averaging: An activity approach. *The Arithmetic Teacher, 37*(7).

Hope, J. (1989). Promoting number sense in school. *The Arithmetic Teacher, 36*(6).

Kenney, M. (1987). Intriguing infinity. In E. M. Maletsky (Ed.), *Teaching with student math notes.* Reston, VA: National Council of Teachers of Mathematics.

Maletsky, E. (1987). Egyptian mathematics. In E. M. Maletsky (Ed.), *Teaching with student math notes.* Reston, VA: National Council of Teachers of Mathematics.

Meconi, L. J. (1992). Numbers, counting, and infinity in middle school mathematics. *School Science and Mathematics, 92*(7).

Rathmell, E. E., and Leutzinger, L. P. (1991). Implementing the standards: Number representations and relationships. *The Arithmetic Teacher, 38*(7).

Sherman, H. J. (1992). Reinforcing place value. *The Arithmetic Teacher, 40*(3).

Sowder, J. (1990). Mental computation and number sense. *The Arithmetic Teacher, 37*(7).

Thompson, C. S. (1989). Implementing the standards: Number sense and numeration in grades K-8. *The Arithmetic Teacher, 37*(1).

Turkel, S., and Newman, C. M. (1988). What's your number? Developing number sense. *The Arithmetic Teacher, 35*(6).

Wearne, D., and Hiebert, J. (1994). Research into practice: Place value and addition and subtraction. *The Arithmetic Teacher, 41*(5).

Whiten, D. J. (1989). Number sense and the importance of asking why. *The Arithmetic Teacher, 36*(6).

Winson, B. (1992). Intermediate focus: Numeration and place value. *Instructor, 102*(2).

Standard 6:

Number Systems and Number Theory

In grades 5-8, the mathematics curriculum should include the study of number systems and number theory so that students can:

- understand and appreciate the need for numbers beyond the whole numbers;
- develop and use order relations for whole numbers, fractions, decimals, integers, and rational numbers;
- extend their understanding of whole number operations to fractions, decimals, integers, and rational numbers;
- understand how the basic arithmetic operations are related to one another;
- develop and apply number theory concepts (e.g., primes, factors, and multiples) in real-world and mathematical problem situations.

Baker, D., Edwards, R., and Marshall, C. (1990). Teaching mathematics with technology: Teaching about exponents with calculators. *The Arithmetic Teacher, 38*(1).

Carraher, T. N., and Schliemann, A. D. (1988). Research into practice, using money to teach about the decimal system. *The Arithmetic Teacher, 36*(4).

Duncan, D. R., and Litwiller, B. H. (1989). Polygons on a number lattice: Sums, products and differences. *The Arithmetic Teacher, 37*(1).

Graviss, T., and Greaver, J. (1992). Extending the number line to make connections with number theory. *The Mathematics Teacher, 85*(1).

Holtan, B., and Dearing, S. (1987). Factors and primes with a t-square. *The Arithmetic Teacher, 34*(8).

Hudson, F. M. (1990). Are the primes really infinite? *The Mathematics Teacher, 83*(3).

Jean, R. V., and Johnson, M. (1989). An adventure into applied mathematics with fibonacci numbers. *School Science and Mathematics, 89*(8).

Lauber, M. (1990). Casting out nines: An explanation and extensions. *The Mathematics Teacher, 83*(3).

Meconi, L. J. (1992). Numbers, counting, and infinity in middle school mathematics. *School Science and Mathematics, 92*(7).

Norman, F. (1991). Figurate numbers in the classroom. *The Arithmetic Teacher, 38*(4).

Peera, Z. (1982). Number patterns and bases. *The Arithmetic Teacher, 30*(2).

Post, T. (1989). Fractions and other rational numbers. *The Arithmetic Teacher, 37*(1).

Rathmell, E. E., and Leutzinger, L. P. (1991). Implementing the standards: Number representations and relationships. *The Arithmetic Teacher, 38*(7).

Simms, A. J. (1987). Repeating decimals into fractions: A microwave recipe. *The Mathematics Teacher, 80*(1).

Steiner, E. E. (1987). Division of fractions: Developing conceptual sense with dollars and cents. *The Arithmetic Teacher, 34*(9).

Sudar, V. K. (1990). Thou shalt not divide by zero. *The Arithmetic Teacher, 37*(7).

Thompson, C. S. (1989). Number sense and numeration in grades K-8. *The Arithmetic Teacher, 37*(1).

Varnadore, J. (1991). Pascal's triangle and fibonacci numbers. *The Mathematics Teacher, 84*(8).

Whitin, D. J. (1986). More patterns with square numbers. *The Arithmetic Teacher, 33*(5).

Whitley, B. V. (1993). From the file: Writing about the importance of numbers. *The Arithmetic Teacher, 40*(5).

Woodward, E., and Gibbs, V. (1990). Finding least common multiples with calculators. *School Science and Mathematics, 90*(9).

Zepp, R. A. (1992). Numbers and codes in ancient peru: The quipu. *The Arithmetic Teacher, 39*(9).

Standard 7:

Computation and Estimation

In grades 5-8, the mathematics curriculum should develop the concepts underlying computation and estimation in various contexts so that students can:

- compute with whole numbers, fractions, decimals, integers, and rational numbers;
- develop, analyze, and explain procedures for computation and techniques for estimation;

- develop, analyze, and explain methods for solving proportions;
- select and use an appropriate method for computing from among mental arithmetic, paper-and-pencil, calculator, and computer methods;
- use computation, estimation, and proportions to solve problems;
- use estimation to check the reasonableness of results.

Coburn, T. (1990). Estimation and mental computation. *The Arithmetic Teacher, 34*(8).

Cramer, K., and Bezuk, N. (1991). Multiplication of fractions: Teaching for understanding. *The Arithmetic Teacher, 39*(3).

Duprey, L. (1994). Reap dividends with stock market math. *Learning, 22*(5).

Erickson, D. K. (1990). Activities: Percentages and cuisenaire rods. *The Mathematics Teacher, 83*(3).

Goldberg, S. (1994). Making a hit with percentages. *Learning, 22*(6).

Harel, G., and Behr, M. (1991). Ed's strategy for solving division problems. *The Arithmetic Teacher, 39*(3).

Harte, S. W., and Glover, M. (1993). Estimation is mathematical thinking. *The Arithmetic Teacher, 41*(2).

Haubner, M. A. (1992). Percents: Developing meaning through models. *The Arithmetic Teacher, 40*(4).

May, L. J. (1994). Benchmarks, estimation skills and the real world. *Teaching PreK-8, 24*(8).

May, L. J. (1989). Estimation: Another view. *Teaching PreK-8, 20*(1).

May, L. J. (1994). Real life math and the world of shopping. *Teaching PreK-8, 24*(4).

May, L. J. (1993). What would you buy. *Teaching PreK-8, 24*(3).

Mick, H. W., and Sinicrope, R. (1989). Two meanings of fraction multiplication. *School Science and Mathematics, 89*(8).

Ott, J. M. (1990). A unified approach to multiplying fractions. *The Arithmetic Teacher, 37*(7).

Ott, J. M., Snook, D. L., and Gibson, D. L. (1991). Understanding partitive division of fractions. *The Arithmetic Teacher, 39*(2).

Payne, J. N., and Towsley, A. E. Implications of NCTM's standards for teaching fractions and decimals. *The Arithmetic Teacher, 37*(8).

Reys, B. (1986). Estimation and mental computation: It's about time. *The Arithmetic Teacher, 34*(1).

Reys, B. J., and Reys, R. E. (1990). Implementing the standards: Estimation—direction from the standards. *The Arithmetic Teacher, 37*(7).

Reys, B. J., and Reys, R. E. (1986). Mental computation and computational estimation—their time has come. *The Arithmetic Teacher, 33*(7).

Reys, R. E. (1985). Testing mental-computation skills. *The Arithmetic Teacher, 33*(3).

Sowder, J. (1989). Research into practice; developing understanding of computational estimation. *The Arithmetic Teacher, 36*(5).

Sowder, J. T. (1990). Mental computation and number sense. *The Arithmetic Teacher, 37*(7).

Sundar, V. K. (1990). Thou shalt not divide by zero. *The Arithmetic Teacher, 37*(7).

Trafton, P. R., and Zawojewski, J. (1987). Estimation and mental computation. *The Arithmetic Teacher, 34*(8).

Watson, J. M. (1991). Models to show the impossibility of division by zero. *School Science and Mathematics, 91*(8).

Standard 8:

Patterns and Functions

In grades 5-8, the mathematics curriculum should include explorations of patterns and functions so that students can:

- describe, extend, analyze, and create a wide variety of patterns;
- describe and represent relationships with tables, graphs, and rules;
- analyze functional relationships to explain how a change in one quantity results in a change in another;
- use patterns and functions to represent and solve problems.

Bidwell, J. K. (1987). Using reflections to find symmetric and asymmetric patterns. *The Arithmetic Teacher, 34*(7).

Bitter, G., and Edwards, N. (1989). Finding number patterns. *The Arithmetic Teacher, 37*(4).

Evered, L. J. (1992). Folded fashions: Symmetry in clothing design. *The Arithmetic Teacher, 40*(4).

Grevsmuhl, U. (1988). Mathematics and modern art. *Mathematics Teaching, 122.*

Hands-on, Inc. (1990). *Patterns and functions: Kindergarten through grade nine.* Solvang, CA: Author.

Holbrook, H., and Van de Walle, J. (1987). Patterns, thinking, and problem solving. *The Arithmetic Teacher, 34*(8).

Howden, H. (1989). Patterns, relationships, and functions. *The Arithmetic Teacher, 37*(3).

Kelly, M. (1986). Elementary school activity: Graphing the stock market. *The Arithmetic Teacher, 33*(7).

Kenny, M. (1987). Spirolaterals. In E. M. Maletsky (Ed.), *Teaching with student math notes.* Reston, VA: National Council of Teachers of Mathematics.

Krulik, S. (1987). 4×4 square arrays. In E. M. Maletsky (Ed.), *Teaching with student math notes.* Reston, VA: National Council of Teachers of Mathematics.

Krulik, S. (1987). Networks. In E. M. Maletsky (Ed.), *Teaching with student math notes.* Reston, VA: National Council of Teachers of Mathematics.

Lauber, M. (990). Casting out nines: An explanation and extensions. *The Mathematics Teacher, 83*(3).

Litwiller, B. H., and Duncan, D. R. (1986). The extended subtraction table: A search for number patterns. *The Arithmetic Teacher, 33*(9).

National Council of Teachers of Mathematics. (1991). *Curriculum and evaluation standards for school mathematics addenda series grades 5-8: Patterns and functions.* Reston, VA: Author.

Onslow, B. (1990). Pentominoes. *The Arithmetic Teacher, 37*(9).

Parker, J., and Widmer, C. C. (1993). Patterns in measurement. *The Arithmetic Teacher, 40*(5).

Russell, S. J., and Corwin, R. B. (1989). Statistics: The shape of the data. A unit of study for grades 4-6. From *Used numbers: Real data in the classroom.* Palo Alto, CA: Dale Seymour Publications.

Seymour, D. (1987). Tessellations: Patterns in geometry. In E. M. Maletsky (Ed.), *Teaching with student math notes.* Reston, VA: National Council of Teachers of Mathematics.

Vissa, J. (1987). Coordinate graphing: Shaping a sticky situation. *The Arithmetic Teacher, 35*(3).

Whitin, D. J. (1986). More patterns with square numbers. *The Arithmetic Teacher, 33*(5).

Woodward, E., and Gibbs, V. (1990). Finding least common multiples with calculators. *School Science and Mathematics, 90*(9).

Zaslavsky, C. (1990). Symmetry in american folk art. *The Arithmetic Teacher, 38*(1).

Standard 9:

Algebra

In grades 5-8, the mathematics curriculum should include explorations of algebraic concepts and processes so that students can:

- understand the concepts of variable, expression, and equation;
- represent situations and number patterns with tables, graphs, verbal rules, and equations, and explore the interrelationships of these representations;
- analyze tables and graphs to identify properties and relationships;
- develop confidence in solving linear equations using concrete, informal, and formal methods;
- investigate inequalities and nonlinear equations informally;
- apply algebraic methods to solve a variety of real-world and mathematical problems.

Berman, B., and Friederwitzer, F. (1989). Algebra can be elementary . . . when it's concrete. *The Arithmetic Teacher, 36*(8).

Berlin, D., and Nesbitt, D. (1990). Time travel: Negative numbers; grades 4-6. *School Science and Mathematics, 90*(5).

Cemen, P. B. (1993). Teacher to teacher: Adding and subtracting integers on the number line. *The Arithmetic Teacher, 40*(7).

Coffield, P. (1987). Codes and counting. In E. M. Maletsky (Ed.), *Teaching with student math notes.* Reston, VA: National Council of Teachers of Mathematics.

Cooke, M. B. (1993). Teacher to teacher: A videotaping project to explore the multiplication of integers. *The Arithmetic Teacher, 41*(3).

Cramer, K., and Post, T. (1993). Making connections: A case for proportionality. *The Arithmetic Teacher, 40*(6).

Miller, D., and England, D. A. (1989). Writing to learn algebra. *School Science and Mathematics, 89*(8).

National Council of Teachers of Mathematics. (1988). *The ideas of algebra, K-12.* (1988 Yearbook). Reston, VA: Author.

Shumway, R. J.(1989). Solving equations today. *School Science and Mathematics, 89*(3).

Silverman, H. (1989). Ideas. *The Arithmetic Teacher, 37*(4).

Thompson, F. M. (1988). Algebraic instruction for the younger child. *The Ideas of Algebra, K-12.* (1988 NCTM Yearbook). Reston, VA: Author.

Van Dyke, R. P. (1990). Expressions, equations and inequalities. *The Mathematics Teacher, 83*(1).

Whitin, D. J. (1992). Activities: Multiplying integers. *The Mathematics Teacher, 85*(5).

Williams, D. E. (1986). Activities for algebra. *The Arithmetic Teacher, 33*(6).

Standard 10:

Statistics

In grades 5-8, the mathematics curriculum should include exploration of statistics in real-world situations so that students can:

- systematically collect, organize, and describe data;
- construct, read, and interpret tables, charts, and graphs;
- make inferences and convincing arguments that are based on data analysis;
- evaluate arguments that are based on data analysis;
- develop an appreciation for statistical methods as powerful means for decision making.

American Statistical Association. (1991). *Guidelines for the teaching of statistics in K-12 mathematics curriculum.* Landover, MD: Corporate Press.

Bright, G. W. (1989). Data bases in the teaching of elementary school mathematics. *The Arithmetic Teacher, 37*(1).

Browning, C. A., and Channell, D. E. (1992). A 'handy' database activity for the middle school classroom. *The Arithmetic Teacher, 40*(4).

Burrill, G. (1987). Correlation: What makes a perfect pair. In E. Maletsky (Ed.), *Teaching with student math notes.* Reston, VA: National Council of Teachers of Mathematics.

Corwin, R. B., and Friel, S. (1990). Statistics: Prediction and sampling. A unit of study for grades 5-6. From *Used numbers: Real data in the classroom.* Palo Alto, CA: Dale Seymour Publications.

Dickinson, C. (1986). Gather, organize, display: Mathematics for the information society. *The Arithmetic Teacher, 34*(4).

Evered, L. J. (1992). Folded fashions: Symmetry in clothing design. *The Arithmetic Teacher, 40*(4).

Fennell, F. (1984). Ya gotta play to win: A probability and statistics unit for the middle grades. *The Arithmetic Teacher, 31*(7).

Fielker, D. (1989). So what do we mean by 'prediction'? *Mathematics Teaching, 127.*

Friel, S. N., and Corwin, R. B. (1990). Implementing the standards: The statistics standards in K-8 mathematics. *The Arithmetic Teacher, 38*(2).

Friel, S., Mokros, J. R., and Russell, S. J. (1992). Statistics: Middles, means, and in-betweens. A unit of study for grades 5-6. From *Used numbers: Real data in the classroom.* Palo Alto, CA: Dale Seymour Publications.

Hands-on, Inc. (1990). *Statistics, probability, and graphing: Kindergarten through grade nine.* Solvang, CA: Author.

Hinders, D. C. (1990). Examples of the use of statistics in society. *The Mathematics Teacher, 83*(2).

Hitch, C., and Armstrong, G. (1994). Daily activities for data analysis. *The Arithmetic Teacher, 41*(5).

Lappan, G. (1988) Research into practice. Teaching statistics: Mean, median, and mode. *The Arithmetic Teacher, 35*(7).

National Council of Teachers of Mathematics. (1991). *Curriculum and evaluation standards for school mathematics addenda series grades 5-8: Dealing with data and chance.* Reston, VA: National Council of Teachers of Mathematics.

National Council of Teachers of Mathematics. (1981). *Teaching statistics and probability.* (1981 Yearbook). Reston, VA: Author.

Newman, C., and Turkel, S. (1985). The class survey: A problem solving activity. *The Arithmetic Teacher, 32*(9).

Olson, A. T. (1987). Exploring baseball data. *The Mathematics Teacher, 80*(7).

Phillips, J. L. Jr., (1992). *How to think about statistics.* New York: W.H. Freeman.

Russell, S. J., and Corwin, R. B. (1989). Statistics: The shape of the data. A unit of study for grades 4-6. From *Used numbers: Real data in the classroom.* Palo Alto, CA: Dale Seymour Publications.

Scheinok, P. A. (1988). A summer program in probability and statistics for inner-city seventh graders. *The Mathematics Teacher, 81*(4).

Vissa, J. (1987). Sampling treats for a school of fish (tagging goldfish crackers to teach estimation; proportions; central tendencies; structured sampling). *The Arithmetic Teacher, 34*(7).

Woodward, E., Frost, S., and Smith, A. (1991). Cemetery mathematics. *The Arithmetic Teacher, 39*(4).

Standard 11:

Probability

In grades 5-8, the mathematics curriculum should include explorations of probability in real world situations so that students can:

- model situations by devising and carrying out experiments or simulations to determine probabilities;
- model situations by constructing a sample space to determine probabilities;
- appreciate the power of using a probability model by comparing experimental results with mathematical expectations;
- make predictions that are based on experimental or theoretical probabilities;
- develop an appreciation for the pervasive use of probability in the real world.

Brahier, D. J., Brahier, A. F., and Speer, W. R. (1992). IDEAS—elections. *The Arithmetic Teacher, 40*(3).

Bright, G. W. (1989). Teaching mathematics with technology: Probability simulations. *The Arithmetic Teacher, 36*(9).

Burns, M. (1988). Dice advice. *Instructor, 97*(5).

Burns, M. (1994). Probability games in a bag. *Instructor, 103*(9).

Burrill, G. (1990). Implementing the standards: Statistics and probability. *The Mathematics Teacher, 83*(2).

Coffield, P. (1987). Pi: The digit hunt. In E. M. Maletsky (Ed.), *Teaching with student math notes.* Reston, VA: National Council of Teachers of Mathematics.

Coffield, P. (1987). Probability: Quantifying chance. In E. M. Maletsky (Ed.), *Teaching with student math notes.* Reston, VA: National Council of Teachers of Mathematics.

Farnsworth, D. L. (1991). Introducing probability. *The Mathematics Teacher, 84*(2).

Fennel, F. (1990). Implementing the standards: Probability. *The Arithmetic Teacher, 38*(4).

Fennell, F. (1984). Ya gotta play to win: A probability and statistics unit for the middle grades. *The Arithmetic Teacher, 31*(7).

Fielker, D. (1989). So what do we mean by 'prediction'? *Mathematics Teaching, 127.*

Green, D. (1993). Puzzling probability problems. *Mathematics Teaching, 145.*

Hands-on, Inc. (1990). *Statistics, probability, and graphing: Kindergarten through grade nine.* Solvang, CA: Author.

Hatfield, L. L. (1992). Activities: Explorations with chance. *The Mathematics Teacher, 85*(8).

Konold, C. (1994). Teaching probability through modeling real problems. *The Mathematics Teacher, 87*(4).

Litwiller, B., and Duncan, D. (1992). Prizes in cereal boxes: An application of probability. *School Science and Mathematics, 92*(4).

Maletsky, E. (1987). Duplication probabilities. In E. M. Maletsky (Ed.), *Teaching with student math notes.* Reston, VA: National Council of Teachers of Mathematics.

Martin, H. M., and Zawojewski, J. S. (1993). Dealing with data and chance: An illustration from the middle school addendum to the standards. *The Arithmetic Teacher, 41*(4).

National Council of Teachers of Mathematics. (1981). *Teaching statistics and probability.* (1981 Yearbook). Reston, VA: Author.

Noone, E. T., Jr. (1988). Chuck-a-luck: Learning probability concepts with games of chance. *The Mathematics Teacher, 81*(2).

Orton, R. (1988). Using subjective probability to introduce probability concepts. *School Science and Mathematics, 88*(2).

Scheinok, P. A. (1988). A summer program in probability and statistics for inner-city seventh graders. *The Mathematics Teacher, 81*(4).

Shulte, A. P. (1987). Learning probability concepts in elementary school mathematics. *The Arithmetic Teacher, 34*(5).

Vissa, J. M. (1988). Probability and combinations for third graders. *The Arithmetic Teacher, 36*(4).

Vissa, J. M. (1987). Sampling treats for a school of fish (tagging goldfish crackers to teach estimation; proportions; central tendencies; structured sampling). *The Arithmetic Teacher, 34*(7).

Yunker, L. (1987). Random walks. In E. M. Maletsky (Ed.), *Teaching with student math notes.* Reston, VA: National Council of Teachers of Mathematics.

Standard 12:

Geometry

In grades 5-8, the mathematics curriculum should include the study of the geometry of one, two, and three dimensions in a variety of situations so that students can:

- identify, describe, compare, and classify geometric figures;
- visualize and represent geometric figures with special attention to developing spatial sense;
- explore transformations of geometric figures;
- represent and solve problems using geometric models;
- understand and apply geometric properties and relationships;
- develop an appreciation of geometry as a means of describing the physical world.

Battista, M. T., and Clements, D. H. (1991). Using spatial imagery in geometric reasoning. *The Arithmetic Teacher, 39*(3).

Brahier, D. J., Hodapp, S., Martin, R., and Speer, W. R. (1992). Ideas—beginning a new school year. *The Arithmetic Teacher, 40*(1).

Bright, G. W. (1989). Teaching mathematics with technology: Logo and geometry. *The Arithmetic Teacher, 37*(1).

Burger, W. F. (1988). An active approach to geometry. *The Arithmetic Teacher, 36*(3).

Butzow, J. W. (1986). Y is for yacht race: A game of angles. *The Arithmetic Teacher, 33*(5).

Claus, A. (1992). Exploring geometry. *The Arithmetic Teacher, 40*(1).

Clements, D. C., and Battista, M. (1986). Geometry and geometric measurement. *The Arithmetic Teacher, 33*(6).

Creamer, K., Ott, J. M., and Sommers, D. P. (1983). But why does $C = \pi rd$? *The Arithmetic Teacher, 31*(3).

Gerve, R. (1990). Discovering pi—two approaches. *The Arithmetic Teacher, 37*(8).

Giganti, P. Jr., and Cittadino, M. J. (1990). The art of tessellation. *The Arithmetic Teacher, 37*(7).

Hands-on, Inc. (1989). *Geometry: Kindergarten through grade nine.* Solvang, CA: Author.

Hawkins, V. (1984). The Pythagorean theorem revised: Weighing the results. *The Arithmetic Teacher, 32*(4).

Hersberger, J., and Talsma, G. (1991). Improving students' understanding of geometric definitions. *The Mathematics Teacher, 84*(7).

Izard, J. (1990). Developing spatial skills with three-dimensional puzzles. *The Arithmetic Teacher, 37*(6).

Jensen, R. J. (1988). Teaching mathematics with technology. Concept formation in geometry: A computer-aided, student-centered activity. *The Arithmetic Teacher, 35*(7).

Juraschek, W. (1990). Get in touch with shape. *The Arithmetic Teacher, 37*(8).

Kaiser, B. (1988). Explorations with tessellating polygons. *The Arithmetic Teacher, 36*(4).

Kriegler, S. (1991). The tangram—more than an ancient puzzle. *The Arithmetic Teacher, 38*(9).

Krulik, S. (1987). Networks. In E. M. Maletsky (Ed.), *Teaching with student math notes.* Reston, VA: National Council of Teachers of Mathematics.

Larke, P. J. (1988). Geometric extravaganza: Spicing up geometry. *The Arithmetic Teacher, 36*(1).

Maletsky, E. (1987). Visualization. In E. M. Maletsky (Ed.), *Teaching with student math notes.* Reston, VA: National Council of Teachers of Mathematics.

Mansfield, H. (1985). Projective geometry in the elementary school. *The Arithmetic Teacher, 37*(7).

Mitchell, C. (1986). Astronomy, geometry, and the ancient greeks. *The Arithmetic Teacher, 33*(9).

Morrow, L. J. (1991). Geometry through the standards. *The Arithmetic Teacher, 38*(8).

National Council of Teachers of Mathematics. (1992). *Curriculum and evaluation standards for school mathematics addenda series grades 5-8: Geometry in the middle grades.* Reston, VA: Author.

Pappas, C. C., and Bush, S. (1989). Facilitating understanding of geometry. *The Arithmetic Teacher, 36*(8).

Periera-Mendoza, L. (1993). What is a quadrilateral? *The Arithmetic Teacher, 41*(4).

Renshaw, B. (1986). Symmetry the trademark way. *The Arithmetic Teacher, 34*(1).

Rowan, T. E. (1990). The geometry standards in K-8 mathematics. *The Arithmetic Teacher, 37*(6).

Seymour, D. (1987). Tessellations: Patterns in geometry. In E. M. Maletsky (Ed.), *Teaching with student math notes.* Reston, VA: National Council of Teachers of Mathematics.

Sgori, R. J. (1990). Communicating about spatial relationships. *The Arithmetic Teacher, 37*(6).

Smith, L. R. (1990). Areas and perimeters of geoboard polygons. *The Mathematics Teacher, 84*(5).

Taylor, L. (1992). Exploring geometry with the *Geometer's Sketchpad. The Arithmetic Teacher, 40*(2).

Whitman, N. (1991). Line and rotational symmetry. *The Mathematics Teacher, 84*(8).

Willcutt, B. (1987). Triangular tiles for your patio? *The Arithmetic Teacher, 34*(9).

Woodward, E., and Brown, R. (1994). Polydrons and three-dimensional geometry. *The Arithmetic Teacher, 41*(8).

Woodward, E., Gibbs, V., and Shoulders, M. (1992). A fifth-grade similarity unit. *The Arithmetic Teacher, 39*(8).

Zaslavsky, C.(1991). Symmetry in american folk art. *The Arithmetic Teacher, 38*(1).

Standard 13:

Measurement

In grades 5-8, the mathematics curriculum should include extensive concrete experiences using measurement so that students can:

- extend their understanding of the process of measurement;
- estimate, make, and use measurements to describe and compare phenomena;
- select appropriate units and tools to measure to the degree of accuracy required in a particular situation;
- understand the structure and use of systems of measurement;
- extend their understanding of the concepts of perimeter, area, volume, angle measure, capacity, and weight and mass;
- develop the concepts of rates and other derived and indirect measurements;
- develop formulas and procedures for determining measures to solve problems.

Bass, H. (1993). Let's measure what's worth measuring. *Education Week, 13*(8).

Coburn, T. G. (1987). Estimation and mental computation (teaching measurement estimation). *The Arithmetic Teacher, 34.*

Coffield, P. (1987). Pi: The digit hunt. In E. M. Maletsky (Ed.), *Teaching with student math notes.* Reston, VA: National Council of Teachers of Mathematics.

Corwin, R. B., and Russell, S. J. (1990). Measuring: From paces to feet. From *Used numbers: Real data in the classroom.* Palo Alto, CA: Dale Seymour Publications.

Drean, T., and Souviney, R. (1992). *Measurement investigations.* Palo Alto, CA: Dale Seymour Publications.

Fay, N., and Tsairides, C. (1989). Metric mall. *The Arithmetic Teacher, 37*(1).

Hands-on, Inc. (1991). *Measurement: Grades three through eight.* Solvang, CA: Author.

Harrison, W. R. (1987). What lies behind measurement? *The Arithmetic Teacher, 34*(7).

Jamber, M. (1993). Make metrics matter? *Teaching PreK-8, 23*(4).

Landers, M. G. (1994). From the file: Conversion of measurements. *The Arithmetic Teacher, 41*(8).

Ligon, H. (1992). Metric mania. *Science Teacher, 59*(7).

Lindquist, M. M., and Rowan, T. E. (1989). Implementing the standards: The measurement standards. *The Arithmetic Teacher, 37*(2).

Markovits, Z., Hershkowitz, R., Taizi, N., and Bruckheimer, M. (1986). Estimeasure. *The Arithmetic Teacher, 34*(4).

National Council of Teachers of Mathematics. (1994). *Curriculum and evaluation standards for school mathematics addenda series grades 5-8: Measurement in the middle grades.* Reston, VA: Author.

Neufeld, K. A. (1989). Body measurement. *The Arithmetic Teacher, 36*(9).

Routledge, J. (1985). What's cooking? *The Arithmetic Teacher, 33*(2).

Smith, R. (1989). Made to measure. *Mathematics Teaching, 128.*

Sovchik, R., and Meconi, L.J. (1994). IDEAS: Measurement. *The Arithmetic Teacher, 41*(5).

AN EXAMPLE OF A CURRICULUM STANDARD*

The National Council of Teachers of Mathematics publication, *Curriculum and Evaluation Standards for School Mathematics,* lists a total of forty standards for grades K-8. These include thirteen standards for grades K-4, thirteen standards for grades 5-8, and fourteen standards of evaluation. The shortened statements of appropriate standards appear earlier in this chapter. The following is a sample complete standard. Those wishing more information are directed to the National Council of Teachers of Mathematics, 1906 Association Drive, Reston, VA 20191.

Standard 10:

Statistics

In grades 5-8, the mathematics curriculum should include the exploration of statistics in real-world situations so that students can:

- systematically collect, organize, and describe data;
- construct, read, and interpret tables, charts, and graphs;
- make inferences and convincing arguments that are based on data analysis;
- evaluate arguments that are based on data analysis;
- develop an appreciation for statistical methods as powerful means for decision making.

Focus

In this age of information and technology, an ever-increasing need exists to understand how information is processed and translated into usable knowledge. Because of society's expanding use of data for prediction and decision making, it is important that students develop an understanding of the concepts and processes used in analyzing data. A knowledge of statistics is necessary if students are to become intelligent consumers who can make critical and informed decisions.

In grades K-4, students begin to explore basic ideas of statistics by gathering data appropriate to their grade level, organizing them in charts or graphs, and reading information from displays of data. These concepts should be expanded in the middle grades. Students in grades 5-8 have a keen interest in trends in music, movies, fashion, and sports. An investigation of how such trends are developed and communicated is an excellent motivator for the study of statistics. Students need to be actively involved in each of the steps that comprise statistics, from gathering information to communicating results.

Identifying the range or average of a set of data, constructing simple graphs, and reading data points as answers to specific questions are important activities, but they reflect only a very narrow aspect of statistics. Instead, instruction in statistics should focus on the active involvement of students in the entire process: formulating key questions; collecting and organizing data; representing the data using graphs, tables, frequency distributions, and summary statistics; analyzing the data; making conjectures; and communicating information in a convincing way. Students' understanding of statistics is also enhanced by opportunities to evaluate others' arguments. This exercise is of particular importance to all students, since advertising, forecasting, and public policy are frequently based on data analysis.

Discussion

Middle-school students' curiosity about themselves, their peers, and their surroundings can motivate them to study statistics. The data to be gathered, organized, and studied should be interesting and relevant; students' interest in themselves and their peers, for example, can motivate them to investigate the "average student" in the class or school. First, students can formulate questions to determine the characteristics of an "average student"—age, height, eye color, favorite music or TV show, number of people in family, pets at home, and so on. Although numerous categories are possible, some discussion will help students to develop a survey instrument to obtain appropriate data. Sampling procedures are a critical issue in data collection. Which students should be surveyed to determine Mr. or Ms. Average? Must every student be questioned? If not, how can randomness in the sampling be assured and how many samples are needed to accumulate enough data to describe the average student?

Random samples, bias in sampling procedures, and limited samples are all important considerations. For instance, would collecting data from the men's and women's basketball teams provide needed information to determine the average height of a college student? Will a larger sample reveal a more accurate picture of the percentage of students with brown hair? The graph in Figure 1 illustrates the results of increasing the sample size.

Data can be presented in many forms: charts, tables, plots (e.g. stem and leaf, box and whiskers, and scatter), and graphs (e.g. bar, circle, or line). See Figure 2. Each form has a different impact on the picture of the information being presented, and each conveys a different perspective. The choice of form depends on the questions that are to be answered. Using the same data, students can develop graphs with different scales to show how the change of scale can dramatically alter the visual message that is communicated.

Computer software can greatly enhance the organization and representation of data. Database programs offer a means for students to structure, record, and investigate information; to sort it quickly by various categories; and to organize it in a variety of ways. Other programs can be used to construct plots and graphs to display data. Scale changes can be made to compare different views of the same information.

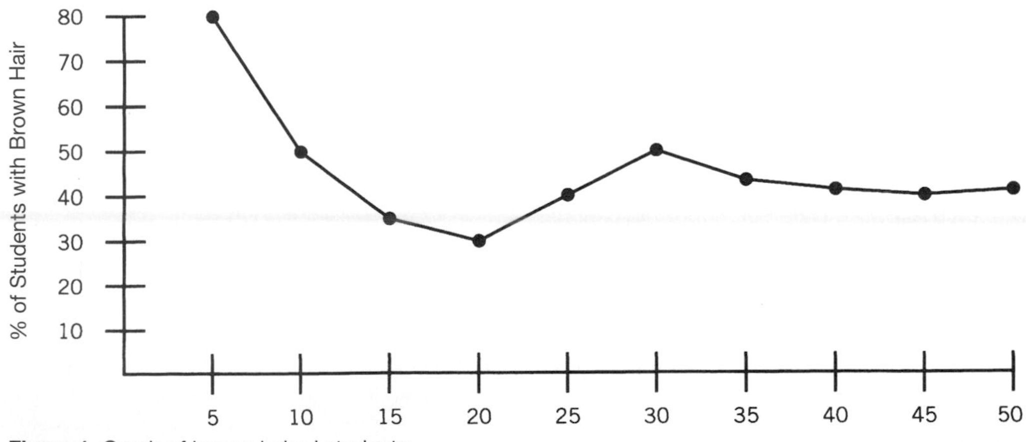

Figure 1. Graph of brown-haired students

Number with Brown Hair	4	5	5	6	10	15	16	17	18	21
Students Sampled	5	10	15	20	25	30	35	40	45	50

Figure 2. Data table

These technological tools free students to spend more time exploring the essence of statistics: analyzing data from many viewpoints, drawing inferences, and constructing and evaluating arguments.

A particular point that should be raised with students is how "average" relates to numerical and nonnumerical data. Although there are several measures of central tendency, students are generally exposed only to the mean or median, yet the mode might be the best "average" for a set of nonnumerical data.

Students also should explore the concepts of center and dispersion of data. The following activity includes all of the important elements of this standard and illustrates the use of box-and-whisker plots as an effective means of describing data and showing variation.

A class is divided into two large groups, and then subdivided into pairs. One student in each pair estimates when one minute has passed and the other watches the clock and records the actual time. All of the students in one group concentrate on the timing task, while half of the students in the second exert constant efforts to distract their partners. The box plots show that the median times for the two groups are about the same, but the times for the distracted group have greater variation. Note that in the distracted group, one data point is far enough removed from the others to be an outlier. See Figure 3.

Sports statistics and other real data provide settings in which students can generate new data and investigate a variety of conjectures. The table in Figure 4 contains some information from an NBA championship game between Los Angeles and Boston.

Using the table, students can generate such new information as: points/minute, rebounds/minute, points/field goals attempted. Who is the best percentage shooter? From another source, they can find the height of each player and determine rebounds/inch of height or points/inch of height.

A problem like this is ideally suited to the curious nature of middle-school students and opens up a world of questions and investigations to them.

Formulating key questions, interpreting graphs and charts, and solving problems are important goals in the study of statistics. Statistics can help answer questions that do not lend themselves to direct measurement. Once data are collected and organized, such questions as the following can guide students in interpreting the data:

What appears most often in the data?
What trends appear in the data?
What is the significance of outliers?
What interpretations can we draw from these data, and can we use our interpretations to make predictions?
What difficulties might we encounter when extending the interpretations or predictions to other, related problems?
What additional data can we collect to verify or disprove the ideas developed from these data?

All media are full of graphical representations of data and different kinds of statistical claims that can be used to stimulate discussion of the message conveyed and the arguments presented in the data.

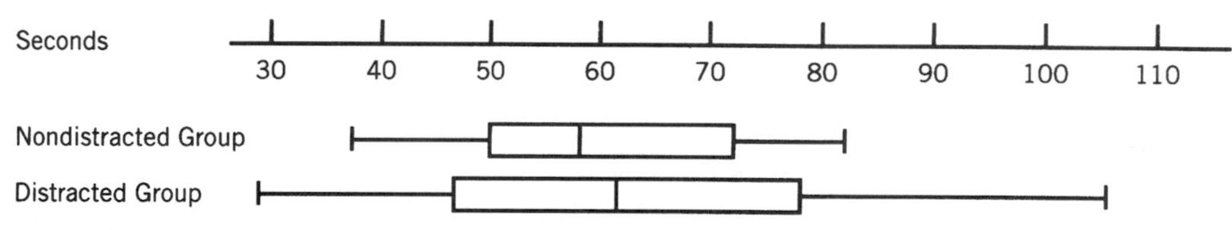

Figure 3. Time estimates

Player	Min.	FG-A	Reb.	Asst.	Pts.
Worthy	37	8–19	8	5	20
Johnson	34	8–14	1	12	19
Bird	31	8–14	6	9	19
McHale	32	10–16	9	0	26

Figure 4. NBA championship series

Suggested Readings

American Association for the Advancement of Science. (1989). *Science for all Americans: A project 2061 panel report on literacy goals in science, mathematics, and technology.* Washington, D.C.: Author.

Atwater, M. M., Radzik-Marsh, K., and Strutchens, M., (Eds.). (1994). *Multicultural education: Inclusion of all, Athens,* GA: The University of Georgia.

Bjork, E. D., and Driscoll, M. (1988). Change in the mathematics curriculum. *The Arithmetic Teacher, 36*(2).

Bodner, G. M. (1986). *Constructivism: A theory of knowledge,* New York: Wiley.

Bruner, J. S. (1968).*Toward a theory of instruction.* New York: W. W. Norton and Company.

California State Department of Education. (1987). *Mathematics: Model curriculum guide, kindergarten through grade eight.* Sacramento, CA: California State Department of Education.

Chambers, D. L. (1990). School mathematics reform: Making the vision a reality. *School Science and Mathematics, 90*(6).

Cobb, P.(1988). The tension between theories of learning and instruction in mathematics education. *Educational Psychologist, 23*(2).

Committee on the Mathematical Education of Teachers. (1991). *A call for change: Recommendations for the mathematical preparation of teachers of mathematics.* Washington, D.C.: The Mathematical Association of America.

Conference Board of the Mathematical Sciences. (1983). The mathematical sciences curriculum K-12: What is still fundamental and what is not. In *Educating americans for the 21st century: Source materials.* National Science Board Commission on Precollege Education in Mathematics, Science, and Technology. Washington, D.C.: National Science Foundation.

Cooney, T. J., (Ed.). (1990). *Teaching and learning mathematics in the 1990s.* Reston, VA: National Council of Teachers of Mathematics.

Crosswhite, F. J. (1990). National standards: A new dimension in professional leadership. *School Science and Mathematics, 90*(6).

Crosswhite, F. J., Dossey, J. A., and Frye, S. M. (1989). Standards for school mathematics: Visions for implementation. *The Arithmetic Teacher, 37*(3).

Crosswhite, F. J., Dossey, J. A., Swafford, J. O., McKnight, C. C., Cooney, T. J., Downs, F. L., Grouws, D. A., and Weinzweig, A. I. (1986). *Second international mathematics study: Detailed report for the united states.* Champaign, IL: Stipes Publishing Company.

Crowley, M. (1987).The van Hiele model of the development of geometric thought. In Lindquist, M. M., and Shulte, A. P., (Eds.). *Learning and teaching geometry, K-12.* Reston, VA: National Council of Teachers of Mathematics.

Davis, R. B., Maher, C. A., and Noddings, N., (Eds.). (1990). *Constructivist views of the teaching and learning of mathematics.* Reston, VA: National Council of Teachers of Mathematics.

Denham, W. F., and O'Malley, E. T., (Eds.). (1985). *Mathematics framework for California public schools, kindergarten through grade twelve.* Sacramento, CA: California State Department of Education.

Dewey, J. (1974). The child and the curriculum. In Archambault, R. D., (Ed.). *John Dewey on education.* Chicago: University of Chicago Press.

Dienes, Z. P. (1960). *Building up mathematics.* London: Hutchinson Educational.

Dossey, J. A., Mullis, I. V. S., Lindquist, M. M., and Chambers, D. (1988). *The mathematics report card: Are we measuring up?* Princeton, NJ: Educational Testing Service.

Flanders, J. R. (1987). How much of the content in mathematics textbooks is New? *The Arithmetic Teacher, 35*(1).

Fosnot, C. T. (1989). *Enquiring teachers, enquiring learners: A constructivist approach for teaching.* New York: Teachers College Press.

Frye, S. M. (1989). The NCTM standards—challenges for all classrooms. *The Arithmetic Teacher, 37*(9).

Fuys, D., Geddes, D., and Tischler, R. (1988). The van Hiele model of thinking in geometry among adolescents. In *Journal for Research in Mathematics Education.* Reston, VA: National Council of Teachers of Mathematics.

Gagne, R. M. (1965). *The conditions of learning.* New York: Holt, Rinehart & Winston.

Harris, M., (Ed.). (1991). *Schools, mathematics and work.* Bristol, PA: Falmer Press.

Hatfield, M. M., and Price, J. (1992). Promoting local change: Models for implementing NCTM's curriculum and evaluation standards. *The Arithmetic Teacher, 39*(5).

Jacobs, H. H. (1993). Mathematics integration: A common-sense approach to curriculum development. *The Arithmetic Teacher, 40*(6).

Johnson, H. C. (1990). How can the curriculum and evaluation standards for school mathematics be realized for all students? *School Science and Mathematics, 90*(6).

Johnston, W. B., and Packers, A. E. (1987). *Workforce 2000: Work and workers for the twenty-first century.* Indianapolis, IN: Hudson Institute.

Kamii, C. (1985). *Young children reinvent arithmetic: Implications of Piaget's theory.* New York: Teachers College Press.

Lapointe, A. E., Mead, N. A., and Askew, J. M. (1991). *Learning mathematics: The international assessment of educational progress.* Princeton, NJ: Educational Testing Service.

Lapointe, A. E., Mead, N. A., and Phillips, G. W. (1989). *A world of differences.* Princeton, NJ: Educational Testing Service.

Lappan, G., and Ferrini-Mundy, J. (1990). Implementing the NCTM curriculum and evaluation standards for school mathematics in grades 5-8: Obstacles and opportunities. *School Science and Mathematics, 90*(6).

Mathematical Sciences Education Board. (1990). *Mathematics education: Wellspring of U.S. industrial strength.* Washington, D.C.: National Research Council.

Mathematical Sciences Education Board. (1990). *Reshaping school mathematics: A philosophy and framework for curriculum.* Washington, D.C.: National Academy Press.

McKnight, C. C., Crosswhite, F. J., Dossey, J. A., Kifer, E., Swafford, J. O., Travers, K. J., and Cooney, T. J. (1987). *The underachieving curriculum: Assessing U.S. school mathematics from an international perspective.* Champaign, IL: Stipes Publishing Company.

Montgomery, M., (Ed.). (1989). *Results from the fourth mathematics assessment of the national assessment of educational progress.* Reston, VA: National Council of Teachers of Mathematics.

National Commission on Excellence in Education. (1983). *A nation at risk: The imperative for educational reform.* Washington, D.C.: U.S. Government Printing Office.

National Council of Supervisors of Mathematics. (1989). Essential mathematics for the twenty-first century: The position of the national council of supervisors of mathematics. *The Arithmetic Teacher, 37*(1).

National Council of Teachers of Mathematics. (1995). *Assessment standards for school mathematics.* Reston, VA: National Council of Teachers of Mathematics.

National Council of Teachers of Mathematics. (1989). *Curriculum and evaluation standards for school mathematics.* Reston, VA: National Council of Teachers of Mathematics.

National Council of Teachers of Mathematics. (1991). *Curriculum and evaluation standards for school mathematics addenda series: Kindergarten book.* Reston, VA: National Council of Teachers of Mathematics.

National Council of Teachers of Mathematics. (1991). *Curriculum and evaluation standards for school mathematics addenda series: First-grade book.* Reston, VA: National Council of Teachers of Mathematics.

National Council of Teachers of Mathematics. (1992). *Curriculum and evaluation standards for school mathematics addenda series: Second-grade book.* Reston, VA: National Council of Teachers of Mathematics.

National Council of Teachers of Mathematics. (1992). *Curriculum and evaluation standards for school mathematics addenda series: Third-grade book.* Reston, VA: National Council of Teachers of Mathematics.

National Council of Teachers of Mathematics. (1992). *Curriculum and evaluation standards for school mathematics addenda series: Fourth-grade book.* Reston, VA: National Council of Teachers of Mathematics.

National Council of Teachers of Mathematics. (1992). *Curriculum and evaluation standards for school mathematics addenda series: Fifth-grade book.* Reston, VA: National Council of Teachers of Mathematics.

National Council of Teachers of Mathematics. (1992). *Curriculum and evaluation standards for school mathematics addenda series: Sixth-grade book.* Reston, VA: National Council of Teachers of Mathematics.

National Council of Teachers of Mathematics. (1992). *Curriculum and evaluation standards for school mathematics addenda series grades K-4: Making sense of data.* Reston, VA: National Council of Teachers of Mathematics.

National Council of Teachers of Mathematics. (1993). *Curriculum and evaluation standards for school mathematics addenda series grades K-4: Number sense and operations.* Reston, VA: National Council of Teachers of Mathematics.

National Council of Teachers of Mathematics. (1993). *Curriculum and evaluation standards for school mathematics addenda series grades K-4: geometry and spatial sense.* Reston, VA: National Council of Teachers of Mathematics.

National Council of Teachers of Mathematics. (1993). *Curriculum and evaluation standards for school mathematics addenda series grades K-4: Patterns.* Reston, VA: National Council of Teachers of Mathematics.

National Council of Teachers of Mathematics. (1991). *Curriculum and evaluation standards for school mathematics addenda series grades 5-8: Dealing with data and chance.* Reston, VA: National Council of Teachers of Mathematics.

National Council of Teachers of Mathematics. (1991). *Curriculum and evaluation standards for school mathematics addenda series grades 5-8: Developing number sense.* Reston, VA: National Council of Teachers of Mathematics.

National Council of Teachers of Mathematics. (1991). *Curriculum and evaluation standards for school mathematics addenda series grades 5-8: Patterns and functions.* Reston, VA: National Council of Teachers of Mathematics.

National Council of Teachers of Mathematics. (1992). *Curriculum and evaluation standards for school mathematics addenda series grades 5-8: Geometry in the middle grades.* Reston, VA: National Council of Teachers of Mathematics.

National Council of Teachers of Mathematics. (1993). *Implementing the K-8 curriculum and evaluation standards.* Reston, VA: National Council of Teachers of Mathematics.

National Council of Teachers of Mathematics. (1991). *Professional standards for teaching mathematics.* Reston, VA: National Council of Teachers of Mathematics.

National Research Council. (1989). *Everybody counts: A Report to the nation on the future of mathematics education.* Washington, D.C.: National Academy Press.

National Research Council. (1990). *Renewing U.S. mathematics: A plan for the 1990's.* Washington, D.C.: National Academy Press.

Ohio Department of Education. (1988). *Mathematics grade level monographs (overview and K-8e).* Columbus: Ohio Department of Education.

Ohio Department of Education. (1990). *Model competency-based mathematics program.* Columbus, OH: Ohio Department of Education.

Papert, S. (1980). *Mindstorms: Children, computers, and powerful ideas.* New York: Basic Books.

Piaget, J. (1954). *The construction of reality in the child.* New York: Basic Books.

Piaget, J. (1965). *The child's conception of number.* New York: Norton.

Piaget, J. (1973). *To understand is to invent.* New York: Grossman Publishers.

Polya, G. (1957). *How to solve it* (2nd ed.). Garden City, NY: Doubleday.

Rathmell, E. C., and Thompson, C. S. (1988). NCTM's standards for school mathematics, K-12. *The Arithmetic Teacher, 35*(9).

Resnick, L. B. (1987). *Education and learning to think.* Washington, D.C.: National Academy Press.

Romberg, T. A. (1990). Evidence which supports NCTM's curriculum and evaluation standards for school mathematics. *School Science and Mathematics, 90*(6).

Romberg, T. A. (1988). NCTM's curriculum and evaluation standards: What they are and why they are needed. *The Arithmetic Teacher, 35*(9).

Schifter, D., and Fosnot, C. T. (1993). *Reconstructing mathematics education: Stories of teachers meeting the challenge of reform.* New York, NY: Teachers College Press.

Shufelt, G., (Ed.). (1983). *The agenda in action.* Reston, VA: National Council of Teachers of Mathematics.

Silver, E. A., Kilpatrick, J., and Schlesinger, B. (1990). *Thinking through mathematics: Fostering inquiry and communication in mathematics classrooms.* New York, NY: The College Board.

Skemp, R. R. (1971). *The psychology of learning mathematics.* Baltimore: Penguin Books.

Speer, W. R., and Brahier, D. J. (1994). Rethinking the teaching and learning of mathematics. In C. A. Thornton, (Ed.). *Windows of opportunity: Mathematics for students with special needs.* Reston, VA: National Council of Teachers of Mathematics.

Stenmark, J. K. (1989). *Assessment alternatives in mathematics.* Berkeley: EQUALS and the California Mathematics Council.

Thompson, P. W. (1994). Concrete materials and teaching for mathematical understanding. *The Arithmetic Teacher, 41*(9).

Thornton, C. A., (Ed.). (1994). *Windows of opportunity: Mathematics for students with special needs.* Reston, VA: National Council of Teachers of Mathematics.

Tobias, S. (1978). *Overcoming math anxiety.* Boston: Houghton Mifflin.

Trafton, P. R., and Bloom, S. J. (1990). Understanding and implementing NCTM curriculum and evaluation standards for school mathematics in grades K-4. *School Science and Mathematics, 90*(6).

U.S. Department of Education. (1991). *America 2000.* Washington, D.C.: U.S. Government Printing Office.

U.S. Department of Labor. (1991). *What work requires of schools: A SCANS report for america 2000.* Washington, D.C.: U.S. Government Printing Office.

van Hiele, P. M. (1986). *Structure and insight.* Orlando, FL: Academic Press.

Vygotsky, L. S. (1978). *Mind in society.* Cambridge, MA: Harvard University Press.

Vygotsky, L. S. (1962). *Thought and language.* Cambridge, MA: M.I.T. Press.

Walsh, J. B. (1990). The NCTM curriculum and evaluation standards for school mathematics: A business perspective. *School Science and Mathematics, 90*(6).

Wheatley, G. J.(1991). Constructivist perspectives on science and mathematics learning. *Science Education, 75*(1).

Wirszup, I., and Streit, R., (Eds.). (1987). *Developments in school mathematics education around the world.* Reston, VA: National Council of Teachers of Mathematics.

Chapter 2

Teaching Mathematics

Overview

In 1991, the National Council of Teachers of Mathematics issued a publication entitled *Professional Standards for Teaching Mathematics.* This companion document to the previously issued *Curriculum and Evaluation Standards for School Mathematics* (1989) represents a set of guidelines designed to address the various aspects of professional mathematics teaching. These professional teaching standards have been grouped into four major categories—standards for teaching mathematics, for evaluation of teaching, for professional development of teachers of mathematics, and for support and development of mathematics teachers and teaching.

Section one, the standards for teaching mathematics, deals with a vision of teaching and learning mathematics that illuminates, supports, and assists the implementation of the *Curriculum and Evaluation Standards for School Mathematics.* Section two, standards for evaluation, describes the nature and purpose of the evaluation of teaching and the roles that should be played by those involved in this evaluation. The third section of standards focuses on guidelines for the preparation of preservice teachers and the continuing education of in-service teachers of mathematics at the K-12 levels. The final section, on support and development, identifies the responsibilities shared by various groups, such as school boards, professional organizations, and policymakers in government, business, and industry, who help shape the environment in which the teachers will teach and the learners will learn mathematics.

Although each of the four categories deserves attention and elaboration, the scope of this book requires that we devote most of our attention to the first set of standards—those focusing on standards for teaching mathematics. Readers who seek a more comprehensive discussion of the full set are encouraged to purchase a copy of the *Professional Standards for Teaching Mathematics* from the National Council of Teachers of Mathematics, 1906 Association Drive, Reston, VA 20191.

NCTM PROFESSIONAL STANDARDS FOR TEACHING

The NCTM teaching standards represent an image of mathematics teaching in which teachers are more proficient in:

- selecting mathematical tasks to engage students' interests and intellect;
- providing opportunities to deepen their understanding of the mathematics being studied and its applications;
- orchestrating classroom discourse in ways that promote the investigation and growth of mathematical ideas;
- using, and helping students use, technology and other tools to pursue mathematical investigations;
- seeking, and helping students seek, connections to previous and developing knowledge;
- guiding individual, small-group, and whole-class work. (*Professional Standards for Teaching Mathematics,* 1991, p. 1)

The six standards that refer to the teaching process are described in the following sections.*

Standard 1:

Worthwhile Mathematical Tasks

The teacher of mathematics should pose tasks that are based on—

- sound and significant mathematics;
- knowledge of students' understandings, interests, and experiences;
- knowledge of the range of ways that diverse students learn mathematics;

and that

- engage students' intellect;
- develop students' mathematical understandings and skills;
- stimulate students to make connections and develop a coherent framework for mathematical ideas;
- call for problem formulation, problem solving, and mathematical reasoning;
- promote communication about mathematics;
- represent mathematics as an ongoing human activity;
- display sensitivity to, and draw on, students' diverse background experiences and dispositions;
- promote the development of all students' dispositions to do mathematics.

*Reprinted with permission from *Professional Standards for Teaching Mathematics,* copyright 1991 by the National Council of Teachers of Mathematics.

Standard 2:

Teachers Role in Discourse

The teacher of mathematics should orchestrate discourse by—

- posing questions and tasks that elicit, engage, and challenge each student's thinking;
- listening carefully to students' ideas;
- asking students to clarify and justify their ideas orally and in writing;
- deciding what to pursue in depth from among the ideas that students bring up during a discussion;
- deciding when and how to attach mathematical notation and language to students' ideas;
- deciding when to provide information, when to clarify an issue, when to model, when to lead, and when to let a student struggle with a difficulty;
- monitoring students' participation in discussions and deciding when and how to encourage each student to participate.

Standard 3:

Students Role in Discourse

The teacher of mathematics should promote classroom discourse in which students—

- listen to, respond to, and question the teacher and one another;
- use a variety of tools to reason, make connections, solve problems, and communicate;
- initiate problems and questions;
- make conjectures and present solutions;
- explore examples and counterexamples to investigate a conjecture;
- try to convince themselves and one another of the validity of particular representations, solutions, conjectures, and answers;
- rely on mathematical evidence and argument to determine validity.

Standard 4:

Tools for Enhancing Discourse

The teacher of mathematics, in order to enhance discourse, should encourage and accept the use of—

- computers, calculators, and other technology;
- concrete materials used as models;
- pictures, diagrams, tables, and graphs;
- invented and conventional terms and symbols;
- metaphors, analogies, and stories;
- written hypotheses, explanations, and arguments;
- oral presentations and dramatizations.

Standard 5:

Learning Environment

The teacher of mathematics should create a learning environment that fosters the development of each student's mathematical power by—

- providing and structuring the time necessary to explore sound mathematics and grapple with significant ideas and problems;
- using the physical space and materials in ways that facilitate students' learning of mathematics;
- providing a context that encourages the development of mathematical skill and proficiency;
- respecting and valuing students' ideas, ways of thinking, and mathematical dispositions;

and by consistently expecting and encouraging students to—

- work independently or collaboratively to make sense of mathematics;
- take intellectual risks by raising questions and formulating conjectures;
- display a sense of mathematical competence by validating and supporting ideas with mathematical argument.

Standard 6:

Analysis of Teaching and Learning

The teacher of mathematics should engage in ongoing analysis of teaching and learning by—

- observing, listening to, and gathering other information about students to assess what they are learning;
- examining effects of the tasks, discourse, and learning environment on students' mathematical knowledge, skills, and dispositions;

in order to—

- ensure that every student is learning sound and significant mathematics and is developing a positive disposition toward mathematics;
- challenge and extend students' ideas;
- adapt or change activities while teaching;
- make plans, both short- and long-range;
- describe and comment on each student's learning to parents and administrators, as well as to the students themselves.

Related Readings

Ball, D. L. (1988). *The subject matter preparation of prospective mathematics teachers: Challenging the myths.* East Lansing, MI: National Center for Research on Teacher Education.

Ball, D. L. (1988). Unlearning to teach mathematics. *For the Learning of Mathematics, 8.*

Ball, D. L., and Feiman-Nemser, S. (1988). Using textbooks and teachers' guides: A dilemma for beginning teachers and teacher educators. *Curriculum Inquiry, 18.*

Ball, D. L. (1991). Implementing the professional standards for teaching mathematics: What's all this talk about discourse? *The Arithmetic Teacher, 39*(3).

Briars, D. J., and Thompson, A. G. (1989). Assessing students' learning to inform teaching: The message in NCTM's evaluation standards. *The Arithmetic Teacher, 37*(4).

Burns, M. (1988). *A collection of math lessons.* New Rochelle, NY: Cuisenaire Company of America.

Burns, M. (1988). Helping your students make sense out of math. *Learning.*

Cooney, T. J., (Ed.). (1990). *Teaching and learning mathematics in the 1990s.* Reston, VA: National Council of Teachers of Mathematics.

Cooney, T. J. (1992). Implementing the professional standards for teaching mathematics: Evaluating the teaching of mathematics: The road to progress and Reform. *The Arithmetic Teacher, 39*(6).

Corwin, R. B. (1993). Implementing the professional standards for teaching mathematics: doing mathematics together: Creating a mathematical culture. *The Arithmetic Teacher, 40*(6).

Crosswhite, F. J. (1986). President's report: Better teaching, better mathematics: Are they enough? *The Arithmetic Teacher, 34*(2).

Davis, R. B., Maher, C. A., and Noddings, N., (Eds.). (1990). *Constructivist views of the teaching and learning of mathematics.* Reston, VA: National Council of Teachers of Mathematics.

Dossey, J. A. (1988). Learning, teaching, and standards. *The Arithmetic Teacher, 35*(8).

Driscoll, M. J. (1981). Learning elementary school mathematics: Individual styles and individual needs. In M. J. Driscoll (Ed.), *Research within reach: Elementary school mathematics.* Reston, VA: National Council of Teachers of Mathematics and CEMREL, Inc.

Driscoll, M. J. (1981). Teaching for remediation in mathematics. In M. J. Driscoll (Ed.), *Research within reach: Elementary school mathematics.* Reston, VA: National Council of Teachers of Mathematics and CEMREL, Inc.

Driscoll, M. J. (1981). The teacher and the textbook. In M. J. Driscoll (Ed.), *Research within reach: Elementary school mathematics.* Reston, VA: National Council of Teachers of Mathematics and CEMREL, Inc.

Fosnot, C. T. (1989). *Enquiring teachers, enquiring learners: A constructivist approach for teaching.* New York: Teachers College Press.

Frank, M. L. (1990). What myths about mathematics are held and conveyed by teachers? *The Arithmetic Teacher, 37*(5).

Friel, S. N., Ball, D. L., Cooney, T. J., and Lappan, G. (1990). Envisioning change in the practice of mathematics teaching: The NCTM's professional standards for teaching mathematics. *School Science and Mathematics, 90*(6).

Greenwood, J. J. (1993). On the nature of teaching and assessing 'mathematical power' and 'mathematical thinking'. *The Arithmetic Teacher, 41*(3).

Grouws, D. A., Cooney, T. J., and Jones, D. (Eds.). (1988). *Perspectives on research on effective mathematics teaching.* Reston, VA: National Council of Teachers of Mathematics.

Johnson, H. C. (1990). How can the curriculum and evaluation standards for school mathematics be realized for all students? *School Science and Mathematics, 90*(7).

Joyner, J. M. (1994). Implementing the professional standards for teaching: Linking teaching, learning, and assessment. *The Arithmetic Teacher, 41*(9).

Keedy, M. L. (1989). Textbooks and curriculum—whose dilemma? *The Arithmetic Teacher, 36*(7).

Lambdin, D. V., Kloosterman, P., and Johnson, M. (1994). Connecting research to teaching. *Mathematics Teaching in the Middle School, 1*(1).

Lampert, M. (1988). What can research on teacher education tell us about improving the quality of mathematics education. *Teaching and Teacher Education, 4*(2).

Leinhardt, G., and Putnam, R. R. (1986). Profile of expertise in elementary school mathematics teaching. *The Arithmetic Teacher, 33*(4).

Lubinski, C. A. (1994). Implementing the professional standards for teaching: The influence of teachers' beliefs and knowledge on learning environments. *The Arithmetic Teacher, 41*(8).

Maher, C. A., and Martino, A. M. (1992). Implementing the professional standards for teaching: Teachers building on students' thinking. *The Arithmetic Teacher, 39*(7).

Mathematical Association of America. (1991). *A call for change: Recommendations for the mathematical preparation of teachers.* Washington, D.C.: Author.

Mathematical Sciences Education Board, National Research Council. (1987). *The teacher of mathematics: Issues for today and tomorrow.* Washington, D.C.: National Academy Press.

National Council of Teachers of Mathematics. (1977). *Organizing for mathematics instruction.* (1977 Yearbook). Reston, VA: Author.

National Council of Teachers of Mathematics. (1991). *Professional standards for teaching mathematics.* Reston, VA: Author.

National Council of Teachers of Mathematics. (1993). *Implementing the K-8 curriculum and evaluation standards.* Reston, VA: National Council of Teachers Mathematics.

Nelson, D., Joseph, G. G., and Williams, J. (1993). *Multicultural mathematics: Teaching mathematics from a global perspective.* Oxford, England: Oxford University Press.

Ohio Mathematics Education Leadership Council. (1989). *Real routes: A handbook for school-based mathematics leaders.* Oberlin, OH: Oberlin College Press.

Parker, R. E. (1993). *Mathematical power: Lessons from a classroom.* Portsmouth, NH: Heinemann.

Pateman, N. (1989). Teachers researching their mathematics classrooms. *The Arithmetic Teacher, 36*(2).

Rathmell, E. C. (1994). Planning for instruction involves focusing on children's thinking. *The Arithmetic Teacher, 41*(6).

Schifter, D., and Fosnot, C. T. (1993). *Reconstructing mathematics education: Stories of teachers meeting the challenge of reform.* New York: Teachers College Press.

Schmalz, R. (1994). The mathematics textbook: How can it serve the NCTM's standards? *The Arithmetic Teacher, 41*(6).

Silver, E. A., and Smith, M. S. (1990). Teaching mathematics and thinking. *The Arithmetic Teacher, 37*(8).

Simon, M. A. (1986). The teacher's role in increasing student understanding of mathematics. *Educational Leadership.*

Speer, W. R., and Brahier, D. J. (1994). Rethinking the teaching and learning of mathematics. In C. A. Thornton (Ed.), *Windows of opportunity: Mathematics for students with special needs.* Reston, VA: National Council of Teachers of Mathematics.

Thornton, C. A. (Ed.). (1994). *Windows of opportunity: Mathematics for students with special needs.* Reston, VA: National Council of Teachers of Mathematics.

Vacc, N. N. (1993). Implementing the professional standards for teaching mathematics: Questioning in the mathematics classroom. *The Arithmetic Teacher, 41*(2).

Vacc, N. N. (1994). Implementing the professional standards for teaching mathematics: Planning for instruction: Barriers to mathematics discussion. *The Arithmetic Teacher, 41*(6).

Wood, T., Cobb, P., and Yackel, E. (1991). Change in teaching mathematics: A case study. *American Educational Research Journal, 28*(3).

Worth, J. (Ed.). (1988). Preparing elementary school mathematics teachers. Readings from *The Arithmetic Teacher.* Reston, VA: National Council of Teachers of Mathematics.

AN EXAMPLE OF A TEACHING STANDARD*

The National Council of Teachers of Mathematics publication, Professional Standards for Teaching Mathematics, includes 24 standards of teaching, evaluation of teaching, development of teachers, and support responsibilities. Chapter 2 (see Part 1) of this text listed the six standards that focus on teaching mathematics.

The following is a sample complete standard from that section, including a vignette that supports the section. Readers who wish more information are directed to the National Council of Teachers of Mathematics, 1906 Association Drive, Reston, VA 20191.

Standard 2:

The Teachers Role in Discourse

The teacher of mathematics should orchestrate discourse by—

- posing questions and tasks that elicit, engage, and challenge each student's thinking;
- listening carefully to students' ideas;
- asking students to clarify and justify their ideas orally and in writing;
- deciding what to pursue in depth from among the ideas that students bring up during discussion;
- deciding when and how to attach mathematical notation and language to students' ideas;
- deciding when to provide information, when to clarify an issue, when to model, when to lead, and when to let a student struggle with a difficulty;
- monitoring students' participation in discussions and deciding when and how to encourage each student to participate.

Elaboration

Like a piece of music, the classroom discourse has themes that pull together to create a whole that has meaning. The teacher has a central role in orchestrating the oral and written discourse in ways that contribute to students' understanding of mathematics.

The kind of mathematical discourse described above does not occur spontaneously in most classrooms. It requires an environment in which everyone's thinking is respected and in which reasoning and arguing about mathematical meanings is the norm. Students, used to the teacher doing most of the talking while they remain passive, need guidance and encouragement in order to participate actively in the discourse of a collaborative community. Some students, particularly those who have been successful in more traditional mathematics classrooms, may be resistant to talking, writing and reasoning together about mathematics.

One aspect of the teacher's role is to provoke students' reasoning about mathematics. Teachers must do this through the tasks they provide and the questions they ask. For example, teachers should regularly follow students' statements with, "Why?" or by asking them to explain. Doing this consistently, irrespective of the correctness of students' statements, is an important part of establishing a discourse centered on mathematical reasoning. Cultivating a tone of interest when asking a student to explain or elaborate on an idea helps to establish norms of civility and respect rather than criticism and doubt. Teachers also stimulate discourse by asking students to write explanations for their solutions and provide justifications for their ideas.

Emphasizing tasks that focus on thinking and reasoning serves to provide the teacher with ongoing assessment information. Well-posed questions can simultaneously elicit and extend students' thinking. The teacher's skill at formulating questions to orchestrate the oral and written discourse in the direction of mathematical reasoning is crucial.

A second feature of the teacher's role is to be active in a different way from that in traditional classroom discourse. Instead of doing virtually all the talking, modeling, and explaining themselves, teachers must encourage and expect students to do so. Teachers must do more listening, students more reasoning. For the discourse to promote students' learning, teachers must orchestrate it carefully. Because many more ideas will come up than are fruitful to pursue at the moment, teachers must filter and direct the students' explorations by picking up on some points and by leaving others behind. Doing this prevents student activity and talk from becoming too diffuse and unfocused. Knowledge of mathematics, of the curriculum, and of students should guide the teacher's decisions about the path of the discourse. Other key decisions concern the teacher's role in contributing to the discourse. Beyond asking clarifying or provocative questions, teachers should also, at times, provide information and lead students. Decisions about when to let students struggle to make sense of an idea or a problem without direct teacher input, when to ask leading questions, and when to tell students something directly are crucial to orchestrating productive mathematical discourse in the classroom. Such decisions depend on teachers' understandings of mathematics and of their students on judgments about the things that students can figure out on their own or collectively and those for which they will need input.

A third aspect of the teacher's role in orchestrating classroom discourse is to monitor and organize students' participation. Who is volunteering comments and who is not? How are students responding to one another? What are different students able to record or represent on paper about their thinking? What are they able to put into words, in what kinds of contexts? Teachers must be committed to engaging every student in contributing to the thinking of the class. Teachers must judge when students should work and talk in small groups and when the whole group is the most useful context. They must make sensitive decisions about how turns to speak are shared in the large group—for example, whom to call on when and whether to call on particular students who do not volunteer. Substantively, if the discourse is to focus on making sense of mathematics, on learning to reason mathematically, teachers must refrain from calling only on students who seem to have right answers or valid ideas to allow a broader spectrum of thinking to be explored in the discourse. By modeling respect for students' thinking and conveying the assumption that students make sense, teachers can encourage students to participate within a norm that expects group members to justify their ideas. Teachers must think broadly about a variety of ways for students to contribute to the class's thinking—using means that are written or pictorial, concrete or representational, as well as oral.

A CLASSROOM TEACHING VIGNETTE

The teacher uses questions to elicit student's thinking, information that he uses to navigate the class's work.

Mr. Luu has been working on probability for a few days with his class of sixth graders. Because his textbook is old, there is little about probability in the book. He has been drawing from a variety of sources as well as making up things himself, based on what he hears in the students' comments. He began by asking students to decide whether a coin-tossing game he presented was fair or not. He found out that although most of the students did consider the possible outcomes, they did not analyze the ways those outcomes could be obtained. For example, they thought that when you toss two coins, it is equally likely to get two heads, two tails, or heads-and-tails. He also learned that many of his students were inclined to decide if a game was fair by playing it and seeing if the players tied: if someone won, then the game might be biased in their favor, they thought.

He decides to present them with two dice-tossing games—the sum game and the product game:

The teacher poses questions and problems that both elicit and challenge students' thinking.

SUM GAME

Two players: Choose one player to be "even" and the other to be "odd." Throw two dice. Add the numbers on the two faces. If the sum is even, the even player gets 1 point. If the sum is odd, the odd player gets 1 point.

PRODUCT GAME

Two players: Choose one to be the "even" player and the other to be "odd." Throw two dice. Multiply the numbers on the two faces. If the product is even, the even player gets 1 point. If the product is odd, the odd player gets 1 point.

After explaining how each game is played, Mr. Luu challenges the students to figure out if the games are fair or not. He begins by holding a discussion about what it means for something to be "fair." Then he presents the rules for each game, telling the students simply that they are to report back on whether or not either of the games is fair or not and to include an explanation for their judgment.

The teacher makes a decision about how much to focus a problem, how much to direct the students. Here, he decides that a common understanding of what makes something "fair" is crucial.

The students pair off and work on the problem. Some play each of the games first, recording their results, as a means of investigating the question. Others try to analyze the games based on the possible outcomes. Mr. Luu walks around and listens to what the students are saying and poses questions:

"What did you say were all the possible totals you could get? How did you know?"
"Why did you decide you needed to throw the dice exactly 36 times?"

The teacher tries to provoke students' thinking. For example, he knows that the students who planned to throw the dice exactly 36 times may be assuming that the experimental results should be the same as their predicted outcomes.

After they have played the game or worked on their analyses for a while, Mr. Luu directs the students to stop, to open their notebooks, and to write in their notebooks what they think about the fairness of the two games.

The teacher appreciates the importance of writing about mathematics, and he provides regular occasions for it.

Next, Mr. Luu opens a whole-class discussion about the games. On the basis of what he saw when he was observing, he calls on Kevin and Rania. Rania beams. She explains that they figured out that the sum game is an unfair game "and we didn't even have to play it at all to be sure."

Kevin provides their proof:"There are six even sums possible—2, 4, 6, 8, 10, and 12—but only five odd ones—3, 5, 7, 9, and 11. So the game is unfair to the person who gets points for the odd sums."

Mr. Luu has called on these two students because on the one hand, they are comfortable with the idea that probabilities can be analyzed, that the game need not actually be played. But on the other hand, these students have made an erroneous conclusion. He thinks that this combination makes their solution a good lead-off for the whole-group discussion.

"What do the rest of you think?" asks Mr. Luu, gazing over the group. Several shake their heads. A few others nod.

"Marcus?" he invites. Marcus's hand was not up, but his face looks up at Mr.Luu. "It don't make sense to me, Mr. Luu. I think that there's more ways to get some of them numbers, like 3—there's two ways to get a 3. But there is only one way to get a 2."

The teacher expects the students to evaluate Kevin and Rania's argument and to decide together whether or not it makes sense.

"Huh?" Several children are openly puzzled by this statement.

"Marcus, can you explain what you mean by saying that 3 can be made two ways?" asks Mr. Luu.

The teacher makes careful decisions about when and how to encourage each student to participate. This time he is rewarded; sometimes when he calls on someone in this way, he gets stony silence.

"Well, you could get a 1 on one die and a 2 on the other, or you could get a 2 on the first die and a 1 on the other. That's two different ways," he explains quietly.

"But how are those different? One plus two equals the same thing as two plus one!" objects a small girl.

"What do you think, Than?" probes Mr. Luu.

Instead of explaining what Marcus has said, the teacher expects Marcus to provide his own clarification and justification.

Than remains silent. Mr. Luu waits a long time. Finally Than says, "But they are two different dices, so it is not same."

"Hmmm," remarks Mr. Luu. "Where are other people on this?"

After three or four more comments on both sides of the issue, time is almost up. Mr. Luu assigns the students, for homework, to repeat the coin-tossing game they had investigated last week, to record their results, and to decide if it is fair when three people play it.

Mr. Luu decides to press this issue, for he knows that understanding the concept of "outcome" is central to understanding probability. He thinks they can resolve this themselves, so he nudges the discussion along.

COIN-TOSSING GAME

Three players: One player is "two heads," one player is "two tails," and one player is "mixed." Toss two coins. If the result is two heads, the "heads" player gets 1 point. If the result is two tails, the "tails" player gets 1 point. If the result is one head and one tail, the "mixed" player gets 1 point.

The teacher extends the discourse by assigning a writing task coupled with more data collection.

Mr. Luu thinks that this game may help them with their thinking about the dice games. He asks them to play the game, to record their results, and to decide if it is fair when three people play it. They are to write about their experiments and explain their conclusion. Mr. Luu suspects that now, if they find out that the "mixed" result person gets about twice as many points as either of the others, they will be able to figure out what is going on and eventually agree with Marcus and Than.

Mr. Luu judges that, mathematically, this is an appropriate question for his students to struggle with. It is closely tied with the dice problem but may make the key concept of "outcome" more accessible.

Suggested Readings

Atwater, M. M., Radzik-Marsh, K., and Strutchens, M. (Eds.). (1994). *Multicultural education: Inclusion of all,* Athens, GA: The University of Georgia.

Ball, D. L. (1988). *The subject matter preparation of prospective mathematics teachers: Challenging the myths.* East Lansing, MI: National Center for Research on Teacher Education.

Ball, D. L. (1988). Unlearning to teach mathematics. *For the Learning of Mathematics, 8.*

Ball, D. L., and Feiman-Nemser, S. (1988). Using textbooks and teachers' guides: A dilemma for beginning teachers and teacher educators. *Curriculum Inquiry, 18.*

Ball, D. L. (1991). Implementing the professional standards for teaching mathematics: What's all this talk about discourse? *The Arithmetic Teacher, 39*(3).

Burns, M. (1988). *A collection of math lessons.* New Rochelle, NY: Cuisenaire Company of America.

Cooney, T. J. (Ed.). (1990). *Teaching and learning mathematics in the 1990s.* Reston, VA: National Council of Teachers of Mathematics.

Cooney, T. J. (1992). Implementing the professional standards for teaching mathematics: Evaluating the teaching of mathematics: The road to progress and reform. *The Arithmetic Teacher, 39*(6).

Corwin, R. B. (1993). Implementing the professional standards for teaching mathematics: Doing mathematics together: Creating a mathematical culture. *The Arithmetic Teacher, 40*(6).

Crosswhite, F. J. (1986). President's report: Better teaching, better mathematics: Are they enough? *The Arithmetic Teacher, 34*(2).

Davis, R. B., Maher, C. A., and Noddings, N. (Eds.). (1990). *Constructivist views of the teaching and learning of mathematics.* Reston, VA: National Council of Teachers of Mathematics.

Dossey, J. A. (1988). "Learning, teaching, and standards. *The Arithmetic Teacher, 35*(8).

Driscoll, M. J. (1981). Diagnosis: Taking the mathematical pulse. In M. J. Driscoll (Ed.), *Research within reach: Elementary school mathematics.* Reston, VA: National Council of Teachers of Mathematics and CEMREL, Inc.

Driscoll, M. J. (1981). Grouping for elementary school mathematics. In M. J. Driscoll (Ed.), *Research within reach: Elementary school mathematics.* Reston, VA: National Council of Teachers of Mathematics and CEMREL, Inc.

Driscoll, M. J. (1981). Learning elementary school mathematics: Individual styles and individual needs. In M. J. Driscoll (Ed.), *Research within reach: Elementary school mathematics.* Reston, VA: National Council of Teachers of Mathematics and CEMREL, Inc.

Driscoll, M. J. (1981).Motivation in mathematics. In M. J. Driscoll (Ed.), *Research within reach: Elementary school mathematics.* Reston, VA: National Council of Teachers of Mathematics and CEMREL, Inc.

Driscoll, M. J. (1981). Teaching for remediation in mathematics. In M. J. Driscoll (Ed.), *Research within reach: Elementary school mathematics.* Reston, VA: National Council of Teachers of Mathematics and CEMREL, Inc.

Driscoll, M. J. (1981). The role of manipulatives in elementary school mathematics. In M. J. Driscoll (Ed.), *Research within reach: Elementary school mathematics.* Reston, VA: National Council of Teachers of Mathematics and CEMREL, Inc.

Driscoll, M. J. (1981). The teacher and the textbook. In M. J. Driscoll (Ed.), Research within reach: Elementary school mathematics. Reston, VA: National Council of Teachers of Mathematics and CEMREL, Inc.

Fosnot, C. T. (1989). *Enquiring teachers, enquiring learners: A constructivist approach for teaching.* New York: Teachers College Press.

Frank, M. L. (1990). What myths about mathematics are held and conveyed by teachers? *The Arithmetic Teacher, 37*(5).

Friel, S. N., Ball, D. L., Cooney, T. J., and Lappan, G. (1990). Envisioning change in the practice of mathematics teaching: The NCTM's professional standards for teaching mathematics. *School Science and Mathematics, 90*(6).

Greenwood, J. J. (1993). On the nature of teaching and assessing 'mathematical power' and 'mathematical thinking.' *The Arithmetic Teacher, 41*(3).

Grouws, D. A., Cooney, T. J., and Jones, D. (Eds.). (1988). *Perspectives on research on effective mathematics teaching.* Reston, VA: National Council of Teachers of Mathematics.

Joyner, J. M. (1994). Implementing the professional standards for teaching: Linking teaching, learning, and assessment. *The Arithmetic Teacher, 41*(9).

Keedy, M. L. (1989). Textbooks and curriculum—whose dilemma? *The Arithmetic Teacher, 36*(7).

Lampert, M. (1988). What can research on teacher education tell us about improving the quality of mathematics education. *Teaching and Teacher Education, 4*(2).

Leinhardt, G., and Putnam, R. R. (1986). Profile of expertise in elementary school mathematics teaching. *The Arithmetic Teacher, 33*(4).

Lubinski, C. A. (1994). Implementing the professional standards for teaching: The influence of teachers' beliefs and knowledge on learning environments. *The Arithmetic Teacher, 41*(8).

Maher, C. A., and Martino, A. M. (1992). Implementing the professional standards for teaching: Teachers building on students' thinking. *The Arithmetic Teacher, 39*(7).

Mathematical Association of America. (1991). *A call for change: Recommendations for the mathematical preparation of teachers.* Washington, D.C.: Author.

Mathematical Sciences Education Board, National Research Council. (1987). *The teacher of mathematics: Issues for today and tomorrow.* Washington, D.C.: National Academy Press.

National Council of Teachers of Mathematics. (1977). *Organizing for mathematics instruction.* (1977 Yearbook). Reston, VA: Author.

National Council of Teachers of Mathematics. (1993). *Professional standards for teaching mathematics.* Reston, VA: Author.

National Council of Teachers of Mathematics. (1993). *Implementing the K-8 curriculum and evaluation standards.* Reston, VA: Author.

Nelson, D., Joseph, G. G., and Williams, J. (1993). *Multicultural mathematics: Teaching mathematics from a global perspective.* Oxford, England: Oxford University Press.

Ohio Mathematics Education Leadership Council. (1989). *Real routes: A handbook for school-based mathematics leaders.* Oberlin, OH: Oberlin College Press.

Parker, R. E. (1993). *Mathematical power: Lessons from a classroom.* Portsmouth, NH: Heinemann.

Pateman, N. (1989). Teachers researching their mathematics classrooms. *The Arithmetic Teacher, 36*(2).

Rathmell, E. C. (1994). Planning for instruction involves focusing on children's thinking. *The Arithmetic Teacher, 41*(6).

Schifter, D., and Fosnot, C. T. (1993). *Reconstructing mathematics education: Stories of teachers meeting the challenge of reform.* New York: Teachers College Press.

Schmalz, R. (1994). The mathematics textbook: How can it serve the NCTM's standards? *The Arithmetic Teacher, 41*(6).

Silver, E. A., and Smith, M. S. (1990). Teaching mathematics and thinking. *The Arithmetic Teacher, 37*(8).

Simon, M. A. (1986). The teacher's role in increasing student understanding of mathematics. *Educational Leadership.*

Speer, W. R., and Brahier, D. J. (1994). Rethinking the teaching and learning of mathematics. In C. A. Thornton (Ed.), *Windows of opportunity: Mathematics for students with special needs.* Reston, VA: National Council of Teachers of Mathematics.

Vacc, N. N. (1993). Implementing the professional standards for teaching mathematics: Questioning in the mathematics classroom. *The Arithmetic Teacher, 41*(2).

Vacc, N. N.. (1994). Implementing the professional standards for teaching mathematics: Planning for instruction: Barriers to mathematics discussion. *The Arithmetic Teacher, 41*(6).

Wood, T., Cobb, P., and Yackel, E. (1991). Change in teaching mathematics: A case study. *American Educational Research Journal, 28*(3).

Worth, J. (Ed.). (1988). Preparing elementary school mathematics teachers. Readings from *The Arithmetic Teacher.* Reston, VA: National Council of Teachers of Mathematics.

Chapter 3

Assessing Mathematics

Overview

In 1995, the National Council of Teachers of Mathematics issued a publication entitled *Assessment Standards for School Mathematics.* This document was written as a third companion document to the previously issued *Curriculum and Evaluation Standards for School Mathematics* (1989) and *Professional Standards for Teaching Mathematics* (1991). The assessment document presents a set of guidelines or benchmarks that assist teachers and other educational decision makers in the development of a meaningful system of assessing student competencies and dispositions. The assessment **standards** document is divided into two main sections—"Mathematics Assessment Standards" and "Use of the Assessment Standards for Different Purposes."

The first section, "Mathematics Assessment Standards," presents a set of six guidelines regarding the design of assessment programs and techniques. The second section, "Use of the Assessment Standards for Different Purposes," outlines four categories for the use of assessment results of student work and dispositions. The document concludes with a short reflection on what it will take to reform assessment practices in mathematics.

Each section of the assessment standards document is important for educators to explore, but the purpose of this book requires that we examine the six assessment standards in particular. Readers who would like to obtain additional information on the assessment standards should contact the National Council of Teachers of Mathematics, 1906 Association Drive, Reston, VA 20191.

NCTM STANDARDS FOR AN EFFECTIVE ASSESSMENT SYSTEM

The six assessment standards that can be used to judge the quality of an assessment system are described in the following sections.*

Standard 1:

The Mathematics Standard

Assessment should reflect the mathematics that all students need to know and be able to do . . . To determine how well an assessment reflects mathematics that students need to know and be able to do, ask questions such as the following:

- What mathematics is reflected in the assessment?
- What efforts are made to ensure that the mathematics is significant and correct?
- How does the assessment engage students in realistic and worthwhile mathematical activities?
- How does the assessment elicit the use of mathematics that it is important to know and be able to do?
- How does the assessment fit within a framework of mathematics to be assessed?
- What inferences about students' mathematical knowledge, understanding, thinking processes, and dispositions can be made from the assessment?

Standard 2:

The Learning Standard

Assessment should enhance mathematics learning . . . To determine how well an assessment enhances learning, ask questions such as these:

- How does the assessment contribute to each student's learning of mathematics?
- How does the assessment relate to instruction?
- How does the assessment allow students to demonstrate what they know and what they can do in novel situations?
- How does the assessment engage students in relevant, purposeful work on worthwhile mathematical activities?
- How does the assessment build on each student's understanding, interests, and experiences?
- How does the assessment involve students in selecting activities, applying performance criteria, and using results?
- How does the assessment provide opportunities for students to evaluate, reflect on, and improve their own work—that is, to become independent learners?

*Reprinted with permission from the *Assessment Standards for School Mathematics,* copyright 1995 by the National Council of Teachers of Mathematics.

Standard 3:

The Equity Standard

Assessment should promote equity . . . To determine how well an assessment promotes equity, ask questions such as the following:

- What opportunities has each student had to learn the mathematics being assessed?
- How does the assessment provide alternative activities or modes of response that invite each student to engage in the mathematics being assessed?
- How does the design of the assessment enable all students to exhibit what they know and can do?
- How do the conditions under which the assessment is administered enable all students to exhibit what they know and can do?
- How does the assessment help students demonstrate their best work?
- How is the role of students' backgrounds and experiences recognized in judging their responses to the assessment?
- How do scoring guides accommodate unanticipated but reasonable responses?
- How have the effects of bias been minimized throughout the assessment?
- To what sources can differences in performance be attributed?

Standard 4:

The Openness Standard

Assessment should be an open process . . . To determine how open an assessment is, ask questions such as these:

- How do students become familiar with the assessment process and with the purposes, performance criteria, and consequences of the assessment?
- How are teachers and students involved in choosing tasks, setting criteria, and interpreting results?
- How is the public involved in the assessment process?
- What access do those affected by the assessment have to tasks, scoring goals, performance criteria, and samples of students' work that have been scored and discussed?
- How is the assessment process itself open to evaluation and modification?

Standard 5:

The Inference Standard

Assessment should promote valid inferences about mathematics learning . . . To determine how well an assessment promotes valid inferences, ask questions such as the following:

- What evidence about learning does the assessment provide?
- How is professional judgment used in making inferences about learning?
- How sensitive is the assessor to the demands the assessment makes and to unexpected responses?
- How is bias minimized in making inferences about learning?
- What efforts are made to ensure that scoring is consistent across students, scorers, and activities?
- What multiple sources of evidence are used for making inferences, and how is the evidence used?
- What is the value of the evidence for each use?

Standard 6:

The Coherence Standard

Assessment should be a coherent process . . . To determine how coherent an assessment process is, ask questions such as these:

- How is professional judgment used to ensure that the various parts of the assessment process form a coherent whole?
- How do students view the connection between instruction and assessment?
- How does the assessment match its purposes with its uses?
- How does the assessment match the curriculum and instructional practice?
- How can assessment practice inform teachers as they make curriculum decisions and determine their instructional practices?

Related Readings

American Association of School Administrators. (1991). *The changing face of testing and assessment: Problems and solutions.* Arlington, VA: American Association of School Administrators.

Bagley, T., and Gallenberger, C. (1992). Assessing students' dispositions: Using journals to improve students' performance. *The Mathematics Teacher, 85*(3).

Baxter, G. P., Shavelson, R. J., Herman, S. J., Brown, K. A., and Valadez, J. R. Mathematics performance assessment: Technical quality and diverse student impact. *Journal for Research in Mathematics Education, 24*(3).

Blume, G. W., and Heid, M. K. (Eds.). (1993). *Alternative assessment in mathematics* (1993 yearbook). University Park, PA: Pennsylvania Council of Teachers of Mathematics.

Brookhart, S. M. (1993). Teachers' grading practices: Meaning and values. *Journal of Educational Measurement, 30*(2).

California State Department of Education. (1989). *A question of thinking: A first look at students' performance on open-ended questions in mathematics.* Sacramento, CA: California State Department of Education.

Campbell, D. (1990). *Arizona student assessment plan, (ASAP).* Phoenix, AZ: Arizona Department of Education.

Charles, R., Lester, F., and O'Daffer, P. (1987). *How to evaluate progress in problem solving.* Reston, VA: National Council of Teachers of Mathematics.

Classroom Assessment in Mathematics Network Project. (1993). *Exploring classroom assessment in mathematics.* Newton, MA: Education Development Center.

Colison, J. (1990). *Connecticut's common core of learning.* Hartford, CT: Performance Assessment Project, Connecticut Department of Education.

Collis, K. F., and Romberg, T. A. (1989). *Assessment of mathematical performance: An analysis of open-ended test items.* Madison, WI: National Center for Research in Mathematical Sciences Education, University of Wisconsin.

Cooney, T. J. (Ed.). (1990). *Teaching and learning mathematics in the 1990s.* (1990 yearbook). Reston, VA: National Council of Teachers of Mathematics.

Csongor, J. E. (1992). Mirror, mirror on the wall . . . Teaching self-assessment to students. *The Mathematics Teacher, 85*(3).

Dossey, J. A., Mullis, I. V. S., and Jones, C. O. (1993). *Can students do mathematical problem solving? Results from constructed-response questions in NAEP's 1992 mathematics assessment.* Washington, D.C.: U.S. Department of Education.

Educational Testing Service. (1993). *Linking educational assessments: Concepts, issues, methods and prospects.* Princeton, NJ: ETS Policy Information Center.

Educational Testing Service. (1993). *Performance assessment sampler —A workbook.* Princeton, NJ: ETS Policy Information Center.

EQUALS. (1989). *Assessment alternatives in mathematics.* Berkeley, CA: University of California, Lawrence Hall of Science.

Fitzpatrick, R., and Morrison, E. J. (1991). Performance and product evaluation. In F. L. Finch (Ed.), *Educational performance assessment.* Chicago: Riverside Publishing Company.

Fraser, B. J., Malone, J. A., and Neale, J. M. (1989). Assessing and improving the psychosocial environment of mathematics classrooms. *Journal for Research in Mathematics Education, 20*(2).

Grace, C., and Shores, E. F. (1991). *The portfolio and its use:*

Developmentally appropriate assessment of young children. Little Rock, AR: Southern Association on Children Under Six.

Graue, H. A., and Smith, S. (1992). *A conceptual framework for instructional assessment.* Madison, WI: National Center for Research in Mathematical Sciences Education.

Hawaii Department of Education. (1991). *Using portfolios: A handbook for the chapter I teacher.* Honolulu, HI: Hawaii Department of Education.

Hynes, M. C. (1991). *Alternative assessment in mathematics.* Orlando, FL: UCF Center for Education Research and Development.

Illinois State Board of Education. (1991). *Defining and setting standards for the Illinois goal assessment program, (IGAP).* Springfield, IL: Author.

Kansas State Board of Education. (1991). *Kansas mathematics standards and 1991 Kansas statewide pilot assessment results.* Topeka, KS: Author.

Kentucky Department of Education. (1992). *Kentucky instructional results information system (KIRIS) open-response released items 1991-92.* Frankfurt, KY: Author.

Kentucky Department of Education. (1992). *Kentucky mathematics portfolio: Teacher's guide.* Frankfort, KY: Author.

Kulm, G. (Ed.). (1990). *Assessing higher order thinking in mathematics.* Washington, DC: American Association for the Advancement of Science.

Larter, S. (1991). *Benchmarks: The development of a new approach to student evaluation.* Toronto, ONT: Toronto Board of Education.

Lehman, M. (1992). *Assessing assessment: Investigating a mathematics performance assessment.* East Lansing, MI: The National Center for Research on Teacher Learning, Michigan State University.

Lesh, R., and Lamon, S. J. (Eds.). (1992). *Assessment of authentic performance in school mathematics.* Washington, D.C.: American Association for the Advancement of Science.

Long, D. J. (1991). *Mathematics proficiency guide, 1991.* Indianapolis: Indiana Department of Education.

Maryland Department of Education. (1991). *Maryland school performance assessment program.* Baltimore: Author.

Massachusetts Department of Education. (1989). *On their own: Student response to open-ended tests in mathematics.* Boston: Author.

Mathematical Sciences Education Board. (1991). *For good measure: Principles and goals for mathematics assessment.* Washington, D.C.: National Academy Press.

Mathematical Sciences Education Board. (1993). *Measuring what counts: A conceptual guide for mathematics assessment.* Washington, D.C.: National Academy Press.

Mathematical Sciences Education Board. (1993). *Measuring up: Prototypes for mathematics assessment.* Washington, D.C.: National Academy Press.

Medrich, E. A., and Griffith, J. E. (1992). *International mathematics and science assessments: What have we learned?* Springfield, VA: National Technical Information Service, US Department of Commerce.

Mitchell, R. (1992). *Testing for learning: How new approaches to evaluation can improve American schools.* New York: The Free Press.

Mumme, J. (1991). *Portfolio assessment in mathematics.* Santa Barbara, CA: California Mathematics Project.

National Council of Teachers of Mathematics. (1993). *Assessment standards for school mathematics* (working draft). Reston, VA: National Council of Teachers of Mathematics.

National Council of Teachers of Mathematics. (1989). *Curriculum and evaluation standards for school mathematics.* Reston, VA: Author.

National Council of Teachers of Mathematics. (1992). *Mathematics assessment* (video program and guide). Reston, VA: Author.

National Council of Teachers of Mathematics. (1991). *Professional standards for teaching mathematics.* Reston, VA: Author.

Pandey, T. (1991). *A sampler of mathematics assessment.* Sacramento, CA: California Department of Education.

Perrone, V. (1995). *Expanding student assessment.* Alexandria, VA: Association for Supervision and Curriculum Development.

Romberg, T. A., and Wilson, L. (1989). *The alignment of six standardized tests with the NCTM standards.* Unpublished manuscript, University of Wisconsin-Madison.

Semple, B. M. (1991). *Performance assessment: An international experiment.* Princeton, NJ: Educational Testing Service.

Stenmark, J. K. (1989). *Assessment alternatives in mathematics: An overview of assessment techniques that promote learning.* Berkeley: University of California (EQUALS, Lawrence Hall of Science).

Stenmark, J. K. (1991). *Mathematics assessment: Myths, models, good questions, and practical suggestions.* Reston, VA: National Council of Teachers of Mathematics.

Stiggins, R. J., and Conklin, N. F. (1992). *In teachers' hands: Investigating the practices of classroom assessment.* Albany: SUNY Press.

Thompson, A. G., and Briars, D. J. (1989). Assessing students' learning to inform teaching: The message in NCTM's evaluation standards. *The Arithmetic Teacher, 37*(4).

U.S. Department of Education. (1991). America 2000: An education strategy. Washington, D.C.: USDOE.

Vermont Department of Education. (1991). *Looking beyond the answer: Vermont's mathematics portfolio assessment program.* Montpelier, VT: Author.

Vermont Department of Education. (1991). *Vermont mathematics portfolio project* (Resource Book and Teacher's Guide). Montpelier, VT: Vermont Department of Education.

Webb, N. L. (Ed.). (1993). *Assessment in the mathematics classroom* (1993 NCTM Yearbook). Reston, VA: National Council of Teachers of Mathematics.

AN EXAMPLE OF AN ASSESSMENT STANDARD*

Standard 6:

The Coherence Standard

Assessment should be a coherent process.

Coherence in assessment involves three types of agreement. First, the assessment process forms a coherent whole; the phases fit together. Second, the assessment matches the purposes for which it is being done. When the design, evidence-gathering, evidence-interpreting, and action phases of the assessment process are consistent with one another and with the purposes of the assessment, it has educational value. Third, the assessment is aligned with the curriculum and with instruction. Students' learning connects with their assessment experiences.

A coherent mathematics assessment system assures that assessors will develop activities and performance criteria tailored to the purposes of each assessment. An assessment framework is useful in judging whether all parts of the process are in harmony, from the design stage to the stage of reporting and using results. The assessment process then unfolds as a logical and coherent whole.

The Coherence Standard has several implications. Just as no single instrument section makes a great orchestra, a coherent mathematics assessment system cannot be based on paper-and-pencil tests alone. Instead, a balance among appropriate and diverse assessment activities can help all students learn.

A coherent mathematics assessment system requires that activities be chosen that are appropriate to the purpose at hand. A teacher would not use a test on linear equations to assess students' knowledge of quadratic equations, or a test of procedural skills to indicate students' conceptual knowledge, or a computation test to assess problem-solving performance.

Coherence in assessment, however, raises broader issues than simply selecting an appropriate test or activity. Coherence relates to all aspects of the assessment process.

External assessment programs are moving away from an extensive reliance on machine-scored multiple-choice items to a greater use of performance tasks and to the use of multiple sources of information. Assessment activities for such programs, however, can be expensive to develop, administer, and score. The programs may entail costs in the form of instructional time taken away from other activities if they are not integrated into instruction. Greater investments of time and funding may be required, which means that people may expect more information from the assessments. As assessment programs change, the pressure to make a single assessment serve multiple purposes is likely to increase. Consequently, special vigilance may be needed to assure that all the uses to which assessment information is being put are in harmony with the purposes of the assessment.

Mathematics teachers organize, conduct, and interpret assessments as part of their ongoing mathematics instruction. When mathematics assessment is a coherent process, teachers and students benefit because they are not confronted by conflicting demands. Attention to coherence underscores the principle that assessment needs to be in step with instruction. When assessment fits the curriculum, students can see that assessment activities not only are related to the mathematics they have learned but also serve clear goals. As students understand how assessment is connected to what they are learning, an increase can be expected in the number of students who will choose to continue their study of mathematics.

Assessment developers in local and provincial or state agencies play a vital role in making sure that the assessments of students' mathematics learning form a harmonious whole as they progress through school. A single assessment touches only a part of the mathematics that students know and can use, but the totality of the assessments students encounter provides a comprehensive picture of their knowledge, skill, and understanding.

To determine how coherent an assessment process is, ask questions such as these:

- How is professional judgment used to ensure that the various parts of the assessment process form a coherent whole?
- How do students view the connection between instruction and assessment?
- How does the assessment match its purposes with its uses?
- How does the assessment match the curriculum and instructional practice?
- How can assessment practice inform teachers as they make curriculum decisions and determine their instructional practices?

*Reprinted with permission from the *Assessment Standards for School Mathematics,* copyright 1995 by the National Council of Teachers of Mathematics.

A CLASSROOM TEACHING VIGNETTE

The vignette that follows illustrates how the interactive nature of assessment and instruction in the classroom can enhance learning. In this story, a sixth-grade student made the incorrect conjecture that all shapes with equal perimeters have equal areas. His teacher decided the misconception was worth exploring in class and changed her lesson plan accordingly.

Inside, Out, and All About

Janna McKnight perched on the edge of her desk at the back of the classroom. Her sixth-grade students were elbowing each other and chatting while parading to the front of the room to place their yellow stickies on a bar chart. They had been finding the area of a salt marsh on a map, a rather irregular shape. Each stickie represented the area (in thousands of square meters) determined by one student.

The portion of the chart from about 85 to 95 was beginning to look like the New York City skyline, with highrise towers huddled close together. Close in, to the left and right of the city, were several lower towers. Off to the right at 196 was one lonely stickie with the initials TP, and down to the left were two other stickies at 55 with the initials BT and AK.

Ms. McKnight called the class to order. "All right, let's see what you've found. Who'd like to make some observations about our data?"

"Ninety-two thousand square meters got the most, but 87 was a close second," Jeremy answered. "It seems like lots of people got answers between 86 and 94."

"The lowest answer was 55—two people got that—and the highest was 196. Those people must have done it wrong, because those answers are, like, too different to be true," Angel offered.

"Bernice, is the 55 with BT on it yours?" Wallace blurted.

"The 196 is mine, and it isn't wrong!" Tyler offered in a defensive tone.

Anthony interrupted, "Bernice and I worked together, but I think our calculator gave us the wrong answer. I just added it up again, and ours should be 85 instead of 55."

"Tyler, would you like to explain how you found 196 as the area of the marsh?"

"Well, you remember how we put string around those circles the other day? You didn't give us any string today. But my sweatshirt has a string in the hood, so I pulled it out and wrapped it around the marsh. Then I straightened it out into a square on top of the plastic, and it was about 14 units long and 14 wide. So its area was about 196. The square wasn't exactly 14, but it was pretty close!"

"So, Tyler found the area of a square he built from reshaping a string that fit around the perimeter of the marsh. I noticed most of the rest of you doing something quite different. Amy?"

Amy explained that her group had put clear plastic graph paper on top of the marsh and counted squares. Dyanne explained how her group counted partial squares as halves or fourths for more accuracy.

"Did anyone approach the problem differently? What do you think about Tyler's procedure?"

"I think it's a lot better," said Richard, "because Tyler didn't have to do all that counting. I wish I'd thought of making it into an easier shape. It would have saved a lot of work."

"But why is Tyler's answer so much bigger?" asked Nancy. I don't know why it's wrong, but Tyler's answer is way too big."

"If the distance around the marsh is a lot, then the area is a lot—wouldn't that be right? Like when one is big, the other is big?" asked Cindy. Numerous heads nodded in agreement, amid a few dissenting frowns.

Pointing to the bulletin board, where dot-paper records of a geoboard activity from the previous week were displayed, Dyanne reminded the class that shapes with equal perimeters could have very different areas.

"All right," said Ms. McKnight, glancing at the clock over the chalkboard. "We're not going to have time today to get to the bottom of this mystery. Let's just write Tyler's conjecture on the board and see whether we can investigate it further tomorrow. Who can use some good mathematical language to say what Tyler's been thinking?"

Janna McKnight wisely did not dismiss Tyler's answer as wrong but probed to discover the source of his confusion. In doing so, she uncovered a common misconception about area and perimeter and made some decisions to adjust her instruction.

What will Ms. McKnight do tomorrow in class? The decisions that she made today have led her to a point where she will have to revise her short-range plans for tomorrow's lesson. She will need to think about ways to follow up on Tyler's conjecture. One of her goals now is to help her students explore the conjecture and decide its validity for themselves, so she wants to plan an activity to make that happen. One idea would be to have them measure the area and perimeter of their own handprints (with fingers spread and with fingers together) and explore the relationship, hoping they will begin to understand why Tyler's conjecture is false. This short-range plan also fits some of her long-range goals for the class. She wants her students to have a sense of what it really means to do mathematics, and she intends to communicate the principle that making conjectures and testing them for validity are important components of mathematical power.

Janna McKnight's understanding of the importance of conjecture and verification in doing mathematics helps her recognize the value of exploring Tyler's conjecture rather than quickly pointing out his error. Teachers are more effective in assessing students' understanding of mathematical ideas when they are knowledgeable about performance standards, familiar with the "big ideas" of mathematics (such as number sense, proportion, and equivalence), confident of their abilities to deal with important mathematical processes (such as problem solving, reasoning, communication, and making connections), and convinced of the importance of dispositions (such as motivation and confidence). Ongoing professional development activities—attending conferences, reading professional journals, and collaborating with other educators—help teachers become aware of, and confident in, their understanding of effective ways to help all students become mathematically powerful.

Suggested Readings

Blume, G. W. & Heid, M. K. (Eds.). (1993). *Alternative assessment in mathematics: 1993 yearbook.* University Park, PA: Pennsylvania Council of Teachers of Mathematics.

California State Department of Education. (1989). *A question of thinking: A first look at students' performance on open-ended questions in mathematics.* Sacramento, CA: California State Department of Education.

Dossey, J. A., Mullis, I. V. S., and Jones, C. O. (1993). *Can students do mathematical problem solving? Results from constructed-response questions in NAEP's 1992 mathematics assessment.* Washington, D.C.: U.S. Department of Education.

Mathematical Sciences Education Board. (1991). *For good measure: Principles and goals for mathematics assessment.* Washington, D.C.: National Academy Press.

Mathematical Sciences Education Board. (1993). *Measuring what counts: A conceptual guide for mathematics assessment.* Washington, D.C.: National Academy Press.

Mathematical Sciences Education Board. (1993). *Measuring up: Prototypes for mathematics assessment.* Washington, D.C.: National Academy Press.

National Council of Teachers of Mathematics. (1989). *Curriculum and evaluation standards for school mathematics.* Reston, VA: National Council of Teachers of Mathematics.

National Council of Teachers of Mathematics. (1991). *Professional standards for teaching mathematics.* Reston, VA: National Council of Teachers of Mathematics.

National Council of Teachers of Mathematics. (1992). *Mathematics assessment* (video program and guide). Reston, VA: National Council of Teachers of Mathematics.

National Council of Teachers of Mathematics. (1995). *Assessment standards for school mathematics.* Reston, VA: National Council of Teachers of Mathematics.

Romberg, T. A., & Wilson, L. (1989). *The alignment of six standardized tests with the NCTM standards.* Unpublished manuscript, University of Wisconsin-Madison.

Stenmark, J. K. (1989). *Assessment alternatives in mathematics: An overview of assessment techniques that promote learning.* Berkeley, CA: University of California (EQUALS, Lawrence Hall of Science).

Stenmark, J. K. (1991). *Mathematics assessment: Myths, models, good questions, and practical suggestions.* Reston, VA: National Council of Teachers of Mathematics.

Vermont Department of Education. (1991). *Looking beyond the answer: Vermont's mathematics portfolio assessment program.* Montpelier, VT: Vermont Department of Education.

Vermont Department of Education. (1991). *Vermont mathematics portfolio project* (Resource Book and Teacher's Guide). Montpelier, VT: Vermont Department of Education.

Webb, N. L. (Ed.). (1993). *Assessment in the mathematics classroom* (1993 NCTM Yearbook). Reston, VA: National Council of Teachers of Mathematics.

Chapter 4

Problem Solving, Decision Making, and Communicating in Mathematics

Overview

For years teachers have indicated that teaching problem solving to children has been a most difficult task. Problem solving *is* more challenging because it is a more complex process than merely writing numerals in a certain pattern and performing certain operations. Students need to bring their mathematical knowledge together and use this information in a thought process to solve problems. Children need encouragement to help them recognize mathematics in their daily environment. Conceptual understanding is developed first, followed by the development of efficient algorithms. These skills are then applied in real life situations.

Reading has been, and probably always will be, one of the major difficulties encountered in solving word problems. Children need specific help in how to read mathematics and how mathematics reading differs from other kinds of reading.

Dramatization is an excellent technique to help children learn how to translate words into mathematical sentences. Encourage children to first read, then dramatize, followed by translating the situation into a mathematical sentence. These two intermediary steps are very often neglected. To help children accurately comprehend the meaning and interpretation of the mathematics, they should be encouraged to reply in a complete sentence that answers the original question.

The calculator can provide computing capabilities for students so that they can concentrate on the mathematics involved in solving problems. The use of calculators to solve problems is part of functioning in society today—children need to know how to use this device in real-life situations. The calculator cannot make decisions about when to add, subtract, multiply, or divide. Students must organize the data themselves and learn to use the calculator as a tool.

SAMPLE LESSON PLAN—"YUMMY FRACTION PROBLEM"

Intermediate Developmental Lesson

Goals:

Investigate problem solving as a process.
Application of fractions to a problem situation.

Objectives:

The students will:

Interpret a problem situation.
Choose an appropriate solution strategy.
Implement a solution strategy.
Verify reasonableness of a solution.

Prerequisite Learning and/or Experiences:

In order to apply a problem solving process to unique problem situations, students should have prior experiences with many problem solving strategies such as modeling, acting, drawing, simplifying, looking for patterns, etc.
Model fractions as part of a whole (regions model).

Materials:

Per cooperative learning group:

fraction manipulatives (fraction circles)
chart paper and markers

Teacher:

chart paper and markers

Procedures:

Students work in cooperative groups of four—coordinators, recorders, reporters and illustrators.

Motivational Introduction

Pose the following problem situation to the class:

- "Jerry came home from a school baseball game and was hungry, as usual. He found a note from his mother telling him to help himself to a piece of pie and a glass of milk. Someone else had already eaten part of the pie, because only $\frac{2}{3}$ of it was left in the pan. After Jerry cut a piece for himself, only $\frac{1}{2}$ of the pie remained. Jerry knows his mother will ask him how much pie he ate. What part of the whole pie did Jerry eat?"

1. Coordinators have groups brainstorm all the details they *know* about the problem. Anticipate a full/complete listing of facts from "$\frac{2}{3}$ of the pie was left before Jerry ate" to "Jerry played baseball after school." Recorders write the information on their groups' chart paper.
2. Reporters will report one fact each group *knows.* The teacher will write each known fact on a class chart. After each group has shared, reporters may add other known facts.
3. Coordinators have groups brainstorm all the details they *do not know* about the problem. Accept responses which will and will not help solve the problem. Recorders write the information on their group's chart paper.
4. Reporters will report one fact each group *does not know.* The teacher will write each unknown fact on a class chart. After each group has shared, reporters may add other unknown facts.
5. Have the students analyze the class chart of knowns and unknowns. Determine what information is relevant and not relevant to solving the problem. Probe for any missing information which might prohibit/limit a solution.

Developmental Activity

6. Coordinators will have groups discuss possible solution strategies for solving the problem. The teacher encourages students to think about using pictures, diagrams, numbers, manipulatives, etc. Recorders will record all possible solution strategies. Coordinators will have groups select the "best" solution strategy. If group consensus cannot be reached, then majority rules.
7. Coordinators will have groups implement their "best" strategy. Illustrators will draw how the problem was solved. Recorders will write about the solution process.

Culminating Activity

8. Coordinators have groups verify their solutions by implementing an alternate solution strategy from their list of all possible solution strategies generated in step 6.
9. Reporters display the group's responses and share their results with the class.

Extension:

Analyze the assessment data to determine future instructional implications. For example, if students are having difficulty interpreting relevant facts (knowns and unknowns), then pose a problem whereby students must generate the data—"How much ice cream do we need?" Such a question should engender more questions. Answers to the questions become a basis for relevant data. Once the data is generated, have students solve the problem.

Student Assessment/Evaluation:

Apply the following rubric to each group's problem solving solution. Use this rubric to determine which components of the problem solving process need additional experiences.

- Interprets the problem through known and unknown facts.

  0 = misinterprets the problem
  1 = misinterprets part of the problem
  2 = correctly interprets the problem

- Chooses an appropriate solution strategy.
  - 0 = no attempt or chooses an inappropriate strategy
  - 1 = chooses a strategy based upon a questionable interpretation
  - 2 = chooses a strategy which could lead to a correct solution
- Implements a solution strategy.
  - 0 = no solution or incorrect solution
  - 1 = partial solution or incorrect due to an error
  - 2 = correct solution
- Verifies reasonableness of solution.
  - 0 = no attempt to verify solution with an alternate strategy
  - 1 = verifies solution with an alternate strategy, but solution still incorrect
  - 2 = verifies solution with an alternate strategy

INSTRUCTIONAL AND ASSESSMENT ACTIVITIES FOR GRADES K-4

1. Problem-solving techniques can be explored and developed before children learn to read. Experience shows that children in kindergarten and first grade have little difficulty working with simple mathematical sentences if careful attention is given to language and symbolism. Problem-solving situations should be set up for student action and participation, with the children constructing meaning and verbalizing the mathematics with the teacher. For example, the teacher might place four chairs at a table and ask a group of five children to sit at the table. The children are now involved in a very real problem, because there are not enough chairs for all students to be seated. The children should discuss the situation and then act out possible solutions they suggest.
2. Writing mathematical sentences in the horizontal form is one way for the first-grade teacher to make use of the "left-to-right" pattern that is so important in beginning reading, writing, and mathematics. Anything that contributes to the development of this pattern is advisable. At the same time, children should be exposed to open sentences in the vertical form so that they do not think the horizontal form is the only way to write a mathematical sentence. Also, be certain to write some horizontal sentences with the sum on the left, e.g., $5 = 2 + 3$, so that children do not develop the notion that such notation is incorrect.
3. Activities in primary grades should begin with groups of real objects, flannel board and chalkboard demonstrations, number line demonstrations, and discussion of these activities. For example, all these activities might be combined in this way: Give three or four children groups of nine objects. Have two or three more children at the chalkboard, one at the flannel board, and one at the number line. Ask the children with the objects to form two groups—one group of five and one group of four. Ask the children at the chalkboard to draw a simple diagram or picture of a group of five and a group of four. Have the child at the flannel board create a group of five and a group of four. Then ask the child at the number line to demonstrate what needs to be done to show a group of five and a group of four.

   Let each child verbalize the situation to illustrate possible variety in the thinking process. The children with the concrete objects might indicate variations such as "I had nine blocks and I took five of them away and that left four" or "I took four blocks and made one group and counted the other group to see if I had a group of five."

   The child at the flannel board might select five felt shapes of one type and four of another. Chalkboard diagrams will vary the same way—some indicating the complete group of nine with a line to separate, others indicating separate groups. The child at the number line has the responsibility for illustrating the numerical symbolism involved.
4. Ask the children what group is formed when they combine a group of five and a group of four. When they reply "nine," ask them how they could write this using numerals so that someone else would know what they mean. Lead the children to write "$5 + 4 = 9$" on the chalkboard and discuss what it means. This is the time to explain the use of the operation and relation symbols. It is also the time to reinforce the idea that $5 + 4$ is just another way of naming 9 (assuming that we are presenting this idea to children exploring the operation of addition).

5. Many elementary mathematics programs give practice from the start in recording addition facts and subtraction facts in vertical and horizontal form.

Vertical	**Horizontal**	**Vertical**	**Horizontal**
$\begin{array}{r} 5 \\ +3 \\ \hline 8 \end{array}$	$5 + 3 = 8$	$\begin{array}{r} 7 \\ -4 \\ \hline 3 \end{array}$	$7 - 4 = 3$

   Encourage frequent practice with basic facts written in both horizontal and vertical form.

6. Write the missing numerals in the frames.

   a) $3 + 3 = \square$ c) $7 + 1 = \square$ e) $\square + 4 = 5$

   b) $\square + 1 - 3$ d) $4 + \square - 6$ f) $1 + \square - 7$

7. Children enjoy making up stories. Write a simple sentence such as $2 + \square = 5$ on the chalkboard. Ask the children to create a story to go with the sentence. (Possible response: I have two marbles in my hand, and I've got more in my pocket. I have five in all. How many marbles do I have in my pocket?) Let several of the children tell the stories they make up. Repeat this activity, using a different sentence each time.

8. Children who are encountering reading difficulties may continue to develop mathematically if a rebus is used in story problem development. A rebus uses pictures in the place of words to tell a story.

9. Children can develop facility in forming open sentences by playing the following game called "Peek-a-boo." A child is given a box containing two blocks with numbers written on their faces. The child then shakes the box and calls out the two numbers on the top of each cube. For example, the pupil may call out "four" and "eight." The first person who can form an appropriate open sentence with those two numbers gets to be the leader. Thus the box is passed to the successful constructor of a number sentence. For the example presented, acceptable responses may be $8 - 4 = \square$, $4 + \square = 8$, or $4 + 8 = \square$, among other variations.

10. Cards marked with numerals and operation symbols can be a useful vehicle for developing open sentences. Children may form several open sentences at their desks and then compare them. A count may be made of how many different open sentences the class formed. Also, pupils may be asked to complete an open sentence that you have written on the chalkboard. Some examples are:

    a) $82 \bigcirc 21 = 61$ c) $4 \bigcirc 4 < 9$

    b) $5 \bigcirc 3 = 15$ d) $3 \bigcirc 3 < 6$

11. Jean and Joan together have fifteen dolls. This is seven more than Jane has. How many dolls does Jane have? Write a number sentence for this problem.

    Possible answers: $\square + 7 = 15$ $15 = 7 + \square$ $15 - 7 = \square$ $15 - \square = 7$

    Children frequently give the erroneous translation "$15 + 7 = \square$." Discussion of the various ways of writing the sentence—why this particular sentence would be incorrect, why one way may be a better interpretation than another—is extremely important. Encourage the children to explain their thinking. It's sometimes difficult to squelch the urge to tell too much—but squelch it.

12. Jayna bought twenty new marbles for her collection. When she counted all the marbles in her collection, she discovered that she now had seventy-four. How many marbles did she have before she bought the new ones? How could we write a number sentence for this problem.

    Possibilities: $20 + \square = 74$ $74 - 20 = \square$ $\square + 20 = 74$ $74 - \square = 20$

    Give the children ample opportunity to explain their thinking processes as they present different ways of writing these sentences.

13. Encourage children to think of similar problems to present to the group orally. Because many children have a speaking vocabulary that is more extensive than their reading and writing vocabulary, it is important to provide this type of "thinking" activity rather than

constantly restrict problem solving to the current reading level. You can act as a recorder, when necessary, to write the dictated story on the chalkboard.

14. True or false?

   a) $4+8=10$ c) $1<6$ e) $4>3$ g) $5<2$

   b) $7+2>8$ d) $10-3<5$ f) $6=3+4$ h) $17-7=10$

15. Styrofoam, sponge, or foam rubber cubes can be used effectively to develop awareness of relations occurring within number sentences. For example, suppose a child rolls three cubes and comes up with the numerals 4, 5, and 7 on the respective faces. The child may be asked to form a number sentence. One possibility might be $4+5>7$; another could be $4<5+7$. What other number sentences can you form? (An advantage of using these cubes is that children can work quietly in a corner of the room.)

16. List all the whole numbers that will make these sentences true.

   a) $\square<4$ c) $2+\square=9$ e) $\square<10$ g) $\square=13$

   b) $15-5=\square$ d) $10-\square=3$ f) $2\times3=\square$ h) $\square\times2=8$

17. Dramatization is an effective method for young children to observe an action, to understand relationships, and to relate mathematics to real situations. For example, the teacher might hand a child (Tonia) a paper sack with some apples inside. A second child (Mary) is requested to place three more apples into the paper sack. The first child is requested to find out how many apples are in the paper sack now. The child may count the apples and find that there are seven apples all together. The teacher may now ask questions such as "How many apples were in the paper sack when it was given to Tonia? How many apples did Mary put into the sack? How many apples are in the sack all together?" After children have observed an action, talked about the situation, and discussed the mathematics, they are then ready to discuss how the idea may be recorded. Help the children write a mathematical sentence: $\square+3=7$. How many apples were in the sack at the beginning? How many apples did Mary put into the sack? How many apples are there all together? How do we solve mathematical sentences like this one? How many apples were in the paper sack when it was given to Tonia?

18. Provide children with specific examples that will require the use of problem-solving techniques that have been taught. If the teacher wants to reinforce the concept of using tables to solve problems, the following situation might be developed: You are a postal clerk and are responsible for selling 32-cent stamps. How can the clerk handle stamp buyers quickly and efficiently? After role playing, in which the same purchases keep recurring, and a discussion, the children might suggest the need for a ready reference chart. Table making can be explored at this time.

Stamp Sales										
Number of stamps	1	2	3	4	5	6	7	8	9	10
Cost of stamps	.32	.64	.96	1.28	1.60	1.92	2.24	2.56	2.88	3.20

19. Children need to learn how to make tables and record data. Obtain many measuring containers, and have children compare the volumes by pouring sand from one container to another. For example, children can discover that a pint container must be filled twice in order to have as much as a quart container filled once. Use metric as well as U.S. customary measuring containers.

20. Using a drinking straw as a ruler, measure many different items. Cut a straw into two equivalent pieces, and measure many objects using the two different straws. Discuss the results with the children.

21. Have each child take a cube; then request that each child place the cube on the pile for the month of his or her birthday. You have started graphing on the concrete level. Children may want to draw pictures on the graph.

Tabletop ____

Jan. Feb. March April May June July Aug. Sept. etc.

22. Obtain a set of colored blocks and have the children sort the blocks by color. Place all of the red blocks into a box that has been covered with red contact paper, the blue blocks into a blue box, and the yellow blocks into a yellow box. Discuss with the children:

    a) blocks that are red, blocks that are blue, and blocks that are yellow.
    b) blocks that are not red, or blocks that are not blue, or blocks that are not yellow.
    c) blocks that are not red or blue, blocks that are not blue or yellow, or blocks that are not red or yellow.
    d) blocks that are not red, yellow, or blue.

23. Use sorting activities that involve other attributes such as shape, size, or thickness. Discuss the different classifications, and also examine the items that do not fit the classifications.

24. Introduce the ideas of conjunction and disjunction to the children by having them select a block that is blue *and* circular, then a block that is red *or* square.

25. The quantifiers *all, some, none,* and *one* can be used with young children. If the attribute blocks have been sorted by color and shape, the children can be asked questions such as:

    a) Are all the squares red?
    b) Are all the red blocks squares?

26. Provide an opportunity for the children to describe certain blocks. For instance, place all the blocks on the table in front of the children. Have a child describe a block, and have another child pick up the block described. The teacher may also want to pick up any other blocks that might also fit the description. For example, one child might say, "a block that is blue and square." If another child picks up a large, blue, square block, the teacher might want to pick up a small, blue, square block and then discuss how the two blocks meet the specifications. Children should learn that they need to be precise in their descriptions.

27. Set up simple sequences of four or five blocks, and then have a child tell what the next block in the sequence should be. Have the child state the reason for selecting that particular block. What should the next block be in this sequence?

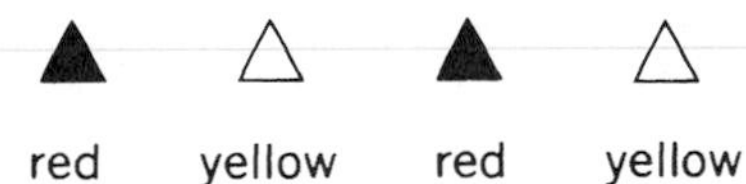

28. Place two large loops of yarn on the table or floor. Two loops should overlap as illustrated in the drawing. Ask children to place attribute blocks into the loops where they belong. In one loop place red blocks. In the other loop place triangles. Discuss the results of the activities. What blocks are in the intersection? Why?

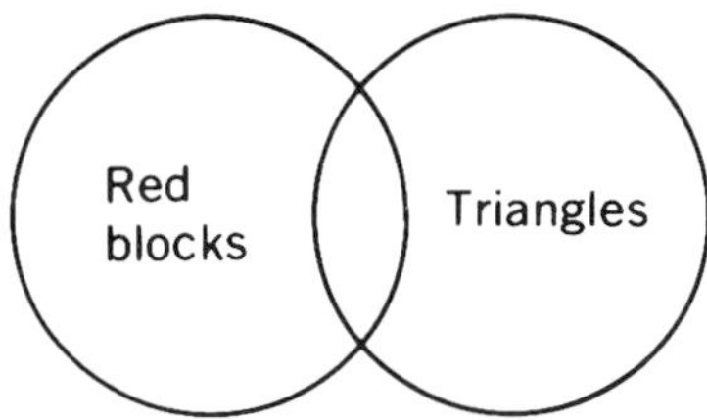

29. Have the children enter certain numbers in the calculator. Ask the children to display

    a) their ages.
    b) the day that was marked on the calendar that morning.
    c) their addresses. (If the children have not memorized their addresses, show their house numbers on the display screen. Clear the screen and have the children copy their own addresses from a paper prepared by the teacher.)
    d) their telephone numbers. (If the children have not memorized their phone numbers, show each child's telephone number on the display screen. The teacher can prepare sheets of paper with one child's telephone number printed on each.)

30. Dramatize problem situations; have the children use calculators to solve the problems and orally give their answers. For example, place seven chairs in a reading circle. Ask the children, "If two more chairs are needed in the library area and are taken from the reading circle, how many chairs will be left in the reading circle?" The children should actually move two chairs from the reading circle to the library area.
31. Set up real-life situations and have the children enter the mathematics into the calculator to obtain a reasonable answer. For example, place three books on Tom's desk and four books on Robin's desk. State the problem situation. Ask the children to use their calculator to show how many books are on Tom's and Robin's desks together. Always spend time discussing the reasonableness of the answers obtained.
32. Children can often be led to discover patterns on the calculator, even when the foundation for those patterns is mathematically beyond their understanding. The children can explore and make simple inferences (and even generalizations) based on their observations and expectations. Remember that even a very young child is quite capable of formulating generalizations. Consider, for example, a preschooler who inappropriately adds "ed" to every verb used in past tense. The child was not taught to do this but has made a generalization.
33. Have the children explore the calculator to determine which keys will make letters when the calculator is inverted. See whether the children can anticipate before pushing the keys.
34. On a calculator, have the children push the [1] key, followed by the [+] key, followed by several presses of the [=] key. Guide the child to a conditional statement of the form, "If I push . . . , then. . . ."
35. Have the children compare and discuss the displays for the following:

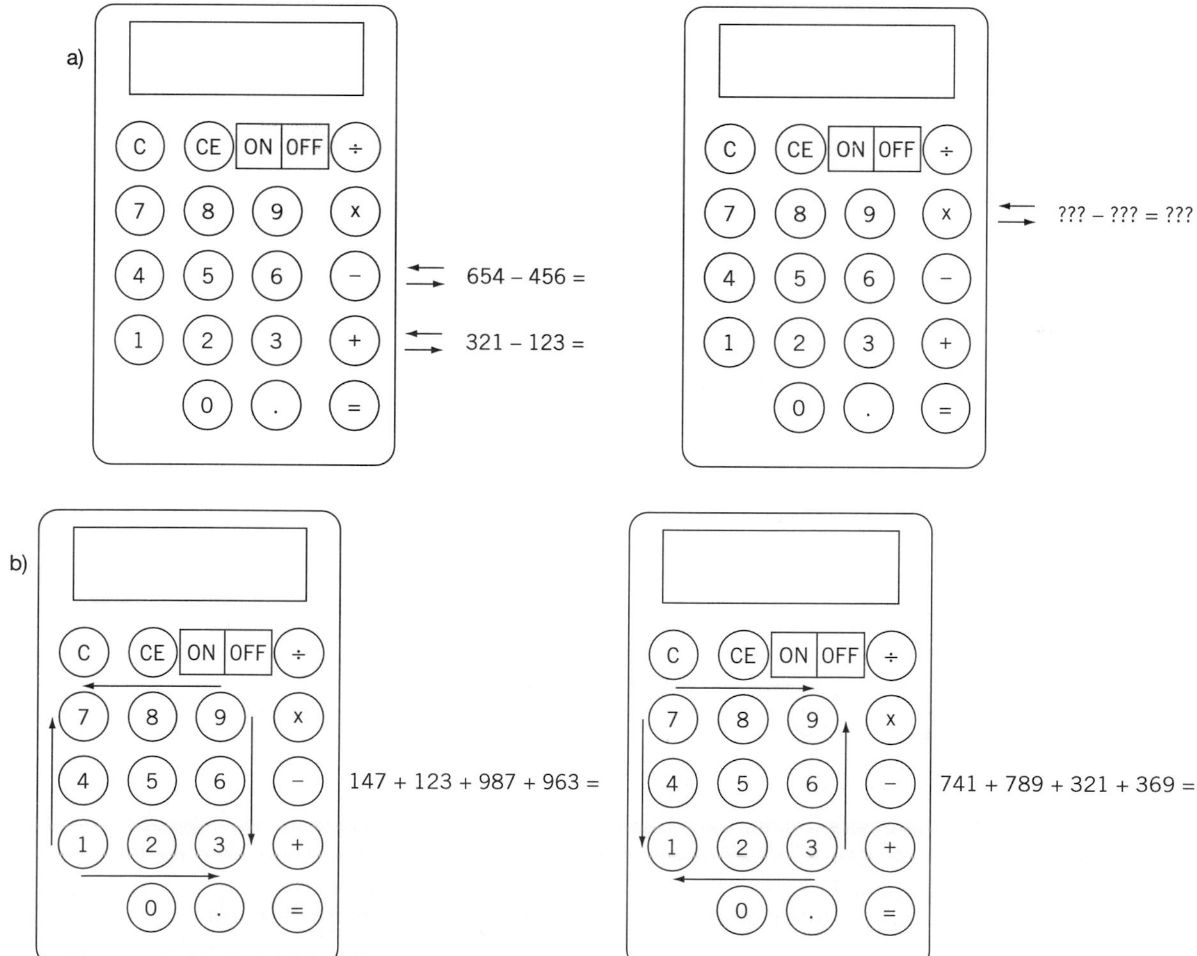

36. Invent your own problem to fit and extend the following given information. Use any units you care to, and write an open sentence describing the problem you have invented.

    a) Jeffrey has 18 ______________________________

       Marge has 12 ______________________________

       ____

    b) Ryan bought 16 ______________________________

       Phyllis bought 26 ______________________________

       ____

37. A useful activity that allows children to practice formulating questions and open sentences is the "Question Game." Pupils are given "answers," such as 639 hats, 69 meters, and 756 hours, and are asked to form open sentences with those numbers as answers.

38. Write the correct relation symbol (<, >, or =) in each ○.

    a) $2 \times 3 \bigcirc 8 - 5$ b) $20 \div 5 \bigcirc 7 - 3$ c) $9 \div 9 \bigcirc 9 \times 0$

39. Place the correct sign (+, –, ×, or ÷) in each △ and ▽. There may be more than one possibility. See how many true statements you can make.

    a) $10 \triangle 2 = 15 \bigtriangledown 3$ c) $9 \triangle 3 = 3 \bigtriangledown 1$

    b) $2 \triangle 5 = 10 \bigtriangledown 3$ d) $8 \triangle 4 = 4 \bigtriangledown 2$

40. Georganna holds her dog as she steps on the scale to weigh herself. Then Georganna weighs herself without the dog. How can Georganna find the weight of her dog?

41. Write mathematical sentences for each puzzle.

    a) I'm thinking of a number. If you add 5 to it, you get 14. What is the number? ($n + 5 = 14$; $n = 9$)
    b) I'm thinking of a number. If you add 4 to it and then add 3, you get 15. What is the number?
    c) I'm thinking of a number. If you subtract 9 from that number, you get 11. What is the number?
    d) If I subtract 4 from a number and then subtract 8, I get 4. What is the number?
    e) I'm thinking of a number. If you add the number to itself and then add 4, you get 12. What is the number?

42. Which of the following are true statements?

    a) $15 - 9 = 25 - 19$ c) $439 - 439 \neq 528 - 528$

    b) $96 - 53 \neq 69 - 35$ d) $241 - 37 \neq 200 - 4$

43. Place the correct relation symbol (>, <, or =) in each ○.

    a) $13 + 26 \bigcirc 31 - 15$ c) $321 + 123 \bigcirc 231 + 213$ e) $2\frac{1}{3} + \frac{1}{3} \bigcirc \frac{10}{3} + \frac{2}{3}$

    b) $86 - 53 \bigcirc 68 - 35$ d) $741 \times 8 \bigcirc 7000 - 1072$ f) $6\frac{1}{3} - 2\frac{1}{6} \bigcirc \frac{19}{3} - \frac{6}{3}$

44. Find the greatest number that will make each sentence true.

    a) $n \times 5 < 47$ c) $n \times 3 < 60$ e) $n \times 7 < 189$

    b) $n \times 8 < 43$ d) $n \times 9 < 66$

45. String beans grow very rapidly and can be used for graphing. Plant bean seeds in paper cups. Give the children strips of paper that they can hold alongside of the bean plant each day, and have them use scissors to cut the strip the same height as the plant. Paste these bars on a graph, and make a bar graph for the growth of a bean plant.

46. Place three large loops of yarn on the floor. Make the loops overlap as illustrated here. Ask the children to place attribute blocks into the appropriate loops.

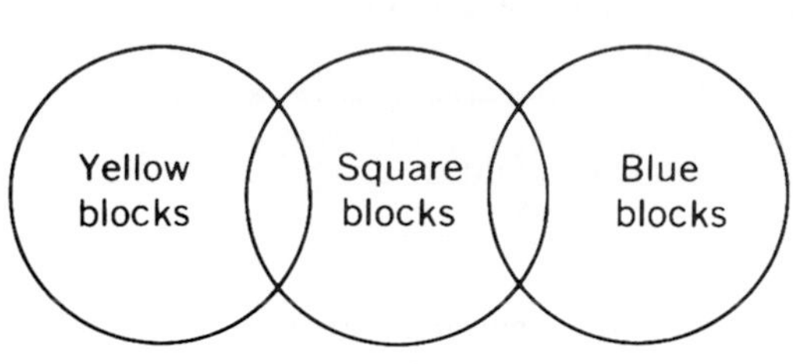

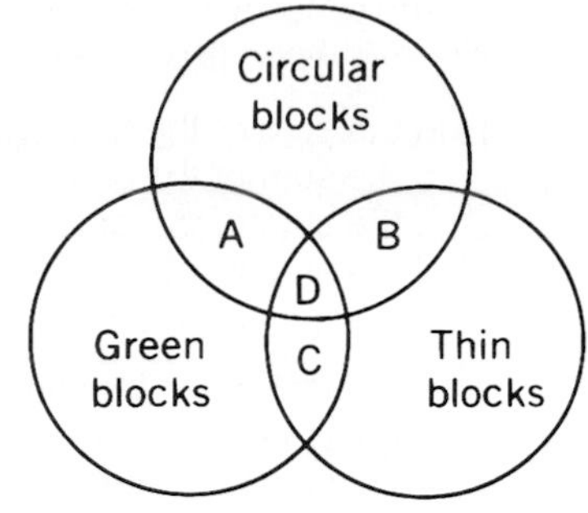

What blocks will be in sections labeled A, B, C, and D? Do you agree with these answers?

A—Green, circular, thick blocks
B—Thin, green blocks that are not circular
C—Circular, thin blocks that are not green
D—Green, circular, thin blocks

INSTRUCTIONAL AND ASSESSMENT ACTIVITIES FOR GRADES 5-8

1. Write a number sentence for each puzzle. What's my number?
   a) When I add 5 to it, I get 13. ($n + 5 = 13$)
   b) When I subtract 3 from it, I get 7.
   c) When I multiply it by 8, I get 24.
   d) I get 19 when my number is subtracted from 26.
   e) When I divide it by 4, I get 12.
   f) When I divide it by 2 and then multiply by 2, I get 34.
2. A helpful technique for developing problem-solving abilities is to involve a picture or drawing. Show the class a picture of an athletic contest, or some other activity. Ask the class to study the picture and to create a story problem about the characters or objects in the picture. Have the pupils solve the story problems they create and then share them with the class.
3. Invent your own problem to fit and extend the following given information. Use any units you care to, and write an open sentence describing the problem you have invented.
   a) Bill had 38 ____________________

      Mary has 23 ____________________

      ____
   b) Jim ordered 16 ____________________

      Jim received 6 ____________________

      ____
4. Write an equation for each sentence. Find the solution.
   a) In 4 years John will be 13 years old. How old is he now?
   b) Peter grew 4 inches during the past year. If he is now 52 inches tall, how tall was he last year at this time?
5. Ask the class to calculate the average number of chews that a student can get from one small Tootsie Roll candy. Provide each student with one small candy, and have each child count the number of chews until the candy is all gone. Collect the data, organize the data into a table or graph, and calculate the average number of chews.
6. Bring a grocery store ad from the local newspaper into the classroom. Have the children create a week's shopping list from the ad, calculate the bill, and figure the sales tax.
7. Ask the local bank to furnish banking material, and have the children create their own bank accounts, learn to write checks, and balance their checkbooks at the end of the month. Children can create their bank statements for the month.

8. All of the following problems can be solved in the same way. Encourage children to find the sum without adding. What techniques can be used?

   Find the sum of the first 100 even numbers.
   Find the sum of the first 100 odd numbers.
   Find the sum of the dates of the days in the month of June.
   Find the sum of the dates of the days in the month of January.
   Find the sum of the dates of the days in the month of February in a leap year.

9. Give the children a box and have them calculate the surface area. Can the children create a formula that would help them? What will happen to the surface area of the box if the measurements are doubled?

10. Obtain a small scale and call the post office for the various postal rates. How much would it cost to mail different items? Children may want to make a table so that they can figure out the cost for mailing different items. If you could mail yourself somewhere, how much would it cost to send you first class?

11. Discuss how to find the weight of 1 file card. For example, children may want to weigh 100 file cards and then calculate the weight of one file card.

12. How many times does your heart beat each day? Each month? Each year? Have children use their dictionaries to find the definition of pulse. Using a watch with a second hand, count your pulse for 30 seconds. How many heartbeats do you have in 1 minute? Count your heartbeats for 1 minute, and check with your calculations above. Use a calculator to calculate the approximate number of heartbeats you have had since your birth.

13. Use a length of string with a washer or metal object tied to the end to make a pendulum. Adjust the length of the string so that it will take 1 second for a complete swing. Each swing from one side to the other will now be 1/2 of a second. Use this pendulum as a timer. What problems arise from this method?

14. Make a pattern that has two or three changes between each pair of blocks in a sequence. Have children take turns selecting a block that could follow in the sequence. Discuss why each block could or could not follow. Study the following example.

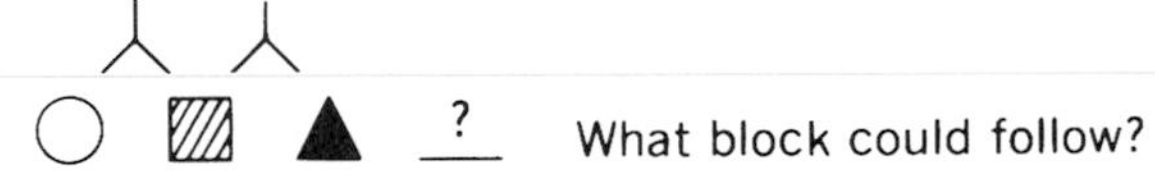
?
What block could follow?

15. Let several children create a sequence of blocks that fit a specific pattern. Have other children describe the pattern. Follow this by having a child state a pattern of a sequence, and have other children create the pattern.

16. Create a sequence that has a predictable, changing pattern. Study the following example.

? ? ?

17. A plumber earns $15.00 per hour and receives time and a half for overtime. Use a calculator to figure the plumber's weekly wages if she worked the normal 40-hour week with 5 hours of overtime.

18. If you earned one dollar every minute, how long would it take you to earn one thousand dollars, one million dollars, and one billion dollars? If a million one-dollar bills were piled one on top of another, how high would the pile reach? Does a calculator help you to focus your attention on the problem?

19. Provide the children with a shoe box. Have the children calculate the number of shoe boxes that could be placed in the classroom. Remember that this may pose some difficulties, because you cannot use half of a shoe box.

20. You have 1 kilometer of fencing and you want to enclose a field containing the most area. Describe the shape of the figure and indicate in square meters the total area that your

figure will enclose. (If children do not include a circle, suggest that they find the area of a circle with a circumference of 1 kilometer.)

21. Calculate the number of minutes in each of the following:

a) one hour	d) one month of May	g) one leap year
b) one day	e) one month of April	h) one decade
c) one week	f) one "regular" year	i) one century

22. How long have you lived? Calculate the total number of seconds you have been alive. Have you had a billionth birthday (in seconds) yet? Calculate the number of days, hours, minutes, and weeks. Calculate the number of years in decimals to the nearest thousandth. Calculate the number of seconds.

23. Get menus from local restaurants. Have the children collect orders and prepare bills.

24. Pattern-searching activities suggested for the lower grades can be expanded and extended for the intermediate grades. Explore the notion of a valid argument by discussing the following:

    Pushing $16 \div 8 =$ puts 2 in the display
    Pushing $6 - 4 =$ puts 2 in the display
    So, $16 \div 8$ must equal $6 - 4$
    Pushing $4 \times 5 =$ puts 20 in the display
    Pushing $3 + 6 =$ doesn't put 20 in the display
    So, 4×5 does not equal $3 + 6$

25. Write a word problem to fit each equation.

    a) $5\frac{1}{2} + n = 10\frac{1}{4}$ b) $\frac{n-3}{3} = 3$ c) $(4 \times n) + 6 = 26$

26. Write an equation for each problem.

    a) The Glen Park school bus has enough room for 34 children. If the driver started with a full load, stopped at North School to let off 18 children, and picked up 9 more children going to South School, how many children were then on the bus?
    b) Jerry came home from a school baseball game and was hungry, as usual. He found a note from his mother telling him to help himself to a piece of pie and a glass of milk. Someone else had already eaten part of the pie, because only $\frac{2}{3}$ of it was left in the pan. After Jerry cut a piece for himself, only $\frac{1}{2}$ of the pie remained. What part of the whole pie did Jerry eat?

27. Present a variety of simple equations using frames or letters as placeholders for missing numerals. Encourage the students to check their solutions by testing to see whether the numbers they obtain make the sentence true.

    a) $2 \times n = 24$ c) $n - 4 = 83$ e) $n \div 7 = 2 \times 14$

    b) $4 \div n = 4$ d) $(5 \times n) + 5 = 20$ f) $(8 + 6) \div 2 = n$

28. Find the solution for each of the following open sentences. Use only counting numbers between 0 and 5.

    a) $\square + 2 = 7$ c) $3 \times \square < 21$

    b) $\square - 2 > 15$ d) $\square + (3 \times \square) = 8$

29. Problem solving in the elementary school can be approached with the use of task cards. These can be constructed by the teacher and often contain a problem for which many strategies and solutions may be appropriate. For example, a card with the following questions can be constructed:

    How long is a minute?
    How many times do you breathe in a minute?
    Estimate; then find out.
    Do you always breathe the same number of times each minute?
    Can you prove your hypothesis?

30. Using only integers, find the solution for each of the following sentences. (Integers will be discussed further in Chapter 8.)

a) $^{-}15+n=13$ c) $4+n={}^{-}3$ e) $n+({}^{-}3)=6$

b) $n+7={}^{-}81$ d) $^{-}20+n={}^{-}90$ f) $n+({}^{-}4)=16$

31. Write an equation for each of the following. Find the solution.

a) Jean is 5 years older than Jane. Sue is 2 years younger than Jean. How much older than Jane is Sue?

b) There are 30 pupils in Roy's class: 16 boys and 14 girls. If $\frac{3}{4}$ of the boys are in the sixth-grade mathematics club and $\frac{1}{2}$ of the girls are in the sixth-grade music club, how many members of the class do not take part in either of these activities?

32. This problem can be posed to the class: "If you had $10.00 to plan a party for the class, what would you buy?" This problem can offer several open-ended directions to explore. Children can estimate costs for the party and then check them with actual prices appearing in stores and newspapers.

33. Compare the height from which a rubber ball is dropped to the height of its first bounce. Then check the height of its subsequent bounces. Show your findings on a graph. Can you form an open sentence that describes the results you obtained?

34. Have children write their name on a piece of paper and then determine how long a piece of paper and how much time would be needed to write their name one million times.

35. If the snow continues to fall at the (constant) rate of .3 an inch per hour, how much snow will fall in 8.5 hours?

36. Connie has 4 pennies, 3 nickels, 2 dimes, and 3 quarters. How many different amounts of money can Connie make by using all the possible combinations of coins?

37. Select a specific pine or "leafy" tree, and have the children calculate the number of needles or leaves on the tree. Discuss with the children the "best" way to estimate the answer. Encourage variety in approaches to this estimation task.

38. Draw a representation of a circle. Place points on the circumference of the circle. Using a straightedge, join all of the points of each drawing. How many regions will each drawing have? What is the number of regions if there are eight points on the circumference of the circle?

a) A circle with one point has one region.
b) A circle with two points will be separated into two regions.
c) A region with three points will have four regions, and so on.

What problem-solving techniques will help find a solution to this word problem? Let's make a table.

Number of points	1	2	3	4	5	6	7	8	9	10
Number of regions	1	2	4							

39. The 32 students in class want to have a round-robin checkers tournament (each child is to play every other child once). How many games will each child play in the first round? If losers are eliminated in each round, how many students will play in the second round? How many games will be played in the second round? In the third round? How many games will be played in all? A table might be helpful.

Number of people	1	2	3	4	5	6	7	8	9	10
Number of games	0	1	3	6	10	15	21	28		
Differences	1	2	3	4	5	6	7			

40. Find the thickness of this page. Would measuring the thickness of 100 pages help in some way?

41. How many pennies would it take to completely fill your classroom? How many dollars would the pennies be worth? How much would the pennies weigh?

42. Calculate the volume of the room. How many cubic feet of air does each student have for breathing? Why are the ceilings higher in auditoriums than in classrooms and houses?

43. Sally had $6.25 in her school savings account. Jeff had $4.98 in his savings account. They both withdrew the same amount of money. Who has the least money left?

44. Betsy is younger than Paul. Paul is younger than Mark. Is Mark older than Betsy?

45. Provide an opportunity for the students to describe verbally a certain set of blocks and then discuss how the blocks meet the specifications. Students should learn that they need to be precise in their descriptions. As students become more adept, you may want to describe a block by telling what it is not. For example, select a block that is not red, not square, and not thick.

46. Group E is the set of numbers divisible by 2.
Group G is the set of even numbers.
Group H is the set of whole numbers.
Group J is the set of odd numbers.
Mark each statement true or false.

    a) Some members of Group J are in Group H.
    b) All members of Group H are in Group J.
    c) No members of Group E are in Group J.
    d) Some members of Group E are in Group G.
    e) All members of Group H are in Group E.
    f) No members of Group G are in Group J.

47. What new fact can you discover by putting two facts together? Here is an example:

    All triangles are polygons.
    All polygons are closed curves.
    Answer: All triangles are closed curves.

    a) All counting numbers are whole numbers.
    25 is a counting number.
    So, . . .
    b) All rectangles are quadrilaterals.
    A square is a rectangle.
    So, . . .
    c) All numbers divisible by 6 are divisible by 3.
    24 is divisible by 6.
    So, . . .

48. Mark each sentence true or false.

    a) All closed curves are circles.
    b) No quadrilaterals are polygons.
    c) Some polygons are quadrilaterals.
    d) All whole numbers are counting numbers.
    e) No even numbers are odd numbers.

49. As children use logic to draw conclusions, they must be careful not to assume anything that is not specifically stated.

    a) Jim and Mike went swimming.
    Did two children go swimming?
    Did Jim and Mike swim all day?
    Did Jim go swimming?
    Did Mike go swimming?
    b) Susan or her sister plays the piano.
    Does at least one girl play the piano?

Does Susan's sister play the piano?
If Susan doesn't play the piano, does her sister play the piano?

c) Some boys like baseball or all boys like baseball.
Does at least one boy like baseball?
Do all boys like baseball?
If some boys do not like baseball, then do all boys like baseball?

d) If the record is playing, then you can hear it.
You cannot hear it.
What can you conclude?

e) If the record is playing, then it is rotating.
Is the conditional true?
Is it true that, if the record is playing, then it is rotating?
Is the antecedent true?
Is the record playing?
What can you conclude?

50. Encourage the children to play games that involve logic and reason—games such as chess, Tower of Hanoi, and Equations.

51. Encourage children to use logic in finding a specific number. As an example, ask the children what is the least number of questions they could ask in order to name a number between 1 and 100 that the teacher is thinking about. Examples of some good questions children could ask are:

    Is it an even number?
    Is the number greater than 50?
    Is the number greater than 75?

    Examples of some poor questions children might ask are:

    Is it 23?
    Is it 78?

    With three good questions we have changed the number of possible answers from 100 to just 20. Can you improve on this?

52. Locate the population and land area for five states. Use a calculator to determine the population per square mile. Which of the five states you chose has the most people per square mile? Calculate the difference in population per square mile among the five states you selected.

53. Have each child in the class count the number of breaths taken per minute. What is the average number of breaths per minute for the children in your classroom? How many combined breaths are taken by all the children in your classroom in one day?

54. A person who lifts 100 pounds on earth could lift 600 pounds on the moon. How much could a person lift on the moon who can lift 135 pounds on earth?

55. Use data from the sports page of your local newspaper and, for example, calculate batting averages for each player on a team.

56. Calculate the percent of your state's population located in each of the larger cities.

57. Use a local newspaper sale advertisement for tires to calculate the percent of savings on each tire on sale. Is the percent of saving on each tire the same as the overall percent of saving if you buy four?

58. Encourage the children to explore patterns and relationships by pushing the keys of a calculator in a certain sequence. Examine the activities suggested for the earlier grades and make appropriate modifications for use with older children.

59. A strategy game for two children can be easily adapted for the calculator. Begin with the calculator displaying a two-digit number such as 47 (any "reasonable" number will do). The children take turns subtracting a single-digit number (except 0) from the number currently in the display. The child who can force another child to display the number 0 at the end of his or her turn is the winner. Help the children to develop a winning strategy, one that will work no matter what the starting number is. (Hint: The strategy depends on who goes first.)

60. One activity that helps to convey how a computer "reasons" and carries out the steps of a program can be used quite successfully with this age group as well as with younger children. Prepare a set of about 10 (or fewer) cards, describing some common activity such as washing a car. Each card should describe only one task associated with this activity. In this example, the cards might include the following: Clean the top; get the water; close the windows; get the soap, brush, and bucket; close the doors; and so on. Have the children work in groups to determine the overall activity by looking only at their own card. This will be easier for some groups because of context clues. The same situation exists when we examine a computer program: Some lines of the program relate directly to the purpose of the program; others are for "cosmetic" purposes, such as clearing the screen or slowing the output.

    When the students have determined the overall activity—perhaps after discussion with other groups whose card(s) were not quite as general—then have the children determine the correct order for carrying out the tasks. In our example, should "close the doors" come before or after "close the windows"? You will find that in some cases the order makes little or no difference, whereas in others the order is critical. This is also an excellent example of how a computer program is structured; some steps could be rearranged without affecting the output, but others must appear in certain locations. This activity could help the children realize that there is often more than one way to carry out a task successfully.

61. While we do not advocate the teaching of programming at the elementary levels, some students might benefit from exploring ways in which a computer reasons by examining short examples of simple programming language. The following program is written in BASIC and can be "walked through" to assess the impact of each line. Describe what each statement of this computer program will do.

```
10 HOME            (Clears the screen)
20 LET A = 5       (Assigns a value of "5" to the variable A)
30 LET B = 8       (Assigns a value of "8" to the variable B)
40 C = A + B       (Adds 5 and 8 and assigns the sum, 13, to C)
50 ?"THE SUM OF ";A;" AND ";B;" IS ";C      (Prints the phrase, "THE SUM OF 5 AND 8
   IS 13" on the screen)
```

Suggested Readings

Bamberger, H. J., & Campbell, P. F. (1990). The vision of problem solving in the standards. *The Arithmetic Teacher, 37*(9).

Bell, A., Greer, B., Grimison, L., & Mangan, C. (1989). Childrens' performance on multiplicative word problems: Elements of a descriptive theory. *Journal for Research in Mathematics Education, 20*(5).

Biggerstaff, M., Halloran, B., & Serrano, C. (1994). Teacher to teacher: Use color to assess mathematics problem solving. *The Arithmetic Teacher, 41*(6).

Bohan, H., & Bohan, S. (1993). Extending the regular curriculum through creative problem solving. *The Arithmetic Teacher, 41*(2).

Bosch, K. A. (1993). Teaching problem-solving strategies. *The Clearing House, 66.*

Brady, R. R. (1991). A close look at student problem solving and the teaching of mathematics. *School Science and Mathematics, 91*(8).

Brown, N. (1993). Teacher to teacher: Writing mathematics. *The Arithmetic Teacher, 41*(1).

Brown, S. (1990). Integrating manipulatives and computers in problem solving experiences. *The Arithmetic Teacher, 38*(2).

Brown, S. I., & Walter, M. I. (1983). *The Art of Problem Posing.* Hillsdale, NJ: Erlbaum.

Carpenter, T. P. (1993). Models of problem solving: A study of kindergarten children's problem-solving processes. *Journal for Research in Mathematics Education, 24.*

Carpenter, T. P. (1994). *Teaching mathematics for learning with understanding in the primary grades.* Madison, WI: National Center for Research in Mathematical Sciences Education.

Carpenter, T. P., Moser, J. M., & Bebout, H. C. (1988). Representation of addition and subtraction word problems. *Journal for Research in Mathematics Education, 19*(4).

Cochener, D., & Cochener, D. (1993). How many miles per hour is that fan going? An experiment to implement problem solving in grades 5-8. *School Science and Mathematics, 93*(3).

Curcio, F. R., & Polya, G. (Eds.). (1987). *Teaching and learning: A problem-solving focus.* Reston, VA: National Council of Teachers of Mathematics.

Davis, R. B. (1991). Research into practice: Giving pupils tools for thinking. *The Arithmetic Teacher, 38*(5).

Driscoll, M. J. (1981). Mathematical problem solving: Not just a matter of words." In M. J. Driscoll (Ed.), *Research within reach: Elementary school mathematics.* Reston, VA: National Council of

Teachers of Mathematics and CEMREL, Inc.

English, L. (1992). Problem solving with combinations. *The Arithmetic Teacher, 40*(2).

Fairbairn, D. M. (1993). Creating story problems. *The Arithmetic Teacher, 41*(3).

Farivar, S., & Webb, N. M. (1994). Helping and getting help—essential skills for effective group problem solving. *The Arithmetic Teacher, 41*(9).

Ford, M. I. (1990). The writing process: A strategy for problem solvers. *The Arithmetic Teacher, 38*(3).

Fulkerson, P. (1992). Getting the most from a problem. *The Arithmetic Teacher, 40*(3).

Garofalo, J., & Mtetwa, D. K. (1990). Mathematics as reasoning. *The Arithmetic Teacher, 37*(5).

Gill, A. J. (1993). Multiple strategies: Product of reasoning and communication. *Arithmetic Teacher, 40.*

Gonzales, N. (1994). Problem posing: A neglected component in mathematics courses for prospective elementary and middle school teachers. *School Science and Mathematics, 94*(2).

Hands-on, Inc. (1990). *Algebra: Kindergarten through grade nine.* Solvang, CA: Author.

Hands-on, Inc. (1989). *Logic: Kindergarten through grade nine.* Solvang, CA: Author.

Hands-on, Inc. (1990). *Patterns and functions: Kindergarten through grade nine.* Solvang, CA: Author.

Harte, S. W., & Glover, M. (1993). Estimation is mathematical thinking. *The Arithmetic Teacher, 41*(2).

Huinker, D. M. (1989). Multiplication and division word problems: Improving students' understanding. *The Arithmetic Teacher, 37*(2).

James, A. (1993). The great escape: Using problem-solving in the classroom. *Mathematics in School, 22.*

Kamii, C., Lewis, B. A. & Livingston, S. J. (1993). Primary arithmetic: Children inventing their own arithmetic. *The Arithmetic Teacher, 41*(4).

Keller, J. D. (1993). Ideas. *Arithmetic Teacher, 40.*

Kersch, M. E., & McDonald, J. (1991). How do I solve thee? Let me count the ways! *The Arithmetic Teacher, 39*(2).

Kloosterman, P. (1992). Non-routine word problems: One part of a problem-solving program in the elementary school. *School Science and Mathematics, 92*(1).

Krulik, S., & Rudnik, J. A. (1994). Reflect . . . for better problem solving and reasoning. *The Arithmetic Teacher, 41*(6).

Lester, F. K., Jr. & Mau, S. T. (1993). Teaching mathematics via problem solving: A course for prospective elementary teachers. *For the Learning of Mathematics, 13.*

Maddon, P. J. (1994). Teacher to teacher: Making story problems relevant. *The Arithmetic Teacher, 41*(9).

Matz, K., & Leier, C. (1992). Word problems and the language connection. *The Arithmetic Teacher, 39*(8).

May, L. (1990). Problem solving: The central focus. *Teaching PreK-8, 21*(1).

May, L. J. (1995). Problem-solving skills. *Teaching PreK-8, 25.*

Meiring, S. P. (1980). *Problem solving . . . a basic mathematics goal. Vol. 1: Becoming a better problem solver.* Columbus, OH: Ohio Department of Education.

Meiring, S. P. (1980). *Problem solving . . . a basic mathematics goal. Vol. 2: A resource for problem solver.* Columbus, OH: Ohio Department of Education.

Moody, W. B. (1990). A program in middle school problem solving, *The Arithmetic Teacher, 38*(4).

National Council of Teachers of Mathematics. (1986). *Estimation and mental computation.* (1986 Yearbook). Reston, VA: Author.

National Council of Teachers of Mathematics. (1993). *Curriculum and evaluation standards for school mathematics addenda series grades K-4: Patterns.* Reston, VA: Author.

National Council of Teachers of Mathematics. (1991). *Curriculum and evaluation standards for school mathematics addenda series grades 5-8: Patterns and functions.* Reston, VA: Author.

National Council of Teachers of Mathematics. (1980). *Problem solving in school mathematics.* (1980 Yearbook). Reston, VA: Author.

O'Daffer, P., & Charles, R. (1989). Problem solving: Tips for teachers: Asking questions to evaluate problem solving. *The Arithmetic Teacher, 35*(5).

Oppedal, D. C. (1995). Mathematics is something good! *Teaching Children Mathematics, 2.*

Otis, M. J., & Offerman, T. R. (1988). How do you evaluate problem solving? *The Arithmetic Teacher, 35*(8).

Piaget, J., & Inhelder, B. (1969). *The early growth of logic in the child.* New York: W. W. Norton and Co.

Polya, G. (1957). *How to solve it.* (2nd ed). Garden City, NY: Doubleday.

Rowan, T. & Marrow L. J. (1993). *Implementing the K-8 curriculum and evaluation standards: Readings from The Arithmetic Teacher. Implementing the K-8 curriculum and evaluation standards.* Reston, VA: National Council of Teachers of Mathematics.

Sanfiorenzo, N. R. (1991). Evaluating expressions: A problem-solving approach. *The Arithmetic Teacher, 38*(3).

Schoenfield, A. H. (1985). *Mathematical problem solving.* Orlando, FL: Academic Press.

Silverman, F., Winograd, K., & Strohauer, D. (1992). Student-generated story problems. *The Arithmetic Teacher, 39*(8).

Sowder, L. (1989). Story problems and students' strategies. *The Arithmetic Teacher, 36*(9).

Thiessen, D. (1987). Problem solving: Tips for teachers: Value lies in writing word problems. *The Arithmetic Teacher, 35*(3).

Thompson, I. (1993). Thirteen ways to solve a problem. *Mathematics Teaching, 144.*

Trahanovsky-Orletsky, A. E. (1991). What's the problem? *Learning, 91.*

Wadlington, E., Bitner, J., Partridge, E., & Austin, S. (1992). Have a problem? Make the writing—mathematics connection. *The Arithmetic Teacher, 40*(4).

Weidemann, W. (1995). Problem solving in math class: "word problems" were never like this. *Middle School Journal, 27.*

Wilde, S. (1991). Learning to write about mathematics. *The Arithmetic Teacher, 38*(6).

Chapter 5

Number Sense, Numeration, and Place Value

Overview

Educators agree that children enter school with widely varying backgrounds. Home environment, travel experiences, stimulating toys, and human communication have had an effect on each child's personality. It is the teacher's responsibility to assess accurately each child's entrance level and to provide experiences that capitalize on inherent curiosity to develop a deeper understanding of the child's environment.

The primary teacher must constantly be aware that children may have vague and somewhat uninformed ideas about mathematics. The teacher is a "question clarifier" rather than a "question answerer." Some teachers find it difficult to comprehend that some children have not grasped relatively simple concepts such as one-to-one correspondence. Resist the temptation to simply tell the students what you want them to know. The primary mathematics program should be geared toward how children learn mathematics and not toward how to listen to a teacher tell you about mathematics. Thus, children should find themselves in situations that require them to discuss and use mathematics to answer their needs.

If our educational system is to prepare children for success, we must teach them to recognize mathematics in the real world. The use of attribute blocks and other manipulative materials provides a valuable vehicle for relating mathematics to the real world. Children need numerous experiences observing, identifying, and verbalizing ideas to others. While basic mathematics concepts are being developed, the children are also developing logical thought processes in mathematics. Children will usually find the concrete level approach to numberness and operations to be an enjoyable and logical approach to mathematics.

Because of daily contact with our base ten numeration system, it isn't long before that exposure causes us to think that our system of numeration is the *only* system and that it has been in existence forever. The Hindu-Arabic numeration system that we use is relatively new compared with many ancient numeration systems.

A comment often heard is, "I understand our base ten system but I certainly do not understand any of the other bases." Comments such as this actually indicate a shallow understanding of base ten. The basic concepts of a place-value system that uses ten as a base are identical to those of a place-value system that uses any other number as a base.

There seems to be little need to translate numerals from one base system to another base system. The value of exploring other bases stems primarily from the development of an in-depth understanding of place value and, to a degree, from an interest in the historical development of numbers.

The development of the concept of place value is very important, beginning in the first grade with the base ten (decimal) system. We are concerned with the structure of our place-value system—understanding, extending, expanding, and comparing what is discovered at each successive step. We should give children an opportunity to apply some of the mathematical concepts they learn to situations that will allow them to think analytically and creatively.

Children are often curious about the past and in knowing what happened before and after a particular event. Ancient numeration systems provide a mental transition for children that should arouse not only curiosity about mathematics but curiosity about history as well. Ancient systems of numeration may be presented as part of a social studies unit that integrates mathematics and social studies. The geographical, social, and economic structure of particular societies could be analyzed so that children can compare these systems from a broader perspective and realize that our system isn't the "one and only," that we might well have had another system, and that we had a great deal of work done for us by ancient cultures we read about in history books.

The activities in this section focus on number sense, numeration, and place value. Children first need to understand the physical representation of groups and one-to-one correspondence and then learn to write numerals as a solid base for developing mathematical concepts. For appropriate activities on other aspects of the beginning mathematics program, please refer to the appropriate chapters.

SAMPLE LESSON PLAN—"I'M A TEN"

Primary Review Lesson

Goal:

Develop real-world connections to numeric values.

Objective:

The students will:

- Communicate everyday uses of the number ten.

Prerequisite Learning and/or Experiences:

- Recognize the numeral ten.
- Write the numeral ten.
- Count to or beyond ten.

Materials:

Teacher:

Chalkboard or chart paper.

Students:

Paper, pencil, and crayons.

Procedures:

Motivational Introduction

We know what it means when someone says they are happy or sad, hungry or full, young or old, and so on. But what does it mean when someone says they are a "ten"?

Tell the following story:

Amanda ran into the house and yelled, "I'm a ten."
"A ten!" her father exclaimed. "How wonderful!"

1. Let's brainstorm a list of reasons why Amanda says she is a ten. Be prepared to discuss what being a ten means. Incorporate how our "definition of a ten" might change if her father had said, "How terrible!" List student ideas on the chalkboard/chart paper.

Developmental Activity

2. Continue brainstorming, but change the parameters to "everyday uses of the number ten." Be prepared to provide examples such as a ten-speed bicycle, ten fingers on two hands, etc. Some students may want to include classroom uses such as base ten blocks. List student ideas on the chalkboard/chart paper.
3. After the class has had an opportunity to add their everyday use of the number ten to the class list, have the students think about their favorite entry. Don't be surprised if each student's favorite entry matches the one he or she brainstormed.
4. Have students draw a picture about their favorite everyday use of the number ten.

Culminating Activity

5. Pair students and have partners tell stories about their pictures to each other. If students need

assistance getting started, be prepared to tell your own ten story.

6. Have students write a story about their picture.
7. Using edited stories and their associated pictures, create a class book entitled, "I'm a Ten." Place the book in the class library for students to read.

Extension:

Repeat this lesson for other values less than twelve. Students may discover some unusual options such as hot dog buns come in packages of 12, but many companies package hot dogs in packages of 8. If applicable, use their discoveries to pose problem situations.

Student Assessment/Evaluation:

Using address labels, record anecdotal notes about each student's everyday uses of ten for portfolio documentation. For example, Mary Kate may draw and write about how her size ten dress is smaller than her mother's size ten dress. Or, Jason explains that ants are small and elephants are big, but 10 ants are equal to 10 elephants because both are 10 things.

Mary Kate
Uses of Ten
Relative magnitude of number — compares adult and child size 10 dresses.

Jason
Uses of Ten
Conservation of number — ten elephants equals ten ants.

INSTRUCTIONAL AND ASSESSMENT ACTIVITIES FOR GRADES K-4

1. Have groups of objects available for children to manipulate and describe. Every classroom has the basic equipment for this task: boxes of crayons, books, pencils, chairs, desks, and, of course, children.
2. Obtain materials from the local fast-food restaurant such as disposable plastic spoons, forks, or cups, and use them as mathematics manipulatives. Use items with which the children are familiar.
3. Some children will probably have collections of small toys such as cars, dolls, dishes, or furniture. Permit them to bring their collections to school and let other children describe them in various ways.
4. Obtain pictures of items (semiconcrete level) for children to separate into groups. Pictures can be cut from old magazines, newspapers, or catalogs and placed in a large brown envelope. Using four old boxes, paste a picture representative of the objects to be placed in each inside the bottom of each box.

Box I furniture
Box II dishes
Box III shoes
Box IV clothing

The child takes a picture from the envelope and places it in the proper box. After all the pictures have been separated, the boxes can be placed on the teacher's desk for checking. The pictures can then be mixed up and put back into the large brown envelope for a different child to separate at another time. Four or five different groups of pictures should be made.

5. A flannel board with felt cutouts and yarn can be used to make groups on a semiconcrete level. Have children take turns making groups, and have another child orally describe the group.

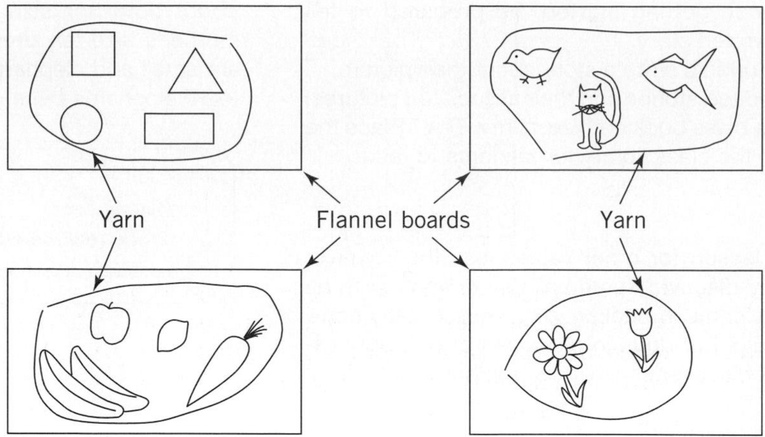

6. Use an overhead projector to project groups of shapes made from different-colored plastic encircled in yarn. Let one child at a time assemble a group on the projector while the rest of the children take turns orally describing the groups.

7. Dictating statements to encourage response from pupils is very useful. Some examples of the type of statements that might be used in first grade are:

   a) all children wearing shoes (the children could stand up so that the real objects—concrete level—composing the group would be seen by all the pupils).
   b) all girls in the room.
   c) all boys in the room.
   d) all children who are wearing red.

   Ask the children to think of statements to dictate for group response; then ask other children to describe the group.

8. Have several covered containers available, such as 1-pound coffee cans, one or two large cardboard boxes, and some small balls, dolls, or wooden blocks. In one container place three items, in another two items, one item in another, and no items in the last container. Give the four containers to four different children, and have each one describe the set of items seen in the container. Discuss how we would describe the container with no members. Use this approach to guide the children into understanding the idea of zero or a group with no members.

9. Discussing questions such as the following can help build a concept of zero. Discuss these, and then encourage the children to think of similar questions.

   a) How many children in the room are taller than the teacher?
   b) How many purple zebras do we have in the classroom?
   c) How many pieces of chalk are there in the empty chalk box?

10. Let children make sets of cards with various numbers of pictures of items pasted on them. Have another set of cards with a numeral written on each card. Beginning with numbers less than four, ask the children to match the card with the proper numeral card.

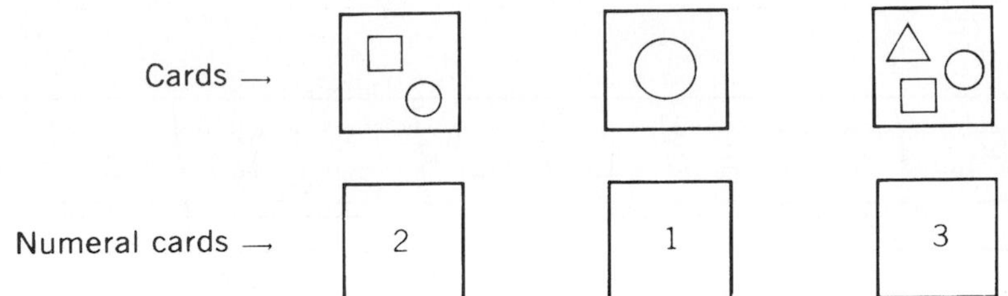

11. After the children have learned how to match the cards with the numeral cards, they can play a game of "Concentration." Turn all the cards face down on a table. Two to four children may play by turning over any two cards during a turn. If the cards are a set and its corresponding numeral card, the child may keep the pair. If the cards do not match, they must again be turned facedown. The child with the most pairs of cards after all the cards have been matched wins the game.
12. Using a length of rope or heavy cord, tie a knot in the rope for each child. The length of the rope will depend on the size of the class. Have each child hold a knot and discuss the one-to-one correspondence of children to the knots in the rope. This activity can be used effectively by taking the class on a walk; variations can be done using additional rope and "left overs."
13. Mark an X on each picture that has one object.

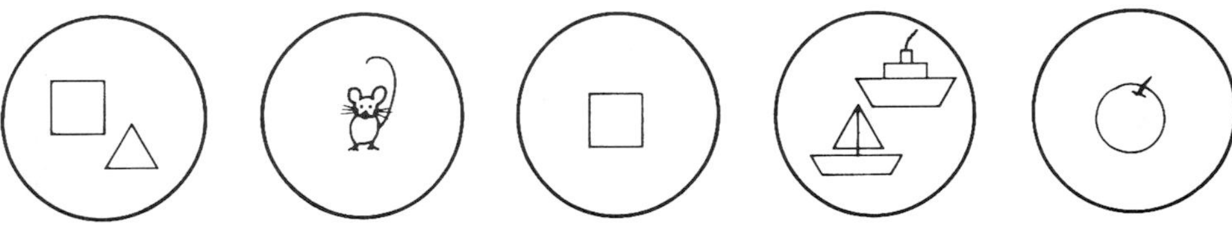

Mark an X on each picture that has three objects.

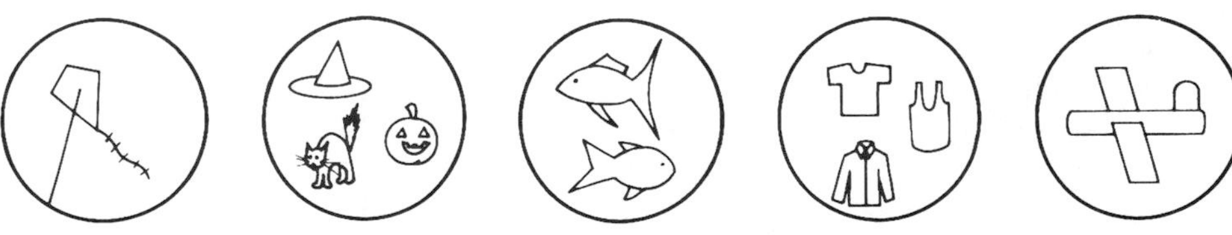

14. As the children begin to recognize groups and numerals through nine, practice can be provided through games. Make bingo cards with numerals on the cards; make markers large enough to cover a numeral. Play the game by showing cards with groups of dots one by one. If a child has the numeral on a bingo card, the child can cover it. Only one numeral may be covered in any one turn. The first child to cover four numerals in a row, across or down, wins the game.

Bingo			
9	3	2	7
5	8	4	1
2	4	7	5
8	1	3	6

Bingo			
1	5	3	6
8	4	2	9
7	8	5	4
6	9	4	7

Bingo			
6	1	9	7
4	8	5	1
6	3	4	7
1	5	9	2

15. Make a walk-on number line by taping a roll of shelf paper to the floor. Mark off spaces that are about equal to a child's pace. Write the numerals so that the child views the numeral correctly as the child walks forward on the number line.

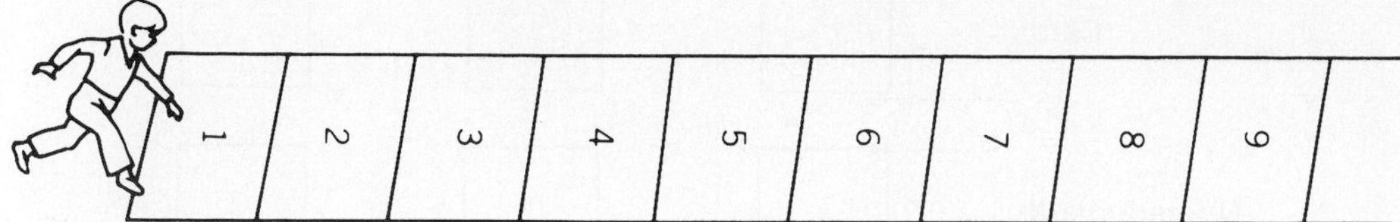

16. If stairs are available, make squares of cardboard about the size of the width of a stair step. Write a numeral on each square and tape it on the proper step. As a child says a number, have another child go to the step with the corresponding numeral on it.

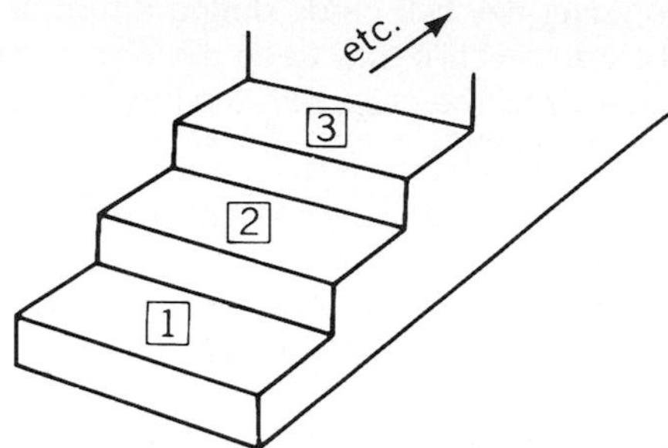

17. Draw line segments to connect the sets with the same number of elements.

18. Draw groups to complete this table.

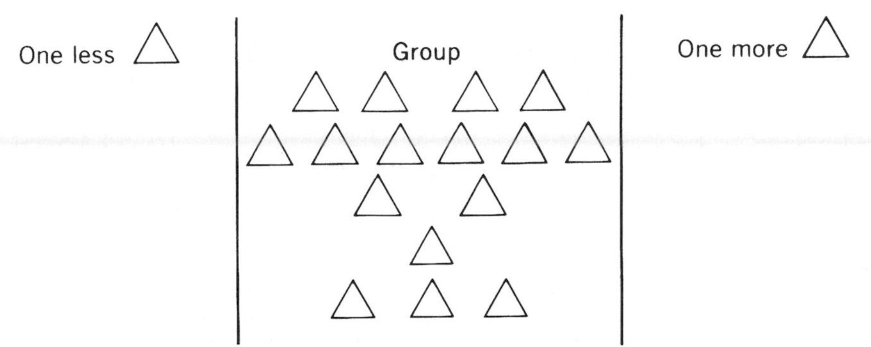

19. Draw a loop around the greater number.

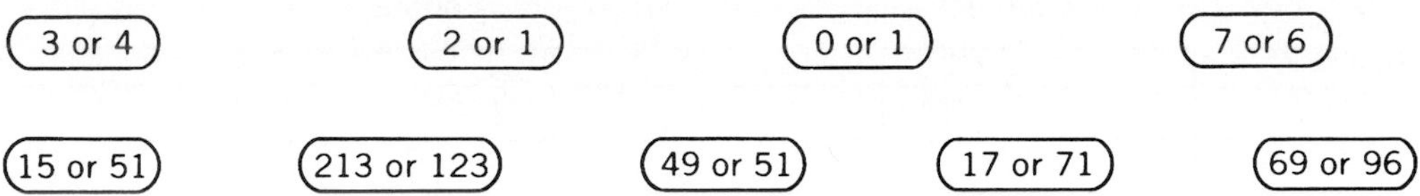

20. Draw a loop around the lesser number.

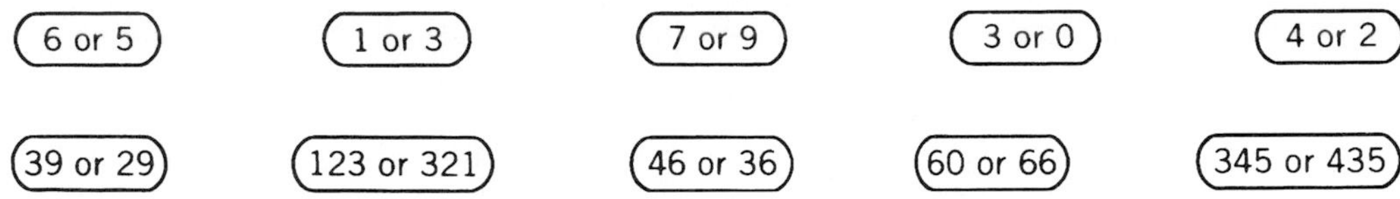

21. For primary children who have not leaned to read, a rebus may be used. In example (a), the children can read that three triangles and four disks make seven triangles and disks. How would you read example (b)?

a) How many? b) How many?

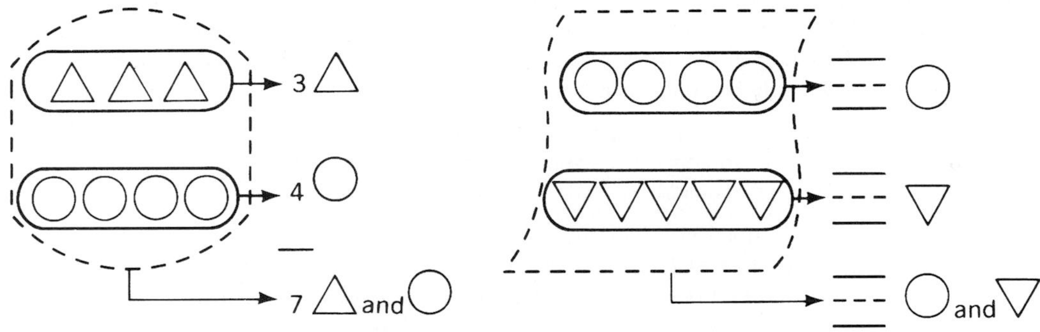

In these examples, children are not adding. They are merely counting the number of triangles, the number of disks, and the number of triangles and disks. This is a readiness activity using groups as a model for addition.

22. Numbers may be used to relate number ideas to two disjoint groups and to the new group created by putting the two groups together. Addition is not used, but counting the objects in each group provides readiness for addition.

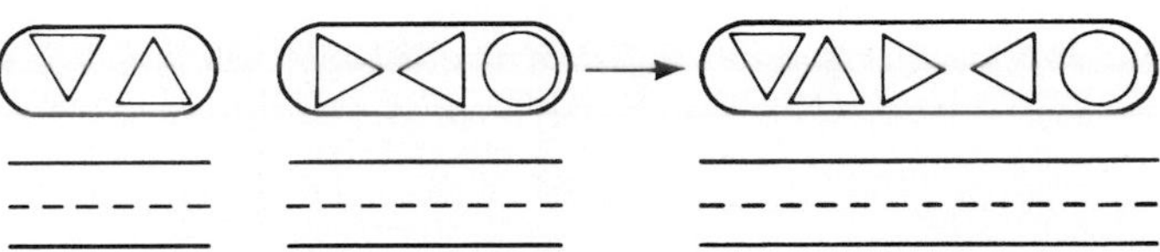

23. Loop the number shown, and complete the table below the groups.

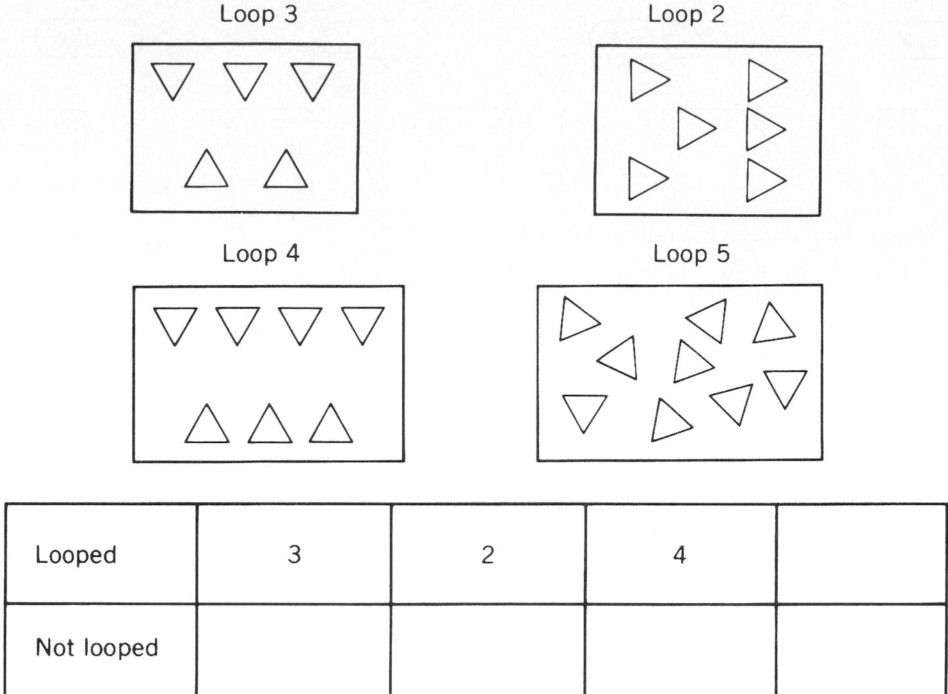

Looped	3	2	4	
Not looped				

24. Make a set of cards by cutting numerals from materials of different textures (such as sandpaper and velvet). Have each child place a finger at the point where one would begin drawing the numeral and then trace the entire numeral. Children can also simulate the motion for forming numerals by "tracing numerals in the air" with their finger.

25. Assign each child a number, and arrange the class in a ring around the teacher. Call out a number; the student who has been assigned that number taps out the correct number and runs around the ring of children.

26. Assign each child a number, which the children keep as a secret. The students then knock on the door a number of times corresponding to their assigned numbers. The class responds, "Come in number seven (number twelve, and so on)." You can also call on the children by "their number" for the remainder of that day.

27. Give each child an egg carton in which a number has been written in each of the indentations. Using pebbles or small pieces of drinking straws, have the children place that number of items in each compartment.

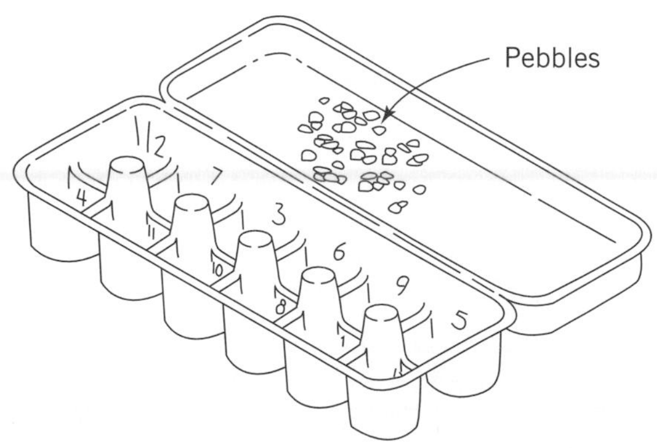

28. Write a numeral for each set. Then place <, >, or = in the ○. (Use the words "less than," "greater than," and "equal to" until the children have a sound understanding of this abstract symbolism.)

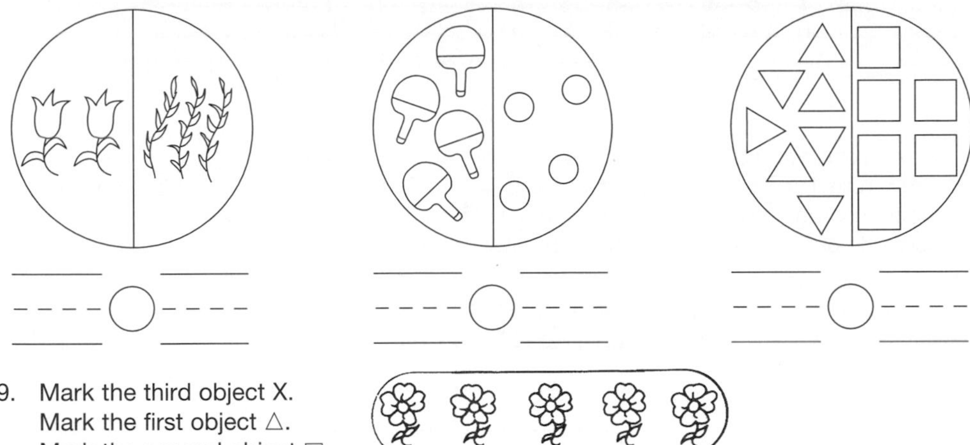

29. Mark the third object X.
Mark the first object △.
Mark the second object □.

30. Request that the children take objects out of their desks and place them in a stated order. For instance, "Place your eraser first, a pencil second, a red crayon third, and a paper clip fourth." After the objects have been placed in order, you may ask them to hold up, for example, the third object. You can check the children's answers very easily.

31. Assign each child an ordinal number, and have the children line up in proper order. This can be done at recess or when the children are being dismissed. Ask children not to tell others what their ordinal number is.

32. Call on children by their "ordinal names" rather than by their given names: for instance, "first one, second row," "third one, first row," or "fifth one, fourth row."

33. Children enjoy drawing dot pictures. Ask them where they think they should begin. When they finish, they should identify the picture.

34. Cut pieces of cardboard 5 centimeters by 10 centimeters for dominoes. Make a set of dominoes with groups on one end and numerals on the other end. Continually add new dominoes as the children develop concepts of numbers. Play the game using the standard rules for the game of dominoes.

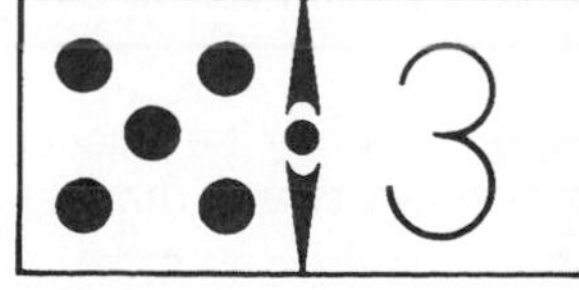

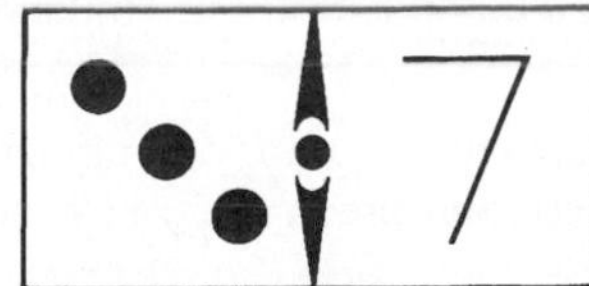

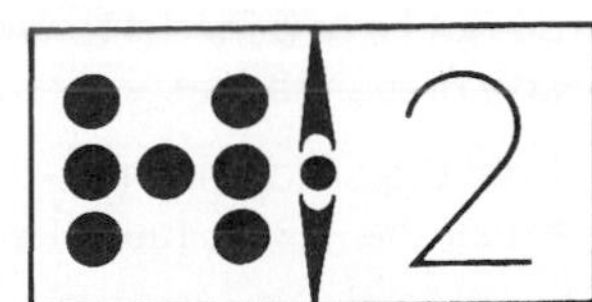

35. Use the number line to help you decide which symbol (<, =, or >) you will put inside each □ to make the sentence true.

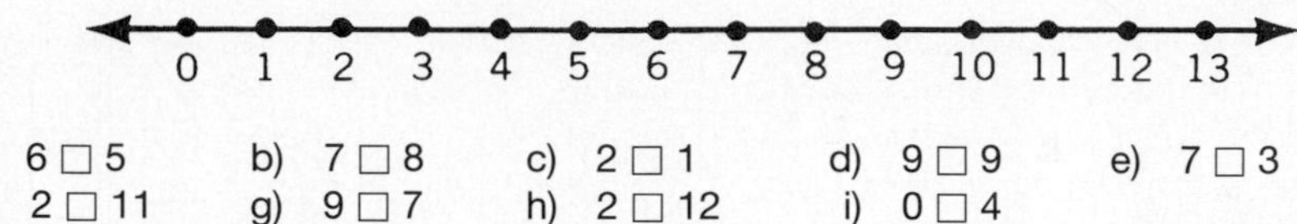

a) 6 □ 5 b) 7 □ 8 c) 2 □ 1 d) 9 □ 9 e) 7 □ 3
f) 2 □ 11 g) 9 □ 7 h) 2 □ 12 i) 0 □ 4

36. Mark a large square piece of cardboard into 100 squares (10 by 10). Make a set of numeral cards from 1 to 99 so that the cards will fit on the board. Have a child begin putting the numeral cards on the board, and ask others to complete the entire board. Have them study the cards on the board and look for number patterns.

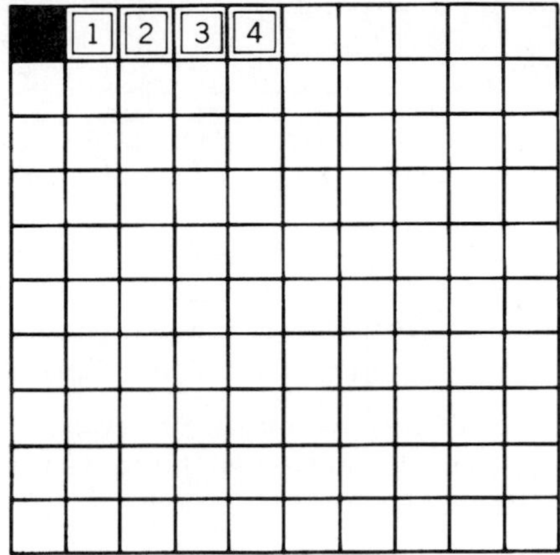

This activity is rich in possibilities for use in many places in the mathematics program. There are many patterns that can be discovered in this table, including those found in even numbers, odd numbers, place value, prime numbers, and addition and subtraction.

37. Mark with an X each train car that names a number that is less than 37.

38. Mark with an X each "body part" that names a number greater than 27 and less than 45.

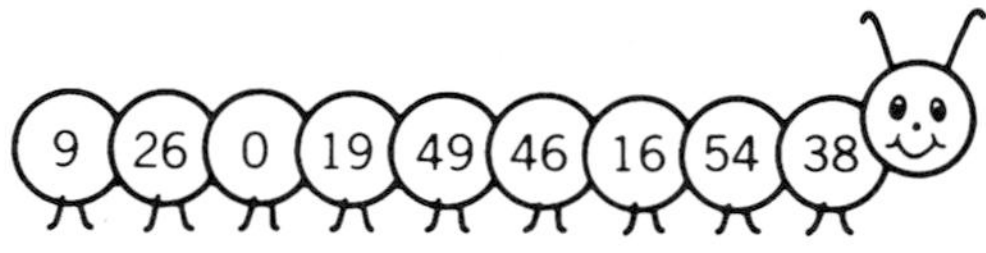

39. The calculator can be used to help children identify the numerals 1 through 10. Write a 2 on the chalkboard, and ask each child to place a finger on the 2 on the number line taped to the front of each child's desk. Have the children locate a 2 on a key on the calculator and then press that key. A "2" should appear on the display screen. Compare the 2 on the number line with the 2 on the keyboard and the 2 on the display screen. Use a similar procedure with all the numbers through 9.

40. State a number, and have the children press that particular key on the calculator. Children can hold up their calculators with the display screen facing the teacher so that the teacher can quickly check to make sure that all children are correct. For this activity the children do not have a model to use as a comparison. They must recognize the numeral word name and press the key.

41. Help the children set up the calculators to be "counting machines." Turn on the calculator, press the + key, the 1 key, and then press the = key ten consecutive times. The display

screen should count from 0 through 10. (*Note:* This will not work on all types of calculators—only those with a "built-in" constant repeat. Use this exercise to check your calculator to see.)

42. Start a pattern on a display screen for a child, and request that the child continue the pattern. For instance, turn on the calculator and press 1, then 2, then 1, then 2; then have the child use the calculator to extend the same pattern. The child should press 1, 2, 1, 2, and so on. The display screen should show 12121212.

43. Try a pattern that repeats itself using three numbers. For instance, turn on the calculator and enter 1, 2, 3, 1. Hand the calculator to a child. The child should enter 2, 3, 1, 2, and the display screen should show 12312312. Try many other patterns, and ask the children to continue these patterns. Can they make up a pattern of their own?

44. Start a pattern of 1, 2, 3, 4, and ask a child to complete the pattern. The child might be expected to press 5, 6, 7, and 8. The display screen should then show 12345678. Press 2 and ask a child to show a counting pattern beginning with 2. The child might then press 3, 4, 5, 6, 7, 8, and 9 in that order. The display screen should show 23456789.

45. Have the children work in pairs. Ask one child to start a pattern and a second child to continue the pattern. Check to make sure that a pattern is apparent on the display screen.

46. Write a numeral for the number of objects shown.

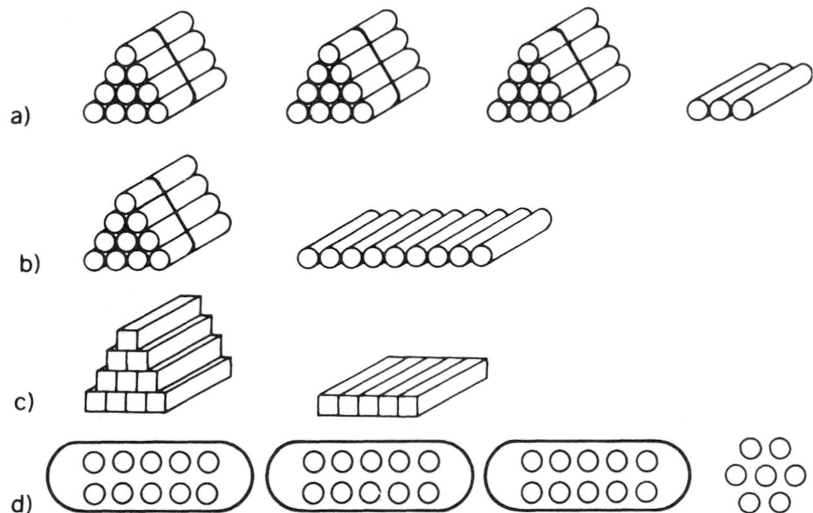

47. Draw a loop around each group of ten. Then write a numeral in each blank that shows how many groups of ten are in that box.

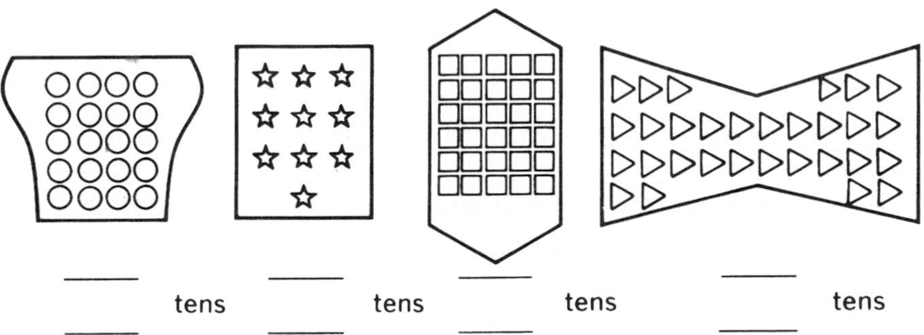

48. Make a set of playing cards. Half the deck should show groups of tens and ones; the other half should be made up of matching cards that show the numeral for each card. Use the cards to play "Go Fish" where a child asks another if he or she has a certain specific card.

49. List the members of each of the following sets:
   a) the set of school days in each week.
   b) the set of numbers greater than five and less than seventeen.
   c) the set of teachers you have this year in school.
   d) the set of months in a year.
   e) the set of days in a week that begin with the letter D.

50. Describe each group in words.
   a) a, e, i, o, u
   b) 2, 4, 6, 8, . . .
   c) 4, 5, 6, 7, 8, 9
   d) 3, 5, 7, 9, 11

51. Find the number for each group.

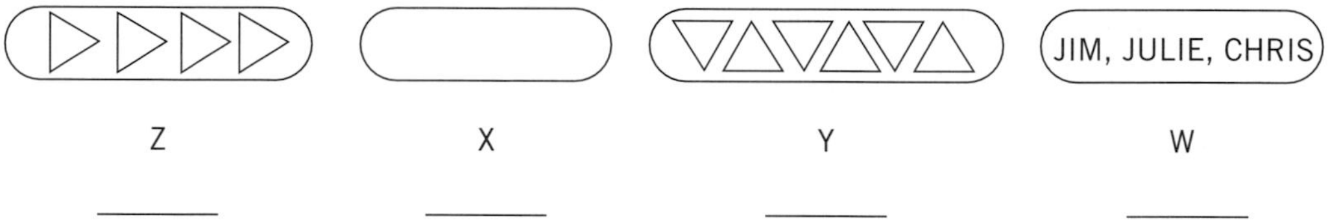

JIM, JULIE, CHRIS

Z ______ X ______ Y ______ W ______

52. Children need to learn to recognize the number of items in a set without counting (subitizing). To help children recognize numbers without counting, make two sets of cards with dots. One set has domino patterns, and the other has randomly placed dots. These cards can be flashed at the children, who then tell how many dots are on each card. Children can check their responses by counting, if necessary.

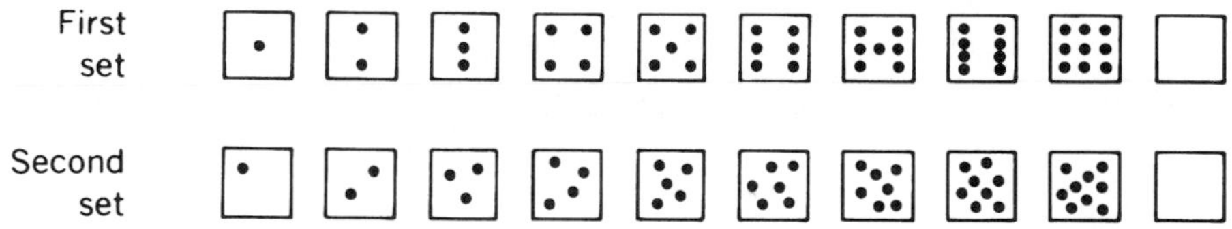

First set

Second set

53. Cards with various numbers of dots are given to each student. The teacher writes a numeral on the board; then the students with the cards just preceding and following the number stand on each side of the written number.

54. Complete columns two and three, then mark the groups as indicated.

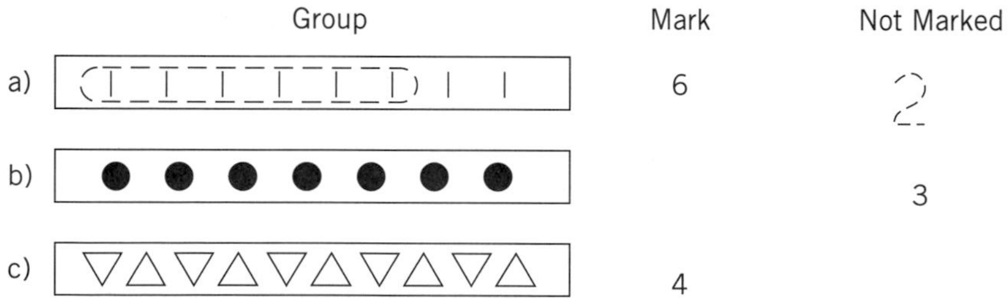

	Group	Mark	Not Marked
a)		6	2
b)			3
c)		4	

55. Find the pattern and fill in the blanks. Children should be asked to justify their response in words.
   a) 10, 12, 14, ______, ______, ______, ______, ______, ______, ______.
   b) 68, 69, ______, ______, ______, ______, ______, ______, ______, ______.
   c) 10, 20, 30, ______, ______, ______, ______, ______, ______, ______.
   d) ______, ______, ______, ______, 58, 59, ______, ______, ______, ______.

e) 19, 9, 8, ____, ____, ____, ____, ____, ____, ____.

f) ____, ____, ____, 18, ____, 22, ____, ____, ____.

g) 239, ____, ____, 242, ____, ____, ____, ____, ____.

h) 147, ____, 151, ____, ____, ____, ____, ____, 163.

i) 17, ____, ____, ____, ____, ____, ____, ____, ____, 35.

56. Place the following numbers in order from the least to the greatest.

a) 19, 22, 17, 20, 18, 21
b) 43, 34, 25, 52, 24, 42, 30
c) 127, 230, 226, 130, 187, 198, 203
d) 78, 76, 68, 85, 87, 67, 58, 65, 57, 86, 75

57. Connect each boat with its ordinal number.

ninth, third, seventh, fourth, eighth, first, fifth, second, tenth, sixth

58. Make a set of cards with two-digit numerals written on them. Have a child arrange the cards in order on the desk from the least value to the greatest. For example:

47 48 49 50 51 52 53 54 55 56 57 58 59 60

59. Give the students a set of cards with numerals on one side and letters on the opposite side, and have them place the cards in order from least to greatest. The students can check the answer by turning the cards over to see if the message is correct.

	78	79	80	81	82	83	84	85
When students turn cards over:	H	A	P	P	Y	D	A	Y

60. Complete the table.

100 Less	10 Less	1 Less		1 Greater	10 Greater	100 Greater
			278 142 369 520 401			

61. Children should understand how to use constants with the calculator and how to use the calculator to count by numbers other than one (see the calculator activities for Chapter 6). Place emphasis on patterns developed counting by numbers other than one.

62. Study the following chart and compare the numerals. Can you find any interesting patterns? Can you think of places or objects where you have seen these numerals used?

Hindu-Arabic	Roman	Hindu-Arabic	Roman	Hindu-Arabic	Roman
1	I	11	XI	21	XXI
2	II	12	XII	22	XXII
3	III	13	XIII	23	XXIII
4	IV	14	XIV	24	XXIV
5	V	15	XV	25	XXV
6	VI	16	XVI	26	XXVI
7	VII	17	XVII	27	XXVII
8	VIII	18	XVIII	28	XXVIII
9	IX	19	XIX	29	XXIX
10	X	20	XX	30	XXX

63. a) What Hindu-Arabic numeral do we write for the following Roman numerals?

III _______ XX _______ XV _______ IV _______ XII _______ VIII _______

XIX _______ IX _______ XXVI _______ XIX _______ XXI _______ I _______

b) Fill in the blanks.

18 = 10 + 8	→	XVIII = X + VIII
14 = 10 + _______	→	XIV = X + _______
25 = 20 + _______	→	XXV = XX + _______
37 = 30 + _______	→	XXXVII = XXX + _______
39 = 30 + _______	→	XXXIX = XXX + _______

Do you notice any similarities between the expanded form of the Hindu-Arabic numerals and the expanded form of the Roman numerals?

64. Place ten objects on a table. Have one child count the objects while another places a tally mark on the chalkboard as each object is counted. Have the children think about the various ways we would group these objects. Encourage them to express some of these ways, such as ten groups of one, two groups of five, five groups of two, and so on. Then ask them to think of these ten objects as one group of ten. Ask how a numeral could be written to record this. Discuss the meaning of the number and the identifying numeral. Extend this kind of activity to help children understand groups of 11 through 19, 20 through 29, and so on.

65. Children beginning to work with "teen" numbers consider them as wholes and not as tens and ones. Each child should have three sets of small cards 2 inches by 3 inches with one digit written on each card. To do this exercise, children should match a digit card with its groups.

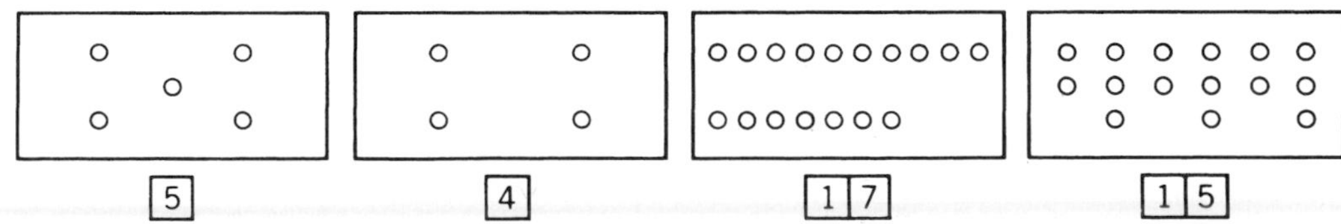

66. Lay out two sheets of paper; print *Ones* on one sheet and *Tens* on the other. Each child should place the *Ones* sheet on the right and the *Tens* sheet on the left. You may use the overhead projector with a transparency showing *Ones* on the right-hand side and *Tens* on the left.

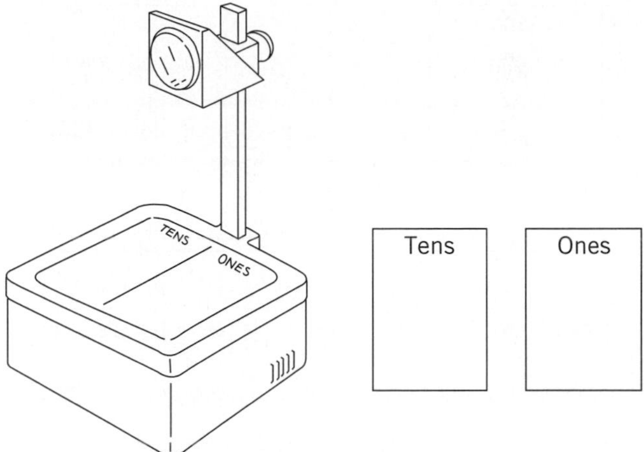

Children may also use small orange juice cans labeled as *Ones* and *Tens.*

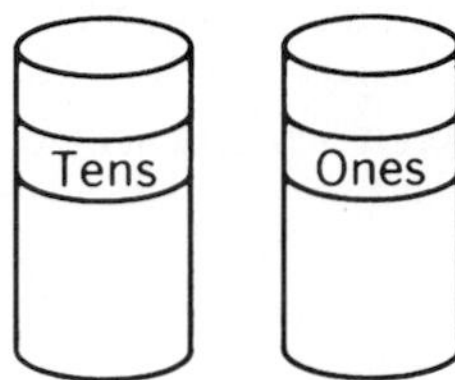

Using the labeled sheets of paper, count objects as they are laid on the *Ones* sheet. Use objects that children are familiar with, such as plastic forks or spoons.

When ten forks are in the ones place, talk about one group of ten and ten groups of one. How are they different? How are they the same?

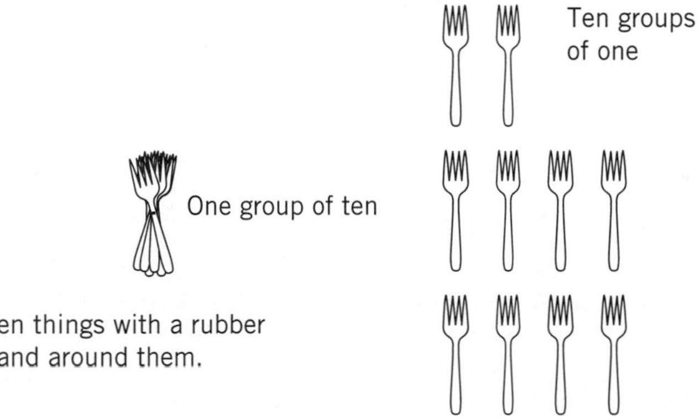

67. Now relate the numeral cards to the groups shown on the papers by having the children lay the correct numeral card on the Ones and the Tens sheets.

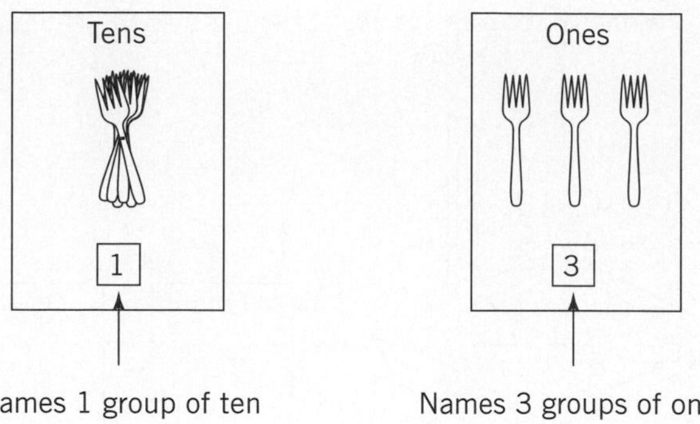

68. Show and discuss how the two numeral cards are brought together to name the number thirteen as follows:

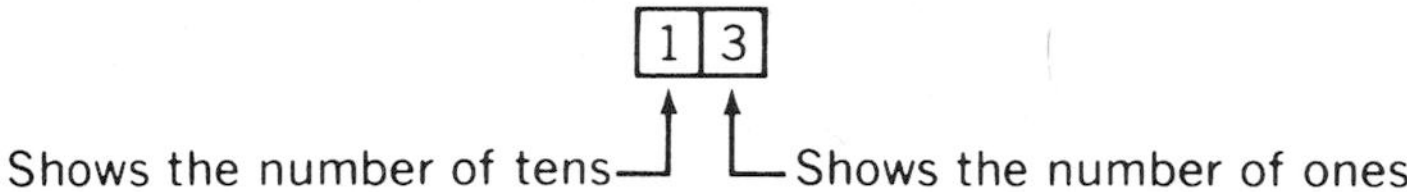

69. Children need many experiences reading and seeing numbers in tens and ones.

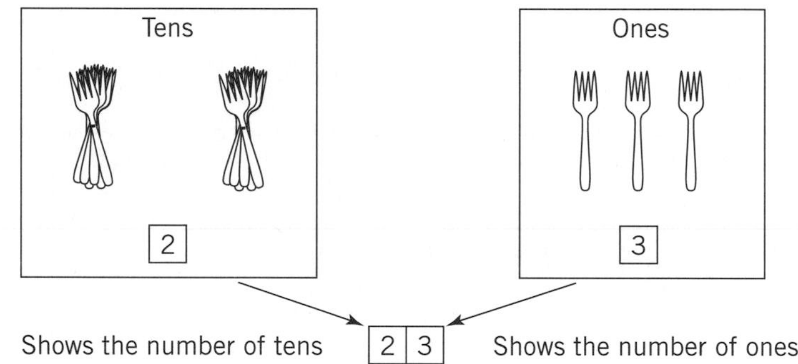

Do not use an abacus or one fork for a group of ten. Children should see packages of tens with rubber bands around them in the tens place.

70. Place numerals on the overhead projector, and have each child lay out the correct number of packages of tens and ones on the place value papers. The orange juice cans can also be used.

71. Instruct children to loop or ring sets of ten objects.

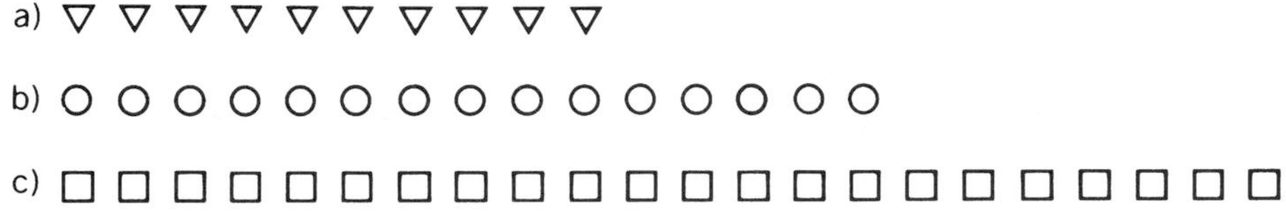

72. How many groups of ten?

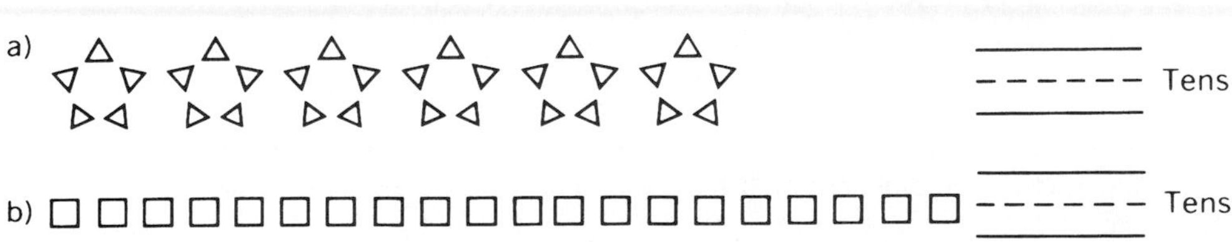

73. How many tens and ones? Loop the groups of ten and write how many tens and ones.

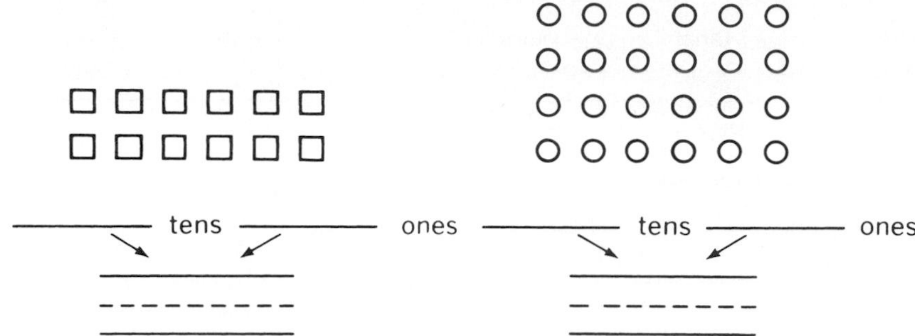

74. Numeral expanders are excellent devices for children to manipulate and for teachers to demonstrate the meaning of place value. The number 124 can be viewed in many different ways. The following are two types of numeral expanders:

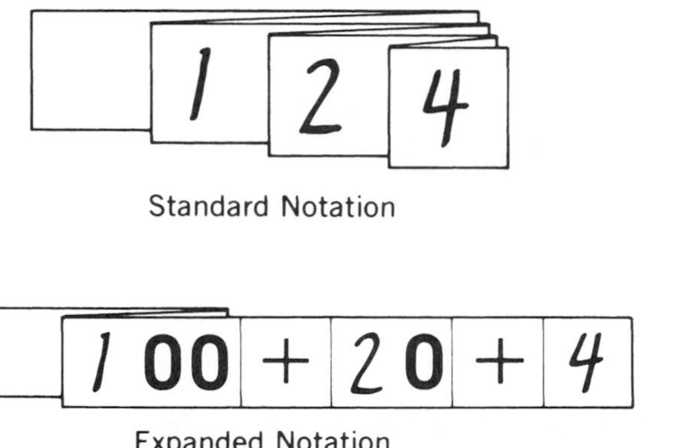

The number 124 can be thought of in many different ways, as the accompanying illustrations show.

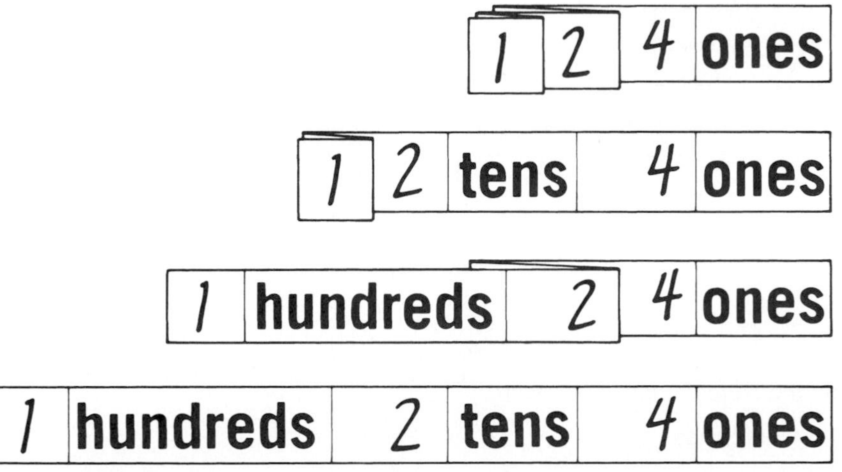

Expanded notation should be used from the very beginning to help the children understand the meaning of the numerals they write. The use of folding numeral expanders will help them readily comprehend the concept.

(*Note:* Numeral expanders with a 24-page teacher's manual and an erasable marking pencil can be purchased directly from William Speer, c/o Prentice Hall Merrill College Publishing, 445 Hutchinson Ave., Columbus, OH 43235.)

75. Name the tens and ones for each number.

    a) 47 = _______ tens _______ ones

    b) 34 = _______ tens _______ ones

    c) 20 = _______ tens _______ ones

    d) 7 = _______ tens _______ ones

76. Write the numeral for each.

    a) 4 tens 2 ones = _______

    b) 1 ten 9 ones = _______

    c) 3 tens 0 ones = _______

    d) 0 tens 8 ones = _______

77. Have each child place the correct number of counters in orange juice cans or on the ones and tens sheets in response to an oral direction:

    a) "Put out 24 counters."

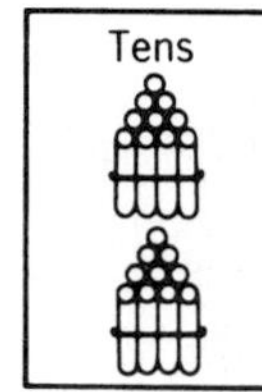

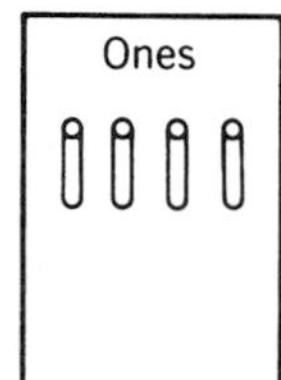

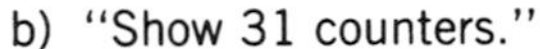

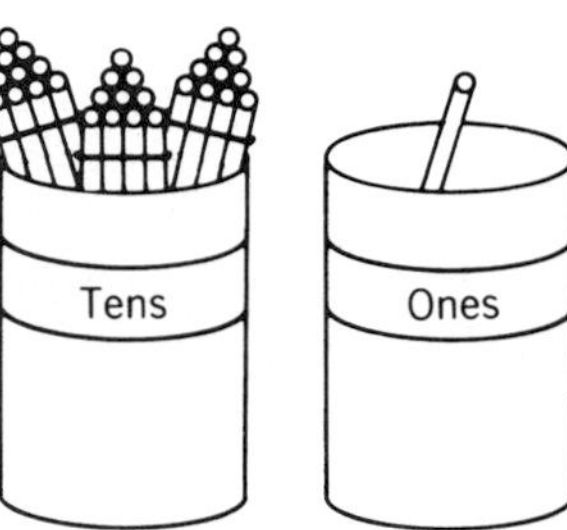

78. Place some counters on the overhead projector, and have the children write the numeral.

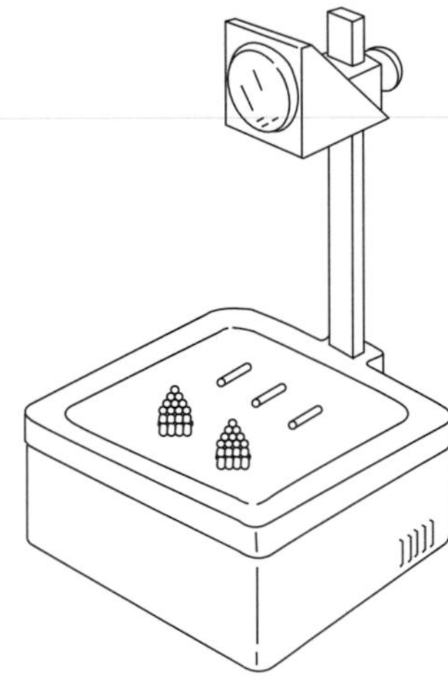

79. Loop the correct numeral for each.

    a) 3 tens 2 ones: 23 32 20

    b) 4 tens 6 ones: 46 64 60

    c) 1 ten 0 ones: 01 10 11

80. Children can write numerals for counters put in a place-value box. Cut a box into two parts along the diagonal. Tape the two parts of the box together, and label one bin *Ones* and the other *Tens.*

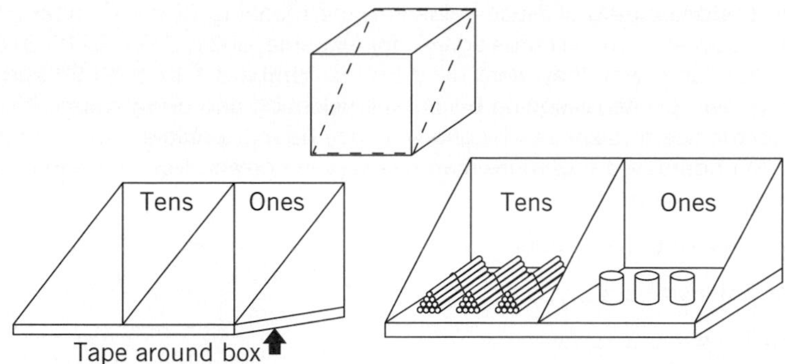

81. Make a set of playing cards to play Rummy. One-fourth of the cards should show groups of tens and ones; one-fourth should show standard notation for the groups; one-fourth should show expanded notation for the groups; and one-fourth should name the tens and ones. For example:

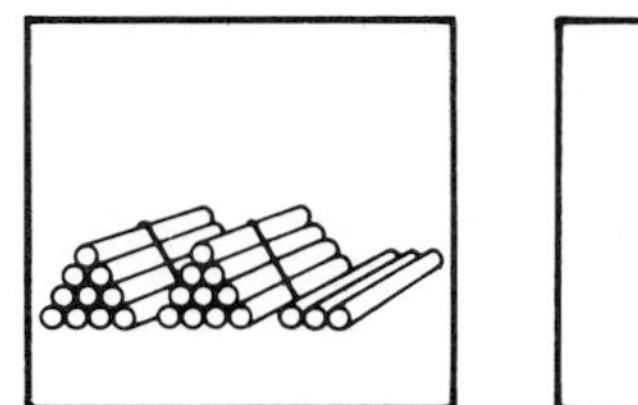

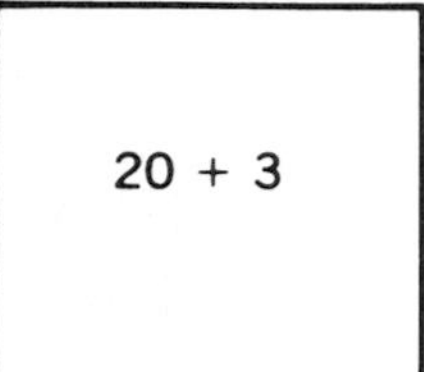

Make twelve sets of four cards for a deck. Play the game in the same manner as regular Rummy.

82. Children may use numeral cards to play the "Greatest Number" game. The cards are randomly dealt among the players. (Begin with two players; then play the game with three or four.) Cards are stacked face down on the table; each child turns over one card at a time. The child with the greatest (or least) value wins the other cards of that round. Cards that are won can be added to the bottom of the winner's pile. At the end of the playing time, the child with the greatest number of cards is the winner.

83. Have four, five, or six children select cards without seeing the numerals on them. Let two children at a time compare cards to see which represents the greater number; then have all the children hold up their cards and line them up in order from least to greatest. Later in the year, cards can be prepared for the numerals 100 through 999 to be used in the same way.

84. Use sets of numeral cards to review basic concepts developed in grades 1 and 2.

43	four tens and three ones	40 + 3
34	three tens and four ones	30 + 4
29	two tens and nine ones	20 + 9
92	nine tens and two ones	90 + 2
17	one ten and seven ones	10 + 7
71	seven tens and one one	70 + 1

Ask one child to display a card. Then have all the children holding cards with different names for the same number stand. Vary the activity by displaying the cards in different places around the room. Ask a child to collect all cards that name the number 43, for example. Continue the activity until all cards have been collected.

85. To extend understanding of place value and the meaning of the numbers 1000 through 9999, use prepared numeral cards again—for example, 3051, 3151, 3115, 3105, 3510, and so on—in the same way they were used for the numbers 1 through 99 and 100 through 999. Always ask for the reasoning behind the selection and comparison. This will present many opportunities to discuss why one way may be more efficient than another. The children should understand that more than one way is correct, but that one way may be the most efficient for them.

86. Write numerals for each number.

a) 7 tens 3 ones = ________

b) 9 tens 1 one = ________

c) 1 hundred 6 tens 4 ones = ________

d) 4 hundreds 5 tens 3 ones = ________

e) 5 thousands 8 hundreds 6 tens 2 ones = ________

f) 4 thousands 5 hundreds 0 tens 0 ones = ________

87. Fill each blank with the correct numeral.

a) 37 = ________ tens ________ ones

b) 70 = ________ tens ________ ones

c) 387 = ________ hundreds ________ tens ________ ones

d) 149 = ________ hundreds ________ tens ________ ones

e) 9370= ________ thousands ________ hundreds ________ tens ________ ones

f) 3907 = ________ thousands ________ hundreds ________ tens ________ ones

88. In the preceding activity, watch for these common misunderstandings of the place-value concept.

38 = 30 tens 8 ones
164 = 100 hundreds 60 tens 4 ones
2728 = 2000 thousands 700 hundreds 20 tens 8 ones

89. By comparing place value, determine which relation symbol (<, =, or >) should be placed in each ○. Have the children explain their reasoning for selecting the symbol.

a) 76 ○ 67
b) 456 ○ 654
c) 58 ○ 57
d) 203 ○ 302
e) 357 ○ 357
f) 409 ○ 410
g) 4554 ○ 4544
h) 3000 ○ 4000

90. Write several rows of numerals on the chalkboard. Then have children write them (or respond orally) in order from least to greatest and then from greatest to least.

a) 69, 68, 70
b) 530, 503, 350
c) 354, 453, 534
d) 989, 999, 1009
e) 346, 364, 436
f) 765, 756, 675, 657
g) 1028, 1258, 342, 585, 854
h) 5021, 512, 5200, 520, 5102

91. Complete the table.

Numbers	Hundreds	Tens	Ones
306			
	6	0	3
596			
		3	2
956			
823			

92. Relate pennies and dimes to the numeral and place value of ones and tens. One dime is one ten. Ten pennies has the same value as one dime.

93. Discuss with the children how each number key that is pressed causes the digit on the display screen to "move over" one place in place value. For example, place a 1 on the display screen; this 1 is in the ones place. Strike the 0 key, and note that the 1 has moved over to the tens place. The 1 now means one set of ten. Demonstrate the concept with a set of plastic spoons—one spoon, ten sets of one, and one set of ten.

94. Place a 9 on the display screen and then add 1. What happens on the display screen? Discuss the place value. Place 99 on the screen and then add 1. Discuss the place value. Later you may also want to try 999 add 1.

95. Demonstrate expanded notation on the calculator. If 10 + 3 is entered into the calculator, when the equal key is struck, 13 will appear on the display screen. What number is 30 + 7? Strike the equal key to verify your guess.

96. Use expanded notation to help you compare each pair of numerals.

a) 10 + 7 = ______ X + VII = ______	c) 23 = 20 + 3 ______ = ______ + III

b) XXX + VI = ______ ______ + 6 = ______	d) XIX = ______ + ______ ______ + ______ = 19

97. Complete the table.

Hindu-Arabic Numeral	Expanded Notation	Roman Numeral	Roman Numeral	Expanded Notation	Hindu-Arabic Numeral
13	10 + 3	XIII	XVII	10 + 7	17
49	______ + ______	XLIX	XL	______ – ______	40
14	______	______	XVIII	______	______
52	______	______	LX	______	______
15	______	______	XIX	______	______
28	______	______	XXXIX	______	______
16	______	______	XX	______	______
73	______	______	XLIV	______	______
21	______	______	XXIII	______	______
70	______	______	XLIX	______	______

98. Color green each balloon with a numeral representing a number less than ten; color red each balloon with numerals represented by numbers between ten and twenty; color yellow each balloon with numerals representing numbers between thirty and forty.

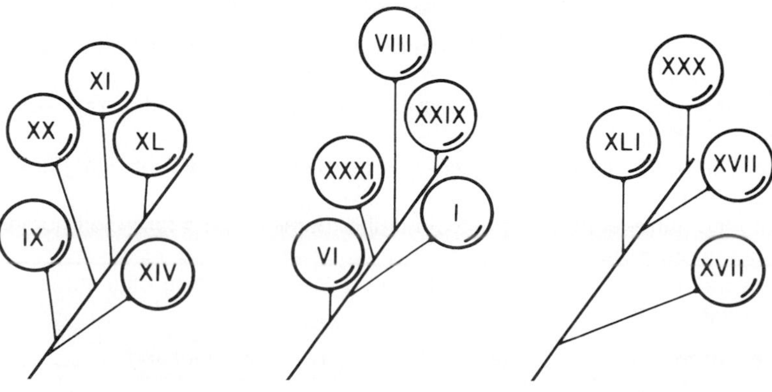

99. Construct several 10-by-10 grids, several 1-by-10 grids, and several 1-by-1 squares for children to manipulate.

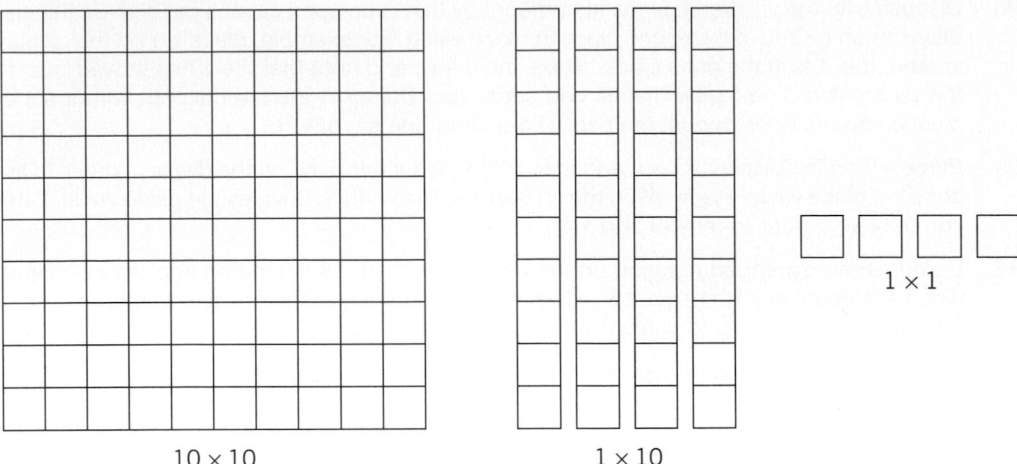

Have the children manipulate these grids to help them understand place value. If base ten blocks are available, they are excellent for helping children understand place value. Cuisenaire rods can also be used to develop place-value concepts.

100. Numbers may be named many different ways. Name the number of tens two ways. Numeral expanders are an excellent device to use with this concept.

a) 347 = 3 hundreds 4 tens 7 ones or 34 tens 7 ones
b) 732 = 7 hundreds 3 tens 2 ones or 73 tens 2 ones
c) 1056 = 1 thousand 5 tens 6 ones or 105 tens 6 ones
d) 4789 = 4 thousands 7 hundreds 8 tens 9 ones or 4 thousands 78 tens 9 ones or 478 tens 9 ones

101. Base ten blocks should be used with intermediate-grade children. Have a student represent a number using base ten blocks; then have each class member write the number for the blocks. Write the number for this block representation:

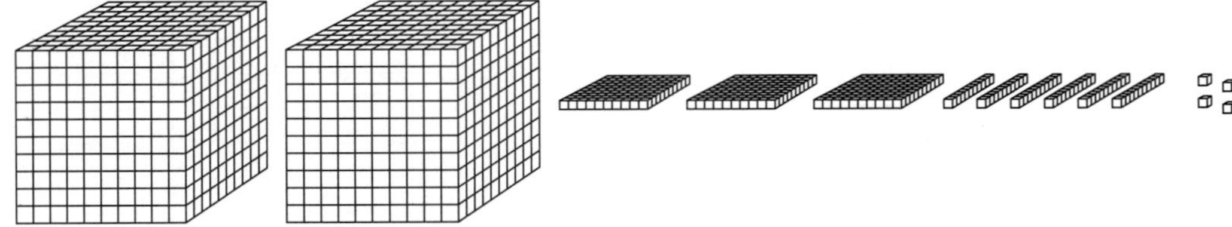

102. In small groups, provide each student with a place-value chart with ones, tens, hundreds, and thousands. Children then take turns rolling a pair of dice. At each roll of the dice, the child takes blocks from the "bank" to represent the number that was rolled. All players must continually turn in blocks so that each always has the least number of blocks possible. The first child to obtain a block representing 1000 is the winner.

103. a) Write the numeral for the greatest number that can be named with a two-digit numeral that has 7 as one of its digits.
b) Write the numeral for the least number named with a two-digit numeral that has 3 as one of its digits.
c) Write the numeral for the greatest number named with a four-digit numeral that has 3 as one of its digits.
d) Write the numeral for the greatest number named with a four-digit numeral that has 4 as one of its digits.
e) Write the numeral for the least number named with a three-digit numeral that has 0 as one digit.

104. a) One hundred is ________ tens. b) One thousand is ________ tens.
c) One thousand is ________ hundreds. d) ________ thousands is one million.

105. Rounding numbers requires a student to have a firm grasp of place value. To round 456 to the nearest hundred, the student must know which is the hundreds place and which is the tens place. Have children solve examples using rounded numbers, and then verify that their answers are approximately correct, using the calculator.

Example	Estimated Answer	Actual Answer
823 + 278	1100	1101
98 × 47	5000	4606
37 × 10	370	370
283 × 100	28300	28300

106. Have children use the expanded form of a number and enter it into the calculator with the proper operations. The results in the display should be the number in standard notation; for example, 2000 + 600 + 40 + 7 = 2647. Enter the 2000, the addition sign, the 600, the addition sign, the 40, the addition sign, the 7, and the equals sign. Now the display should read 2647.

INSTRUCTIONAL AND ASSESSMENT ACTIVITIES FOR GRADES 5-8

Although much of the material in this chapter focuses on mathematics developed in grades K-4, much of the content discussed can be and should be expanded throughout the curriculum. Suggested activities that extend the concepts of this chapter to upper grades can be found in appropriate chapters throughout the text. Some selected examples follow.

1. Describe each group in words.

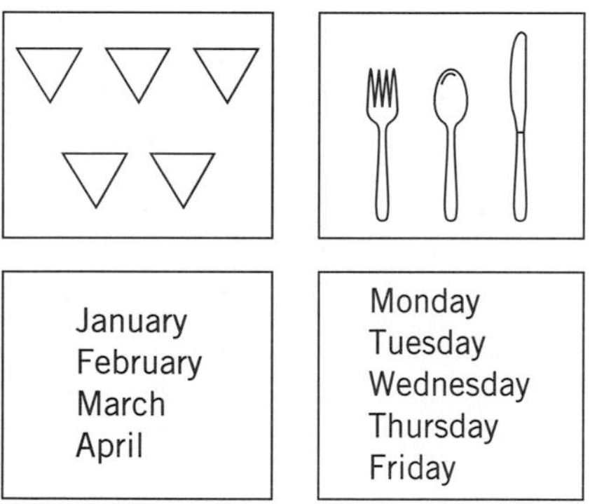

2. State a single sentence that describes each collection.

   a) 2, 4, 6, 8   b) rectangles and squares
   c) $\frac{3}{4}, \frac{6}{8}, \frac{24}{32}$ d) BOB, TOT, MOM, POP, WOW

3. Make a deck of cards with a set pictured on each card. Place all cards face down on a table and play a game of "Concentration." If the two cards turned over are equivalent, the player keeps the pair. If the two cards are not equivalent, they must be replaced face down on the table. The player with the most pairs wins. The number of players may vary from two to four, depending on how many cards are in the deck.

4. Study the patterns and fill in the blanks. Children should be asked to justify their response in words.

   a) 19, 24, 29, ____, ____, ____, ____, ____, ____, 64

   b) 91, 84, 77, ____, ____, ____, ____, ____, ____, ____

   c) ____, ____, ____, 136, 150, 164, ____, ____, ____, ____

   d) 323, 333, ____, ____, ____, ____, ____, ____, 403

e) _____, _____, _____, _____, _____, _____, 473, 485, 497

f) 42, _____, _____, 51, _____, _____, 60, _____, _____, 69

g) _____, 184, _____, 170, _____, _____, _____, _____, _____, 128

5. Use quantifying statements to expand students' analysis of the mathematical meanings common in everyday language. Some examples of the type of statements that might be used are:

   a) all children wearing red (the children could stand up so that the real objects—concrete level—composing the group would be seen by all the pupils).
   b) all girls in the room.
   c) all boys in the room.
   d) all students with a math book on the desk.

   Ask the students to think of statements to dictate for group response; then ask other students to describe the group.

6. As an introductory activity for coordinate graphing, call on children by using ordered pairs consisting of their "ordinal names" and ordinal position rather than their given names: for instance, "first one, second row," "third one, first row," or "fifth one, fourth row."

7. Mark a large square piece of cardboard into 100 squares (10 by 10). Make a set of numeral cards from 1 to 99 so that the cards will fit on the board. Have a child begin putting the numeral cards on the board, and ask others to complete the entire board. Have them study the cards on the board and look for number patterns.

	1	2	3	4	5	6	7	8	9
10	11	12	13	14	15	16	17	18	19
20	21	22	23	24	25	26	27	28	29
30	31	32	33	34	35	36	37	38	39
40	41	42	43	44	45	46	47	48	49
50	51	52	53	54	55	56	57	58	59
60	61	62	63	64	65	66	67	68	69
70	71	72	73	74	75	76	77	78	79
80	81	82	83	84	85	86	87	88	89
90	91	92	93	94	95	96	97	98	99

   This activity is rich in possibilities for use in many places in the mathematics program. There are many patterns that can be discovered in this table, including those found in even numbers, odd numbers, place value, prime numbers, and in addition and subtraction.

8. Older students can be asked to "think like a calculator." Have the children examine the following counting algorithm and then describe what each statement will do:

```
20 X = 0                     (Assigns a value of "0" to X)
30 X = X + I                 (Redefines X as one more than X)
40 ?X                        (Prints the current value of X)
50 IF X > 20 THEN END        (When X is more than 20, it stops)
60 GOTO 30                   (When X is less than 20, add 1 again)
```

   Change line 30 to each of the following. How will this change the algorithm ?

a) X = X + 2 (Redefines X as two more than X)
b) X = X + 3 (Redefines X as three more than X)
c) X = X + X (Redefines X as twice X)

Why did X = X + X print only 0? What other statement must be changed in the algorithm? Change line 20 to X = 1. How did this change the algorithm ? Why?

9. The study of systems of numeration other than our own emphasizes the structure of our decimal system and the meaning of our numerals by comparison and contrast. The study of place value and the examination of the strengths and weaknesses of several systems of numeration sharpen children's interest in the history of our Hindu-Arabic numerals and the development of decimal numeration.

Hindu-Arabic	1	10	100	1000	10,000
Egyptian	|	∩	𓍢	𓆼	𓂭

Write a Hindu-Arabic numeral for each Egyptian numeral.

a) ∩∩∩ ||| |||
b) ∩∩∩∩∩ |||| ∩∩∩∩ ||||
c) 𓍢𓍢𓍢 𓍢𓍢𓍢 |||
d) 𓆼 𓍢𓍢 |||
e) 𓆼 𓍢𓍢𓍢 ∩ |||
f) 𓂭𓂭𓆼 ||| |||

Write an Egyptian numeral for each Hindu-Arabic numeral.

g) 123 ________
h) 24 ________
i) 1001 ________
j) 1111 ________
k) 223 ________
l) 1214 ________

10. Complete the table.

Roman Numerals	I		III		V		VII		IX		XI	
Hindu-Arabic Numerals		2		4		6		8		10		12

11. Write three different names for these numbers. One of the three names must be a Roman numeral.

6 14 21 29 34 35

12. a) Write the Roman numeral for: 300 ________ 92 ________ 505 ________.
b) Write the Hindu-Arabic numeral for: CI ________ CDXX ________ XCIX ________.

13. Write the correct symbol (<, >, or =) in each □ to make true statements.

a) XXX □ III
b) 23 □ XXXII
c) IV □ IV
d) XXXIV □ 30 + 4
e) 20 + 6 □ XXIV
f) XXXIX □ XXXI
g) IX □ 10 − 1
h) XVII □ 7 + 10

14. Suppose that a recent excavation near Rome unearthed a secret code that was "cracked" after the code-breakers found a translation from Roman numerals to Roman letters. Using English letters and Hindu-Arabic numerals for our example, can you break the code found on the next page?

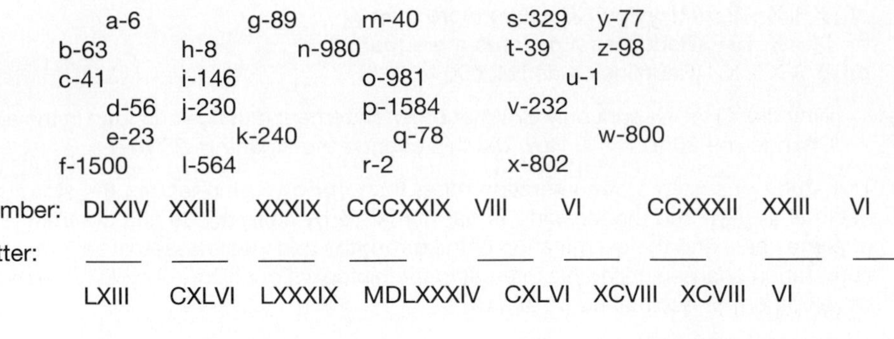

a-6 g-89 m-40 s-329 y-77
b-63 h-8 n-980 t-39 z-98
c-41 i-146 o-981 u-1
d-56 j-230 p-1584 v-232
e-23 k-240 q-78 w-800
f-1500 l-564 r-2 x-802
Number: DLXIV XXIII XXXIX CCCXXIX VIII VI CCXXXII XXIII VI
Letter:
LXIII CXLVI LXXXIX MDLXXXIV CXLVI XCVIII XCVIII VI

15. Provide the children with numbers written on a worksheet, and have the children model each number using base ten blocks. Model each of these examples with base ten blocks.

    a) 359 b) 641 c) 47 d) 2317

16. Use as many different combinations of base ten blocks as you can to represent the number 107.

17. Numeral expanders are excellent devices for children to manipulate and for teachers to demonstrate the meaning of place value. The number 124 can be viewed in many different ways; following are two types of numeral expanders:

Standard Notation

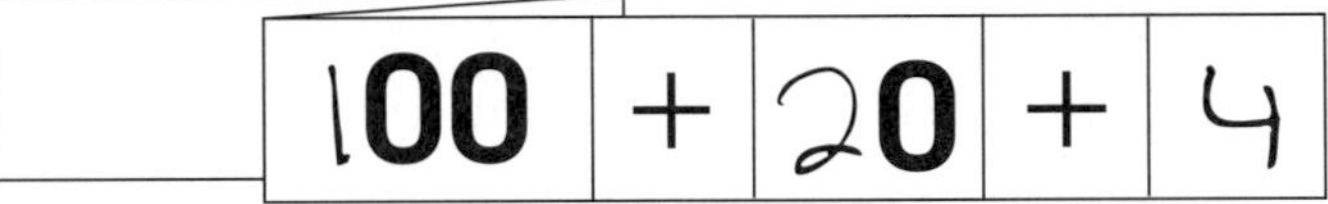

Expanded Notation

The number 124 can be thought of in many different ways, as the accompanying illustrations show.

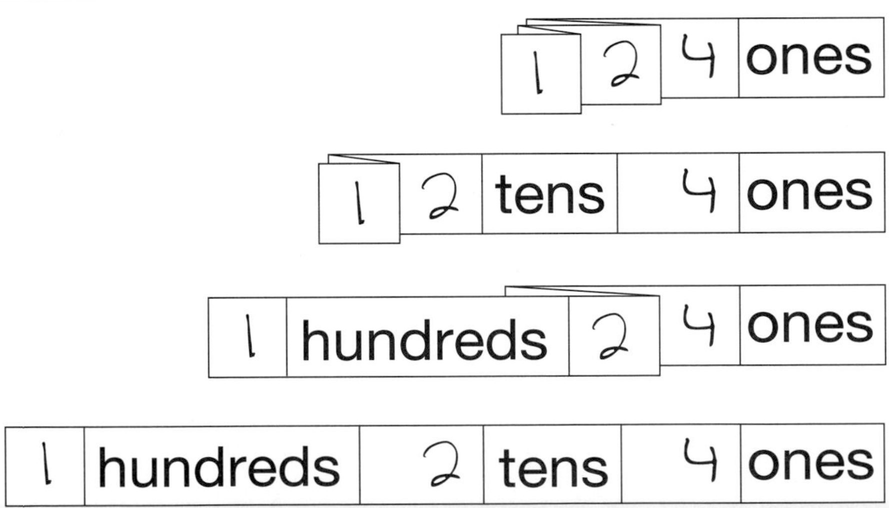

Expanded notation should be used from the very beginning to help the children understand the meaning of the numerals they write. The use of folding numeral expanders will help them readily comprehend the concept.
(*Note:* Numeral expanders with a 24-page teacher's manual and erasable marking pencil can be purchased directly from William Speer, c/o Prentice Hall Merrill College Publishing, 445 Hutchinson Ave., Columbus, OH 43235.)

18. Draw rings around groups of five; then fill in the blanks.

______ fives ______ ones	______ fives ______ ones

19. With thirty-seven objects I can make:

    ______ groups of seven and ______ ones left over

    ______ groups of eight and ______ ones left over

    ______ groups of twelve and ______ ones left over

    ______ groups of ten and ______ ones left over

    ______ groups of nine and ______ ones left over

20. a) A gum manufacturer has decided to place five sticks of gum in each pack. What base system can be used to describe the packaging process?

    b) What number could be represented by the following pictures of gum?

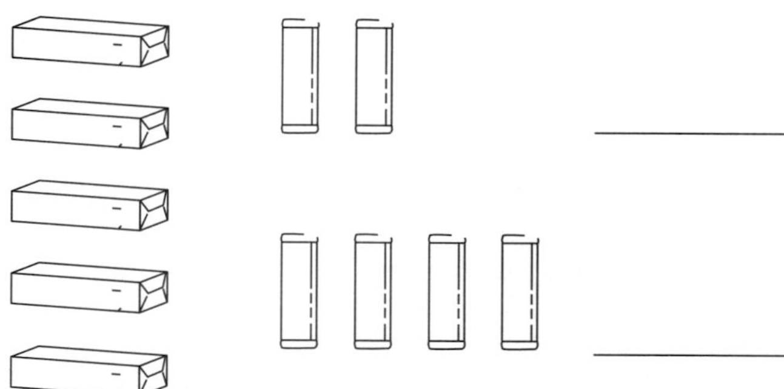

21. Have children toss four beanbags into four large cans. Label one can 125, one can 25, one can 5, and one can 1. As the children toss the beanbags into the cans, have them record the base five numeral they score.

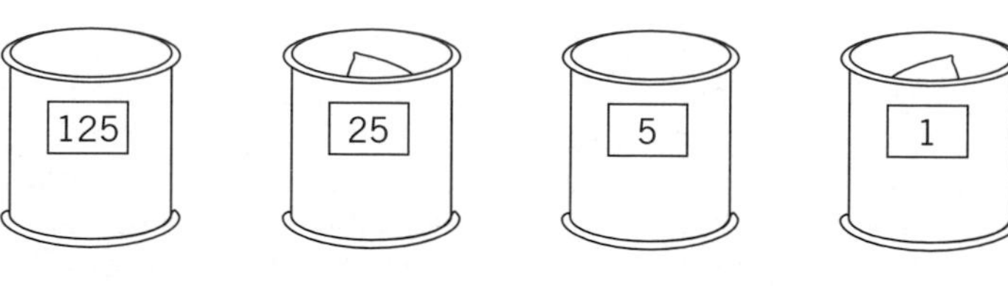

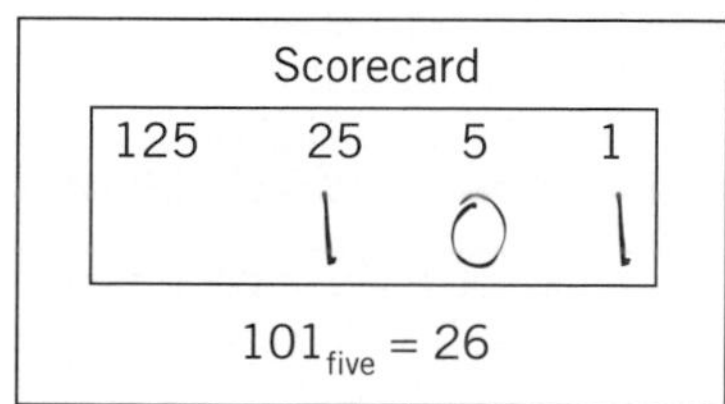

This child would receive a score of 26.

22. Draw a loop around all the numerals that could be used to make each sentence a true statement.

a) 14,621 > ________	14,261	12,421	16,124	14,612
b) 76,543 = ________	76,543	76,435	76,453	76,534
c) 80,010 < ________	81,000	80,100	80,001	80,110
d) 49,052 < ________	49,520	49,025	49,502	49,205
e) 35,093 > ________	35,039	35,930	35,390	35,309

23. In deciding what relation symbol should be used between each pair of numerals, first compare place value. Write the proper symbol in the □, and then give the place value of the digit that helped you decide. For example:

83762 [=] 83762—hundreds place

a) 342,432 □ 345,342	d) 90,000 □ 90,909
b) 68,723 □ 67,832	e) 505,525 □ 502,555
c) 234,572 □ 245,372	f) 89,901 □ 89,899

24. Have the children carefully observe what happens as they enter digits into the calculator. Enter the number 123 into the calculator. Push the 1 key; the 1 is placed in the ones place. Next push the 2 key; the 1 immediately moves to the tens place, and the 2 is placed in the ones place. If the 3 key is pushed next, the 1 moves to the hundreds place, the 2 moves to the tens place, and the 3 is then in the ones place. Discuss with the children how the place value changes continually as digits are entered into the calculator.

25. Have the children work in pairs with one calculator between them. One student should enter a large number into the calculator. Then, handing the calculator back and forth, each child requests the other to remove one digit by placing a 0 in its place. As an example, suppose the number 12345 is entered into the calculator. The first child asks the second child to remove the 2. The second child must know that the 2 is in the thousands place and that, to remove the 2, we must subtract 2000 from the number. NOW, the number becomes 10345. The second child may now request that the first child remove a digit. Continuing in this manner, the children can demonstrate their understanding of place value.

26. Provide many experiences for the children to multiply a given number by 1, 10, 100, 1000, and so on, using a calculator. Have the children discuss how the place value changes when multiplying by a number with a given number of zeros. For example, multiplying 23 by 1, 10, and 100 changes the place value of the 2 and the 3. Do not tell the children that you "add a zero" to the number. When you multiply by 10, the place value is changed. Children have a different idea of what "adding a zero" means.

27. Have the children enter one million into their calculators so that they know what the numeral for one million looks like. Clear the calculator display. Now enter the number 1000. What number should 1000 be multiplied by to obtain one million again on the display? Have children try their guesses. Provide many such experiences with large numbers so that children begin to realize the relationship that exists among the place values of very large numbers.

28. Have two children work together with their own calculators. Roll a die, and have the children enter the digit into any place value they want, in order to obtain the greatest number possible. Only one nonzero digit may be entered into any one place. Roll the die eight times. The student with the greatest number displayed on the calculator wins that round. Continue for a set number of rounds. For example, if the first roll of a die is 4, which place value should that digit be placed in so that the greatest number can be obtained? One child may place the 4 in the millions place, and the other child may place the 4 in the thousands place, hoping that a greater number will be rolled in the next roll. Since eight rolls are used in each round, each of the eight places on the calculator display will show a number other than zero.

29. Make a counting chart to compare the symbols that would be used in base two, base five, base eight, and base ten systems.

Base Ten	Base Eight	Base Five	Base Two
1	1	1	1
2	2	2	
3			
4			
5			
6			
7			
8			
9			
10			
11			
12			
13			
14			
15			
16			

Can you find any interesting patterns in this chart? Could you make a counting chart for other bases from what you have discovered by examining this chart?

10,000	1000	100	10	1	$\frac{1}{10}$	$\frac{1}{100}$

30. a) Each place in the grid has __________ times the value of the place to its right.

    b) Each place in the grid has __________ times the value of the place to its left.

    c) Make a decimal grid and fill in the following numerals:

    473 83,079

    1006 20,000.09

    476.54 113.27

    d) Write each numeral in part (c) in expanded notation.

31. Write the numeral for the greatest number you can name using only the digits 6, 0, 8, 1, and 2.

32. Write the numeral for the least number you can name using only the digits 9, 8, 7, 4, and 5.

33. Place value systems based on groupings other than ten are receiving much different emphasis in mathematics programs today than they did 20 years ago. A study of other place-value systems in different bases can help you understand some of the difficulties that children have in understanding the decimal system. Bases other than ten are a part of some elementary school mathematics programs because of the historical value of studying them and for the comparison to the base ten system.

Study the following place-value grid for 142_{five}:

Twenty-Fives	Fives	Ones
1	4	2

Make similar place-value grids for each of the following numerals:

a) 34_{five} b) 11_{two} c) 212_{five} d) 101_{two}
e) 1234_{five} f) 1011_{two} g) 42_{eight} h) 643_{eight}

34. a) A traveler went on vacation for two weeks and three days. How many days was the vacation? ($23_{seven} = 17_{ten}$)
 b) How is example (a) related to base seven?
 c) 1 week 4 days can be written __________$_{seven}$, and 11 days can be written 11__________.
 d) Complete the following table:

Vacation	Base Seven	Base Ten	Days
3 weeks 1 day			
	16_{seven}		
			43 days
		17_{ten}	
4 weeks 5 days			
		36_{ten}	
4 weeks 3 days	43_{seven}		
			65 days

35. a) I purchased one dozen eggs and found five eggs in the refrigerator. How many eggs were there all together? ($15_{twelve} = 17_{ten}$)
 b) How is example (a) related to base twelve?
 c) Complete the following table:

Dozen	Base Twelve	Base Ten	Eggs
2 dozen 11 eggs			
	34_{twelve}		
		26_{ten}	
			42 eggs
	19_{twelve}		
3 dozen 7 eggs			
			60 eggs
		36_{ten}	

36. a) Sara wanted to buy some candy. She had 2 quarters, 1 nickel, and 4 pennies. How much money did she have? ($214_{five} = 59_{ten}$)
 b) How is example (a) related to base five?

c) Complete the following table:

Coins	Base Five	Base Ten	Total Money
1 quarter 2 nickels			
	43_{five}		
		83_{ten}	
			79 cents
	342_{five}		
		42_{ten}	
			92 cents
3 quarters 4 nickels 3 pennies			

37. A light switch in a classroom can be used as a model of the binary numeration system. Assign zero to the "off" position, and one to the "on" position. Suppose the light is off and you flick the light switch 2^7 or 128 times. Would this light be on or off? Justify your answer.

38. Encourage the students to create and develop number systems of their own. Students can present their systems to the class for discussion and further exploration.

39. With proper understanding of place value, grouping, and expanded notation, the use of exponential notation comes naturally at this level. The student is able to see the practical value of exponential notation and has reached the point where it can be placed in proper perspective.

    As one example, have a child write 5,432,216 in expanded notation:

    $$5{,}000{,}000 + 400{,}000 + 30{,}000 + 2000 + 200 + 10 + 6$$

    The children may groan—and well they should at this point. Now write the same example in this form:

    $$(5 \times 1{,}000{,}000) + (4 \times 100{,}000) + (3 \times 10{,}000) + (2 \times 1000) + (2 \times 100) + (1 \times 10) + (6 \times 1)$$

    Ask the children whether they think this method is any better and why. Give them an opportunity to compare the two forms and to express any pertinent observations they may have. It is possible a child might suggest that there is a still more efficient way of writing the numeral so that the meaning can be understood. However, it is also possible that you may have to initiate the idea in some way.

    Begin with 10:

    $10 \times 1 =$ __________

    $10 \times 10 =$ __________

    $10 \times 10 \times 10 =$ __________

    $10 \times 10 \times 10 \times 10 =$ __________

    Children will soon see the familiar pattern. Then ask if anyone would like to express an idea about the products written in this form:

    $10^1 \quad 10^2 \quad 10^3 \quad 10^4$

40. When the children can make a generalization about what is happening, it will be necessary to explain to them the meanings of the words *base* and *exponent.* They can then make these words a part of their vocabularies.

    Check their understanding by using various numbers for the base factor and a variety of exponents. When children first begin using exponents, the tendency is to multiply the base factor by the exponent. For example, 5^3 is likely to elicit a response of 15 rather than 125. When this happens, ask the child to write the meaning of the numeral without the exponent: $5 \times 5 \times 5$.

41. Chalkboard activity: Write various numerals on the chalkboard.

26	335	4167	53,248
1207	80,933	2979	450

Have children write these in the expanded form, such as $335 = (3 \times 100) + (3 \times 10) + 5$. Seek a generalization about renaming each numeral using exponents. Let children work examples of their own at the chalkboard, and have other members of the class explain and verify each example.

42. a) Rewrite each of the following using exponents:

$4 \times 4 \times 4 \times 4 \times 4 \qquad 5 \times 5 \times 5 \times 5 \times 5 \times 5 \times 5$

b) In each of the following, how many times is 5 used as a factor?

$5^3 \qquad 5^7 \qquad 5^{10} \qquad 5^{12} \qquad 5^{20}$

c) Rename each of the following numbers without exponents:

$4^3 \qquad 3^4 \qquad 7^7 \qquad 175^2$

43. Use a calculator to multiply by 1, 10, 100, and so on. Then divide that product by 1, then by 10, 100, 1000, 10000, 100000, and so forth. Study this sequence of examples:

9 × 1 =	9000 ÷ 1 =	9 ÷ 1 =
9 × 10 =	9000 ÷ 10 =	9 ÷ 10 =
9 × 100 =	9000 ÷ 100 =	9 ÷ 100 =
9 × 1000 =	9000 ÷ 1000 =	9 ÷ 1000 =
9 × 10000 =	9000 ÷ 10000 =	9 ÷ 10000 =
9 × 100000 =	9000 ÷ 100000 =	9 ÷ 100000 =

44. Use a calculator to multiply decimal numbers by 1, 10, 100, 1000, and so on, and discuss the effect on the numbers. Consider these examples:

a)	b)
3.476 × 1 =	1 × .0931 =
3.476 × 10 =	10 × .0931 =
3.476 × 100 =	100 × .0931 =
3.476 × 1000 =	1000 × .0931 =
3.476 × 10000 =	10000 × .0931 =

45. Use a calculator to add decimal numbers expressed in expanded notation and to see how they are put together into standard notation. Add these examples:

a) .3 + .05 + .007 =
b) .08 + .9 + .001 =
c) .02000 + .00005 + .10000 + .0004 + .00300 =
d) .1 + .02 + .003 + .0004 + .00005 =
e) 8 + 90 + .70 + .06 =

46. Use a calculator to solve this sequence of examples. Record your answers. To begin, enter the number .2456.

.02456 × 10 = ________ × 10 = ________ × 10 = ________ × 10 = ________

× 10 = ________ × 10 = ________ × 10 = ________ ÷ 10 = ________ ÷ 10 =

________ ÷ 10 = ________ ÷ 10 = ________ ÷ 10 = ________ ÷ 10 =

________ ÷ 10 = ________ ÷ 10 = ________ ÷ 10 = ________ ÷ 10 =

________ ÷ 10 = ________ ÷ 10 = ________ ÷ 10 = ________ ÷ 10 =

________ ÷ 10 = ________ ÷ 10 =

Discuss with the children the sequence of answers to these examples. Create other similar examples.

47. Use the calculator to multiply and divide many different numbers by 10. Use both whole numbers and decimals.

Suggested Readings

Beougher, C. (1994). Making connections with teddy bears. *The Arithmetic Teacher, 41*(7).

Bohan, H., & Bohan, S. (1993). Extending the regular curriculum through creative problem solving. *The Arithmetic Teacher, 41.*

Boulton, L., & Gillian, M. (1993). An analysis of the relation between sequence counting and knowledge of place value in the early years of school. *Mathematics Education Research Journal, 5.*

Bruckheimer, M., Hershkowitz, R., & Markovits, Z. (1989). Number sense and nonsense. *The Arithmetic Teacher, 36*(6).

Buschman, L. (1993). The versatile number line. *The Arithmetic Teacher, 40*(8).

Carpenter, T. (1994). *Teaching mathematics for learning with understanding in the primary grades.* Madison, WI: National Center for Research in Mathematical Sciences Education.

Carpenter, T. P., Peterson, P. L., Chiang, C., & Loef, M. (1989). Using knowledge of children's mathematics thinking in classroom teaching. *American Educational Research Journal, 26.*

Crites, T., & Dougherty, B. J. (1989). Applying number sense to problem solving. *The Arithmetic Teacher, 36*(6).

Davydov, V. V. (1991). *Psychological abilities of primary school children in learning mathematics.* Reston, VA: National Council of Teachers of Mathematics.

Derrington, M. L. (1993). Enrichment in the mathematics and science curriculum in the primary grades. *School Science and Mathematics Journal, 93*(1).

Dienes, Z. P. (1965). *Modern mathematics for young children.* Essex, England: The Educational Supply Association Limited.

Driscoll, M. J. (1981). Counting strategies. In M. J. Driscoll, (Ed.), *Research within reach: Elementary school mathematics.* Reston, VA: National Council of Teachers of Mathematics and CEMREL, Inc.

Driscoll, M. J. (1981). Mathematics in kindergarten. In M. J. Driscoll, (Ed.), *Research within reach: Elementary school mathematics.* Reston, VA: National Council of Teachers of Mathematics and CEMREL, Inc.

Dutton, W. H., & Dutton, A. (1991). *Mathematics children use and understand: Preschool through third grade.* Mountain View, CA: Mayfield.

Eves, H. (1976). *An introduction to the history of mathematics.* 4th ed. New York, NY: Holt, Rinehart & Winston.

Fennell, F. (1992). Ideas. *The Arithmetic Teacher, 39.*

Fitzgerald, W. M., & Boyd, J. U. (1994). Teacher to teacher: A number line with character. *The Arithmetic Teacher, 41*(7).

Flexer, R. J. (1986). The power of five: The step before the power of ten. *The Arithmetic Teacher, 34*(3).

Ford, M. S., and Crew, C. G. (1991). Table-top mathematics—A home study program for early childhood. *The Arithmetic Teacher, 38*(8).

Frank, A. R. (1989). Counting skills—A foundation for early mathematics. *The Arithmetic Teacher, 37*(1).

Gluck, D. H. (1991). Helping students understand place value. *The Arithmetic Teacher, 38*(7).

Greenes, C., Schulman, L., & Spungin, R. (1993). Developing sense about numbers. *The Arithmetic Teacher, 40*(5).

Greeno, J. G. (1991). Number sense as situated knowledge in a conceptual domain. *Journal for Research in Mathematics Education, 22*(3).

Hands-on, Inc. (1992). *Number and operations.* Solvang, CA: Author.

Heddens, J. W. (1974). *Numeral expanders.* Kent, OH: James W. Heddens.

Hiebert, J. (1989). The struggle to link written symbols with understandings: An update. *The Arithmetic Teacher, 36*(7).

Hiebert, J., & Behr, M., (Eds.). (1988). *Number concepts and operations in the middle grades.* Reston, VA: National Council of Teachers of Mathematics.

Hiebert, J., & Wearne, D. (1992). Links between teaching and learning place value with understanding in first grade. *Journal for Research in Mathematics Education, 23.*

Hope, J. (1989). Promoting number sense in school. *The Arithmetic Teacher, 36*(6).

Hope, J. A., Leutzinger, L., Reys, B. J., & Reys, R. E. (1988). *Mental math in the primary grades.* Palo Alto, CA: Dale Seymour Publications.

Howden, H. (1989). Teaching number sense. *The Arithmetic Teacher, 36*(6).

Hurd, S. P. (1991). Egyptian fractions: Ahmes to Fibonacci, to today. *Mathematics Teacher, 84.*

Jones, G. A. (1994). A model for nurturing and assessing multidigit number sense among first grade children. *Educational Studies in Mathematics, 27.*

Jones G. A., & Thornton, C. A. (1993). Children's understanding of place value: a framework for curriculum development and assessment. *Young Children, 48.*

Joseph, L., & Kamii, C. (1988). Teaching place value and double-column addition. *The Arithmetic Teacher, 35*(6).

Joslyn, R. D. (1990). Using concrete models to teach large-number concepts. *The Arithmetic Teacher, 38*(3).

Kamii, C. (1985). *Young children reinvent arithmetic.* New York, NY: Teachers College Press.

Kamii, C., & Lewis, B. (1990). Constructivism and first grade arithmetic. *The Arithmetic Teacher, 38*(1).

Kamii, C., Lewis, B. A., & Livingston, S. J. (1993). Primary arithmetic: Children inventing their own procedures. *The Arithmetic Teacher, 41*(4).

Keller, J. D. (1993). Ideas. *The Arithmetic Teacher, 40.*

Leushina, A. M. (1991). *The development of elementary mathematical concepts in preschool children.* Reston, VA: National Council of Teachers of Mathematics.

Lilburn, P., & Rawson, P. (1994). *Let's talk math: Encouraging children to explore ideas.* Portsmouth, NH: Heinemann.

Meconi, L. J. (1990). Number bases revisited. *School Science and Mathematics, 90*(9).

Meconi, L. J. (1992). Numbers, counting, and infinity in middle school mathematics. *School Science and Mathematics, 92*(7).

Merenda, R. C. (1995). A book, a bed, a bag: Interactive homework for "10"! *Teaching Children Mathematics, 1.*

Metina, L. S. (1991). *Mathematics in preschool: An aid for the preschool educator.* Reston, VA: National Council of Teachers of Mathematics.

National Council of Teachers of Mathematics. (1975). *Mathematics learning in early childhood.* 37th Yearbook. Reston, VA: National Council of Teachers of Mathematics.

National Council of Teachers of Mathematics. (1991). *Curriculum and evaluation standards for school mathematics addenda series: Kindergarten book.* Reston, VA: National Council of Teachers of Mathematics.

National Council of Teachers of Mathematics (1991). *Curriculum and evaluation standards for school mathematics addenda series: First-grade book.* Reston, VA: National Council of Teachers of Mathematics.

National Council of Teachers of Mathematics. (1992). *Curriculum and evaluation standards for school mathematics addenda series: Second-grade book.* Reston, VA: National Council of Teachers of Mathematics.

National Council of Teachers of Mathematics. (1993). *Curriculum and evaluation standards for school mathematics addenda series grades K-4: Number sense and operations.* Reston, VA: National Council of Teachers of Mathematics.

National Council of Teachers of Mathematics. (1978). *Developing computational skills.* 1978 Yearbook. Reston, VA: National Council of Teachers of Mathematics.

National Council of Teachers of Mathematics. (1986). *Estimation and mental computation.* 1986 Yearbook. Reston, VA: National Council of Teachers of Mathematics.

National Council of Teachers of Mathematics. (1991). *Curriculum and evaluation standards for school mathematics addenda series grades 5-8: Developing number sense.* Reston, VA: National Council of Teachers of Mathematics.

Parker, J., & Widmer, C. (1991). Teaching mathematics with technology: How big is a million? *The Arithmetic Teacher, 39*(1).

Passarello, L. M., & Fennell, F. (1992). Ideas. *The Arithmetic Teacher, 39.*

Piaget, J. (1965). *The child's conception of number.* New York, NY: Norton.

Rathmell, E. E, & Leutzinger, L. P. (1991). Implementing the standards: Number representations and relationships. *The Arithmetic Teacher, 38*(7).

Reys, B. J. (1994). Promoting number sense in the middle grades. *Mathematics Teaching in the Middle School, 1.*

Ross, S. H. (1989). Parts, wholes, and place value: A developmental view. *The Arithmetic Teacher, 36*(6).

Rowan, T. E., & Morrow, L. J. (1993). *Implementing the K-8 curriculum and evaluation standards: Readings from The Arithmetic Teacher. Implementing the K-8 curriculum and evaluation standards.* Reston, VA: National Council of Teachers of Mathematics.

Sharma, M. C. (1993). Place value concept: how children learn it and how to teach it. *Math Notebook, 10.*

Sherman, H. J. (1992). Reinforcing place value. *The Arithmetic Teacher, 40*(3).

Slovin, H. (1992). Number of the day. *The Arithmetic Teacher, 39*(7).

Sowder, J., & Schappelle, B. (1994). Research into practice: Number sense-making. *The Arithmetic Teacher, 41*(7).

Steffe, L. P., von Glaserfield, E., Richards, J., & Cobb, P. (1983). *Children's counting types: Philosophy, theory, and application.* New York, NY: Praeger.

Thiessen, D., & Matthias, M. (1992). *The wonderful world of mathematics: A critically annotated list of children's books in mathematics.* Reston, VA: National Council of Teachers of Mathematics.

Thompson, C. S. (1989). Number sense and numeration in grades K-8. *The Arithmetic Teacher, 37*(1).

Thompson, V. (1992). How to win people and influence friends: Calculators in the primary grades. *The Arithmetic Teacher, 39*(5).

Venger, A. L., & Gorbov, S. F. (1993). Psychological foundations for an introductory course of mathematics for six year olds. *Focus on Learning Problems in Mathematics, 15.*

Wearne, D., & Hiebert, J. (1994). Research into practice: Place value and addition and subtraction. *The Arithmetic Teacher, 41*(5).

Wheatley, G. H., & Yackel, E. (1990). Promoting visual imagery in young pupils. *The Arithmetic Teacher, 37*(6).

Whitin, D. J. (1989). Number sense and the importance of asking 'why'? *The Arithmetic Teacher, 36*(6).

Whitley, B. V. (1993). From the file: Writing about the importance of numbers. *The Arithmetic Teacher, 40*(5).

Wood, T., Cobb, P., Yackel, E., & Dillon, D. (1993). *Rethinking elementary school mathematics: Insights and issues.* Reston, VA: National Council of Teachers of Mathematics.

Wright, B. (1990, July). Research for teaching: A constructivist investigation of number learning in the kindergarten year. *Australian Mathematics Teacher.*

Wright, B. (1994). Mathematics in the lower primary years: a research-based perspective on curricula and teaching practice. *Mathematics Education Research Journal, 6.*

Zaslavsky, C. (1989). *Zero: Is it something? Is it nothing?* New York, NY: Orchard Books.

Zazkis, R., & Khoury, H. A. (1993). Place value and rational number representations: Problem solving in the unfamiliar domain of non-decimals. *Focus on Learning Problems in Mathematics, 15.*

Zepp, R. A. (1992). Numbers and codes in ancient Peru: The Quipu. *The Arithmetic Teacher, 39*(9).

Chapter 6

Addition and Subtraction of Whole Numbers

Overview

As you study this chapter, budget your time carefully according to your needs. Your familiarity with the topics may lead you to overlook some important details in the teaching/learning process as it relates to addition and subtraction. Compare how mathematics was taught when you were in elementary school to the techniques as suggested in Parts 1 and 2. Concentrated effort should be devoted to the activities section and the question of how children develop the necessary understanding and skills. Become well versed in the concepts, the materials used in teaching the concepts, and the methodology used in teaching the concepts.

This chapter exposes you to effective methods and procedures for teaching children, for helping children discover ideas and generalizations, and for developing skills. When you have concluded the study of this chapter you should have an intuitive meaning of and a formal definition for addition and its inverse operation, subtraction. The basic properties of addition for the whole numbers should be understood and functional.

Addition and subtraction should be initiated with primary-age children and be reviewed and extended every year in the elementary school. For example, the six-year-old child can learn what addition is and apply it to one- and two-place numbers. The seven-year-old child should memorize the basic facts and extend addition to three-, four-, and five-place numbers. The eight-year-old child might extend the concept of addition into another number system such as integers or rational numbers expressed as fractions. The nine-year-old child should review addition of whole numbers and extend the idea to any number of places and/or extend the idea of addition to another system of numbers.

The spiral curriculum approach can be extended through the various age levels of the child. A systematic, cyclic approach to concept and skill development is essential. The activities for this chapter follow a consistent pattern of presentation and reinforcement.

As children develop and become more complex individuals, the problems that they encounter also become more complex. We suggest starting the mathematics program for each grade level with new concepts and ideas and then reinforcing the operations when the need arises. Children quickly become bored when each grade level is begun with an examination of addition, subtraction, multiplication, and division.

Children need practice and drill to maintain skills and concepts that they have previously developed. However, practice and drill need not be boring. Positive results can be obtained in many interesting and unique ways. Experiences for children should progress from the concrete through the semiconcrete and from the semiabstract to the abstract. Remember that many types of materials are available and should be used in developing children's concepts of addition and subtraction. Materials that should be explored at this time include, but should not be limited to, base ten blocks, Cuisenaire rods, calculators, and computers.

The operation of addition and its inverse have always been part of the child's work in mathematics. The objective is still to find a shorter way than counting to determine a total or a part, but the child's understanding must precede the presentation of conventional algorithms.

SAMPLE LESSON PLAN—"REGROUPING UP AND DOWN"

Primary Review/Direct Instruction

Goal:

Develop conceptual understanding of regrouping as it relates to algorithmic procedures.

Objective:

The students will:

- Model regrouping as the trading of ten for one/one for ten.
- Connect the regrouping process to algorithmic procedures.

Prerequisite Learning and/or Experiences:

- Exploration of face value, place value, and total value with base ten blocks.
- Conceptual understanding of addition as combining and subtraction as separating.

Materials:

Per learning group:

- tub of base ten blocks (units, longs, flats)
- one game die
- place value mat for each student

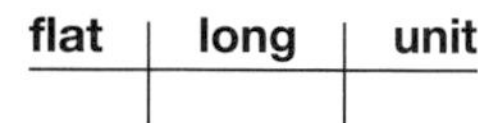

Per class:

- large, soft, sponge die

Procedures:

Motivation

Drop about 6 popsicle sticks on the overhead. Ask students to tell "How many?" Clear off the overhead and drop a handful (more than 15) of popsicle sticks. Repeat the "How many?" query. Explore possible solutions such as counting by ones or making small manageable groups. Guide the discussion toward rubberbanding groups of ten and determining the amount through the use of _____ tens and _____ ones. If feasible, substitiute real-life experiences for popsicle sticks whereby students determine the amount through groups of ten. For example, how many students in the cafeteria, how many cars drive by the classroom window in ten minutes, or how many pennies are in a jar. The point to be made is that grouping can help us count and add numbers. "Now, let's learn a game that helps us regroup by tens!"

Introduction

1. Divide the class into two teams, but have students remain in their learning group seats. Explain the rules for the regrouping game: For round one team "A" (ASTROS) will toss the large die toward team "B" (BEARS); each player on the ASTROS will collect as many units (ones) as the die indicates and place them on the place value mat in the units column; play then passes to the BEARS for their round one turn. Continue playing rounds. During each round the two teams toss the die to the opposing team, collect as many units as the die indicates, and trade ten units (ones) for one long (ten) whenever possible. The first team to trade ten longs for one flat (100) wins the game. Encourage individual participation by having different team members toss the die for each round. Repeat the game until students can verbalize the rules for the regrouping game.

Developmental Activity

2. Once students demonstrate confidence with the rules for the regrouping game, provide many opportunities for small groups to play the game. Anticipate possible misplacement of the counters on the place value mat. Also be prepared to coach the transfer of ten units to one long for some groups.
3. When students play in small groups, each student plays against the other group members. Each student in the group rolls the die. The student with the highest (or lowest) number starts. After the first player rolls the die, collects as many units

(ones) as the die indicates, and places the units on the place value mat, then round one play passes to the second, third, and fourth students. Continue playing rounds. Be sure to encourage individual participation by having students closely watch as each player collects units and regroups, if needed, before another student begins play. The first student to trade ten longs for one flat wins the game.

Culminating Activity

4. For those at the appropriate developmental level, have students connect the regrouping process to an algorithmic procedure for addition. After each roll, have players keep a written record of the additions and regroupings. If students apply a "traditional" algorithmic approach, then recordings may indicate regrouping with a "carry." For example:

Round one:	5	Round two:	$\begin{array}{r} 5 \\ +3 \\ \hline 8 \end{array}$
Round three:	$\begin{array}{r} 8 \\ +6 \\ \hline 14 \end{array}$	Round four:	$\begin{array}{r} 14 \\ +5 \\ \hline 19 \end{array}$
Round five:	$\begin{array}{r} {\scriptstyle 1} \\ 19 \\ +4 \\ \hline 23 \end{array}$	Round six:	$\begin{array}{r} 23 \\ +2 \\ \hline 25 \end{array}$

Student Assessment/Evaluation:

Observe students' regrouping strategies. For example, if a student has eight units and rolls a five, then how is the regrouping of ones to tens handled? Does the student place five units on the board and then make a group of ten units to trade for a long? Or, does the student automatically reach for a long and take two units off the board? Talk to students. Find out not only *how* but also *why* they regroup. Assess student recordings of the additions and regroupings. Apply rubric scoring as follows:

0 = no attempt
1 = does not demonstrate an algorithmic procedure which indicates addition with regrouping.
2 = demonstrates an algorithmic procedure which indicates addition with regrouping

Extension:

If students are able to demonstrate an algorithmic procedure which indicates addition with regrouping, then have students begin a concrete subtraction with a flat on their mats and play to zero. After deciding which student begins the round, the first player rolls the die and removes as many units (ones) as the die indicates. The student will need to trade one flat for ten longs and one long for ten units in order to remove units. Play then passes on the second, third and fourth students. Each round the students roll and remove units (ones). The first player to remove all of the units is the winner.

Have students connect the concrete regrouping process to an algorithmic procedure for subtraction. After each roll, have players keep a written record of the subtractions and regroupings. If the students apply a "traditional" algorithmic approach, then recordings may indicate regrouping with a "borrow."

INSTRUCTIONAL AND ASSESSMENT ACTIVITIES FOR GRADES K-4

1. Use many concrete situations in teaching the understanding of addition and its inverse, subtraction, at this level: counting sticks, plastic spoons, plastic forks, paper cups, flannel board, cutout shapes, and anything available from the child's everyday world. For example:

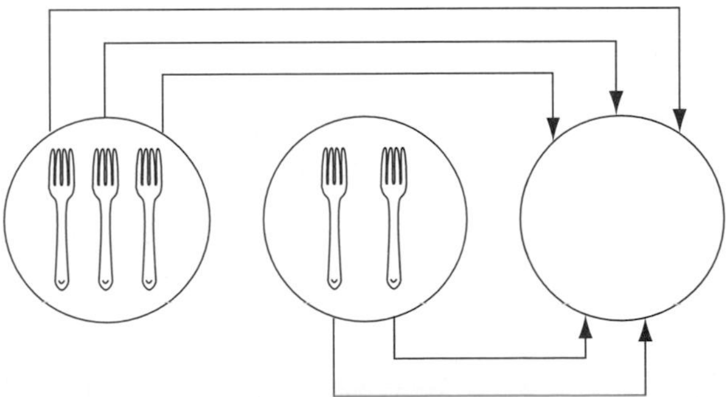

Place plastic forks on a table and encircle them with yarn to indicate groups. Use another piece of yarn to make the outline of another set. Move the three forks and the two forks into the new group. This is a model for the concept $3 + 2 = 5$. A group of three elements joined with a group of two other elements forms a new group of five elements.

Many of these experiences with groups should be used to teach the children what actually happens when two groups are joined. Then introduce the sign of operation (+) and the relation symbol (=) in developing mathematical sentences.

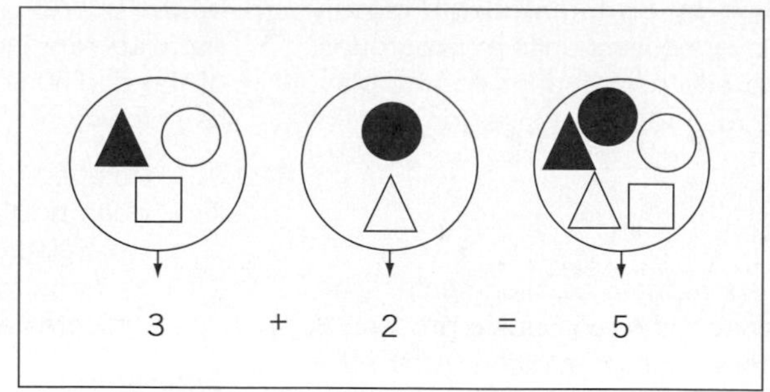

2. Make three sets of numeral cards with the numerals 0 to 9. Also make cards with the symbols +, =, and –. Have the children construct addition sentences for groups shown on the flannel board or overhead projector. For example, if you display a group of two stars and a group of five discs, the numeral-card addition sentence would look like this:

3. Make a set of cards with the words *Addend, Addend,* and *Sum* on them. Using the symbol cards, children can show an addition sentence.

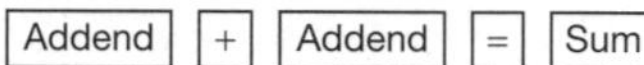

4. The cards from Activities 2 and 3 above can be used for many games. You can omit the card for either the addend or the sum and let one of the children put in the missing card. Change the sentence and repeat the activity. Children can play this game in groups of two or three.

5. On a set of cards about 2 inches by 3 inches write the numerals 0 through 9. Place the cards face down, and draw two cards to use as addends. Model the addition example on the number line. Exercises of this type provide practice in addition facts by using number line diagrams.

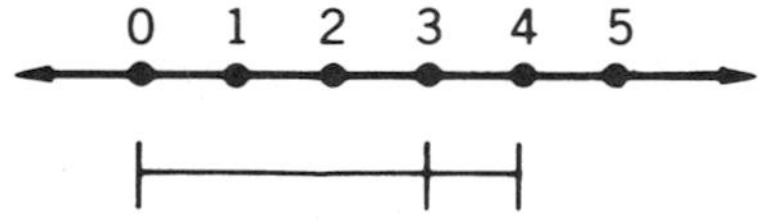

Children can label the addends and the sum. For this example, they can write the addition sentence 3 + 1 = 4.

Model 1 + 4 on the number line.

6. Make a set of dominoes with a pair of addends on one end of the domino and a sum on the other. Play the game of dominoes by using the cards in which only a sum may be matched with a pair of addends. Some of the dominoes might look like this:

7. Make bingo cards of sums for each child in the classroom. At random, draw flash cards, and have the children place markers on the sums. The first child with five in a row (across or down) wins.

2	4	5	7	1
12	7	8	4	13
3	6	9	2	10
9	2	15	1	6
6	12	1	9	8

4	13	8	2	16
10	7	5	14	9
5	6	13	9	11
3	6	10	17	5
15	8	12	4	7

10	5	12	6	18
17	8	11	13	3
16	12	2	9	14
11	7	5	4	6
6	18	15	12	9

8. Help children memorize the basic addition facts by the following means:

   a) Make flash cards of a set of cardboard keys that can be put on key chains.

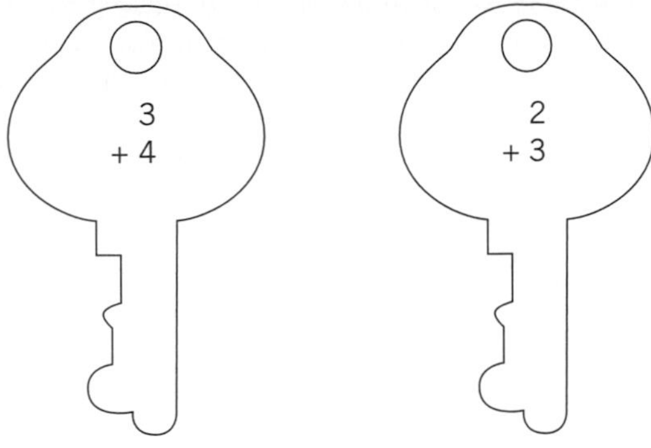

   b) Make flash card necklaces with yarn and paper medallions.

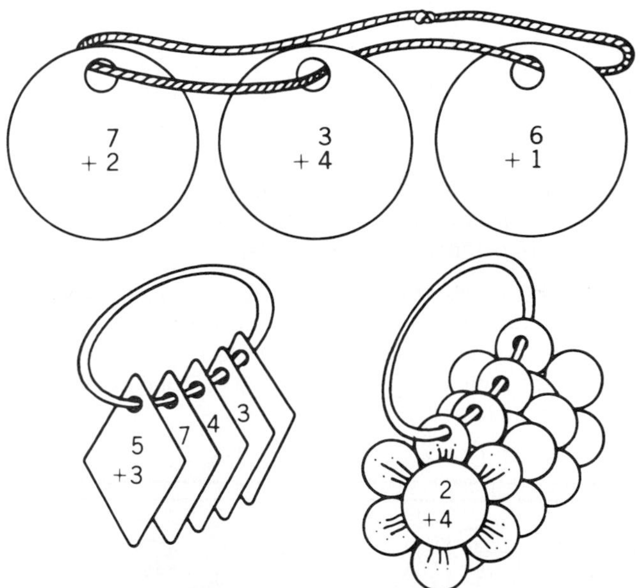

While the children memorize the basic facts, have them "live" with the flash cards (as designed above) all day long. Have the children wear the keys on a chain attached to their belt loops or wear necklaces of cardboard medallions. Parents, other teachers, and siblings can reinforce the flash cards when they see a child wearing them. Classroom teachers can reinforce the flash cards as children are lining up for recess, a change of activities, lunch period, or dismissal. Children will enjoy seeing the packet of medallions grow as they memorize the facts.

9. Write the sums in the outer regions.

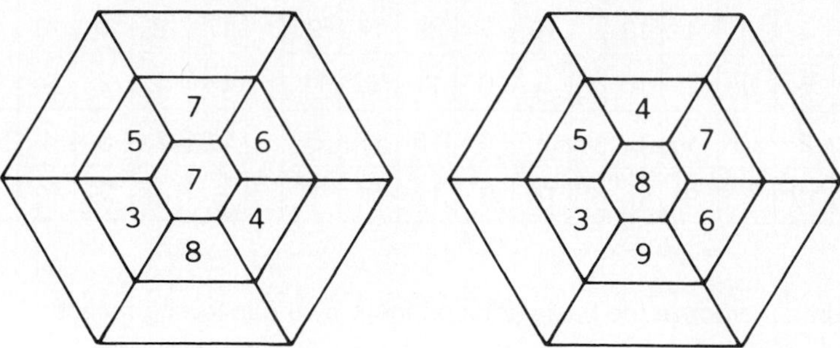

10. Using cubes or other concrete materials, place a group of objects on the overhead projector so that the entire class can observe the group. Have the children write a numeral for the cardinal number of the group. Remove some of the cubes, and have them write a numeral for the cardinal number of the cubes removed. For example:

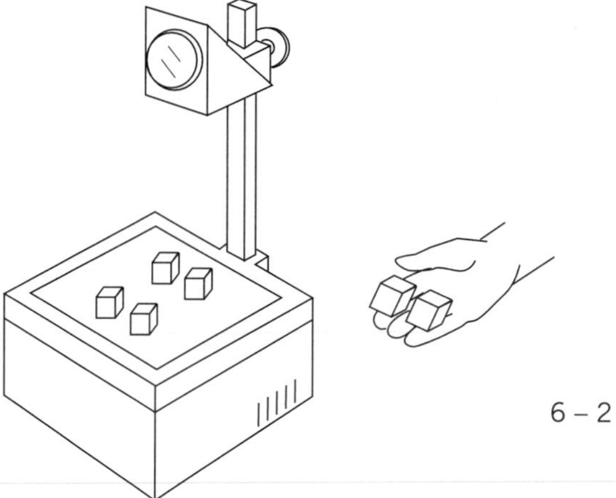

Discuss the operation, relate it to the concept of subtraction, and introduce the subtraction symbol (–). Thus the mathematical sentence 6 – 2 = _____ emerges. Proceed the same way with many different concrete materials.

11. Use the flannel board to display two disjoint groups with different cardinal numbers. Discuss how the two groups are different. Use yarn to connect the objects in the two disjoint groups to show one-to-one correspondence. Write a comparison subtraction sentence. Discuss the subtraction sentence that can be written. Then place a numeral for the cardinal number of the group under that group.

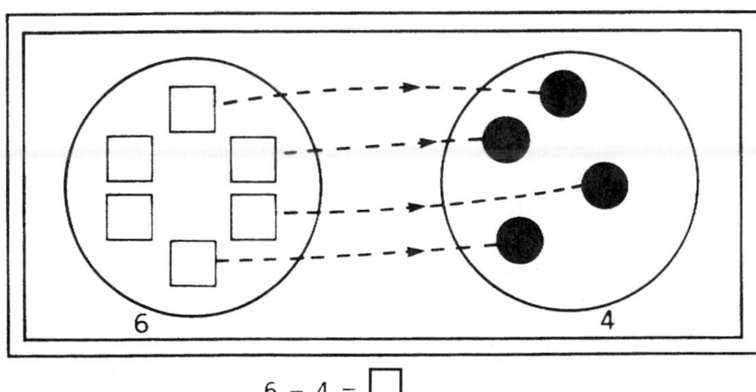

6 – 4 = □

12. Present group pictures similar to those shown in Activity 11. Have the children fill in the boxes with the correct numerals.

$3 - 1 = \square$	$2 - 1 = \square$	$3 - 2 = \square$
$\square - 1 = 2$	$2 - \square = 1$	$\square - 2 = 1$
$3 - \square = 2$	$\square - 1 = 1$	$3 - \square = 1$

13. Give each child a group of blocks. Provide for individual differences by giving different-sized groups of blocks to different children. Have the children separate the group of blocks into two subgroups in as many different ways as they can, and have them write mathematical sentences to record their findings.

$6 - 1 = 5$	$6 - 4 = 2$	$6 - 0 = 6$ (This example may be difficult for some children.)
$6 - 2 = 4$	$6 - 5 = 1$	
$6 - 3 = 3$	$6 - 6 = 0$	

Eventually the children should discover all possible combinations for the numbers 1 to 10.

14. Use the word cards mentioned in activity 3 with *Addend* and *Sum* on them to develop the relation between addition and subtraction.

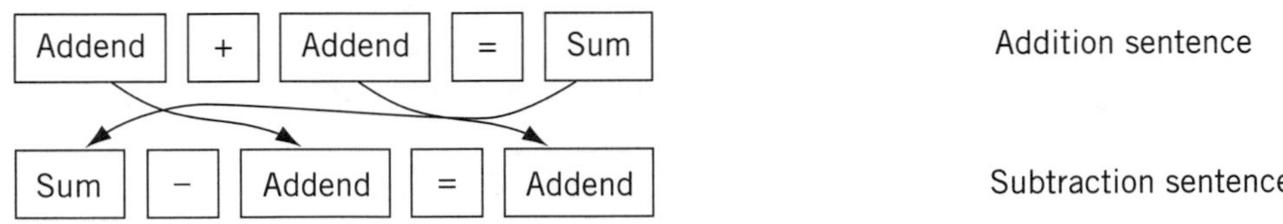

Use concrete examples in conjunction with this development.

15. With a group of objects and the word cards, children should be able to write four related sentences. For example:

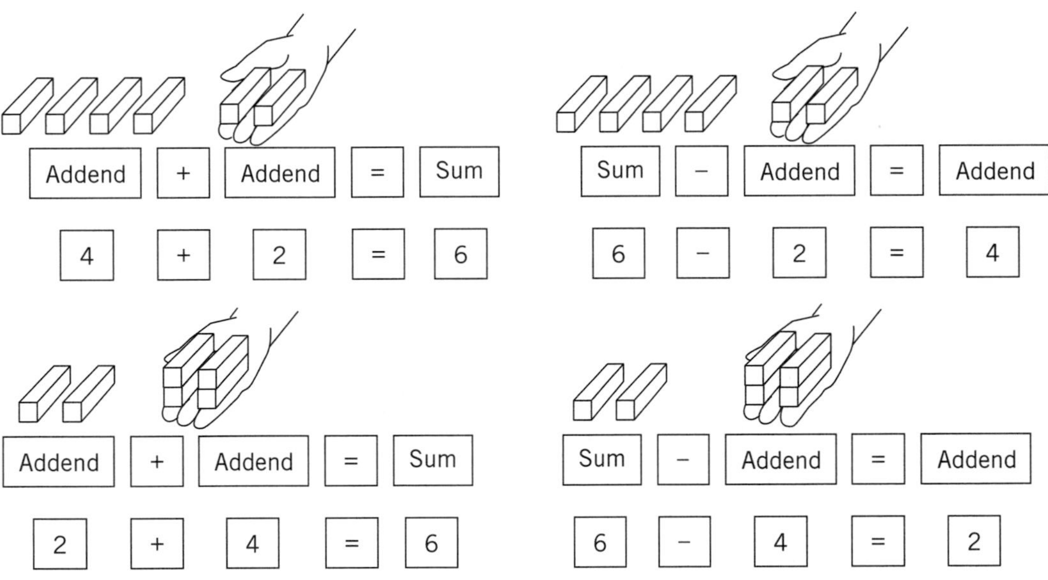

16. Solve each example.

a) $\begin{array}{r} 4 \\ +\square \\ \hline 9 \end{array}$ b) $\begin{array}{r} 6 \\ +\square \\ \hline 8 \end{array}$ c) $\begin{array}{r} 8 \\ -\square \\ \hline 5 \end{array}$ d) $\begin{array}{r} 9 \\ -\square \\ \hline 3 \end{array}$ e) $\begin{array}{r} \square \\ +5 \\ \hline 10 \end{array}$ f) $\begin{array}{r} 2 \\ +\square \\ \hline 10 \end{array}$

g) $\square + \triangle = 7$ h) $\triangle + \square = 8$ i) $\square + \triangle = 6$

17. Make a set of cards of various basic addition facts. Have the children match these cards with numeral cards for the addition facts.

2 + 3	4 + 1	6 + 2	4 + 4	1 + 5	5 + 3
5	5	8	8	6	8

18. The preceding activity might also be done with the addends written on a disk (12-inch diameter) and the sums written on pie-shaped pieces that fit on top.

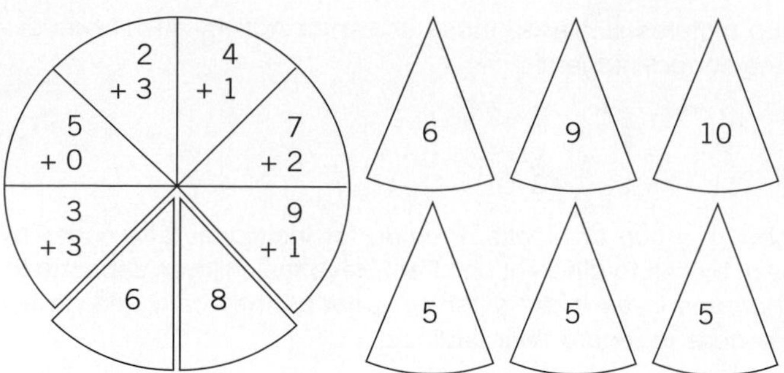

An example written on a pie-shaped piece can also be matched with a disk that has the sum written on it.

19. Practice can be made more interesting by making "practice worms." Cut disks with a 3-inch radius out of light-colored construction paper. Give each child a disk, and have him or her draw a worm face on it. Write one practice example on each plain disk (these may be dittoed on a sheet of paper, and each child may cut one out). The practice sheet can meet individual needs by having sheets with different examples for different children. As the children solve the examples and get them correct, they may staple the discs together to make a practice worm. The worms may be posted on the bulletin board for display.

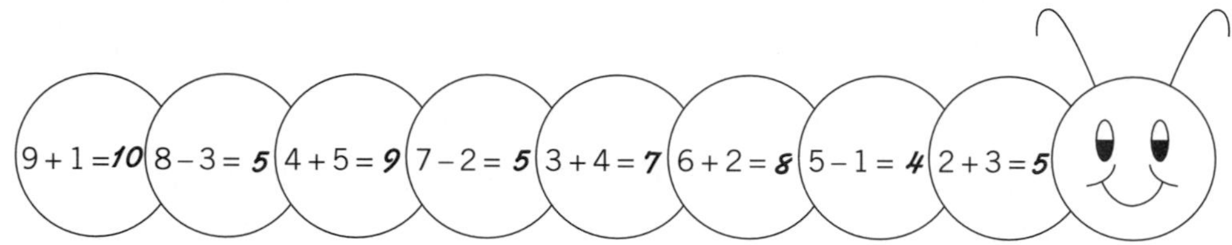

20. The procedure for making worms described in Activity 19 can also be used for making trains. The child receives an engine, a caboose, and a series of boxcars with examples to solve. As the examples are completed correctly, they may be stapled together. Which group of children can get the longest train during mathematics period today? The trains may be posted on the bulletin board.

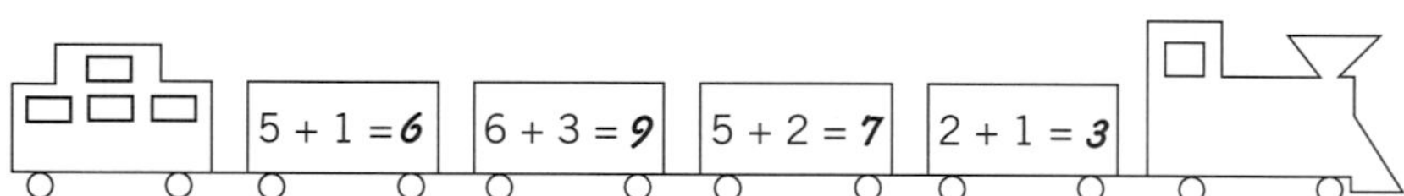

21. In the fall, a large tree branch may be placed in the corner of the classroom, perhaps in a holiday tree stand. Worksheets of colored construction paper may be made showing examples on leaves. Have the children cut out the leaves and solve the examples. Examples with correct answers are tied on the tree. Different shapes, such as apples or flowers, could be used the next week.

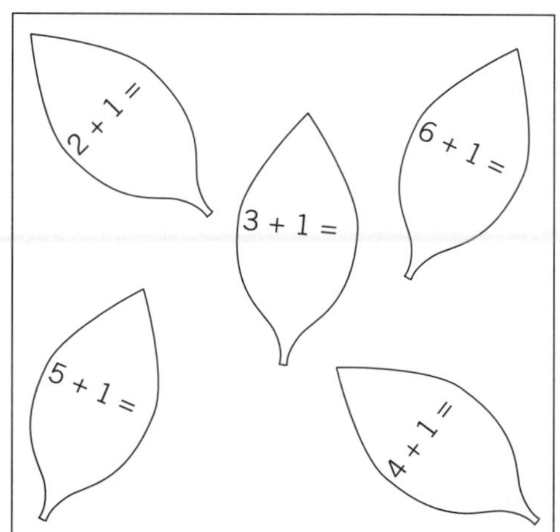

22. A racetrack may be used for addition and subtraction practice. It is easy to construct a board like the one illustrated.

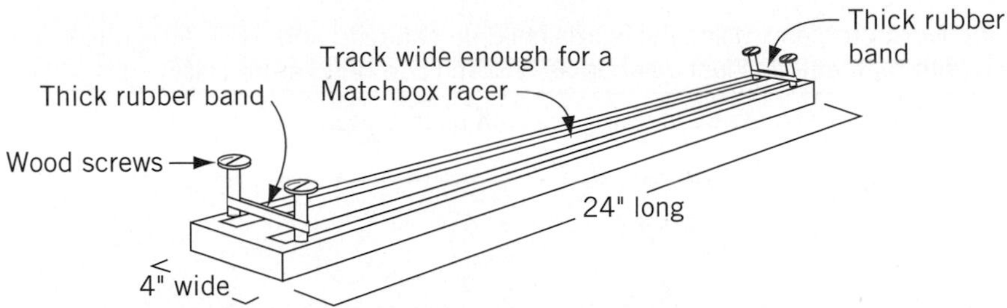

A 1-inch-thick board approximately 4 inches wide and 24 inches long can be used to make a racetrack. Use 1-inch wood screws at each end; place thick rubber bands around the screws at each end of the board. Glue a heavy strip of white cardboard the length of each side of the board, just wide enough for a Matchbox car to move freely. Mark off each strip of cardboard in squares, and alternate the lines on each side of the track. Cover the white cardboard with clear contact paper. Use a china marker to write addends on the contact paper. The addends can be varied to meet the children's needs.

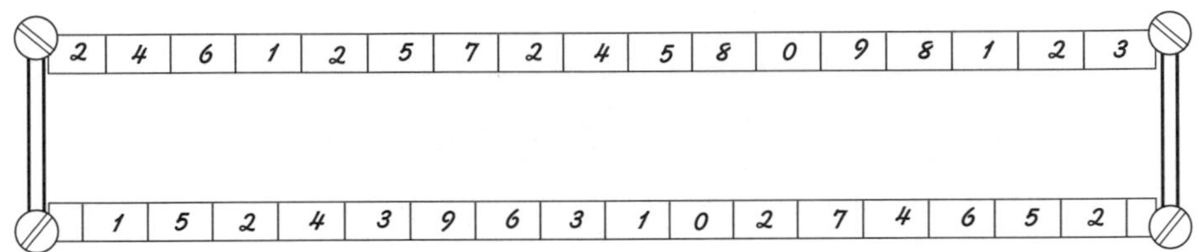

Place the car on the track; let the children push it against a rubber band and let it bounce back. Use the number in front of the car as an addend. Repeat to get a second addend. The same procedure may be used for subtraction by writing sums on one side and addends on the other. The race track may be used for multiplication, division, fractions, and decimals, and in many other places in the mathematics program.

23. A "diffy board" is an excellent device to use for subtraction practice.

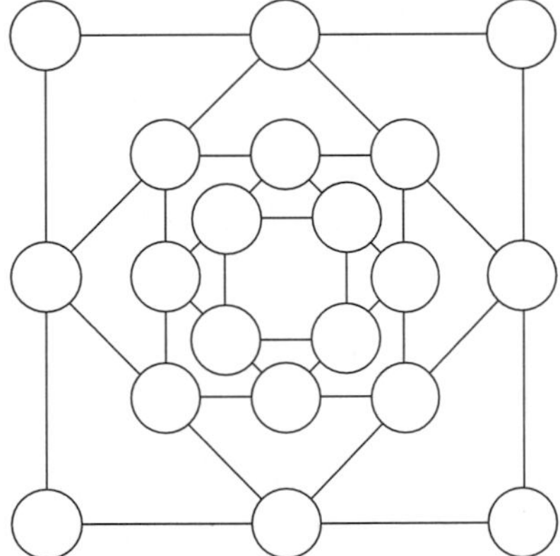

With the diffy board, place any number in each of the four corners. Subtract the smaller number from the larger on any one line, and write the difference between the two in the loop between the two numbers. Continue the process as you work toward the center of the square.

24. Introduce simple word problems. Begin on the concrete level and discuss the example. Early in the year use some words and rebuses for word problem development.

I have $$. You have $$$
How many $ in all?
The child should write $2 + 3 = \square$
The child should solve the problem and write, "We have 5 $."

"Betty has three toys. Tom has one toy. How many toys are there in all?"
The children can write $3 + 1 = \square$.
The child should answer with a complete sentence. "There are four toys in all."

Develop word problems using the words children can read and write. Integrate reading and writing with mathematics just as soon as children can handle the skills.

25. Complete the addition example that goes with each picture.

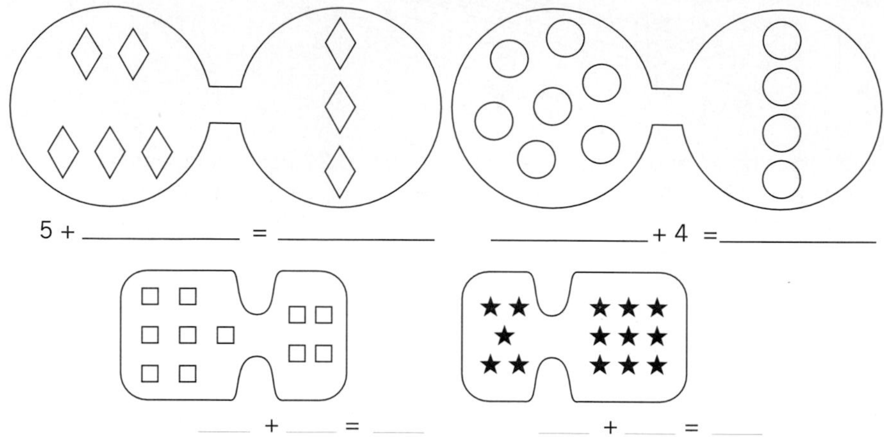

26. The following activity can be used to find missing addends. Construct a cardboard garage from a milk carton. Ten small cars will be needed. The students are shown the ten cars and are asked to close their eyes while the "mechanic" takes several cars into the garage. The students open their eyes, see how many cars are *outside* the garage, and then are requested to tell how many cars are *inside* the garage, by subtraction.

27. Have the children model addition and subtraction examples on the number line. Then have them write number sentences from number line models. For example, $9 + 5 =$ ______

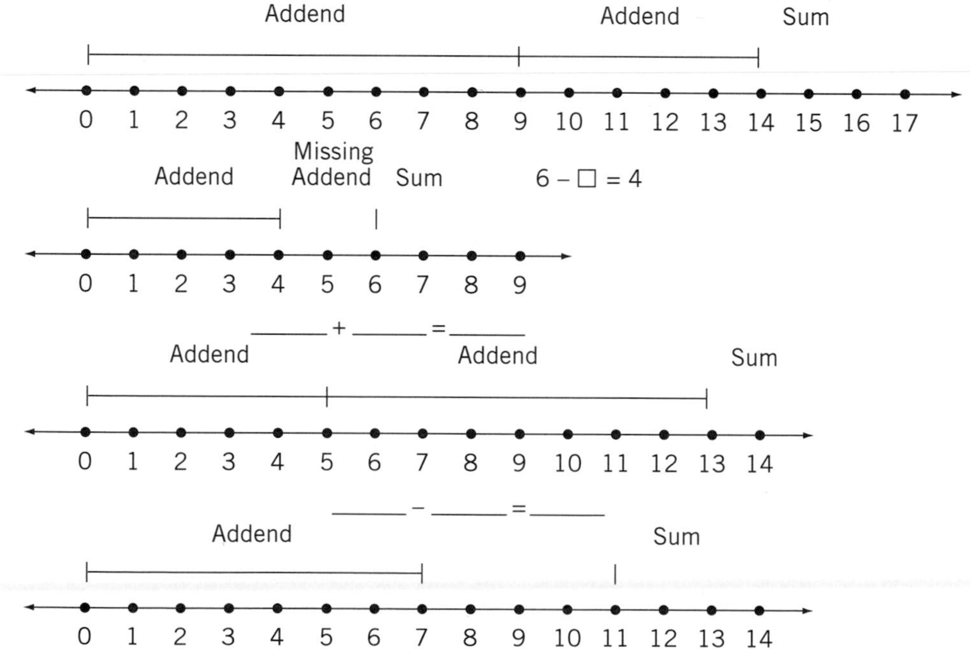

28. Fill in the missing numerals.

a) 32 = 3 tens 2 ones
+ 54 = +5 tens 4 ones
___ = ___ tens ___ ones

b) 27 = 2 tens 7 ones
+ 51 = +5 tens 1 one
___ = ___ tens ___ ones

c) 42 = 4 tens 2 ones
+35 = +3 tens 5 ones
___ = ___ tens _ ones

e) 63 = 6 tens 3 ones
−41 = −4 tens 1 one
___ = ___ tens _ ones

d) 39 = 3 tens 9 ones
−25 = +2 tens 5 ones
___ = ___ tens _ ones

f) 84 = 8 tens 4 ones
−32 = −3 tens 2 ones
___ = ___ tens _ ones

29. Complete the examples.

a) 73	b) 3_	c) _9	d) 98	e) 87
+ ___	+ _2	− 2_	− _6	− _2
93	56	65	72	5_

30. When the children are well grounded in the basic addition facts and the basic ideas of place value, they should be able to explore column addition with three one-place addends. The following examples can be used for practice. Observe that in several examples, if you group properly, you can get a sum of ten for two of the addends. This can be used to simplify the computation greatly.

a)	c)	e)	g)	i)
2	9	3	4	6
3	1	2	5	4
+7	+8	+6	+4	+8

b)	d)	f)	h)	j)
5	6	8	9	5
2	7	3	6	8
+5	+9	+7	+4	+7

31. Have children estimate answers to addition or subtraction examples, and then have them use a calculator to check how close their answers are. Discuss and agree as a class what "close" might be.

EXAMPLE	ESTIMATION	CALCULATOR	CLOSE?
21 + 38	60	59	yes
49 + 32	80	81	yes
19 + 28	40	47	no

32. Children in the primary grades can learn to add a constant using the calculator. When adding a constant, you can add the same number to many numbers without reentering the constant number. For instance, if the constant number is 3 and we want to add 3 to many different numbers, we would use the following procedure:

ANY NUMBER		ENTER THE CONSTANT		DISPLAY READS
[1]	[+]	[3]	[=]	4

The calculator is now set up to add the constant 3 to any number that is entered. If you press the 2 key and the equals key, the display will show 5. We can now enter any number and then hit the equals key, and the calculator will add 3 to the entered number and display the new sum.

EXAMPLE	KEYS PUSHED	DISPLAY SHOWS
7 + 3 =	[7] [=]	10
12 + 3 =	[1] [2] [=]	15
37 + 3 =	[3] [7] [=]	40

33. A similar procedure to that described in Activity 36 can be used to subtract a constant using the calculator. Subtracting a constant means to subtract a given number from many numbers without reentering the constant. For example, if the constant is 4 and we want to subtract 4 from many different numbers, we would use the following procedure:

ENTER ANY NUMBER		ENTER THE CONSTANT		DISPLAY READS
[7]	[−]	[4]	[=]	3

The calculator is now set up to subtract 4 from any number that is entered.

EXAMPLE	KEYS PUSHED	DISPLAY SHOWS
9 − 4 =	[9] [=]	5
47 − 4 =	[4] [7] [=]	43
82 − 4 =	[8] [2] [=]	78

34. Provide practice exercises with some numbers missing. For example:

1□57	□394	3□58
+ 4731	+ 5602	+ 26□1
5988	999□	5989

35. Have the children use base ten blocks to demonstrate the concepts of regrouping in both addition and subtraction. The children may work in small groups; one member is the banker, and the children must exchange the blocks at the bank.

36. Have the children illustrate examples by manipulating concrete materials on the overhead projector. Use small sheets of colored transparent plastic to represent different groups of materials.

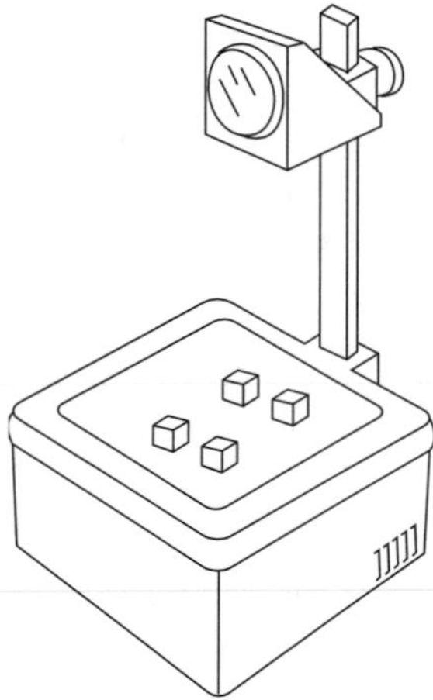

37. Use the place-value box for demonstrating the regrouping process in both addition and subtraction.

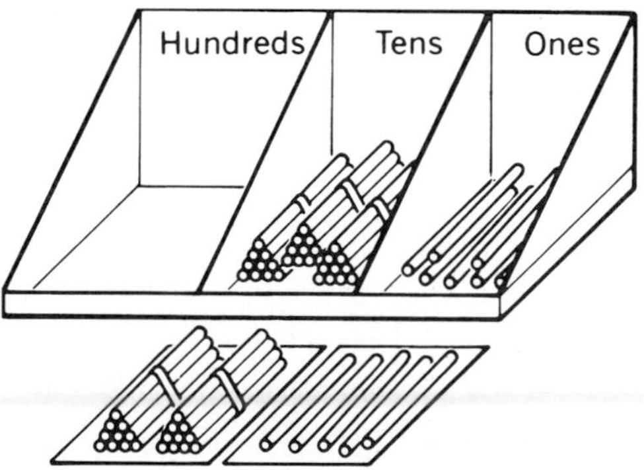

38. An elliptical adding machine can be used to practice addition with two or more addends. Construct the adding machine out of cardboard. Three or more strips of thin cardboard 2 centimeters wide should be cut. These strips can be marked off into 2-centimeter squares.

Choose appropriate addends for the student to practice. The student inserts these strips into the elliptical adding machine and manipulates the strips to arrive at various addends.

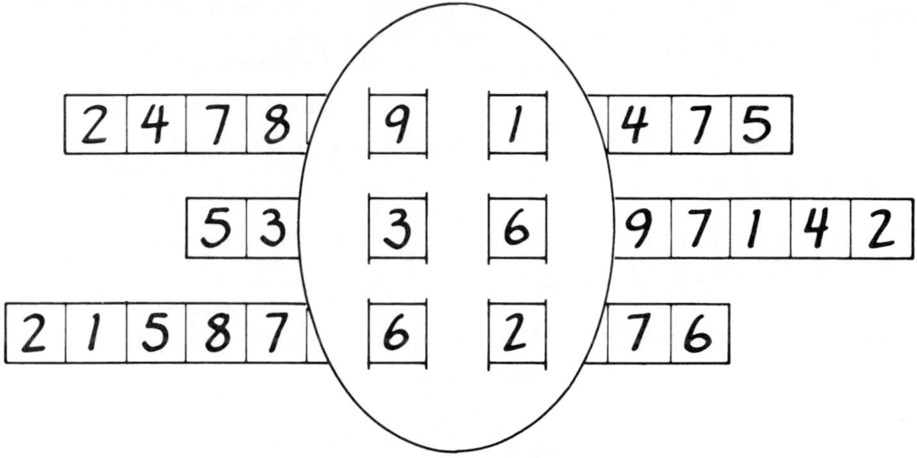

39. Cut a piece of cardboard of any geometric shape into puzzle pieces. On each edge place an addition or subtraction example, so that the matching edges yield the same answer.

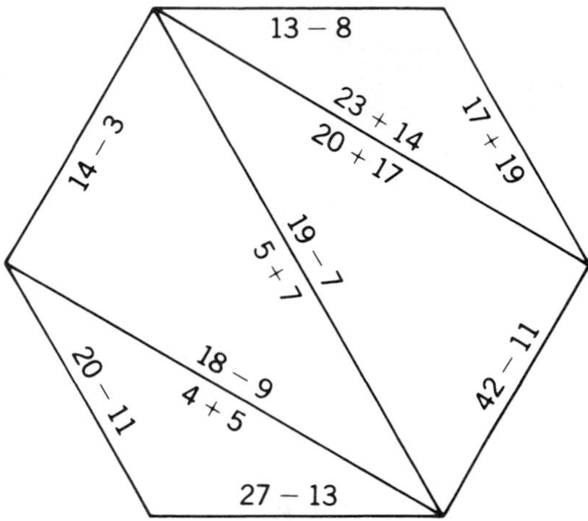

40. For the following activity, you will need a deck of cards with the face cards removed. Before the game begins, a sum is chosen (such as 10). Each student is dealt five cards. Four cards are turned face up, with the remainder of the deck placed in the middle (see illustration). The students take turns playing their cards on one of the four cards face up to obtain the predetermined sum. If a student does not have a card to play, he or she draws from the deck to see if it can be played; this is continued until a play can be made. In the following example, proper plays would be 7, 9, 2, and 6, respectively:

Changing the sum is one of many ways of varying this activity.

41. Cards with addition and subtraction examples can be used in the game of "Concentration." Students must match cards that have the same difference or sum.

42. Place the sum of each example in the proper column or row. Only one number may be put into any one square, and you may check the sum of verifying the number both horizontally and vertically.

Down	Across
1. 9 + 5 + 9 + 8 = _____	1. 8 + 3 + 7 + 5 + 9 = _____
2. 7 + 5 + 15 + 19 = _____	2. 6 + 12 + 5 + 7 + 11 = _____
3. 23 + 14 + 9 + 8 = _____	3. 9 + 14 + 11 + 7 + 15 = _____
4. 8 + 7 + 8 = _____	4. 7 + 9 + 7 = _____
5. 54 + 63 + 15 = _____	6. 19 + 15 + 12 + 7 = _____
6. 13 + 9 + 12 + 8 + 9 + 7 = _____	7. 31 + 23 + 5 + 4 = _____
7. 27 + 18 + 15 + 14 = _____	8. 126 + 53 + 31 + 17 + 15 = _____

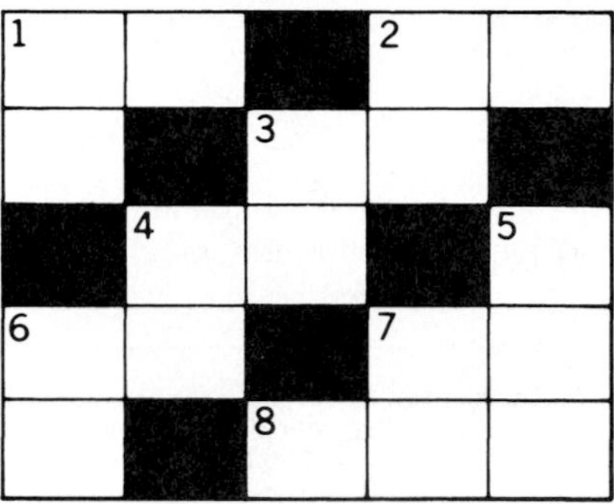

43. Palindromes are useful devices to practice addition skills. A palindrome reads left to right the same as it does right to left. Choose any two- or three-digit number, reverse the digits, and add until the sum is a palindrome. The following examples illustrate how palindromes can be used:

```
 23                                   37
+32  (Reverse digits and add;        +73   (Reverse digits and add.)
 55  the result is a palindrome.)    110
                                    +011   (Reverse digits and add;
                                     121   the result is a palindrome.)
```

Some numbers will have to be manipulated many times to arrive at a palindrome; for example, try 649.

44. You can check a student's understanding of basic subtraction facts by having him or her sort small flash cards into cups. Place a digit (0-9) on each of ten small paper drinking cups.

Cut cards large enough to fit on the bottom of the cups horizontally. Write a basic subtraction fact on each card. A child may sort the cards by placing each one in the cup that has the difference written on its side. The cups will stack because the cards all fit flat on the bottom of each cup. The cups can be put on the teacher's desk, where they can be checked for accuracy at a later time.

45. In the following activity, 81 cards are used, each 6 centimeters by 3 centimeters or 2 inches by 3 inches. Each set of 9 cards should be composed of the numbers 1 through 9. Shuffle the entire deck and place the cards face down. A sum greater than 9 is chosen before the beginning of the game. Each player draws 15 cards. The first puts down 2 or more cards to add up to the predetermined sum. The following players place their cards in such a way that the sum of the cards is equal to the predetermined sum. The play continues until

one of the players is out of cards or until no other play can be made. In the latter case, the player with the lowest sum on the cards in his or her hand is declared the winner. In the following illustration a sum of 12 is used:

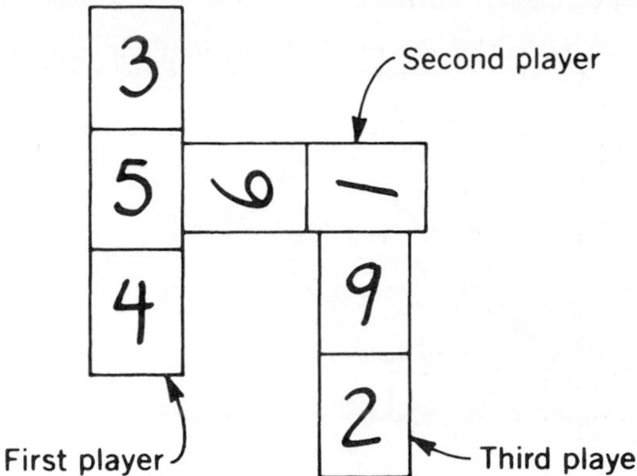

46. Children may use the calculator to check addition and subtraction examples that have been completed using standard algorithms. Perhaps more importantly, they can use a calculator to identify a different way to arrive at the answer.

47. Children can examine a sequence of numbers, determine the pattern, and then complete the pattern. The calculator is a convenient device to use in checking such sequences. Use the concept of adding a constant as developed in the primary section, and extend these sequences. Begin using only addition sequences, try subtraction sequences, and then combine addition and subtraction sequences. Study the following examples:

    a) 1, 3, 5, 7, _____, _____, _____, _____, _____, _____.

    After studying this sequence, the child should clear the calculator and then enter 1. Since the student thinks that the pattern is add 2, he or she should push the keys in order as suggested: 1 + 2 = = = = = = = = =. The calculator display should show 1, 1, 2, 3, 5, 7, 9, 11, 13, 15, 17, 19.

    b) 73, 70, 67, 64, 61, _____, _____, _____, _____, _____, _____.

    Study this sequence, and determine the operation and the numerical amount. Use your calculator to verify the sequence. The student should clear the calculator and then enter the following values: 73 – 3 = = = = = = = = = = =. The calculator will display 7, 73, 73, 3, 70, 67, 64, 61, 58, 55, 52, 49, 46, 43.

    c) 5, 9, 6, 10, 7, 11, _____, _____, _____, _____, _____, _____.

    Note that this sequence first adds 4 and then subtracts 3. The students should clear the calculator and then enter the following values: 5 + 4 = – 3 = + 4 = – 3 = + 4 = – 3 = + 4 = – 3 = + 4 = – 3 =.

48. Software and courseware packages appropriate for primary and/or intermediate grades are available on the commercial market.

49. Many software or courseware programs are available to provide drill and practice in addition and subtraction for primary school children. Many programs focus on specific basic facts or mathematical concepts. Programs of this sort will add interest and motivation to a mathematics program. Generally, computers should be used for objectives that cannot be easily accomplished using traditional classroom methods. For some children timed practice provides an excellent boost to memorize the basic facts—especially when the competition is to beat a personal best, not other children in the class. Children should not be competing against each other; they should compete against themselves to improve accuracy and speed. There is no substitute for memorizing the basic addition and subtraction facts.

INSTRUCTIONAL AND ASSESSMENT ACTIVITIES FOR GRADES 5-8

1. Many of the activities that we have suggested for the primary grades may be adapted for intermediate and middle grade children. Do not hesitate to use manipulative materials with

older children when they do not comprehend a concept. Select the materials carefully so that the children do not feel that they are using "childish" material. Select new sets of materials that are real to these children (for instance, use money, baseball cards, popular toys, or sticks of gum in individual wrappers).

2. A "diffy board" is an excellent device to use for subtraction practice.

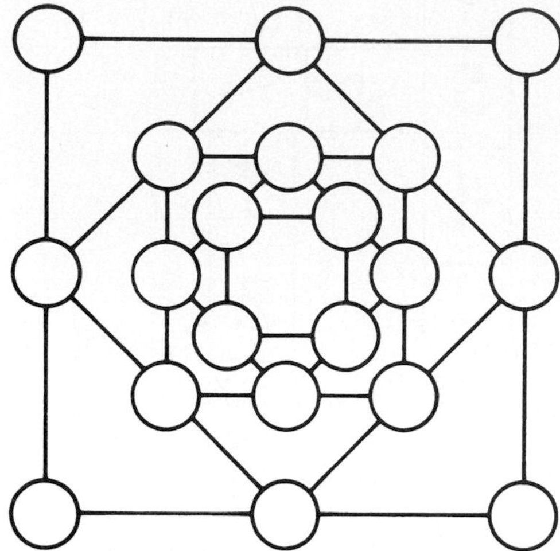

With the diffy board, place *any number* in each of the four corners. Subtract the smaller number from the larger on any one line, and write the difference between the two in the loop between the two numbers. Continue the process as you work toward the center of the square. The diffy board can be used with whole numbers, fractions, decimals, money amounts, measurements of the same type (e.g., linear, capacity, etc.), or any numbers that can be compared by subtraction.

3. Many variations on cross-number puzzles can be used to further develop students' addition and subtraction skills. Place the numbers 1, 3, 5, 7, 9, 11, 13, 15, and 17 into the table so that the sum is the same in each row, column, and diagonal.

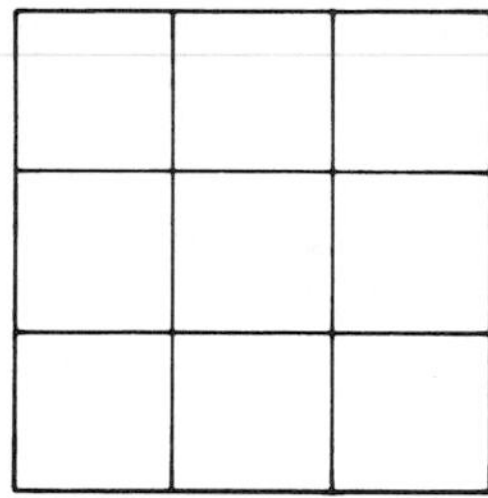

4. Construct a magic square out of cardboard. Place clear self-adhesive contact paper over the board so that the student can write on the magic square with a china marker. In the following magic square, all numbers in a row, column, or diagonal add to 15. Many variations on the magic square can be devised.

2	9	4
7	5	3
6	1	8

5. This is a game played by two children using one calculator. The children take turns by passing the calculator back and forth. The rules of the game define a set of one-place

numbers to be used with the operation of addition. The winner of the game is the player who causes a preselected sum to appear on the display. For example, in this game, children will use addition and the digits 1, 2, 3, 4, 5, 6, and 7. The winner must display the sum of 31. Suppose that the first player enters the digit 3 and passes the calculator to the second player. The second player enters the operation + and a selected digit such as 7; 10 will appear on the display. The calculator is then passed back to the first player. For the second turn the child presses + and a selected digit such as 4; 14 will appear on the display. This process continues until the preselected number (31 in this case) appears on the display.

6. Using whole numbers for the sides of a rectangle, write the dimensions of all rectangles that could be constructed having a perimeter of 8 meters.
7. Complete the following addition table:

Addends

Addends

+			81
33	50		
			94
52		67	
	61		98
49			

8. Using numbers 1 through 25, place one numeral in each loop of the following figure so that adding the three numbers on any one line will always produce the same sum.

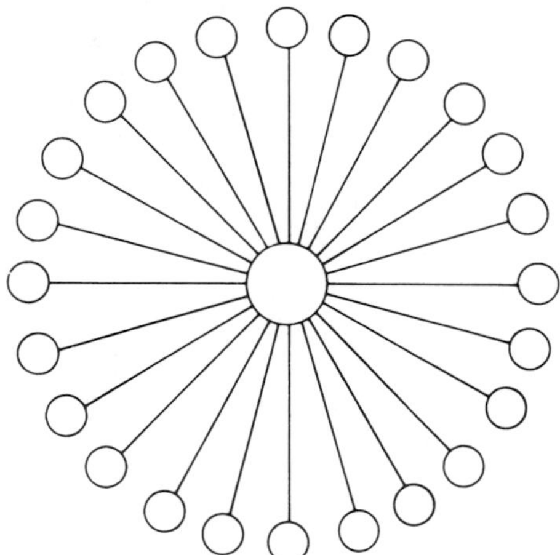

9. The children should use no paper or pencils until they are ready to write their answer for this activity. Tell them to begin with number 43, and continue to subtract 4 mentally until the number is in the twenties. Have them write their answer in large numerals, and hold it up so that the teacher can check the answer. Children could check themselves by subtracting the constant 4 on their calculators.
10. Provide many opportunities for mental addition and subtraction. Whenever some time is available, the teacher might say, "Follow me. Ready? 7 add 9, add 5, subtract 6 add 23, the sum is 0." The teacher should create examples that are appropriate for the students in the class.
11. Have the children take turns passing the calculator back and forth. Each player subtracts 1, 2, 3, or 4 from the display number on the calculator. Begin with number 43 on the display. The first person to display 0 is the winner. Play additional games using different digits and another sum.

12. Estimate the sum of each example by rounding each number to the nearest hundred. The children can use a calculator to find the sum.

Example	Estimate	Example	Estimate
318 + 432	300 + 400	789 + 207	
196 + 469		578 + 623	

13. Children should have a great deal of fun exploring palindromes on a calculator. Palindromes are numbers that read the same from left to right as they do from right to left. Here are some examples of palindromes: 12321, 242, 6357536, and 131. To find a palindrome, add to any number the digits in reverse order; continue until a palindrome is found. For instance, place 37 on your calculator display. Now add 73 to the 37. Your display should now read 110. Now, reverse the digits of 110 and add again: 110 + 011. The sum is 121, and 121 is a palindrome. You can now reverse the digits of 121 and add this to 121; the sum is 242, which is also a palindrome. By adding, change these numbers into palindromes: 49, 79, 182, and 386.

Suggested Readings

Ashlock, R. B. (1990). *Error patterns in computation.* Columbus, OH: Merrill Publishing.

Baroody, A. J. (1989). Kindergartners' mental addition with single-digit combinations. *Journal for Research in Mathematics Education, 20*(2).

Boulton, L., & Gillian, M. (1993). An assessment of the processing load of some strategies and representations for subtraction used by teachers and young children. *Journal of Mathematical Behavior, 12.*

Campbell, M. D. (1989). Basic facts drill—Card games. *The Arithmetic Teacher, 36*(8).

Carey, D. A. (1991). Number sentences: Linking addition and subtraction word problems and symbols. *Journal for Research in Mathematics Education, 22*(4).

Cooper, R. (1994). *Alternative math techniques instructional guide.* Bryn Mawr, PA: Center for Alternative Learning.

Couch, J. P. (1994). The fabulous fact fan. *Teaching PreK-8, 24.*

Driscoll, M. J. (1981). Algorithms in elementary school mathematics. In M. J. Driscoll, (Ed.), *Research within reach: Elementary school mathematics.* Reston, VA: National Council of Teachers of Mathematics and CEMREL, Inc.

Driscoll, M. J. (1981). Estimation and mental arithmetic. In M. J. Driscoll, (Ed.), *Research within reach: Elementary school mathematics.* Reston, VA: National Council of Teachers of Mathematics and CEMREL, Inc.

Feinberg, M. M. (1990). Using patterns to practice basic facts. *The Arithmetic Teacher, 37*(8).

Fuson, K. C., & Briars, D. J. (1990). Using a base ten blocks learning/teaching approach for first- and second-grade place-value and multi-digit addition and subtraction. *Journal for Research in Mathematics Education, 21*(3).

Gill, A. J. (1993). Multiple strategies: product of reasoning and communication. *The Arithmetic Teacher, 40.*

Harrison, N., & Van Devender, E. M. (1992). The effects of drill and practice computer instruction on learning basic mathematics facts. *Journal of Computing in Childhood Education, 3.*

Heddens, J. W. (1981). A theoretical study of the organization of basic addition facts for memorization. *1981 Research Monograph.* Kent, OH: Research Council for Diagnostic and Prescriptive Mathematics.

Hiebert, J., & Behr, M., (Eds.) (1988). *Number concepts and operations in the middle grades.* Reston, VA: National Council of Teachers of Mathematics.

Hiebert, J., & Wearne, D. (1992). Links between teaching and learning place value with understanding in first grade. *Journal for Research in Mathematics Education, 23.*

Hope, J. A., Reys, B. J., & Reys, R. E. (1987). *Mental math in primary grades.* Palo Alto, CA: Dale Seymour Publications.

Hope, J. A., Reys, B. J., & Reys, R. E. (1988). *Mental math in junior high.* Palo Alto, CA: Dale Seymour Publications.

Hope, J. A., Reys, B. J., & Reys, R. E. (1988). *Mental math in the middle grades.* Palo Alto, CA: Dale Seymour Publications.

Kamii, C., & Joseph, L. (1988). Teaching place value and double-column addition. *The Arithmetic Teacher, 35*(6).

Kamii, C., Lewis, B. A., & Livingston, S. J. (1993). Primary arithmetic: Children inventing their own procedures. *The Arithmetic Teacher, 41*(4).

May, L. J. (1994). Teaching math: extending the meaning of addition and subtraction. *Teaching PreK-8, 25.*

McKillip, W. D., & Stanic, G, M. A. (1989). Developmental algorithms have a place in elementary school mathematics instruction. *The Arithmetic Teacher, 36*(5).

National Council of Teachers of Mathematics. (1978). *Developing computational skills.* 1978 Yearbook. Reston, VA: National Council of Teachers of Mathematics.

National Council of Teachers of Mathematics. (1986). *Estimation and mental computation.* 1986 Yearbook. Reston, VA: National Council of Teachers of Mathematics.

Ohlsson, S. (1992). The cognitive complexity of learning and doing arithmetic. *Journal for Research in Mathematics Education, 23.*

Page, A. (1994). Helping students understand subtraction. *Teaching Children Mathematics, 1.*

Pearson, E. S. (1986). Summing it all up: Pre-1900 algorithms. *The Arithmetic Teacher, 33*(7).

Romberg, T. A., & Collis, K. F. (1987). *Learning to add and subtract.* Reston, VA: National Council of Teachers of Mathematics.

Smith, P. J., & Thornton, C. A. (1988). Action research: Strategies for learning subtraction facts. *The Arithmetic Teacher, 35*(8).

Sowder, J. (1990). Mental computation and number sense. *The Arithmetic Teacher, 37*(7).

Starky, M. A. (1989). Calculating first graders. *The Arithmetic Teacher, 37*(2).

Thompson, F. (1991). Two-digit addition and subtraction: What works? *The Arithmetic Teacher, 38*(5).

Thornton, C. A. (1989). 'Look ahead' activities spark success in addition and subtraction number-fact learning. *The Arithmetic Teacher, 36*(8).

Trafton, P. R., & Zawojewski, J. S. (1990). Implementing the standards: Meaning of operations. *The Arithmetic Teacher, 38*(3).

Usnick, V. E. (1991). It's not drill AND practice, it's drill OR practice. *School Science and Mathematics, 91*(8).

Usnick, V. E. (1992). Multidigit addition: a study of an alternate sequence. *Focus on Learning Problems in Mathematics, 14.*

Van de Walle, J. A. (1991). Implementing the standards: Redefining computation. *The Arithmetic Teacher, 38*(5).

Van Houten, R. (1993). Rote vs. rules: A comparison of two teaching and correction strategies for teaching basic subtraction facts. *Education and Treatment of Children, 16.*

Wearne, D., & Hiebert, J. H. (1994). Research into practice: Place value and addition and subtraction. *The Arithmetic Teacher, 41*(5).

Chapter 7

Multiplication and Division of Whole Numbers

Overview

Multiplication and division are fundamental tools of mathematics. Many children (and some adults) are able to perform these functions mechanically but have little understanding of the underlying concepts. Students need to give particular attention to readiness activities for multiplication and division, models for developing meaning for multiplication and division, basic properties, and algorithms. Because of different entrance levels, considerable variance in ability and understanding will be apparent among the students. Irrespective of the prerequisites the students possess, the exit level of comprehension must emphasize correct use of the mathematical language, appropriate symbolic representation, and an understanding of the uses of multiplication and division in real-world situations.

Multiplication can be thought of as an efficient way of counting or adding, yet it has uniqueness as an operation on a number of equal-sized sets. Division has two distinctly different meanings that must be developed. Division is modeled by separating a given number of elements into equal-sized groups, or it can mean the separation of a given number of elements into a certain number of groups.

Children should receive multiplication and division development at each grade level. Readiness activities must begin with the five-year-old child and then be extended each year thereafter. By the end of elementary school, children should be able to function successfully with both multiplication and division. During that period of time children must develop a sound understanding of multiplication and division, master the basic facts of multiplication and division, apply the principles of place value, understand the interrelatedness of the basic structures, and understand and apply the basic ideas of regrouping.

As with addition and subtraction, the concepts of multiplication and division are not new, but the methods that we use to teach these concepts to children have been reexamined. Manipulating concrete objects from the real world, using the number line, and studying illustrations allow children to build an understanding of the computational process *before* conventional algorithms are presented. Understanding must precede skill; when understanding and skill are properly developed, children will have a great deal of power in mathematics.

Students should be introduced to multiplication and division with concrete materials from the real world. They should see these concepts in many different modes to help them think about the meaning of multiplication and division. Children should memorize the basic multiplication facts and become acquainted with the distributive property of multiplication over addition and its use in solving multiplication examples. At the intermediate level, the meaning of division should be developed and the children should memorize many division facts. The study of division is expanded in the upper elementary levels.

SAMPLE LESSON PLAN—"REMAINDER REMINDER"

Intermediate Review/Application

Goal:

Develop understanding of the role of the remainder in the division quotient.

Objectives:

The students will:

- Compare whole number, decimal, and fraction remainders.
- Create real-world problems which correlate with a specific remainder format (whole number, decimal, and fraction).

Prerequisite Learning and/or Experiences:

- Conceptual understanding of division as measurement (repeated subtraction of equal-sized groups) and partition (sharing to form equal-sized groups).
- Experience using the Math Explorer or similar calculator which has the option of displaying remainders as either whole numbers, decimals, or fractions.
- Conversion of decimals to fractions and fractions to decimals.

Materials:

- Paper and pencil
- Various manipulatives to use in the problem-solving process
- Chart paper or blank overhead transparency (optional)

Procedures:

Motivational Introduction

Describe to the class a dilemma you have after reviewing division problems that were solved by students with the Math Explorer calculator. Share the following three answers to $54 \div 4 = \square$:

Lindsay:	$54 \div 4 = 13$ r2
Jaime:	$54 \div 4 = 13.5$
Max:	$54 \div 4 = 13\frac{1}{2}$

Pose the question, "Who's right?" Use the "think-pair-share" model of cooperative learning to explore the question.

Introduction Activity

1. Have individual students *think* about their answer to the question, "Who's right?" Encourage students to write down their thoughts.

Developmental Activity

2. Pair students with a neighbor. Have *pairs* talk to each other about their responses. Encourage students to defend their thinking.
3. Have pairs *share* their responses with the class. Be sure the class discussion incorporates as many viewpoints as possible. You might use chart paper or an overhead transparency to record their ideas.
4. Conclude the whole group discussion with reasons why all three answers have the potential to be the correct answer. Lead the discussion to examples of real-life situations in which each solution is an appropriate response.

Culminating Activity

5. Have *pairs* create and write real-world problems for $36 \div 8 = \square$ such that all three solutions, i.e., whole number remainder, decimal remainder, and fraction remainder, are addressed. Watch for students who use the new numbers but simply copy a problem discussed in step 4. Be careful to use this activity to encourage creativity over mimicry. Also suggest that students use either manipulatives and/or drawings to verify their solutions.
6. Have pairs *share* their problems with the class. Create a bulletin board display with the title "Division Remainders" and three subheadings labeled for Whole Numbers, Decimals, and Fractions. Display student-generated problems under the appropriate heading. Students might also elect to decorate the bulletin board with illustrations of their problems.

Extension:

If students are able to determine appropriate remainder situations for the bulletin board display, then challenge them to determine real-world problems for which the correct answer to the situation requires that any remainder be ignored. Also, ask them to describe a real-world problem where a remainder is ignored and the quotient is increased by one.

Student Assessment/Evaluation:

Assess the content of students' real-world problems to determine if all three remainder situations (whole number, decimal, and fraction) are addressed. Apply rubric scoring as follows:

0 = no attempt
1 = one correct remainder situation
2 = two correct remainder situations
3 = three correct remainder situations

INSTRUCTIONAL AND ASSESSMENT ACTIVITIES FOR GRADES K-4

1. Multiplication and division activities for primary children are readiness activities; abstract teaching does not take place until the intermediate grades. Many situations that indicate multiplication can be discussed with first-grade children. For instance, if you have four tables and six children are sitting at each, the children can count to find out how many are seated at the tables. Do not refer to multiplication as such; it isn't needed at this point. Make use of occasions when children line up in pairs, or by threes, or fours, and again discuss the multiplication situation.

2. In primary grades, the number line provides a natural readiness activity for children. Run a strip of masking tape the length of the classroom. About one pace apart, place small strips of masking tape perpendicular to the strip. Write numerals on the cross strips to make a number line. Have the children walk on the number line and say, for example, the number that the right foot steps on—2, 4, 6, 8, 10, and so on. These numbers are the multiples of two.

3. Place groups of plastic forks on small cards (5 inches by 8 inches, or 15 centimeters by 25 centimeters). Put two forks on each card.

Ask questions such as:

a) How many groups? (3)
b) How many forks in each group? (2)
c) How many altogether? (6)

Then state, "We have 3 groups of 2, or 6 in all."
After many experiences similar to this example, the symbol "×" for multiplication may be introduced.

4. Plastic clothespins may also be put on cards to model multiplication.

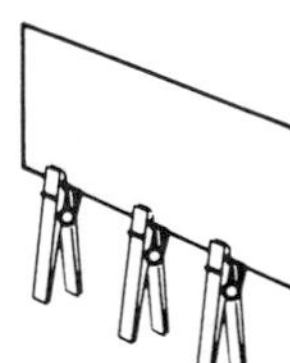

How many groups? (2)
How many pins in each group? (3)
How many in all? _________ (6)

Then state, "We have 2 groups of 3, or we have 6 in all."

How many pairs of shoes? _________ (3)
How many shoes in a pair? _________ (2)
How many shoes? _________ (6)

5. Give the children a group of counters and 15-centimeter-by-25-centimeter (or 5-inch-by-8-inch) cards. Have the children model many multiplication facts.

3×4

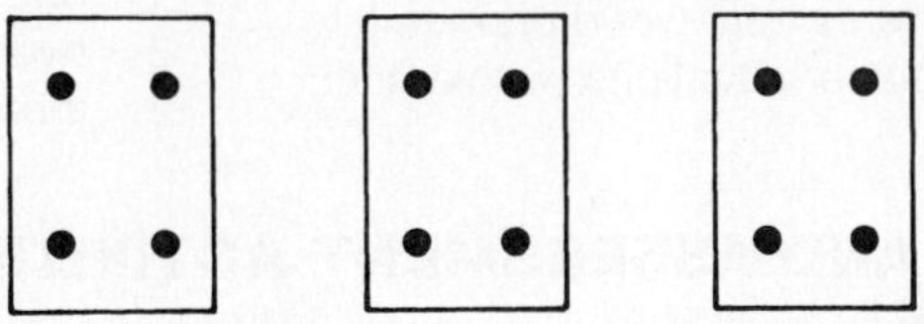

6. Using checkers on construction paper, have the child model 2 rows of 3. Discuss this with the child. Rotate the paper 90 degrees. Discuss the result of 3 rows of 2.

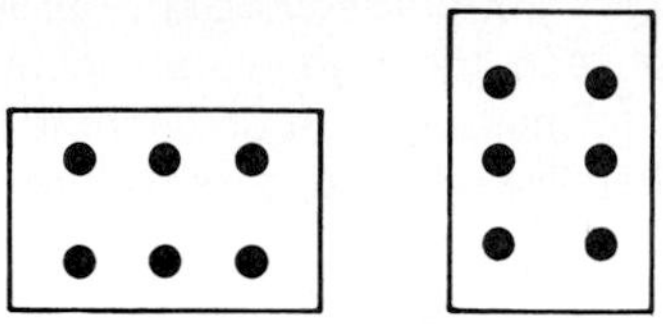

(turned 90°)

7. 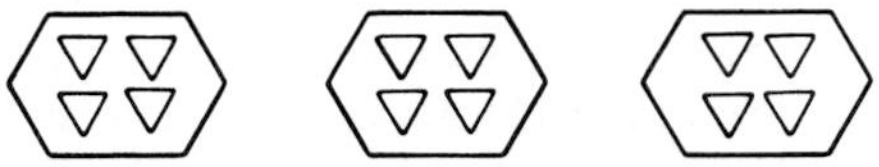 How many groups? ________

How many in each group? ________

How many in all? ________

8. 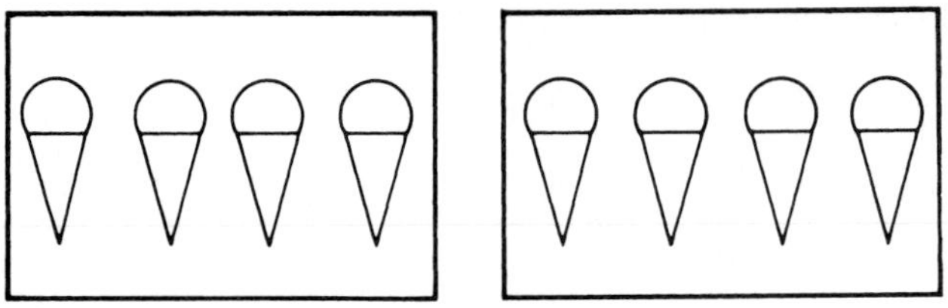 How many groups? ________

How many in each group? ________

How many in all? ________

9. ________ ________ ________

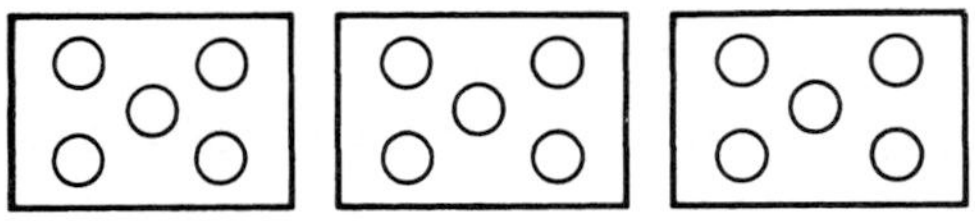

________ groups of ________ = ________

10. a) Draw a ring around 3 groups of 2.

How many?

$3 \times 2 =$ ________

b) Draw a ring around 2 groups of 3.

How many?

$2 \times 3 =$ ________

11. Model each example on a number line

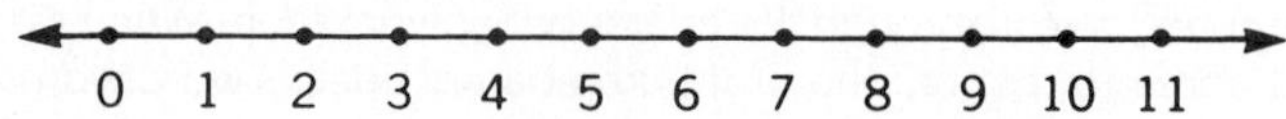

a) $2 + 2 + 2 + 2 =$ ________ b) $4 \times 2 =$ ________

c) $3 + 3 + 3 + 3 =$ ________ d) $4 \times 3 =$ ________

12. Ring groups of 2.

a) △△ ______ sets of 2 = ______ or ______ × ______ = ______

b) △△△△ ______ sets of 2 = ______ or ______ × ______ = ______

c) △△△△△△ ______ sets of 2 = ______ or ______ × ______ = ______

d) △△△△△△△△ ______ sets of 2 = ______ or ______ × ______ = ______

e) △△△△△△△△△△ ______ sets of 2 = ______ or ______ × ______ = ______

f) △△△△△△△△△△△△ ______ sets of 2 = ______ or ______ × ______ = ______

13. Fill in the missing numerals in each sequence.

a) 2, 4, 6, 8, ______, ______, ______, ______, ______, ______

b) 5, 10, 15, ______, ______, ______, ______, ______, ______, ______

c) 3, 6, 9, ______, ______, ______, ______, ______, ______, ______

14. Fill in each blank.

a) $3 + 3 + 3 + 3 =$ ______ or $4 \times 3 =$ ______

b) $2 + 2 + 2 + 2 + 2 =$ ______ or $5 \times 2 =$ ______

c) $1 + 1 + 1 =$ ______ or 3×1

15. Write +, −, or × in each □.

a) 5 □ 6 = 11 b) 7 □ 4 = 3 c) 2 □ 3 = 6 d) 9 □ 4 = 5

e) 3 □ 4 = 12 f) 7 □ 3 = 10 g) 8 □ 5 = 3 h) 5 □ 4 = 20

16. Write a multiplication sentence for each number line model.

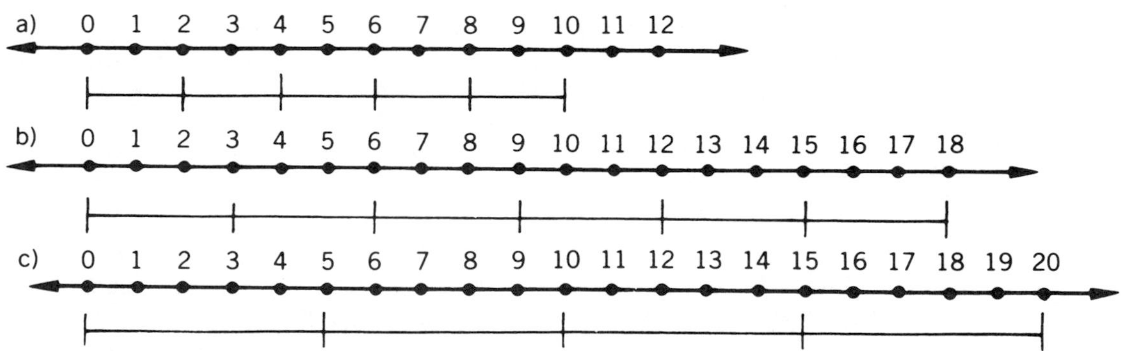

17. Write a multiplication sentence for each array.

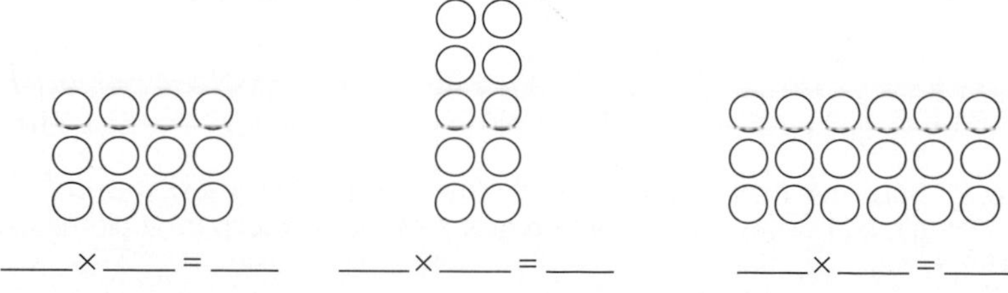

____ × ____ = ____ ____ × ____ = ____ ____ × ____ = ____

18. Cut two octagons about 6 inches across out of heavy cardboard. With a felt-tip marker draw all the diagonals, and print a different numeral on each sector of the octagon. Place a short, sharpened pencil through the center of each octagon. When the pencil is spun, the octagon will come to rest on one of the numbered sides. Two children can play by each spinning an octagon on a pencil and using the numbers on the side they land on as the factors. The children can take turns saying the product. If the octagons are covered with clear contact paper, a china marker may be used to change the numerals so that each child can practice on the multiplication facts he or she needs. For example, to begin, one could use numbers 1, 2, 3, 4, 5, 6, 7, and 8 on one octagon and numbers 1, 2, 3, 1, 2, 3, 1, 2 on the other. More advanced students might use numbers 2, 3, 4, 5, 6, 7, 8, 9 on one octagon and 7, 8, 9, 7, 8, 9, 6, 9 on the other. Vary the examples to provide the practice that a given pair of children might need.

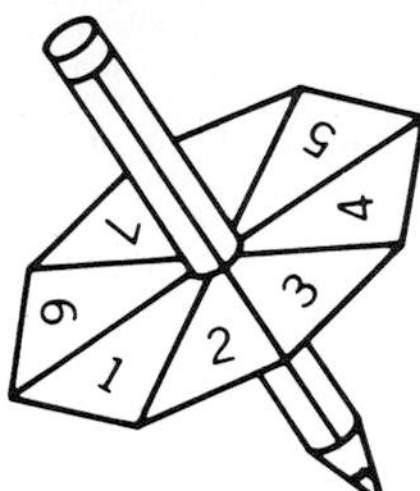

19. Make a pair of cubes out of wood, foam rubber, or sponges, and write numerals on each side to be used as factors. The children can take turns rolling the dice, saying the products, and checking each other. If the product is correct, they may place a card with a 0 or X on the tic-tac-toe board.

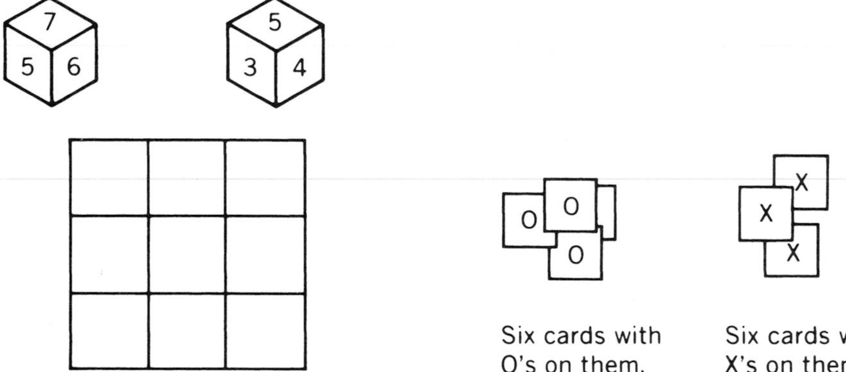

20. String twelve wheel macaroni on a string about 1 meter long (about 3 feet long). Tie the string between two chairs.

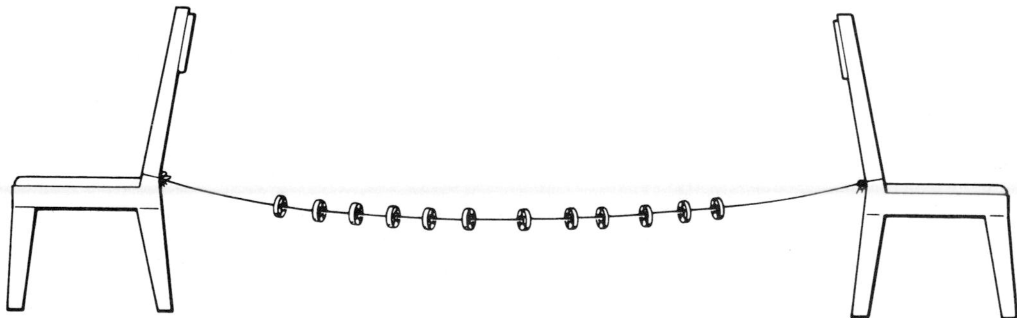

Say, "There are twelve macaroni on the string. How many groups of four can we make?" Begin by having a child count a group of four and clip on a clothespin; then count another group of four and place another clothespin. This shows there are three groups of four in twelve.

21. Give the children 15-centimeter-by-25-centimeter (or 5-inch-by-8-inch) cards on which to place groups.

If we separate the six forks into three equal groups, how many forks will be in each group? After the children discuss the problem, distribute the forks. Now the children can see that six forks placed into three groups makes two forks in each group. Thus $6 \div 3 = 2$.

22. Use the overhead projector and objects such as pennies, checkers, or quarters to make arrays. Have the children write a multiplication sentence on a transparency. Then turn the transparency 90 degrees, and have them write another multiplication sentence.

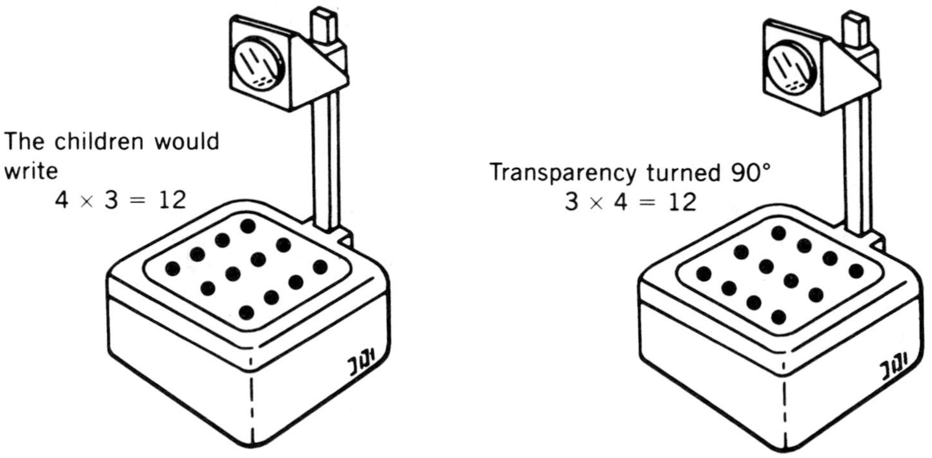

Discuss the two different sentences made from the one array, and relate them to the commutative property of multiplication. Have different children make arrays for class members to write multiplication sentences

23. Write the multiplication sentence suggested by each number line diagram.

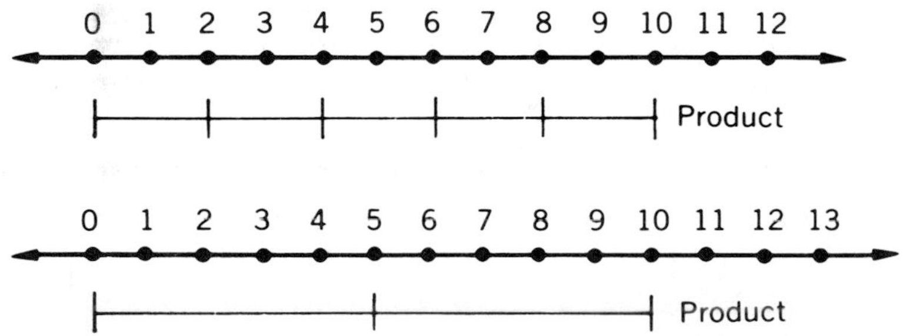

Compare the two multiplication sentences on the following page. Note that the products are the same but the factors are interchanged.

$5 \times 2 = 10$ and $2 \times 5 = 10$
Thus, $5 \times 2 = 2 \times 5$

Again, discuss the commutative property of multiplication.

24. To help establish the basic idea of a multiplication sentence, introduce and teach the words *Factor* and *Product* in the same way that you would teach new words in reading. Make cards of the words and symbols for a multiplication sentence, and manipulate the cards to show a multiplication sentence. Have each child make his own set of cards to manipulate.

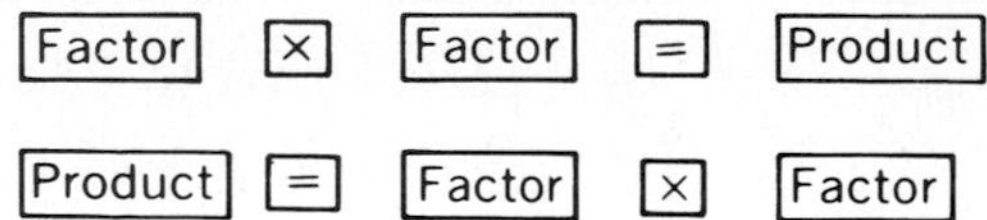

Relate the multiplication sentence to models for multiplication.

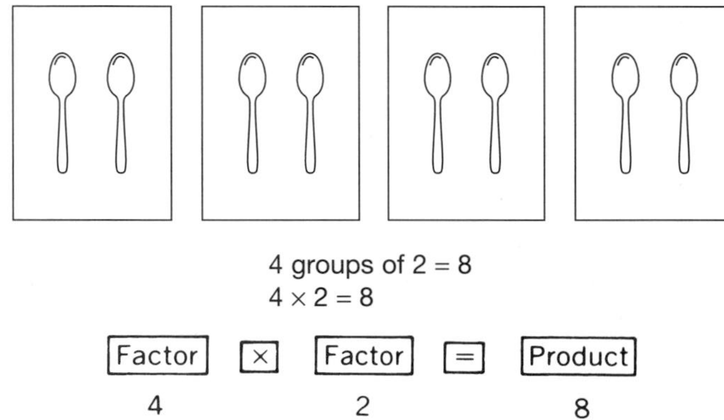

25. Develop the zero property of multiplication by using empty boxes. Each box can represent a group. Thus these two boxes can represent:

2 groups of 0 = 0 $\qquad$ $2 \times 0 = 0$

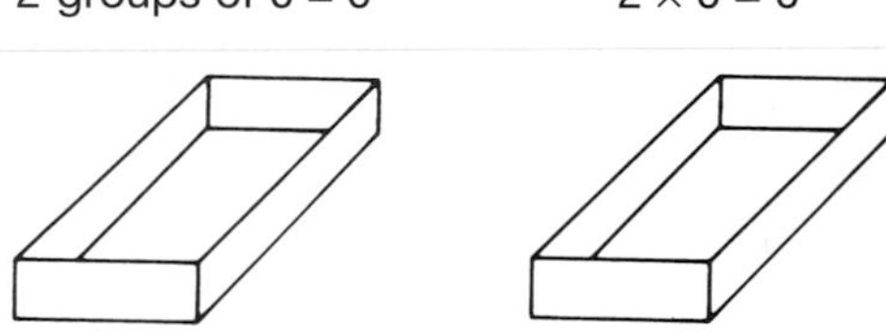

Then place a third box with the other two. The children should write $3 \times 0 = 0$. Continue until the children generalize that zero multiplied by any number is zero.

26. Use groups as a model to develop the identity element of multiplication.

Model of groups $\qquad$ Multiples of 1

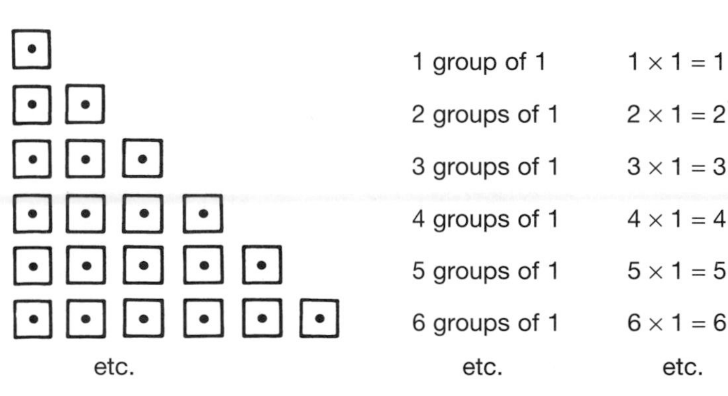

1 group of 1 1 × 1 = 1
2 groups of 1 2 × 1 = 2
3 groups of 1 3 × 1 = 3
4 groups of 1 4 × 1 = 4
5 groups of 1 5 × 1 = 5
6 groups of 1 6 × 1 = 6
etc. etc. etc.

It is essential to use the commutative property of multiplication at this point. Using the commutative property of multiplication, the children should generalize that one times any number equals that number. Now fill in the second row and second column of the multiplication table.

27. Develop tables of multiples for each number by using groups as models.

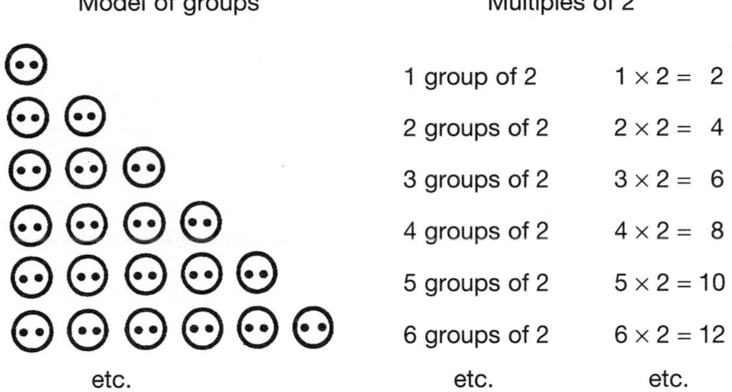

Model of groups	Multiples of 2	
(1 group)	1 group of 2	1 × 2 = 2
(2 groups)	2 groups of 2	2 × 2 = 4
(3 groups)	3 groups of 2	3 × 2 = 6
(4 groups)	4 groups of 2	4 × 2 = 8
(5 groups)	5 groups of 2	5 × 2 = 10
(6 groups)	6 groups of 2	6 × 2 = 12
etc.	etc.	etc.

Study the multiplication table to discover where each set of multiples will fit in.

28. Because children sometimes have difficulty using charts of basic facts, the following procedure might be used. Construct two plastic strips of different colors so that the strips are slightly wider and longer than a row of the chart. Glue the two strips together at a 90 degree angle. At the overlapped end, cut out a rectangle the size of one of the rectangles on the chart. The student can use this device to find the product of two numbers on the basic fact chart. This guide can also be used for addition.

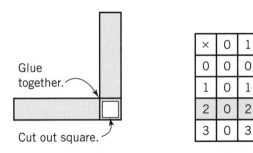

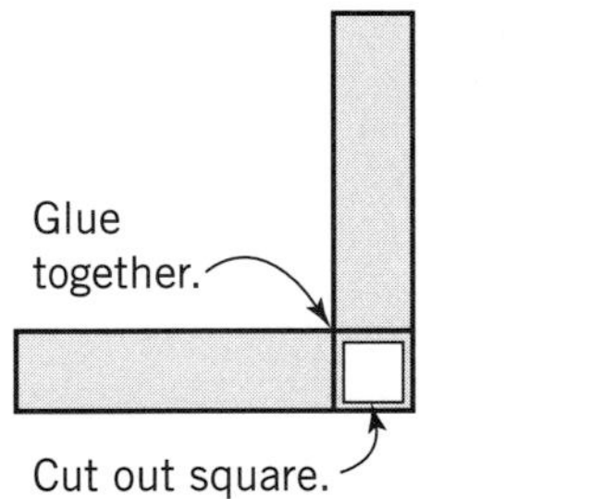

×	0	1	2	3
0	0	0	0	0
1	0	1	2	3
2	0	2	4	6
3	0	3	6	9

29. To make memorization of basic facts more interesting, Edmund the Eel might be used. An eel is drawn on cardboard or construction paper. Irregularly shaped cards with basic facts written on them can be placed on the eel as the student memorizes them.

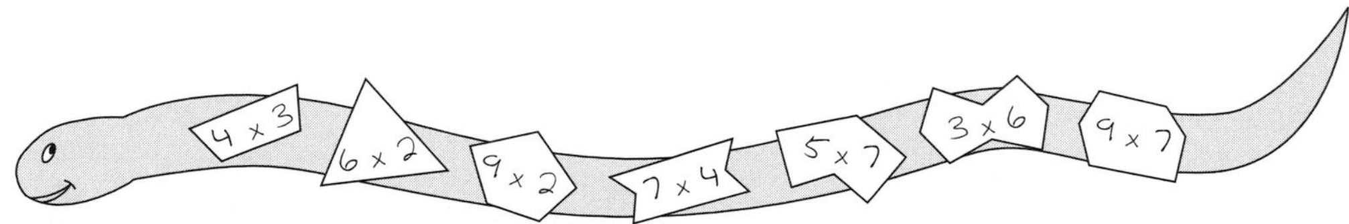

30. Fill in the blanks.

a) ________ × 2 = 6 b) ________ × 4 = 16 c) 5 × ________ = 15

d) 6 × ________ = 24 e) 6 ÷ 2 = ________ f) 16 ÷ 4 = ________

g) 15 ÷ 5 = ________ h) 24 ÷ 6 = ________

31. Use groups to extend the basic multiplication facts.

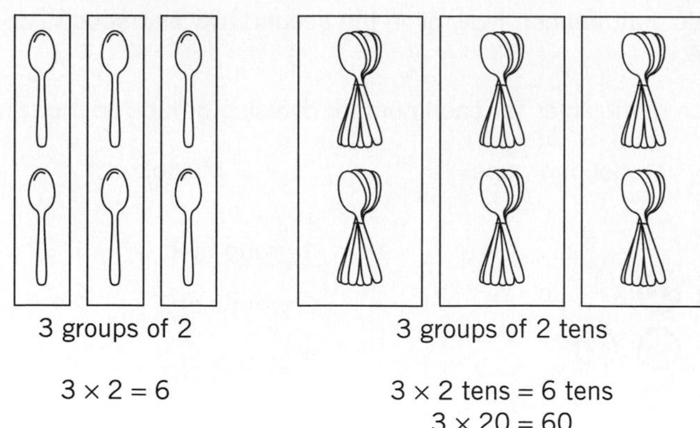

32. Study the following to see how basic facts are extended and combined to solve multi-step exercises.

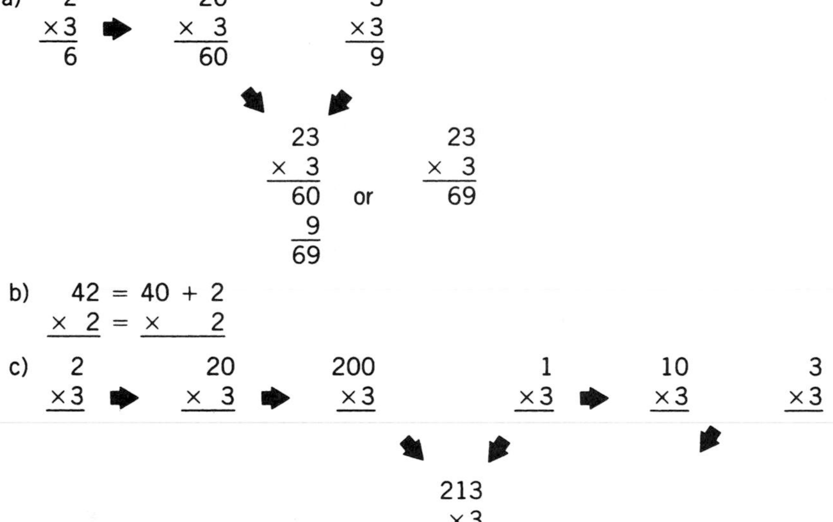

33. Use concrete materials for children to see how regrouping in multiplication works. They may need to use expanded notation before becoming familiar with the algorithm and being able to use the conventional short form. Base ten blocks could be put to excellent use here.

a) $\begin{array}{r} 23 \\ \times\ 4 \\ \hline \end{array}$ b) $\begin{array}{r} 36 \\ \times\ 2 \\ \hline \end{array}$ c) $\begin{array}{r} 48 \\ \times\ 3 \\ \hline \end{array}$ d) $\begin{array}{r} 426 \\ \times\ 5 \\ \hline \end{array}$

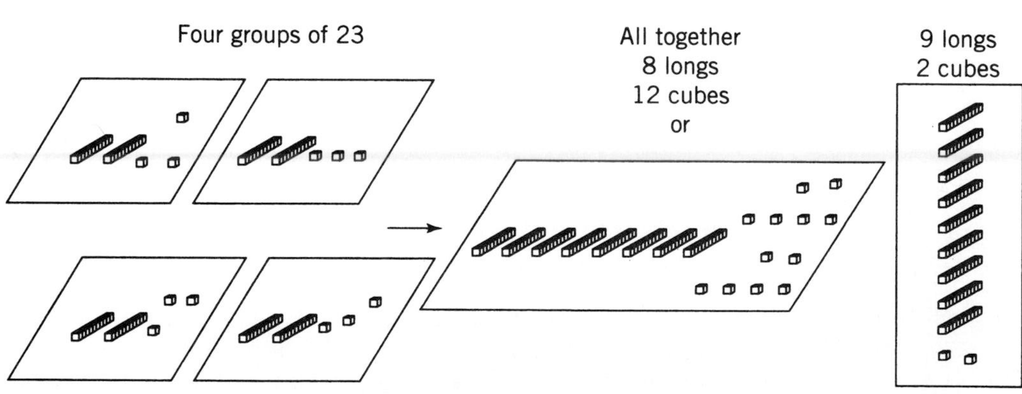

34. Children need to learn how to multiply quickly using 10, 100, or 1000. Do not stress "adding" zeros, but emphasize place value.

a) $\begin{array}{r} 1 \\ \times 2 \\ \hline \end{array}$ $\quad \begin{array}{r} 10 \\ \times\ 2 \\ \hline \end{array}$ $\quad \begin{array}{r} 100 \\ \times\ \ 2 \\ \hline \end{array}$ $\quad \begin{array}{r} 1000 \\ \times\ \ \ 2 \\ \hline \end{array}$

b) $\begin{array}{r} 1 \\ \times 5 \\ \hline \end{array}$ $\quad \begin{array}{r} 10 \\ \times\ 5 \\ \hline \end{array}$ $\quad \begin{array}{r} 100 \\ \times\ \ 5 \\ \hline \end{array}$ $\quad \begin{array}{r} 1000 \\ \times\ \ \ 5 \\ \hline \end{array}$

c) $\begin{array}{r} 14 \\ \times 1 \\ \hline \end{array}$ $\quad \begin{array}{r} 14 \\ \times 10 \\ \hline \end{array}$ $\quad \begin{array}{r} 14 \\ \times 100 \\ \hline \end{array}$ $\quad \begin{array}{r} 14 \\ \times 1000 \\ \hline \end{array}$

35. Give each child 24 counters and several 5-inch-by-8-inch cards. Have the student model a variety of problems, such as, "How many groups of 6 can be made from 24 counters?" Then have the student model four equal groups from 24 counters.

36. For each multiplication sentence, write two related division sentences.

a) $3 \times 6 = 18$ b) $7 \times 5 = 35$ c) $4 \times 9 = 36$ d) $7 \times 8 = 56$

37. Use the arrays to help you complete each example.

a)
○○○○○○○○○○ ¦ ○○
○○○○○○○○○○ ¦ ○○
○○○○○○○○○○ ¦ ○○
○○○○○○○○○○ ¦ ○○

$4 \times 12 = 4 \times (10 + 2)$
$= (4 \times \quad) + (4 \times \quad)$
$=$ ________ + ________
$=$ ________

b)
○○○○○○○○○○ ¦ ○○○
○○○○○○○○○○ ¦ ○○○
○○○○○○○○○○ ¦ ○○○
○○○○○○○○○○ ¦ ○○○
○○○○○○○○○○ ¦ ○○○
○○○○○○○○○○ ¦ ○○○

$6 \times 13 = 6 \times$ (________ + ________)
$= (6 \times$ ________) + (6 × ________)
$=$ ________ + ________
$=$ ________

38. Place six items on the overhead projector, and ask the children, "How many groups of 2 can be made from the six items?"

Place small, colored plastic squares on the overhead projector. As the squares are placed, put two plastic spoons on each square.

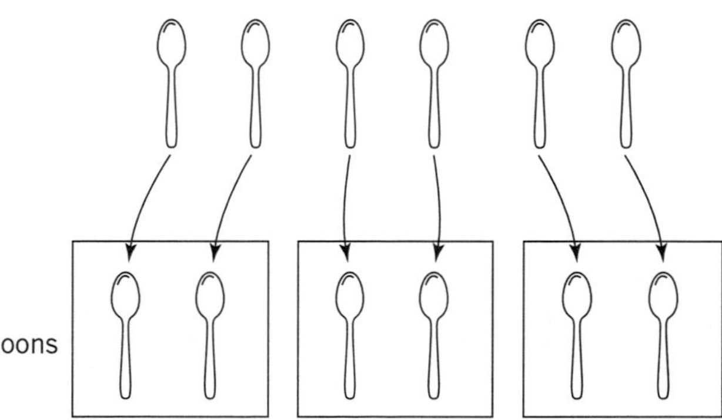

Thus, there are three groups of 2 in 6. Children need many of these types of experiences using tangible objects.

39. Separate a group of plastic cups into two groups. If there are eight plastic cups, for instance, how many would go into each of two groups? Place two sheets of paper on the

desk, one for each group. Now separate the eight plastic cups into the two groups. How many cups belong in each group?

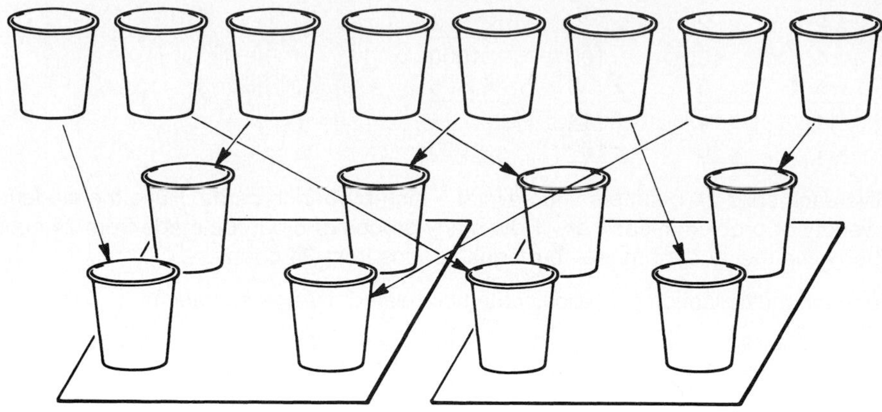

The children need many experiences on the concrete level manipulating materials for both measurement and partition division.

40. Write division sentences for each number line model.

a)

b)

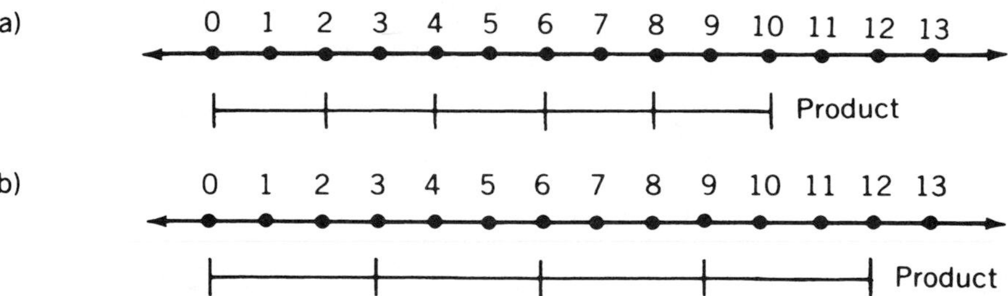

41. Complete each example.

a) $28 \div 2 = (20 + 8) \div 2$
$= (20 \div 2) + (\_\_\_\_\_\_ \div 2)$
$= 10 + \_\_\_\_\_\_$
$= \_\_\_\_\_\_$

b) $842 \div 2 = (800 + \_\_\_\_\_\_ + 2) \div 2$
$= (800 \div \_\_\_\_\_\_) + (40 \div \_\_\_\_\_\_) + (2 \div \_\_\_\_\_\_)$
$= \_\_\_\_\_\_ + \_\_\_\_\_\_ + \_\_\_\_\_\_$
$= \_\_\_\_\_\_$

c) $96 \div 3 = (90 + \_\_\_\_\_\_) \div 3$
$= (\_\_\_\_\_\_ \div 3) + (\_\_\_\_\_\_ \div 3)$
$= \_\_\_\_\_\_ + 2$
$= \_\_\_\_\_\_$

d) $105 \div 5 = (100 + 5) \div \_\_\_\_\_\_$
$= (\_\_\_\_\_\_ \div 5) + (\_\_\_\_\_\_ \div 5)$
$= 20 + \_\_\_\_\_\_$
$= \_\_\_\_\_\_$

42. The place-value box is an excellent device to use for beginning division because it can be used to model as many as three places in the dividend.

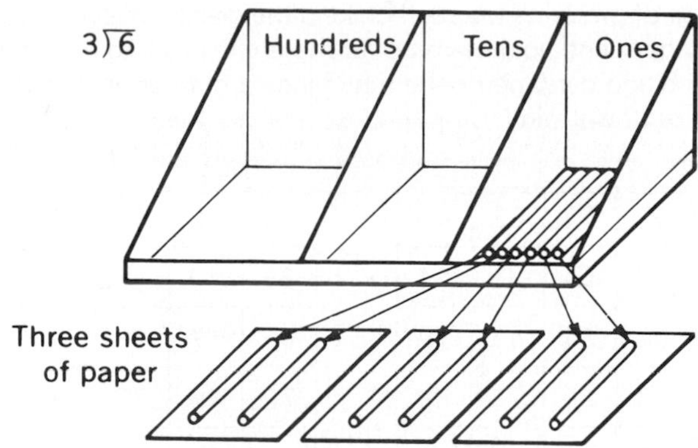

If six things are separated into three groups, how many things go into each group?

43. The previous example can be expanded to 6 tens divided by 3.

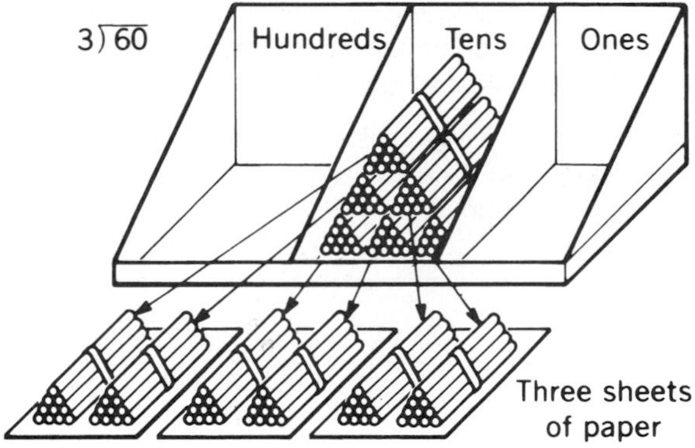

44. Division having a remainder must be presented using tangible objects.

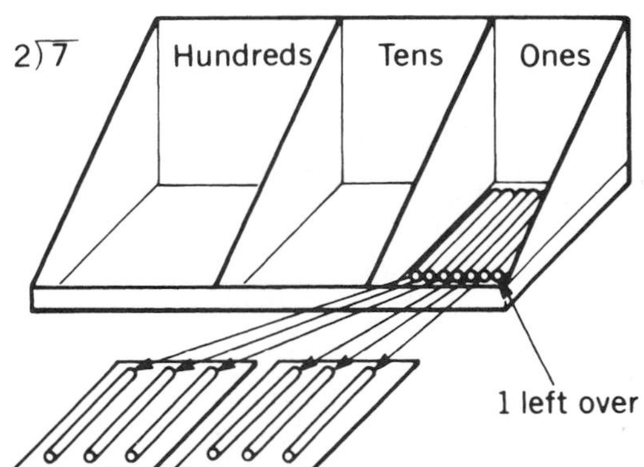

45. Invent a story using array cards, such as "Last night, I had just finished making a set of array cards when I heard a strange sound and saw many colorful flashing lights. I quickly ran into the yard carrying my array cards. A strange machine was parked in the yard. Upon investigation, a hungry Wookie with square teeth grabbed my array cards. Here's all that's left. What can we do?"

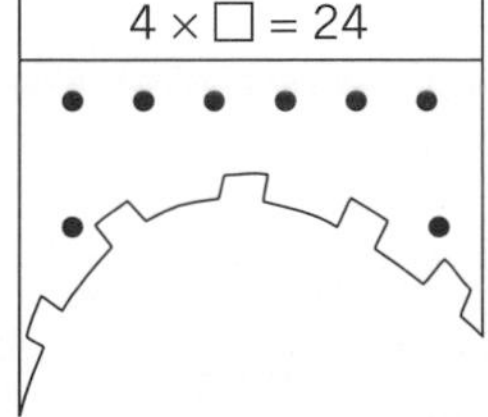

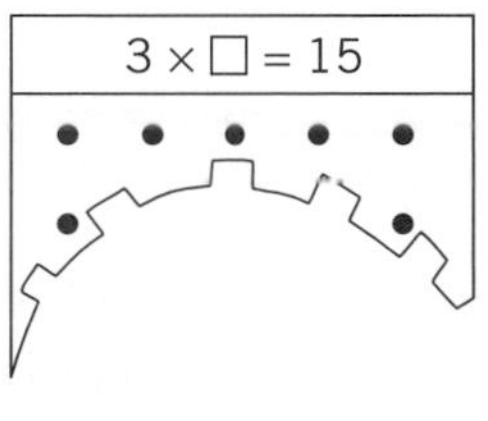

46. Make bingo cards of products for each child in the class. Let one child draw multiplication flash cards at random and hold them up for the entire class to see. If a child has the product on his or her bingo card, he or she may place a marker on it. The first child to get five in a row (across or down) wins.

12	45	42	63	40
36	7	54	25	64
81	56	24	45	18
40	16	9	72	30
27	48	32	5	28

9	12	35	54	20
28	40	8	14	42
45	7	16	24	64
72	56	30	6	27
18	36	4	48	5

47. Make a playing board for a trip to the moon. Make small cardboard rockets to move on the board. Make three different-colored cards.

Red cards (worth 5 jumps)—more difficult facts, such as 7×8.
Blue cards (worth 3 jumps)—moderately difficult facts, such as 5×6.
Yellow cards (worth 1 jump)—easier facts, such as 2×3.

Each child takes a turn drawing a red, blue, or yellow card of his or her choice. The other children check the answer, and, if correct, the child can move 1, 3, or 5 places, depending on the card selected. The first one to arrive at the moon wins.

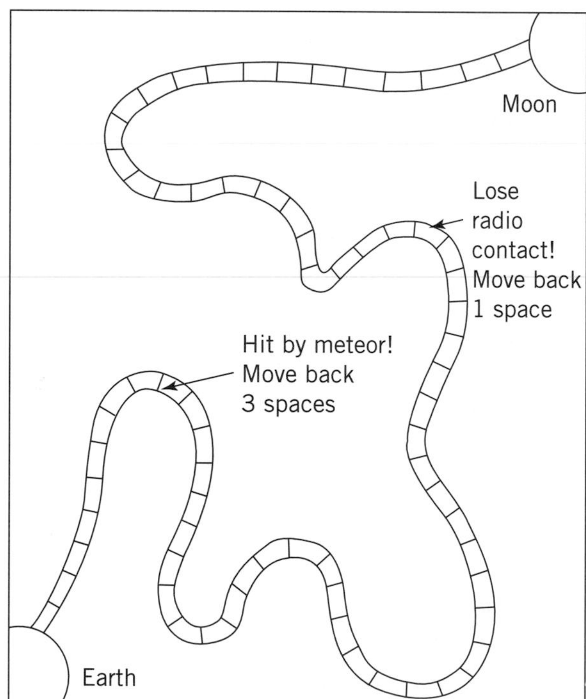

48. Fill in the blanks.

a) $1 \times 6 =$ ________
$10 \times 6 =$ ________
$100 \times 6 =$ ________

b) $1 \times 8 =$ ________
$10 \times 8 =$ ________
$100 \times 8 =$ ________

c) $1 \times 14 =$ ________
$10 \times 14 =$ ________
$100 \times 14 =$ ________

d) $1 \times 56 =$ ________
$10 \times 56 =$ ________
$100 \times 56 =$ ________

49. Find the missing factor

a) $m \times 5 = 25$ b) $6 \times m = 54$ c) $w \times 32 = 96$ d) $7 \times z = 63$

50. Rewrite each division sentence as a related multiplication sentence; then find the product.

a) $n \div 7 = 5$ b) $c \div 9 = 7$ c) $d \div 9 = 8$ d) $m \div 7 = 6$

51. Cut octagons with diagonals about 10 inches long out of cardboard. Draw the line segments as shown in the diagram. With a felt marking pen write the numerals as shown. Cover the entire cardboard octagon with clear contact paper. Use a china marker to write a factor inside the center circle. The children may write the products in the outer part of each segment. The octagon can be easily erased and used many times.

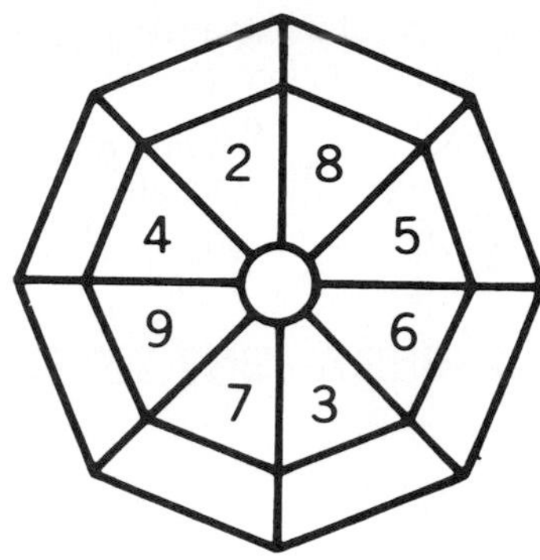

52. Using a number line, numbered by tens and/or hundreds, and a set of cards with two- and three-digit numbers, have the students place the numbers to the nearest ten, then to the nearest hundred.

53. Again use short, simple word problems to give students practice in translating problem situations into mathematical sentences. Write an equation for each problem, then find the solution.

a) Thirty-eight books on each shelf. Five shelves. How many books?
b) Ten pairs of socks on each section of the clothesline. Four sections of clothesline. How many socks?
c) Nine players on each team. Eight teams in the league. How many players in the league?
d) Five school days in each week. How many school days in four weeks?
e) Eight wieners in each plastic pack. Twelve packs. How many wieners?
f) Twenty-four hamburger buns. Eight in a package. How many packages?
g) Sixteen scouts. Four scouts per boat. How many boats will be needed?

54. Children can learn to use a constant for multiplication on the calculator. Procedures may vary with different calculators; some calculators require the constant to be entered first, and some calculators require the constant to be entered second. The use of a constant in multiplication allows many multiplications by a given number without having to enter that given number each time. For instance, if the constant number is 3 and we want to multiply many numbers by 3, we use the following procedure:

CONSTANT	OPERATION	ANY NUMBER	EQUALS	DISPLAY READS
[3]	[×]	[2]	[=]	[6]

Now the calculator has been set up to multiply any number by 3. If you strike the 7 key and the equals key, the display will read 21; if you strike the 9 key and the equals key, the display will read 27.

Example	Keys Struck	Display Shows
$8 \times 3 =$	[8] [=]	24
$4 \times 3 =$	[4] [=]	12
$17 \times 3 =$	[1] [7] [=]	51
$29 \times 3 =$	[2] [9] [=]	87

55. Look for patterns in a series of numbers, and then verify the pattern and extend it using the calculator. Study this example: 2, 6, 18, 54, 162, ________, ________, ________, ________, ________, and so on. Children should discover that each number is three times the number that precedes it. This example can be set up in the calculator; enter 3, then ×, then 2, and then continue to push the equals key. The sequence generated should be the same as indicated in this example; then it can be extended. Create other patterns for the children to study, and generate other numbers in the sequence.

56. Many software programs are available to provide drill and practice for memorizing the basic multiplication and division facts. Children can compete against themselves, rather than each other, for greater accuracy or speed.

INSTRUCTIONAL AND ASSESSMENT ACTIVITIES FOR GRADES 5-8

1. Mark the numeral naming the greatest multiple of ten that will make each sentence a true statement.

a) $3 \times n < 146$	20	30	40	50	60
b) $5 \times n < 234$	20	30	40	50	60
c) $4 \times n < 111$	20	30	40	50	60
d) $6 \times n < 2354$	100	200	300	400	500

2. Use the greatest multiple of 1, 10, 100, or 1000 to make each sentence a true statement.

a)	b)
________ $\times 40 < 500$	________ $\times 70 < 2100$
________ $\times 40 < 100$	________ $\times 70 < 1000$
________ $\times 40 < 80$	________ $\times 70 < 9000$
________ $\times 40 < 12{,}000$	________ $\times 70 < 500$
________ $\times 40 < 200$	________ $\times 70 < 40{,}000$

3. Mark each true or false; then list a property for each.

a) $82 \times 39 = 39 \times 82$
b) $5 \times (6 \times 7) = (5 \times 6) \times 7$
c) $8 \times (7 \times 9) = (7 \times 9) \times 8$
d) $2354 \times 1 = 2354$
e) $0 \times 4782 = 0$
f) $(23 \times 14) \times 36 = 23 \times (14 \times 36)$
g) $(9 \times 37) \times 18 = 18 \times (9 \times 37)$

4. Study the following to see how basic facts are extended and combined to solve multi-step exercises. Solve each.

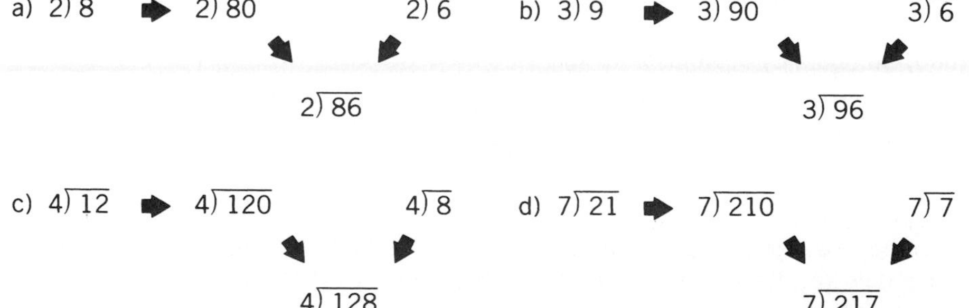

5. True or false?

   a) $8 \div 4 = 4 \div 8$ b) $24 \div 3 = 3 \div 24$
   c) $15{,}827 \div 19 = 19 \div 15{,}827$ d) $(8 \div 4) \div 2 = 8 \div (4 \div 2)$

6. Children should practice with many division examples that have one-place divisors. Once they understand such examples well and have acquired reasonable skill in solving them, the children should be ready to move on to examples with two-place divisors. Encourage the children to check answers to division examples by using this idea:

   Dividend = (Quotient × Divisor) + Remainder

   Complete these examples, and check your answers.

   a) $2\overline{)449}$ b) $30\overline{)935}$

   400 ← ________ × 2 900 ← ________ × 30

   40 ← ________ × 2 30 ← ________ × 30

   8 ← ________ × 2

7. Complete the table.

	+	−	×	÷
533 △ 13				
782 △ 34				
901 △ 53				
1645 △ 47				
899 △ 29				
837 △ 31				
1596 △ 42				
1118 △ 26				

8. The children might use the calculator to check multiplication and division examples that they have solved. More importantly, they should use the calculator to explore alternative ways to arrive at the answer to an exercise. This serves as a more reasoned way of checking than simply pressing keys.

9. If we need to find the circumferences of many wheels, pi (π) can be set up in the calculator as a constant. Then we need only strike the key(s) for the diameter and the equals key; the circumference will appear on the display screen.

   Set up the calculator for pi:

Pi		Any Number		Circumference
3.14	×	1	=	3.14

   Now the calculator is set up to compute circumferences of circles. If the diameter of a circle is 7, just strike the 7 key and the equals key; 21.98, the circumference of a circle with a diameter of 7, will appear on the display screen.

Diameter	Keys Struck	Display Shows
8	[8] [=]	25.12
10	[1] [0] [=]	31.4
23	[2] [3] [=]	72.44

10. The multiples of any given number can be generated using a constant. For instance, to generate the multiples of 4, set up the calculator with the constant 4. By entering the set of whole numbers one at a time and striking the equals key each time, the multiples of 4 will be displayed.

EXAMPLE	KEYS STRUCK	DISPLAY WILL GENERATE THE MULTIPLES OF 4
0 × 4	[0] [=]	0
1 × 4	[1] [=]	4
2 × 4	[2] [=]	8
3 × 4	[3] [=]	12
4 × 4	[4] [=]	16
5 × 4	[5] [=]	20
6 × 4	[6] [=]	24
7 × 4	[7] [=]	28
and so on		

Have the children explore by generating sets of multiples for any given number.

11. Have the children estimate answers to multiplication examples, and then have them verify their estimates using a calculator. Provide space on a worksheet for the children to write the estimated answer and the calculated answer. Example questions are:

    a) How much money would you spend in a year if you spend a thousand dollars a day?
    b) If you spend a dollar a minute, how much money would you spend in a year?
    c) If you drop a penny in your piggy bank each hour, how much money would you have in your bank at the end of a leap year?
    d) If you buy a new car every five years, how much money do you think you will spend on cars during your lifetime?
    e) How many minutes are there in a regular year? In a leap year?
    f) How many minutes old are you?
    g) How many seconds old are you?

12. Through generalizations, children can find answers to exercises that are too large for their calculators. For instance, solve as many of the following examples on your calculator as you can. Study the patterns; then write the answers to the remaining examples.

1 × 1 =	9 × 2 =
11 × 11 =	99 × 2 =
111 × 111 =	999 × 2 =
1111 × 1111 =	9999 × 2 =
11111 × 11111 =	99999 × 2 =
111111 × 111111 =	999999 × 2 =
1111111 × 1111111 =	9999999 × 2 =
11111111 × 11111111 =	99999999 × 2 =
and so on	and so on

Create similar examples for children to solve.

13. Solve problems such as the following: 480 children attend our school. If all the children attend an assembly, how many chairs will be needed in each of the 15 rows?

14. The symbolism used on a computer for multiplication and division is different than we are normally used to using. In pencil-paper arithmetic, the × sign is used to indicate multiplication; on many computers, the * (asterisk) is used to symbolize multiplication. In pencil-paper arithmetic, we use the ÷ sign or the $\overline{)\quad}$ sign to indicate division; on many computers, we use /, a slash, to symbolize division.

15. Provide the students with cards having incorrect computations of quotients. Challenge the students to locate and correct the errors. For example:

$$5\overset{81}{\overline{)4005}}$$

Give the following directions to the student: “Calamity Kate had committed careless computations. Each card has a computational error. See whether you can find the error and correct it for Calamity Kate.”

16. Using 3-inch-by-5-inch (or 8-centimeter-by-13-centimeter) number and symbol cards, as shown, have the students write as many mathematical sentences as they can from the set of cards.

24	6	4	3	8	×	÷	=

17. Begin with a magic square. Have the student multiply each number in the magic square by a given number. Is the result also a magic square?

18. Use a deck of cards with the face cards removed. Deal two cards to each player. Have the players multiply the numbers of the two cards together. A point is given for each correct answer.

19. For this activity a deck of 52 cards with the numbers 1 through 25 is needed: three cards each of the numbers 1 through 10, two each of the numbers 11 to 17, and one each of the numbers 18 through 25. Five cards are turned face up. A sixth card is turned up on top of the deck. Players my add, subtract, multiply, or divide the numbers on the five cards in any order to attain the number on the sixth card.

20. Division can be used to compute the distance of lightning from an observer. Since it takes approximately five seconds after the lightning flash for the sound of thunder to travel one mile, the student can count the number of seconds between the flash and the sound then divide by 5 to see how far away the lightning is.

21. Choose any three-place number (for example, 234), repeat the three digits, and use this number (in our example, 234234) as the dividend. Use 91 as the divisor. The quotient will be the product of 11 and the three-place number ($11 \times 234 = 2574$). There will never be any remainder. This is based on elementary number theory and the factors of 1001 (7, 13, and 11).

22. The teacher writes the number 12345679 on the board and then asks a student, “What's your favorite number?” If the student responds “5,” the teacher directs him/her to multiply 12345679 by 45 ($9 \times$ the favorite number). What's the resulting product?

$$\begin{array}{r} 12345679 \\ \times 45 \\ \hline 555555555 \end{array}$$

If the student had given 3 as a favorite number, the teacher would have asked him/her to multiply 12345679 by 27 (9×3):

$$\begin{array}{r} 12345679 \\ \times 27 \\ \hline 333333333 \end{array}$$

23. Using only the operation keys and digit keys 2 and 3, make the calculator display screen read 57. What is the least number of key punches necessary to reach 57?

24. Using only the operation keys and digit keys 2 and 4, make the calculator display read 73. What is the least number of key punches necessary to arrive at 73?

25. Using only the operation keys and the digit keys 7 and 2, make the calculator display screen read 93 with the least number of key punches.

26. Use the calculator to solve each example. What can you discover about the products?

$76923 \times 1 =$
$76923 \times 10 =$
$76923 \times 9 =$
$76923 \times 12 =$
$76923 \times 3 =$
$76923 \times 4 =$

Now multiply 76923 by all other numbers between 0 and 13 (2, 7, 5, 11, 6, and 8). What can you discover about these products?

76923 × 2 =
76923 × 7 =
76923 × 5 =
76923 × 11 =
76923 × 6 =
76923 × 8 =

27. Solve the following multiplication examples. First estimate the answers, and then check them on your calculator.

1 × 8 + 1 =
12 × 8 + 2 =
123 × 8 + 3 =
1234 × 8 + 4 =
12345 × 8 + 5 =
123456 × 8 + 6 =
1234567 × 8 + 7 =
12345678 × 8 + 8 =
123456789 × 8 + 9 =

28. Using only digits 1, 2, 3, 4, and 5, place numbers in the boxes of each example so that you will have the greatest possible product. Use each digit only once in each example. Use your calculator to check these answers.

```
  □ □ □ □        □ □ □        □ □ □
×       □      ×   □ □      ×     □
---------      ---------    ---------
                            _ _ _ _
                            ×     □
                            ---------
```

29. Use only digits 5, 6, 7, 8, and 9. Place numbers in the boxes of each example so that you will have the greatest possible product. Use each digit only once in each example. Use your calculator to check your reasoning.

```
  □ □ □ □        □ □ □        □ □ □
×       □      ×   □ □      ×     □
---------      ---------    ---------
                            _ _ _ _
                            ×     □
                            ---------
```

30. Use only digits 0, 1, 2, 3, and 4. Place numbers in the boxes of each example so that you will have the least possible product. Use each digit only once in each example. Use your calculator to check your reasoning.

```
  □ □ □ □        □ □ □        □ □
×       □      ×   □ □      ×   □
---------      ---------    -------
                            _ _ _
                            ×   □
                            -------
                            _ _ _
                            ×   □
                            -------
```

31. Have the children use the calculator to multiply numbers by 1, 10, 100, and 1000. Study the place-value relationship in each example. This will help children to understand why the partial products must be properly placed in multiplication. Multiplying by 10 causes the place value to change. Why? Do not say, "We add a zero," because the process of "adding zero to a number" does not change the value of the number.

```
  4563      4563      4563       4563
×    1    ×   10    ×  100    × 1000
------    ------    ------    -------
  4563     45630    456300    4563000
```

32. Have the children explore the properties of multiplication, using the calculator. For instance, multiply 34 × 56 and then multiply 56 × 34. The commutative property of multiplication works for every multiplication example. Try the associative property or the distributive property of multiplication over addition.

Suggested Readings

Abel, J., Allinger G. D., & Andersen, L. (1987). Popsicle sticks, computers, and calculators: Important considerations. *The Arithmetic Teacher, 34*(9).

Broadbent, F. W. (1987). Lattice multiplication and division. *The Arithmetic Teacher, 34*(5).

Burns, M. (1994). Across the curriculum: math in action; hands-on science; ready to write; the art lesson. *Instructor, 103.*

Burns, M. (1991). Introducing division through problem-solving experiences. *The Arithmetic Teacher, 38*(8).

Cooper, R. (1994). *Alternative math techniques instructional guide.* Bryn Mawr, PA: Center for Alternative Learning.

Curcio, F. R., Sicklick, F., & Turkel, S. B. (1987). Divide and conquer: Unit strips to the rescue. *The Arithmetic Teacher, 34*(4).

Englert, G. R., & Sinicrope, R. (1994). Making connections with two-digit multiplication. *The Arithmetic Teacher, 41*(8).

Graeber, A. O. (1993). Research into practice: Misconceptions about multiplication and division. *The Arithmetic Teacher, 40*(7).

Graeber, A. O., & Baker, K. M. (1990). Curriculum materials and misconceptions concerning multiplication and division. *Focus on Learning Problems in Mathematics, 13*(2).

Graeber, A. O., & Baker, K. M. (1992). Little into big is the way it always is. *The Arithmetic Teacher, 39*(8).

Hall, W. D. (1983). Division with base-ten blocks. *The Arithmetic Teacher, 31*(3).

Hall, W. D. (1981). Using arrays for teaching multiplication. *The Arithmetic Teacher, 29*(3).

Harel, G., & Behr, M. (1991). Ed's strategy for solving division problems. *The Arithmetic Teacher, 39*(3).

Harel, G., & Confrey, J. (1994). *The development of multiplicative reasoning in the learning of mathematics.* Albany, NY: State University of New York Press.

Harrison, N., & Van Devender, E. M. (1992). The effects of drill and practice computer instruction on learning basic mathematics facts. *Journal of Computing in Childhood Education, 3.*

Hiebert, J., & Behr, M., (Eds.). (1988). *Number concepts and operations in the middle grades.* Reston, VA: National Council of Teachers of Mathematics.

Hope, J. A., Reys, Barbara J., & Reys, R. E. (1988). *Mental math in junior high.* Palo Alto, CA: Dale Seymour Publications.

Hope, J. A., Reys, Barbara J., & Reys, R. E. (1988). *Mental math in the middle grades.* Palo Alto, CA: Dale Seymour Publications.

Huinker, D. M. (1989). Multiplication and division word problems: Improving students' understanding. *The Arithmetic Teacher, 37*(2).

Jensen, R. J. (1987). Teaching mathematics with technology: Division in the early grades. *The Arithmetic Teacher, 35*(2).

Killion, K., & Steffe, L. P. (1989). Research into practice: Children's multiplication. *The Arithmetic Teacher, 37*(1).

May, L. J. (1994). Teaching math: extending the meaning of multiplication and division. *Teaching PreK-8, 25.*

McKillip, W. D., & Stanic, G. M. A. (1989). Developmental algorithms have a place in elementary school mathematics instruction. *The Arithmetic Teacher, 36*(5).

National Council of Teachers of Mathematics. (1978). *Developing computational skills.* 1978 Yearbook. Reston, VA: National Council of Teachers of Mathematics.

National Council of Teachers of Mathematics. (1986). *Estimation and mental computation.* 1986 Yearbook. Reston, VA: National Council of Teachers of Mathematics.

Remington, J. (1989). Introducing multiplication. *The Arithmetic Teacher, 37*(3).

Robold, A. I. (1983). Grid arrays for multiplication. *The Arithmetic Teacher, 30*(5).

Soles, M. E. (1989). Finding the average with frisbee tosses. *The Arithmetic Teacher, 36*(5).

Stefanich, G. P., & Rokusek, T. (1992). An analysis of computational errors in the use of division algorithms by fourth-grade students. *School Science and Mathematics, 92*(4).

Sundar, V. K. (1990). Thou shalt not divide by zero. *The Arithmetic Teacher, 37*(7).

Tierney, C. C. (1985). Patterns in the multiplication table. *The Arithmetic Teacher, 32*(7).

Trafton, P. R., & Zawojewski, J. S. (1990). Implementing the standards: Meaning of operations. *The Arithmetic Teacher, 38*(3).

Vest, F. (1985). Physical models to explain a division algorithm. *School Science and Mathematics, 85*(3).

Watson, J. M. (1991). Models to show the impossibility of division by zero. *School Science and Mathematics, 91*(8)

Chapter 8

Number Theory and Number Systems

Overview

Elementary number theory is a very valuable tool to help children develop understanding and meaning as they learn mathematics. This chapter provides an opportunity to develop fundamental understanding of basic number theory. Knowledge of prime numbers and factorization provides a tool for the child to use in developing number sense, especially in work with fractional numbers to find common denominators and rewrite fractions in simplest form. The study of prime numbers and factorization can also introduce children to the exciting topic of number theory. The Fundamental Theorem of Arithmetic is an important foundation for further work. This chapter provides a solid base on which a future understanding of mathematics may be built.

The student of mathematics may want to research some of the historical aspects of the development in this chapter. The history of the sieve of Eratosthenes is interesting for some, as is the study of some prominent Greek mathematicians. Long an intriguing topic to mathematicians and nonmathematicians alike, the study of number lore can be a motivating topic for children to consider. For example, in Greek numerology, two was considered to be a "female number," while three was considered "male." Research into this subject can be as fascinating as the answer itself—you never know what you'll find along the way! Did you know that some numbers have been given "supernatural" connotations? According to St. Augustine, God created the world in six days because six is a *perfect* number (that is, six is the sum of all its divisors except itself, $1 + 2 + 3$).

SAMPLE LESSON PLAN— "THE EVEN/ODD DEBATE"

Primary Developmental Lesson

Goal:

Investigate number theory concepts related to even and odd numbers.

Objectives:

The students will:

- Generate outcome rules for the sums of even and odd addends.

Prerequisite Learning and/or Experiences:

Concrete experiences comparing even and odd single digit numbers whereby students match counters in one to one correspondence:

□□□□□ □□□□□	□□□□ □□□
Ten is even.	Seven is odd.

Application of even and odd to multidigit values, i.e.,

numbers ending in 0, 2, 4, 6, 8, are even and numbers ending in 1, 3, 5, 7, 9, are odd.

Ability to use a calculator to add.

Materials:

Per groups of three students:

- unifix cubes
- calculator
- paper and pencil

For the teacher:

- counters for the overhead
- transparencies of two-digit addends (even add even, odd add odd, and even add odd, odd add even)

Procedures:

Motivational Introduction

During calendar time every morning we have been exploring what makes a number even and what makes a number odd. Ask a student to come to the overhead and demonstrate why ten is even? Have counters available. Watch for awareness of one-to-one correspondence in that each counter used has a match. Ask for a volunteer to demonstrate why seven is odd. Look for one-to-one correspondence such that one counter does not have a match. Compare and discuss the results.

Challenge the class to a thinking contest. Tell the students if they give you two numbers to add, you will tell them if the sum is even or odd. Since some students may try to stump you with "big" numbers, allow the class to use calculators to check your responses. Of course, you already know the rules of even add even is even, odd add odd is even, even add odd is odd, and odd add even is odd. Your task is to impress them with your ability to quickly tell whether the sum is even or odd to the point where many will undoubtedly want to know how the "trick" works. Now is the teachable moment.

1. Display a transparency of two digit, even addends. Have students work in cooperative groups of three. The first student builds one-to-one correspondence towers of unifix cubes for each of the even addends. This will result, for example, in a tower for each addend similar to the example shown.

□□ □□ □□ □□	□□ □□ □□
8	6

   The two towers for the two even addends should then be snapped together. The group should note that an even tower snapped to an even tower creates a longer even tower (in this case, a "14 tower").

   The second student then uses the calculator to determine the sum. The third student labels a recording sheet *Even add Even* and records the sum as even or odd. Continue roles until all sums on the transparency are found.

2. Ask groups to study their examples and describe in their own words what they see. Accept any and all responses which equate to the mathematical rule that an even number add an even number yields an even sum. Record on the transparency:

   even number + even number = even number

Developmental Activity

3. Display a transparency of two digit, odd addends. Have groups predict on their recording sheets now labeled *Odd add Odd* if the sums will be even or odd. Have groups verify their predictions by returning to their roles of building towers, using the calculator, and recording the sum as even or odd. Be prepared to help the tower builders deal with the two extra cubes for each odd addend which will need to be matched up for the sum.
4. Ask groups to compare their examples to their predictions and describe in their own words what they see. Have the class develop a rule for adding two odd numbers. Accept any responses which equate to the mathematical rule that an odd number add an odd number yields an even sum. Record on the transparency:

   odd number + odd number = even number

5. Repeat steps 3 and 4 for even add odd/odd add even. The process should produce the rule that an odd number add an even number or an even number add an odd number yields an odd sum. The rule should be recorded on the transparency as:

   odd number + even number = odd number
   even number + odd number = odd number

Culminating Activity

6. Challenge the groups to apply these rules to any two addends. Have one student write two addends. Don't be surprised if students start trying three- and four-digit numbers. Another student applies the rules and predicts if the sum will be even or odd. The third student enters the addends into the calculator and compares the sum to the prediction. Students alternate roles so everyone in the group has an opportunity to write addends, predict the sum as even or odd, and check the prediction with the calculator.

Extension:

Encourage students to use their knowledge on parents and/or siblings at home. Have them play your motivational introduction activity at home. Either a parent or older brother or sister should write down two addends. The student should then tell them if the sum is even or odd. The parent or sibling checks by calculating the answer and comparing the results to the child's prediction of even or odd.Just in case parents or siblings want to know the "trick," students should be prepared to state the rules in their own words.

Student Assessment/Evaluation:

Observe students during the culminating activity to determine if they are applying the rules generated during the lesson. Apply the following rubric to the groups as they work:

0 = no attempt
1 = predicts sum as even or odd, but guesses
2 = predicts sum as even or odd, but applies rule inconsistently
3 = predicts sum as even or odd and applies rule consistently

INSTRUCTIONAL AND ASSESSMENT ACTIVITIES FOR GRADES K-4

1. Have children stack ten cubes into two stacks, alternating between stacks. Then have them stack seven cubes. If the two stacks of cubes are the same height, the number is even. If the two stacks of cubes are uneven, then the number of cubes is odd.

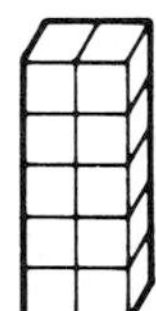

Ten is even.

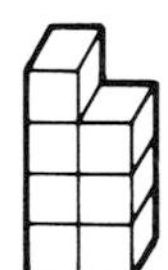

Seven is odd.

Using the same procedure, have the children examine the sum of two even numbers, the sum of two odd numbers, and the sum of one even and one odd number.

2. Look for a pattern that will help you fill in the blanks.

   a) 2, 4, 6, 8, _____, _____, _____, _____

   b) 3, 6, 9, _____, 15, _____, _____, _____

   c) 4, 8, 12, _____, _____, 24, _____, _____

   d) 5, _____, 15, 20, _____, _____, _____, _____

   e) 10, 100, 1000, _____, _____, _____, _____

3. A puzzle game can be used to develop facility with the factorization of numbers. A homemade puzzle game may be made by cutting out a magazine picture, dry mounting it to a cardboard base, covering it with clear contact paper, cutting it into several jigsaw puzzle pieces, and then writing numerals on the backs of the pieces. Children play this game in the following way. A child takes a puzzle piece, say, one with the numeral 18. If the child can name all the factors of 18, he or she gets to use the puzzle piece in an attempt to construct the puzzle. If the child is unable to state the factors of 18, then he or she must try again with another piece.

4. If children's experiences with mathematical concepts are developed through an organized systems approach, then many topics, including integers, may be introduced much earlier than they might be in traditional programs. When we look at a thermometer and observe that the temperature has dropped below zero, we begin to see the need for negative numbers. If integers are used to describe concrete situations in mathematical terms, they may be introduced easily in the primary and intermediate grades. Some elementary mathematics programs provide the opportunity for children to have experiences with integers beginning in first grade. To lay a good foundation, it is important to draw on situations in

which children can see a real need or use for integers. Problems dealing with the thermometer, the altitude with respect to sea level, and simple statistics of gain and loss can be easily discussed with the aid of integers.

5. Children may draw "maps" such as the following on long sheets of paper. Questions about the "maps" may be either printed on cards (for independent study) or asked orally by the teacher.

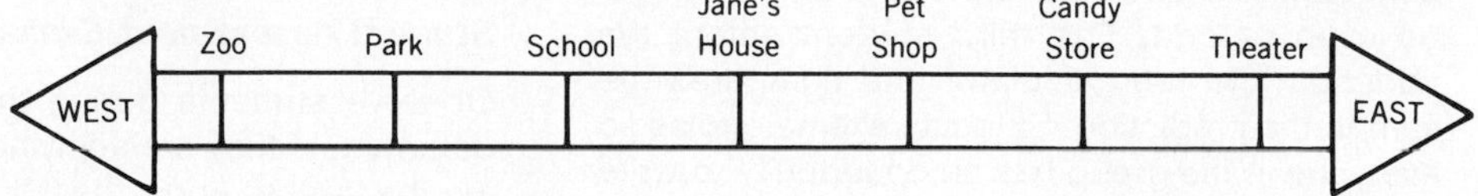

Questions such as the following can be asked:

a) How many blocks will I travel going from Jane's house to the theater?
b) If I go 3 blocks east starting from Jane's house, where will I land?
c) How many blocks will I travel going from Jane's house to the pet shop?
d) If I want to go to the zoo from Jane's house, how many blocks will I go? Which direction?
e) If I start at Jane's house and go 3 blocks west and then 5 blocks east, where will I be? How many blocks from Jane's house will I be? Which direction from Jane's house will I be?

(*Note:* To stress the idea of an origin, always use Jane's house as the starting point.)

6. Make copies of a number line such as the one shown so that each child has one to use.

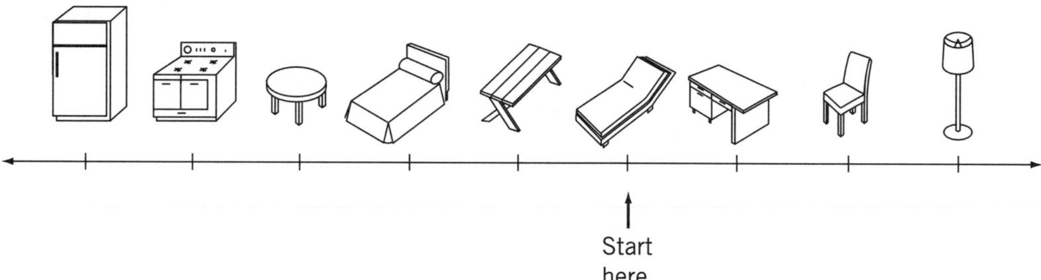

Using the overhead projector, have children locate items of furniture shown on the number line. For example, write on the overhead transparency "Move 3 →". Let a child explain that this would take us to the floor lamp if we moved 3 → to the right. After many oral experiences as described above, the child could work on a worksheet. For example, "Mark the object designating your location with an X."

Move	Land on			
← 2				
→ 2				
← 4				
← 1				
→ 3				

7. Number lines may be drawn with numerals of a different color on each side of "our house."

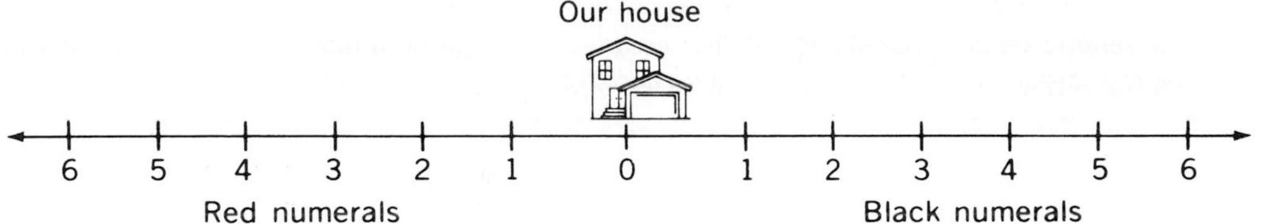

Discuss with the children how many blocks you would be from home if you walked 4 →. Where are you? Four blocks in the black. If you walk 2 ← where are you? In the red 2 →. If you walk 3 → then 4 ←, where are you?

8. Make an integer number line on the floor with masking tape for the children to walk on.

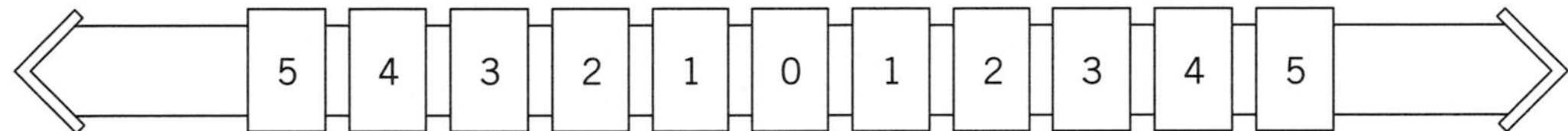

Each side of the number line may be made from different colors of tape. Provide many opportunities for the children to walk on this number line.

9. Have the children use calculators to add many even numbers. Ask the children to study the examples and generalize a rule. (An even number added to another even number will yield an even sum.)

10. Have the children use their calculators to add odd numbers. Ask the children to generalize a rule for adding two odd numbers. (An odd number added to another odd number will yield an even sum.)

11. Have the children use their calculators to add an even number to an odd number. Ask the children to generalize a rule for adding an odd number to an even number. (An odd number added to an even number will yield an odd sum.)

12. Request that the children use their calculators to multiply many numbers by zero and then generalize a rule for multiplying by zero. Use the same procedure, and generalize a rule for multiplying by 1.

13. Have the children use their calculators to add zero to many numbers. The children should then be asked to generalize a rule for adding zero to a number.

14. Have the children place a number on the calculator display screen. Subtract 1 from the number on the display screen. Continue to subtract 1; the display screen will soon show numbers with a negative sign in front of them. Discuss with the children why this happens, and relate the discussion to the number line. Model the number line on the overhead projector. Extend numeral labels to the left of zero.

15. Set up the calculator for a constant. Subtract one (–1), and continue to just push the equals key. That is, first press any number key followed by a subtraction sign and the number 1; then continuously press the equals key. For instance, try entering this sequence of key punches:

[7] [−] [1] [=] [=] [=] [=] . . . .

What happens when the equals key is pushed eight times? Nine times? What appears on the display screen each time the equals key is pushed after the eighth time?

16. Turn on the calculator, and display zero on the screen. For this activity, set up the calculator by entering:

Record each number in a column as it appears on the display screen. Then clear the screen. Again, begin with zero on the display screen and enter:

[+] [1] [–] [=] [=] [=] [=] [=].

In a second column parallel to the first column, write the numbers as they appear on the display screen. Your record should look like this:

0	0
–1	+1
–2	+2
–3	+3
–4	+4
–5	+5
–6	+6

Discuss the two output columns with the children. How are these outputs alike? How are they different? What can the children discover about integers?

17. Wooden cubes and a sheet of paper with the headings *Numeral, Dimensions of Rectangles,* and *Number of Rectangles* are used for this activity. Beginning with one cube, the student records the numeral 1 under the column marked *Numeral,* records the dimensions of the rectangle (1 × 1) formed by the cube, and records the number of rectangles formed (1). Have the children record the numbers with only two rectangles, the numbers with more than two rectangles, and the numbers with less than two rectangles. Continue recording information until children have enough information to make a generalization.

Numeral	Dimensions of Rectangle	Number of Rectangles
1	1 × 1	1
2	1 × 2, 2 × 1	2
.	.	.
.	.	.
.	.	.
6	1 × 6, 6 × 1, 2 × 3, 3 × 2	4
.	.	.
.	.	.
.	.	.

18. Write each number as the product of two whole numbers in as many ways as you can.

    a) 28 b) 42 c) 63 d) 72 e) 124 f) 108

19. Complete the following table:

Number	Whole-Number Factors	Prime Number?
9		
14		
19		
55		
73		

20. Given just a little experience, children can often make up interesting stories and can be encouraged to be imaginative with the situations they invent. Some of the stories may be dramatized to show the process necessary to solve the problem. For example: John started at the top of a flight of stairs and walked down 8 stairs, then down 7 more stairs, and then back up 15 stairs. What stair was he on then? Why would John ever make such a trip on the stairs?

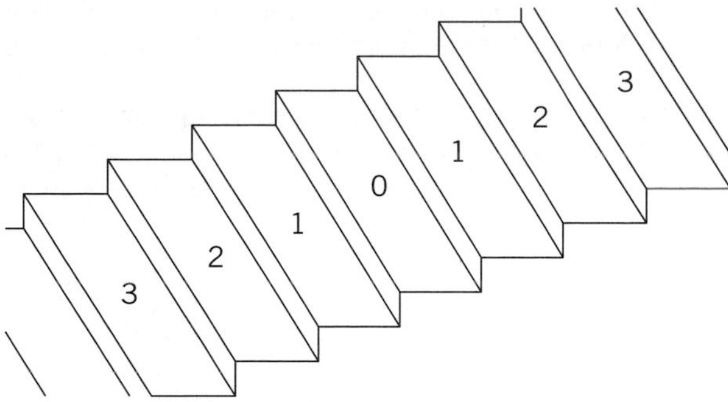

(*Note:* You may want to number the middle step zero and then number the steps both ways from the zero step.)

21. The calculator can be easily used to generate a set of multiples for any given number. For instance, what are the multiples of 7? You can set the calculator up for this example by pressing

The first number to appear on the display screen is 7, which is the result of 1×7. Each time the equals key is pressed, the next multiple of 7 is displayed. The screen should show 7, 14, 21, 28, and so on.

INSTRUCTIONAL AND ASSESSMENT ACTIVITIES FOR GRADES 5-8

1. Divide children into groups of four or five and have them play "Buzz" by taking turns counting; in place of prime numbers, however, they say "buzz." Taking turns, children might say 1, buzz, buzz, 4, buzz, 6, buzz, 8, 9, 10, buzz, 12, buzz, 14, 15, 16, buzz, and so forth. "Buzz" is said in place of the prime numbers, 2, 3, 5, 7, 11, 13, 17, and so on. A variation of this game is to change the direction of play (clockwise to counterclockwise around the circle or vice versa) every time someone says "buzz."
2. Children can play a game called "Road Race." This game provides practice in identifying prime numbers and correct factorizations. Make a board showing a winding road consisting of a series of squares. Two players start off by flipping a coin and placing their tokens at the start position. The winner starts by drawing a card from the card deck illustrated. If the question on the card is answered correctly, the student moves one space. If the question is missed, the student goes back one space (a flat tire or pit stop has been ordered). Some sample questions that could be pulled from the card deck are "Name all the factors for 72" or "Is 13 a prime number?"
3. When children see a need for integers in real situations, understanding comes naturally and rapidly. If the integers are developed before rational numbers, a completely different type of elementary mathematics program exists. Some elementary school mathematics programs have developed a rather extensive approach to the system of integers for the intermediate grades. Rational numbers, which are then taught following the integers, stressing both positive and negative value, can be taught almost simultaneously.
4. The following activity helps to develop ideas of distance and direction—important aspects of the understanding of integers. The children should be divided into two teams—the Reds and the Blues, for example. Each member of the Reds is paired with a team member from the Blues. Each pair of opponents should have a playing board. The board may be a copy of the racetrack shown. The children on each team each have a marker that corresponds to the color of their team. You should prepare a deck of cards with instructions for moves written on them. Each instruction card should give a distance to travel and a direction of travel. For example, a card with +4 written on it might mean "Travel 4 miles toward the finish line." A card with –2 written on it would then mean "Travel 2 miles toward the repair shop." The Reds alternate with the Blues in making the moves called by the teacher as

cards are drawn from the pile. The game ends when the first cars reach the finish line. If a team's cars enter the repair shop first, then that team is declared out of the race and the other team wins.

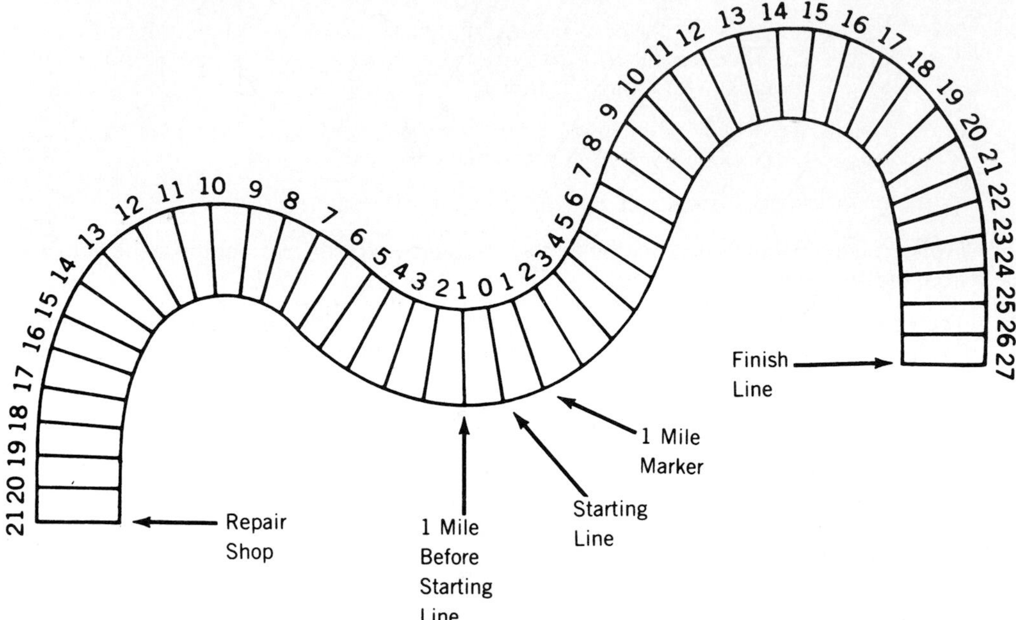

5. Children should realize that a number line may be oriented in any position—vertically or diagonally as well as the common horizontal orientation. A thermometer is a real-life example of a vertical number line. A speedometer is often a "circular" number line.

   Use a large demonstration thermometer, if one is available, otherwise, sketch one on the chalkboard. Ask questions such as the following:

   a) If the thermometer reads 72 degrees and the temperature drops 15 degrees, what is the reading on the thermometer then?
   b) If the thermometer reads 54 degrees after it has dropped 7 degrees, what was the original reading?
   c) If the thermometer reads 12 degrees below zero and rises 20 degrees, what is the temperature then?
   d) If the thermometer reads 3 degrees below zero and drops 8 degrees, what is the temperature reading then?

6. Use your calculator to find the prime factors for each of the following numbers. Check the prime numbers in order, beginning with 2. The divisibility rules will also help you make good estimations. The teacher will want to use the calculator to generate examples for children to solve. Here are some sample beginning examples:

   a) 3570 b) 789 c) 5083 d) 510 e) 27,761 f) 13,860

7. Children can learn to use the constant feature of a calculator for exponents. For example, 3^5 means $3 \times 3 \times 3 \times 3 \times 3$, which equals 243. Using the calculator, we would enter

   [3] [×] [=] [=] [=] [=]

   and the display screen would read 243. Provide the children with examples for practice and generalization. Discuss with the children how this procedure functions.

8. Numbers can be easily factored and the results expressed in exponential form. For example, $256 = 2^{\square}$. To find the exponent for this example, use the following procedure on the calculator:

   [2] [5] [6] [÷] [2] [=] [=] [=] [=] [=] [=] [=] [=]

In this example, 256 is divided by 2 continuously until the display screen shows 1. Since the equals key was pressed eight times, eight is the power of two necessary to equal 256. Discuss this procedure with the children. (The procedures suggested in Activities 3 and 4 can be used as checks for each other.)

9. Generate and list multiples for 63 and 42; then locate the least common multiple for the two numbers. You should locate the least common multiple as 126. Provide other practice for children to locate least common multiples.

10. Use a calculator to identify the greatest common factor for a given pair of numbers. What is the greatest common factor for 1548 and 1505?

11. Use the calculator to generate a series of numbers in which each number differs from the previous by a constant of –2. Set up the calculator by pressing the following keys

[+] [−] [2] [=] [=] [=] . . . .

Now the calculator will add a negative two each time the equals key is pressed.

12. Discuss the relation between subtraction and negative numbers on a calculator. Some calculators have a +/– key that allows you to assign a negative value. How can you display –5 on your personal calculator?

13. Set up the calculator as illustrated:

Why are the numbers alternately negative and positive? Have the children experiment with many examples, using negative numbers and multiplication. Discuss with the class the numerical value and the sign value.

14. A puzzle game can be used to develop facility with the factorization of numbers. A home-made puzzle game may be made in the following way: (a) cut out a magazine picture, (b) dry mount it to a cardboard base, (c) cover it with clear contact paper, and (d) cut it into several jigsaw puzzle pieces, and (e) write numerals on the backs of the pieces. Children can play this game in the following way. A child takes a puzzle piece, say, one with the numeral 18. If the child can name all the factors of 18, he or she gets to use the puzzle piece in an attempt to construct the puzzle. If the child is unable to state the factors of 18, then he or she must try again with another piece.

15. What pairs of prime numbers will result in each of the following products?

a) 14 b) 35 c) 18 d) 22 e) 55 f) 86

16. Complete the factor trees so that you have only prime factors on the bottom row.

a)

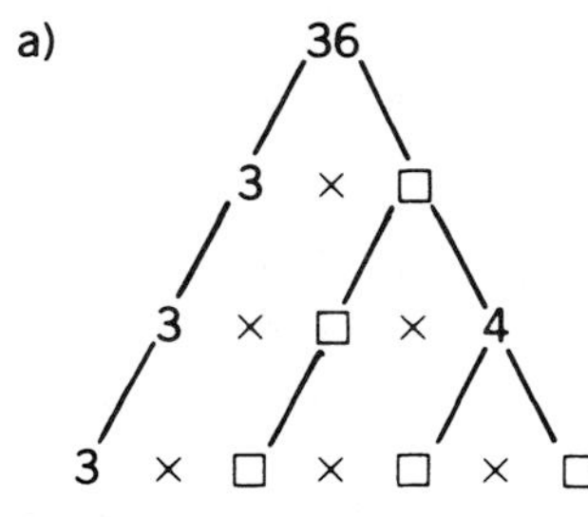

b)

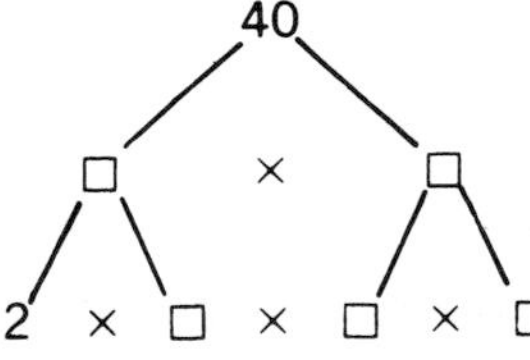

c)

98
2 × 49
2 × □ × □

d)

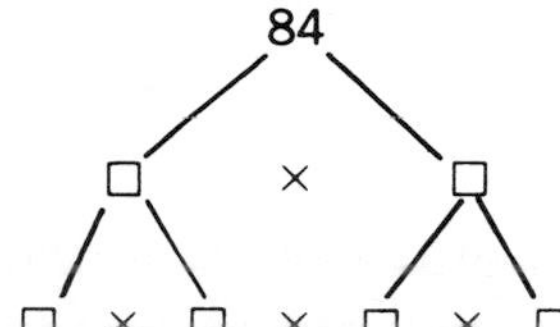

17. One game for finding prime factors is called "Prime Spin." Cut out a large (24-inch diameter) cardboard circular region, and mark it into sections as shown. Mount a cardboard arrow in the middle with a brass fastener.

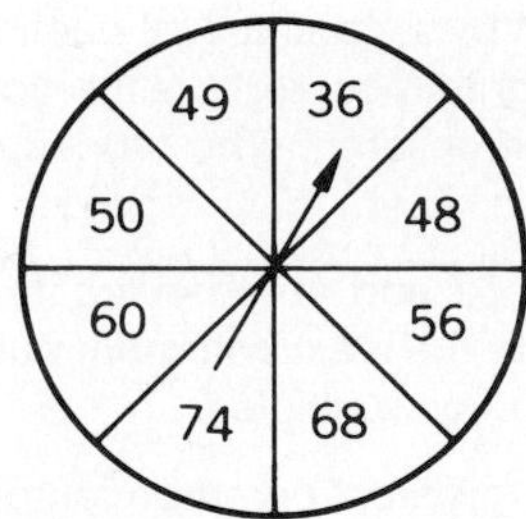

For more efficient use, the region could be covered with clear contact paper so that numerals could be written with a grease pencil and then erased. This would provide greater variety to the game.

To play the game, separate the class into two teams. Have each team member alternately spin the wheel. A member of the rival team must then provide the prime factors of the number spun. If this student is correct, then the team scores the number that has been spun. If the same number is spun twice, another spin should be performed so that new numbers will be factored. The team with the highest point total is declared the winner.

18. a) What number is a factor of every number?

    b) Every prime number has exactly ________ factors.

    c) Every prime number is odd except ________.

    d) What is the only prime number between 61 and 71? Between 113 and 131? Between 79 and 89? Between 103 and 109?

19. List all the whole number factors of each number

    a) 90 b) 144 c) 220 d) 420 e) 275

20. a) List the set of even numbers between 3 and 55.
    b) List the set of prime numbers between 1 and 55.
    c) Is it possible to write a name for any even number, 4 or more, that is the sum of two of the primes in the list for part a?

    Example: Is 4 in the list? Is 2 in the list? Is $2 + 2 = 4$? Is this the sum of two of the primes in the list? How many more can you find?

1 13 5 8 18 4
3 9 11 15 7
2 17 16
14 6 12 10

21. A game called "Name that Prime" can be used to help practice finding prime numbers. Numerals may be drawn on the chalkboard as shown above. The class is then separated into two teams. The teacher calls out a number—for example, 35. The first team that reports the correct prime factors (from the original set of numerals placed on the chalkboard) gets a point. If the number cannot be factored with the numerals on the board, the first team that states this gets a point. Again, the team with the most points is the winner.

22. Use the sieve of Eratosthenes to name the prime numbers between 1 and 200.

23. Cross-number puzzles may be used for practice in locating greatest common factors; the students fill in the squares of the table with the greatest common factor of the two numbers on the vertical and horizontal axes. The following is an example of a cross-number puzzle:

	18	35	24	32
6	6	1	6	2
28		7		
54				
12				

24. Write the set of factors for each number in the given pair. Then write the set of common factors of the given numbers.

    a) 14 and 20 b) 36 and 24 c) 15 and 25 d) 40 and 16 e) 18 and 36

25. What is the greatest common factor (GCF) of each pair of numbers in Activity 24?

26. Write each number as the product of primes.

    a) 90 b) 144 c) 220 d) 420 e) 275

27. a) List the multiples of 16: __________

    List the multiples of 24: __________

    What is the LCM of 16 and 24? __________

    b) List the multiples of 42: __________

    List the multiples of 4: __________

    What is the LCM of 4 and 42? __________

    c) List the multiples of 12: __________

    List the multiples of 9: __________

    What is the LCM of 12 and 9? __________

28. Find the LCM of each of these pairs:

    a) (6, 10) b) (16, 18) c) (15, 6) d) (60, 36) e) (64, 54)

29. A baseball game can be played to practice the concept of least common multiples. Two teams of pupils are formed. One team is given a set of cards with two numerals on them (for example, 18, and 36). This team is the defensive team. The team in the field selects a pitcher who then shows one of these cards to the offensive team. If the offensive team can find the LCM for the given numbers, they have a man on first base. If they answer incorrectly, they have one out. After three outs, the teams switch sides and play continues. The team that scores the most runs is the winner.

30. Which number (or numbers) less than 100 has (have) the greatest number of factors?

31. What two numbers less than 100 have the greatest number of common multiples?

32. Make a table for the sieve of Eratosthenes by placing only six numbers in a row. Make the table to at least 100. Study the patterns in the table, and list any interesting discoveries about these patterns.

33. Maps may be used as number lines to develop a feeling for magnitude and direction. Children may use different techniques for recording directions. Some suggestions are:

    L2 or R2 for left 2 or right 2,
    N3 or S3 for north 3 or south 3,
    E4 or W4 for east 4 or west 4, and
    U5 or D5 for up 5 or down 5.

34. Make copies of a number line without numerals; the children can then label the points representing positive and negative integers. Use the number line to help you decide which relation symbol (< or >) you should write in each loop.

    a) $^{+}3 \bigcirc {}^{+}5$
    b) $^{-}8 \bigcirc {}^{+}6$
    c) $^{-}1 \bigcirc {}^{+}1$
    d) $^{-}999 \bigcirc {}^{+}6$
    e) $0 \bigcirc {}^{-}7$
    f) $^{+}6 \bigcirc {}^{-}3$
    g) $^{+}5 \bigcirc {}^{-}5$
    h) $^{+}8 \bigcirc 0$
    i) $^{-}3 \bigcirc {}^{-}5$
    j) $^{-}4 \bigcirc 6$
    k) $^{+}17 \bigcirc {}^{-}20$
    l) $^{-}8 \bigcirc 0$

35. For each child, make a large integer number line (about 10 centimeters by 50 centimeters) from cardboard, allowing about 2 centimeters between the numbers. Cover the number line with clear contact paper or else laminate it, and provide china marking pencils so that the children can model examples on it.

36. Bend two different colors of pipe cleaners into crescent-shaped curves to represent positive and negative integers. For instance, one white pipe cleaner would be $^{+}1$, and one red pipe cleaner would be $^{-}1$. Matching the two half-circles together (one red and one white) would form a 0. To represent the sum of $^{+}4 + {}^{-}5 = {}^{-}1$, use the pipe cleaners as shown.

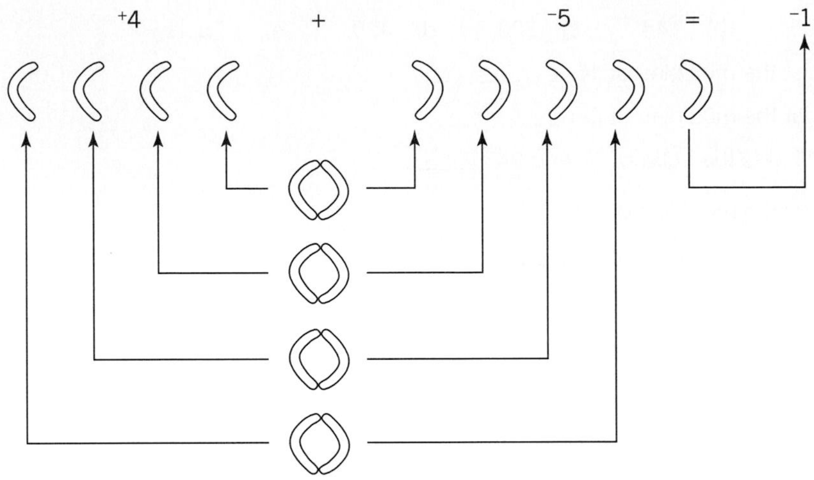

37. Model each integer addition example on the number line.

    a) Begin with examples of like signs of direction.

    $^{+}3 + {}^{+}7 = \square$ $\quad$ $^{-}4 + {}^{-}5 = \square$

    b) Follow like signs of direction in examples with examples of unlike signs of direction.

    $^{-}3 + {}^{+}4 = \square$ $\quad$ $^{+}6 + {}^{-}9 = \square$ $\quad$ $^{+}5 + {}^{-}3 = \square$

38. After many integer addition examples have been solved, have the children study them and look for patterns. Through guided discovery, they should develop some generalizations about how to add integers.

39. Rewrite each subtraction example as a missing addend sentence.

    a) $^{+}7 - {}^{+}3 = \square$ $\quad$ c) $^{+}6 - {}^{-}3 = \square$ $\quad$ e) $^{+}11 - \square = {}^{-}15$
    b) $^{-}8 - {}^{+}5 = \square$ $\quad$ d) $^{-}9 - \square = {}^{+}4$ $\quad$ f) $^{-}19 - \square = {}^{-}23$

40. Rewrite each subtraction example as a missing addend sentence; then model it on the number line.

    a) $^{+}9 - {}^{+}7 = \square$ $\quad$ c) $^{-}5 - {}^{-}3 = \square$ $\quad$ e) $^{-}12 - \square = {}^{-}15$
    b) $^{-}8 - {}^{+}5 = \square$ $\quad$ d) $^{-}6 - {}^{+}9 = \square$ $\quad$ f) $^{+}17 - \square = {}^{-}2$

41. After many integer subtraction examples have been solved, encourage the children to study them for patterns. Through guided discovery, help the children develop some generalizations that will help them subtract integers.

42. List the integers that are

    a) less than $^{-}5$ and greater than $^{-}10$ $\quad$ c) less than $^{+}4$ and greater than $^{-}1$
    b) greater than $^{-}2$ and less than $^{+}4$ $\quad$ d) greater than $^{-}10$ and less than $^{+}1$

43. Write the opposite of each integer.

    a) 112 $\quad$ b) $^{+}270$ $\quad$ c) 0 $\quad$ d) $^{+}256$

44. Write the correct operation sign (+ or –) in each $\triangle$.

    a) $^{-}5 \triangle {}^{-}9 = {}^{+}4$ $\quad$ c) $^{+}26 \triangle {}^{+}11 = {}^{+}15$ $\quad$ e) $^{-}1 \triangle {}^{+}8 = {}^{+}7$
    b) $^{+}10 \triangle {}^{-}10 = 0$ $\quad$ d) $^{-}9 \triangle {}^{+}5 = {}^{-}4$ $\quad$ f) $^{+}18 \triangle {}^{-}3 = {}^{+}21$

45. Complete the following chart:

Integers	$^{+}7$, □	□, $^{-}6$	$^{-}9$, $^{-}7$	$^{+}18$, $^{-}18$	$^{-}3$, $^{+}6$	$^{+}9$, $^{-}9$	□, $^{-}4$
Result	$^{-}5$	$^{+}9$	$^{-}16$	0			$^{-}9$
Operation	Addition	Subtraction			Addition	Subtraction	Subtraction

46. Solve each equation. If you wish, draw a number line and use it for help.

a) $^{+}2 + {}^{-}5 = n$ d) $^{+}2 + {}^{+}4 = n$ g) $^{-}3 + {}^{-}2 = n$
b) $^{-}7 + {}^{+}3 = n$ e) $^{+}8 + {}^{-}6 = n$ h) $^{-}6 + {}^{+}4 = n$
c) $^{-}4 + {}^{+}9 = n$ f) $0 + {}^{-}5 = n$ i) $^{+}4 + 0 = n$

47. Football situations offer excellent opportunities for children to work with integers. A gain of yardage is considered as a positive number, and a loss of yardage is considered a negative one.

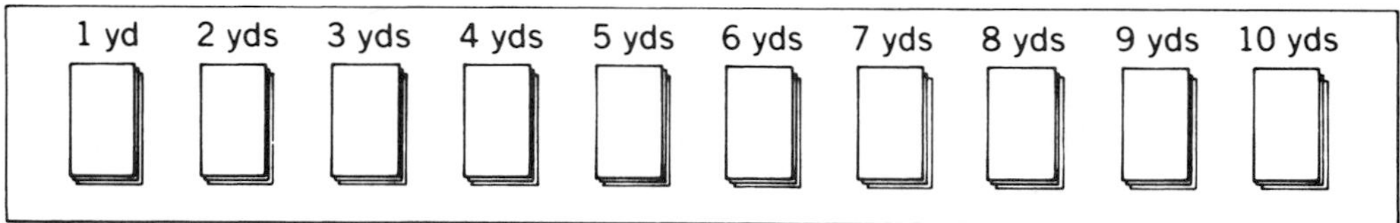

The children can make game boards as scale models of real football fields and prepare cards with examples on them. Separate stacks of cards can be made for the various amounts of yardage possible, so that children can collect yardage cards. More difficult examples should be worth more yards than the easy examples, and the example cards should be labeled with the amount of yardage they are worth.

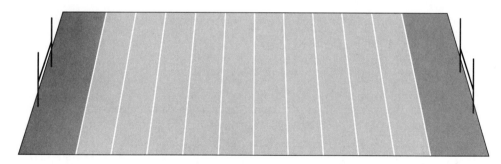

A child must make 10 yards in four downs (attempts) or lose the ball. If a student misses his or her example, he or she loses the yardage on the example card. The child who gets the ball over the goal line receives 6 points. Other rules can be made for your specific classroom situations.

48. Make a set of cubes with integers written on the faces. As children roll the dice, use the top two numbers as an addition or subtraction example to solve.

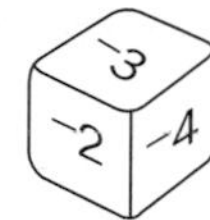

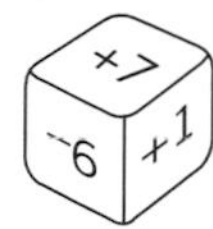

49. The dice from Activity 48 could also be used for addition of integers in a game to be played on an open manila folder. In this game, students begin by putting playing pieces on Tee 1. For each correct example they get to move the piece one space forward. The

first one to arrive at the green wins. If students want to continue the game, they move to Tee 2, and so forth.

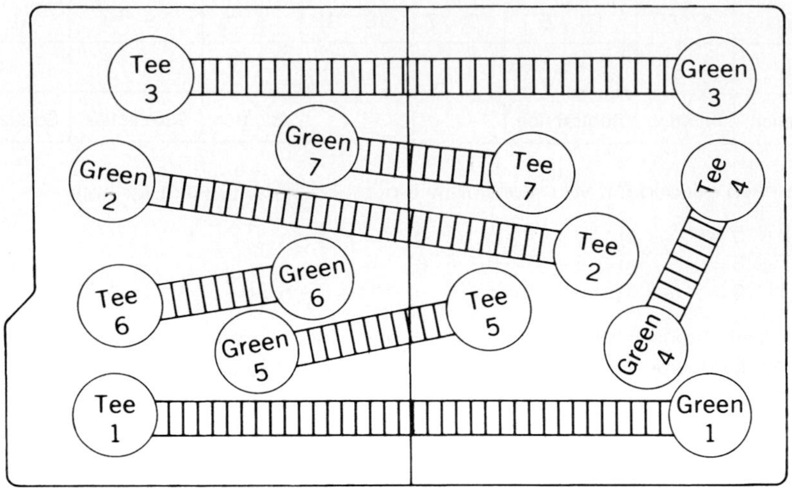

50. After all the operations and inverse operations have been developed, three dice may be used. The third die should provide the method of selecting the operation for each turn.

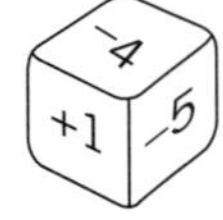

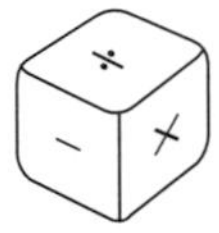

51. Make a number line diagram to illustrate each of these equations.

a) $^{+}3 + {}^{-}4 = {}^{+}1$ c) $^{-}6 + {}^{-}2 = {}^{-}8$ e) $^{+}4 + {}^{-}4 = 0$
b) $^{-}6 - {}^{+}8 = {}^{-}14$ d) $^{+}3 + {}^{+}7 = {}^{+}10$ f) $^{-}8 - {}^{-}1 = {}^{-}7$

52. Rewrite each subtraction equation as a missing addend equation, then find the solution.

a) $^{+}9 - {}^{+}4 = n$ d) $^{+}6 - {}^{-}3 = n$ g) $^{-}2 - {}^{+}3 = n$
b) $^{-}3 - {}^{-}2 = n$ e) $^{+}10 - {}^{+}2 = n$ h) $^{+}10 - {}^{+}10 = n$
c) $^{+}9 - {}^{-}4 = n$ f) $^{-}8 - {}^{+}1 = n$ i) $^{-}6 - {}^{-}9 = n$

53. A profit and loss game may be played after addition and subtraction have been presented. Prepare sets of cards with P or L on them. Cards of two different colors may also be used (for example, red cards for loss and white cards for profit). Some example cards follow:

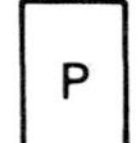
P P L L L
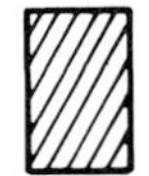
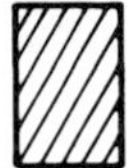

Profit cards   Loss cards   White cards   Red cards

Now make a set of operation cards such as the following:

$^{+}5 + {}^{-}3$ $^{-}2 + {}^{+}4$ $^{+}5 - {}^{-}3$ $^{-}1 - {}^{+}4$

In the example on the left $^{+}5$ means to take five P cards; $^{-}3$ means to take three L cards. The operation sign + means to take the cards as indicated. The player would take five P cards ($^{+}5$) and three L cards ($^{-}3$).

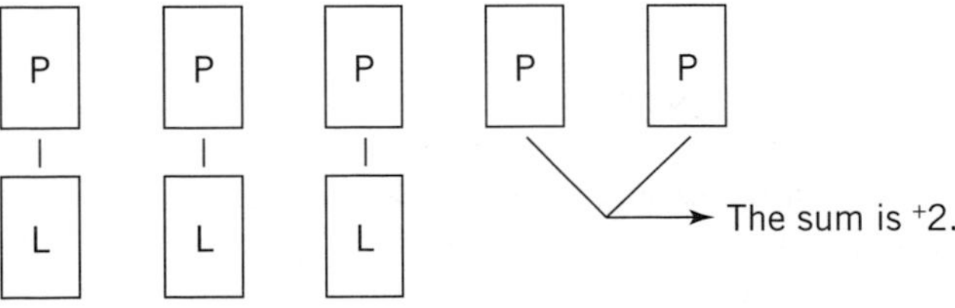

Now let's examine the third card from the left; $^{+}5$ means that the player takes five P cards. Here we have the operation sign –, which means the player takes the opposite of the next number indicated. Therefore $^{-}3$ means to take three P cards.

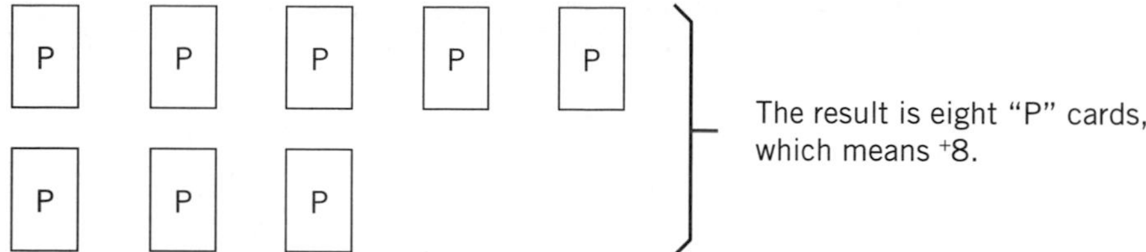
P
P
P
P
P
P
P
P
The result is eight "P" cards, which means +8.

54. Find the products.

a) $^{+}2 \times {}^{-}3 = \square$ d) $^{+}3 \times {}^{-}5 = \square$ g) $^{+}3 \times {}^{-}1 = \square$
b) $^{+}3 \times {}^{-}4 = \square$ e) $^{+}6 \times {}^{+}2 = \square$ h) $^{+}10 \times {}^{-}3 = \square$
c) $^{+}8 \times {}^{-}3 = \square$ f) $^{+}7 \times {}^{-}8 = \square$ i) $^{+}4 \times 0 = \square$

55. Complete the tables.

a) Factors (rows: Factors)

×	0	+2	+4	+6	+8
0			0		
−2					
−4				−24	
−6					
−8					

b) Factors (rows: Factors)

×	+1	−1	+2	−2	+3
+1					
−1					
+2			+4		
−2					−6
+3					

56. Complete the second column of each table.

a)

n	$^{-}2 \times n$
+2	
+1	−2
0	
−1	
−2	
−3	
−4	

b)

n	$n \times {}^{+}3$
+10	
+5	
0	
−5	
−10	−30
−15	
−20	

c)

n	$^{-}5 \times n$
+4	−20
+2	
0	
−2	
−4	
−6	
−8	

57. Find the missing factors.

a) $^{-}2 \times n = {}^{+}8$ c) $^{-}3 \times n = {}^{-}12$ e) $^{+}1 \times n = {}^{-}9$
b) $^{+}4 \times n = {}^{-}20$ d) $^{+}4 \times n = {}^{+}20$ f) $^{+}7 \times n = {}^{-}14$

58. For this activity, use several 3-by-3 grids. You may want to laminate the grids and have the children use grease pencils for writing on them. Place four numbers in four squares of the grid as shown. Have the students add across and down the rows and place their sums in the empty squares. This activity can also be used for subtraction, multiplication, and division of integers.

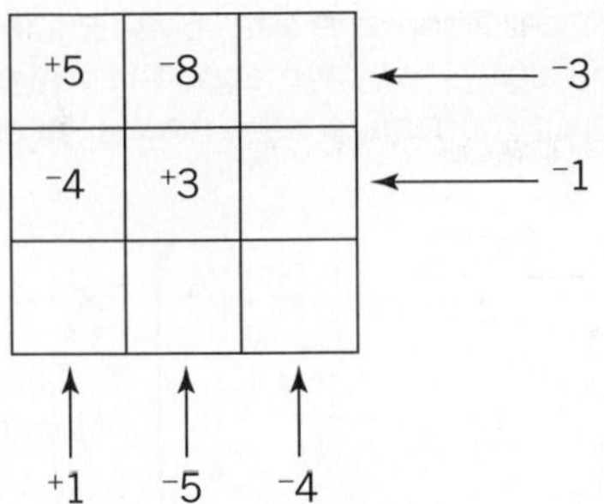

59. On the floor, form a large square (2 feet on a side) by using masking tape. Divide the square into eight equivalent squares. Place a different integer in each square. Construct a large die, and place an operation sign on each of the six sides of the die: addition, subtraction, multiplication, or division. Give the student two counters. The student tosses the die to determine the operation to be used. The student then takes the counters and tosses them onto the square, with directions to add, subtract, multiply, or divide the given numbers according to the results of the die toss.

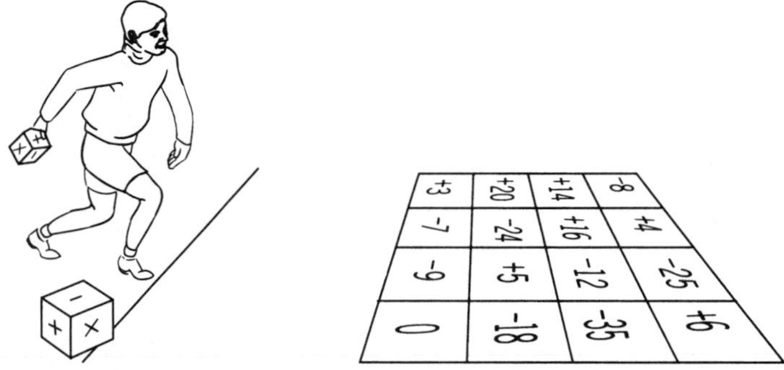

60. Study this sequence of numbers: 2, 4, 6, ... Use your calculator to generate the next twenty numbers in the sequence. The calculator should be set up by pressing

[2] [+] [2] [=] [=] [=] [=], and so on.

How many numbers in this series are prime numbers?

Study this sequence of numbers: 5, 11, 17, 23, ... Use your calculator to generate the next twenty numbers in the sequence. Set up the calculator by pressing the following keys:

[5] [+] [6] [=] [=] [=] [=] · · ·, and so on.

How many numbers in the series are prime numbers? Experiment with other sequences. Can you find the sequence with the most prime numbers?

61. The number 37 can be a strange number! Can you determine the product of 37 × 333 without using your calculator? (*Hint:* Multiply 37 by the multiples of 3, beginning with 3.) When you think you know the product of 37 and 333, write the answer. Check this on your calculator. Write the answer for 37 × 3333; then check on your calculator. Then try 37 × 33333 and 37 × 333333.

62. Use your calculator to experiment with these examples. Write the answers and look for patterns.

9 × 6 = __________

99 × 6 = __________

999 × 6 = __________

9999 × 6 = __________

Using the pattern you just discovered, write the answers for these examples; then check your guesses on your calculator.

9999999 × 6 = ________

9999999 × 9 = ________

9999999 × 3 = ________

63. Some calculators have a +/– "change sign" key. This key changes the sign of the number on the display screen. Have the children experiment with this key. For example:

a) [–] [8] [5] [:] [5] [+/–] [=]

b) [9] [1] [:] [3] [+/–] [=]

c) [–] [4] [8] [:] [2] [+/–] [=] [=] [=] [=] [=] [=] . . .

Suggested Readings

Battista, M. T. (1983). A complete model for operations on integers. *The Arithmetic Teacher, 30*(9).

Berlin, D., & Nesbitt, D. (1990). Time travel: Negative numbers; grades 4-6. *School Science and Mathematics, 90*(5).

Bezuska, S. J. (1985). A test for divisibility by primes. *The Arithmetic Teacher, 33*(2).

Boyd, B. V. (1987). Learning about odd and even numbers. *The Arithmetic Teacher, 35*(2).

Brown, G. W. (1984). Searching for patterns of divisors. *The Arithmetic Teacher, 32*(4).

Burton, G. M., & Knifong, J. D. (1980). Definitions for prime numbers. *The Arithmetic Teacher, 27*(6).

Cemen, P. B. (1993). Teacher to teacher: Adding and subtracting integers on the number line. *The Arithmetic Teacher, 40*(7).

Chang, L. (1985). Multiple methods of teaching the addition and subtraction of integers. *The Arithmetic Teacher, 33*(4).

Cooke, M. B. (1993). Teacher to teacher: A videotaping project to explore the multiplication of integers. *The Arithmetic Teacher, 41*(3).

Dirks, M. K. (1984). The integer abacus. *The Arithmetic Teacher, 31*(7).

Edwards, F. M. (1987). Geometric figures make the LCM obvious. *The Arithmetic Teacher, 34*(7).

Esty, W. W. (1991). One point of view: The least common denominator. *The Arithmetic Teacher, 39*(4).

Ewbank, W. A. (1987). LCM—Let's put it in its place. *The Arithmetic Teacher, 35*(3).

Fitzgerald, W., Winter, M. J., Lappan, G., & Phillips, E. (1986). *Factors and multiples (middle grades mathematics project).* Menlo Park, CA: Addison-Wesley.

Graviss, T., & Greaver, J. (1992). Extending the number line to make connections with number theory. *The Mathematics Teacher, 85*(1).

Hiebert, J., & Behr, M., (Eds.). (1988). *Number concepts and operations in the middle grades.* Reston, VA: National Council of Teachers of Mathematics.

Hope, J. A., Reys, B. J., & Reys, R. E. (1988). *Mental math in junior high.* Palo Alto, CA: Dale Seymour Publications.

Hudson, F. M. (1990). Are the primes really infinite? *The Mathematics Teacher, 83*(3).

Hurd, S. P. (1991). Egyptian fractions: Ahmes to Fibonacci to today. *The Mathematics Teacher, 84.*

Jean, R. V., & Johnson, M. (1989). An adventure into applied mathematics with Fibonacci numbers. *School Science and Mathematics, 89*(8).

Lauber, M. (1990). Casting out nines: An explanation and extensions. *The Mathematics Teacher, 83*(3).

Lester, F. K., Jr., & Mau, S. T. (1993). Teaching mathematics via problem solving: A course for prospective elementary teachers. *For the Learning of Mathematics, 13.*

Meconi, L.J. (1992). Numbers, counting, and infinity in middle school mathematics. *School Science and Mathematics, 92*(7).

National Council of Teachers of Mathematics. (1978). *Developing computational skills.* 1978 Yearbook. Reston, VA: National Council of Teachers of Mathematics.

National Council of Teachers of Mathematics. (1986). *Estimation and mental computation.* 1986 Yearbook. Reston, VA: National Council of Teachers of Mathematics.

National Council of Teachers of Mathematics. (1993). *Curriculum and evaluation standards for school mathematics addenda series grades K-4: Patterns.* Reston, VA: National Council of Teachers of Mathematics.

National Council of Teachers of Mathematics. (1991). *Curriculum and evaluation standards for school mathematics addenda series grades 5-8: Patterns and functions.* Reston, VA: National Council of Teachers of Mathematics.

Norman, F. (1991). Figurate numbers in the classroom. *The Arithmetic Teacher, 38*(4).

Olson, M. (1991). Activities: A geometric look at greatest common divisor. *The Mathematics Teacher, 84*(7).

Padberg, F. F. (1981). Using calculators to discover simple theorems—An example from number theory. *The Arithmetic Teacher, 27*(8).

Sarver, V. T. Jr. (1986). Why does a negative times a negative produce a positive? The Mathematics Teacher, 79(7).

Shilgalis, T. W. (1994). Are most fractions reduced? *The Mathematics Teacher, 87.*

Sowder, J. T. (1990). Mental computation and number sense. *The Arithmetic Teacher, 37*(7).

Thompson, P. W., & Dreyfus, T. (1988). Integers as transformations. *Journal for Research in Mathematics Education, 19*(2).

Vance, J. H. (1992). Understanding equivalence: A number by any other name. *School Science and Mathematics, 92*(5).

Varnadore, J. (1991). Pascal's triangle and Fibonacci numbers. *The Mathematics Teacher, 84*(8).

Werner, M. (1973). *Teaching the set of integers to elementary school children.* Dubuque, IA: Kendall Hunt.

Whitin, D. J. (1986). More patterns with square numbers. *The Arithmetic Teacher, 33*(5).

Whitin, D. J. (1992). Activities: Multiplying integers. *The Mathematics Teacher, 85*(5).

Whitman, N. C. (1992). Activities: multiplying integers. *The Mathematics Teacher, 85.*

Winson, B. (1992). Operations and number relations. *Instructor, 102*(3).

Wood, E. F. (1989). More magic with magic squares. *The Arithmetic Teacher, 37*(4).

Chapter 9

Algebraic Reasoning: Generalizing Patterns and Relationships

Overview

When asked to recall experiences with algebra, most people think back to a first-year algebra course, ordinarily studied in the freshman year of high school. The content of that course generally included equation-solving, some graphing, and a great deal of manipulation of symbols, including variables. Historically, algebra content has been relegated to one or two high school courses, which often take students by surprise as they explore topics that are seemingly unrelated to elementary school and are certainly more abstract.

In the contemporary view of the teaching and learning of mathematics, we acknowledge that algebra is a critical content strand that should be developed for all students across all grade levels. National reports, such as one written by the National Research Council (1989), have pointed out that the vast majority of jobs available today require proficiency in algebra. Furthermore, traditional elementary school textbooks have contained little "new" information in the middle grades (Flanders, 1987); whereas, algebra books typically contain what the student perceives to be all "new" material, so it is no surprise that students are often put off by the course. Consequently, the National Council of Teachers of Mathematics (1989) established Standards that emphasize the development of algebraic thinking throughout the elementary school years. Just as a topic such as number sense or geometry constitutes a part of the mathematical content at each grade level, algebra can also be explored each year.

While "algebra," per se, is difficult to define, it is important to realize that algebra is used to generalize and to abstract patterns and relationships. Algebra contains a number of content strands that need to be addressed, including patterns and models, variables, exponents, graphing, and functions. We use algebraic thinking anytime we look at a table, a graph, or an equation, acknowledge a trend, and use this trend to predict future events.

When presented with developmentally-appropriate learning activities, algebraic thinking can be developed throughout the K-8 grade range. Early experiences with algebra include logical, "if . . . then" discussions, as well as verbalizing and extending patterns and using "more than" and "less than" to compare sets. As children explore both visual and numerical patterns, they should learn to put data into a table, to graph it on a coordinate grid, and, eventually, to write an equation that relates the numbers in the table.

The processes of equation-solving and working with variables need to be firmly-rooted in concrete activities, gradually working students toward symbolic processes typically associated with "traditional" algebra courses. We believe that algebra is best learned through active teaching methods that involve students developing their own methods and procedures to solve problems, rather than being "told" how to use abstract procedures to solve equations and simplify expressions. The product of this type of active teaching and learning is not only the eventual mastery of procedures to manipulate variables but the development of an algebraic "way of thinking" about mathematics.

SAMPLE LESSON PLAN— "GENERALLY SPEAKING: THE SEARCH FOR PATTERNS"

Intermediate Developmental/ Direct Instruction

Goal:

Develop skills of finding and generalizing patterns.

Objectives:

The students will:

- Create a table of numerical values.
- Describe a pattern as it emerges in a table.
- Extend and generalize a numerical pattern.

Prerequisite Learning and/or Experiences:

- Experience with placing data in table form.
- Experience at searching a table for patterns and verbalizing the patterns to extend them.
- Experience with using unifix cubes and interpreting bar graphs.

Materials:

- a catalogue, such as from a mail-order company
- a set of unifix cubes for each small group of students
- a calculator for each student
- overhead unifix cubes

Procedures:

Motivational Introduction

Hold up a mail-order catalogue and ask the students if anyone in their family has ever purchased an item, such as a toy or clothing, through a catalogue. Then, ask if any of their parents belong to a record/CD, book, or video club. Explain that these clubs send a monthly statement that assumes you will buy the "book of the month," for example, and that unless you return the card, the book is automatically sent to you in the mail, and you have to pay for it.

1. Tell the students that, today, we will be looking at a mail-order company called Toys Galore that sends out a "toy of the month" to its members. The club works like this: In January, you are mailed the "toy of the month." Then, in February, you are mailed 2 new toys plus another January toy. In March, you are mailed 3 new toys, plus another set of the 2 February toys and the January toy. This process continues throughout the year.
2. The problem to be solved is: How many "new" toys do you receive each month, and how many toys will you have received altogether by the end of the year?

Developmental Activity

3. Distribute a set of unifix cubes to each table of 3-4 students. Ask the students to lay out cubes that would represent how many toys were received each of the first three months. (Each unifix cube equals one toy received.) Children might lay their cubes out like this:

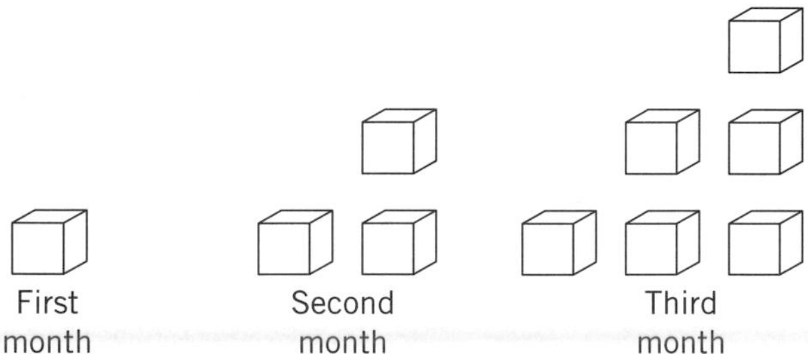

First month   Second month   Third month

Ask students to share their responses and demonstrate them on the overhead projector with overhead unifix cubes.

4. Have the students snap the unifix cubes together so that one tower of cubes represents toys received in January, while the other two towers stand for toys received in February and March, as shown:

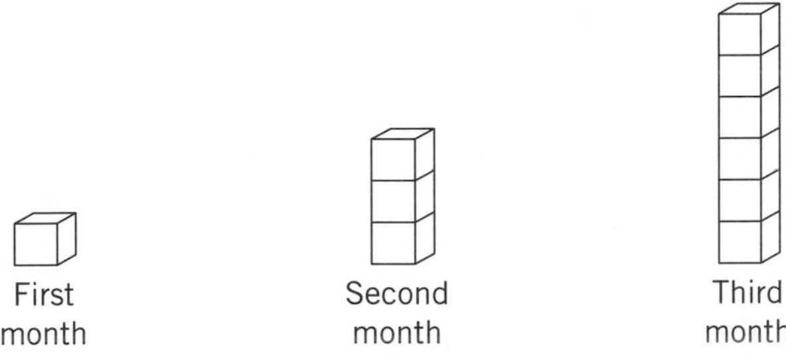

5. Ask the students to explain how they decided the number of cubes to place in each tower. They should describe that January had 1 toy, but February had 3 (i.e., 2 "new" toys, plus another January toy), and March had 6 toys (i.e., 3 "new toys," plus more of the 2 February and 1 January toys).
6. On the chalkboard, set up a table of values that includes the following information:

Month Number	Toys Sent	Total Toys Sent
1	1	*1*
2	3	*4*
3	6	*10*

Using their unifix cubes, the students should determine the number of Total Toys Sent by the end of each month.

7. Ask the students to predict the numbers that would go in the 4th row of this table and to defend their answers with unifix cubes. Discuss the student responses until an agreement is reached (Month Number = 4, Toys Sent = 10, and Total Toys Sent = 20).
8. In teams, have the students use their calculators to extend the pattern to 12 months to complete the table and solve the problem posed in the Motivation. They might want to use unifix cubes for the first few months, but they should discover that it becomes impractical and unnecessary to continue this way as the pattern becomes clear and numbers become large.
9. Ask students to share their responses and to verbalize the patterns that they found in the table. They should discover that a total of 78 toys would be mailed in December, yielding a total of 364 toys sent during the year.

Culminating Activity

10. After discussing the results from the table above, ask the students to determine how many of the January toys were mailed during the year. Students should determine that there was 1 January toy mailed each of 12 months for a total of 12 January toys. Similarly, two February toys were mailed for each of the next 11 months, totaling 22 February toys. Ask students to continue this process to determine the number of toys from each month that was mailed. How does this answer compare to the answers described by students in step 9 above? What other patterns do you see when you list the number of toys received in each month?

Extensions:

The process described above is the same as the gift-giving procedure in the song "The Twelve Days of Christmas." During the holiday season, have the students sing the song and determine how many partridges, calling birds, French hens, and so forth, are received over the 12-day period. A similar activity could center around gift-giving over the 8 days of Hanukkah.

Have the students substitute modern-day gifts in place of the gifts mentioned in "The Twelve Days of Christmas," such as "2 calculators," "3 boats of French fries," or "10 CDs playing." Then, approximate the cost of each "gift" and, with a calculator, have children determine the cost of actually giving these gifts over the holiday season.

Use the data in the table to draw a graph and analyze its characteristics. Is it linear? Why or why not?

Student Assessment/Evaluation:

Ask students to react to the activity in their journals. Provide them with the following prompts: (a) How did your team solve the problem? What patterns did you find? (b) If the year had 15 months, how many gifts would be given in the 15th month, and how many would you receive altogether? Explain how you got your answer.

Read the journal entries the following day and examine the patterns described by students as well as their ability to extend the pattern to a "15th month."

INSTRUCTIONAL AND ASSESSMENT ACTIVITIES FOR GRADES K-4

1. Distribute sets of pattern blocks to tables of children. Ask each child to build a kite by placing a yellow hexagon and two green triangles together as shown:

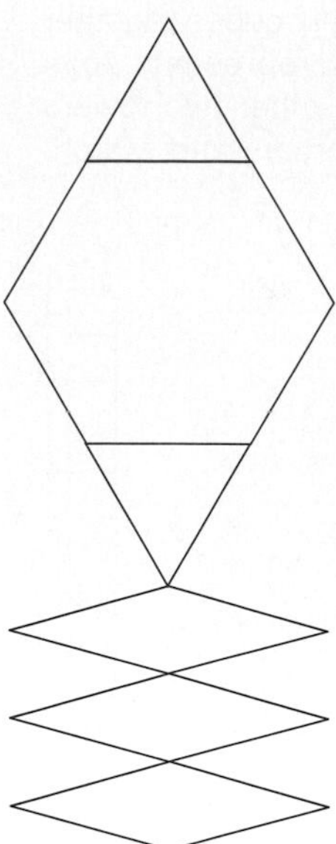

The tan rhombuses represent bows on the tail of the kite. Children should generate a table of values that relate the number of bows on the tail to the total number of pattern blocks required to build the picture.

Number of Bows	Total Number of Blocks
0	3
1	4
2	5

Through analyzing the table, children should be able to address questions such as:

a) What patterns do you see?
b) How many blocks will it take to build a kite that has 16 bows on its tail?
c) If a picture was made that required 40 blocks, how many bows would the kite have in its tail?
d) Let the number of bows on the tail be represented by the variable "t." Write an expression that generalizes the number of blocks required to build the picture.

Lastly, children can be challenged to build the kite by using a different combination of blocks (for example, the hexagon can be rebuilt by using three of the blue rhombuses, so the kite would require a total of five blocks). Then, a new table of values can be constructed and the four questions above can be re-explored. How many different ways can children find to build the kite? Note that each new kite construction will produce a new table of values.

2. Have the children write or orally communicate several "If . . . then" stories. For example, they might share that "If it is Saturday, then my mommy and daddy are both at home. Tomorrow is Saturday, so mommy and daddy will both be at home." These stories can be written on pieces of posterboard and displayed in the classroom.

3. Some of children's earliest experiences with variables come from using an empty "box" in equations and asking children to fill the "box" with a number that makes a sentence or equation true. For example:

   $\square + 3 = 7$ $\quad \square - 5 = 11$ $\quad 10 - \square = 4$ $\quad 7 + \square = 15$

4. Count the number of boys and the number of girls in the classroom and have the children represent these two quantities by placing blocks representing boys on one side of their desk and blocks representing girls on the other side. Then, ask the students to come up with as many statements that compare the number of boys and girls that they can devise.
   For example, if the class has 16 girls and 12 boys, children might say that there are four more girls than boys, that there are four less boys than girls, that the number of girls is the

number of boys plus four, and so forth. Children can also visit another classroom or two and collect data from those rooms to make similar comparisons.

5. As children are learning their multiplication facts, several patterns involving factors and products can be explored. One example is to make a list of the numbers 1 to 20 in a table and determine the total number of factor pairs that result in that product:

Product	Number of Factor Pairs
1	1 (1×1)
2	2 (1×2, 2×1)
3	2 (1×3, 3×1)
4	3 (1×4, 2×2, 4×1)

Children can determine the factor pairs by using color tiles to form arrays that require the number of tiles in the “Product” column. After listing the number of factor pairs for all of the products from 1 to 20, children should examine the table and verbalize all patterns that they see. Some numbers, for example, only have two pairs of factors and are the prime numbers. Products that have an odd number of factors can always form a square and are referred to as perfect squares. What other patterns can be identified?

6. Have one child raise his or her hand and ask the class how many fingers they see. Then, have a second child raise his or her hand and ask how many fingers are being held up altogether. Continue this process using several children. Then, generate a table of values and a graph of the data:

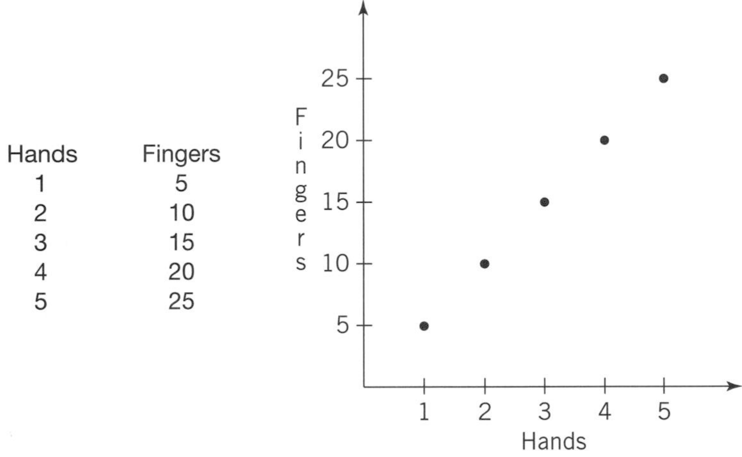

Hands	Fingers
1	5
2	10
3	15
4	20
5	25

Finally, children should be challenged to write a variable expression in which the number of hands is represented by “h,” and they come up with a formula for determining the number of fingers (e.g., 5h).

7. Distribute color tiles or blocks to pairs of children. Ask them to build the smallest square that they can by using the tiles/blocks. They should determine that the smallest square is formed by using one tile. Then, leaving the first square on the table, ask the children to build the next largest square next to it, which they will find to be a 2 × 2 square that requires four tiles. Continue this process until they have built six squares.

   Ask the students to compare the number of tiles required to build the first square to the number for the second square and so on. By counting the blocks, they should notice that 3 blocks were added as they went from the smallest to the next and that 5 blocks were added to this arrangement, then 7, and so forth. Ask children to use this information to predict how many tiles it would take to build the tenth square. Also, which square would require using 64 tiles? Can a square be constructed out of 90 tiles? Why or why not?

8. Construct a function machine for use with the whole class or small groups of children seated at a learning station. To build the machine, you will need an empty half-gallon milk carton and posterboard. In the front of the milk carton, cut two slots and insert a curved, rectangular piece of posterboard on the inside of the carton that connects the two slots.

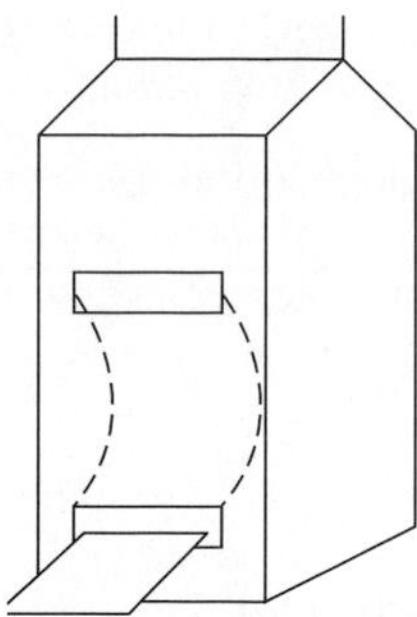

Finally, construct some cards that fit in the slots that have an input value on one side and an output value, upside down, on the other side (e.g., 2 with 3, 4 with 5, 5 with 6). Then, when a card is inserted in the slot on the top of the carton, it should slide through the "machine" and come out on the reverse side at the bottom of the carton.

The role of the student is to decide what the machine is doing to the input value to produce the output. Children should be encouraged to express their answers as, for example, "the function adds 1 to the input," "the output is one more than the input," and so forth. Students at the upper grades can be given more complex functions, such as functions which divide the input by three or double the input before adding 1.

9. As children are learning the addition, subtraction, multiplication, and division facts, they should have experiences with representing facts with variables.

    a) Represent addition facts as, for example, $x + y = 9$ (the 9 family) and ask children to determine the value of y when the value of x is given. For example, tell the students that $x = 4$ and ask them to determine the value of y.
    b) Represent subtraction facts as, for example, $x - y = 4$ and ask children to determine the value of y when the value of x is given. For example, tell students that $x = 7$ and ask them to determine the value of y.
    c) Represent multiplication facts as, for example, $a \times b = 12$ or $ab = 12$ and ask children to determine the value of b when the value of a is given. For example, tell students that $a = 2$ and ask them to determine the value of b.
    d) Represent division facts as, for example, $a/b = 7$ and ask children to determine the value of y when the value of x is given. For example, tell students that $a = 56$ and ask them to determine the value of b.

10. Make sure that each child has a calculator programmed with arithmetic logic. Then, have children predict exactly what their calculator will display as they press each button in sequence, such as:

11. Present the following scenario to a class:

    We are going to an ice cream store, and each person is going to buy a cone with two scoops of ice cream. We need to decide how many cones and how many scoops of ice cream will be purchased.

    Make a table, as shown:

No. of Children	No. of Cones	No. of Scoops
1	1	2
2	2	4
3	3	6

    Ask the students to describe any patterns that they see in the table. Allow them to predict how many cones and ice cream scoops will be needed for the entire class. For upper primary students, they could draw a graph relating the number of children to the number of scoops of ice cream and write an equation that relates these variables as well (e.g., $s = 2c$, where s = the number of scoops, and c = the number of children).

12. Supply each pair of children with a calculator, a set of counters (such as colored plastic chips), and a Hundreds Chart. The 10×10 grid below is a picture of a Hundreds Chart:

0	1	2	3	4	5	6	7	8	9
10	11	12	13	14	15	16	17	18	19
20	21	22	23	24	25	26	27	28	29
30	31	32	33	34	35	36	37	38	39
40	41	42	43	44	45	46	47	48	49
50	51	52	53	54	55	56	57	58	59
60	61	62	63	64	65	66	67	68	69
70	71	72	73	74	75	76	77	78	79
80	81	82	83	84	85	86	87	88	89
90	91	92	93	94	95	96	97	98	99

Ask children to enter a sequence in their calculators, such as [5] [+] [5] [=] [=] [=] [=]. Each time that they hit the equals sign, the repeated addition function (common to most calculators) will continue to add 5 to the previous sum. As the calculator displays a new number, one student should place a counter on that number on the hundreds chart. After all of the squares are covered that are possible, have children generalize their results and describe any visual or numerical patterns that they see. Have children try this for the following sequences:

a) [5] [+] [5] [=] [=] [=] [=]
b) [3] [+] [3] [=] [=] [=] [=]
c) [4] [+] [7] [=] [=] [=] [=]
d) [5] [+] [1] [0] [=] [=] [=] [=]

13. Have children place one color tile on their desks and ask them to find its perimeter. Perimeter can be described as "the number of people that can sit up to the table to eat." Since a square table could readily seat four people, the perimeter is four. When two tiles are laid on a table such that they share one side, six people could sit at the table, so its perimeter is six. Continue this process.

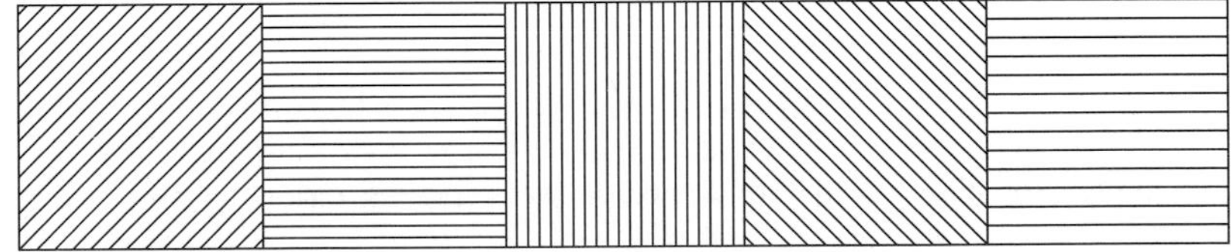

a) What would be the perimeter if 100 tiles were lined-up?
b) How many tiles would be required to form a rectangle whose perimeter is 50?
c) Is it possible to form a rectangle with a perimeter of 65? Why or why not?
d) Express the perimeter, P, with a variable expression that uses the number of color tiles, C.
e) Draw a simple graph that relates the number of tiles (x) to the perimeter (y).

14. Give each student a set of cubes, such as unifix cubes. Then, challenge the children to solve the following number puzzles by using their cubes. They should be required to explain their reasoning and to demonstrate their problem-solving process for the class.

a) I'm thinking of a number that is 5 more than 31.
b) My number, divided by 6, is 7.

c) If you double my number and add three, you get 15.
d) Three less than my number is 18.
e) If you take away 5 from half of my number, you get 1.
f) If you take my number away from 14, you get 6.

15. Present a sequence of numbers to the children and ask them to describe the pattern and make predictions about future terms in the sequence. The following examples illustrate how to do this:

    a) Consider the sequence of numbers: 2, 5, 8, 11, 14, . . . (i) Extend the pattern to 10 terms; (ii) use a calculator to find the 20th term; (iii) decide whether or not the number 200 is in the sequence. Finally, children can describe the rule for how each term in the sequence can be determined by using the previous term.
    b) Answer the questions above for the following numerical sequence: 6, 5, 7, 6, 8, 7, 9, . . .

16. Have the children draw graphs of the multiplication facts, where "x" represents one of the factors, and "y" represents the product. For example, if they were graphing the 4's table, they would plot the points (0,0), (1,4), (2,8), (3,12), (4,16), (5,20), (6,24), (7,28), (8,32), and (9,36).

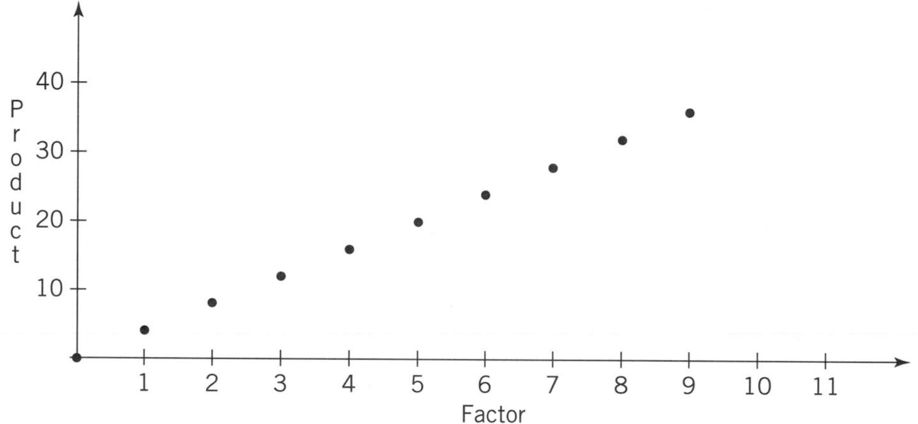

Do the points all lie on a line? Why? Would this be true for the graphs of all of the tables? Graph them and find out.

17. The study of functions is rooted in an understanding that changes in one variable bring about changes in another variable. Have children generate a list of "real life" situations in which changes in one event bring about changes in another. For example, they might say that "the number of hours of sleep I get at night depends on what time I go to bed" or that "the number of times I get to go down the slide on the playground depends on how many children are in line to ride it."

18. In the upper primary grades, children explore measurement and determine that there are 3 feet in each yard. If there are 3 feet in 1 yard, then there are 6 feet in 2 yards, and so forth. Have children make a table and a graph that relates the number of yards to the number of feet.

19. There is some excellent computer software on the market that helps children analyze and continue patterns. One such program is *Millie's Math House,* which has children extending patterns of pictures, such as horse-dog-horse-dog, etc. If computers are available, obtain a piece of software that develops patterning and allow students to explore and create their own patterns using the technology.

INSTRUCTIONAL AND ASSESSMENT ACTIVITIES FOR GRADES 5-8

1. Analyzing data for the purpose of making predictions is an important skill to develop in the upper grades. Following is a list of the prices of a first-class postage stamp for letters over the past several years:

1973—8¢	1985—22¢	1987—22¢	1990—25¢	1992—29¢
1984—20¢	1986—22¢	1988—25¢	1991—29¢	1995—32¢

Students should do the following:

a) Graph the data, with the x-values being the years and the y-values representing the cost of the stamp. (Hint: It may be helpful to use x-values from 0 to 22, where "year 0" is 1973, and "year 22" is 22 years later in 1995.)
b) Describe what you notice about the data. Do the rates appear to be "fairly" raised over the years? Why or why not?
c) Use the data to predict what you think the price of a stamp was in 1980. Then, consult an almanac to compare your answer to the actual.
d) Use the data in the table and on the graph to predict the price of a stamp in the year 2010. Explain how you determined your answer.

2. Make a master copy of a sheet containing small squares, rectangles, and large squares, as shown:

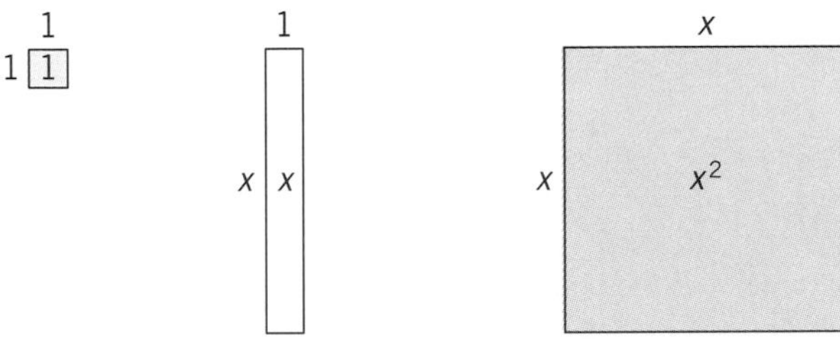

Children should cut out the tiles with scissors and put them into an envelope with their names on them. Then, anytime that tiles are required or preferred to solve a problem, every child has easy access to the tiles. Note that base ten blocks can be used for the same purpose, except that children need to be cautious not to attempt to "trade in" 10 units for an "x," since the rectangular piece does not always stand for the number 10.

3. Provide each child with a monthly calendar, such as that of January, 1996, below:

S	M	T	W	T	F	S
	1	2	3	4	5	6
7	8	9	10	11	12	13
14	15	16	17	18	19	20
21	22	23	24	25	26	27
28	29	30	31			

Ask the students to choose and box-in any "square" of nine numbers (such as 14, 15, 16, 21, 22, 23, 28, 29, and 30). Locate the largest number in the box and subtract 8 from it. Then, multiply this result by 9. Now, find the sum of all of the numbers in the square. The two results should be equal.

Students should determine why this works by exploring the underlying algebraic principles. They might begin by calling the number in the "upper-left" corner of their square "x." That would make the other numbers x+1, x+2, x+7, x+8, x+9, x+14, x+15, and x+16. By working with algebra tiles, the "trick" can be explained.

4. Provide small groups of students with a tape measure, several round objects, such as lids to plastic bowls, and graph paper. Children should measure the diameter and the circumference of each circle and record the data in a table. A sample is shown below:

Diameter (x)	Circumference (y)
4 cm	12.5 cm
6 cm	18 cm
21 cm	67 cm

Then, students should take the data from the table and use it to produce a graph which shows how the circumference depends upon the diameter.

a) Is the graph roughly a straight line? Why or why not?
b) If you believe that the graph should contain data points that lie on a line (are linear), why aren't the points that you graphed "exactly" on a line?

c) Starting from any point on your graph, count the number of units up and the number of units over to get to the next point on the graph. Divide the "rise" up by the "run" over—this value is called the slope of your line. What is your slope? Based on what you know about circles, what "should" be the slope of the line? Why? (Note: Students should recognize that the slope of the line would be π—slightly more than 3—because the circumference of a circle is found by multiplying the diameter by π.)

5. Children can play the game of "I have . . . who has" with algebra concepts. To play the game, a set of cards needs to be designed so that each student receives one card. A sample of 10 possible cards is shown below:

I have 10. Who has only a variable?
I have x. Who has three more than my number?
I have x + 3. Who has twice my number?
I have 2x + 6. Who has the solution to the equation 3x – 1 = 5?
I have 2. Who has an expression that can be represented by two algebra tile rectangles and 5 small squares?
I have 2x + 5. Who has two less than my number?
I have 2x + 3. If my expression is equal to 10, who has my value for x?
I have 3.5. Who has an equation with two variables?
I have x + 2y = 10. Who has my "y" value if x is 4?
I have 3. Who has 7 more than my number?

The cards are shuffled and distributed, one to each student. Any student in the room can begin by reading what he or she "has" and asking the "who has" question. Play continues until the last student is able to play his or her card. This game can be extended to any mathematical concept and be designed for as many students as are in a class.

6. If students have access to graphing calculators or to computers with graphing capabilities, they can conduct mathematical explorations of graphing patterns. For example, students can enter the equations $y = x$, $y = 2x$, and $y = 3x$ into the calculator and describe how the lines are similar and how they are different (e.g., the lines all pass through the origin—the point (0,0)—but they have different slopes). Students can also compare, for example, the graphs of $y = x$, $y = x + 1$, $y = x + 5$, and $y = x - 3$ to find similarities and differences.

7. Articles frequently appear in the newspaper in which data, such as crime statistics or sales totals, are reported in a table to show changes over time. Encourage students to bring newspaper clippings to class and analyze the data from the tables. Look for trends and allow students to predict future statistics based upon past trends. Remember that a key concept in the study of algebra is to get students to think about how changes in one variable (such as the year) will bring about changes in another variable (such as the cost or profits).

8. Students are often fascinated by mathematical "tricks" that have explanations for why they work rooted in algebra. For example, ask students to write down a number, add 4, triple the result, subtract 6, divide by 3, and subtract the original number. Tell them that you can read their minds and that their answers must be 2. Use algebra tiles to demonstrate the underlying mathematics.

   Then, ask each student to create his or her own puzzle for the rest of the class to analyze. Have the students write their puzzles on index cards and place them in a box.

Draw a card from the box a couple times a week to give students practice in using variables to analyze these "tricks."

9. Using a scale balance, have students weigh a paper cup filled with a type of cereal. Then, have them place a second cup filled with the same type of cereal on the pan and find the total weight of the two cups. Continue this process up to five cups of cereal and record the data in a table, as shown:

   Cups of Cereal #1 *Total Weight*

   Then, repeat the process with a second brand of cereal to create a new table:

   Cups of Cereal #2 *Total Weight*

   Finally, students should use a single piece of graph paper to graph the data from both tables on the same set of axes. Ask them to describe what they see. What does the "steepness" or the "slope" of the line tell us about the cereal? Which type of cereal would have a steeper graph—Grape Nuts or Cheerios? Conduct the experiment to verify your conjecture.

10. Distribute wooden cubes or some other type of blocks to the class. Ask the students to find the volume and surface area of one cube. Then, they should build the next largest cube and record the same data. Continue this process four times and put the data into a table form:

Cube	Volume	Surface Area
1	1	6
2	8	24
3	________	________
4	________	________
n	________	________

   Have the students predict the volume and surface area of the 8th cube and explain their reasoning. Then, challenge students to write a general expression for determining the volume and the surface area of a cube if the cube number is known. The problem can also be extended to exploring how many blocks are nested entirely "inside" of a constructed square and how this number can be determined.

11. In a science lab area, give each pair of students a birthday candle mounted to a nonflammable plate. Light the candle, and, with a ruler, measure the height of the candle every 30 seconds until it burns down. Put the data into a table and draw a graph in which the height (y) depends on the amount of time the candle burns (x). Use the data to predict how long it might take a taller candle or one with a larger diameter to burn down.

12. Suppose that you had an important message that you wanted every student in your school to know. You tell two students on the first day and ask each of them to tell two more students the next day and continue this process until the whole school knows the message. A table can be generated to think about what happens:

Day No.	New Students Told	Total Students Told
1	2	2
2	4	6

   a) How many days would it take for the message to get around to everyone in a school of 250 students?
   b) How many days would it take for the message to get around to everyone in a school of 800 students?
   c) Write a variable expression that would allow you to determine the number of new students told and total students told if you only know the day number.

13. In teams of three, give each group of students a ball (like a superball), a tape measure, and a roll of masking tape. Standing next to a wall, have one student drop the ball from a given height, such as six feet. When the ball bounces, another student should place a piece of tape on the wall at the highest point the ball bounces. When it bounces a second time, another piece of tape should be placed on the wall representing its maximum height. Continue this process until the ball stops bouncing, as possible. The third student should

measure the height of each bounce, and a table can be constructed that compares the number of bounces to the maximum height of each bounce.

a) What patterns occur in the data?
b) Graph the data, by hand or with a graphing calculator. What visual patterns appear?
c) Predict how might this graph be different for a different type of ball or the same ball dropped from a different height.
d) Conduct the experiment again, either using a different ball or a different starting height and compare the data to the first experiment and your prediction.

14. Algebraic thinking can be connected with probability explorations since there is often a great deal of patterning involved with finding permutations and combinations. Suppose that you were going to toss one coin. In this case, the coin could either come up Heads or Tails—2 outcomes. If you toss two coins, there are 4 possible outcomes—HH, HT, TH, or TT.

a) Have students list and count all of the possible outcomes for tossing 1, 2, 3, 4, and 5 coins.

Coins Tossed	Outcomes
1	2 (H, T)
2	4 (HH, HT, TH, TT)
3	______________

b) Predict the number of possible outcomes when 10 coins are tossed.
c) Find the probability of tossing exactly one Head when 1, 2, 3, 4, or 5 coins are tossed.

No. of Coins	Outcomes	Probability of 1 Head
1	2	$\frac{1}{2}$
2	4	$\frac{2}{4}$ (HT or TH)
3	8	$\frac{3}{8}$ (HTT, THT, or TTH)

d) Describe the patterns you see in part c. Write a variable expression that could be used to determine the probability of tossing exactly one head if you know how many coins have been tossed.
e) Graph the data from the table in part c. Describe the visual pattern that is formed. Is the graph linear? Why or why not?

15. Discuss how one calculates 7×22 or 4×98 mentally. Connect this with the distributive property by getting students to think of 7×22 as:

$$7\ (22) = 7\ (20 + 2) = 7\ (20) + 7\ (2) = 140 + 14 = 154$$

and

$$4\ (98) = 4\ (100 - 2) = 4\ (100) - 4\ (2) = 400 - 8 = 392$$

This process of analyzing mental arithmetic will make it much easier to discuss what happens when, for example, an expression such as $3x\ (x + 5)$ is multiplied because a connection can be made to arithmetic.

16. Distribute calculators to all of the students in the class, but deliberately give some students calculators that "think" arithmetically (left-to-right) and give other students algebraic calculators (that follow the proper order-of-operations). Ask the students to key the following sequence into their calculators:

Ask the students what answers their calculators are displaying. Students with arithmetic calculators will be showing "53," since the calculator worked left-to-right, while students with algebraic calculators will have the answer "8," because their calculators "knew" to multiply before adding or subtracting.

a) Discuss the difference in these answers and encourage students to determine whether their own calculator uses arithmetic or algebraic logic.
b) Give the students another expression, such as:

$$3 + 12 \div 2 - 4$$

and ask them to predict what the arithmetic calculator will do with the problem and compare this to what they expect that the algebraic calculator will do.
c) By the time a student reaches approximately the sixth grade, he or she should be able to explain the difference between calculators with arithmetic and algebraic logic and demonstrate the difference by using a specific example.

17. While a hundreds chart is typically used for analyzing simple patterns at the lower grade levels (see the activities for grades K-4), it can be powerful at the upper grade levels as well.

a) Give each student a hundreds chart, a calculator, and several plastic chip counters. Have them key into the calculator the following sequence:

[2] [+] [1] [1] [+] [=] [=] [=]

The repeat function will generate the numbers 2, 13, 24, etc. Have the students cover these numbers on their charts using the chips. Then, leaving the counters in place, have the students create another sequence.

They should also cover these numbers on the chart. Describe the patterns that have been formed. What is the relationship between these two lines?
b) Have the students devise their own pair of calculator keystroke sequences that would create another set of parallel lines.
c) The students should be able to create another pair of calculator sequences that would create a set of perpendicular lines.
d) Discuss patterns on the hundreds chart as going from one counter "up" or "down" and "over" to another to develop a basic understanding of finding the slope of a line.

18. When working with measurement or geometry, the use of formulas can help students to work with variable equations and expressions.

a) The area of a rectangle can be found by multiplying length times width, or $A = l \times w$. If $A = 32\ cm^2$ and $w = 8$ cm, find the length.
b) The area of a square can be found by "squaring" the length of a side, or $A = s^2$. If the area of a square is 50 in^2, estimate the length of each side.
c) The area of a circle can be determined by multiplying pi times the square of the radius, or $A = \pi \times r^2$. Suppose that the area of a pizza is 154 in^2. Find the radius and diameter of the pizza.
d) The area of a triangle can be found by taking half of the base times the height, or $A = \frac{1}{2} b \times h$. If the height of a triangle is 14 mm and the area is 84 mm^2, find the length of the base.
e) The total surface area of a rectangular prism can be found by using this formula: $TSA = 2\ (lw + hw + lh)$. Students should be able to explain why this formula works. Then, suppose that the total surface area is 100 cm^2 and that the height is 6 cm and the width is 2 cm. Find the length.

19. A 13-year-old wants to invest a $1,000 savings for 30 years. Assuming that interest is compounded once every year, use a calculator or a computer to explore the difference between investing the money at 5%, 7%, and 10% interest. What patterns do you notice?

20. A checkerboard is generally a square grid with each side measuring 8 units, as shown:

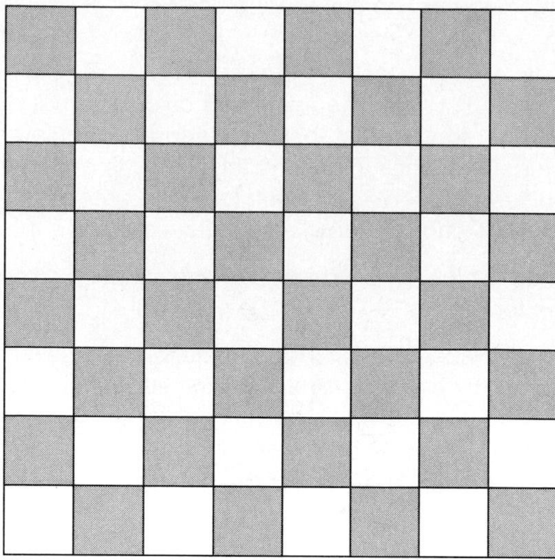

   a) How many squares can you find on the checkerboard?
   b) Describe any patterns you encountered while trying to solve this problem.
   c) Generalize your answer by explaining how you could use your process and answer to find the number of squares on a checkerboard that was 10×10, rather than 8×8.

21. Present the following problem to your students:

   At a local county fair, you have two choices when you go through the entrance gate. You can either pay \$5.00 at the door and then pay \$1.75 for each ride, or you can pay \$17.00 at the door and ride all day for "free."

   a) Determine which plan you would choose and defend your solution with mathematics.
   b) Draw a graph in which the x-values represent the number of rides, and the y-values stand for the amount of money spent. Where do these lines intersect (cross) one another, and what does this tell you?

It is important to give students the problem and little, if any, "coaching" at first. Let them deal with it in their own ways, and you may discover that some students choose to guess-and-check, while others prepare an organized table, and still others may decide to draw a graph to display the options. One of the key concepts in algebra is to develop multiple representations of the same problem—sometimes, an equation is better, while other times, a graph is more helpful. Students need to become comfortable with working a problem using several different models.

22. The Fibonacci numbers are a sequence of numbers in which each term can be found by taking the sum of the previous two numbers, as follows:

   1, 1, 2, 3, 5, 8, 13, 21, . . .

   a) Without explaining the "rule," give students the first 7 or 8 terms and ask them to determine the rule.
   b) Have students generate the first 20 terms of the sequence.
   c) Is the 100th Fibonacci number even or odd? Explain your pattern and how you know.

23. Sing the song "The Twelve Days of Christmas." Students should determine (a) how many gifts are given on each of the 12 days and (b) the total number of gifts given over the time period. A table is useful for exploring this problem:

Day Number	Gifts Today	Total Gifts
1	1	1
2	3 (2 + 1)	4 (3 + 1)
3	6 (3 + 2 + 1)	10 (4 + 6)

Students should describe any patterns they encounter while solving this problem. Can a formula using a variable be written for determining the Gifts Today and Total Gifts if the Day Number is known? Do you recognize the sequence of numbers appearing in the Gifts Today column?

24. Have a small group of students, at a learning center, fill a transparent water jug (such as a sun tea jug) that has a valve. Then, one student should hold open the valve, draining the water into a bucket, while a second student measures the "height" of the water in the jug with a meter stick. A third student should record the data every 30 seconds. The water level should be put into a table and graphed either by hand or with a graphing calculator or computer. Have students analyze the data to determine what patterns they see. Is the graph linear? Why or why not? What would happen if the jug were twice as high or twice as wide?

25. If the school has computers with spreadsheet programs available, the use of a spreadsheet can be an excellent way to promote algebraic thinking and to solve problems that involve algebra. Any of the problems in this section that involved the creation of a table can be laid out on a computer. Students can write spreadsheet formulas and use the "fill down" or "fill right" functions to make predictions about the data.

Suggested Readings

Barber, H. C. (1932). Present opportunities in junior high school algebra. In W.D. Reeve (Ed.), *The teaching of algebra.* New York, NY: Teachers College, Columbia University.

Bennett, A., Maier, L., & Nelson, T. (1988). *Math and the mind's eye.* Portland, OR: The Mathematics Learning Center, Portland State University.

Clark, A., Grzesiak, K., Hansbarger, M., Johnston, A., Stewart, J., & Thomas, C. (1990). Algebra activities, K-9. *Monographs of the Michigan council of teachers of mathematics* (Serial No. 23).

Coburn, T. G., Bushey, B. J., Holton, L. C., Latozas, D., Mortimer, D., & Shotwell, D. (1993). *Patterns* (from the NCTM Curriculum and Evaluation Standards Addenda Series, Grades K-6). Reston, VA: National Council of Teachers of Mathematics.

Committee on the Mathematical Education of Teachers. (1991). *The call for change.* Washington, DC: Mathematical Association of America.

Edwards, E. L. (Ed.). (1990). *Algebra for everyone.* Reston, VA: National Council of Teachers of Mathematics.

Flanders, J. R. (1987). How much of the content in mathematics textbooks is new? *The Arithmetic Teacher, 35.*

Gardella, F. J., Glatzer, D., Glatzer, J., Hirschhorn, Rosenberg, C., & Walsh, M. A. (1994). Making sense of Algebra. In C. A. Thornton & N. S. Bley (Eds.), *Windows of opportunity: Mathematics for students with special needs.* Reston, VA: National Council of Teachers of Mathematics.

Heid, M. K., Choate, J., Sheets, C., & Zbiek, R. M. (1995). *Algebra in a technological world* (from the NCTM Curriculum and Evaluation Standards Addenda Series, Grades 9-12). Reston, VA: National Council of Teachers of Mathematics.

Howden, H. (1985). *Algebra tiles for the overhead projector.* New Rochelle, NY: Cuisenaire Company of America.

Kaput, J. J. (1995). A research base supporting long term algebra reform. In D. T. Owens, M. K. Reed, & G. M. Millsaps (Eds.), *Proceedings of the seventeenth annual meeting of the north american chapter of the international group for the psychology of mathematics education.* Columbus, OH: ERIC Clearinghouse for Science, Mathematics, and Environmental Education.

Kieran, C. (1992). The learning and teaching of school algebra. In D. A. Grouws (Ed.), *Handbook of research on mathematics teaching and learning.* New York, NY: NCTM/Macmillan.

Kieran, C. (1990). Cognitive processes involved in learning school algebra. In P. Nesher & J. Kilpatrick (Eds.), *Mathematics and cognition: A research synthesis by the international group for the psychology of mathematics education.* Cambridge: Cambridge University Press.

Kieran, C. (1989). The early learning of algebra: A structural perspective. In S. Wagner & C. Kieran (Eds.), *Research issues in the learning and teaching of algebra.* Reston, VA: Lawrence Erlbaum Associates/NCTM.

Lodholz, R. D. (1990). The transition from arithmetic to algebra. In E. L. Edwards, Jr. (Ed.), *Algebra for everyone.* Reston, VA: National Council of Teachers of Mathematics.

Mathematical Sciences Education Board. (1993). *Measuring up: Prototypes for mathematics assessment.* Washington, DC: National Academy Press.

Meiring, S. (Ed.) (1992). *A core curriculum: Making mathematics count for everyone.* Reston, VA:

National Council of Teachers of Mathematics.

National Council of Teachers of Mathematics. (1992). *Algebra for the twenty-first century: Proceedings of the 1992 conference.* Reston, VA: Author.

National Council of Teachers of Mathematics. (1991). *Professional standards for teaching mathematics.* Reston, VA: Author.

National Council of Teachers of Mathematics. (1990). *Algebra for everyone* (video program and guide). Reston, VA: Author.

National Council of Teachers of Mathematics. (1989). *Curriculum and evaluation standards for school mathematics.* Reston, VA: Author.

National Research Council. (1989). *Everybody counts: A report to the nation on the future of mathematics education.* Washington, DC: National Academy Press.

Ohio Department of Education. (1990). *Model competency-based mathematics program.* Columbus, Ohio.

Phillips, E., Gardella, T., Kelly, C., & Stewart, J. (1991). *Patterns and functions* (from the NCTM Curriculum and Evaluation Standards Addenda Series, Grades 5-8). Reston, VA: National Council of Teachers of Mathematics.

Rasmussen, P. *Mathtiles manual: A concrete approach to arithmetic and algebra.* Berkeley, CA: Key Curriculum Press, 1977.

Resnick, L. B., Cauzinille-Marmeche, E., & Mathieu, J. (1987). Understanding algebra. In J. Sloboda & D. Roger (Eds.), *Cognitive process in mathematics.* New York, NY: Oxford University Press.

Steen, L. A. (Ed.). (1990). *On the shoulders of giants: New approaches to numeracy.* Washington, DC: National Academy Press.

Thompson, P. W. (1989). Artificial intelligence, advanced technology, and learning and teaching algebra. In S. Wagner & C. Kieran (Eds.), *Research issues in the learning and teaching of algebra.* Reston, VA: Lawrence Erlbaum Associates/NCTM.

Thorpe, J. A. (1989). Algebra: What should we teach and how should we teach it? In S. Wagner & C. Kieran (Eds.), *Research issues in the learning and teaching of algebra.* Reston, VA: Lawrence Erlbaum Associates/NCTM.

U.S. Department of Labor. (1991). *What work requires of schools: A SCANS report for America 2000.* Washington, DC: U.S. Government Printing Office.

Usiskin, Z. (1988). Conceptions of school algebra and uses of variables. In A. F. Coxford (Ed.), *National council of teachers of mathematics 1988 Yearbook: The ideas of algebra K-12.* Reston, VA: National Council of Teachers of Mathematics.

Usiskin, Z. (1988). Why elementary algebra can, should, and must be an eighth-grade course for average students. *The Mathematics Teacher, 80.*

Chapter 10

Rational Numbers Expressed as Fractions: Concepts

Overview

Students must be exposed to fraction concepts at each grade level. In the primary grades, the teacher should concentrate on providing an intuitive approach to fractional numbers involving explorations dealing with continuous and discrete models. Groups of objects, number lines, and regions are three models that should be used to develop an understanding of fractional numbers. More emphasis needs to be placed on the basic understanding of fractions so that less time will need to be devoted to the operations on fractions. Many elementary teachers begin teaching operations on fractional numbers before children have internalized the prerequisite fraction concepts. It is important to remember that concrete and semiconcrete experiences and demonstrations should be used frequently to provide a background of understanding necessary for working with the more abstract concepts later.

The contemporary approach to elementary school mathematics provides a consistent pattern of experiences designed to extend the child's understanding of concepts with each successive step. A basic understanding of fraction concepts beginning in the primary grades not only meets the mathematical needs of the child, but also gives the child a proper perspective of number structure. The child who is introduced to concepts of fractional numbers at the primary grades sees their relation to whole numbers at an advantageous time. When the child reaches the point of operations with fractional numbers, they are then not thought of as something completely new and different.

Since so many children want the "biggest half of the candy bar," there is a need to provide many situations that will help children understand the meaning of the denominator and the numerator in a fraction. This understanding must precede any computation with fractional numbers. Manipulation of real objects, demonstrations on the felt board with regions separated into fractional parts, and simple exercises involving folding and cutting paper not only will increase understanding of fractional parts but also introduce computational skills as well. Use Cuisenaire rods, base ten blocks, pattern blocks, and fraction bars in presenting the concept of fractions.

Using transparent colored plastic, cut out circular regions about 6 centimeters in diameter. Using a different color for each set of fractions, make five circular regions of each color. Cut one set of five circular regions into halves, and cut the remaining sets into thirds, fourths, fifths, sixths, sevenths, eighths, ninths, tenths, and twelfths. Keep each set in a small envelope marked to indicate the type of pieces inside. The pieces can be easily manipulated on the overhead projector by both teacher and students, and students can easily see the relationships among the pieces.

At the primary grade levels it is particularly important to establish visual perception of the concept of fractional parts. Use of the number line will help in establishing the idea of $\frac{1}{2}$, $\frac{1}{4}$, and so on, and the fact that a fractional number has many names.

0								1
$\frac{0}{2}$				$\frac{1}{2}$				$\frac{2}{2}$
$\frac{0}{4}$		$\frac{1}{4}$		$\frac{2}{4}$		$\frac{3}{4}$		$\frac{4}{4}$
$\frac{0}{8}$	$\frac{1}{8}$	$\frac{2}{8}$	$\frac{3}{8}$	$\frac{4}{8}$	$\frac{5}{8}$	$\frac{6}{8}$	$\frac{7}{8}$	$\frac{8}{8}$

Use the chalkboard or pictures of articles to give children opportunities to talk about fractions. For example:

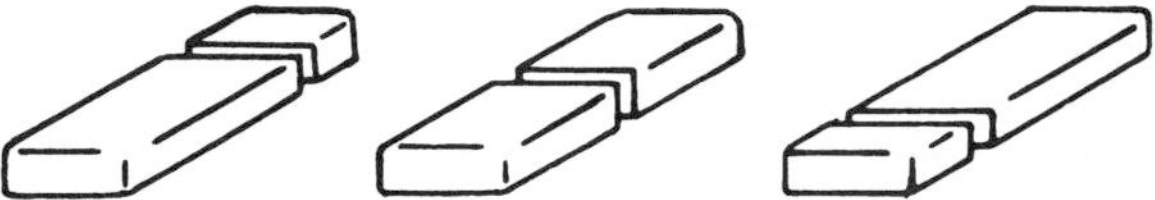

Jimmy and Johnny were playing together at Johnny's house. Johnny's sister came home with a candy bar for Johnny. She didn't know that Jimmy was going to be there, too. She cut the candy bar into two pieces so that Jimmy and Johnny could each have one-half. Have a child come to the chalkboard and point out the candy bar that is cut into halves (or to the proper picture, if pictures are used).

Using this same kind of activity, have children make up stories about the pictures. They should be encouraged to write sentences that describe the fractional parts represented by the objects in the picture. This activity can be extended to include one-fourth, one-third, and so on.

The teacher can make the following models to demonstrate the relationships among fractions and equivalent fractions.

Using heavy cardboard or posterboard, make a fraction chart similar to the one shown.

1 Unit

$\frac{1}{2}$ | $\frac{1}{2}$

$\frac{1}{3}$ | $\frac{1}{3}$ | $\frac{1}{3}$

$\frac{1}{4}$ | $\frac{1}{4}$ | $\frac{1}{4}$ | $\frac{1}{4}$

$\frac{1}{5}$ | $\frac{1}{5}$ | $\frac{1}{5}$ | $\frac{1}{5}$ | $\frac{1}{5}$

Make the same type of fraction model on plywood. Construct a frame from a piece of plywood on which narrow strips of wood are nailed or glued. Construct rectangles of plywood so that the rectangles will fit between the wooden strips. Cut each rectangle into different fractional parts.

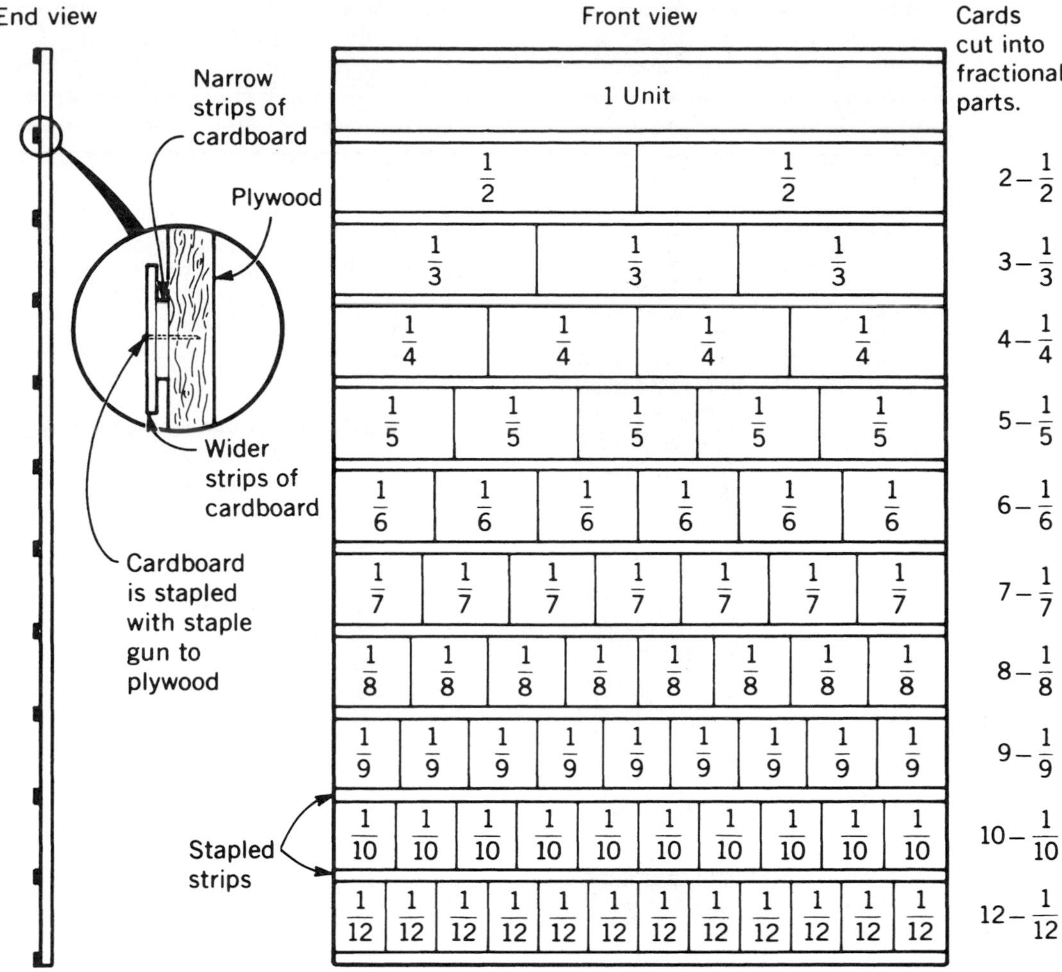

Attach a long string (the length of the fraction board) to a thumbtack. The children can see which fractions are related by placing the thumbtack on the top edge of the fraction board and drawing the string taut. For instance, place the thumbtack in the top of the fraction board directly above the split between the two one-half pieces. Tighten the string down the center of the board so that the children can see that two one-fourths, three one-sixths, four one-eighths, five one-tenths, and six one-twelfths are the same in length as one-half. Thus one-half is equivalent to two-fourths, three-sixths, four-eighths, five-tenths, and six-twelfths. A similar procedure can be used with the other fractional parts.

To construct a circular fraction kit, trace 16 large circles on construction paper (or use paper plates if available). Cut them as follows: three regions intact (units), two regions in two parts (halves), two regions in three parts (thirds), two regions in four parts (fourths), two regions in five parts (fifths), two regions in six parts (sixths), two regions in eight parts (eighths), and one region in twelve parts (twelfths). The teacher may want to make a fraction kit out of colored transparencies to use on an overhead projector.

SAMPLE LESSON PLAN—"THE PIZZA SLICE DECISION"

Intermediate Developmental Lesson

Goal:

Investigate the way the size of a fractional part corresponds to the original whole region.

Objectives:

The students will:

- Compare the sizes of unit fractions with like denominators to their original whole region.

Prerequisite Learning and/or Experiences:

- Relating region model parts to fractional language.

- Ability to connect region model parts to abstract notation.

Materials:

For each student:

- Two construction paper circles—one 10 inch diameter and one 12 inch diameter
- Access to a tub of Cuisenaire rods

Procedures:

Motivational Introduction

Relate the following story to your students: Last evening I was invited to a party. The hostess served pizza for the main course. I have been making an effort to eat fewer calories, so I really didn't want very much pizza, but I was too hungry not to eat anything. I decided I could eat one slice of pizza. When I went to the serving table, I noticed the pepperoni pizzas were on 12 inch diameter plates and cut into eight equal-sized slices. The cheese pizzas were on 10 inch diameter plates and also cut into eight equal-sized slices. I chose a slice of cheese pizza. Did I make the correct choice? Why? Be prepared at this point for student responses that are spontaneous and, consequently, not based on reason connected to the problem. Some, for example, may say "No, because I like pepperoni pizza better." Use the Think, Pair, Share strategy with the following activity to determine the answer.

1. Provide each student with two construction paper circles, one 12 inches in diameter and the other 10 inches in diameter. Challenge the students to use the circles to answer the pizza slice question. Give each student a short time to think and work alone.
2. Have partners share their thoughts and solution strategies with each other. Now is the time to observe potential solutions. If pairs decide the cheese slice has the least calories because pepperoni is high in fat content, then change the parameters to just cheese on both pizzas. Or, if pairs decide the cheese slice has the fewest calories because a 10-inch pizza is smaller than a 12-inch pizza, have them defend their reasoning with fractional parts.
3. Have pairs share their solution strategies. Although other solutions have merit, call special attention to solutions which physically show that one-eighth of a 10 inch pizza is less than one-eighth of a 12 inch pizza.

Developmental Activity

4. Based upon the pizza slice question, state the following hypothesis: Two fractions with the same numerator and denominator may not be the same size. Using Cuisenaire rods and a carefully planned experiment, have pairs determine if the hypothesis is true or false.
5. Provide each pair of students with a small tub of Cuisenaire rods. Have everyone hold an orange rod in their hands. Tell them that for this activity the orange is worth one. Have each pair of students complete the following chart:

Rod color	Rod Value
orange	1
blue	
brown	
black	
dark green	
yellow	
purple	
light green	
red	
white	

Be prepared to help some groups begin. Have them line up a train of whites equal to the orange rod. Ask how many whites altogether? (10). Hold up one of the whites. Ask how many whites out of the total? (1 of 10). So, a white rod is worth one tenth of an orange rod. Beside *white* on the chart write 1/10. Encourage use of this value to help determine the fractional names for the other color rods.

6. Have pairs volunteer answers to fill in the chart. Due to the nature of equivalent fractions, expect more than one response for some rods. Whenever more than one fraction for a color is proposed, have the pair defend their answer. The chart should ultimately resemble this:

Rod color	Rod Value
orange	1
blue	$\frac{9}{10}$
brown	$\frac{8}{10}$; $\frac{4}{5}$
black	$\frac{7}{10}$
dark green	$\frac{6}{10}$; $\frac{3}{5}$
yellow	$\frac{5}{10}$; $\frac{1}{2}$
purple	$\frac{4}{10}$; $\frac{2}{5}$
light green	$\frac{3}{10}$
red	$\frac{2}{10}$; $\frac{1}{5}$
white	$\frac{1}{10}$

7. Add a third column to the chart and have pairs repeat the same process, but this time name the brown rod as one. The resulting chart should resemble this:

Rod color	Rod Value	Rod Value
orange	1	$\frac{10}{8}$; $1\frac{2}{8}$; $1\frac{1}{4}$
blue	$\frac{9}{10}$	$\frac{9}{8}$; $1\frac{1}{8}$
brown	$\frac{8}{10}$; $\frac{4}{5}$	1
black	$\frac{7}{10}$	$\frac{7}{8}$
dark green	$\frac{6}{10}$; $\frac{3}{5}$	$\frac{6}{8}$; $\frac{3}{4}$
yellow	$\frac{5}{10}$; $\frac{1}{2}$	$\frac{5}{8}$
purple	$\frac{4}{10}$; $\frac{2}{5}$	$\frac{4}{8}$; $\frac{1}{2}$

light green	$\frac{3}{10}$	$\frac{3}{8}$
red	$\frac{2}{10}, \frac{1}{5}$	$\frac{2}{8}, \frac{1}{4}$
white	$\frac{1}{10}$	$\frac{1}{8}$

Culminating Activity

8. Have pairs of students compare and contrast the fractional data on the chart. Have students find two fractions the same, but different color rods (e.g. $\frac{1}{2}$ is yellow when orange is one, but $\frac{1}{2}$ is purple when brown is one). Have students find two rods the same color, but with different fraction names (e.g., black is worth $\frac{7}{8}$ when brown is one, but worth $\frac{7}{10}$ when orange is one). Have a class discussion of the results.
9. Return to the hypothesis. Have the class compare the results of the Cuisenaire rod activity to the hypothesis statement of "two fractions with the same numerator and denominator may not be the same size."
10. Have individual students write if the hypothesis is true or false and describe why.

Extension:

Apply the hypothesis statement to the "groups of objects" model for rational numbers. Pose the following scenerio: "I have two bags of M&M candies. One bag weighs 8 ounces and the other bag weighs 12 ounces. You are allowed to devour one-eighth of either bag. Which bag will you choose and why?" Look for a responses which relate one-eighth of 12 ounces as having more M&Ms than one-eighth of 8 ounces. Of course, students who are not chocolate lovers may opt for the fewer number of candies.

Student Assessment/Evaluation:

Score the content of the students' writings related to the hypothesis being true or false and why. Apply the following rubric:

0 = no attempt
1 = statement false, no defense
2 = statement false, defended reasoning
3 = statement true, no defense
4 = statement true, defended reasoning

INSTRUCTIONAL AND ASSESSMENT ACTIVITIES FOR GRADES K-4

1. Open a manila file folder and write the fraction $\frac{1}{2}$ on one side; on the other write the fraction $\frac{1}{4}$. Cut out a number of geometric shapes, and color either $\frac{1}{4}$ or $\frac{1}{2}$ of each. Make five or ten folders so that many children can sort the shapes by placing them on the proper side of the folder.

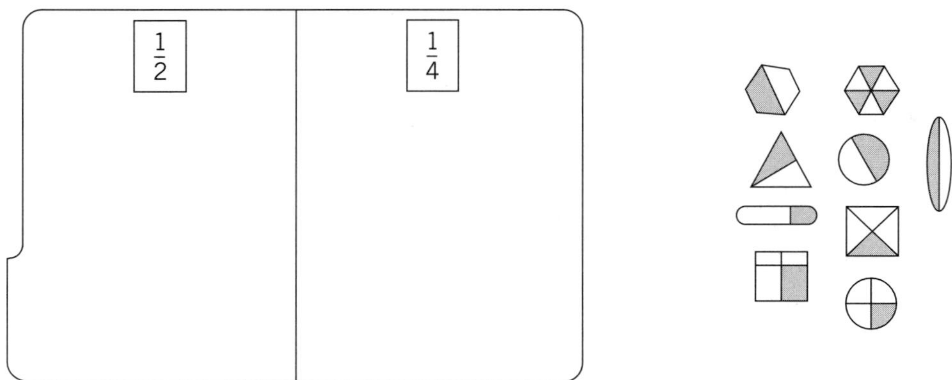

2. Tape another piece of cardboard to some of the folders, and put the fraction $\frac{1}{3}$ on this section. Make figures with $\frac{1}{3}$ on them colored to add to the set.

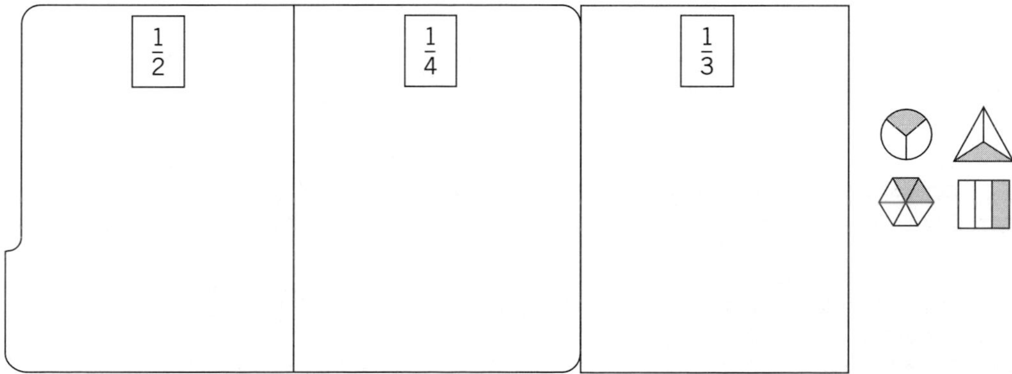

3. Mark each figure that has $\frac{1}{2}$ of the region shaded. How many did you mark? If you left some unmarked, why?

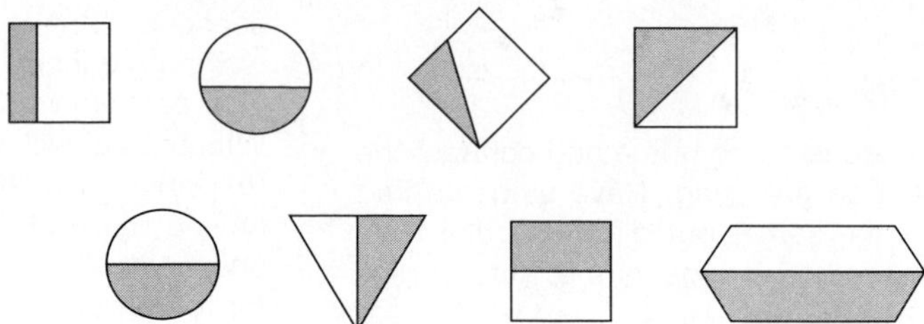

4. Mark each figure that has $\frac{1}{4}$ of the region shaded.

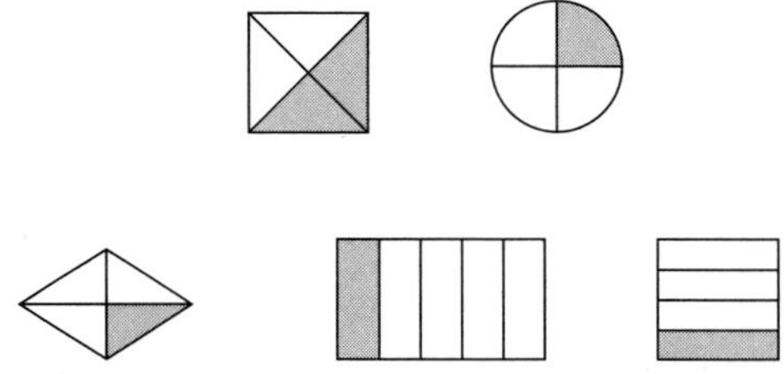

5. Shade $\frac{1}{3}$ of the figure.

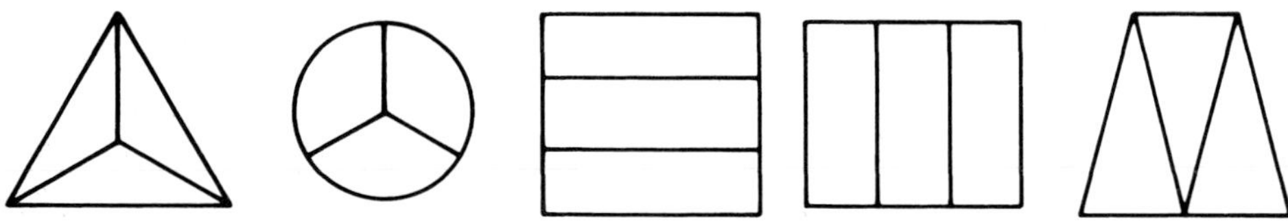

6. Make a set of cardboard dominoes. Draw a figure on both ends of each domino, and shade $\frac{1}{2}$, $\frac{1}{3}$, or $\frac{1}{4}$ of the figure. Play regular dominoes by matching shapes that have the same fractional part shaded.

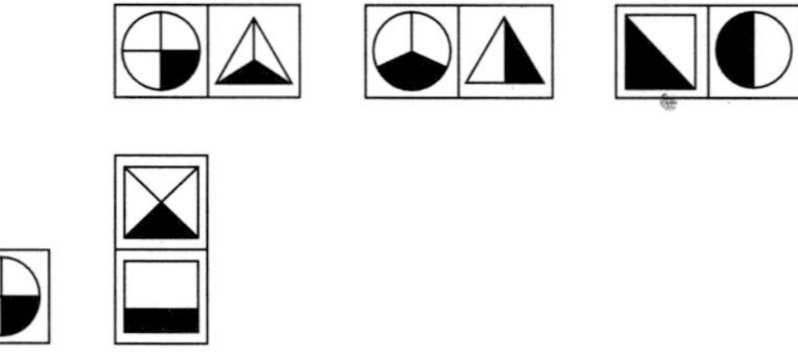

7. Use the felt board or chalkboard for simple diagrams. Ask a child to draw a loop around $\frac{1}{2}$, $\frac{1}{3}$, or $\frac{1}{4}$ of the objects pictured.

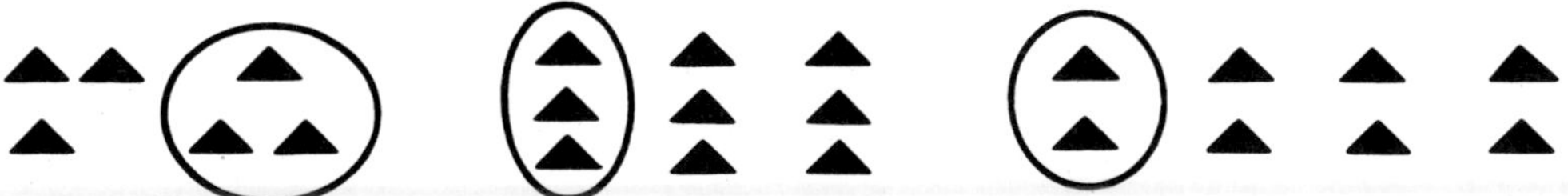

8. Give each child two congruent circles of different colors cut from construction paper. Instruct the children to fold one circle in half and cut with scissors along the fold. Fit both halves over the other circle. Have the children trade halves with another student to see if two halves still make a whole. Use a third circle with a larger diameter than the other two. Fold it in half; have the children discuss why this half doesn't match the halves from the other circles. This is an important activity to emphasize the attention that must be paid to unit size.

9. Give each child two squares of construction paper of different colors. Instruct the children to fold one square in half and cut along the fold (do not demonstrate this). Have them fit both halves over the other square and trade halves with another student. Often, some students will cut a square along the diagonal, which provides excellent material for discussion.

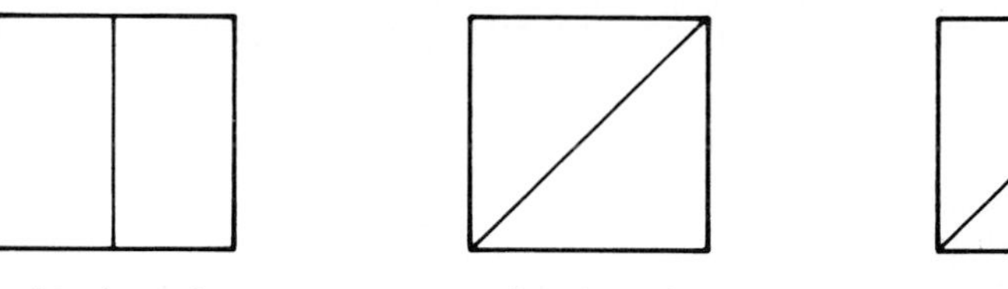

Student A

Student B

Results when Student A and Student B exchange halves

10. Give a student eight checkers: five red and three black. Have the student write the fraction for the part of the set that is red and the part of the set that is black. You may use disks cut from colored transparencies and placed on the overhead projector. Have the children orally tell the fraction for a given part of the set.

11. Draw a loop around the correct fraction representing the shaded portion.

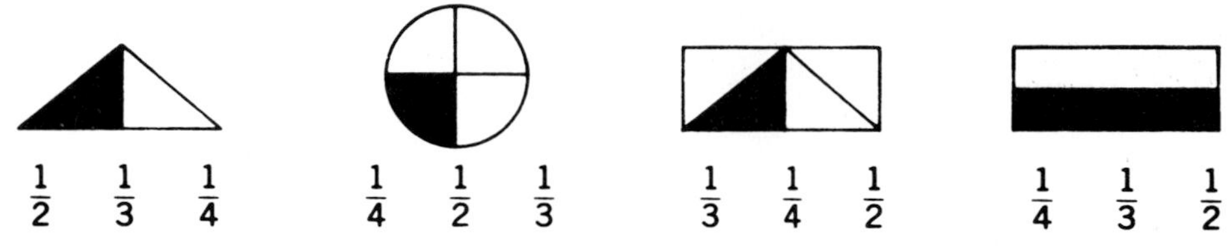

12. Color $\frac{1}{4}$ of each picture.

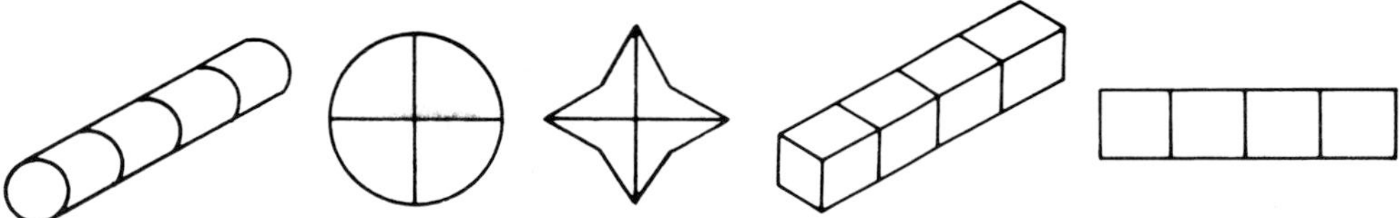

13. Draw a loop around the correct fraction representing the shaded portion.

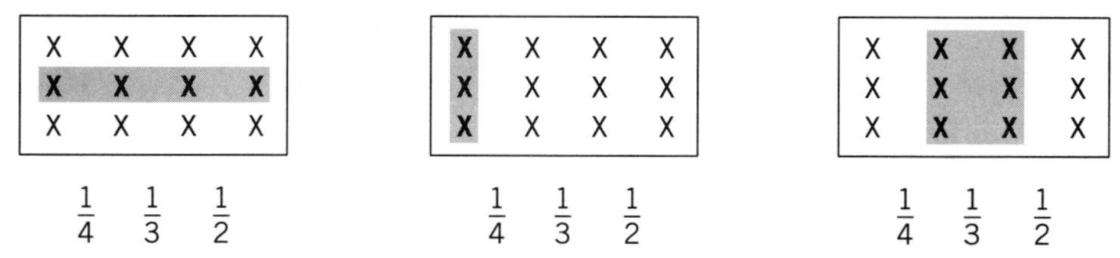

14. Color $\frac{1}{2}$ of each set.

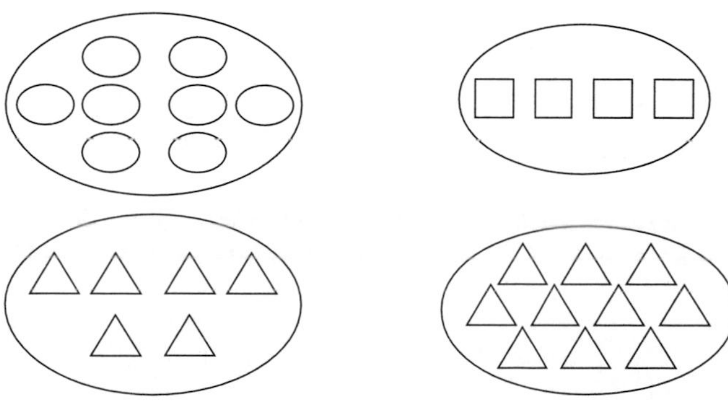

15. Color $\frac{1}{4}$ of each set.

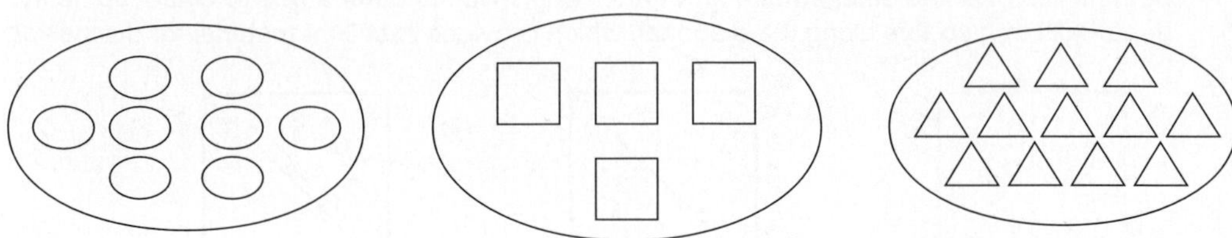

16. a) Color $\frac{1}{3}$ of each picture. b) Color $\frac{2}{3}$ of each picture.

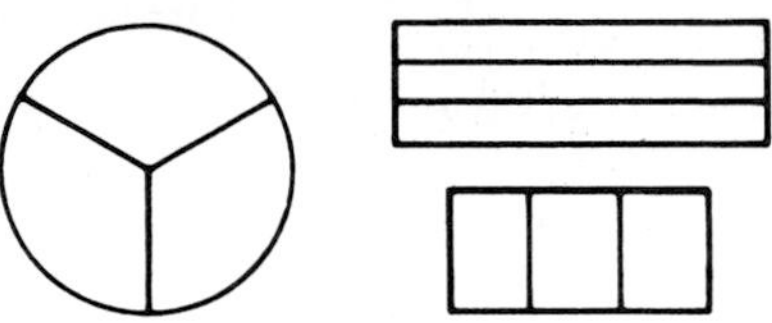

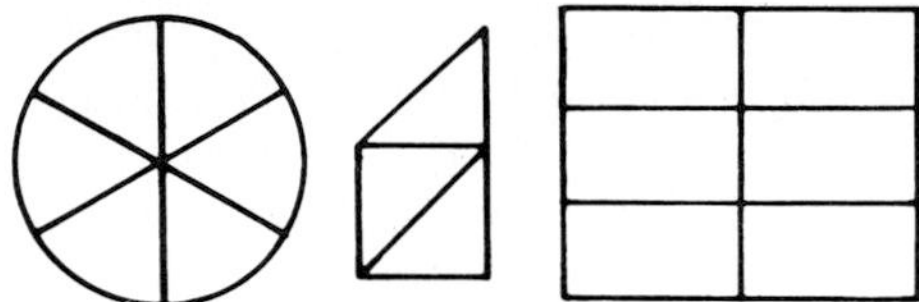

c) Color $\frac{3}{4}$ of each picture. d) Color $\frac{1}{3}$ of each group.

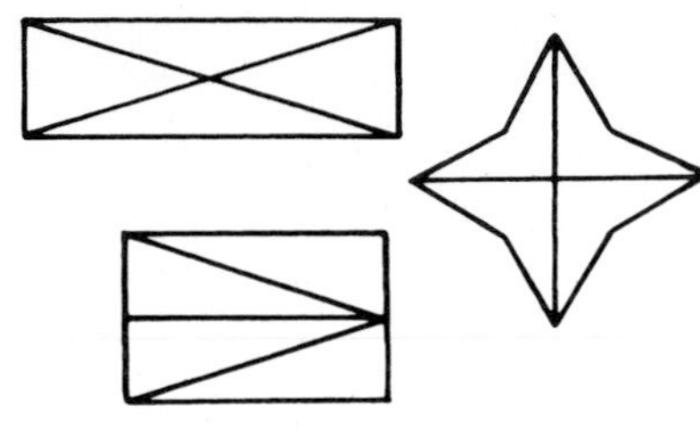

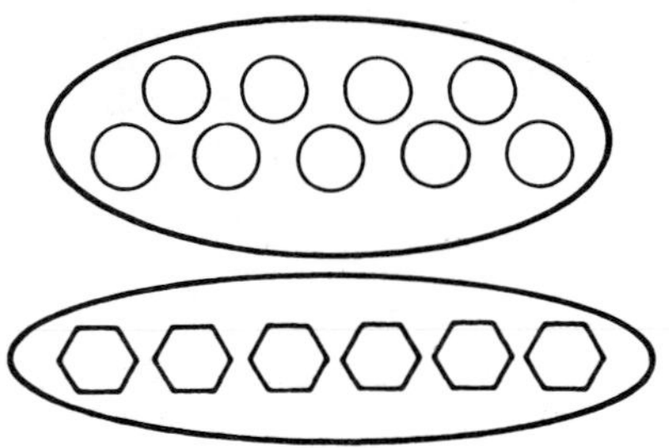

17. Loop the correct fraction for each bar.

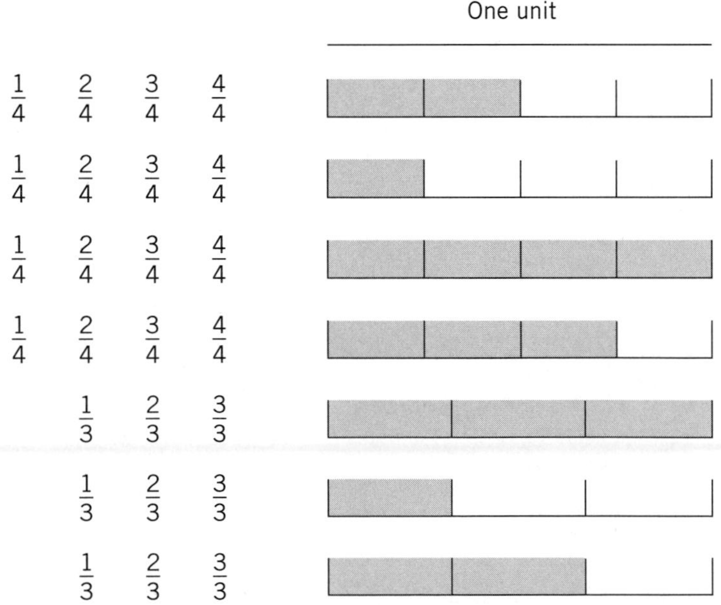

18. Write the correct fraction for each.

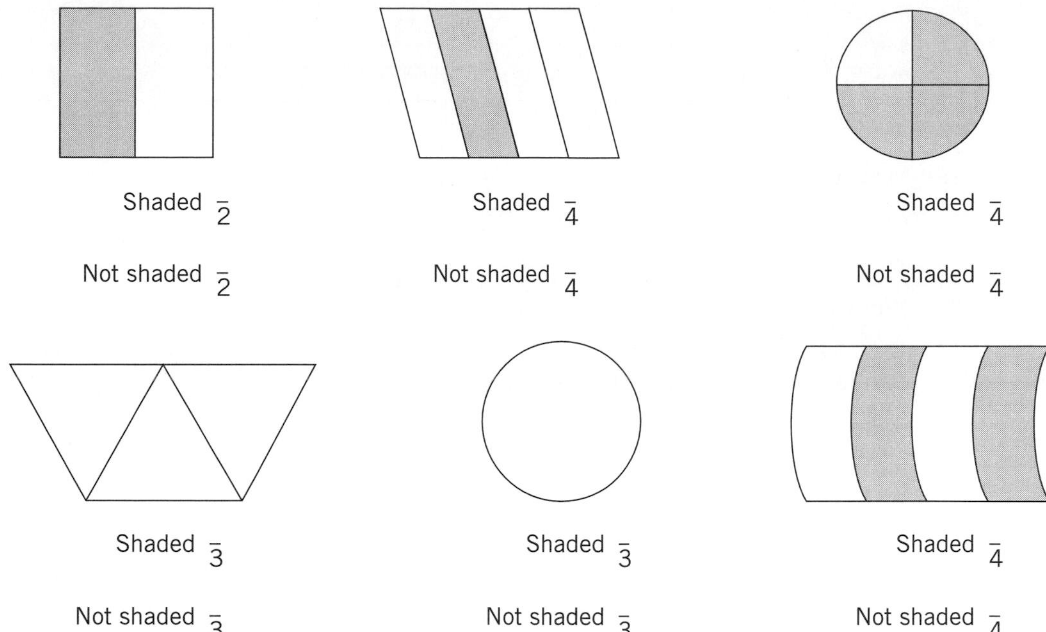

19. Give the student two yellow buttons, eight blue buttons, and five cards. Ask the student to tell what fraction of the buttons is yellow $\left(\frac{2}{10}\right)$ and what fraction is blue $\left(\frac{8}{10}\right)$. Have the student place two buttons on each card with the two yellow ones together. Now ask which fraction of the cards with buttons is yellow $\left(\frac{1}{5}\right)$ and which is blue $\left(\frac{4}{5}\right)$. Variations of this activity can be done by changing the number of buttons and cards.

20. Give each child a copy of the following chart; the children can cut out strips, or rows, to answer the questions that follow.

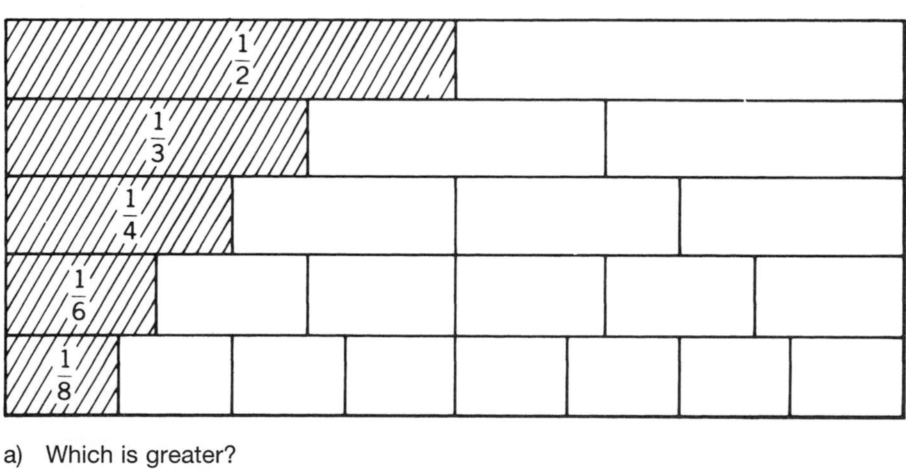

a) Which is greater?

$\frac{1}{2}$ or $\frac{1}{4}$ $\quad$ $\frac{1}{2}$ or $\frac{1}{6}$ $\quad$ $\frac{1}{8}$ or $\frac{1}{4}$ $\quad$ $\frac{1}{6}$ or $\frac{1}{3}$ $\quad$ $\frac{1}{2}$ or $\frac{2}{3}$ $\quad$ $\frac{2}{3}$ or $\frac{5}{6}$ $\quad$ $\frac{3}{8}$ or $\frac{1}{4}$ $\quad$ $\frac{5}{8}$ or $\frac{3}{4}$

b) Which is less?

$\frac{1}{3}$ or $\frac{1}{2}$ $\quad$ $\frac{1}{4}$ or $\frac{1}{6}$ $\quad$ $\frac{1}{8}$ or $\frac{1}{6}$ $\quad$ $\frac{3}{4}$ or $\frac{5}{6}$ $\quad$ $\frac{3}{4}$ or $\frac{2}{3}$ $\quad$ $\frac{1}{2}$ or $\frac{3}{4}$ $\quad$ $\frac{3}{8}$ or $\frac{1}{4}$

c) Which are equivalent?

$\frac{1}{2}$ and $\frac{2}{4}$ $\quad$ $\frac{2}{3}$ and $\frac{3}{4}$ $\quad$ $\frac{3}{8}$ and $\frac{2}{4}$ $\quad$ $\frac{1}{4}$ and $\frac{1}{6}$ $\quad$ $\frac{4}{6}$ and $\frac{2}{3}$ $\quad$ $\frac{6}{8}$ and $\frac{3}{4}$

21. Write the correct fraction for the shaded part of each figure.

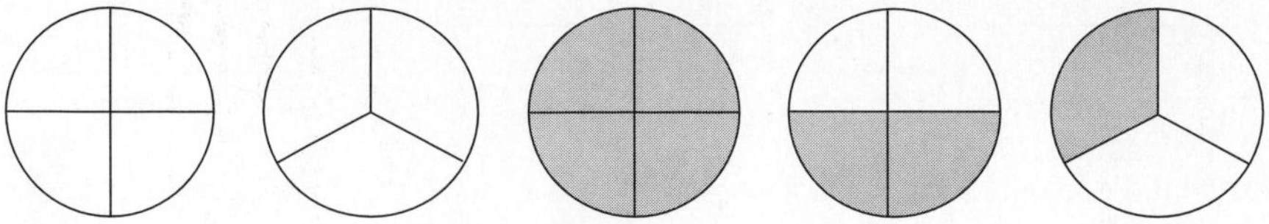

22. Write the correct symbol (<, >, or =) in each ○.

    a) $\frac{1}{3}$ ○ $\frac{1}{4}$ c) $\frac{2}{4}$ ○ $\frac{1}{2}$ e) $\frac{3}{8}$ ○ $\frac{4}{8}$

    b) $\frac{1}{6}$ ○ $\frac{1}{4}$ d) $\frac{2}{4}$ ○ $\frac{1}{8}$ f) $\frac{1}{6}$ ○ $\frac{2}{6}$

23. Write four fractions that are names for, or equal to, 1.

24. Examine these figures. Write a fraction for the shaded part of each figure. Then write a fraction for the unshaded part of each figure.

    a)

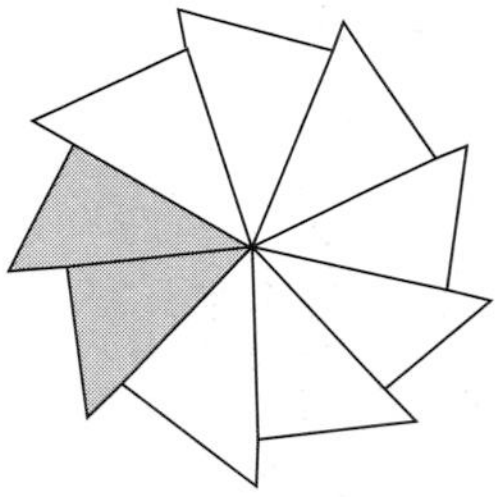

    b)

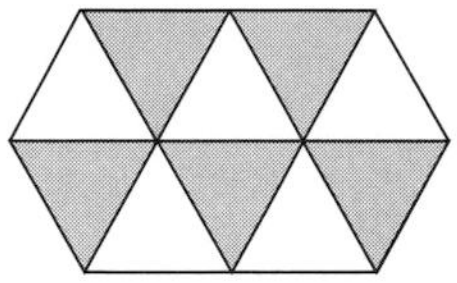

    c)

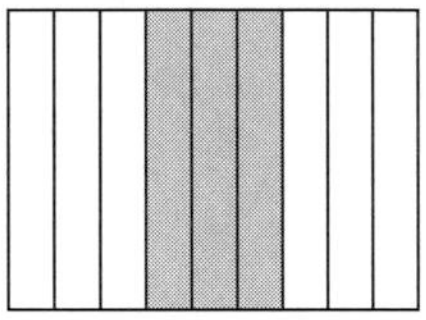

25. Write the correct fraction below each point labeled with a letter.

    a)

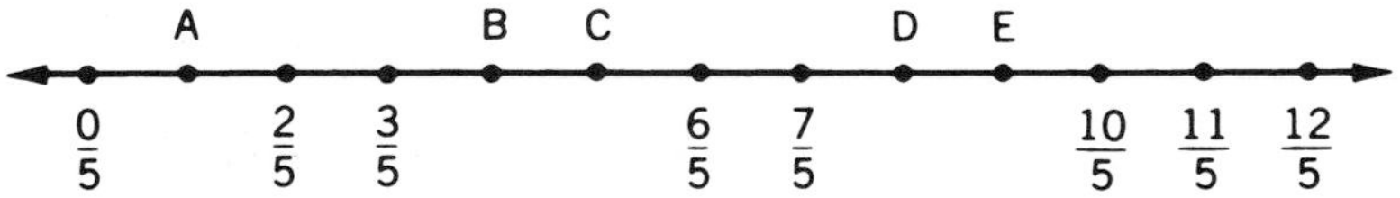

    b)

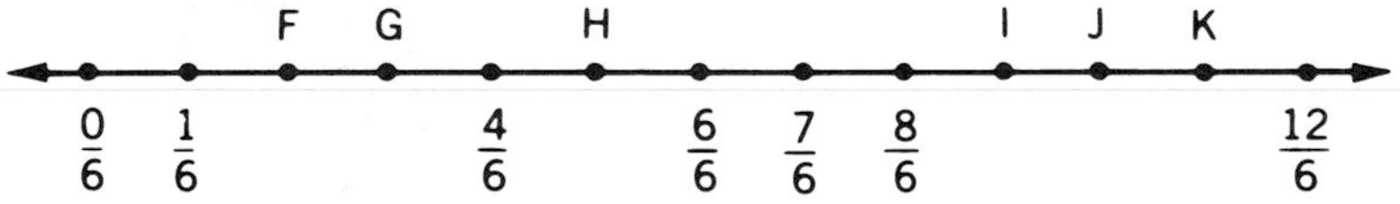

    c)

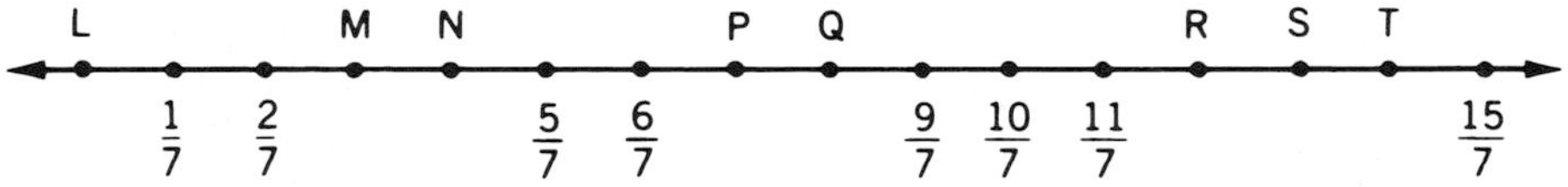

26. Use the number lines in Activity 25 to help you answer these questions.

    a) What whole number is named by $\frac{5}{5}$, $\frac{6}{6}$, and $\frac{7}{7}$?

    b) What whole number is named by $\frac{10}{5}$, $\frac{12}{6}$ and $\frac{14}{7}$?

27. For this activity, cardboard cutouts of circles, squares, rectangles, triangles, and diamond shapes (rhombuses) are cut into halves, thirds, and fourths. Construct a die with the fractions $\frac{1}{2}$, $\frac{1}{3}$, and $\frac{1}{4}$. Roll the die. The person with the largest fraction rolls first. Roll the die in turn, and select a corresponding region to match the die. With the cardboard cutout regions, try to form one whole figure. The first person to get one whole figure can be declared the winner, or the score can be kept and the game played for a certain time period with the high scorer declared the winner. Vary this game by trying to get one of each of the shapes listed.

INSTRUCTIONAL AND ASSESSMENT ACTIVITIES FOR GRADES 5-8

1. Most calculators do not display fractions on the screen, but calculators can be used to change fractions to decimal form, if fractions are interpreted as division. The numerator divided by the denominator will produce a decimal on the display screen. An interesting

discussion can arise from comparing the indicated division (for example, $\frac{1}{3}$ or 1 divided by 3) to the decimal display (.33333333) and the fraction it represents (33333333/100000000).

2. Students in the intermediate grades may wish to examine calculators that do display rational numbers as fractions. They can use these relatively inexpensive calculators to explore equivalent fractions, mixed numerals, improper fractions, naming fractions as decimals, and naming decimals as fractions, as well as to begin as operations on fractions. Study the potential of such a device and the many ways it can assist in the development of fraction concepts.
3. Teachers can use the computer to assist them with both curricular and instructional decisions about rational numbers expressed as fractions. Of course, programs are readily available to provide drill and practice for the individual child or small groups. Perhaps more importantly, software that promotes problem solving and concept development is also obtainable. Much of this software makes use of the computer's graphics and animation capabilities to model fractions rather than emphasize the symbolic notation. Search out available resources and compile information on software packages that may prove useful.
4. Examine a ruler or measuring cup, and discuss how each is marked and why.
5. Give the students paper plates, graph paper, or construction paper; then ask them to shade various fractional regions of the materials.
6. Using several rectangular regions with the same dimensions, have the student find as many ways as possible to illustrate a given fraction (for instance, $\frac{1}{4}$).

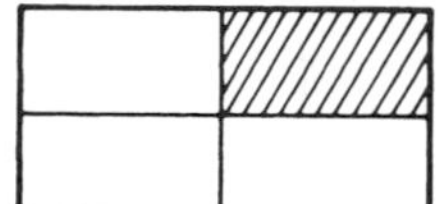
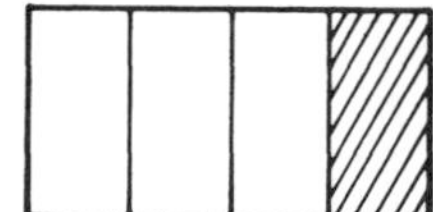
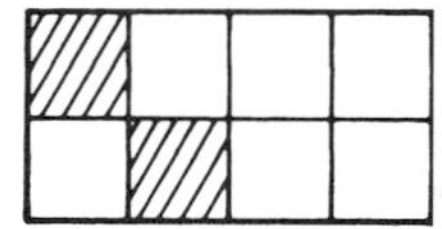

7. On graph paper, have the students model $\frac{1}{2} = \frac{2}{4}$, $\frac{2}{3} = \frac{4}{6}$, $\frac{1}{4} = \frac{2}{8}$, and $\frac{2}{5} = \frac{4}{10}$. This requires the students to think at a sophisticated level.

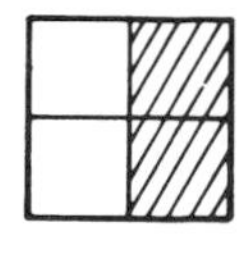
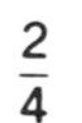
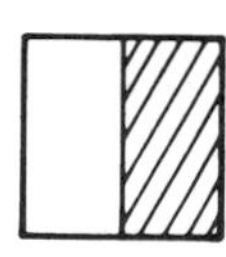

$$\frac{2}{4} = \frac{1}{2}$$

8. For this demonstration activity, draw a number line on the chalkboard. Label the points.

a) Which point is $\frac{1}{2}$ the distance between points A and I?
b) Which point is $\frac{1}{4}$ the distance between points E and I?
c) Which point is $\frac{3}{4}$ the distance between points A and I?
d) Which point is $\frac{6}{8}$ the distance between points A and I?
e) Which point is $\frac{4}{8}$ the distance between points A and I?
f) The distance from C to D can be named by what fraction?
g) The distance from E to G can be named by what fraction?

This activity can be used with sketches of number lines that include points labeled with various sets of fractions. Other questions can be included to reinforce the concept. Children should be given the opportunity to pose questions of their own to other members of the group.

9. Complete the following table.

Group	Number of the Group	Parts Shaded	Fraction Shaded	Parts Not Shaded	Fraction Not Shaded
a) ○●○●○					
b) ▲▽▲▽▲▽▲					
c) ○●○●○○					
d) ●○●○●○●○●○					
e) ⬢⬡⬡⬡					
f) ○●●○○●●○					
g) ●●○●●●○●●●○					

10. Hand each child a page of number lines. Give the children the name of the first and last points on each number line. Have the children name all the points marked on each line.

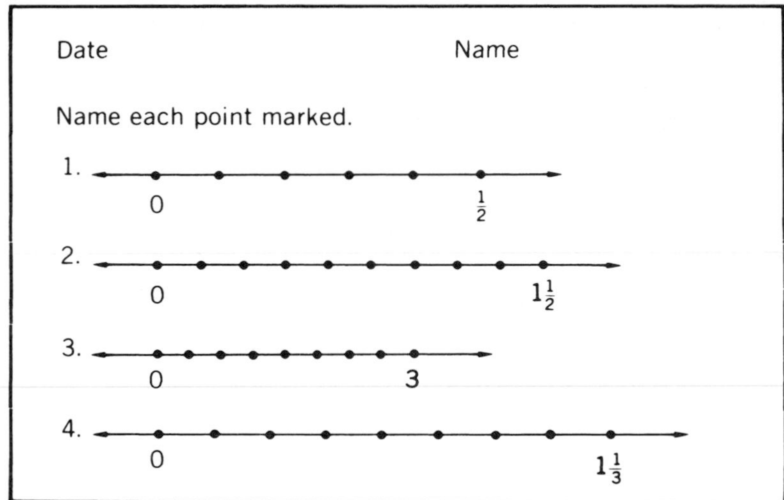

Date
Name
Name each point marked.
1.
0
$\frac{1}{2}$
2.
0
$1\frac{1}{2}$
3.
0
3
4.
0
$1\frac{1}{3}$

11. Construct a deck of about sixty cards. Write a fraction on each card. You may start by using fractions with the denominators of 2, 3, 4, 6, and 8. Five cards are dealt to each player and are placed face up in front of the player in the order in which they are dealt. For example:

$\boxed{\frac{5}{8}}$ $\boxed{\frac{1}{4}}$ $\boxed{\frac{5}{6}}$ $\boxed{\frac{1}{8}}$ $\boxed{\frac{3}{4}}$

Each player draws a card or takes a discard from the pile in order. The first person to have five fractions in order from least to greatest is the winner. For instance, the player's first draw is $\boxed{\frac{2}{3}}$, so he or she discards $\boxed{\frac{1}{8}}$

$\frac{5}{8}$	$\frac{1}{4}$	$\frac{5}{6}$	$\frac{2}{3}$	$\frac{3}{4}$

The fraction $\frac{5}{8}$ must be replaced by some fraction less than $\frac{1}{4}$, and $\frac{5}{6}$ must be replaced by some fraction more than $\frac{1}{4}$ and less than $\frac{2}{3}$ for the player to win.

12. Identify a pattern and complete the sequence.

    a) 3, $2\frac{1}{2}$, 2, ____, ____, ____, ____ c) 8, 4, 2, 1, ____, ____, ____, ____

    b) 1, $1\frac{1}{2}$, 2, ____, ____, ____, ____ d) 18, 12, 8, $5\frac{1}{3}$, ____, ____, ____

13. Arrange the fractions in each of the following groups of fractional numbers in order from least to greatest:

    a) $\frac{1}{2}, \frac{6}{6}, \frac{6}{3}, \frac{3}{4}$ b) $\frac{2}{3}, \frac{3}{2}, \frac{4}{3}, \frac{3}{4}$ c) $\frac{9}{10}, \frac{2}{5}, \frac{2}{10}, \frac{3}{6}$ d) $\frac{5}{8}, \frac{2}{3}, \frac{5}{6}, \frac{3}{4}$

14. Draw a number line or diagram, if you need it, to help you fill in the blanks.

    a) $\frac{1}{2}$ is 4 times as great as _____.

    b) $\frac{1}{4}$ is _____ times as great as $\frac{1}{8}$.

    c) $\frac{1}{8}$ is _____ times as great as $\frac{1}{16}$.

    d) $\frac{1}{5}$ is 2 times as great as _____.

    e) $\frac{1}{2}$ is 5 times as great as _____.

    f) $\frac{1}{3}$ is 3 times as great as _____.

15. The following activity can be used to reinforce the students' understanding of equivalent fractions. Construct a deck of 42 cards with the following sets of fractions: halves, thirds, fourths, fifths, sixths, eighths, and tenths. One card should also be constructed for each of the whole numbers 1, 2, 3, and 4. The cards are then $\frac{1}{2}, \frac{2}{2}; \frac{1}{3}, \frac{2}{3}, \frac{3}{3}; \frac{1}{4}, \frac{2}{4}, \frac{3}{4}, \frac{4}{4}; \frac{1}{5}, \frac{2}{5}, \frac{3}{5}, \frac{4}{5}, \frac{5}{5}; \frac{1}{6}, \frac{2}{6}, \frac{3}{6}, \frac{4}{6}, \frac{5}{6}, \frac{6}{6}; \frac{1}{8}, \frac{2}{8}, \frac{3}{8}, \frac{4}{8}, \frac{5}{8}, \frac{6}{8}, \frac{7}{8}, \frac{8}{8}; \frac{1}{10}, \frac{2}{10}, \frac{3}{10}, \frac{4}{10}, \frac{5}{10}, \frac{6}{10}, \frac{7}{10}, \frac{8}{10}, \frac{9}{10}, \frac{10}{10}$; 1, 2, 3, 4. Each player is dealt seven cards. The deck is placed in the middle of the playing area, and a card off the deck is turned face up. Players take turns playing their cards. A card with the same denominator or a card with an equivalent fraction is discarded on top of the card that is face up, on the discard pile. If a player has a card with a whole number, he or she can play the card and change the denominator to be played next. If a player does not have a card that can be played, he or she must draw from the deck and lose a turn. The game ends when one player gets rid of all of his or her cards.

16. Using graph paper, draw diagrams of rectangular or square regions to model each fraction.

    a) $\frac{1}{4}$ b) $\frac{2}{3}$ c) $\frac{5}{6}$ d) $\frac{7}{8}$ e) $\frac{3}{5}$ f) $\frac{5}{2}$

17. Write ten fractions for the number 1.

18. Using many names for 1, generate a group of equivalent fractions for each.

Names for 1	$\frac{2}{2}$	$\frac{3}{3}$	$\frac{4}{4}$	$\frac{5}{5}$	$\frac{6}{6}$	$\frac{7}{7}$	$\frac{8}{8}$	$\frac{9}{9}$
Fractions for $\frac{1}{2}$								
Fractions for $\frac{2}{3}$								
Fractions for $\frac{3}{4}$								

19. Have each child make two sets of multiple strips (as shown) for each number 1 through 10. Cut the strips apart. Consider the fraction $\frac{2}{3}$. If you place the *two* strip over the *three* strip,

you have a set of equivalent fractions that names the fractional number $\frac{2}{3}$. A set of equivalent fractions can be shown for fractions with denominators of less than 10 by putting the appropriate two strips together.

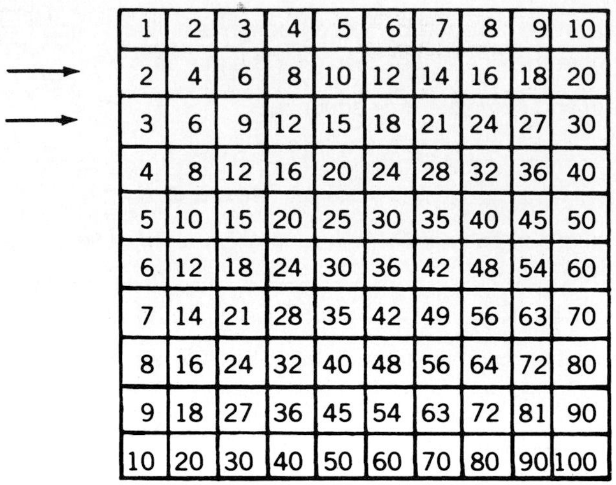

1	2	3	4	5	6	7	8	9	10
2	4	6	8	10	12	14	16	18	20
3	6	9	12	15	18	21	24	27	30
4	8	12	16	20	24	28	32	36	40
5	10	15	20	25	30	35	40	45	50
6	12	18	24	30	36	42	48	54	60
7	14	21	28	35	42	49	56	63	70
8	16	24	32	40	48	56	64	72	80
9	18	27	36	45	54	63	72	81	90
10	20	30	40	50	60	70	80	90	100

20. Which pairs of fractions are equivalent?

a) $\frac{9}{25}, \frac{4}{10}$ c) $\frac{8}{10}, \frac{40}{50}$ e) $\frac{17}{25}, \frac{9}{12}$

b) $\frac{13}{16}, \frac{9}{10}$ d) $\frac{11}{22}, \frac{72}{144}$ f) $\frac{2}{6}, \frac{20}{60}$

21. Place the correct relation symbol (<, =, or >) in each circle.

a) $\frac{2}{3} \bigcirc \frac{5}{6}$ c) $\frac{3}{8} \bigcirc \frac{3}{4}$ e) $\frac{4}{5} \bigcirc \frac{4}{7}$ g) $\frac{2}{5} \bigcirc \frac{4}{10}$

b) $\frac{3}{4} \bigcirc \frac{6}{8}$ d) $\frac{8}{15} \bigcirc \frac{8}{14}$ f) $\frac{0}{3} \bigcirc \frac{0}{6}$ h) $\frac{2}{3} \bigcirc \frac{3}{4}$

22. Prepare a set of cards and a call sheet with the fractions $\frac{1}{2}, \frac{1}{3}, \frac{2}{3}, \frac{1}{4}, \frac{3}{4}, \frac{1}{5}, \frac{2}{5}, \frac{3}{5}, \frac{4}{5}, \frac{1}{6}, \frac{5}{6}, \frac{1}{8}, \frac{3}{8}, \frac{5}{8}, \frac{7}{8}, \frac{1}{9}, \frac{2}{9}, \frac{4}{9}, \frac{5}{9}, \frac{7}{9}, \frac{8}{9}$. Prepare bingo cards with equivalent fractions of $\frac{2}{4}, \frac{3}{6}, \frac{4}{8}, \ldots; \frac{2}{6}, \frac{3}{9}, \frac{4}{12}, \ldots$; and so on. Play proceeds according to the usual bingo rules.

23. Complete the following table:

Fraction	Prime Factors	Fraction in Simplest Form
$\frac{10}{12}$	$\frac{2 \times 5}{2 \times 6}$	$\frac{5}{6}$
$\frac{27}{36}$		
$\frac{78}{117}$		
$\frac{85}{51}$		

24. Complete the following chart. Use the example as a guide.

Fraction	Factors of the Numerator	Factors of the Denominator	Greatest Common Factor	Simplest Form
$\frac{6}{8}$	2, 3, 6, 1	2, 4, 8, 1	2	$\frac{3}{4}$
$\frac{8}{12}$				
$\frac{5}{15}$				
$\frac{14}{10}$				
$\frac{4}{3}$				
$\frac{16}{9}$				

25. Students in the upper elementary grades can use the calculator to explore the notion of a fraction as an indicated division. When discussing whole number division, children should be exposed to notations such as "12 divided by 3," "12 ÷ 3," and "$\frac{12}{3}$." This last form leads in a natural way to considering $\frac{3}{4}$ and "3 divided by 4." On a standard calculator, this can be keyed in as

   [3] [÷] [4] [=]

   yielding an answer of .75. (Children who have been introduced to decimal notation can readily see that "three divided by four" = .75 = $\frac{75}{100}$ = $\frac{3}{4}$ or "three-fourths.")

26. The calculator can serve as a cursory introduction to decimal notation by first emphasizing the whole number, place-value pattern in which each place to the immediate right is one-tenth the value of the place to its immediate left. That is, the hundreds place is one-tenth the value of the thousands place, the ones place is one-tenth the value of the tens place, and so on. This pattern extends to the right of the decimal point, with the tenths place having one-tenth the value of the ones place, the hundredths place having one-tenth the value of the tenths place, and so on. With this brief introduction, an upper-grade student can be given, for example, a one-, two-, or three-place decimal and be asked to write it as a fraction with a denominator of 10, 100, or 1000. Then the student should write this fraction in simplified form and enter it into the calculator as an indicated division. If the student successfully completes these steps, the answer to the indicated division should be the initial decimal.

27. Students in the upper grades should certainly explore the use of calculators that can display rational numbers in fraction form. An overhead projector version exists that can be effectively used for large-group discussion of such topics as simplifying fractions, generating equivalent fractions, rewriting improper fractions as mixed numerals (and vice versa), rewriting decimals as fractions (and vice versa), and, at this point, exploring addition and subtraction of fractions with the same denominators. (More challenging addition and subtraction, as well as multiplication and division, will be examined in Chapter 11).

Suggested Readings

Akaishi, A., & Saul, M. (1991). Exploring, learning, sharing: Vignettes from the classroom. *The Arithmetic Teacher, 39*(3).

Bezuk, N. S. (1988). Fractions in the early childhood mathematics curriculum. *The Arithmetic Teacher, 35*(6).

Bright, G. W., Behr, M. J., Post, T. R., & Wachsmuth, I. (1988). Identifying fractions on number lines. *Journal for Research in Mathematics Education, 19*(3).

Buschman, L. (1993). The versatile number line. *The Arithmetic Teacher, 40*(8).

Conaway, B., & Midkiff, R. B. (1994). Connecting literature, language, and fractions. *The Arithmetic Teacher, 41*(8).

Cooper, R. (1994). *Alternative math techniques instructional guide.* Bryn Mawr, PA: Center for Alternative Learning.

Cramer, K., & Post, T. (1987). Children's strategies in ordering rational numbers. *The Arithmetic Teacher, 35*(2).

Esty, W. W. (1991). The least common denominator. *The Arithmetic Teacher, 39*(4).

Ewbank, W. A. (1987). LCM—Let's put it in its place. *The Arithmetic Teacher, 35*(3).

Hiebert, J., & Behr, M., (Eds.). (1988). *Number concepts and operations in the middle grades.* Reston, VA: National Council of Teachers of Mathematics.

Hope, J. A., Reys, B. J., & Reys, R. E. (1988). *Mental math in junior high.* Palo Alto, CA: Dale Seymour Publications.

Hunting, R. P., & Sharpley, C. F. (1988). Fraction knowledge in preschool children. *Journal for Research in Mathematics Education, 19*(2).

Lappan, G., Fitzgerald, W., Winter, M. J., & Phillips, E. (1986). *Similarity and equivalent fractions* (Middle Grades Mathematics Project). Menlo Park, CA: Addison-Wesley.

Lilburn, P., & Rawson, P. (1994). *Let's talk math: Encouraging children to explore ideas.* Portsmouth, NH: Heinemann.

Mack, N. K. (1990). Learning fractions with understanding: Building on informal knowledge. *Journal for Research in Mathematics Education, 21*(1).

National Council of Teachers of Mathematics. (1978). *Developing computational skills.* 1978 Yearbook. Reston, VA: NCTM.

Payne, J. N., & Towsley, A. E. (1990). Implications of NCTM's standards for teaching fractions and decimals. *The Arithmetic Teacher, 37*(8).

Post, T. R. (1989). Fractions and other rational numbers. *The Arithmetic Teacher, 37*(1).

Pothier, Y., & Sawada, D. (1990). Partitioning: An approach to fractions. *The Arithmetic Teacher, 38*(4).

Rees, J. M. (1987). Two-sided pies: Help for improper fractions and mixed numbers. *The Arithmetic Teacher, 35*(4).

Rowan, T. E., & Morrow, L. J. (1993). *Implementing the K-8 curriculum and evaluation standards: Readings from The Arithmetic Teacher. Implementing the K-8 curriculum and evaluation standards.* Reston, VA: National Council of Teachers of Mathematics.

Shilgalis, T. W. (1994). Are most fractions reduced? *The Mathematics Teacher, 87.*

Steffe, L. P. & Olive, J. (1991). The problem of fractions in the elementary school. *The Arithmetic Teacher, 38*(9).

Quinter, A. H. (1987). Helping children understand ratios. *The Arithmetic Teacher, 34*(9).

Witherspoon, M. L. (1993). Fractions: In search of meaning. *The Arithmetic Teacher, 40*(8).

Woodward, E., and Gibbs, V. (1990). Finding least common multiples with a calculator. *School Science and Mathematics, 90*(6).

Zazkis, R., & Khoury, H. A. (1993). Place value and rational number representations: Problem solving in the unfamiliar domain of nondecimals. *Focus on Learning Problems in Mathematics, 15.*

Zeman, M. (1991). The part-whole schema in the conceptualization of fractions. *Journal of Mathematical Behavior, 10.*

Chapter 11

Rational Numbers Expressed as Fractions: Operations

Overview

At this point in their mathematical development, children have studied the operations of addition and multiplication and the inverse operations, subtraction and division, using whole numbers. The students should have the basic facts of addition and subtraction memorized and the basic facts of multiplication and division nearly memorized. The basic structure (properties) should be understood and operable. With the introduction of operations on fractions, we are applying what the students already know to another set of numbers—an extension of known concepts to an extension of our number system.

Finding an effective approach to addition and subtraction of fractions has been a difficult task for some teachers. Rather than trying to develop an understanding of the concepts, we too often resort to providing a mechanical technique that will obtain a correct answer. Explaining several examples and providing practice has been viewed as an acceptable technique for teaching both multiplication and division of fractions. The question, then, centers on whether this provides the students with a solid foundation for mathematics. We need to reiterate that concrete models must be used to help children visualize what is really happening when they multiply and divide fractions.

Most adults have a vague understanding of what division of fractions means in the real world and it is true that the occasions to use division of fractions in the real world are rare. This text suggests models that clearly illustrate what the division of fractions means. However, it becomes very difficult to model examples other than the most simple ones. Yet, the concepts can be clearer after seeing a few examples solved by manipulating sectors of circular shaped regions.

Children need many examples of addition, subtraction, multiplication, and division of fractions before they can perform these operations themselves. Such examples should be on concrete, semiconcrete, and semiabstract levels first, in that order. Real objects should be used to show parts of groups and regions. The number line is also an excellent model to help children understand addition of fractions.

Children need many experiences with diagrams—shading fractional parts and determining the intersection of these parts. It is important to remember that as long as children need to refer to diagrams to understand a concept, they should be encouraged to do so. It is also important to allow children who already understand a concept to apply what they have learned; holding them back or barraging them with pictures can be just as harmful as pushing them into abstractions before they are ready.

Children should not be presented with shortcuts to operations with fractions before they completely understand how the operations work; this can confuse them and rob them of the joy of discovering for themselves why the operations function as they do. If they understand the basic concepts involved, they can develop true proficiency in working with fractions.

SAMPLE LESSON PLAN—"SWEET FRACTIONS"

Intermediate Developmental Lesson

Goal:

Apply repeated addition concept of multiplication to fraction situations.

Objective:

The students will:

- Explore solution strategies for repeated addition with fractions.
- Connect the solution process to algorithmic procedures.

Prerequisite Learning and/or Experiences:

- Exploration of fractions with regions, number lines, and sets.
- Conceptual understanding of multiplication as repeated addition.
- Experience with problem-solving strategies which include modeling and drawing.

Materials:

Per individual:

- paper and pencil
- access to fraction manipulatives

Per class:

- one bag of regular molasses cookies (1 cup of each sweetener)
- one bag of reduced-calorie molasses cookies ($\frac{2}{3}$ cup of each sweetener)

Recipe: Molasses Cookies

1 $\left(\frac{2}{3}\right)$ cup molasses	pinch of salt 1 cup shortening
1 $\left(\frac{2}{3}\right)$ cup granulated sugar	1 Tbsp. soda dissolved in 1 cup boiling water
1 $\left(\frac{2}{3}\right)$ cup brown sugar	1 tsp. vanilla
1 tsp. allspice	

Cream shortening with sugars and add molasses. Next, add the soda dissolved in boiling water, allspice, salt, and vanilla. Add enough flour (approximately 5 cups) to roll into one-inch balls. Flatten and place on cookie sheet sprayed with vegetable oil. Bake at 350° for 8-10 minutes. Let cool on cookie sheet before removing. Yields 5-6 dozen.

Procedures:

Motivational Introduction

Hold up two bags of homemade molasses cookies. Tell the students that one bag holds regular cookies and the other bag holds reduced calorie cookies. Instead of the typical amounts of sweeteners, you cut back on the sweet ingredients (molasses, brown sugar and granulated sugar) in order to reduce the calories. Tell the class that you need their help to determine the total amount of sweeteners in each batch of cookies. After generating the sweetener information, they will conduct a taste test comparison of the regular and reduced-calorie cookies.

1. Pose the following question: "If a regular batch of molasses cookies were baked with 1 cup granulated sugar, 1 cup brown sugar, and 1 cup molasses, how much total sweetener was used?" Have students think about potential solution strategies and share their thoughts with a neighboring student.
2. Have students discuss their ideas. Most students will readily say that 3 cups of sweeteners were used. Be sure students defend their reasoning. Typical responses will probably be $1 + 1 + 1 = 3$ or $3 \times 1 = 3$. Ask why both explanations are correct. Lead discussion to the interpretation of repeated addition as multiplication.

Developmental Activity

3. Now pose the following question: "If this calorie-reduced batch of molasses cookies was made with $\frac{2}{3}$ cup brown sugar, $\frac{2}{3}$ cup granulated sugar, and $\frac{2}{3}$ cup of molasses as sweeteners, how much total sweetener is used? Have individual students solve the problem situation. Encourage the use of pictures and drawings as well as multiplication as repeated addition.
4. While students are working, walk around the classroom and observe students' responses. Be sure to talk with students about their process for

solving this particular situation. Begin to determine a potential student-sharing sequence which will begin with a least sophisticated response and ends with the most sophisticated response. Sophisticated responses are those in which a multiplicative mathematical sentence are connected to a representational model.

Culminating Activity

5. Have students share solution strategies. Remember, sharing should proceed in the sequence determined in step 4. Look for some of the following solution strategies:

   Kevin: Thought about 3 sets of $\frac{2}{3}$. Used drawings of rectangular regions.

   Shawn: Wrote the mathematical sentence $3 \times \frac{2}{3} = \square$. Found three groups of $\frac{2}{3}$ by adding $\frac{2}{3} + \frac{2}{3} + \frac{2}{3}$.

   Nicole: Wrote the same mathematical sentence as Shawn. Used the number line to find the answer of 2 cups.

   Rhonda: Rewrote the mathematical sentence as 3 × 2 thirds. Worked the problem like whole number multiplication—3 × 2 thirds is 6 thirds or $\frac{6}{3}$.

   Dennis: Found the solution of 2 cups with the number line. Studied the mathematical sentence $3 \times \frac{2}{3} = \square$. Determined a numeric solution by multiplying the whole number times the numerator for an answer of 6 and then dividing by the denominator of 3 for a final answer of 2.

   Be ready to discuss why $\frac{6}{3}$ and 2 are acceptable solutions as well as which one is most appropriate for this problem situation.

6. Use Dennis' solution to develop a workable algorithmic procedure of whole number times numerator divided by denominator. Possibly call it "Dennis' Algorithm" to instill a sense of ownership and pride in discovery.

Extensions

Conclude with a taste test comparison of regular molasses cookies made with 3 cups of sweeteners and reduced-calorie molasses cookies made with 2 cups of sweeteners. Use the data to generate a graph. Be sure to consider three potential categories—regular, reduced-calorie, or no difference/taste the same.

To explore the understanding of fractions with the set model pose the following problem situation: "Mom bought a 6-pack of soda pop. After school Ronnie and his friends drank $\frac{2}{3}$ of the soda pop. Mom wants to know if there is enough soda pop left for her and Dad to have one soda apiece. How much soda pop did Ron and his friends drink?" Have students solve the problem situation using models and drawings.

Compare their representational solutions to a slight modification of Dennis' alogorithm. This time multiply the numerator times the whole number (instead of the whole number times the numerator) and divide by the demoninator. Have students discuss why this modification is mathematically acceptable. Lead discussion toward the application of the commutative property for multiplication.

Student Assessment/Evaluation:

Observe students' solutions. Carefully determine how the concept of multiplication as repeated addition is applied to both the representations (models, pictures, drawings) and mathematical sentences. Use this information to determine a sequence (least to most sophisticated application) for sharing purposes. If no one discovers a multiplicative algorithmic procedure for fractions, then be ready to ask leading questions such that the class generates a workable procedure.

INSTRUCTIONAL AND ASSESSMENT ACTIVITIES FOR GRADES K-4

1. In the primary grades we use activities to prepare children to work with fractions; they should not, of course, be expected to perform operations with abstract fraction symbols. Instead, the children should manipulate concrete objects to show the relations involved in discovering that equivalent fractions exist, how they relate to one another, and how they compare. Provide models, such as Cuisenaire rods and base ten blocks, to *prepare* children to add, subtract, multiply, and divide fractions.

2. Discuss with the children the idea of one-half of a class. After several discussions they should begin to realize that one-half and one-half make up the entire class. This is particularly apparent when you choose teams for games.

3. Discuss how many of certain pieces of something make up the whole—that is, that it takes 3 one-thirds (for instance) to make one whole item.

4. Give children groups of objects and ask them to show one-fourth of the group.

5. Using the fraction kit described in Chapter 10, ask the child to model:

   a) $\frac{1}{3} + \frac{1}{3}$ b) $\left(\frac{1}{3} + \frac{1}{3}\right) + \frac{1}{3}$ c) $\frac{1}{2} + \frac{1}{4}$ d) $\frac{3}{6} + \frac{1}{2}$

6. Give a child two egg cartons, each half full of counters. Ask the child what part of each egg carton is full. Have the child put the "eggs" all in one carton. Now ask the child what part of the egg carton is full. The teacher should write the mathematical sentence $\frac{1}{2} + \frac{1}{2} = 1$.
7. Give children egg cartons and counters and ask them to show one-half dozen. Have them model $\frac{1}{4}$ of the group of 12 counters.
8. Using a ruler marked in eighths of an inch, have the child add $\frac{1}{8}$ and $\frac{5}{8}$.
9. Divide a paper plate into sixths. Color $\frac{2}{6}$ blue and $\frac{3}{6}$ green. Show that:

   a) $\frac{2}{6} + \frac{3}{6} = \frac{5}{6}$ b) $\frac{6}{6} - \frac{5}{6} = \frac{1}{6}$ c) $\frac{5}{6} - \frac{2}{6} = \frac{3}{6} = \frac{1}{2}$ d) $\frac{5}{6} - \frac{3}{6} = \frac{2}{6} = \frac{1}{3}$
10. Using the fraction kit described in Chapter 10, have the children model:

   a) $\frac{5}{8} - \frac{2}{8}$ b) $\frac{1}{2} - \frac{1}{4}$ c) $\frac{5}{6} - \frac{1}{2}$
11. Have the children study and discuss a simple addition example such as the following:

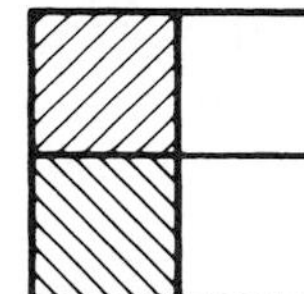

How many fourths shaded  ?

How many fourths shaded ?

How many fourths shaded and ?

   Relate how $\frac{1}{4} + \frac{1}{4} = \frac{2}{4}$ records the idea.
12. Children who have used the number line as a model for addition of whole numbers will find little difficulty in relating it to fractions. For example:

$$\frac{1}{2} + \frac{1}{2} = \square$$

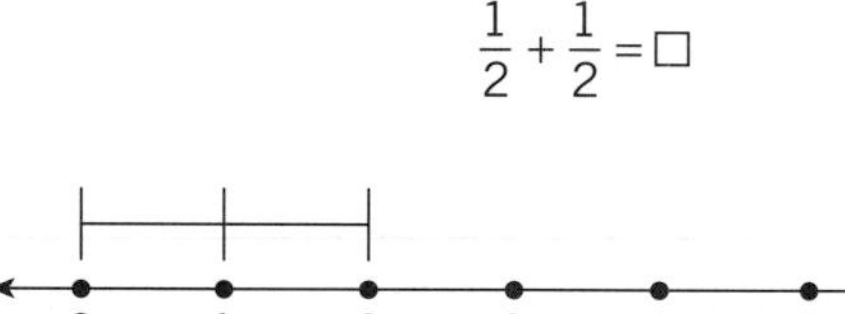

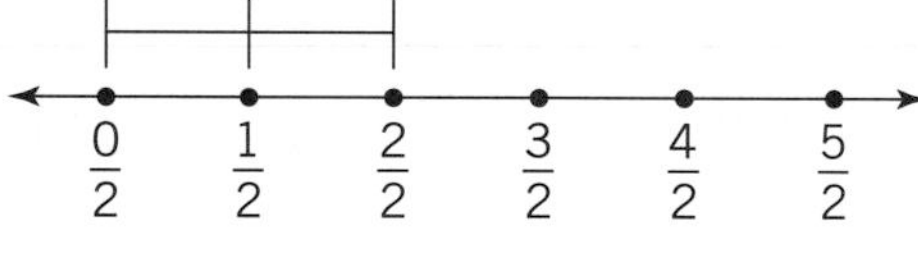

$$\frac{1}{2} + \frac{1}{2} = \frac{2}{2} = 1$$

13. Make number line diagrams to help solve the following examples:

   a) $\frac{1}{4} + \frac{1}{4} = \square$ c) $\frac{2}{4} + \frac{1}{4} = \square$ e) $\frac{3}{4} - \frac{1}{4} = \square$ g) $\frac{4}{6} + \frac{1}{6} = \square$

   b) $\frac{1}{6} - \frac{1}{6} = \square$ d) $\frac{2}{6} + \frac{1}{6} = \square$ f) $\frac{3}{6} + \frac{1}{6} = \square$ h) $\frac{5}{6} - \frac{1}{6} = \square$
14. Find the differences.

   a) $9\frac{6}{7} - 3\frac{2}{7}$ b) $5\frac{4}{9} - 1\frac{1}{9}$ c) $6\frac{13}{15} - 4\frac{11}{15}$ d) $10\frac{8}{11} - 5\frac{2}{11}$ e) $3\frac{17}{20} - 2\frac{3}{20}$

INSTRUCTIONAL AND ASSESSMENT ACTIVITIES FOR GRADES 5-8

1. Children who have had experience using measuring cups will be ready to use such measuring cups as models for addition of rational numbers expressed as fractions. For example:

$$\frac{1}{4} + \frac{1}{4} = \frac{2}{4} = \frac{1}{2}$$

   1 fourth
   + 1 fourth

   2 fourths $= \frac{2}{4} = \frac{1}{2}$

2. Use the following number line to help you find the sums. Label the points on the number line to show halves, fifths, and tenths.

a) $\frac{3}{10} + \frac{4}{10} = \square$ c) $\frac{7}{10} - \frac{3}{10} = \square$ e) $\frac{1}{2} + \frac{1}{5} = \square$

b) $\frac{2}{5} - \frac{2}{5} = \square$ d) $\frac{0}{5} + \frac{3}{5} = \square$ f) $\frac{2}{5} - \frac{3}{10} = \square$

3. Draw diagrams to help you complete each equation.

a) $\frac{1}{4} + \frac{1}{2} = \square$ d) $\frac{5}{8} + \frac{1}{4} = \square$ g) $\frac{1}{2} + \frac{1}{3} = \square$

b) $\frac{3}{8} + \frac{2}{8} = \square$ e) $\frac{1}{2} + \frac{0}{4} = \square$ h) $\frac{5}{8} + \square = \frac{3}{4}$

c) $\frac{1}{2} + \square = \frac{4}{6}$ f) $\frac{2}{4} + \square = \frac{3}{4}$ i) $\frac{1}{6} + \square = \frac{1}{3}$

4. Find the missing addends. Draw a number line diagram for each example.

a) ________ $+ \frac{2}{4} = \frac{3}{4}$ c) $\frac{2}{5} +$ ________ $= \frac{5}{5}$

b) $\frac{3}{4} - \frac{2}{4} =$ ________ d) $\frac{5}{5} - \frac{2}{5} =$ ________

5. Write the fraction that represents the shaded area. The unit region is the large rectangular region. A, B, C, and D represent the number of shaded squares in the corresponding rows.

A ________ B ________ C ________ D ________

A + B + C + D = ________

a) Write an addition sentence expressing the sum of A and B.
b) Write a subtraction sentence using A and B.
c) Write an addition sentence using C and D.
d) Write a subtraction sentence using C and D.

6. Allow children to test addition of fractions for commutativity and associativity. Let them discuss their results and justify their reasoning. For example:

Is $\frac{1}{4} + \frac{2}{4} = \frac{2}{4} + \frac{1}{4}$?

Is $\left(\frac{1}{5} + \frac{2}{5}\right) + \frac{2}{5} = \frac{1}{5} + \left(\frac{2}{5} + \frac{2}{5}\right)$?

7. Emphasis on the inverse relation is evident in the use of equations with missing addends. For example:

$$\frac{3}{5} - \frac{1}{5} = \square \text{ or } \frac{1}{5} + \square = \frac{3}{5}$$

8. Children in the intermediate grades should be able to translate some simple problem situations that involve fractions into mathematical sentences. Write a mathematical sentence for each problem found on the following page; then solve the problems.

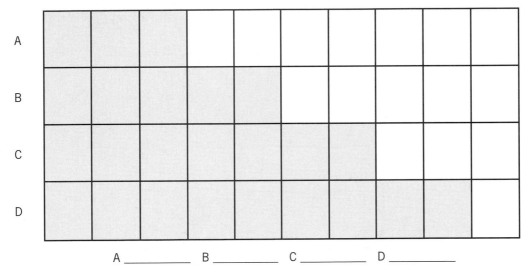

a) It took Lewis $2\frac{1}{2}$ hours to mow Mrs. Huffie's lawn. It took him $1\frac{3}{4}$ hours to mow Mrs. Martin's lawn. How much more time did he spend on Mrs. Huffie's lawn?

b) Linda's library books weighed $2\frac{1}{4}$ pounds. Diane's weighed $3\frac{1}{4}$ pounds. Henry carried both stacks of books for the girls. How many pounds of books did he carry?

c) Fred fed $2\frac{1}{4}$ bags of peanuts to the elephants and $3\frac{3}{4}$ bags to the monkeys. He kept 1 bag for himself. How many bags of peanuts did Fred buy?

d) Michelle picked 3 rows of corn on Monday and 8 rows on Tuesday. There were 18 rows of corn in the garden. What fractional part of the corn did she have left to pick?

9. Make a set of 50 cards about 2 inches by 3 inches. Write one fraction on each card. Some fractions may be repeated. Shuffle the cards and deal five to each player. The object is to put together a set of fraction cards that add up to 1. Two or more cards may be used. During a turn a child draws a card and lays down as many sets of cards that add up to 1 as possible. The pupil who has the most sets wins.

10. Use a file folder to make a game board as shown. Using two different colors of cardboard, make about 25 cards of each color, each just a little smaller than the squares drawn on the board. On the cards, write addition and subtraction examples whose answers are the same as the fractions written on the board. Two individuals may play the game. Randomly place the cards face down. One player uses one color set, and the other player uses the other. Players take turns drawing one of their own cards, solving it, and placing it on the game board on its proper answer The players check each other. Once a card is placed on the game board and judged correct, it cannot be moved to view the fraction beneath the card. If the other player has a card with the same answer, that card is placed on top of the first player's card. Each player tries to get three of his or her cards in a row or column. The first to do so wins the game.

Write sums on board

$\frac{5}{8}$	$\frac{2}{3}$	$\frac{3}{8}$
$\frac{1}{3}$	$\frac{1}{6}$	$\frac{1}{2}$
$\frac{7}{8}$	$\frac{3}{4}$	$\frac{5}{6}$

11. Use sponge-rubber or wooden cubes to make a set of dice with fractions written on the faces.

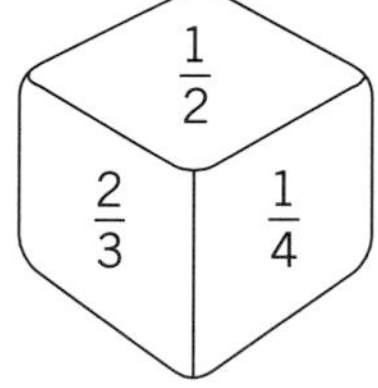

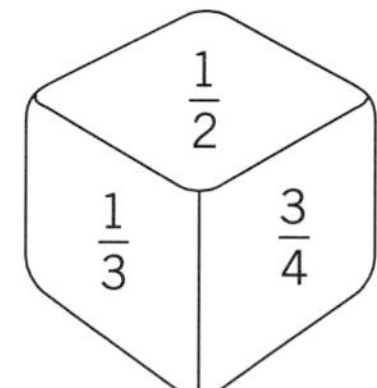

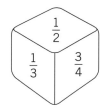

Have the children roll the dice and use the fractions on the top side as addends to find the sum.

12. Use the dice from Activity 11. After rolling them, the child should compare the two and then subtract the lesser value from the greater.

13. In the intermediate grades the major emphasis is on preparing students to multiply fractions and on multiplication examples in which one of the factors is a whole number. The children need to understand that when we find $\frac{1}{5}$ of a group, we are partitioning or separating the

group into five equivalent groups. If we separate a group of 20 objects into five equivalent groups, each group will contain 4 objects. We therefore say that $\frac{1}{5}$ of 20 = 4 or $\frac{1}{5} \times 20 = 4$. Do not, however, teach children that *of* "means" multiply.

14. Have children use their fraction kits to solve the following examples:

a)  

3 groups of $\frac{1}{4} = \square$

$3 \times \frac{1}{4} = \frac{3}{4}$

b)   

4 groups of $\frac{2}{3} = \square$

$4 \times \frac{2}{3} = \square$

c)  

3 groups of $\frac{3}{8} = \square$

$3 \times \frac{3}{8} = \square$

15. Which part of each region is shaded?

a) 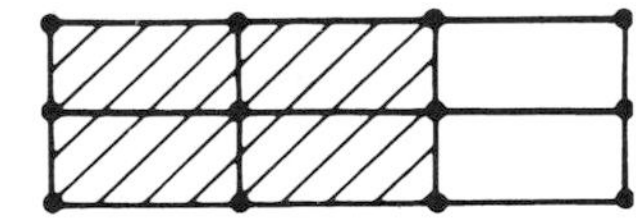

b) 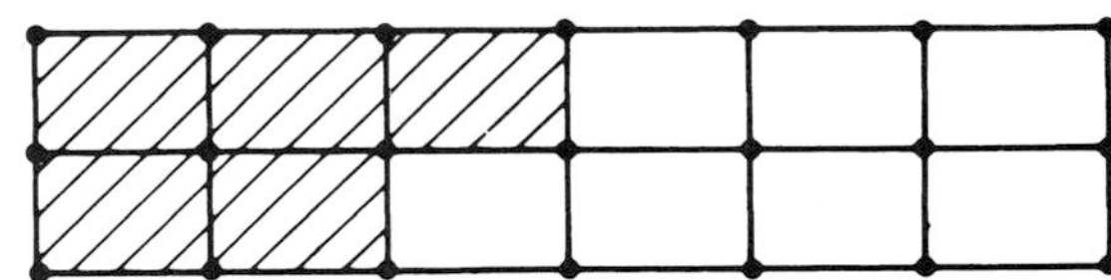

c) 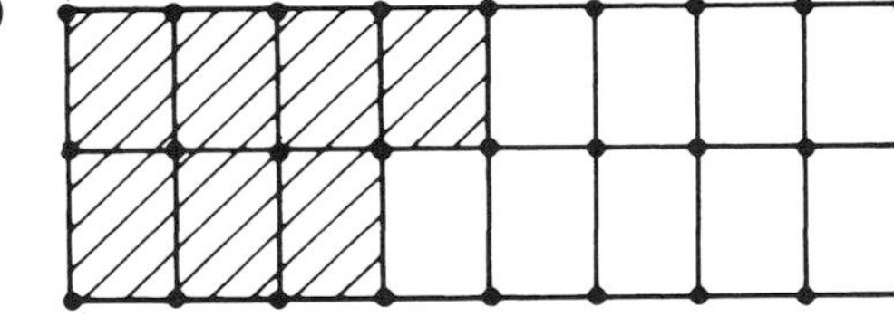

d) 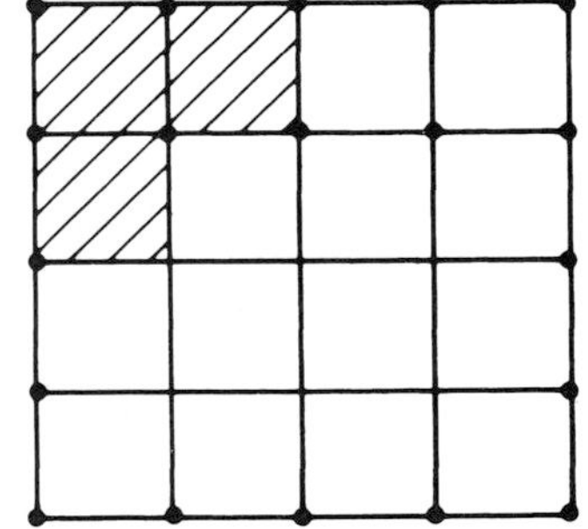

16. What part of each region is double-shaded?

a) 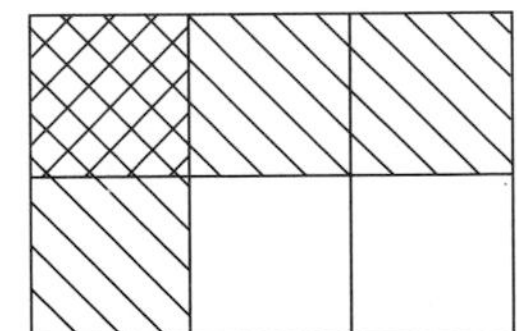

____ is double-shaded.

$\frac{1}{2}$ of $\frac{1}{3}$ is ____.

b) 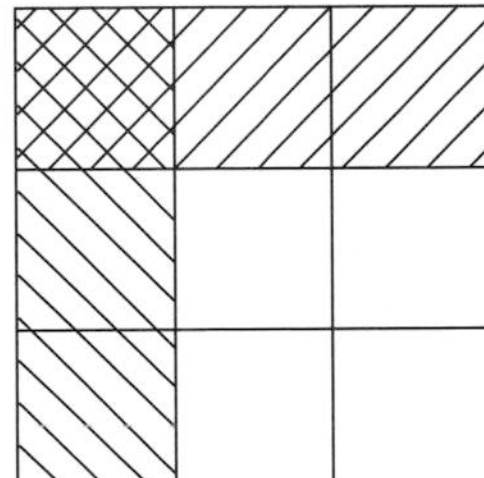

____ is double-shaded.

$\frac{1}{3}$ of $\frac{1}{3}$ is ____.

17. What part of the region has been colored twice?

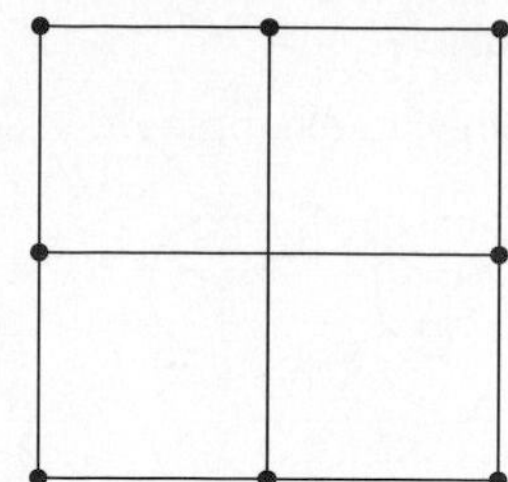

Color $\frac{1}{2}$ of the region blue.

Color $\frac{1}{2}$ of the blue region red.

$\frac{1}{2}$ of $\frac{1}{2}$ is ____.

18. Complete the sentence under each diagram.

a) 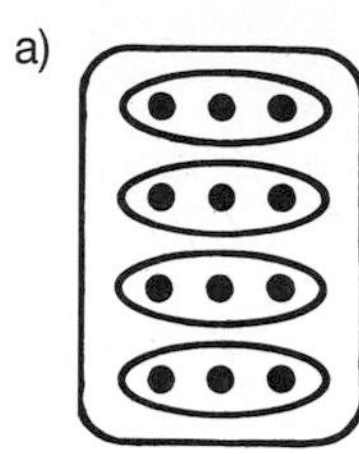

$\frac{1}{4}$ of 12 = ____

b) 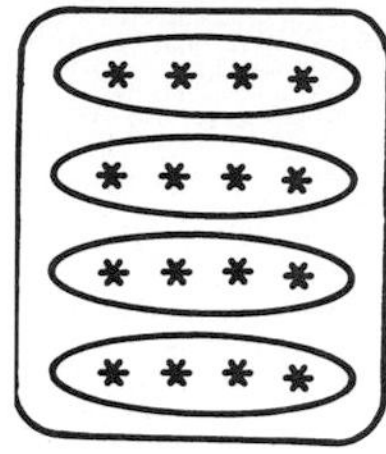

$\frac{1}{4}$ of 16 = ____

c) 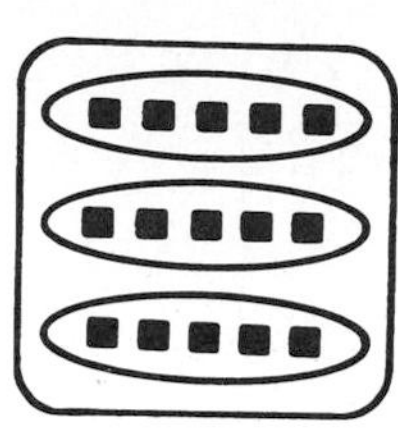

$\frac{1}{3}$ of 15 = ____

d) 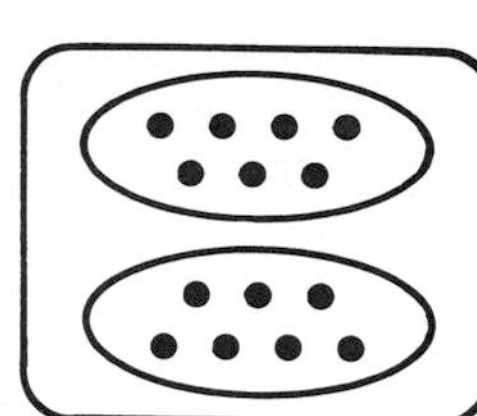

$\frac{1}{2}$ of 14 = ____

19. The number line model will help you understand multiplication of rational numbers expressed as fractions. For example:

a) 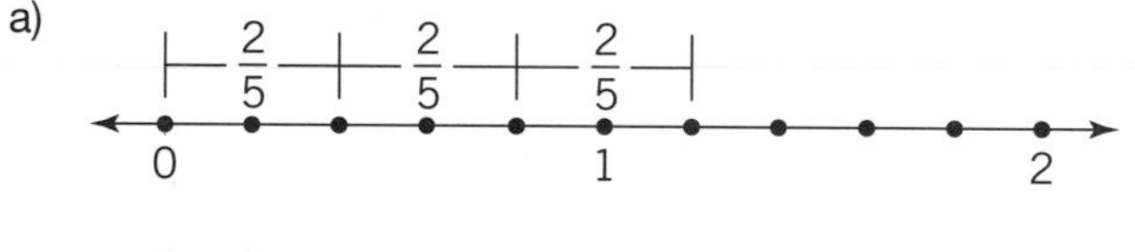

$\frac{0}{5}$ $\frac{1}{5}$ $\frac{2}{5}$ $\frac{3}{5}$ $\frac{4}{5}$ $\frac{5}{5}$ $\frac{6}{5}$ $\frac{7}{5}$ $\frac{8}{5}$ $\frac{9}{5}$ $\frac{10}{5}$

3 jumps of $\frac{2}{5} = \square$

$3 \times \frac{2}{5} = \square$

b) 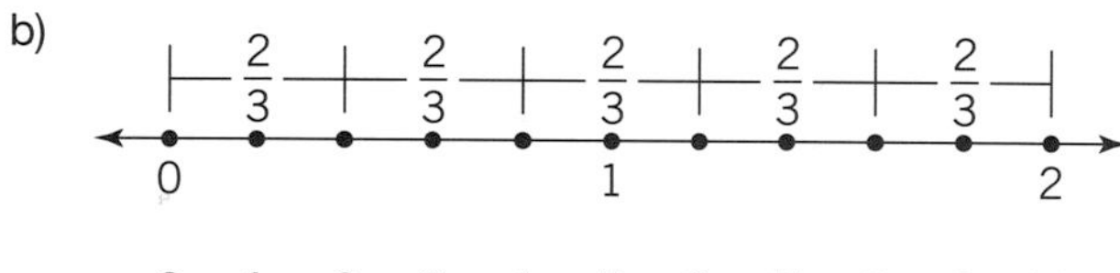

$\frac{0}{3}$ $\frac{1}{3}$ $\frac{2}{3}$ $\frac{3}{3}$ $\frac{4}{3}$ $\frac{5}{3}$ $\frac{6}{3}$ $\frac{7}{3}$ $\frac{8}{3}$ $\frac{9}{3}$ $\frac{10}{3}$

5 jumps of $\frac{2}{3} = \square$

$5 \times \frac{2}{3} = \square$

20. Further readiness activities can be presented by giving the children practice with repeated addition of fractional numbers.

a) $\frac{2}{3} + \frac{2}{3} + \frac{2}{3} = \square$
$\therefore 3 \times \frac{2}{3} = \square$

b) $\frac{3}{8} + \frac{3}{8} + \frac{3}{8} = \square$
$\therefore 3 \times \frac{3}{8} = \square$

c) $\frac{2}{7} + \frac{2}{7} + \frac{2}{7} = \square$
$\therefore 3 \times \frac{2}{7} = \square$

d) $\frac{4}{5} + \frac{4}{5} + \frac{4}{5} + \frac{4}{5} = \square$
$\therefore 4 \times \frac{4}{5} = \square$

e) $\frac{1}{9} + \frac{1}{9} + \frac{1}{9} + \frac{1}{9} = \square$
$\therefore 4 \times \frac{1}{9} = \square$

f) $\frac{7}{6} + \frac{7}{6} + \frac{7}{6} = \square$
$\therefore 3 \times \frac{7}{6} = \square$

21. Complete the following:

a) $\frac{1}{2}$ of 6 = 3 or $\frac{1}{2} \times 6 =$ ______

b) $\frac{1}{2}$ of 8 = ______ or $\frac{1}{2} \times 8 =$ ______

c) $\frac{1}{5}$ of 10 = ______ or $\frac{1}{5} \times 10 =$ ______

d) $\frac{1}{3}$ of 12 = 4 or $\frac{1}{3} \times 12 =$ ______

e) $\frac{1}{4}$ of 12 = ______ or $\frac{1}{4} \times 12 =$ ______

f) $\frac{1}{3}$ of 9 = ______ or $\frac{1}{3} \times 9 =$ ______

22. On a sheet of cardboard draw a figure as shown. Make each diagonal about 6 to 8 inches long; laminate the card. Use a china marker to write examples on the figure. The children may write the products in the outside ring.

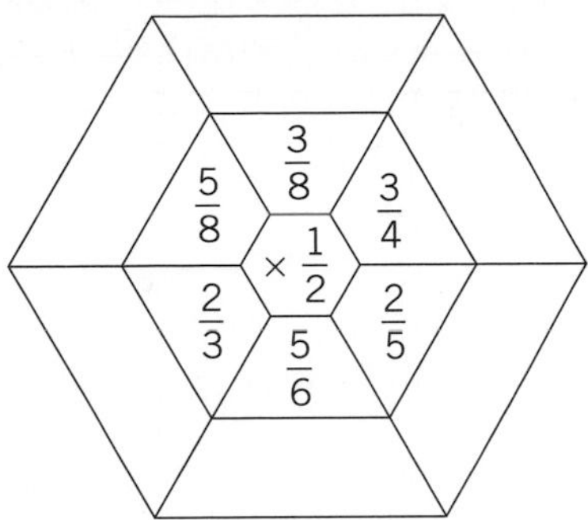

23. Using the fraction kit described in the activities for Chapter 10, have the student model:

a) $\frac{5}{8} + \frac{2}{8}$ b) $\frac{5}{6} - \frac{2}{6}$ c) $\frac{7}{10} + \frac{1}{5}$ d) $\frac{1}{2} - \frac{1}{4}$

24. Use the geoboard and establish that the entire area is called one (1). What is the value of each small square? $\left(\frac{1}{36}\right)$ (Answers will vary with the size of the geoboard.) What is the value of 6 small squares?

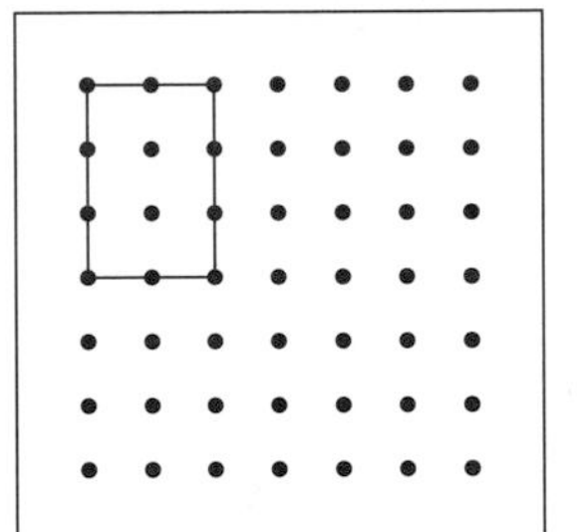

$\left(\frac{6}{36} \text{ or } \frac{1}{6}\right)$

Have students use geoboards or dot paper to represent the following fractions:

$\frac{1}{3}$ $\frac{2}{6}$ $\frac{1}{2}$ $\frac{3}{6}$

On a 5-by-5 geoboard have the student model $\frac{1}{2} + \frac{1}{8}$. The task is to count the squares to arrive at a sum.

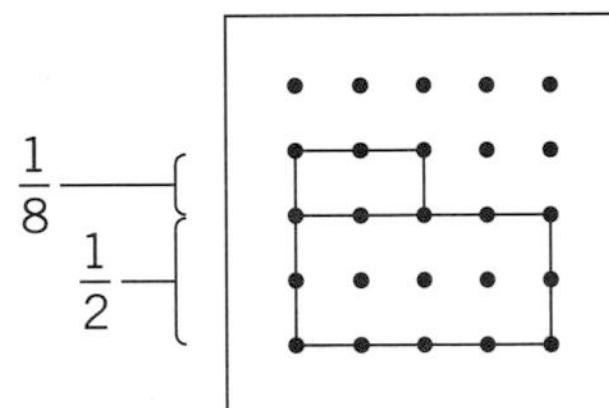

25. Using construction paper of different colors, construct a rectangle so that two unit squares fit over it. Next construct two triangles by cutting another unit square along the diagonal. This will give you triangle A. Take the other half of the unit square and cut in it half. This will give you triangle B. Questions such as the following can be asked: "What part of the square is triangle A? What part of triangle A is triangle B?"

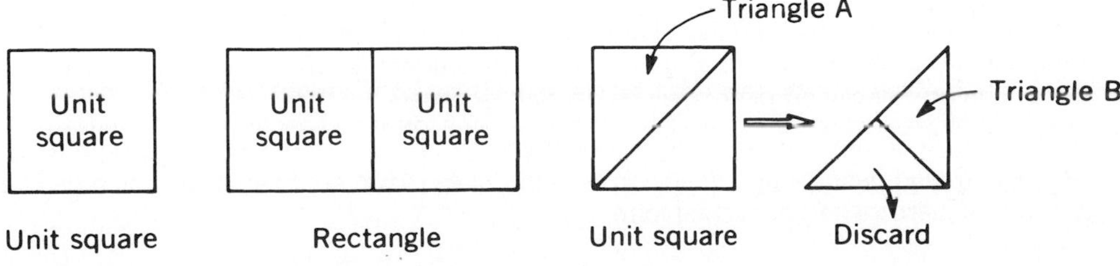

26. Using a number line, have the student diagram examples such as:

a) $\frac{5}{8}+\frac{7}{8}$ b) $\frac{7}{4}-\frac{5}{4}$ c) $\frac{4}{5}+\frac{3}{10}$ d) $\frac{5}{6}-\frac{2}{3}$

27. Complete the tables.

+	$\frac{1}{3}$	$\frac{5}{6}$	$7\frac{1}{8}$
$\frac{1}{2}$			
$2\frac{1}{3}$			
$2\frac{1}{4}$			

−	$\frac{1}{2}$	$\frac{2}{3}$	$\frac{7}{12}$
$\frac{5}{6}$			
$\frac{25}{12}$			
$7\frac{2}{3}$			

28. Have the student fill in the missing numbers.

Addend	Addend	Sum
	$\frac{1}{2}$	$\frac{7}{8}$
$\frac{1}{3}$	$\frac{4}{6}$	
$\frac{3}{10}$		$\frac{4}{5}$

29. Use what you have learned about whole numbers and fractions to complete each sentence.

a) If $\frac{1}{2}+\frac{1}{2}=1$, then $1\frac{1}{2}+\frac{1}{2}=$ ______.
b) If $\frac{1}{4}+\frac{3}{4}=1$, then $2\frac{1}{4}+\frac{3}{4}=$ ______.
c) If $\frac{1}{4}+\frac{1}{4}=\frac{1}{2}$, then $3\frac{1}{4}+1\frac{1}{4}=$ ______.
d) If $\frac{1}{3}+\frac{2}{3}=1$, then $2\frac{1}{3}+\frac{2}{3}=$ ______.
e) If $\frac{1}{2}+\frac{1}{4}=\frac{3}{4}$, then $2\frac{1}{2}+\frac{1}{4}=$ ______.
f) If $\frac{1}{2}+\frac{1}{3}=\frac{5}{6}$, then $4\frac{1}{2}+2\frac{1}{3}=$ ______.

30. Place the correct sign of operation in each △.

a) $\frac{9}{12}\triangle\frac{3}{6}=1\frac{1}{4}$ b) $\frac{4}{5}\triangle\frac{3}{10}=\frac{1}{2}$ c) $\frac{6}{16}\triangle\frac{3}{8}=\frac{3}{4}$ d) $\frac{3}{4}\triangle\frac{11}{12}=1\frac{2}{3}$

31. Make each statement true or false.

a) $\frac{1}{4}+\frac{2}{3}=\frac{2}{3}+\frac{1}{4}$
b) $1-\frac{3}{8}=\frac{3}{8}-1$
c) $\frac{3}{4}-\frac{4}{4}=\frac{4}{4}-\frac{3}{4}$
d) $\frac{1}{8}+0=0-\frac{1}{8}$
e) $\frac{1}{3}+0=0+\frac{1}{3}$
f) $\frac{1}{6}+1=\frac{7}{7}+\frac{2}{12}$

32. Find the prime factors of the numerator and denominator of each fraction.

a) $\frac{6}{10}$ b) $\frac{9}{12}$ c) $\frac{4}{8}$ d) $\frac{12}{25}$ e) $\frac{15}{25}$

In each fraction above, did you find a common prime factor for the numerator and denominator? Are any of the fractions in simplest form? Rename each fraction in simplest form.

33. Are the following fractions in simplest form? If not, rewrite them in simplest form.

a) $\frac{7}{30}$ b) $\frac{10}{12}$ c) $\frac{4}{6}$ d) $\frac{15}{16}$ e) $\frac{7}{8}$ f) $\frac{24}{27}$

34. Find the greatest common factor of the numerator and denominator of each fraction.

a) $\frac{6}{9}$ b) $\frac{8}{12}$ c) $\frac{16}{12}$ d) $\frac{25}{15}$ e) $\frac{8}{8}$ f) $\frac{64}{80}$

35. Construct several cardboard flash cards. On each card place several fractions with unlike denominators. Show the card to the student. The student should state the least common denominator. Pencil and paper may be used if necessary.

36. Find the least common multiple of the denominators. Express the fractions using the LCD as the common denominator; then add or subtract as indicated. Examples should be written in both vertical and horizontal form.

Example: $\frac{1}{2} + \frac{1}{4}$ LCD = 4 $\frac{1}{2} + \frac{1}{4} = \frac{2}{4} + \frac{1}{4} = \frac{3}{4}$

a) $\frac{2}{5} + \frac{4}{3} =$ ________ c) $\frac{1}{2} - \frac{1}{4} =$ ________ e) $\frac{8}{10} + \frac{15}{20} =$ ________

b) $\frac{3}{8} + \frac{3}{16} =$ ________ d) $\frac{5}{6} - \frac{1}{2} =$ ________ f) $\frac{5}{12} + \frac{6}{15} =$ ________

37. Rewrite the following mixed numerals as improper fractions. Use either example 1 or example 2 as a guide.

Example 1	Example 2
$3\frac{1}{3} = 1 + 1 + 1 + \frac{1}{3}$	$3\frac{1}{3} = 3 + \frac{1}{3}$
$= \frac{3}{3} + \frac{3}{3} + \frac{3}{3} + \frac{1}{3}$	$= \frac{9}{3} + \frac{1}{3}$
$= \frac{9}{3} + \frac{1}{3}$	$= \frac{10}{3}$
$= \frac{10}{3}$	

a) $2\frac{3}{5}$ c) $1\frac{3}{8}$ e) $2\frac{3}{11}$ g) $5\frac{3}{7}$

b) $3\frac{5}{6}$ d) $1\frac{4}{7}$ f) $3\frac{6}{13}$ h) $9\frac{2}{5}$

38. Use examples like the following to reinforce children's understanding of addition and subtraction. (Some children will have difficulty with the + sign in the middle of a subtraction example. They will add the fractions and subtract the whole numbers. If so, replace the + sign with the word *and*.)

Addition

$$\begin{aligned} 3\tfrac{5}{6} &= \left(3 + \tfrac{5}{6}\right) = \left(3 + \tfrac{10}{12}\right) \\ +1\tfrac{3}{4} &= +\left(1 + \tfrac{3}{4}\right) = +\left(1 + \tfrac{9}{12}\right) \\ &= \left(4 + \tfrac{9}{12}\right) \\ &= 4 + \left(\tfrac{12}{12} + \tfrac{7}{12}\right) \\ &= (4 + 1) + \tfrac{7}{12} \\ &= 5\tfrac{7}{12} \end{aligned}$$

Subtraction

$$\begin{aligned} 3\tfrac{5}{6} &= \left(3 + \tfrac{5}{6}\right) = \left(3 + \tfrac{10}{12}\right) \\ -1\tfrac{3}{4} &= -\left(1 + \tfrac{3}{4}\right) = -\left(1 + \tfrac{9}{12}\right) \\ &= \left(2 + \tfrac{1}{12}\right) \\ &= 2\tfrac{1}{12} \end{aligned}$$

39. Find the sum or difference.

a) $6\frac{2}{3} + 2\frac{1}{4} = \square$ c) $2\frac{7}{16} - 1\frac{3}{8} = \square$ e) $5\frac{1}{2} + 3\frac{1}{4} = \square$

b) $12\frac{1}{2} - 8 = \square$ d) $7\frac{5}{6} + 4\frac{3}{3} = \square$ f) $9\frac{1}{6} - 5\frac{3}{4} = \square$

40. On a sheet of white cardboard, draw a figure as shown. Cover the drawing with clear contact paper so that you can use a china marker to write on it.

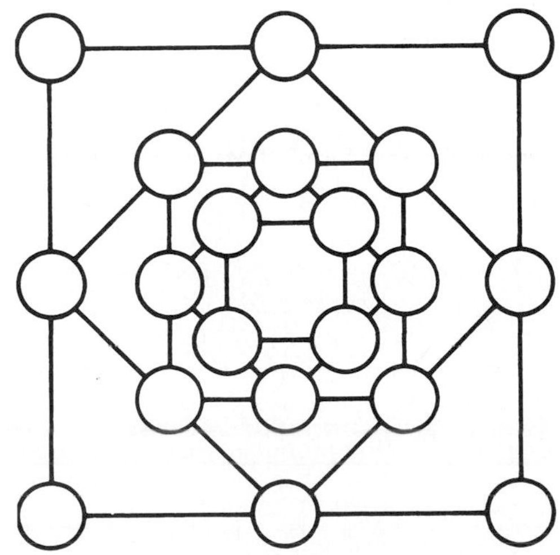

Write a fraction in each circular region in the four corners of the outermost square. Find the difference between the larger fraction and the smaller one, and write the difference in the circular region between the fractions subtracted. Continue this process, moving toward the center of the figure. Can you find four fractional numbers to put in the first four circular regions so that you end with zeros in the innermost circular regions?

41. For this activity, construct two decks of cards from cardboard of different colors. On each card, write an addition or subtraction example with one of the following answers: $\frac{1}{2}$, $\frac{3}{4}$, $\frac{7}{10}$, $\frac{5}{8}$, $\frac{4}{5}$, $\frac{5}{6}$, $\frac{3}{5}$, $\frac{3}{8}$, or $\frac{1}{4}$. On a file folder, place a 3-by-3 grid on the inside of one page. Place the listed fractions in squares of the grid.

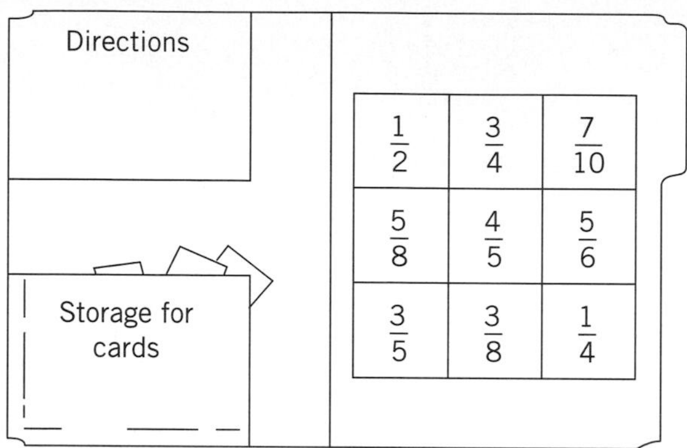

Place the folder between two players. One player uses a deck all of one color, and the other player uses the deck of the other color. The players take turns drawing a card and solving the example. The other player checks the example after the player places his or her card on the answer board. One player may place cards on top of cards played by the other player. After cards are placed on the board, the players may not look at the answers underneath. The first player to get three in a row or column wins the game.

42. Present a variety of word problems that involve addition and subtraction of fractions. Have the students write and solve an appropriate mathematical sentence for each problem. Word problems of this kind provide valuable experience in analyzing problems, and they provide practice in performing operations on fractions. Perimeter problems offer a chance to review various ideas of geometry while giving practice in computation.

43. Draw equal-size squares on a series of transparencies for the overhead projector. On each transparency shade a different sector of the square. Place two transparencies on top of each other to model different multiplication examples. Make two transparencies for each model.

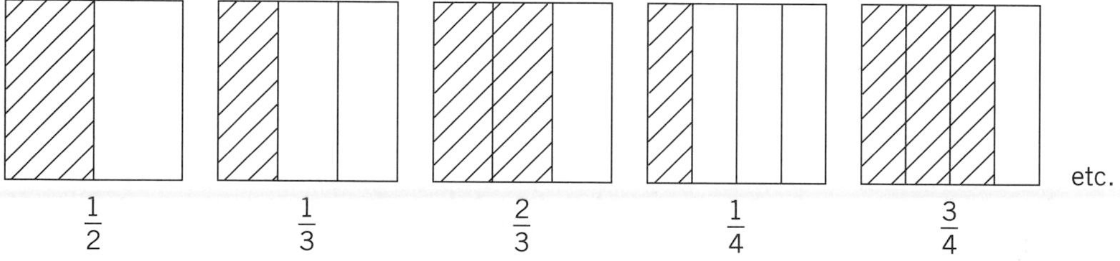

44. Use the diagrams to help you find the products. Also use the overhead transparencies of Activity 42.

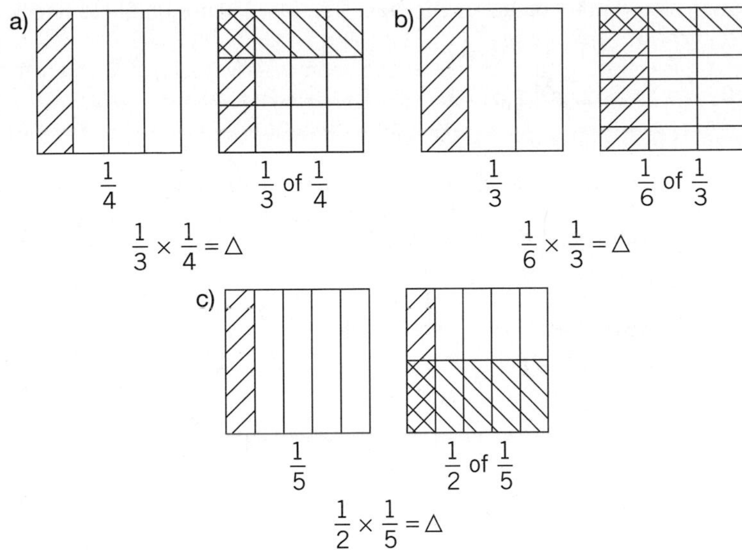

45. Using the fraction kit and sheets of paper to represent groups, have the student model three groups of $\frac{2}{5}$. Have the student manipulate the regions and write the multiplication sentence.

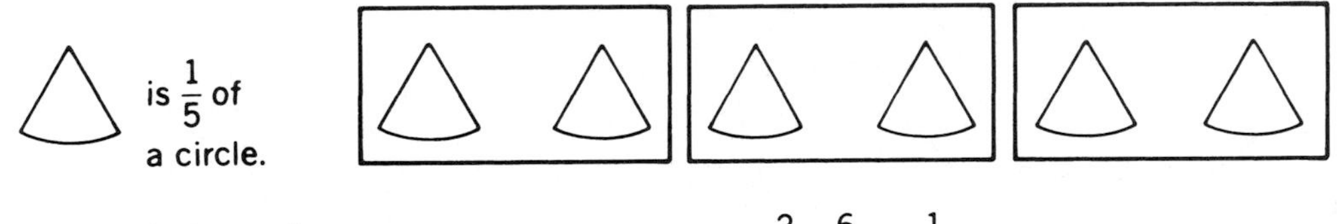

A sheet of paper is used for each group.

$$3 \times \frac{2}{5} = \frac{6}{5} \text{ or } 1\frac{1}{5}$$

46. Have the children shade parts of regions to solve examples such as the following:

a) $\frac{1}{2} \times \frac{1}{7} = \square$ b) $\frac{2}{3} \times \frac{1}{2} = \square$ c) $\frac{4}{5} \times \frac{1}{3} = \square$ d) $\frac{3}{4} \times \frac{1}{5} = \square$

47. The number line should also be used for modeling examples such as $3 \times \frac{2}{5} = \frac{6}{5}$.

48. Solve each of the following sentences:

a) $\frac{7}{8} \times \frac{2}{3} = n$ c) $\frac{3}{7} \times \frac{2}{3} = n$ e) $\frac{4}{5} \times \frac{3}{7} = n$ g) $\frac{3}{4} \times \frac{4}{5} = n$

b) $\frac{5}{6} \times \frac{1}{3} = n$ d) $\frac{1}{4} \times \frac{5}{8} = n$ f) $\frac{2}{5} \times \frac{3}{5} = n$ h) $\frac{3}{7} \times \frac{4}{9} = n$

49. Factor the numerator and denominator of each fraction before multiplying. Then use what you know about other names for 1 and the multiplication property of 1 to express the product in simplest form.

Example:
$$\frac{7}{10} \times \frac{2}{3} = \frac{7 \times 2}{2 \times 5 \times 3}$$
$$= \frac{2 \times 7}{2 \times 5 \times 3}$$
$$= \frac{2}{2} \times \frac{7}{5 \times 3}$$
$$= 1 \times \frac{7}{15}$$
$$= \frac{7}{15}$$

a) $\frac{5}{6} \times \frac{2}{3}$ c) $\frac{3}{8} \times \frac{3}{4}$ e) $\frac{3}{10} \times \frac{5}{25}$

b) $\frac{21}{35} \times \frac{42}{64}$ d) $\frac{6}{10} \times \frac{0}{15} \times \frac{11}{30}$ f) $\frac{9}{49} \times \frac{7}{56}$

50. Rewrite each mixed numeral as an improper fraction. Then multiply to find *n*.

a) $1\frac{7}{8} \times 2\frac{1}{5} = n$ c) $1\frac{2}{7} \times 8\frac{1}{4} = n$ e) $4\frac{1}{6} \times 5\frac{1}{2} = n$

b) $3\frac{1}{7} \times 2\frac{1}{5} = n$ d) $5\frac{1}{3} \times 5\frac{1}{3} = n$ f) $8\frac{1}{3} \times 2\frac{2}{5} = n$

51. Which product is not another name for 1?

a) $1\frac{1}{2} \times \frac{2}{3}$ b) $\frac{7}{8} \times \frac{8}{7}$ c) $\frac{1}{10} \times 1$ d) $1\frac{5}{6} \times \frac{6}{11}$

52. Write the reciprocal of each fractional number.

a) $\frac{5}{8}$ b) $\frac{1}{2}$ c) $\frac{9}{8}$ d) $\frac{4}{9}$ e) $\frac{12}{10}$ f) $9\frac{1}{2}$ g) 0

53. Complete each table.

a)

n	$\frac{2}{3} \times n$
0	
1	
2	$\frac{4}{3}$
3	
4	

b)

n	$\frac{1}{5} \times n$
$\frac{1}{2}$	
$\frac{2}{3}$	
$\frac{3}{4}$	
$\frac{4}{5}$	
$\frac{5}{6}$	

c)

n	$2 \times n$
$1\frac{1}{2}$	
2	
$2\frac{1}{2}$	
3	
$3\frac{1}{2}$	

54. Trying to demonstrate division of fractions *concretely* presents difficulties in interpretation. However, it is not impossible. At this point children are accustomed to seeing an example in division written in four ways:

$$8 \div 4 = n \qquad 4\overline{)8} \qquad n \times 4 = 8 \qquad \frac{8}{2} = n$$

It is not difficult for them to understand that if we begin with a group of eight objects, we can divide this group into two groups of four objects or four groups of two objects. With this reasoning as a reference point, division of fractions can be demonstrated in a way that makes sense.

$$\text{Example: } \frac{8}{9} \div \frac{4}{9} = n \qquad \frac{4}{9}\overline{)\frac{8}{9}} \qquad n \times \frac{4}{9} = \frac{8}{9}$$

Let's examine the concept in terms of regions. Consider the example $2 \div \frac{1}{3} = n$. We are asking how many one-thirds there are in 2.

$$\frac{1}{3}\overline{)2} = \frac{1}{3}\overline{)\frac{6}{3}} \quad (6)$$

Clearly, there are 6 one-thirds in 2. Now, suppose that we have 1 unit region divided into fourths. How many three-fourths are contained in 1 unit region?

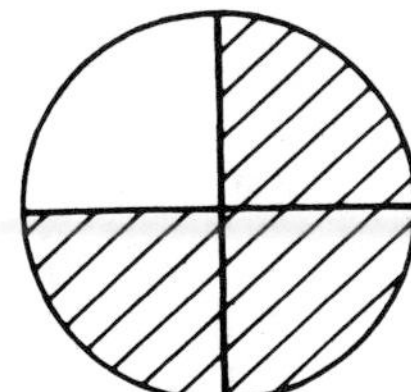

The shaded area is three-fourths of the unit region, but there is part of the unit region left over.

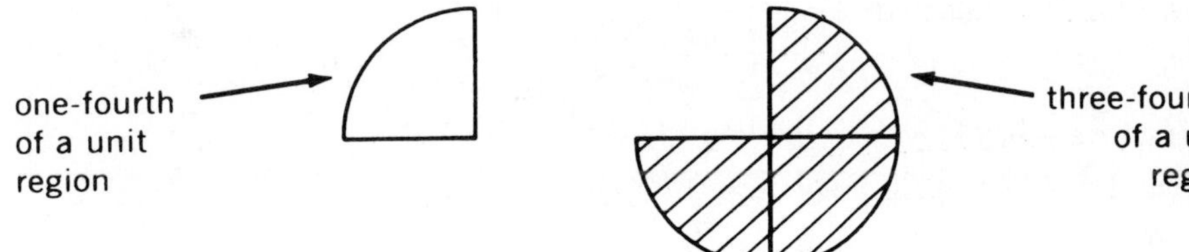

The part left over is one-third of the three-fourths region. So there are $1\frac{1}{3}$ three-fourths in the one-unit region.

$$1 \div \frac{3}{4} = 1\frac{1}{3}$$

Several different approaches to division of fractions are possible. One excellent method that stresses structure and properties of operation is the method just explained. The sensitive teacher will be aware of the difficulties that individual children are experiencing and whenever possible will vary the approach to meet individual needs. Children should eventually discover the usual algorithm for division of fractions, but it is essential that the algorithm be used only after the children understand why it works.

55. The number line is an excellent device to use for developing an understanding of the division of fractions.

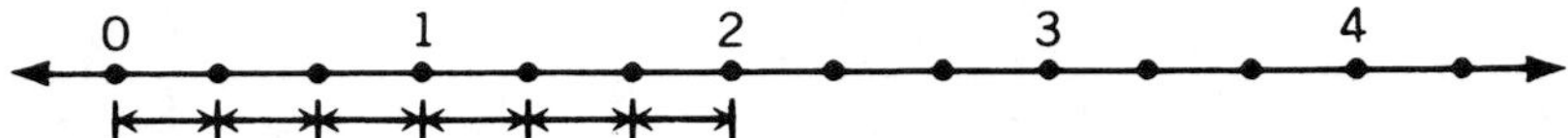

How many one-thirds are there in 2? You can readily see that there are 6 one-thirds in 2. Thus 2 divided by $\frac{1}{3}$ is 6. Draw a number line and show how many three-fourths are in 1.

56. Throughout their study of division of whole numbers, the children have been made aware of the inverse relationship between multiplication and division. This relationship should again be stressed to help the children understand division of fractions. It is also important for the children to understand that every expression of the form $a \div b$ can be written in the form $\frac{a}{b}$, and vice versa. A factor multiplied by a factor equals a product, or a product divided by a factor equals a missing factor.

57. Complete the following:

    a) Because $\frac{2}{3} \times 6 = 4$, we know that $4 \div \frac{2}{3} =$ ________ and $4 \div 6 = \frac{2}{3}$.
    b) Because $\frac{3}{5} \times 5 = 3$, we know that $3 \div \frac{3}{5} = 5$ and $3 \div 5 =$ ________.
    c) Because $\frac{4}{7} \times 7 = 4$, we know that $4 \div \frac{4}{7} =$ ________ and $4 \div 7 =$ ________.
    d) Because $\frac{8}{5} \times 5 = 8$, we know that $8 \div \frac{8}{5} =$ ________ and $8 \div 5 =$ ________.
    e) Because $\frac{13}{16} \times 16 = 13$, we know that $13 \div \frac{13}{16} =$ ___ and $13 \div 16 =$ ________.

58. Complete each of the following:

    a) $1 \div \frac{1}{3} =$ _____   c) $1 \div \frac{2}{3} =$ _____   e) $1 \div \frac{3}{4} =$ _____   g) $1 \div \frac{5}{6} =$ _____
    b) $1 \div \frac{7}{6} =$ _____   d) $1 \div \frac{10}{3} =$ _____   f) $1 \div \frac{4}{9} =$ _____   h) $1 \div \frac{13}{8} =$ _____

59. Solve each sentence for *n*.

    a) $\frac{6}{7} \div \frac{7}{6} = n$ c) $\frac{3}{5} \div \frac{8}{7} = n$ e) $\frac{5}{4} \div \frac{9}{10} = n$ g) $\frac{13}{6} \div \frac{1}{4} = n$
    b) $\frac{1}{9} \div \frac{7}{15} = n$ d) $\frac{4}{9} \div \frac{7}{12} = n$ f) $\frac{35}{64} \div \frac{7}{8} = n$ h) $\frac{6}{5} \div \frac{14}{15} = n$

60. Solve each sentence.

    a) $2\frac{1}{6} \div \frac{1}{3} = n$ b) $2\frac{5}{7} \div \frac{1}{14} = n$ c) $1\frac{3}{8} \div \frac{6}{24} = n$ d) $5 \div 4\frac{1}{2} = n$

61. Rewrite each of the following as a multiplication sentence and solve:

    a) $\frac{4}{5} \div \frac{5}{9} = \square$ b) $\frac{2}{2} \div \frac{7}{8} = \square$ c) $\frac{3}{2} \div \frac{5}{3} = \square$ d) $8\frac{3}{4} = \square$

62. Write <, >, or = in each circle.

a) $5\frac{1}{2} - 4\frac{11}{12}$ ○ $2\frac{3}{4} \div 11$

b) $7\frac{1}{3} \div 2\frac{1}{5}$ ○ $5 - 1\frac{2}{3}$

c) $\frac{5}{6} \div \frac{5}{12}$ ○ $17\frac{8}{10} \div \frac{9}{10}$

d) $\frac{5}{2} \times \frac{2}{5}$ ○ $\frac{2}{3} \times \frac{2}{3}$

e) $1\frac{1}{2} \div \frac{3}{3}$ ○ $\frac{5}{3} \times \frac{3}{4}$

f) $10 \div \frac{4}{9}$ ○ $5 \div \frac{2}{9}$

g) $\frac{8}{3} \times \frac{1}{4}$ ○ $\frac{8}{3} \div \frac{1}{4}$

h) $5 \div 3\frac{1}{2}$ ○ $\frac{1}{5} \times \frac{7}{2}$

63. Write only the answer to the following examples. Do all computation mentally.

a) $5 \times 15 =$ ________

b) $2 \times 3\frac{1}{2} =$ ________

c) $7 \times 13 =$ ________

d) $3 \times 2\frac{2}{3} =$ ________

e) $6 \times 6 =$ ________

f) $4\frac{1}{4} \times 4 =$ ________

g) $4 \times 18 =$ ________

h) $5\frac{3}{4} \times 2 =$ ________

64. Complete the following chart. The first example has been done for you.

Example	Unknown Factor Is between:	Unknown Factor Is between:	Unknown Factor Is Closer to:
$24 \div 3\frac{5}{6}$	$24 \div 3$ and $24 \div 4$	8 and 6	6
$16 \div 2\frac{2}{3}$			
$18 \div 3\frac{1}{3}$			
$9 \div 2\frac{3}{4}$			

65. Write a mathematical sentence for each problem. Then solve the sentence.

a) Richard went to a movie that was $1\frac{1}{2}$ hours long. He watched only $\frac{2}{3}$ of the movie. How long did he stay?

b) Mrs. Mosley traveled for $4\frac{1}{4}$ hours at a constant speed of 40 miles an hour. How many miles did she go?

c) A rectangle is $2\frac{3}{8}$ inches long and $1\frac{1}{4}$ inches wide. What is its area in square inches?

d) A rectangle has an area of 60 square inches. It is $3\frac{3}{4}$ inches wide. How long is it?

e) In a class of 30 students, $\frac{1}{6}$ of the boys have brown hair. The boys make up $\frac{3}{5}$ of the class. How many boys are there with brown hair?

66. Complete the following table by finding fraction pairs:

Sum	Fraction Pair	Product
1	$\frac{1}{2}, \frac{1}{2}$	$\frac{1}{4}$
$\frac{14}{48}$		$\frac{1}{48}$
$\frac{17}{12}$		$\frac{1}{2}$
$1\frac{7}{30}$		$\frac{2}{6}$
$\frac{11}{8}$		$\frac{7}{16}$
$1\frac{7}{15}$		$\frac{8}{15}$
$1\frac{5}{24}$		$\frac{7}{24}$
$\frac{61}{56}$		$\frac{15}{56}$

67. Prepare 48 cards with a fraction example on each card (addition, subtraction, multiplication, and division). Deal all the cards. Each player places his or her cards face down. Taking the top card of the deck, the player solves the example on that card. The player whose example yields the greatest answer wins all the cards played. At the end of the period, the person with the most cards is declared the winner.

68. Use three small wooden or sponge-rubber cubes. Write a fraction on each face of two of them. On the third put operation signs. Let the children take turns rolling the dice and solving the examples.

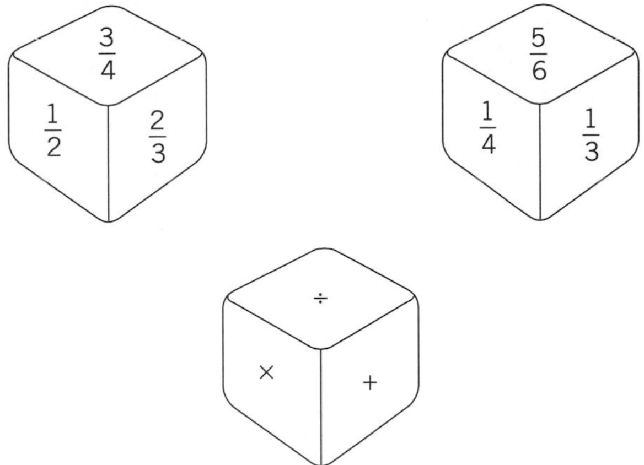

69. A student familiar with decimal notation for fractions can explore the result of adding (or subtracting) such numbers as .25 + .75, or .3 + .7, or even .25 + .5 + .25. The total need not always equal one whole. Much can be gained from such examples as .2 + .3 or .25 + .5. It can also be quite interesting to discuss, at this level, why $\frac{1}{3} + \frac{1}{3} + \frac{1}{3} = \frac{3}{3}$ but on some calculators, when the indicated divisions are performed, the result is .99999999.

70. Multiplication can be explored with decimal-display calculators, but the examples should be limited to those in which a fraction with a terminating decimal equivalent is being multiplied by a whole number, for example, $3 \times \frac{1}{4}$ or $5 \times \frac{3}{10}$. Division may not be advisable at all on such calculators at this level, but there is one application that may prove worthwhile. When exploring the notion of division of fractions, children can use the calculator to provide feedback regarding such questions as, "How many two-fifths are there in ten?" or "How many three-eighths are there in three-fifths?" Of course, it is important to carefully select the fractions for such examples to avoid repeating decimals.

71. Perhaps most useful of all at this grade level is a calculator that is capable of displaying rational numbers in fraction form. When the student has had considerable experience with modeling fraction operations and has grasped the meaning underlying these operations, then fraction calculators can be used to provide a means of exploring the abstract algorithms and forming hypotheses on procedures that will yield a correct result without the use of the calculator.

72. A number of microcomputer software packages are available to assist children with fraction concepts. Many deal exclusively with the concepts presented in Chapters 8, 9 and 10, and most of those focus solely on drill and practice. Nevertheless, a few programs do make effective use of graphics and animation to attend to the concept development needs of the children. Readers are advised to explore local resources for available software.

Suggested Readings

Bezuk, N. S., & Armstrong, B. E. (1993). Activities: understanding division of fractions. *The Mathematics Teacher, 86.*

Blaeuer, D. A. (1984). Fractions, division, and the calculator. *School Science and Mathematics, 84*(2).

Cramer, K., & Bezuk, N. (1991). Multiplication of fractions: Teaching for understanding. *The Arithmetic Teacher, 39*(3).

Fennell, F. (1992). Ideas. *The Arithmetic Teacher, 39.*

Grossnickle, F. E., & Perry, L. M. (1985). Division with common fraction and decimal divisors. *School Science and Mathematics, 85*(7).

Hope, J. A., Reys, B. J., & Reys, R. E. (1988). *Mental math in junior high.* Palo Alto, CA: Dale Seymour Publications.

Kalman, D. (1985). Up fractions! Up n/m! *The Arithmetic Teacher, 32*(8).

Lehman, J. R., & Kandl, T. M. (1995). Smiles: Popcorn investigations for integrating mathematics, science, and technology. *School Science and Mathematics, 95*

May, L. J. (1994). Teaching math: Get cookin' with fractions. *Teaching Pre K-8, 24.*

McKillip, W. D., & Stanic, G. M. A. (1989). Developmental algorithms have a place in elementary school mathematics instruction. *The Arithmetic Teacher, 36*(5).

Mick, H. W., & Sinicrope, R. (1989). Two meanings of fraction multiplication. *School Science and Mathematics, 89*(8).

Moses, B. E., & Proudfit, L. (1992). Ideas. *The Arithmetic Teacher, 40.*

National Council of Teachers of Mathematics. (1978). *Developing computational skills.* 1978 Yearbook. Reston, VA: Author.

Ott, J. M. (1990). A unified approach to multiplying fractions. *The Arithmetic Teacher, 37*(7).

Ott, J. M., Snook, D. L., & Gibson, D. L. (1991). Understanding partitive division of fractions. *The Arithmetic Teacher, 39*(2).

Payne, J. N., & Towsley, A. E. (1990). Implications of NCTM's standards for teaching fractions and decimals. *The Arithmetic Teacher, 37*(8).

Post, T. R. (1989). Fractions and other rational numbers. *The Arithmetic Teacher, 36*(1).

Sinicrope, R., and Mick, H. W. (1992). Multiplication of fractions through paper folding. *The Arithmetic Teacher, 40*(2).

Chapter 12

Rational Numbers Expressed as Decimals: Concepts and Operations

Overview

As our country continues to use and adapt to the metric system, we must rethink the need and value of rational numbers expressed as fractions and those expressed as decimals. Since the metric system is based on ten—the same as our decimal number system—undoubtedly more emphasis needs to be placed on decimals and less emphasis on fractions. However, for many years to come it will be necessary to relate fractions and decimals—parents will always cut candy bars in "half," and the business world will continue to use percent and relate percents to fractions and decimals.

Too often teachers begin teaching decimals on the abstract level and children become lost very quickly. More emphasis needs to be placed on the concrete level as children develop an understanding of what rational numbers expressed as decimals really are. If a better foundation is developed, less time will need to be devoted to the operations with respect to decimals. Since the basic facts of addition, subtraction, multiplication, and division are the same for decimals as for whole numbers, the study of decimals presents only a new application of concepts the children already understand.

The concepts developed with whole numbers can easily be extended to decimals. Children soon realize that the basic facts they have memorized also apply to decimals, and thus there are no new basic facts to memorize. The place value generalization is simply extended to the right of the decimal point.

Children should realize, with the aid of a teacher's focused questions, that the fraction-decimal-percent relation is merely a matter of renaming. This approach eliminates a great deal of the confusion and misunderstanding that was common in many "disconnected" elementary school mathematics programs.

Children already have an understanding of fractions, and the number line provides an excellent visual presentation of the relation between fraction and decimal forms. The place-value grid, or chart, and squared, graph paper are other aids used to present this relationship.

Another way of preparing children to understand decimals is to use real money; dollars and cents are expressed in decimals. You can "buy" some item such as shoes or books from the children at the beginning of the class period with real money; then they can buy them back at the end of the class period.

SAMPLE LESSON PLAN—"THE DECIMAL QUEST"

Intermediate Developmental/ Direct Instruction

Goal:

Develop an understanding of decimal numbers.

Objectives:

The students will:

- Read, write, and model money notation.
- Connect money notation to decimal notation.
- Model, read, and write decimal notation.

Prerequisite Learning and/or Experiences:

- Experience modeling the relationships between pennies, dimes, one dollar bills, ten dollar bills, etc.; i.e., 10 pennies = 1 dime; 10 dimes = 1 dollar; 10 one dollar bills = 1 ten dollar bill, etc. and connecting models to money notation.
- Experience modeling whole numbers with base ten numeration blocks and connecting models to numerical notation.
- Experience modeling fractional numbers and connecting models to fractional notation.

Materials:

For whole group presentation:

- overhead money (coins and bills)
- overhead base ten numeration blocks

For pairs of students:

- access to a container of base ten numeration blocks

Procedures:

Motivational Introduction

Have students generate a list of some of their favorite technology dependent purchases (CDs, videos, game cartridges, etc.) and the cost of each item. Circle all of the money amounts which include four digit values such as $25.32. (You may have to provide appropriate "cents" amounts because most students will list prices for these items only in dollars.) Ask for volunteers to restate one of the amounts (stress correct format such as twenty-five dollars and thirty-two cents). On the overhead challenge the volunteers to model the cost using the least amount of coins and bills, but only have pennies, dimes, one dollar bills, and ten dollar bills available. Relate the model to the following *value* chart:

Tens 10	Ones 1	Dimes .10	Pennies .01
20	5	.30	.02

Continue reading and modeling costs as deemed necessary. Then erase all the dollar signs from the values written on the board. Without any dollar signs, have students discuss how to read the results. Accept any and all responses. Tell students these are called decimal numbers and today we will explore how to model decimals with base ten numeration blocks and connect the model to reading/writing decimal numbers.

1. Have students select a flat from the base ten numeration blocks. Tell students that today the flat has a value of one. Using their knowledge of fractional numbers, have students work in pairs to identify the value of the long, small cube, and block.
2. Have pairs share their thinking strategies and fractional names. Use the student-generated data to produce a chart similar to the money value chart in the motivational introduction:

	Block	Flat	Long	Cube
Fraction	10	1	$\frac{1}{10}$	$\frac{1}{100}$

Developmental Activity

3. Have students compare the money chart to the fraction chart and discuss how they think fraction numbers can be rewritten as decimal numbers.
4. Use this information to complete the chart as follows:

	Block	Flat	Long	Cube
Fraction	10	1	$\frac{1}{10}$	$\frac{1}{100}$
Decimal	10	1	.1	.01

5. Discuss how the fractional number and the decimal number are both read the same, i.e., $\frac{1}{10}$ and .1 are one tenth; $\frac{1}{100}$ and .01 are one hundredth.

Culminating Activity

6. Return to the former money values written on the board during the motivational introduction. Remember, the dollar signs have been erased. Remind the students of how they modeled these values as money. Now challenge each pair of students to use the base ten numeration blocks to model each value and fill in the chart with the decimal notation.

	Block	Flat	Long	Cube
Decimal	10	1	.1	.01
	20	5	.3	.02

7. Have pairs share their models for each decimal number at the overhead. Use this opportunity to

discuss how to read decimal numbers, i.e., 25.32 = twenty five and thirty-two hundredths.

8. Since all the values generated for this activity include hundredths, have students discuss how to read decimal numbers with only one decimal place instead of two decimal places. Have students explore with models the similarities and differences between 25.3 and 25.30, etc. Relate this to trading ten hundredths for one tenth.

Extension:

A. Write the following chart on the board:

Thousands	Hundreds	Tens	Ones	?	?	?

Have students use their understanding of place value to complete the chart. Using ones as the central focus, encourage students to discuss their ideas. Be sure to clarify that all the places to the right of the ones place represent fractional parts of 1. This is also a good time to talk about how the decimal point separates whole number values from fractional number parts in a decimal numeral and should always be read as *and,* not as *point.*
B. Refer to the trading up/trading down game in Chapter 6. Have the students play the same game, but substitute decimal numbers for whole numbers. Remember, for the decimal version the flat is worth one. In the decimal version ten hundredths are traded for one tenth and ten tenths are traded for one when trading up. When trading down, one is traded for ten tenths and one tenth is traded for ten hundredths.

Student Assessment/Evaluation:

Observe students' modeling of decimal numbers and their ability to read and write decimal notation. Use a checklist to note students' observable behaviors:

✓ observed X not observed

Decimal numbers—tenths

_______ Models value

_______ Reads notation

_______ Writes notation

Decimal numbers—hundredths

_______ Models value

_______ Reads notation

_______ Writes notation

INSTRUCTIONAL AND ASSESSMENT ACTIVITIES FOR GRADES K-4

1. Construct a deck of cards with the numerals .10 through .99. Shuffle the deck and deal the cards face down. Players turn one card over at a time. The player with the greatest number on the cards gets to take the cards from the other players. The player who has the most cards at the end of the period is declared the winner.
2. Point out to the children ratios they have seen or see every day, such as one flower to six petals, one car to four wheels, two wheels to one bicycle, two feet to one child, and so forth. Materials on a flannel board and semiconcrete materials can be used for illustration.
3. When children play with a calculator, they will press keys just to experiment. In this process, they will eventually divide a smaller number by a larger number. Many calculators will display the results of 1 ÷ 6 as .1666666, so this result can be used to initiate questions about decimals.
4. Using the newspaper, have the children prepare shopping lists and compute the totals of their grocery bills.
5. Use the calculator for computing change to be given to a customer. Play store; have the cashier use the calculator.
6. Use a 10-by-10 grid cut from graph paper to illustrate .5, .05, .60, and .68.

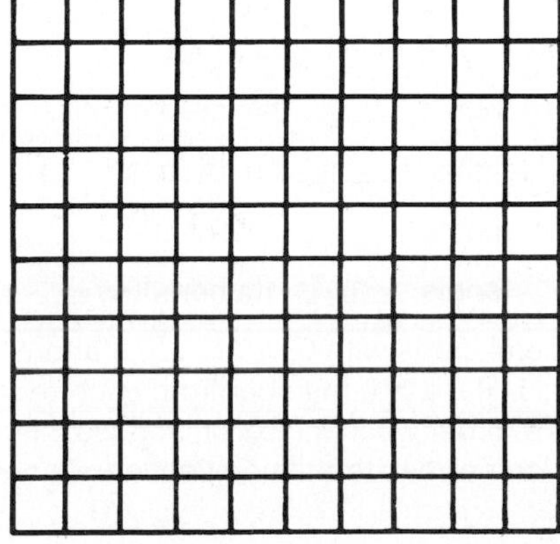

7. A game using teacher-made cardboard dominoes can be helpful in learning to recognize equivalent fractions and decimals. A set of 28 dominoes is required. Each domino should show numerals for positive rational numbers as fractions, decimals, or both. For example:

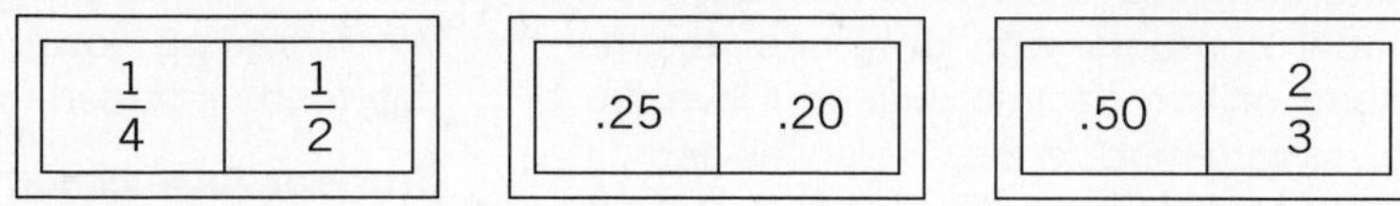

Some of the cards should be doubles. For example:

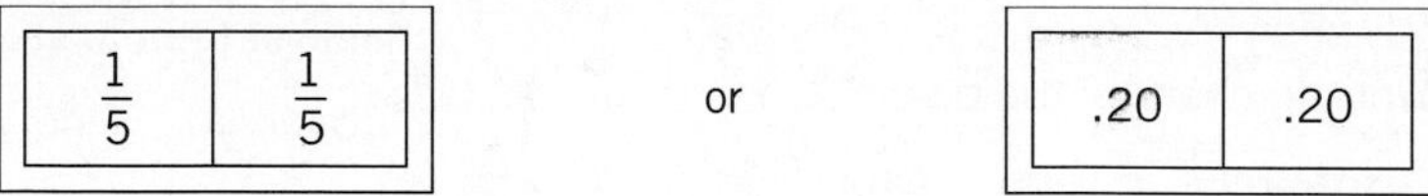

Place dominoes face down on the table and shuffle. Each player selects five dominoes; the remaining dominoes are left on the table in a pile. The player with the greatest double begins by placing it on the table. The player to the left may play a domino if he or she has one with a numeral equal to the sum of the two on the double or one with a numeral naming a fraction or decimal equivalent to the original domino. If the child cannot play, he or she must draw from the pile until a play results. The next player may play either on the other side of the double, if he or she has the sum, or on the last domino played, if he or she has a fraction or decimal equal to the open end or equal to the sum of the two fractions or decimals. The game is ended when one player has no more dominoes. To score this game, each player gets one point per play.

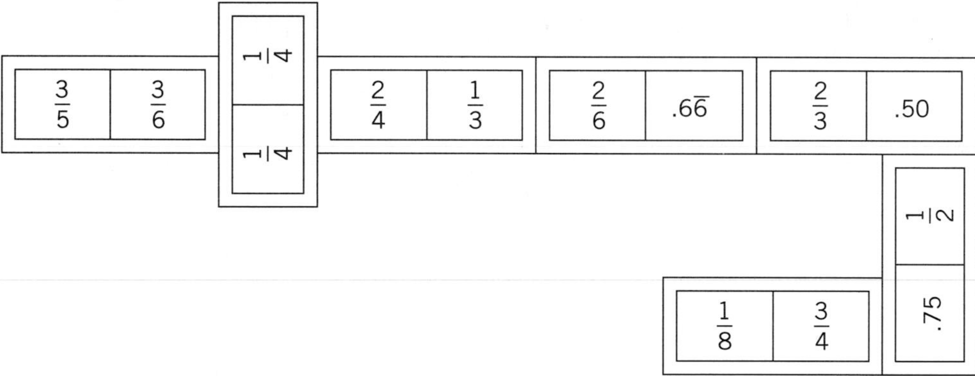

8. Label the remaining points on the number line.

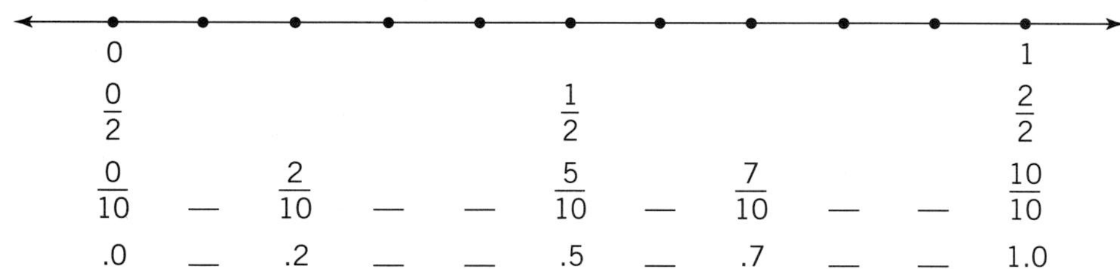

9. Write the correct numeral in each blank space.

a) .58 means _______ tenths _______ hundredths.

b) .06 means _______ tenths _______ hundredths.

c) .309 means _______ tenths _______ hundredths _______ thousandths.

d) .572 means _______ tenths _______ hundredths _______ thousandths.

10. Prepare two sets of numeral cards with 0, 1, 2, . . . , 9 and a card with a decimal point on it for each set of numerals. Have one member from each team come to the table or chalk rack and place the cards in order when the caller dictates a number (for example, 1325.76). Additional sets of cards can eliminate the competition element. If there is enough space,

the game can be made more active: Each student can be given a numeral or decimal point; then the students, in teams, arrange themselves to form the numeral.

11. Complete the sequences.
    a) .14, .16, .18, ________, ________
    b) .43, .49, .55, ________, ________
    c) .56, .50, .44, ________, ________
    d) .80, .40, .20, .10, ________, ________
12. Mark 40 cards with numerals expressed as decimals. For example:

    | .06 | .8 | .25 |

    One person mixes the cards and deals one at a time, face down, until each player has three cards. When the dealer says "Grab," each player then picks up his/her cards and arranges them in the correct order. The first person to declare "Between" and display the correct sequence wins a point. A person who says "Between" first but illustrates an incorrect sequence loses two points. The first person to get twelve points is the winner.
13. Which of the following statements are true?
    a) $.84 > .76$ b) $\frac{40}{100} = .04$ c) $.23 < \frac{23}{100}$ d) $\frac{4}{100} \neq .04$ e) $.07 = \frac{7}{10}$ f) $.72 > .8$
14. Write the correct relation symbol (<, >, or =) in each □.
    a) .8 □ 1 c) .02 □ .8999 e) 1 □ .001 g) 1 □ .999 i) .0901 □ 1
    b) .2 □ 1 d) 1.1 □ 1 f) 1 □ $\frac{1}{10}$ h) 1.01 □ 1
15. Tell whether the first number is to the left or right of the second number on the number line.
    a) .48 is to the __________ of .61
    b) 3.98 is to the __________ of 2.876
    c) .094 is to the __________ of 4.0
    d) 4.0 is to the __________ of 2.989
    e) 4.301 is to the __________ of 4.3001
    f) .11 is to the __________ of .9
16. Rename each of the following as a decimal:
    a) $\frac{3}{10}$ b) $\frac{85}{100}$ c) $\frac{14}{100}$ d) $\frac{89}{10}$ e) $\frac{5}{100}$ f) $3\frac{4}{10}$
17. Rename each of the following as a proper fraction or a mixed numeral:
    a) .13 c) 4.15 e) 4.87 g) .09 i) 6.70
    b) 1.06 d) 8.9 f) 6.05 h) .101
18. A game can be developed for practice in renaming fractions as decimals and vice versa. Make a set of 40 cards. Mark 20 with fractions and the other 20 with the equivalent decimal numerals. The cards are shuffled and then placed face down on a table (in the manner of a "Concentration" board). The first player turns up any two cards; if they are equivalent names (one fraction and one decimal) for the same number, the player keeps the pair of cards and takes another turn. If the cards do not name equivalent decimals and fractions,

the player places the cards back on the table face down and the next player takes a turn. When all the cards have been paired, the game is over. The player with the most pairs (one fraction and one decimal) is the winner.

19. Complete each pair of equations.

a) $\frac{6}{10}+\frac{9}{10}=\triangle$	b) $1\frac{4}{10}+\frac{3}{10}=\triangle$	c) $3+\frac{9}{10}=\triangle$	d) $\frac{11}{10}+\frac{3}{10}=\triangle$
$.6+.9=\square$	$1.4+.3=\square$	$3+.9=\square$	$1.1+.3=\square$

20. Fill in the blanks to complete each example.

a) .37 =		_____ tenths	_____ hundredths	c) .06 =		_____ tenths	_____ hundredths
+ .82	+	8 tenths	2 hundredths	+ .24	+	2 tenths	_____ hundredths
						_____ tenths	10 hundredths
						3 tenths	_____ hundredths

b) 2.6 =		_____ ones	_____ tenths	d) 4.3 =		_____ ones	_____ tenths
+ 4.7	+	4 ones	7 tenths	+ .9	+		9 tenths
		_____ ones	13 tenths			4 ones	_____ tenths
		7 ones	_____ tenths			_____ ones	2 tenths

INSTRUCTIONAL AND ASSESSMENT ACTIVITIES FOR GRADES 5-8

1. Find the following sums and differences. Show your work in vertical form. Be sure that the digits are lined up according to place-value positions.

   a) $7.38+5.16$ c) $32.1+9.46$ e) $4.0+.905$ g) $663.4+8$
   b) $73.2-8.0$ d) $3.72-.5$ f) $130-2.4$ h) $18-.42$

2. A magic square for decimals might prove to be a useful vehicle for practice with addition and subtraction. Remember that in a magic square, the sum of each row horizontally, vertically, and diagonally should be the same. In the following magic square, the sum of each row is 7.5:

3.25	1.5	2.75
2.0	2.5	3.0
2.25	3.5	1.75

3. Use a dollar sign and a decimal point to express each of the following amounts of money:

   a) 6 dimes, 4 pennies
   b) $3\frac{1}{2}$ dollars
   c) 1 quarter, 3 dimes, 2 pennies
   d) 8 dimes, 2 nickels, 7 pennies
   e) 2 dimes, 4 pennies
   f) 3 quarters, 1 nickel
   g) 23 pennies
   h) 1 half-dollar, 1 quarter

4. How much change would you get if you bought a quart of oil for $1.05 and then filled your gas tank with 15 gallons of gasoline at 98.9¢ a gallon and paid for all of this with a $20 bill?

5. A variety of problems can be presented that will reinforce basic concepts of measurement and help children understand some of the uses and advantages of decimal notation. For example, have the children draw polygons on pieces of paper. Ask them to measure the

sides of the polygons to the nearest centimeter and to the nearest inch. Which measurements are "easier" to make? Have the children calculate the perimeters of the polygons they drew in centimeters and in inches (using the measurements they have obtained). Which measurements are "easier" to add?

6. Draw sets to show that the following ratios are equivalent:

8 to 10	3 to 9	4 to 12	3 to 1
4 to 5	9 to 27	8 to 24	12 to 4

7. Children may be given directions to construct two sets, one containing 4 red counters and the other containing 5 black counters. The ratio of red to black counters is thus $\frac{4}{5}$. They should then be asked to place 4 more red counters and 5 more black counters on the table. Now the ratio of red to black counters is $\frac{8}{10}$. It should be noted that these two ratios are equivalent because for every 4 red counters there are 5 black counters.

8. Express the following as ratios in fraction form:

a) 1 inch to 1 foot
b) 1 quart to 1 gallon
c) 2 runs in 3 innings
d) 2 cookies for 5 cents
e) 1 millimeter to 1 decimeter
f) 6 milligrams to 1 kilogram

9. Write an equivalent ratio for each given ratio.

a) $\frac{8}{12}$ = ________
b) $\frac{4}{6}$ = ________
c) $\frac{14}{21}$ = ________
d) $\frac{12}{18}$ = ________
e) $\frac{32}{24}$ = ________
f) $\frac{2}{3}$ = ________
g) $\frac{15}{10}$ = ________
h) $\frac{27}{18}$ = ________
i) $\frac{3}{8}$ = ________

10. Study the following table:

Father's Age	Son's Age	$\frac{\text{Son's Age}}{\text{Father's Age}}$
24	0	0
26	2	$\frac{1}{13}$
28	4	$\frac{1}{7}$
32	8	$\frac{1}{4}$
36	12	$\frac{1}{3}$
48	24	$\frac{1}{2}$

What can you say about the ratio of the son's age to the father's as each gets older?

11. Have children write simple verbal problems involving ratios. This is an excellent way to find out whether they understand the basic ideas. Give them opportunities to discuss the problems and explain their thinking.

12. Have the children divide fractions and study the patterns of the decimals. For example:

1 divided by 11	6 divided by 11
2 divided by 11	7 divided by 11
3 divided by 11	8 divided by 11
4 divided by 11	9 divided by 11
5 divided by 11	and so on.

13. When 9 is divided by 17, the calculator display screen will read .5294117. How can the example be entered into the calculator so that it will have eight decimal places?

14. Provide many experiences for children to change rational numbers written in fraction form to decimal form by interpreting fractions as division.

15. Select any two-digit number; multiply that number by 10 two consecutive times. Now divide the number on the display screen by 10 four consecutive times. Discuss what happens to the number on the display screen after each multiplication or division.

16. Have the children change decimal names for numbers into decimals and then add the numbers. Check the exercise against a given sum. Study the following example:

Thirty-one and forty-two-thousandths	=	________
Sixty and four-tenths	=	________
Twenty-six and seven-hundredths	=	________
Total	=	________
Check		117.512

17. Count on your calculator, using decimal values. For instance, begin with the number 7.8 and add .1 ten consecutive times. Observe what happens as each number is added; discuss the results with the class.

18. Solve each example given in the first column of the following table. Write the answer in the second column. Write the digit in the appropriate place in the last column, and add the numbers in the last column. If the sum is the same as the sum written below the example, the work is correct. If the sums are not the same, the student must check his or her work to find the mistake. Study the example.

Example	Answer	Place	Number	
4.35 + 7.8 =	________	Tenths		________
9.84 – 6.37 =	________	Hundredths		________
10.7 – 3.58 =	________	Ones		________
			Total	________
			Check	7.07

19. Teachers can easily construct a place-value pocket chart by using a piece of tag board 24 inches by $5\frac{1}{2}$ inches, folded $1\frac{1}{2}$ inches and stapled or sewn as marked.

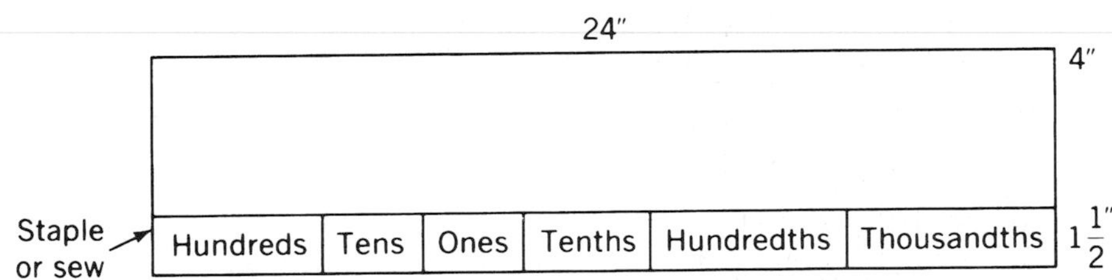

The teacher can use this place-value pocket chart by calling a number, such as 258.025. Using cards labeled with numerals 2, 5, 8, 0, and 2, the student is to place the proper card in its correct pocket.

20. Tell the place value of each of the individual digits of these numbers.

a) 71.57 b) 4.666 c) 122.32

21. Write the decimal numeral for each of the following:

a) 89 and 4 tenths
b) 9 and 798 thousandths
c) 6 and 6 thousandths
d) 584 and 24 hundredths
e) 42 and 59 hundredths
f) 33 and 547 thousandths

22. Display the two numbers .310 and .0300 and ask students to read them with the appropriate place-value names. Discuss the need to emphasize the appropriate parts of these names. (The first is "three hundred ten *thousandths*;" the second is "three hundred *ten-thousandths*.")

23. Mark the decimal in each column that represents the greatest fractional number.

A	B	C	D
3.6	.065	1.003	35.505
3.4	.65	1.133	35.550
4.4	.0605	1.303	35.555
2.9	.0655	1.330	35.500

24. Write five decimals that name numbers that fit the description.

a) greater than .11 and less than .2
b) greater than .09 and less than .1
c) greater than .01 and less than .1
d) greater than .9 and less than 1.0

25. Complete each sequence.

a) 1.78, 2.88, 3.98, ________, ________

b) 8.5, 9.0, 9.5, ________, ________

c) 3.5, 3.4, 3.3, ________, ________

d) 3.076, 3.086, 3.096, ________, ________

26. A game providing practice with order relations of decimals can easily be developed by using three different-colored dice. Each die represents place value of a decimal numeral. For example, a red die could stand for tenths, blue for hundredths, and green for thousandths. One pupil rolls the die and records the numeral represented. Another repeats the process. The pupil with the greatest value of decimal numeral is the winner.

27. A modification of rummy can be a helpful game that provides valuable practice in renaming fractions as decimals and vice versa. A pack of cards, each marked with a fraction or decimal, is needed. For each number, there must be three cards, each with the number shown in different forms; for example, $\frac{1}{2}$, .50, and .500. There should be approximately 20 of these sets.

Two to four players may play the game. Deal five cards to each player. Place the remainder of the deck face down with the top card turned face-up. The player to the left of the dealer begins. The player may take either the turned-up card or the top card of the face-down deck. If the player has three cards showing equivalent fractions or decimals, these are laid down on the table. When finished, one card is discarded face-up. Play continues. When one player has no cards, the game ends, and the player with the most sets of three wins.

28. Rename as decimals.

a) $\frac{33}{200}$ b) $\frac{19}{20}$ c) $\frac{27}{500}$ d) $\frac{16}{50}$ e) $\frac{17}{25}$ f) $3\frac{5}{6}$

29. Rewrite each decimal as a fraction.

a) .7 b) 1.67 c) .064 d) .06 e) 5.5 f) 2.25

30. Complete the table. What pattern do you find?

Factors	Number of Decimal Places	Product	Number of Decimal Places
.36 and .2			
3.56 and .08			
.345 and .8			
.1245 and .18			

31. Use 10-by-10 squares cut from graph paper to model the addends and sum of the following exercises;

a) .23 + .45 b) .34 + .5 c) .89 + .47 d) 1.6 + .7

32. Stress the comparison between fraction and decimal notation frequently as children begin to extend their working knowledge in the operations of arithmetic. This is not to imply that every example must be translated from one form into the other, which would defeat the

purpose. When a child understands the relation and can select the notation that is most efficient in a given situation, then the purpose has been accomplished.

This is particularly true in the operations of multiplication and division involving decimals. The memorized rules of "counting the decimal places" and "moving the decimal point" should be replaced by sound mathematical reasoning that can be justified.

Study and complete the following examples:

a) $.1 \times 6 = \frac{\square}{10} \times 6$

b) $.25 \times .3 = \frac{25}{\square} \times \frac{3}{\triangle}$

c)
```
  .36 =            3 tenths  6 hundredths
 ×  4         ×              4 ones
              ------------------------------
                  12 tenths 24 hundredths
                  14 tenths __ hundredths
         __ ones __ tenths __ hundredths
```

d)
```
  .26 =            2 tenths  6 hundredths
 × .4         ×    4 tenths
              ----------------------------------------------
                         8 hundredths 24 thousandths
                        __ hundredths __ thousandths
              __ tenths __ hundredths __ thousandths
```

e)

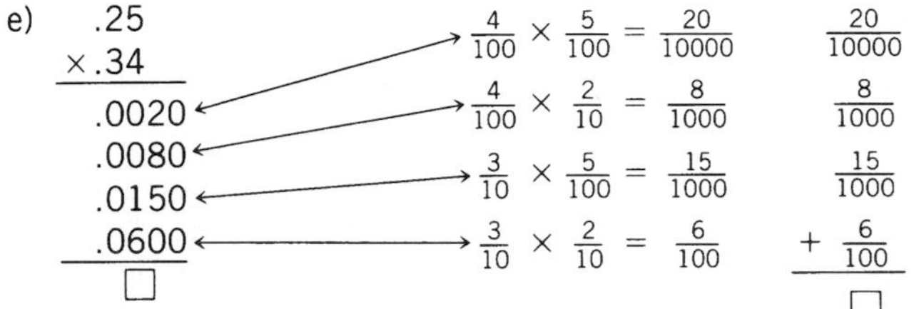

f)
```
  .34
 ×.08
```

33. Multiply each of the following by $\frac{10}{10}$, $\frac{100}{100}$, or $\frac{1000}{1000}$ to make the denominator a whole number:

a) $\frac{6.72}{3.2}$ b) $\frac{8.51}{.23}$ c) $\frac{1.59}{.4}$ d) $\frac{69.3}{.31}$ e) $\frac{45}{1.5}$

34. Rewrite each example in fraction form, and find the quotient.

a) $7 \div 4$ b) $.44 \div .4$ c) $172.8 \div .12$ d) $38.6 \div 6.8$

35. Construct bingo cards with a variety of numbers expressed as percentages, decimals, and fractions in the nine squares. Make a list of fractions and their equivalent decimals and percentages.

.60	15%	$\frac{1}{4}$
37.5%	FREE	.05
$\frac{2}{3}$	.8	75%

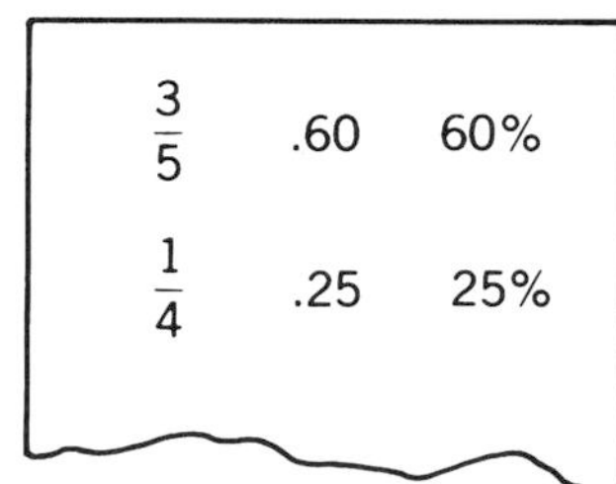

The caller chooses one of the numbers, and students may cover any equivalent number on their cards. The first person to get three in a row or column is the winner.

36. Write a message; then construct a grid on the inside of a file folder with a space for each letter of the message. Make a set of cards with a fraction on one side of each card and a letter on the other side. Have the student take one card at a time and change the fraction written on the card to its decimal equivalent. Find the decimal equivalent on the board. Turn the card over, and place the card on the board so that the letter is showing. If the child has placed each card correctly, he or she will receive a message.

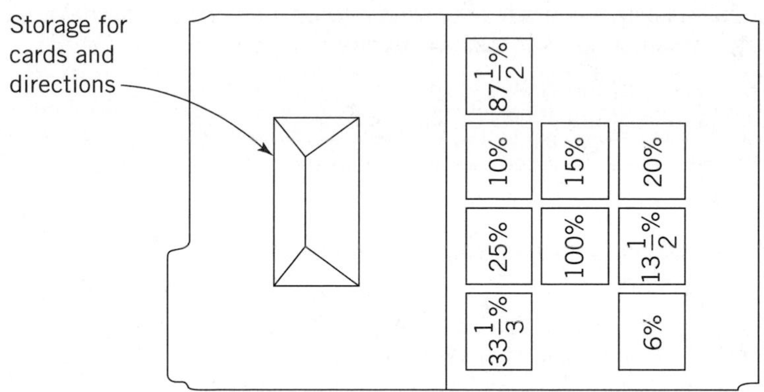

37. A shoe box can be used to facilitate practice with equivalent fractions, decimals, and percents. Take the lid off the shoe box and cut out eight rectangular slits.

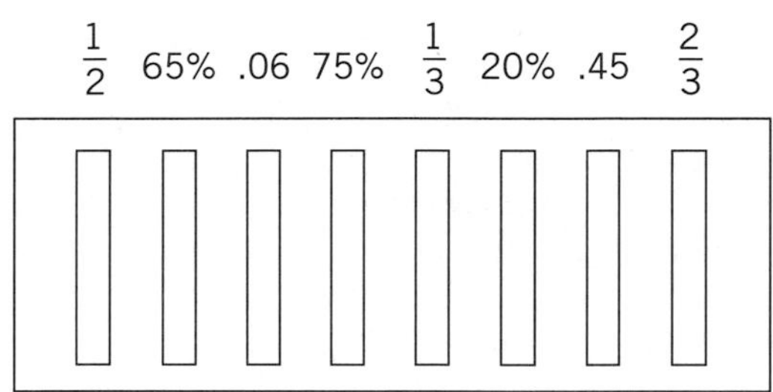

Write a fraction, decimal, or percent above each slit and then partition the shoe box into eight sections and replace the lid. Make cards representing the value in at least three ways. For example, for the slit marked $\frac{1}{2}$, the following cards should be made.

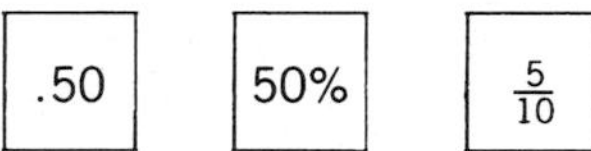

Make approximately fifty to sixty cards. The student's task is to place the appropriate card in a slit named by an equivalent decimal, fraction, or percent. After students have finished, they may open the box and check the bottom of the shoe box where the correct representations are listed.

38. Write the correct relation symbol (<, >, or =) in each loop.

a) $\frac{2.54}{100}$ ○ $\frac{2.54}{10}$
b) $16 \div .4$ ○ $.4 \div 16$
c) $62.4 \times \frac{10}{24}$ ○ $62.4 \div 2.4$
d) $\frac{5}{6} \div \frac{5}{12}$ ○ $\frac{178}{10} \div \frac{89}{10}$
e) .6 ○ 6%
f) 1 ○ 100%
g) 50% ○ $\frac{1}{2}$
h) 2 ○ 200%
i) $25.5 \div 5.1$ ○ $255 \div 51$
j) $\frac{174}{1000}$ ○ $\frac{17.4}{1000}$
k) $7 \div .75$ ○ $.75 \div 7$
l) 7 ○ 7%
m) .04 ○ 4%
n) $\frac{1}{2}$ ○ $\frac{1}{2}$%

39. Use your knowledge of scientific notation to complete each of the following:

a) $780 = 7.8 \times$ ________
b) $4800 = 4.8 \times$ ________
c) $6790 = 6.79 \times$ ________
d) $23{,}800 =$ ________ $\times 10^4$
e) ________ $= 4.98 \times 10^4$
f) $495{,}000 =$ ________ 10^5

40. Collect a variety of inexpensive materials and place them in a shoe box or other container. For example:

15 nails	9 circular regions
24 paper clips	12 triangular regions
18 straws	6 cup hooks

Prepare a question sheet that may be laminated for students to write on, or else provide a separate answer sheet. Ask such questions as:

What is the ratio of the straws to the paper clips? (8:24 or 1:3)
What is the ratio of the straws to the cup hooks? (8:6 or 4:3)

41. Find the number represented by the letter in each of the proportions.

a) $\frac{2}{1} = \frac{24}{n}$ b) $\frac{5}{m} = \frac{9}{27}$ c) $\frac{13}{a} = \frac{17}{17}$ d) $\frac{16}{18} = \frac{24}{y}$

42. Write a mathematical sentence for each problem. Then solve the sentence and answer the question:

a) If a space capsule travels at a speed of 28,800 kilometers per hour, how many kilometers does it travel in 1 minute? How many kilometers per second?
b) A car can travel 33 kilometers on 1 liter of gasoline. How far will it go on 5 liters of gasoline?
c) David's mother drives 104 kilometers in 1 hour. At this speed, how many hours will it take her to drive 520 kilometers?
d) George can run 75 meters in 12 seconds. How long will it take him to run 175 meters if he doesn't change his pace?

43. Repeating decimals have some interesting aspects that are worth exploring. For example, $.\overline{9} = 1$, that is, a decimal expression of an infinite string of 9's is equal to 1—not approximately 1, but equal to 1. How can this be? Surely, such a decimal expression will always be "short of 1," even if we continue billions of places to the right. But that's just the point: *billions of places* implies an end, while *infinitely many* does not. The equality between $.\overline{9}$ and 1 could be demonstrated by a number of methods. Consider this logical argument:

$$\begin{array}{r} \frac{1}{3} = .\overline{3} \\ +\frac{2}{3} = .\overline{6} \\ \hline \frac{3}{3} = .\overline{9} \end{array}$$

44. A meter stick (or any region that is easily divided into either 10 or 100 equal parts) can be a useful tool when studying percents. Consider this exercise: "12 is 40% of some number. What is that number?" To find the number, let the meter stick represent 100% of the number.

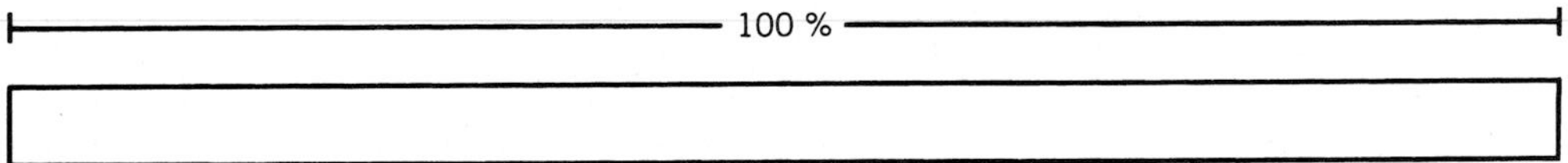

We know from the statement of the exercise that 12 is 40% of the meter stick.

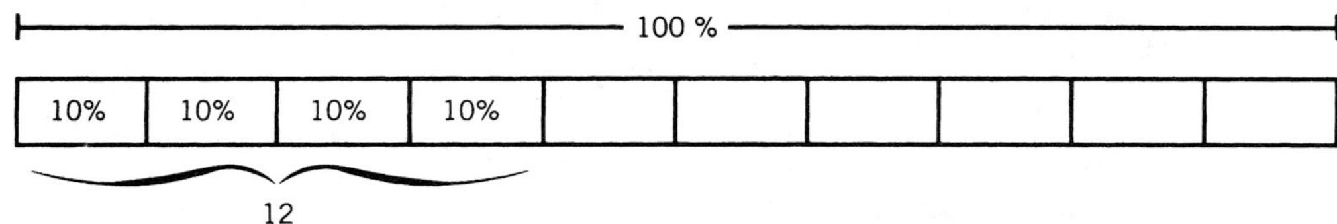

Because the meter stick is already divided into centimeters, we know that the 12 represents 40 centimeters. As the illustration shows, 24 represents a total of 80 centimeters. The remaining 20 centimeters, one-half of 40, must be represented by one-half of 12, or 6. Thus the entire meter stick (100%) must be 12 + 12 + 6, or 30.

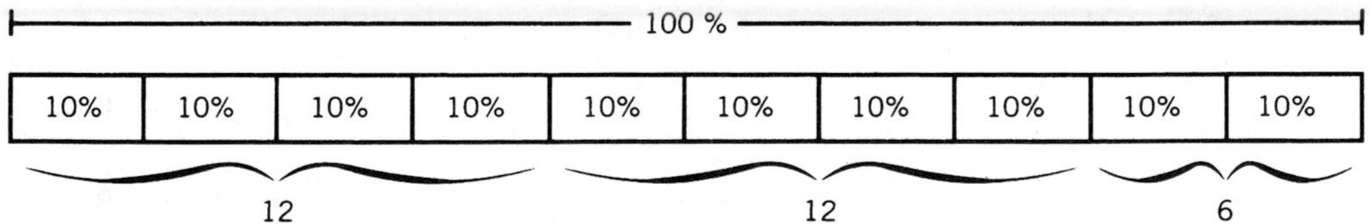

45. Have children use the calculator to check decimal exercises by finding a different way to perform the indicated operation.

46. Assume that a sheet of paper measures .001 inch thick. How thick will the paper be if it is folded in half? In fourths? In eighths? How many sheets of paper will it take to make a stack 1 inch thick?
47. On a calculator, use the repeated add function discussed in Chapter 6 and a constant of .1. What is the answer after the equals key is pressed 20 times? 25 times? 50 times?
48. Provide children with decimal multiplication examples that have been solved numerically without decimal points. Have the children provide the decimal points and then check answers using a calculator.
49. Have children use the calculator to multiply a given number by .1 and then .01, .001, and so on. Compare the answers. Discuss with the children the effect of multiplying by tenths, hundredths, and thousandths. Also try multiplying decimals by 1, 10, 100, and 1000; discuss the effects with the class.
50. Have children use the calculator to divide a given number by .1, .01, .001, and so on. Compare the answers. Discuss with the class the effects of dividing by tenths, hundredths, and thousandths. Also try dividing a decimal number by 1, .1, .01, .001, and so on. Discuss the effects with the class.
51. Provide children with decimal division examples solved numerically without decimal points. Have the children supply the necessary decimal points in the answers and check the results on a calculator.
52. Teach children how to change a number on a calculator to a percent using the percent key. For instance, place the number 250 on the screen; then press the % key. Now what appears on the screen? How do you describe what happened? How do you explain what happened?
53. The combination of the percent key and the add-on function on a calculator is very useful in the business world. The best way to explain this is by carefully examining a problem. If a suit that regularly sells for $175 is on sale at 20% off, what will a customer have to pay for the suit (including a 5% sales tax)? Solve the problem by pressing the following keys:

    [1] [7] [5] [−] [2] [0] [%] [=] [+] [5] [%] [=]

    Study this example, and discuss with the class how the add-on and percent key combination works. Create additional examples for the children to solve before you ask them to generalize.
54. Using data from the sports page of the newspaper, calculate batting averages, percent of wins, and percent of losses for a baseball team. Use football data to calculate the percent of passes completed, and so on. Basketball data can be used to calculate field goal and free throw percentage. Discuss appropriate data for other sports such as tennis, soccer, golf, etc.
55. Walk 100 meters three times; calculate the average length (to the nearest hundredth of a meter) of one pace during these walks. How many steps must you take to walk 1,000,000 meters?
56. How many aluminum cans will be needed to make a stack 1,000,000 meters high?
57. "Guess-My-Number Game": Set up the calculator by selecting a number between 1 and 100; key it into the calculator, followed by [÷] [=]. This makes the selected number a constant divisor, but don't reveal this to the students. Hand the calculator to another student, and ask the student to guess the number that was entered. Enter another number and hit the [=] key. A decimal will appear on the display screen. Students should be able to discover the hidden number by analyzing the numbers that appear on the display screen after several trials.
58. Check software catalogs for programs that provide the drill and practice needed for the upper elementary grades. Many software programs also keep records for the teacher. In these cases, the teacher can easily check the computer to find out how many examples each child has practiced, the number of correct and incorrect answers, the percent of accuracy, and the amount of time consumed.

Suggested Readings

Battista, M. T. (1993). Mathematics in baseball. *The Mathematics Teacher, 86*(4).

Behr, M. J., Harel, G., Post, T. T., & Lesh, R. (1992). Rational number, ratio, and proportion. In Grouws, D. A. (Ed.), *Handbook of Research on Mathematics Teaching and Learning,* New York, NY: Macmillan.

Clason, R. G. (1986). How our decimal money began. *The Arithmetic Teacher, 33*(5).

Cooper, R. (1994). *Alternative math techniques instructional guide.* Bryn Mawr, PA: Center for Alternative Learning.

Cramer, K., Bezuk, N., & Behr, M. (1989). Proportional relationships and unit rates. *The Mathematics Teacher, 82*(2).

Cramer, K., & Post, T. (1993). Making connections: A case for proportionality. *The Arithmetic Teacher, 40*(6).

Duprey, L. (1994). Reap dividends with stock market math. *Learning, 22*(5).

Erickson, D. K. (1990). Activities: Percentages and cuisenaire rods. *The Mathematics Teacher, 83*(3).

Goldberg, S. (1994). Making a hit with percentages. *Learning, 22*(6).

Grossnickle, F. E., & Perry, L. M. (1985). Division with common fractions and decimal divisors. *School Science and Mathematics, 85*(7).

Haubner, M. A. (1992). Percents: Developing meaning through models. *The Arithmetic Teacher, 40*(4).

Hiebert, J., & Behr, M., (Eds.). (1988). *Number concepts and operations in the middle grades.* Reston, VA: National Council of Teachers of Mathematics.

Hope, J. A., Reys, B. J., & Reys, R. E. (1988). *Mental math in junior high.* Palo Alto, CA: Dale Seymour Publications.

Klein, P. A. (1990). Remembering how to read decimals. *The Arithmetic Teacher, 37*(9).

Levain, J. P. (1992). Solutions to multiplying problems at the end of the primary cycle. *Educational Studies in Mathematics, 23.*

May, L. (1993). What would you buy? *Teaching PreK-8, 24*(3).

May, L. (1994). Real life math and the world of shopping. (1994). *Teaching PreK-8, 24*(4).

May, L. J. (1995). Using models to extend the meaning of decimals. *Teaching PreK-8, 25.*

Meyer, R. A., & Riley, J. E. (1984). Investigating decimal fractions with the hand calculator. *School Science and Mathematics, 84*(7).

Payne, J. N., & Towsley, A. E. (1990). Implications of NCTM's standards for teaching fractions and decimals. *The Arithmetic Teacher, 37*(8).

Post, T. R. (1989). Fractions and other rational numbers. *The Arithmetic Teacher, 36*(1).

Quintero, A. M. (1987). Helping children understand ratios. *The Arithmetic Teacher, 34*(9).

Rowan, T. E., & Morrow, L. J. (1993). *Implementing the K-8 curriculum and evaluation standards: Readings from The Arithmetic Teacher. Implementing the K-8 curriculum and evaluation standards.* Reston, VA: National Council of Teachers of Mathematics.

Schliemann, A. D., & Carraher, T. N. (1988). Using money to teach about the decimal system. *The Arithmetic Teacher, 36*(4).

Winson, B. (1992). Intermediate focus: Numeration and place value. *Instructor, 102*(2).

Chapter 13

Data Analysis: Graphs, Statistics, and Probability

Overview

Many college students preparing to teach in elementary schools may recall little or no introduction to either statistics or probability in their own elementary mathematics development. The topics of statistics and probability are sometimes placed as the last chapter in a mathematics textbook, and many classes never "get to them." Because of the lack of content knowledge coupled with little opportunity to develop competency with statistics and probability, some college students may find this short introduction unit to be a challenge. However, many also find the introduction of these concepts to be intriguing and motivating—particularly with many experiences explored on the concrete level and systematically moving through the semiconcrete, semiabstract, and abstract levels of development.

The underlying concepts of statistics will probably be more familiar to students than those of probability. Many of us are ill-prepared to function successfully with statistics, and yet the basic concepts are not difficult to comprehend or calculate. Approaching statistics with real data, studying the data, and then arriving at generalizations seem to offer less frustration to students than using a deductive approach. Often, students can be well into the study of statistics before they realize it. Probability, although commonly used, is less well recognized and many will probably approach this topic in a less biased manner than statistics.

This chapter may be easily coordinated with science or social studies topics, as well as topics from other school disciplines. The uses for statistics and probability are becoming more familiar to children through television and newspapers. Space travel has posed new problems in probability. What are the chances that a shuttle will achieve a given orbit? What are the chances that the weather will be suitable for liftoff? Industry has used statistics and probability to determine the chances that certain products are defective; the Department of Labor publishes statistics on employment. Many other sources of data are available for interesting class activities.

An experimental approach to statistics and probability is perhaps the most beneficial for elementary children. Situations that can be reenacted in the classroom provide motivation and enjoyment. Children should be encouraged to design and perform their own experiments and keep careful records of data. Many statistics and probability activities can be placed on activity cards or prepared for a laboratory approach to mathematics.

Many elementary school mathematics programs begin the study of graphs by teaching children how to read graphs. We suggest that children will develop a better understanding of graphs and graphing if they are actively involved in *constructing* the graphs they are asked to read and interpret. These early experiences, as well as later ones, should involve concrete graphing before the formal graphs in this chapter are discussed. That is, children should have many opportunities to use real objects set out in rows or columns. For example, the children in one class might be asked to stand behind birth-month signs while the children of another class use this human graph to make statements about the data.

SAMPLE LESSON PLAN—"COLORFUL M&M'S"

Intermediate Developmental Lesson

Goal:

Develop conceptual understanding of averaging.

Objective:

The students will:

- Determine averages by leveling concrete bar graphs.
- Draw conclusions from data.

Prerequisite Learning and/or Experiences:

- Constructing concrete and pictorial bar graphs.
- Interpreting concrete and pictorial bar graphs.

Materials:

Per cooperative learning group:

- 4 bags of individual-sized (<2 oz.) M&M candies
- cm graph paper
- chart paper and markers

Per class:

- 2 inch construction paper circles in red, yellow, blue, green, orange, and dark brown (approx. 10-15 of each color)
- large graphing mat

Colors of M&M's

red	□	□	□	□	□	□	□	□
yellow	□	□	□	□	□	□	□	□
blue	□	□	□	□	□	□	□	□
green	□	□	□	□	□	□	□	□
orange	□	□	□	□	□	□	□	□
brown	□	□	□	□	□	□	□	□

- overhead cm graph paper transparency
- chart paper and marker

Procedures:

Students work in cooperative groups of four—coordinators, recorders, reporters, and illustrators.

Motivational Introduction

Begin by asking if the class believes that everyone likes the same "things." What sports do they like the best? What television programs? What foods? What school subjects? Even if we don't all pick the same thing we can still try to find the class' favorite by collecting data and drawing graphs.

1. Begin by holding up a bag of M&M candy. Have each student name his or her favorite color M&M candy and record it on a slip of paper. Match each student choice with a colored construction paper circle representing his or her favorite color.
2. Use the construction paper circles to create a "Favorite Color of M&M Candy" class graph. Display the large graphing mat. Have each student individually attach his or her colored circle to the appropriately labeled column on the graphing mat.
3. Have the class discuss the resulting data display. Incorporate descriptive (yellow has five), comparative (two more yellows than blues), and interpretive (brown is the class' least favorite color) conclusions. Be sure to determine the "most favorite" color of M&M for the class.

Developmental Activity

4. Coordinators supply each member of their group with a bag of M&M candies.
5. Each student carefully opens the bag of M&M's and removes only the "red" pieces.
6. Illustrators have groups build "red" towers on cm graph paper and label each tower with the students' initials. Coordinators have groups level the towers (to determine a group average). For example:

		○						
○		○		→	○	○	○	
○	○	○	○	→	○	○	○	○
○	○	○	○	→	○	○	○	○
○	○	○	○	→	○	○	○	○
GU	MH	JF	RM	→	GU	MH	JF	RM

7. Recorders record their group averages for "red" (to the nearest whole number) on their group chart. For example:

M&M Color Averages for Ginny's Group

Color	Average
red	4
yellow	
orange	
blue	
green	
brown	

8. Reporters share groups' averages for "red." Teacher models by building a "red" tower for each group on an overhead cm graph transparency. As the "red" towers are leveled, a class average is determined, and the average is recorded on a class "Color Averages" chart.
9. Each student eats his or her "red" tower. Steps #4-8 are repeated for each remaining color of M&M.

Culminating Activity

10. Refer to the class "Favorite Color" graph and "Color Averages" chart. Compare and contrast the data. Note similarities or differences between the class' favorite color and the color with the highest average recorded for the class.

Extension:

As a connection to language arts, have each student write a letter to the President of the M&M/Mars Candy Company (address is on the candy wrapper). The letter should address how the class voted on its favorite color of M&M, how the class determined the color with the highest average, what the class decided when the two sets of data were compared, and how the candy company should consider this data when packaging M&M candies.

Student Assessment/Evaluation:

Assess completion of the graphs and the quality and quantity of the descriptive, interpretive and comparative statements they create. Apply a rubric scoring to both individual and class performance as follows:

0 = no attempt
1 = able to generate/interpret statements of only one type
2 = able to generate/interpret statements of only two types
3 = able to generate/interpret statements of all three types

Assess the content of individual letters prepared for the extension. Each letter should contain four distinctive parts based upon the requirements listed. Apply a rubric scoring responses as follows:

0 = no attempt
1 = competently responds to one of the four requirements
2 = competently responds to two of the four requirements
3 = competently responds to three of the four requirements
4 = competently responds to four of the four requirements

INSTRUCTIONAL AND ASSESSMENT ACTIVITIES FOR GRADES K-4

1. Provide the children in the classroom with wooden cubes to represent each of their pets. (*Note:* We are asking the children to function on the semiabstract level, since cubes will be used to represent pets.) Place a chart in front of the children with columns labeled for each type of pet. The chart might look like the one illustrated here.

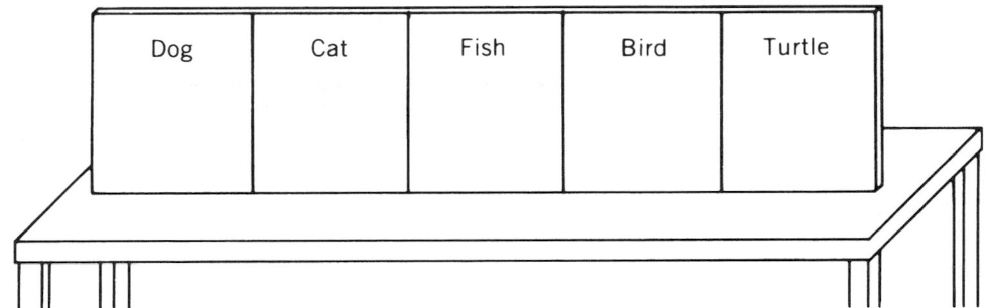

Ask children who have pets to place a cube in the proper column. The children should stack cubes one at a time. Discuss with the children the placement of each cube. The completed activity might be illustrated by the following drawing:

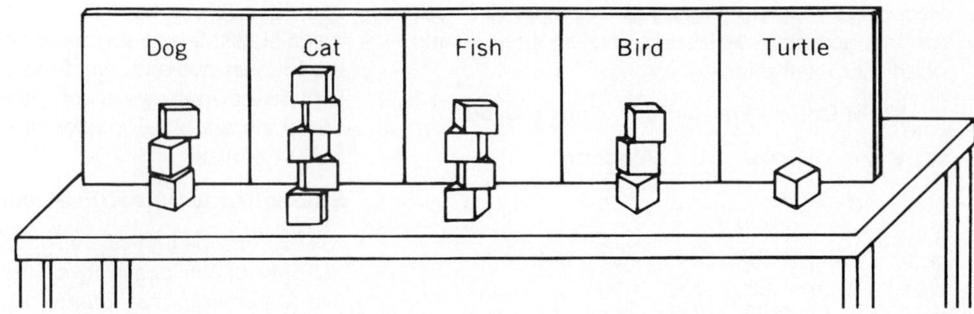

Discuss with the children how the graph shows the number of each type of pet. Ask the children how we might make a picture of the actual graph. Talk about a beginning line (baseline), and suggest that we could draw bars to represent the number of cubes in each stack. Draw a picture of the graph, and post this graph on the bulletin board. Compare the number of pets with both the actual graph and the drawn graph.

2. Primary children can visit other classrooms in the school and record the number of children who have birthdays during each month. Make a bulletin board using a line graph to show the birthdays of all the children in the school.

3. Young children often wear name tags to help them learn the names of their classmates. Prepare a classroom bulletin board with an attractive background and separate it into twelve columns labeled for each month of the year. Ask the children to bring up their name tags one at a time and tell the month of their birthdays. Place the name tags in the proper column and build a bar graph showing the children and their months of birth.

Our Birthdays

Jan	Feb	March	April	May	June	July	Aug	Sept	Oct	Nov	Dec
											Jim
	Kay			Ted							Ole
	Mary			Peg		Leo					Ruth
	Jon			Bill		Ruth	Betty		Sak		Eli
May	Bob	Don	Al	Liz		Carol	Helen	Mike	Ned	Rod	Jake

4. After a few days, gather the children around the bulletin board described in Activity 3. Use yarn to connect the center of each bar, and then remove the name tags. The bar graph has now been changed into a line graph. Discuss the two types of graphs with the children. With older children you should lead a discussion as to whether this is an appropriate type of graph for these data.

5. This is a game for two players or teams. You'll need a "track" similar to that shown, and a coin. Both teams start at the beginning and alternate turns flipping the coin. If heads comes up, then the team moves ahead one space. If tails comes up, then the team moves ahead two spaces. Each team tries to be the first one to reach the end. Mark the paths with H's and T's as heads and tails are flipped. Does the same team win this game if it's played several times? Does the "best" team win? What can be said about the tosses of the winning team?

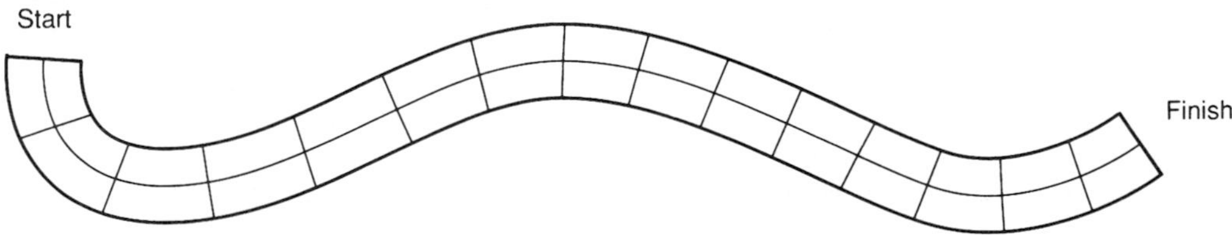

6. Although the calculator and computer both have limited application in the primary grades with respect to statistics and probability, keep in mind that calculators and computers are both designed as data handlers. For example, the calculator may be used for "number crunching" to avoid having attention taken away from the concept under discussion. Data collections that include many measures can still be explored if the calculator is used effectively and wisely as a tool, not a crutch.

7. The computer may prove to be more useful than the calculator in the context of manipulation of data because the "data" that it is capable of handling include words as well as numbers. Database software is readily available for all grade levels. This software allows the user to search data for common characteristics or traits. These common elements can then often be tallied, and sometimes graphed, within the software itself. When this is not the case, the information can be translated into graph form by the user. Children can gather and enter their own data, or the teacher can find precollected data packages. Readers are encouraged to examine database software locally available for the microcomputer system they are using.

8. If there are seven books in one stack, two books in the second stack, and three books in the third stack, how can I adjust them so that the same number of books will be in each of the three stacks?

9. Find the average of each collection of numbers.

a)

3, 7, 4, 1, 1 7, 8, 3 9, 3, 6, 4, 3

b)

65, 25, 52, 37, 46 0, 8, 3, 9, 6, 4 68, 114, 94, 88

10. Have the children collect and bring into the classroom graphs from newspapers and magazines to put on a bulletin board.

11. Collect data on a specific topic, say a favorite wild animal. Make a table of the results of the data collection. Using this same data, make a bar graph, a line graph, and a circle graph.

12. Make simple graphs from classroom data. Avoid data that directly compare the children. Have each child make a graph showing his or her own personal progress. For instance, graph spelling grades of one particular child for each week or the results of memorizing the basic subtraction or multiplication facts. Again, avoid *sharing* data that might embarrass individuals.

13. What is the average number of days per month? Discuss with the children what the calculator answer of 30.416666 means.

14. Roll a die ten times. Record the top number on the die each time, and calculate the average for the ten rolls. Could you tell the average without dividing by 10? How? Could you use the same procedure if the die is rolled 25 times? Explain.

15. Discuss with children the advantages of using a calculator when exploring such topics as statistics and probability. When is the calculator most useful in this context? When is it of little use?

16. Encourage the children to collect information about school lunches for a period of time. They should identify different beverages available, different main items, different vegetables, different fruits, different breads, and different desserts. The children can then enter the data into a database program and analyze the data by using the various aspects of the database. For example, children can use the database to determine the fruit most commonly offered. Follow-up "studies" can be done regarding the favorite dessert of the class and the frequency with which it is served. The children could also explore the probability of certain items appearing together or on certain days of the week.

17. Use the "find" or "search" capability of a word processing package to identify how many times certain words appear in a previously typed passage. Can you find the "mode"? If your word processor has a word count capacity, can you find the average number of words per paragraph? How could the phrase "average paragraph" be interpreted?

18. a) If you flip a coin, the chances are one out of two that the coin will land heads up. What are the chances that it will land tails up? Why? (When we say, "What are the chances that a particular event will occur?" we are asking, "What is the probability that the event will occur?")
    b) Does the fraction $\frac{1}{2}$ represent this probability?
    c) Can you write five more fractions that represent the same probability as $\frac{1}{2}$?

INSTRUCTIONAL AND ASSESSMENT ACTIVITIES FOR GRADES 5-8

1. Suppose you are blindfolded and a friend places two different pairs of shoes in front of you and tells you to choose one pair. What is the probability that the first two shoes you pick up will be a matched pair? Why?
2. Choose a number at random from this collection:

   {2, 3, 4, 5, 12, 13, 14, 15, 22, 23, 24}

   a) What are the chances that the number would be an even number?
   b) What are the chances that the number would be an odd number?
   c) What are the chances that it would be an even number and a multiple of 5?
   d) What are the chances that it would be an odd number and a multiple of 5?
3. The following diagram is a simple map of three towns and the highways between them:

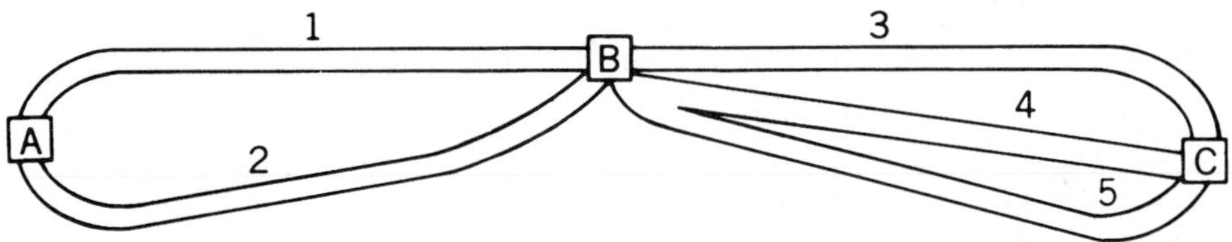

   a) List all the possible routes you could use to get from town A to town C.
   b) How many possible routes did you find?
   c) If we say that taking any one of the routes is equally likely, what is the probability of taking highways 1 and 4?
4. Suppose you have five red poker chips, four blue chips, and three white chips in a bag.
   a) What is the probability of getting a blue chip on the first draw?
   b) What is the probability of getting a white chip on the first draw?
   c) What is the probability of *not* getting a white chip on the first draw?
   d) Suppose you got a red chip on the first draw. What is the probability of getting another red chip on the next draw?
   e) If you know that the probability of getting a blue chip is 0, what does this tell you about the colors of the chips in the bag?
   f) Write fractions (probability ratios) to represent the probabilities for parts a-d.
5. Flip a coin 25 times and keep a record of the number of times heads appear and the number of times tails appear. From your experiment, what do you think is the probability of getting heads? Now flip the coin 50 times, and record the results the same way. How do the two charts compare? Do you think there is any change in the probability of the number of times heads will appear?
6. Many games such as Monopoly or Parchessi use two dice with a certain number of dots on each face of each die. Usually these dots number from 1 to 6 on each face.

   Toss a die 60 times and record the number of times each of the numerals 1, 2, 3, 4, 5, or 6 appears.

Numeral	Occurs
1	II
2	~~IIII~~
3	I
4	III
5	II
6	I

Can you think of a way to record the results of this kind of experiment using two dice at a time? Try it!

7. Make a set of cards with the letters A, B, C, D, and E.

A	B	C	D	E

Make a total of 14 "A" cards, 8 "B" cards, six "C" cards, 6 "D" cards, and 2 "E" cards.

If you shuffle the cards and draw one card, what are the chances of getting an A card? What are the chances of getting an E card? Which cards would have equal chances?

Make a simple chart to record this experiment. Guess which type of card you will get. Write it down. Draw a card and write down the letter of the card you actually got. See how many times you win.

8. You have probably played games that have a spinner like the one pictured. If you do not have one, make one similar to it with cardboard, a paperclip, and a thumbtack. Use stiff, flat cardboard and make sure the spinner turns freely.

If you spin the spinner just one time, what are the chances of landing on 6? What are the chances of landing on 3?

Spin the spinner 20 times and keep a record of the results.

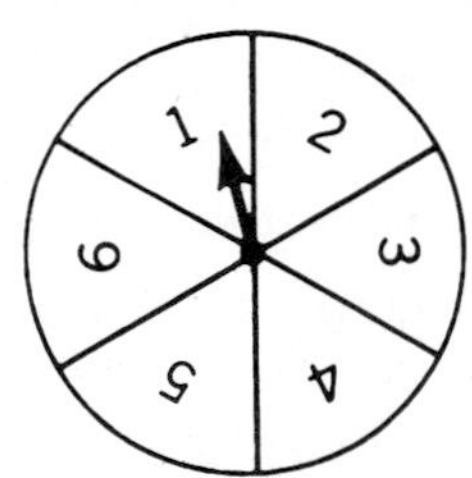

Numeral	1	2	3	4	5	6
Occurs						

a) Which numeral occurred the greatest number of times?
b) Which numeral occurred the least number of times?
c) Which numerals occurred about the same number of times?
d) According to your experiment, which numeral seems most likely to occur?
e) Which numeral seems least likely to occur?
f) Try this experiment two more times; compare the three records you now have. Have you changed your opinion?

9. Make a chart showing the number of students who are present in class for a two-week period. What is the average or mean number of students present? What is the median? The mode?

10. Last month the temperatures recorded in Bloom City at 5:00 p.m. were 75, 62, 54, 68, 72, 52, 62, 63, 71, 72, 65, 80, 74, 69, 64, 72, 82, 80, 69, 70, 59, 64, 69, 72, 67, 75, 62, 71, 74, and 54.

a) Make a chart with the above information, giving the temperature and the tally (the number of times each temperature was recorded). What is the range?
b) Find the mean, the median, and the mode.
c) What is the best indicator of the measure of central tendency for this information?
d) Check your newspaper each day and graph the maximum and minimum temperatures for a week or a month.

11. The mean age of the people attending a picnic at the fairgrounds was 18. Does this mean that most of the people there were teenagers? Why or why not?

12. I have five puppies. These are their weights, in ounces:

Puff	37
Red	45
Ginger	54
Daisie	62
Molly	27

What is the average weight of my dogs?

13. Francine has been keeping a record of the amount of homework she has done each night for eight nights. About how much time does Francine spend on homework each night?

1st night	30 min
2nd	45 min
3rd	10 min
4th	70 min
5th	43 min
6th	21 min
7th	0 min
8th	53 min

How many different ways can you think of to answer the question? Which way seems "best"?

14. Select one or two stocks from those listed in a newspaper and graph the quotations from the paper each day for a month.

15. Children can keep a running line graph showing increases (hopefully) in their own spelling grades or mathematics grades.

16. The children can keep a large graph in the hall for projects undertaken by the entire school or PTA. Children should accept responsibility for collecting the data, recording the data, and keeping the graph up-to-date.

17. Ask students to construct a bar graph, line graph, circle graph, pictograph, stem-and-leaf plot, and box-and-whisker plot from the same set of data. What characteristics must be present in the data to make all of these different graphs?

18. Assuming that Americans eat 43,200,000 hot dogs every day, what is the average number of hot dogs eaten every hour? Every minute? Every second?

19. Bob drove 406 miles in 72 hours. What was Bob's average driving speed? Does that mean he drove that speed constantly?

20. At this level, take full advantage of the data-handling and data-analyzing capabilities of the microcomputer, the database, and the word processing programs available in your situation.

21. Some upper elementary children might be ready to explore computer spreadsheet software. Spreadsheet programs allow the user to enter and manipulate numbers according to user-defined formulas. If the child is ready, spreadsheets can provide an excellent way to explore statistical concepts.

Suggested Readings

American Statistical Association. (1991). *Guidelines for the teaching of statistics in K-12 mathematics curriculum.* Landover, MD: Corporate Press.

Boruch, R. F., & Zawojewski, J. S. (1987). Coupling literature and statistics. *Teaching Statistics, 9.*

Brahier, D. J., Brahier, A. F., & Speer, W. R. (1992). IDEAS—Elections. *The Arithmetic Teacher, 40*(3).

Bright, G. W. (1989). Teaching mathematics with technology: Probability simulations. *The Arithmetic Teacher, 36*(9).

Browning, C. A., & Channell, D. E. (1992). A 'handy' database activity for the middle school classroom. *The Arithmetic Teacher, 40*(4).

Bruni, J. V., & Silverman, H. J. (1986). Developing concepts in probability and statistics—and much more. *The Arithmetic Teacher, 33*(6).

Bryan, E. H. (1988). Exploring data with box plots. *The Mathematics Teacher, 81*(3).

Burns, M. (1988). Dice advice: With a toss of the die, you can teach a lesson on probability. *Instructor, 97*(5).

Burns, M. (1994). Four great math games. *Instructor, 103*(8).

Burns, M. (1994). Probability games in a bag. *Instructor, 103*(9).

Burrill, G. (1990). Implementing the standards: Statistics and probability. *The Mathematics Teacher, 83*(2).

Chancellor, D. (1991). Calendar mathematics: Taking chances. *The Arithmetic Teacher, 39*(3).

Cook, M. (1993). Ideas: Combinations. *The Arithmetic Teacher, 41*(4).

Corwin, R. B., & Friel, S. (1990). Statistics: Prediction and sampling. A Unit of Study for Grades 5-6. From *Used numbers: Real data in the classroom.* Palo Alto, CA: Dale Seymour Publications.

Corwin, R. B. & Russell, S. J. (1990). Graphs that grow. *Instructor, 99*(8).

Crites, T. (1994). Using lotteries to improve students' number sense and understanding of probability. *School Science and Mathematics, 94.*

Curcio, F. (1989). *Developing graph comprehension: Elementary and middle school activities.* Reston, VA: National Council of Teachers of Mathematics.

Drake, B. M. (1993). Sharing teaching ideas: Exploring 'different' dice. *The Mathematics Teacher, 86*(9).

Edwards, N. T., Bitter, G. G., & Hatfield, M. M. (1990). Teaching mathematics with technology: Data base and spreadsheet templates with public domain software, *The Arithmetic Teacher, 37*(8).

English, L. (1992). Problem solving with combinations. *The Arithmetic Teacher, 40*(2).

Farnsworth, D. L. (1991). Introducing probability. *The Mathematics Teacher, 84*(2).

Fennel, F. (1990). Implementing the standards: Probability. *The Arithmetic Teacher, 38*(4).

Fielker, D. (1989). So what do we mean by prediction? *Mathematics Teaching.*

Friel, S. N., & Corwin, R. B. (1990). Implementing the standards: The statistics standards in K-8 mathematics. *The Arithmetic Teacher, 38*(2).

Friel, S., Mokros, J. R., & Russell, S. J. (1992). Statistics: Middles, means, and in-betweens. A Unit of Study for Grades 5-6. From *Used numbers: Real data in the classroom.* Palo Alto, CA: Dale Seymour Publications.

Garfield, J. (1994). Student reaction to learning about probability and statistics. *School Science and Mathematics, 94*(2).

Garfield, J., & Ahlgren, A. (1988). Difficulties in learning basic concepts in probability and statistics: Implications for research. *Journal for Research in Mathematics Education, 19*(1).

Glicksberg, J. (1990). Taste that graph. *The Arithmetic Teacher, 38*(4).

Goldman, P. (1990). Teaching arithmetic averaging: An activity approach. *The Arithmetic Teacher, 37*(7).

Green, D. (1993). Puzzling probability problems. *Mathematics Teaching, 145.*

Hands-on, Inc. (1990). *Statistics, probability, and graphing: Kindergarten through grade nine.* Solvang, CA: Author.

Hatfield, L. L. (1992). Activities: Explorations with chance. *The Mathematics Teacher, 85*(8).

Hinders, D. C. (1990). Examples of the use of statistics in society. *The Mathematics Teacher, 83*(2).

Hitch, C., & Armstrong, G. (1994). Daily activities for data analysis. *The Arithmetic Teacher, 41*(5).

Huff, D. (1954). *How to lie with statistics.* New York, NY: W.W. Norton.

Johnson, E. M. (1981). Bar graphs for first graders. *The Arithmetic Teacher, 29*(4).

Keller, J. D. (1993). Ideas. *The Arithmetic Teacher, 40.*

Konold, C. (1994). Teaching probability through modeling real problems. *The Mathematics Teacher, 87*(4).

Korithoski, T. P., & Korithoski, P. A. (1993). Mean or meaningless. *The Arithmetic Teacher, 41*(4).

Landwehr, J. M., & Watkins, A. E. (1985). Stem and leaf plots. *The Mathematics Teacher, 78*(2).

Litwiller, B., & Duncan, D. (1992). Matching garage-door openers. *The Mathematics Teacher, 85*(3).

Litwiller, B., & Duncan, D. (1992). Prizes in cereal boxes: An application of probability. *School Science and Mathematics, 92*(4).

Martin, H. M., & Zawojewski, J. S. (1993). Dealing with data and chance: An illustration from the middle school addendum to the standards. *The Arithmetic Teacher, 41*(4).

Mosteller, F. (1988). Broadening the scope of statistics and statistical education. *The American Statistician, 42*(2).

National Council of Teachers of Mathematics. (1981). *Teaching statistics and probability.* 1981 Yearbook.

Reston, VA: National Council of Teachers of Mathematics.

National Council of Teachers of Mathematics. (1991). *Curriculum and evaluation standards for school mathematics addenda series grades 5-8: Dealing with data and chance.* Reston, VA: National Council of Teachers of Mathematics.

National Council of Teachers of Mathematics. (1992). *Curriculum and evaluation standards for school mathematics addenda series grades K-4: Making sense of data.* Reston, VA: National Council of Teachers of Mathematics.

Pagni, D. L. (1989). A television programming challenge: A cooperative group activity that uses mathematics. *The Arithmetic Teacher, 36*(1).

Parker, J., & Widmer, C. C. (1992). Statistics and graphing. *The Arithmetic Teacher, 39*(8).

Passarello, L. M., & Fennell, F. (1992). Ideas. *The Arithmetic Teacher, 39.*

Paull, S. (1990). Not just an average unit. *The Arithmetic Teacher, 38*(4).

Paulos, J. A. (1989). *Innumeracy.* New York, NY: Hill and Wang.

Phillips, E., Lappan, G., Winter, M. J., & Fitzgerald, W. (1986). *Probability* (middle grades mathematics project). Menlo Park, CA: Addison-Wesley.

Phillips Jr., J. L. (1992). *How to think about statistics.* New York, NY: W.H. Freeman.

Ramondetta, J. (1994). Graph it! and make numbers make sense. *Learning, 22*(8).

Rowan, T. E., & Morrow, L. J. (1993). *Implementing the K-8 curriculum and evaluation standards: Readings from The Arithmetic Teacher. Implementing the K-8 curriculum and evaluation standards.* Reston, VA: National Council of Teachers of Mathematics.

Russell, S. J., & Corwin, R. B. (1989). Statistics: The shape of the data. A Unit of Study for Grades 4-6. From *Used numbers: Real data in the classroom.* Palo Alto, CA: Dale Seymour Publications.

Russell, S. J., & Corwin, R. B. (1990). Sorting: Groups and graphs. A Unit of Study for Grades 2-3. From *Used numbers: Real data in the classroom.* Palo Alto, CA: Dale Seymour Publications.

Schwartzman, S. (1993). An unexpected expected value. *The Mathematics Teacher, 86*(2).

Shielack, J. F. (1990). Teaching mathematics with technology: A graphing tool for the primary grades. *The Arithmetic Teacher, 38*(2).

Vissa, J. (1987). Sampling treats from a school of fish. *The Arithmetic Teacher, 34*(7).

Vissa, J. (1988). Probability and combinations for third graders. *The Arithmetic Teacher, 36*(4).

Watson, J. O. (1993). America's pastime. *The Mathematics Teacher, 86.*

Woodward, E. (1983). A second grade probability and graphing lesson. *The Arithmetic Teacher, 3*(7).

Woodward, E., Frost, S., & Smith, A. (1991). Cemetery mathematics. *The Arithmetic Teacher, 39*(4).

Zawojewski, J. S. (1988). Research into practice: Teaching statistics: Mean, median, and mode. *The Arithmetic Teacher, 35*(7).

Chapter 14

Measurement

Overview

Engineers and scientists have considerable need for measuring instruments. Should these instruments be calibrated in U.S. customary units or in metric units? The average American adult needs measurement to consider "which is longer?", "which is the best buy?", "which is heavier?", etc. Should the average American use U.S. customary or metric measurements as they make these decisions?

Most people are able to use a ruler to measure length and a scale to measure weight, but does the average American have a solid understanding of what measurement is? If an individual understands measurement as a comparison of a standard to an object of unknown length, then does it make any difference if the units are metric or U.S. customary? Through use, we develop an understanding of foot, pound, and gallon. The same should also be true for a meter, gram, and liter. More emphasis should be placed on measurement and less emphasis on which set of units we should use.

The concepts of measurement should begin with the young child's experiences with real measures. Children need many experiences experimenting with measuring devices such as rulers, scales, containers, clocks, and thermometers. As measurement is developed in the intermediate grades, children should develop tables of equivalences. They should decide on the precision and the accuracy of measure needed for different tasks. New units of measure are continually inserted into the program, including standard units for measuring area and standard units for measuring volume.

The exploration of measurement is well-suited to a laboratory approach. Children learn measurement best by measuring. Provide many materials for children to use in experimenting and discovering relationships. Children can begin to measure with very crude instruments and then continually refine the instruments as more precise measurements are required. Children enjoy making their own measuring instruments. The teacher might construct a ruler and set up a place in the room called the "Bureau of Standards" to house the ruler the teacher constructed. From the standard ruler at the Bureau of Standards, each child may construct his or her own measuring device. Standard units for surface measure and volume can also be developed and placed in the Bureau of Standards.

To young children, the concept of measurement is most meaningful when it is expressed in terms of concepts such as "longer," "shorter," "taller," "later," and "farther." In the spring they realize that the days are longer and they are allowed to play outside later. In winter, the days are shorter, and it seems that they must go to bed earlier. They know that some children are taller than others, that some stores are farther away than others, and that some people are older than others. All of these familiar situations create a perfect setting for developing the concepts of measurement.

In learning and teaching metric measurement, children, teachers, and parents are in a unique position, because children can learn the metric system in school and then go home and teach their parents some mathematics they probably do not know as well as they should.

When faced with a simple situation that demands measurement of length, a child should understand the need for measuring and be able to decide on the proper units to use and perform the measurement with a degree of accuracy appropriate to the child's age and maturity.

SAMPLE LESSON PLAN—"DECIMETER SCAVENGER HUNT"

Primary Developmental/Discovery Lesson

Goal:

Develop physical reference points for standard linear units of measure.

Objectives:

The students will:

- Find objects whose measure is approximately one decimeter.
- Employ physical references to estimate to the nearest decimeter.
- Use denominate numbers to describe actual measures.

Prerequisite Learning and/or Experiences:

Experience measuring objects linearly (length, width, height, and distance) using nonstandard units of measure.

Materials:

- a piece of non-stretchy string, one decimeter long (or a strip of posterboard with dimensions of one decimeter long by one centimeter wide) for each student
- paper and pencil
- chart paper or overhead transparency (optional)

Procedures:

Motivational Introduction

Begin the lesson by stating "Our principal has asked each teacher to complete a classroom furniture inventory which must include measurements. I will need your help, so let's begin by measuring our desktops."

Pose the question, "What's the distance across the bottom of your desktop?" Have students share their ideas for answering this query. Accept responses including both nonstandard and standard measurement ideas, but guide discussion toward the two components central to this lesson, namely, *a numeric value* associated with *a unit of measure.*

To spur discussion about the need for standard measures ask each student to measure the distance across the bottom of his or her desk using *knuckle spans.* Describe a knuckle span as the distance across all four knuckles on your hand when you make a fist. Once the students have measured their desks in knuckle spans, have individuals report results. Be sure students report results as ________ (a numeric value) knuckle spans. Encourage students to tell how they arrived at a solution as this will set the stage for using the same measuring device over and over again. Chart several results and compare the variety of answers. Discuss differences and why these differences occurred. Use this information to develop a rationale for standard units of measure.

1. Have each student search for ONE other student that has a "knuckle span" that is a different size than his or her own. Provide each student with a piece of string which measures one decimeter. Have the pairs of students compare their knuckle spans to the length of string. One student makes a fist while the other student holds the string taut between the thumb and pointing finger; pairs change roles. Now have pairs compare their strings. Pairs should notice the strings are almost as long as their individual knuckle spans and that both strings are the same length. If it seems appropriate to define this length now, tell the students that society has agreed to call this "one decimeter." Be certain students realize that this refers to the length represented by the string and that any object of the same length is also a decimeter in length. (The reason for using a decimeter as the reference length is that an inch or centimeter is too small—at this point it is preferred to use a measure that the students can

easily physically hold and manipulate. In any case, this lesson is more concerned with the process of measurement than with the name of the measure.)

Developmental Activity

2. While remaining at their desks, have students look around the classroom for objects which they believe are about one decimeter long, tall, wide, across, etc. Ask students to write down the names of three objects they think will fit this "length" requirement.
3. Have students compare the length of their string to each object they wrote down. Students are to note if the object is *close* to being one decimeter long, *too long,* or *too short.* Next to the name of each object, have students write "too long", "close", or "too short". In order to gather information students will need to be out of their seats, so set a time limit for measuring and recording.
4. Have students share which objects were close to being one decimeter long. Chart their responses. Some typical responses may include a piece of unused chalk, a new crayon, a filing cabinet handle, a single light switch plate, etc. Have students clearly explain which portion of each object they measured. For example, the height of the light switch plate is about one decimeter.
5. Have students take home a decimeter string and locate three different objects at home which are about one decimeter long. Have students record their findings and bring them to school the next day.
6. Include the "at home" measurements in the chart begun in step 4.

Culminating Activity

7. Now, have students estimate the length of the bottom of their desktop in decimeters. Encourage students to imagine an object from the chart repeatedly laid across the bottom of their desk. Use this mental image to "guesstimate" how many decimeters would fit across the bottom of their desk.
8. Have each student write down his or her estimate and then use the string to actually measure the bottom of the desks. (Have extra strings available for those students that left theirs at home from the homework assignment.) Some students may not know how to repeatedly use the string to measure a distance longer than the string, so be prepared to offer suggestions and assistance. It may be necessary to use several decimeter strings laid end-to-end as a model compared to the same string used repeatedly. Have students record measurements to the nearest decimeter.
9. Because we are using a standard unit of measure, most students should have the same response to the question, "How many decimeters long is the bottom of your desk?" If major discrepancies occur, then repetition technique is most likely the problem. Have those with unusual answers demonstrate the process used.
10. Have students compare estimates to actual measures. During the discussion encourage students to describe how the physical reference they imagined helped them estimate before they measured.

Extension:

Provide opportunities for students to estimate and measure several real objects (*not pictures* of objects from activity pages) to the nearest decimeter. For example, determine the measurement data to complete the principal's furniture inventory request. Generate a form which lists the classroom furniture along with required dimensions such as length, width, and/or height. Encourage students to use a physical reference as an estimate tool before actually measuring. Each student will eventually self-select physical referents to which they best relate through personal experience.

Student Assessment/Evaluation:

Observe students' classroom and at-home responses for objects which are close to one decimeter. If students' responses tend to be too long or too short, then encourage students to look for objects which relate to them personally. The length of a new crayon which students often hold is probably a better physical reference than a piece of new chalk which is more likely to be held by the teacher.

INSTRUCTIONAL AND ASSESSMENT ACTIVITIES FOR GRADES K-4

1. Stimulating interest in measuring objects or people in the student's real world is a logical starting point in the early grades. Many activities result from appropriate questions asked by the teacher. For example:

   Who is the tallest?
   Who can reach the widest?
   Who is heaviest?
   Who can jump the highest?
   Which is longer, the chalk tray or the windowsill?
   Which is later in the day—breakfast or bedtime?
   Which holds more—a milk glass or a coffee cup?

2. To measure the chalk tray, for example, have a long stick available to use as a unit. Have children measure the length of the tray in "stick units." It is advisable to have two children work together. This kind of measuring activity can be performed by several pairs of children and the results compared. The sticks used should not have markings of any sort.
3. Have sticks of various lengths available. Ask children to measure the width of the room in stick-length units. Repeat the activity using sticks of greater length and sticks of shorter length. Have children compare and discuss the results; then decide which stick length is the most practical to use for this project. Give children ample time to follow through on this activity. Have groups of three or four children work together measuring various objects or distances in the classroom. Let them compare their results and present their findings to the class for discussion.
4. Select an object in the room for children to measure, one that does not allow the stick length to fit an even number of times. Have children estimate the amount of a unit (or stick length) left over, and lead them into the idea of rounding to the nearest whole unit. (If the object measured is approximately one-half of a unit, children may call it this.)
5. Select groups to work together measuring objects that you have already measured. Have each group record their results and then check to see if their measurements are reasonably correct. Many children may lack the dexterity and coordination needed to obtain precise results, and this should be taken into account.
6. Have a child stretch his or her arms horizontally; measure the distance from the tip of the middle finger of the right hand to the tip of the middle finger of the left hand. Record the distance. Then measure and record the same child's height. Repeat the activity with enough children to indicate whether or not, for each child, these two measurements tend to be similar.
7. Distribute several unmarked foot rulers (wooden, plastic, or stiff cardboard straightedges, all 1 foot long). Ask the children to compare these rulers and find out if they are the same length. Have them compare the foot ruler with the yardstick. Encourage them to think about various uses for each. For example, "Which one would you use to measure the bookcase?" "Which one would you use to measure the length of a sheet of paper?"
8. Have children use heavy cardboard to make rulers 1 decimeter long. Create a "Bureau of Standards" that is in charge of deciding what length each unit will be on the cardboard rulers (1 meter, 1 centimeter, and so on); the students model their rulers after those of the "Bureau of Standards." Each child can mark his or her ruler into centimeters. Discuss reasons for the formation of the U.S. Bureau of Standards and the variety of duties the bureau might perform.
9. Place strips of masking tape of various lengths in different parts of the room. Use lengths between 1 foot and 8 feet, preferably. Have children use their foot rulers to measure these lengths, and have them record and compare their results.

   After this activity, have a child use his or her foot ruler to measure a 10-inch strip. Rounded to the nearest foot, this would be recorded as 1 foot. Ask another child to measure a 3-inch strip with his or her foot ruler. Rounded to the nearest foot, this would be recorded as zero feet. At this point, the children should be asked to think about the notion of "zero feet." Is it really zero or not? This should generate the idea of using smaller units.
10. Distribute 1-inch cubes to the children, and let them use these to discover how many will fit on their foot ruler. (Remember, we have been using sticks for foot rulers, with no calibrations up to this point.) They will discover that 12 of these 1-inch "units" will fill the foot ruler; consequently we can say that 1 foot unit of measure is equivalent to twelve 1-inch units of measure. The children should now be able to use standard rulers with inch or even half-inch markings. Discuss the convenience of using this kind of ruler, and let them practice measuring objects.
11. Draw several triangles or quadrilaterals, at least 1 foot on each side, on 24-inch-by-36-inch newsprint or tagboard. Have children measure the lengths of the line segments forming the sides of the figures. Use both a foot ruler and a meter stick.

12. Have the children line up one at a time, tallest to shortest. Discuss who is the tallest and who is the shortest. On another day, have them line up shortest to tallest, and discuss the relationship.
13. Have children name objects that are longer than their reading books. Then have them name objects that are shorter than the tops of their desks.
14. Ask the children, "Who lives farthest from school?" Have children who walk to school count their steps as they walk. Children must be able to count at least to several hundred to do this activity.
15. Present a variety of activities related to the number line from 0 to 12. You can present many addition and subtraction activities that will develop readiness for telling time.

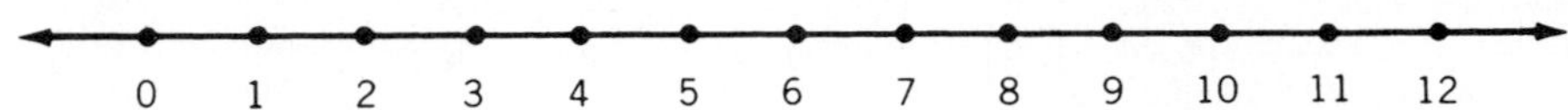

After these activities, review counting by fives, and present many experiences counting by fives from 0 to 55. Supplement these activities with work on the number line from 0 to 59. Label only those points that correspond to multiples of five.

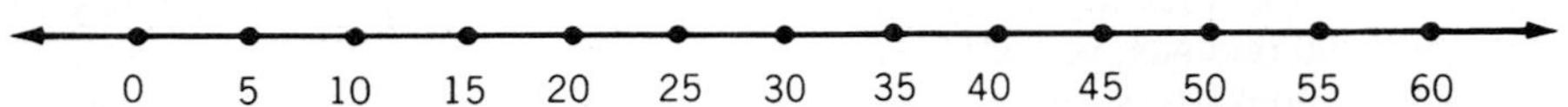

Relate the two number line diagrams. Be sure that children do not become confused by the use of different unit lengths in the two number line diagrams.

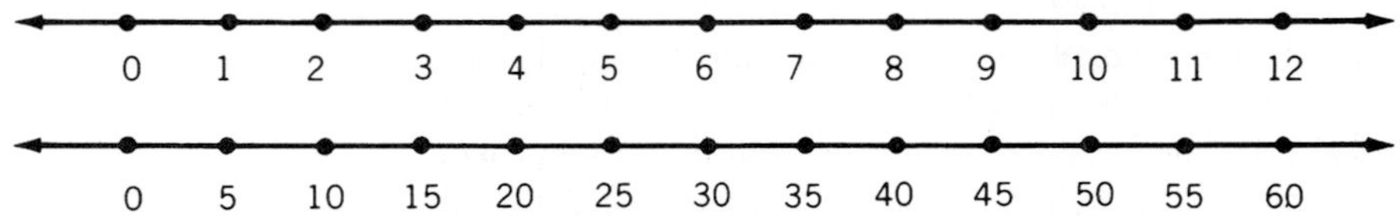

16. Now make the number lines into "number circles" by cutting off the excess portions at the ends of the diagrams and forming a circle (so that the 12 falls on top of the 0). To do this, you can use number lines made of cardboard segments that are hinged at the places where the numerals go. First work with the "number circle" that shows numerals from 1 to 12 (remember the 12 has covered the 0). Introduce the hour hand, and have children tell which numeral it points to as you move it from one position to another. In a similar manner, make a "number circle" from a number line model that is marked in intervals of five from 0 to 55. Introduce the minute hand, and let the children practice reading the numeral to which the minute hand is pointing.
17. Have the children discuss the difference between A.M. and P.M. Throughout the year, discuss the calendar, the day of the week, and the month.
18. Place a large clock in the room, and set the hands of the clock for a certain activity—for instance, a snack. The clock is not running. When the hands of the clock on the wall (the clock you use to tell time) are the same as the hands on the activity clock, it will be time for the snack. Have the children observe that the long hand must go around the clock once for the short hand to move to the next number.
19. Children in the primary grades should explore the use of a digital clock. They can use a real digital clock to practice reading the time displayed. For large-group practice, it may be necessary to make a set of digital flash cards. Take 12 large index cards, and write the numerals 1 through 12 on the left half of individual cards. On eleven other large index cards, write the numerals 5 through 55, in multiples of five, on the right half. Remember to write the 5 as 05. Cut the left half off the "minute" cards. The children can then use the two sets to model different five-minute intervals. Make additional minute cards to model such times as 9:23.
20. Multiple-use overhead transparencies are very valuable in working with children. Make two transparencies, one with clock faces and one with the hands of the clock. The centers of

the clocks and the hands should be positioned at the vertices of a square, as in the following example:

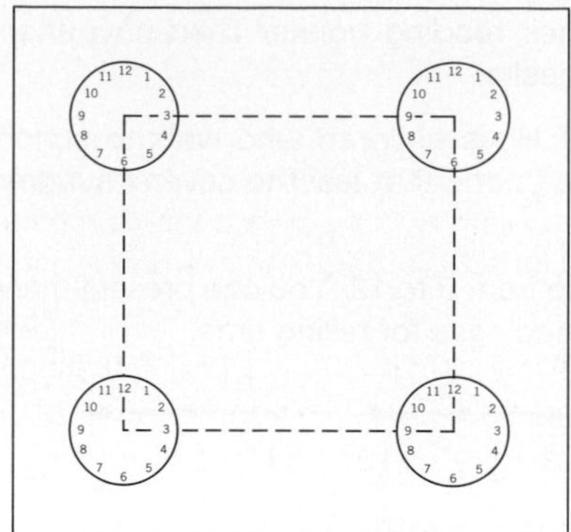

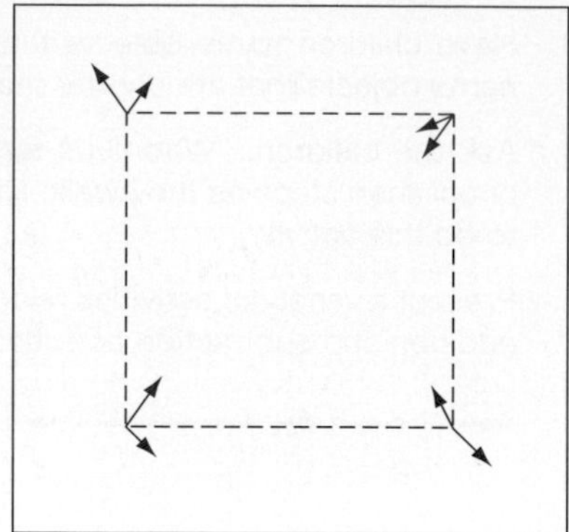

The dotted lines should not be on the transparency; these are only shown to help you make the transparency. Note that the transparency with the hands can be rotated so that it can be placed on the clock faces four different ways. If you rotate the transparency with the clock hands 90 degrees, you will have four more clock faces for children to read. This will provide four clocks to read in each position, and with four positions you have sixteen clocks to read.

Now you can flip the transparency over and place it on the clocks again. Rotate the transparency; you will have another sixteen clocks for the children to read. This will provide a total of thirty-two clock faces for the children.

21. Allow children to explore various measures for liquids by comparing the capacities of different containers with those of gallon, quart, pint, and liter containers. To avoid a "liquid mess" you may use sand instead of water for this activity.

22. Allow the children to compare the weight of various objects in the classroom to a 1-pound weight or a 1-ounce weight. Use this activity only to compare weights, not to determine the actual weight of an object. You may also want to have the children use metric weights such as a kilogram, but, as with U.S. customary measures, the emphasis should be exclusively on "heavier or lighter," not on actual measure.

23. Construct a pan balance so that the children can place items in the pans and determine if the items have the same or different weights. Drill three holes through a narrow stick as shown in the diagram.

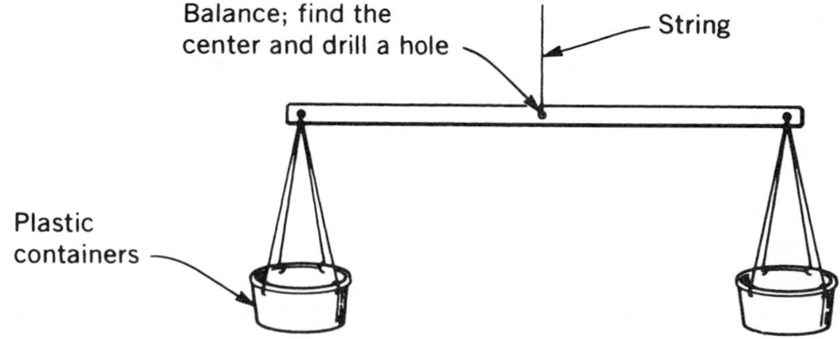

One hole should be in the center of the stick, the other two placed at an equivalent distance from the two ends. Hang the balance from a table or tall piece of furniture by a string attached to the center hole. The pans can be made of plastic containers and hung by string as shown.

24. In teaching children about money, teachers should use real money, since if play money is used, the children must jump to one more level of abstraction to associate each unit of play money with the corresponding unit of real money. To avoid loss of money, try "buying"

something from the child (like a shoe) for a fixed amount (say, 75 cents). Place a large box in the room, and have each child put one shoe in it; then give the child 75 cents. At the end of the period when the child returns the 75 cents, he or she gets the shoe back.

25. Have children sort money into different denominations. Then discuss with them why they sorted the coins as they did. Study each coin and describe its characteristics.

26. Place a coin under a sheet of paper on a table. Describe the coin to a group of children sitting around the table; when they think they know what the coin is, they should raise their hands. Note how many clues are needed for different children to recognize the coin being described. After everyone is sure what the coin is, turn the sheet of paper over to see if the children are correct.

27. Use the calculator to make a chart for the ticket seller at the movie theater. Tickets sell for $4.50 for adults and $3.25 for children. Make one chart for adults and another chart for children.

Adults' Tickets	
Number of Tickets	Cost
1	$4.50
2	
3	
4	
5	
6	
7	
8	
9	
10	

Children's Tickets	
Number of Tickets	Cost
1	$3.25
2	
3	
4	
5	
6	
7	
8	
9	
10	

28. Use your calculator to fill each space in the table:

Cost of Item	Money Given	Change
$1.79	$2.00	
3.49	5.00	
2.19	3.00	
1.28		.22
3.31		1.69

29. Provide the children with newspaper ads, and have them prepare a shopping list from the ads. Find the total amount of the bill.

30. Using catalogs, calculate the costs of a variety of orders.

31. Provide many opportunities for the children to measure various items. Use U.S. customary rulers marked only in inches and metric rulers marked only in centimeters. Children seem to find too many markings on a ruler to be confusing. As children become competent at measuring, add the $\frac{1}{2}$-inch line and the millimeter markings. Children need a great deal of experience estimating measurements and then measuring to check their estimates.

32. Use string to measure objects or things that are not "in a straight line." For example, have the children take measurements of their waists, wrists, necks, heads, arms, and so forth. Have the children estimate the lengths before they measure.

33. Have the children use straightedges to draw line segments of a given length (say, 5 centimeters). Then have them use a ruler to check how close their measurements really were to what was requested.

34. Children can now begin adding and subtracting denominate numbers. Give the children two cards of different sizes. They should measure each card and tell how much longer or how much wider one card is than another.

35. Through various experiences, children will discover the need for a measuring instrument that is longer than a foot. Again, appropriately initiated discussion questions can provide a point of departure. For example:

    How long do you think the room is?
    How long is the fence along the soccer field?
    How long is the bulletin board?
    Could you measure the length of any of these with the measuring units we have been using?
    Does anyone know another way we would measure these things?

    If children suggest that the measurement could be made in yards or meters, encourage further response to check for understanding. Then present the uncalibrated yardstick, the foot ruler, and the 1-inch cubes for observation and comparison. Also introduce the uncalibrated meter stick and the decimeter.

36. Have one child measure the length of the bulletin board with a yardstick. Have another measure the length of the same bulletin board with a foot ruler. Use several activities of this kind involving comparisons to establish the idea of selecting an appropriate unit of measure. Use this same activity with metric measures.

    It is important to provide experiences such as these that will constantly reinforce awareness of the relation between the 1-inch, 1-foot, and 1-yard units. If this understanding is developed in the early grade levels, then linear measurement will present little problem as the child progresses to the more abstract kinds of measurement at the intermediate and middle grade levels.

37. While the concept of a mile is difficult for a small child to comprehend, there are many ways of creating an intuitive understanding. Almost every child rides in an automobile and realizes that distance traveled is measured in miles on the odometer. Many groups take walks that measure 1 mile or more in length. In some areas, a familiar place or certain building, such as the library, may be a distance of 1 mile from the school. Any practical experiences that can be interpreted by the child can be valuable in helping the child to understand the meaning of mile. The same approach can be used to develop a sense of kilometer, as well as the notion that a kilometer is less than a mile.

38. Have the children play a question-and-answer game. One question might be, "What unit of measure would I use to measure the length of my desk?" The child who responds with an appropriate unit is then asked to think of another question to present.

    As a variation of this activity, have one child select a unit of measure—the 1-inch cube, the foot ruler, or the yardstick—and ask, "What three lengths could I measure with this?"

39. In a school hallway, use small strips of masking tape every ten dekameters to mark the length of a kilometer. Have the children walk the distance. They will probably be surprised at how many times they will need to walk down the same hall in order to walk a kilometer. If you have the space outdoors, you might mark off a square that is 25 meters on each side. To illustrate the length of a kilometer, have the children walk around the square ten times during recess.

40. Allow the children to discover the relationships between standard units of liquid measure (gallon, quart, pint). Provide the children with standard-size containers, and let them pour sand from the smaller containers into the larger containers. Be sure to have the children keep records of their findings.

41. Obtain a large metal ball bearing and a large piece of styrofoam (such as the kind sometimes used as packing in a box). Have the children place the ball bearing in one hand and the styrofoam in the other hand and guess which is heavier. Use a pan balance to show which object really is the heavier.

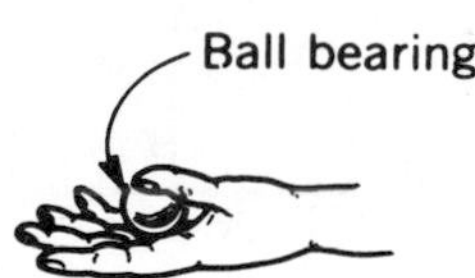

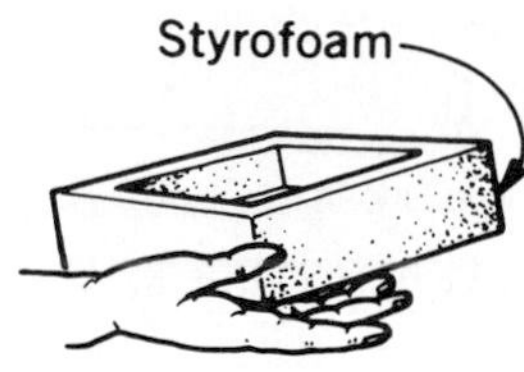

An important point here is to be certain the child does not automatically associate the greater weight with the larger object.

INSTRUCTIONAL AND ASSESSMENT ACTIVITIES FOR GRADES 5-8

1. In the intermediate grades, children should be able to determine the approximate weight of an object by using a balance scale and various combinations of pound, ounce, gram, and kilogram weights.

2. Have the children guess the weight of a variety of objects; then place the objects on a scale and weigh them to see how close the estimates really are to the actual weight. Children need many experiences like this with both metric and U.S. customary measurements. Do not convert from one system to the other; work either entirely in the metric system or entirely in the U.S. customary system.

3. Follow the "number line" procedure described in this chapter to teach children various ways to read a clock. Review the relationship between the two number lines, this time using the two clocks. Reintroduce the hour hand and the minute hand on the clock face. At this level (assuming that the children can read the clock to minute intervals), the concepts of "quarter past," "half past," and "quarter to" can be presented. Relate the concepts to fractional numbers. You may even wish to discuss how these terms seem to lose their literal translations when reading a digital clock.

4. Use the calculator to find the price of one item when you know the price for several items. For example, if three items sell for $1.79, what is the price per item? Some children will have difficulty rounding the number into a value that they can understand. Using the calculator, 1.79 divided by 3 is 0.5966666. What does this number mean in terms of money?

5. Extend the preceding concept into unit price. If 4 ounces sell for $1.35, what is the price per ounce? Using the calculator, divide 1.35 by 4; the display screen will show .3375. Discuss with the children what this means.

6. The grocery store has three brands of soup.

   Brand A has 539 grams for $.69.
   Brand B has 305 grams for $.32.
   Brand C has 553 grams for $1.29.

   Which brand is the best buy? Use the unit price to make a valid comparison.

   Brand A .69/539 = .0012801
   Brand B .32/305 = .0010491
   Brand C 1.29/553 = .0023327

   Brand B seems to be the best buy, since you pay .0010491 cent (less than a penny) per ounce for the soup.

7. Compare each sentence:

   a) Our family drinks 3 quarts of milk each day.

      The unit of measure is __________.

      The measure is __________.

      The amount of milk is __________.

b) My desk is 9 chalk pieces long.

Its length is __________.

Its measure is __________.

The unit of measure is __________.

8. Answer the questions in each column.

	Which is longer?	How much longer?
a) 23 inches or 1 foot	______________	______________
b) 18 inches or 2 feet	______________	______________
c) 4 feet or 1 yard	______________	______________
d) 1 foot 8 inches or 19 inches	______________	______________
e) 1 yard 4 inches or 42 inches	______________	______________
f) 1 yard 2 feet or 7 feet	______________	______________
g) 1 mile or 3495 feet	______________	______________

9. Answer each question. The symbol $\overset{m}{=}$ means "has the same measure as." The first example has been worked for you.

a) 24 in. $\overset{m}{=}$ __2__ ft	g) 6 ft $\overset{m}{=}$ _____ yd
b) 27 in. $\overset{m}{=}$ _____ ft _____ in.	h) 9 ft $\overset{m}{=}$ _____ yd
c) 32 in. $\overset{m}{=}$ _____ ft _____ in.	i) 7 ft $\overset{m}{=}$ _____ yd _____ ft
d) 18 in. $\overset{m}{=}$ _____ ft _____ in.	j) 5 ft $\overset{m}{=}$ _____ yd _____ ft
e) 78 in. $\overset{m}{=}$ _____ ft _____ in.	k) 10 ft $\overset{m}{=}$ _____ yd _____ ft
f) 108 in. $\overset{m}{=}$ _____ ft _____ in.	l) 30 ft $\overset{m}{=}$ _____ yd _____ ft

10. Activities dealing with the metric system should stress the relationship of various metric units of linear measure to decimal notation, as well as the *relationships* between U.S. customary and metric units. Remember: Compare measures but do *not* convert from one measuring system to another.

11. Distribute several meter sticks so that each group of four or five children has one. Then pass a yardstick around the class. Have children compare the length of the meter stick with that of the yardstick. Do not convert meters to yards or yards to meters.

    Have one group of children measure the length of the classroom in yards and another group measure it in meters. Have other groups of children find the width of the room in yards and in meters.

12. Children might also be asked to measure and cut various shapes from construction paper according to lengths expressed in centimeters. This would provide an opportunity to compare the centimeter with the inch. Have the children measure lengths of some objects in inches and in centimeters. Ask them to compare an inch with a centimeter. Which is longer? Measure the height of several children in centimeters and in inches.

13. In the following exercises, use $\overline{RS}$ as a unit. Since your unit is the centimeter, express your answers to the nearest centimeter. Estimate the lengths before beginning. After measuring the first segment, adjust your estimates, if necessary.

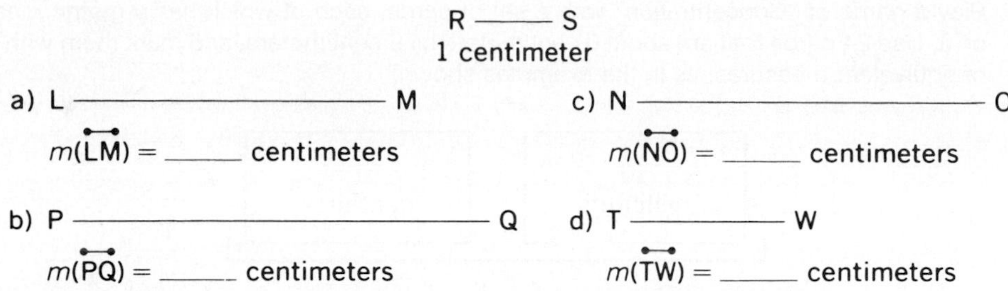

14. Make a set of ten cards, and on each one paste a picture of an object to be measured. Have the children measure the objects in at least two ways so that the objects can be compared. If you laminate the cards, they can easily be erased. For example:

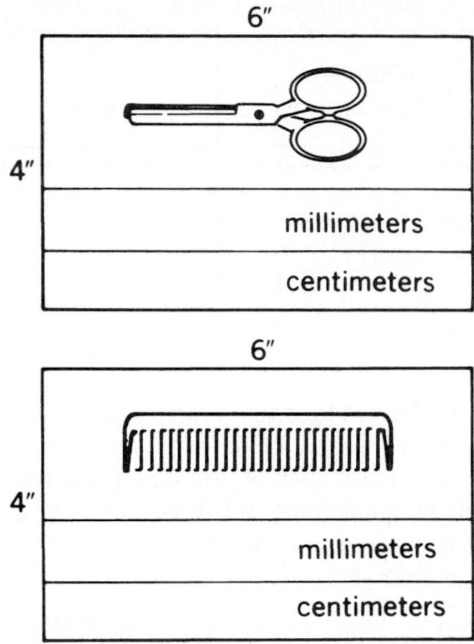

15. Play metric bingo. You will need to make a set of cards with metric measures on them for the caller to use. You will also need a set of bingo cards with metric measures on them. Play the game like regular bingo. Here are some sample cards:

2 milliliters

1 centimeter

100 centimeters

Metric bingo				
2 l	.8 l	.1 m	7 m	10 ml
6 km	2 g	10 m	35 cm	.1 cm
100 cm	5 dm	1 kg	.1 km	68 cm
.01 km	.7 cm	5 m	1 cm	55 g
2 kg	2 ml	40 l	.5 dm	10 m

Metric bingo				
1 cm	10 ml	.7 cm	2 ml	2 kg
.5 dm	.1 l	2 g	7 m	.1 m
68 cm	5 m	1 kg	.1 km	55 g
100 mm	.8 l	.1 m	35 cm	6 km
40 l	.01 km	5 dm	.1 cm	100 cm

Metric bingo				
1 kg	6 km	1 m	2 kg	5 dm
.1 cm	.5 dm	10 ml	10 mm	35 cm
.1 km	.7 cm	100 cm	78 cm	.1 m
2 g	10 l	1 cm	2 ml	5 m
55 g	7 m	.8 l	.01 km	40 l

16. Play a game of "Concentration" with a set of cards, each of which has a metric measure on it. Use 24 cards that are about 6 centimeters by 9 centimeters, and mark them with pairs of equivalent measures, as in the examples shown.

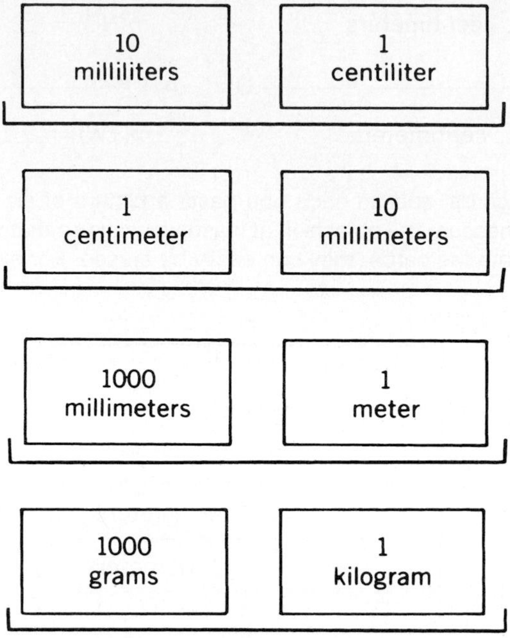

Place all cards face down. Players take turns turning over pairs of cards. If the cards have equivalent measures, the player keeps the set of cards. If the cards are not equivalent, they are replaced. The game continues until all the cards are picked up. The player with the most cards is the winner. As the children learn the game, you can increase the number of cards to 50. *Do not* play this game as if the object is to find two equivalent measures from the U.S. customary and metric systems.

17. Have the children construct metric measurement instruments out of heavy cardboard. Make a ruler marked in millimeters that is 10 centimeters long. Then construct a cube that is 10 centimeters on a side. A pattern is shown. Tape each of the seams.

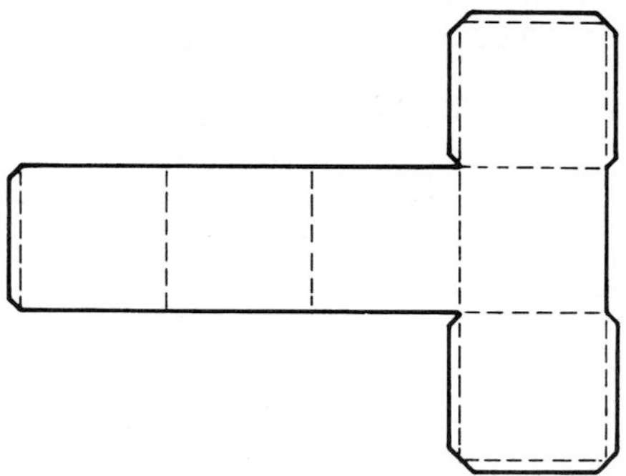

This cube is 1000 cubic centimeters. It will hold 1 liter. Its mass is 1 kilogram when it is full of water. One interesting aspect of the metric system is that length, mass, and volume are all related. This is not the case with the U.S. customary system.

18. The heart pumps an average of 80 milliliters of blood per second. Use your calculator to compute the amount of blood pumped:

a) per hour
b) per day
c) per week
d) in the month of January
e) in the month of February
f) in the month of April
g) in a year

19. Use the calculator to change 12 feet into an equivalent number of yards. Use the calculator to change 12 yards into an equivalent number of feet.

20. Use the constant key and set up the calculator to solve many examples of changing feet to yards. Enter the following into the calculator:

   [1] [2] [÷] [3] [=]

   Now you can enter any number of feet and press the equals key; the display screen will show the number of yards. Try using

   [2] [4] [=]

   An 8 should appear on the display screen. This is the number of yards that equals 24 feet. Try several more examples.

21. Set up the calculator constant so that it will change yards to feet.

22. Set up the calculator constant so that it will change grams to kilograms.

23. Experiment with the constant key to change units. Remember: Do not convert measures between the U.S. customary and metric systems. Convert measures only within one measuring system.

Suggested Readings

Anderson, A. (1994). Mathematics in context: Measurement, packaging, and caring for our environment. *School Science and Mathematics, 94*(3).

Andrade, G. S. (1992). Teaching students to tell time. *The Arithmetic Teacher, 39*(8).

Bass, H. (1993). Let's measure what's worth measuring. *Education Week, 13*(8).

Beaumount, V., Curtis, R., & Smart, J. (1986). *How to teach perimeter, area, and volume.* Reston, VA: National Council of Teachers of Mathematics.

Burns, M. (1978). *This book is about time.* James and Carolyn Robertson (Eds.). Covelo, CA: Yolla Bolly Press.

Burton, G., & Edge, D. (1985). Helping children develop a concept of time. *School Science and Mathematics, 85*(2).

Campbell, P. F. (1989). Young children's concept of measure. In Leslie P. Steffe, (Ed.), *Transforming early childhood mathematics education.* Hillsdale, NJ: Lawrence Erlbaum Associates.

Chancellor, D. (1992). Calendar mathematics: Time and time again. *The Arithmetic Teacher, 39*(5).

Classon, R. (1986). How our decimal money began. *The Arithmetic Teacher, 33*(5).

Corwin, R. B., & Russell, S. J. (1990). *Measuring: From paces to feet. Used numbers: Real data in the classroom.* Palo Alto, CA: Dale Seymour Publications.

Drean, T., & Souviney, R. (1992). *Measurement investigations.* Palo Alto, CA: Dale Seymour Publications.

Driscoll, M. J. (1981). Measurement in elementary school mathematics. In Mark J. Driscoll, (Ed.), *Research within reach: Elementary school mathematics.* Reston, VA: National Council of Teachers of Mathematics and CEMREL, Inc.

Fay, N., & Tsairides, C. (1989). Metric mall. *The Arithmetic Teacher, 37*(1).

Hands-on, Inc. (1991). *Measurement: Grades three through eight.* Solvang, CA: Author.

Harrison, W. R. (1987). What lies behind measurement? *The Arithmetic Teacher, 34*(7).

Hildreth, D. J. (1983). The use of strategies in estimating measurements. *The Arithmetic Teacher, 30*(5).

Hovey, L., & Hovey, K. (1983). The metric system—An overview. *School Science and Mathematics, 83*(2).

Jamber, M. (1993). Make metrics matter? *Teaching PreK-8, 23*(4).

Kastner, B. (1989). Number sense: The role of measurement applications. *The Arithmetic Teacher, 36*(6).

Keller, J. D. (1993). Ideas. *The Arithmetic Teacher, 40.*

Landers, M. G. (1994). From the file: Conversion of measurements. *The Arithmetic Teacher, 41*(8).

Ligon, H. (1992). Metric mania. *Science Teacher, 59*(7).

Lindquist, M. M. (1987). Estimation and mental computation: Measurement. *The Arithmetic Teacher, 34*(5).

Lindquist, M. M. (1989). Implementing the standards: The measurement standards. *The Arithmetic Teacher, 37*(2).

May, L. (1990). Measurement is a happening. *Teaching PreK-8, 20*(8).

May, L. (1994). Benchmarks, estimation skills and the real world. *Teaching PreK-8, 24*(8).

National Council of Teachers of Mathematics. (1976). *Measurement in school mathematics,* 1976 Yearbook. Reston, VA: National Council of Teachers of Mathematics.

National Council of Teachers of Mathematics. (1994). *Curriculum and evaluation standards for school mathematics addenda series grades 5-8: Measurement in the middle grades.* Reston, VA: National Council of Teachers of Mathematics.

Neufeld, K. A. (1989). Body measurement. *The Arithmetic Teacher, 36*(9).

Nunes, T. (1993). Tools for thought: The measurement of length and area. *Learning and Instruction, 3.*

Parker, J., & Widmer, C. C. (1993). Patterns in measurement. *The Arithmetic Teacher, 40*(5).

Rowan, T. E., & Morrow, L. J. (1993). *Implementing the K-8 curriculum and evaluation standards: Readings from The Arithmetic Teacher. Implementing the K-8 curriculum and evaluation standards.* Reston, VA: National Council of Teachers of Mathematics.

Shaw, J. M. (1983). Student-made measuring tools. *The Arithmetic Teacher, 31*(3).

Shaw, J. M. & Puckett Cliatt, M. J. (1989). Developing measurement sense. In Trafton, Paul R. (Ed.), *New directions for elementary school mathematics,* 1989 Yearbook of the National Council of Teachers of Mathematics. Reston, VA: National Council of Teachers of Mathematics.

Shroyer, J., & Fitzgerald, W. (1986). *Mouse and elephant: Measuring growth* (Middle Grades Mathematics Project). Menlo Park, CA: Addison-Wesley.

Sovchik, R., & Meconi, L. J. (1994). IDEAS: Measurement. *The Arithmetic Teacher, 41*(5).

Stevenson, C. L. (1990). Teaching money with grids. *The Arithmetic Teacher, 37*(8).

Zanelotti, G. (1989). Metric olympics. *The Arithmetic Teacher, 36*(5).

Chapter 15

Geometry: Basic Concepts and Structures

Overview

This chapter presents geometric terms and concepts that are the fundamental building blocks for the study of geometry. To function successfully in geometry, a firm foundation and a basic vocabulary need to be developed. Students need to learn the symbolism that corresponds with terminology and how to put these symbols together to construct geometric ideas and hypotheses.

In daily conversation, many geometric terms are misused. For instance, the term *line* is often incorrectly used as a synonym for line segment or ray. Because of such confusion in the use of terms, many students find geometry more difficult than some other areas of mathematics. Also, geometry is too often associated with the process of memorizing a series of steps in a proof that must be repeated word for word.

Many of today's teachers were introduced to geometry at the secondary level in a traditional geometry course that utilized formal proof. Because of this narrow view of what geometry is, some teachers find it difficult to acknowledge that many basic ideas of geometry have an important place in the elementary school curriculum.

Many of the concepts of this chapter have been presented to the reader as abstractions, but it is clear that young children cannot work easily with such abstract notions as point, line, line segment, and so on. Any consideration of these concepts at elementary or middle grade levels should be based on the child's intuitive understanding of the concepts and not on textbook descriptions or formal characterizations by means of axioms or postulates. An intuitive approach to geometry permits you to use a wealth of activities that can be exciting and mathematically sound. Rather than memorizing a set of formulas with little or no meaning, the student needs to understand what a formula means and how it was developed. In presenting geometric concepts, it is important to consider the maturity, coordination, and attention span of the learner.

SAMPLE LESSON PLAN—"OPPOSITE DAY IN MATHEMATICS"

Primary Developmental Lesson

Goal:

Exploration of transformational geometry.

Objectives:

The students will:

- Construct transformations (flips, slides, and turns).

Prerequisite Learning and/or Experiences:

Ability to recognize three-sided figures as triangles.

Materials:

For the teacher:

- the poem "Opposite Day in Old Bombay" by Maurice Poe
- overhead transparencies

For each student:

- two pieces of construction paper (9 by 12)—two different colors
- glue, scissors, and pencil

Procedures:

Motivational Introduction

Read the following poem:

There is a day in old Bombay,
I think it is the tenth of May,
When everything works the opposite way.

When some one says IN,
they really mean OUT.
And when they say WHISPER,
they really mean SHOUT.

If some one says GO,
you know you should STOP.
And it's on the BOTTOM,
means it's on the TOP.

This day can be confusing
you must be alert.
Absolutely clean
means it's full of dirt.

If some one says GOOD,
they really mean BAD.
And when they say HAPPY,
they really mean SAD.

You've got to distinguish,
the DO'S from the DON'TS.
And remember that I WILL,
really means I WON'T.

It's essential to remember
that RIGHT means WRONG.
That DAY means NIGHT,
and SHORT means LONG.

Oh, it's very confusing,
there's no doubt about that.
When TALL means SHORT,
and THIN means FAT.

There is a day in OLD Bombay,
I think it is the tenth of May,
When everything works the
OPPOSITE WAY!

Have students brainstorm other real-life, opposite ideas. Tell students that today in mathematics we will explore some geometry opposites called transformations.

1. Since many young children may have experienced toys which can be transformed into other shapes, begin by having students describe "transformation" in their own words.
2. Use the students' descriptions of "transformation" to explore the geometric transformations of flip, slide, and turn. Have students sit on the floor in rows with space in front to demonstrate each transformation. Ask for "gymnastic" volunteers and select three students to perform demonstrations for the children sitting on the floor.
3. Have three children lay on their backs. Ask one child to flip over into another position. The child might somersault head over heals or roll over onto his or her stomach. Have the second child keep one part of his or her body stationary while turning the rest of the body. The child might keep the head, buttocks, or feet stationary. Have the third child slither like a snake, but remain on his or her back. The child might decide to slither up, down, or over. Discuss and demonstrate many possible placements for flipping, turning and sliding. Did any two transformations create the same body position?

Developmental Activity

4. As students return to their desks, hand out two different colored pieces of construction paper to each student. Once students are sitting in their seats, they should have access to a pencil, scissors, and glue, too. Most students will have these supplies in their desks.
5. Have each student select one piece of construction paper and fold it in half horizontally. Each student should open the construction paper so that there is a top half and a bottom half laying on the desktop:

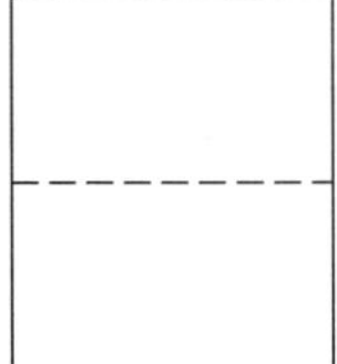

6. Have each student select the other piece of construction paper and fold it in half also. With the paper still folded, have each student draw a triangle on the front of one of the halves. If students ask, any kind of triangle is acceptable. Encourage large drawings. After every student has drawn a triangle, have them cut it out with the paper still folded. This method should produce two congruent triangles.
7. Have each student lay one of the triangles on the top half of the open piece of construction paper. Now, lay the other triangle on the bottom half of the construction paper so it looks like a flip. If necessary, remind students of the earlier demonstrations with students' bodies. Walk around the room and observe students' work. Have volunteers show their solutions at the overhead.
8. Repeat step 7 for both turns and slides.

Culminating Activity

9. Have students select their favorite transformation (flip, turn, or slide).
10. Once each student has selected his or her favorite, the student should glue down the triangles to model that choice.
11. Use the students' work to create a "Transformation" bulletin board with the subheadings of FLIP, SLIDE, and TURN. Challenge students to place their final product in the appropriate space.

Extension:

Try a similar activity, but this time create symmetrical opposites instead of transformational opposites.

Student Assessment/Evaluation:

Assess placement of students' work on the "Transformation" bulletin board. Since two transformations might create the same position in space, have students orally defend their placement. Apply the following rubric:

0 = no attempt
1 = improper placement
2 = proper placement

INSTRUCTIONAL AND ASSESSMENT ACTIVITIES FOR GRADES K-4

1. Provide the children with large sheets of construction paper, flattened drinking straws, and paste. Have them arrange the straws in various geometrical patterns and paste them on the construction paper. Colored string or yarn can be dipped in paste and arranged on construction paper in the same way.
2. Copy and distribute "join the dots" puzzles. These puzzles involve joining dots in consecutive order (by number) to obtain a picture. These puzzles are very useful in developing a visual awareness of line segments and shapes.
3. Use large sheets of squared paper and let children trace over the lines on the paper to create pictures made up of line segments.
4. Use any easy-to-obtain, inexpensive materials you can think of that will give children experiences in forming simple figures: toothpicks, drinking straws, pipe cleaners, and so on.
5. Some first graders have sufficient motor development to be able to work with a geoboard. Let the children explore how different shapes and lines can be modeled on the geoboard. Provide time for the children to experiment with the boards.
6. Children will enjoy working with tangrams and simple designs as they explore spatial relations. First allow the children to become acquainted with the materials through free play. Provide the children with some outlines of simple designs and ask them to place the tangrams to "fill-in" the outline provided. Teachers can relate this activity to putting materials back into their storage boxes or special locations.
7. Some young children will have the motor development necessary for drawing segments with the aid of a straightedge. They may be asked, for example, to draw angles of different types.
8. Have two children sit so that they cannot observe each other. Provide both children with identical sets of blocks. As one child builds with the blocks, he or she is to describe what is being built and give instructions to the other child to imitate; for example, "Place a cube in front of you, place a cone on top of the cube, place the ball to the left of the cube. . . . " After all the blocks have been used, compare the two displays of blocks to see if they are alike. (Be careful not to use the terminology of two-dimensional geometry when discussing three-dimensional objects.)

9. Teachers should provide many opportunities for children to use vocabulary that has to do with location or position. Place a box on a table, and have the children follow directions such as "Place a sheet of paper under the box, place the doll behind the box, place a comb in the box, place a pencil to the side of the box . . . ," and so forth.

10. The computer language called Logo is appropriate for geometric activities in the early grades. Use Logo for drawing basic geometric shapes, thereby advancing the level of abstraction from the concrete to the semiconcrete level. Children can learn to give commands such as FORWARD, BACK, RIGHT, and LEFT to direct a Logo turtle around a microcomputer screen. Students will acquire and develop language skills as they develop some rudimentary programming skills. (Should spelling lists for language arts programs be revised in view of the computer?)

11. Using you or a student as the "turtle," have children verbally describe and dramatize what they want the Logo turtle to do. Soon children will associate their own movements with the movements of the turtle.

12. Seat the children on the floor in the shape of a square. Provide each child with different models of squares and discuss the figures with the children. After the children have developed a clear mental image of a square, have them try to draw a square on the video screen. Use the children's suggestions as a "trial-and-success" opportunity. A final program might look something like this:

```
FORWARD 50
LEFT 90
FORWARD 50
LEFT 90
FORWARD 50
LEFT 90
FORWARD 50
LEFT 90
```

13. Begin with a question to promote discussion. For example, "I'm thinking of a certain point on the chalkboard. How could I show you the point?" The usual response will be "Make a dot with the chalk." If this is the reaction, show children a sheet of paper with a tiny pinhole. Then make a large dot on the chalkboard. This may stimulate some pupils to make a mental comparison. Direct their thinking toward the idea of a geometric point by encouraging this comparison of physical representation.

14. Children enjoy drawing some of the many possible paths between two points and creating stories about the path from one point to the other. For example:

    Johnny started to walk to his friend Joe's house. He walked by the pond and saw Arthur fishing. He stopped in the park to play on the swings for a while. Then he passed the ice-cream man, but he didn't have any money with him so he couldn't buy anything. He went on to Joe's house, but Joe wasn't home, so Johnny decided to go back home the shortest way possible. Which path did Johnny take?

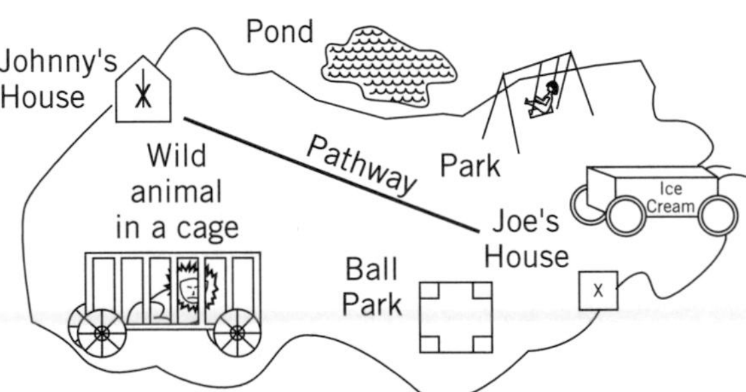

    This is obviously a simplified situation. Children have the imagination to create much more involved and complex stories.

15. How many different objects can you think of that could be models of line segments? A pencil could be one model. What others can you think of?

16. Draw two dots on the chalkboard and connect them.

Ask whether the line could be longer or shorter and still connect the points. Lead the children to think about a "part of a line" in comparison with a "line." Draw a dot with a line through the point represented by the dot. Ask whether any other lines could be drawn through this point. Have children give you directions until the idea is established that there are infinitely many lines that can be drawn through the point.

17. Use the geoboard to show open and closed curves. Examine each model made by the children and discuss why it is an open or closed curve.

18. Provide the children with many drawings of curves and ask them to classify all of the drawings as either open or closed.

19. Have the children reproduce on paper specific patterns displayed on a geoboard. Can children observe and reproduce a specific design? Children who cannot reproduce the pattern should be allowed to trace over the rubber bands on the geoboard.

20. The following can be used successfully as a group activity. Give the directions orally:

Draw a picture of line segment AB, and A and B as end points.

Draw a longer line segment, but keep A as one end point.

Place an arrow at the end of the line segment that goes through point B. What does the arrow mean?

21. a) Mark two points on your paper. Name the points E and F. Draw line segment EF.
    b) Mark two points on your paper. Name the points G and H. Draw line GH.
    c) Mark one point on your paper. Name it N. Draw a ray having N as the end point.

22. How would you describe this picture? Does the figure have an inside and an outside? Label the inside and the outside.

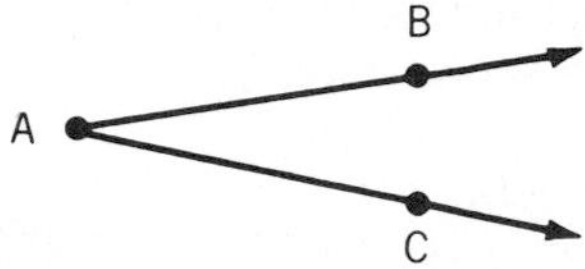

23. How would you describe this picture? How many things can you find in your classroom that are models of this figure?

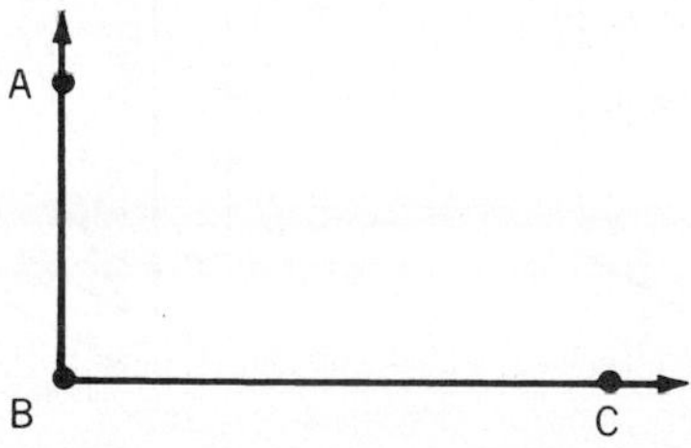

24. Make a shape on the geoboard and turn the board halfway around. Does the shape still look the same? Two examples are shown:

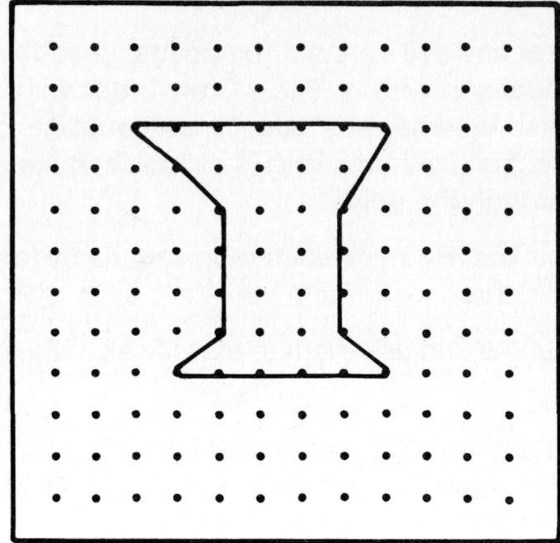

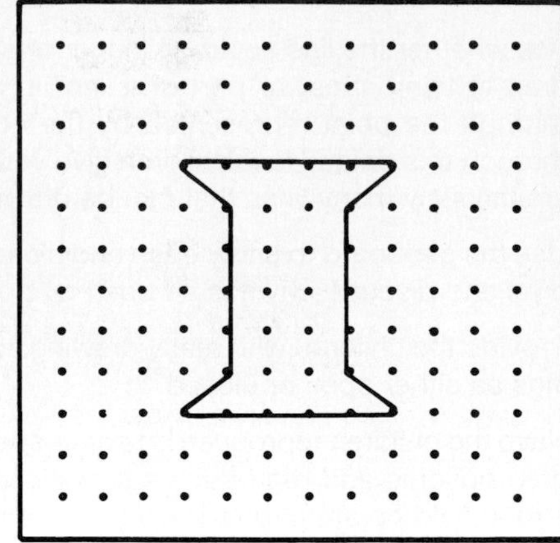

25. The children can use rubber bands to represent different geometric shapes on a geoboard.

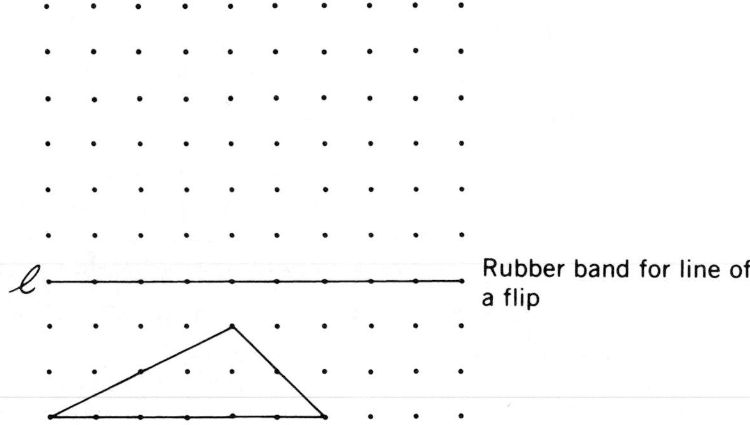

a) Place a rubber band on the board to show how the figure will look after it is flipped over the line ℓ.
b) Use a rubber band to make a square. Use more rubber bands to show all of the lines of symmetry.
c) Make a regular hexagon with a rubber band.

26. Introduce line symmetry by folding pieces of paper and having the children cut out familiar shapes. Two examples are shown here.

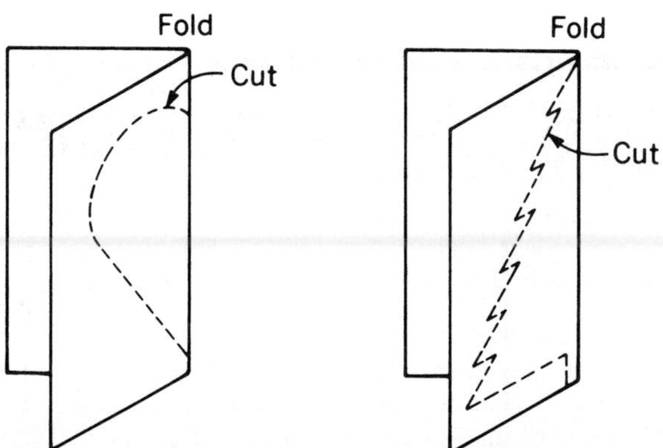

27. Let each child fold sheets of paper and cut out various shapes.

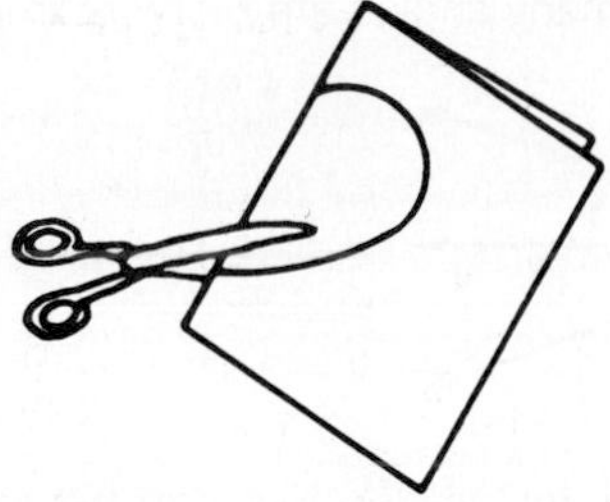

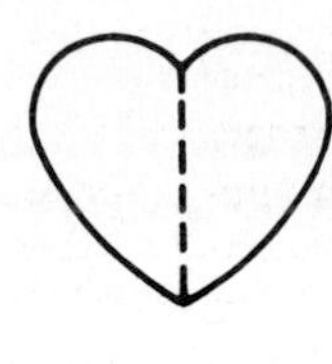

When the paper is unfolded, the child will have a figure symmetric with respect to the line along which the paper is creased.

Fold a sheet of paper into fourths and cut out the various shapes that have two different lines of symmetry.

INSTRUCTIONAL AND ASSESSMENT ACTIVITIES FOR GRADES 5-8

1. Draw two dots on the chalkboard. Ask which dot is larger. Then ask which dot is the better representation of a geometric point, and why.

2. Which of the objects that you named are the best models of line segments? Is a pencil a better model than a tree? Why? Can you make a mark with your pencil that is a better picture of a line segment than the mark you make with your crayon?

3. At intermediate grade levels, it may be easier for children to think of a line segment as "part of a line" and end points as a "starting point" and an "ending point." Children should be allowed to use the vocabulary that is easiest for them in describing concepts. Also, they should be provided with a strip of cardboard to use as a straightedge. Since coordination varies considerably in children of this age, some children will have difficulty drawing line segments neatly.

   Have children use cardboard straightedges to draw line segment AB.

   A •   • B

4. With the use of a straightedge and a pencil that is well sharpened, have the children draw angles. Some activities that can be use in drawing angles are as follows:

   a) How many different kinds of right angles can you draw? Children will respond that ┘ is a different kind of right angle from └. They need to place many right angles on top of each other to realize that there is only one type of right angle.
   b) How many different acute angles can you draw? Children should begin to realize that there are an infinite number.
   c) How many different obtuse angles can you draw?

5. Use a geoboard to make an angle with the greatest number of degrees possible. Compare different models and discuss which fits the criterion. Using the geoboard, make an angle with the fewest possible degrees.

6. Make many different curves on a geoboard and have the children tell whether or not they are simple closed curves.

7. Have the children reproduce on paper specific shapes and/or designs displayed on a geoboard. Do the children observe and reproduce specific aspects of the figures such as angle sizes and lengths of component parts?

8. Mark a point on your paper and name it S. Draw a ray having S as the end point. Draw another ray having S as the end point. Describe your drawing.

9. Draw pictures of four different angles on your paper. How many points will you need to make to name each angle?

10. Study the following diagram carefully. How many angles are pictured in this diagram?

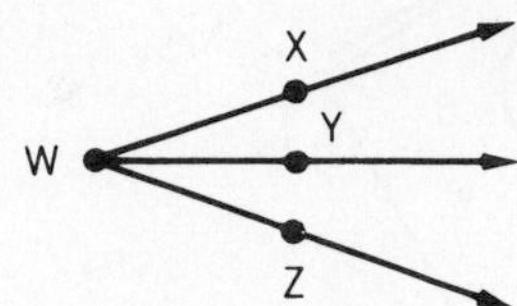

11. Microcomputer activities suggested earlier for grades K-4 can be easily adapted for grades 5-8.
12. Obtain a software package for the Logo language that is compatible with your computer. Introduce the command TO. The command TO BOX, described below, should cause the computer to draw a square. Try this program:

TO BOX	TO PINWHEEL
REPEAT 4(FD30RT90)	REPEAT 4(BOX)
END	END

We will use an asterisk (*) preceding the name of every entry. Try this program:

*SQUARE	*PENS
REPEAT 4(FD40RT90)	REPEAT 2(*SQUARE)
FD10	
END	

Now try these programs:

REPEAT 3(*SQUARE)   REPEAT 4(*SQUARE)

13. To begin an activity that develops vocabulary and descriptive abilities, have two students sit so that they cannot observe each other. Provide both with an identical, but arbitrary, set of six Cuisenaire rods. As one student builds with the rods, he or she is to describe what is being built and give instructions to the other child to imitate; for example, "Place the red rod in front of you, place a blue rod on top of the red one, place the orange rod to the left of the dark green one. . . ." After all the rods have been used, compare the two displays of rods to see if they are alike.
14. Teachers should provide many opportunities for children to use vocabulary that has to do with location or position. Place a box on a table and have the children follow directions such as "Place a sheet of paper under the box, place the red pattern block behind the box, place a triangular pattern block in the box, place a four-sided pattern block to the side of the box . . . ," and so forth.
15. Some children's toys include a built-in computer. Often these are in the form of a remote-control vehicle or robot that can be programmed to complete simple tasks. Obtain such a controllable toy and allow the children to observe how it moves. Have the children sit on the floor in the shape of a circle. Place the robot/vehicle in front of the teacher and have a discussion about it. Program the toy so that it will move to the center of the circle, turn toward a previously selected student, and then move toward that student, stopping in front of him or her. Have that student program the toy so that it will use the same procedure, moving toward and stopping in front of another child. Continue the process until the children become proficient. Programmable robots should be available in a work space during work time. Young children can become very effective programmers of these toys. They provide an opportunity for children to experiment on the concrete level.
16. Have students dramatize programming the Logo turtle by directing you on a trip around the classroom. Only certain defined words should be allowed, such as FORWARD, LEFT, RIGHT, BACKWARD, along with a number of steps to take. Soon children will associate their "commands" of your movements with the commands necessary to move the turtle.
17. Have the students arrange their desks in the shape of a triangle. Also provide the students with models of triangles and discuss the characteristics of a triangle. Ask a child to walk

so that his or her path is in the shape of a triangle. Request that the children experiment by drawing a triangle using Logo commands. A completed program might look something like this:

```
FORWARD 50
RIGHT 120
FORWARD 50
RIGHT 120
FORWARD 50
RIGHT 120
```

18. Draw a large dot on the chalkboard. Then ask the following questions for class discussion:
    a) Is this a point? If I erase the chalk mark, does the point move?
    b) How many points are covered by a dot you make with a pencil?
    c) Does a big dot represent a larger point than a small dot?
    d) Did you ever see a real point?
19. Draw a representation of a line and of a line segment on the chalkboard. Then use the following questions for class discussion:
    a) What is a line?
    b) What is a line segment?
    c) How many end points does a line have?
    d) How many end points does a line segment have?
    e) Can you find three objects in the room that are examples of line segments?
20. Name all the different line segments you can find in this figure. One is $\overline{AC}$.

21. Name all the line segments you see represented in this figure.

22. Draw two line segments each having point A as one end point. Draw three line segments each having point A as one end point. How many different line segments can you draw each having A as an end point?
23. Show another way to name each line segment.

    $\overline{AB}$ $\overline{AC}$ $\overline{CB}$ $\overline{CD}$ $\overline{AE}$ $\overline{CA}$ $\overline{EF}$ $\overline{DC}$ $\overline{FB}$

24. Draw a dot on your paper and label it point A.
    a) Use your straightedge to draw one line through point A.
    b) Draw a different line through point A.
    c) Draw three more lines through point A.
    d) Using the letters B, C, D, E, and F, label one point other than point A on each of these lines.
    e) Can you draw still more lines through point A?
25. Use your straightedge and pencil to help you answer the following questions:
    a) How many line segments can you draw having end points A and B?
    b) How many line segments can you draw that are extensions of $\overline{AB}$?
    c) How many lines contain both A and B?
    d) Is a line segment all of a line?
    e) Is a line segment part of a line?
    f) Is a line part of a line segment?

26. Find ten different names for the following line:

27. Draw a picture of a line on your paper. Let A be a point on this line.
    a) Choose a point on the line different from A and label it B.
    b) Choose another point on the line in the opposite direction from A and label it C.
    c) Name two rays that are part of this line and have A as an end point.
    d) Are there any more rays on this line that have A as an end point?

28. Mark a point on your paper and label it A.
    a) Draw one ray having end point A.
    b) Draw another ray having end point A.
    c) Draw four more rays having end point A.
    d) How many rays are there having A as an end point?

29. Name all the angles you can find in the following figure. Do five different rays with a common end point always form this same number of angles? Explain.

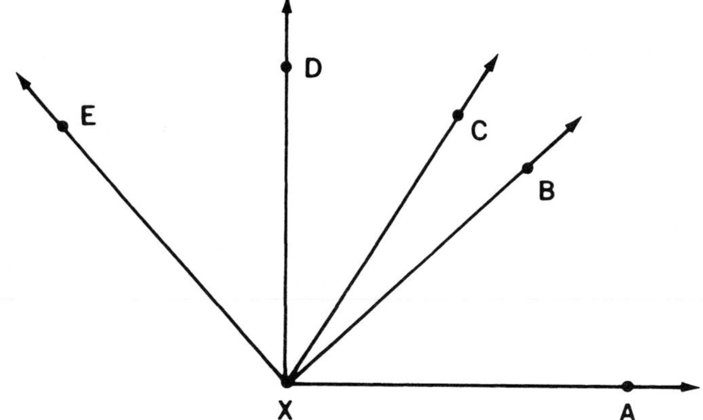

30. Without using your protractor, tell whether the angles shown appear to be acute angles or obtuse angles.

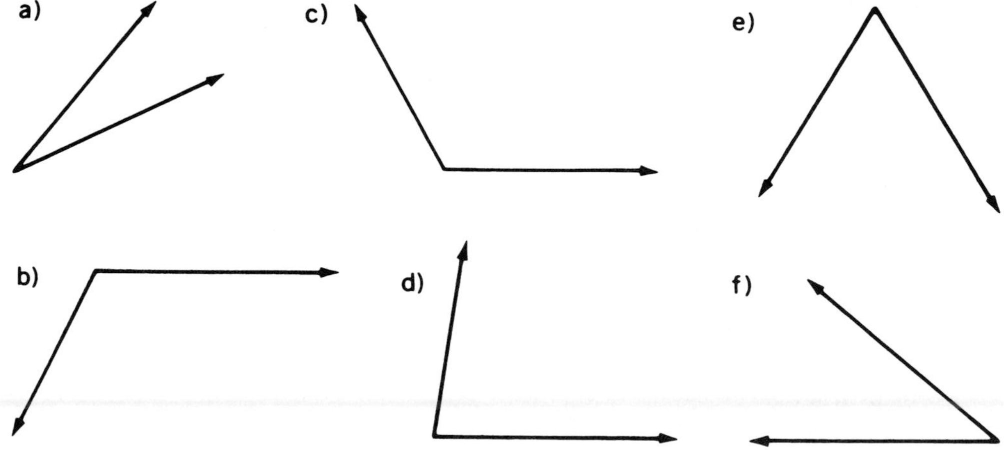

31. Use your protractor to draw angles with the following measures:

    a) 35° b) 160° c) 90° d) 33° e) 179°

32. Use your compass to draw a circle. Then mark five points on the circle. How many line segments can you draw using pairs of these five points as end points?

33. a) Draw a line on a sheet of paper. Mark a point on the line and label it A. Now mark a point not on the line and label it B. Draw ray AB. Use your compass and straightedge to bisect each of the two adjacent angles.
    b) Measure the angle formed by the rays that are the bisectors. What is the measure of the angle? If you had marked point B in a different position, what would be the measure of the angle formed by the two bisectors?

34. Study the following letters of the alphabet:

    A B C D E F G H I J

    a) Which of these letters are symmetric with respect to a line?
    b) Do any of these letters have more than one line of symmetry? If so, which ones?
    c) What other letters can you think of that are symmetric with respect to a line?

35. Use your compass to draw a circle (any size) on your paper.
    a) Use your ruler to draw two lines of symmetry for the circle.
    b) Can you draw more lines of symmetry? How many lines of symmetry do you think a circle has?

36. Trace each figure and the line shown with it. After you have done this, draw the flip image of the figure in the line.

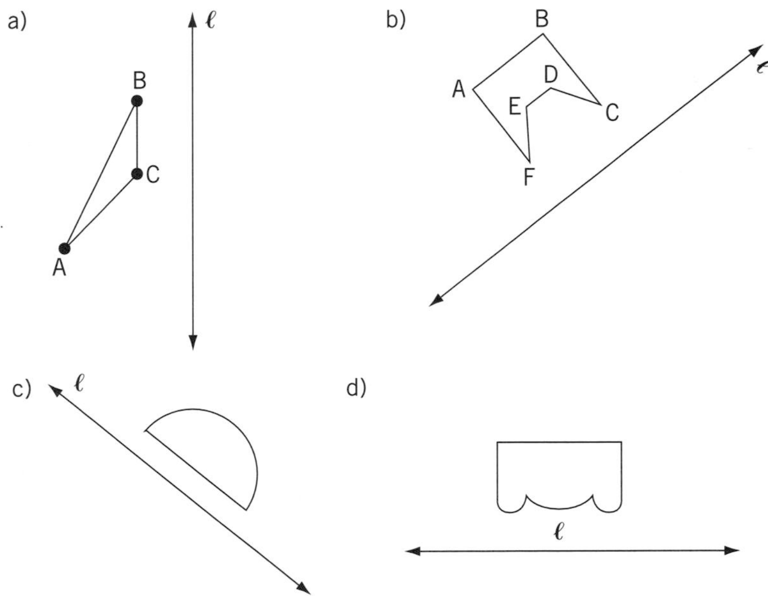

37. Students can study rotations conveniently by using tracings of figures on overhead transparencies. Have students do a number of experiments to sketch the images of various figures under rotations of one-quarter turn, one-third turn, one-half turn, and so on. Have the students consider questions such as the following:
    a) Does a clockwise rotation through one-half turn give the same image as a counterclockwise rotation through one-half turn? (Assume that the "center of rotation" stays the same.)
    b) Around what point can a circle be rotated through a one-half turn clockwise so that the image of the circle is the circle itself?
    c) Draw a square. Draw dotted line segments to join both pairs of opposite vertices. Label the point where the segments intersect with the letter C. What is the image of

the square under a one-quarter turn clockwise around point C? Under a one-half turn clockwise around C? Under a three-quarter turn clockwise around C?

d) Draw other geometric figures that are their own images under one-quarter turns, one-half turns, and three-quarter turns.

38. In which cases is the figure labeled ② a slide image (that is, an image under a translation) of the figure labeled ①?

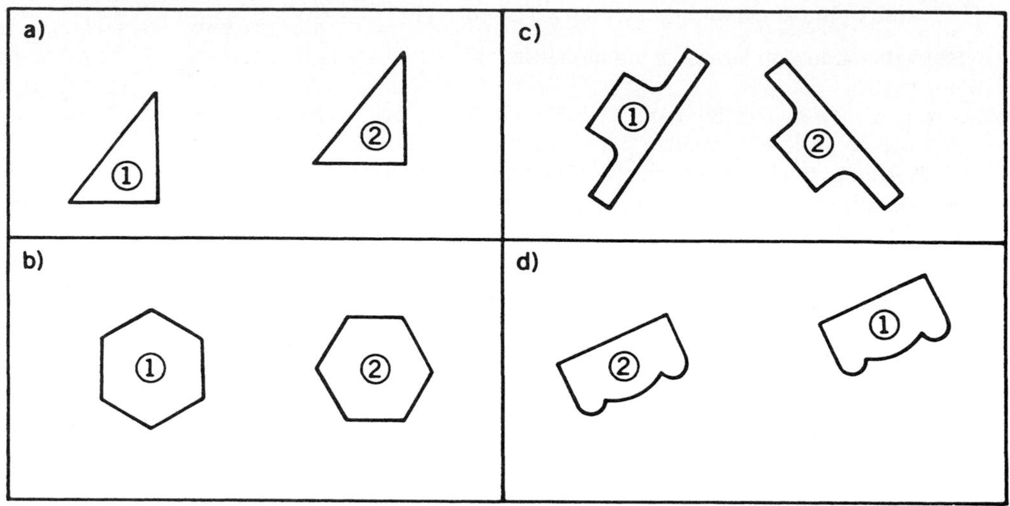

Suggested Readings

Amir-Moez, A. R. (1988). Variations on Pythagoras' theorem. *School Science and Mathematics, 88*(8).

Bidwell, J. K. (1987). Using reflections to find symmetric and asymmetric patterns. *The Arithmetic Teacher, 34*(7).

Brahier, D. J., Hodapp, S., Martin, R., & Speer, W. R. (1992). Ideas—Beginning a new school year. *The Arithmetic Teacher, 40*(1).

Bright, G., & Harvey, J. (1988). Learning and fun with geometry games. *The Arithmetic Teacher, 35*(8).

Burger, W. F. (1988). An active approach to geometry. *The Arithmetic Teacher, 36*(3).

Burger, W. F., & Shaughnessy, M. (1986). Characterizing the van Hiele levels of development in geometry. *Journal for Research in Mathematics Education, 17*(1).

Claus, A. (1992). Exploring geometry. *The Arithmetic Teacher, 40*(1).

Dunkels, A. (1990). Making and exploring tangrams. *The Arithmetic Teacher, 37*(6).

Ellington, B. (1983). Star trek: A construction problem using compass and straightedge. *The Mathematics Teacher, 76*(9).

Evered, L. J. (1992). Folded fashions: Symmetry in clothing design. *The Arithmetic Teacher, 40*(4).

Fuys, D., Geddes, D., & Tischler, R. (1988). The van Hiele model of thinking in geometry among adolescents. *Journal for Research in Mathematics Education.* Reston, VA: National Council of Teachers of Mathematics.

Grevsmuhl, U. (1988). Mathematics and modern art. *Mathematics Teaching, 122.*

Hands-on, Inc. (1989). *Geometry: Kindergarten through grade nine.* Solvang, CA: Author.

Hersberger, J., & Talsma, G. (1991). Improving students' understanding of geometric definitions. *The Mathematics Teacher, 84*(7).

Johnson, A., & Boswell, L. (1992). Geographic constructions. *The Mathematics Teacher, 85*(7).

Keller, J. D. (1993). Ideas. *The Arithmetic Teacher, 40.*

Kriegler, S. (1991). The tangram—More than an ancient puzzle. *The Arithmetic Teacher, 38*(9).

Larke, P. (1988). Geometric extravaganza: Spicing up geometry. *The Arithmetic Teacher, 36*(1).

May, L. J. (1995). Teaching math. Understanding geometry. *Teaching PreK-8, 25.*

McDonald, J. L. (1989). Cognitive development and the structuring of geometric content. *Journal for Research in Mathematics Education, 20*(1).

May, B. A. (1985). Reflections on miniature golf. *The Mathematics Teacher, 78*(9).

Morrow, L. J. (1991). Geometry through the standards. *The Arithmetic Teacher, 38*(8).

National Council of Teachers of Mathematics. (1987). *Geometry for grades K-6* (Readings from *The Arithmetic Teacher*), Jane M. Hill, (Ed.). Reston, VA: National Council of Teachers of Mathematics.

National Council of Teachers of Mathematics. (1987). *Learning and teaching geometry, K-12.* 1987 Yearbook. Reston, VA: National Council of Teachers of Mathematics.

National Council of Teachers of Mathematics. (1993). *Curriculum and evaluation standards for school mathematics addenda series grades K-4: Geometry and spatial sense.* Reston, VA: National Council of Teachers of Mathematics.

National Council of Teachers of Mathematics. (1992). *Curriculum and evaluation standards for school mathematics addenda series grades 5-8: Geometry in the middle grades.* Reston, VA: National Council of Teachers of Mathematics.

Navarro, C. F. (1990). *Early geometry: A visual, intuitive introduction to plane geometry for elementary school children.* Alexandria, VA: Smart Smart Books.

Newman, C. M., & Turkel, S. B. (1988). Integrating arithmetic and geometry with numbered points on a circle. *The Arithmetic Teacher, 36*(5).

Norman, F. (1991). Figurate numbers in the classroom. *The Arithmetic Teacher, 38*(7).

Pappas, C. C., & Bush, S. (1989). Facilitating understandings of geometry. *The Arithmetic Teacher, 36*(8).

Piaget, J., & Inhelder, B. (1964). *The child's conception of geometry.* New York, NY: Harper Torchbooks (Harper & Row).

Pohl, V. (1986). *How to enrich geometry using string designs.* Reston, VA: National Council of Teachers of Mathematics.

Prentice, G. (1989). Flexible straws. *The Arithmetic Teacher, 37*(3).

Rowan, T. E. (1990). The geometry standards in K-8 mathematics. *The Arithmetic Teacher, 37*(6).

Rowan, T. E., & Morrow L. J. (1993). *Implementing the K-8 curriculum and evaluation standards: Readings from The Arithmetic Teacher. Implementing the K-8 curriculum and evaluation standards.* Reston, VA: National Council of Teachers of Mathematics.

Rubenstein, R. N. (1993). Angle sense: A valuable connector. *The Arithmetic Teacher, 40.*

Sawada, D. (1985). Symmetry and tesselations from rotational transformations on transparencies. *The Arithmetic Teacher, 33*(4).

Sicklick, F., Turkel, S. B., & Curcio, F. R. (1988). The transformational game. *The Arithmetic Teacher, 36*(2).

Smith, R. F. (1986). Let's do it: Coordinate geometry for third graders. *The Arithmetic Teacher, 33*(8).

Souza, R. (1988). Golfing with a protractor. *The Arithmetic Teacher, 35*(8).

Taylor, L. (1992). Exploring geometry with the *Geometer's Sketchpad. The Arithmetic Teacher, 40*(2).

Teppo, A. (1991). van Hiele levels of geometric thought revisited. *The Mathematics Teacher, 84*(7).

Thiessen, D., & Matthias, M. (1989). Selected children's books for geometry. *The Arithmetic Teacher, 37*(4).

van Hiele, P. (1986). *Structure and insight: A theory of mathematics education.* New York, NY: Academic Press.

Wheatley, G. H. (1991). Enhancing mathematics learning through imagery. *The Arithmetic Teacher, 39*(1).

Wheatley, G. H., & Yackel, E. (1990). Promoting visual imagery for young pupils. *The Arithmetic Teacher, 37*(6).

Whitman, N. (1991). Line and rotational symmetry. *The Mathematics Teacher, 84*(8).

Wilson, P. S. (1990). Understanding angles: Wedges to degrees. *The Mathematics Teacher, 90*(8).

Wilson, P., & Adams, V. (1992). A dynamic way to teach angle and angle measure. *The Arithmetic Teacher, 39*(5).

Woodward, E., & Buckner, P. G. (1987). Reflections and symmetry—A second-grade miniunit. *The Arithmetic Teacher, 35*(2).

Woodward, E., Gibbs, V., & Shoulders, M. (1992). A fifth-grade similarity unit. *The Arithmetic Teacher, 39*(8).

Zaslavsky, C. (1991). Symmetry in American folk art. *The Arithmetic Teacher, 38*(1).

Chapter 16

Geometry: Polygons and Polyhedra

Overview

Renewed emphasis on geometry has become a part of most elementary school mathematics programs. However, teachers sometimes feel that with some limited attention given to identifying squares, rectangles, triangles, and circles they can "skip geometry" in favor of emphasis on the fundamental operations of addition, subtraction, multiplication, and division. Of course, this approach does not provide children with a well-balanced mathematics program. It also does not provide them with background experiences needed those aspects geometry explored at the secondary level.

Young children's mathematics comes from the real world, and geometry certainly is a part of everyday life. Geometry is all around us and needs to be integrated with the mathematics of whole numbers and rational numbers. Exploring area and perimeter provides an excellent opportunity to bring together addition, multiplication, area, and perimeter. Measuring for carpet, paint, lawn fertilizer, or some other common need offers a real situation involving the children and their parents.

Space figures are more familiar to young children than two-dimensional figures. Blocks, boxes, and many toys are space figures, and these are the objects from the child's environment. From the faces of space figures children can identify the shape of a square, the shape of a rectangle, or the shape of a triangle. From this real-world approach children then draw pictures of the shapes. As children mature, their drawings begin to take on more of the characteristics of three-dimensional drawings.

When children play with blocks, they operate in a three-dimensional world. The teaching of geometric concepts must begin with having children manipulate concrete objects. Children need help in "seeing" the objects and their properties. Attribute blocks, Cuisenaire rods, Dienes Multibase Blocks, and other materials all begin a mathematics program with manipulatory space figures. The geoboard is a device for use on the semi-concrete level for modeling geometric shapes. The Mira can be used on the semiabstract level where children can begin drawing models. String art, straw shapes, and other manipulatives can be used on the more abstract levels, when curves, perimeter, and volume are presented to the class. Many other mathematics concepts are also explored as the children learn the characteristics of the shapes merely because the materials are used as manipulatives. The concepts of thick and thin, big and little, and large and small can be learned, as can color, shape, and size.

As you study the mathematics programs available for elementary school children you will notice that there is a wide variation in grade placement of geometric concepts. Decisions as to what geometric concepts should be taught at specific grade levels must be made with attention to developmental readiness. The van Hieles' work with geometry and the young child, as well as that of others listed in the bibliography of this and the previous chapter, provide evidence that children can explore many geometric ideas at an early age.

SAMPLE LESSON PLAN—"PENTOMINO ADVENTURE"

Intermediate Developmental Lesson

Goals:

Visualize the relationships between 2-D and 3-D shapes. Develop spatial sense.

Objectives:

The students will:

- Form different shape configurations having equal areas.
- Use transformational geometry to identify congruent shapes.
- Construct/model all possible pentominos.
- Identify/construct all possible pentomino boxes.

Prerequisite Learning and/or Experiences:

Experiences comparing and contrasting the properties of plane geometry shapes and solid geometry figures.

Materials:

For the teacher:

- a cubical box carefully wrapped in a manner that allows easy unwrapping

Per student:

- at least 2 empty half pint milk cartons
- one pair of scissors
- math journal

Per cooperative learning group:

- bag of color tiles
- one-inch graph paper
- markers

Procedures:

Motivational Introduction

Engage the students in a discussion about wrapping presents for birthdays. Specifically, call their attention to a wrapped package that is shaped like a cube. Ask them to visualize the shape the wrapping paper was BEFORE you wrapped the present. Was it cubical? Was it even three-dimensional? Carefully unwrap the box and fold the wrapping paper flat to discover the answer.

To explore this "wrapping and unwrapping" notion further, have students cut empty milk cartons to form lidless boxes/cubes. The bottom square should be used as a guide for the size of the four sides. Once students have cut these lidless boxes, challenge them to cut one three-dimensional, lidless milk carton into the following flat, two dimensional shape:

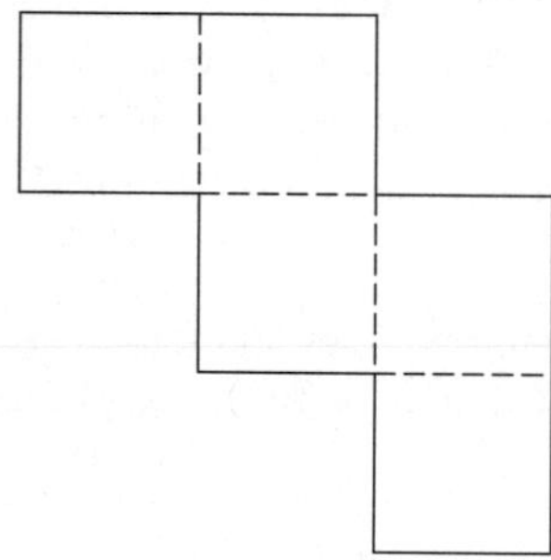

Be prepared for students to request the chance to cut more than one box. Have students write in a journal how many cutting attempts they made before they were successful and what they thought when asked to perform the task of cutting a 3-D shape into a specific 2-D shape. Have students share their reactions. Tell the class that the following activities will help them in discovering relationships between 2-D and 3-D shapes.

Have students form cooperative groups of four and determine who will be coordinator, recorder, reporter, and illustrator.

1. Ask each group to find all possible shapes which can be made from two square color tiles placed flat on a desk top. One at a time have reporters share findings of their group on the overhead projector. Be ready to discuss flips and rotations as well as slide changes. For example,

   THIS IS A FLIP OF THIS   THIS IS A SLIDE OF THIS

   After several shapes are displayed using exactly two tiles, ask which shapes follow the rule of "two full sides touching." Determine there is only one shape, known as a *domino.*

2. Using three color tiles, ask coordinators to have their group apply the rule of "two full sides touching" to three squares. Reporters should share the two possible *triominoes* on overhead.

   Again, be ready to discuss shapes which have been transformed, i.e., the same shape but in a different position due to a flip (or turn).

   THIS IS A FLIP (OR TURN) OF THIS

3. Using four color tiles, have groups apply the rule of "two full sides touching" to four squares. Reporters should share the five possible *tetrominoes* on the overhead projector.

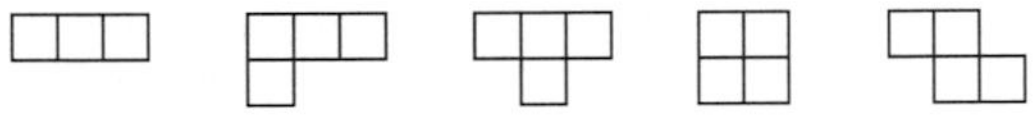

   Some students may recognize four of these shapes from tetris computerized games.

Developmental Activity

4. Using five color tiles, coordinators engage groups in finding all possible pentominos having an area of five square units in which every square borders at least one other square along a full side. As each pentomino is found, the illustrators should carefully color in the shape on one-inch graph paper. Recorders should challenge everyone to help them watch for any shapes which may be the same if flipped (reflected) or turned (rotated).

   THIS IS A FLIP OF THIS THIS IS A TURN OF THIS

5. When groups feel certain they have found all possible pentominos, have reporters share how many their group found and how they know all pentominos have been determined. (*Note to teacher:* Accept all responses at this time, but know there are 12 possible pentominoes.)
6. One at a time, reporters should share a possible pentomino on the overhead until all 12 have been modeled. As each pentomino is modeled, recorders check to verify if their group has that pentomino. If not, then illustrators should add that shape to their groups' graph paper. It is not uncommon for groups to have some difficulty discovering some of the following pentominos.

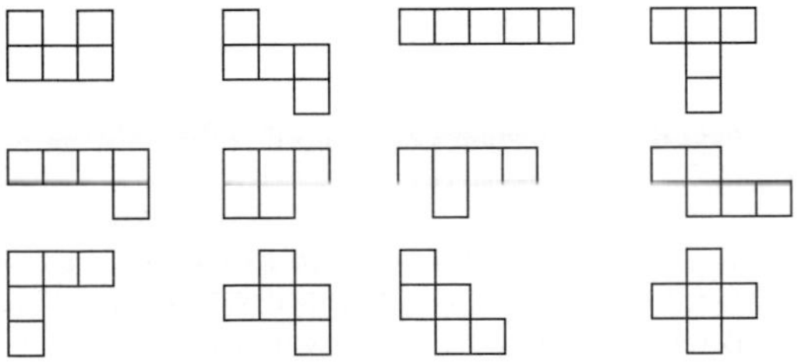

Culminating Activity

7. Coordinators should have their group look at the 12 pentominoes drawn on the graph paper while thinking about the shape of the lidless milk carton box. Each group should determine which pentominoes will fold into a lidless box. Recorders should mark those shapes with an "X".
8. As the illustrators and recorders cut out each pentomino, the coordinator and reporter should verify which ones will and will not fold into a lidless box. The coordinators should then have their group compare predictions and results by checking the folded boxes against shapes marked with an "X".
9. Reporters should share lidless box results by reporting their groups' predictions and actual results. (*Note:* eight of the pentominoes will fold into a lidless box.)
10. Have each student individually repeat the motivational introduction by cutting a milk carton into a lidless box, cutting the lidless box into a specific pentomino, and writing in their journal about the attempts and reactions. Individuals should share results. Have students conclude their journal entries by describing the geometry ideas they discovered while doing the pentomino activities.

Extension:

Write the following chart on the board:

Omino name	Number of squares used	Number of shapes made
Domino	2	1
Triomino	3	2
Tetromino	4	5
Pentomino	5	12
Hexomino	?	??

Challenge students to predict the values for the hexominoes row. Challenge groups to model all possible hexominoes and record them on graph paper. They should predict which ones will fold into boxes, cut out the hexominoes, and verify their predictions by folding into boxes.

Some students may feel they have found a number pattern they can use to predict the number of hexominoes. Don't be surprised by the tenacity of some students to try to apply their rule to septominoes. *Note to the teacher:* It has been determined that there is no function that describes a generalization of this relationship.

A related extension would be to examine area/perimeter relations of dominoes, triominoes, etc. Chart out conclusions in a manner similar to that shown for the omino table above. Students may be surprised that shapes with the same area may not have the same perimeter. Students may note that the more "compact" the shape, the less perimeter it will have. Ask the students to generate a working definition of "compact."

Student Assessment/Evaluation:

Observe students' willingness to be risk takers when constructing ominoes and boxes. Note students which:

1. immediately reach for materials and begin constructing
2. reflect before constructing with materials
3. hesitate using materials; require assistance with constructions
4. refuse to participate

Assess content of students' journal writings which describe what geometry ideas they discovered while doing the pentomino activities. Look for responses that reflect area measurement, transformational geometry, relationships between 2-D and 3-D shapes, etc. Apply the following scoring rubric to students' responses:

0 = no attempt
1 = responses do not reflect geometric thinking
2 = only one geometric idea reported
3 = 2-3 geometric ideas reported
4 = 4 or more geometric ideas reported

INSTRUCTIONAL AND ASSESSMENT ACTIVITIES FOR GRADES K-4

1. Remember that children at the primary level need many experiences with familiar objects and materials. Formal definitions of terms such as *triangle, rectangle,* or *parallelogram* mean very little to a young child. Developing visual imagery is vital. One reason to present figures in elementary mathematics is to develop the children's ability to perceive space relationships on an increasingly abstract level. Perhaps one of the most difficult tasks for a young child is to perceive a three-dimensional figure in a two-dimensional diagram. Children need many experiences observing, drawing, cutting, and folding geometric models.
2. Attribute blocks that are used in the primary grades for patterning and sequencing provide an excellent introduction to geometric shapes. Children need many experiences sorting the blocks according to shape, number of corners, and number of sides.
3. Make a set of bingo cards with different shapes in each square. Have the children play bingo: One child holds up a block, and the other children cover that shape on their cards with a marker. Two sample bingo cards are:

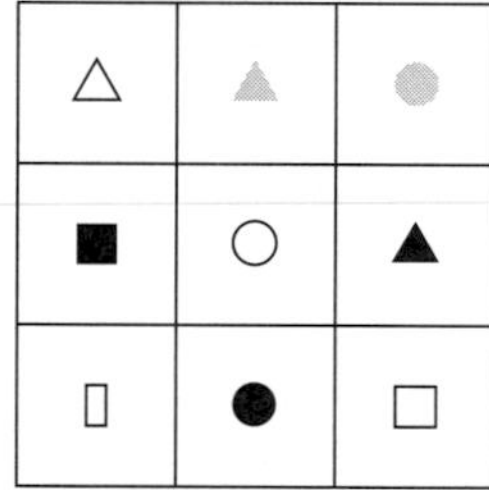

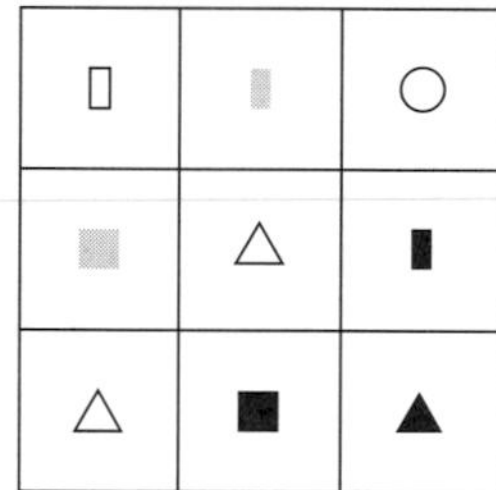

4. Write the numeral that tells the number of sides in each figure.

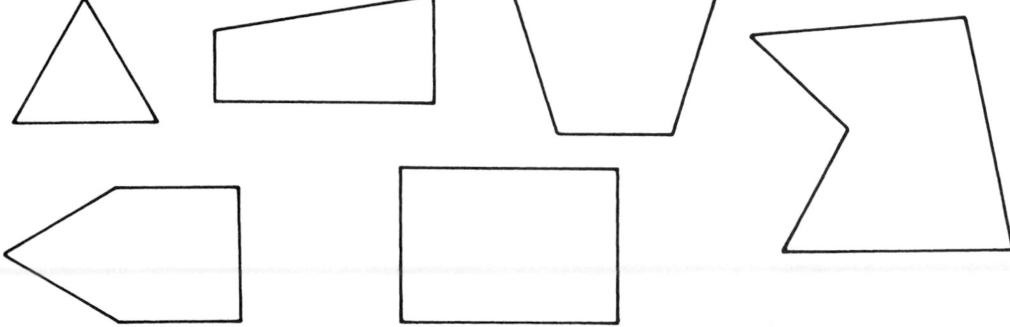

5. Provide the children with cutout shapes that they can paste on construction paper. Start a pattern and have them paste the next shape in place.
6. Give the children sheets of paper to draw pictures of curves. Talk about simple curves, closed curves, and open curves. Transparencies and marking pencils may be used so that you can project the children's drawings on the screen and discuss them.

7. Have the children cut out various shapes (circular, rectangular, square, and triangular). Discuss and compare the shapes of the cutouts. This activity can be extended with activities such as the following:

   a) Place several circle cutouts of various sizes on the chalk tray or flannel board. Have children take turns arranging these in order from largest to smallest, or from smallest to largest. This can also be done with cutouts of triangles, rectangles, and squares.
   b) Place four or five of these cutouts on the chalk tray or flannel board. Ask one child to examine carefully the order of the shapes. Have another child scramble the order of the cutouts. Ask the first child to see whether he or she can replace the cutouts in their original order.
   c) Provide heavy cardboard triangles, squares, and circles. Have the children cut copies of these from construction paper and make designs with the copies.
   d) Draw an X on the circle.

      Draw an X on the triangle.

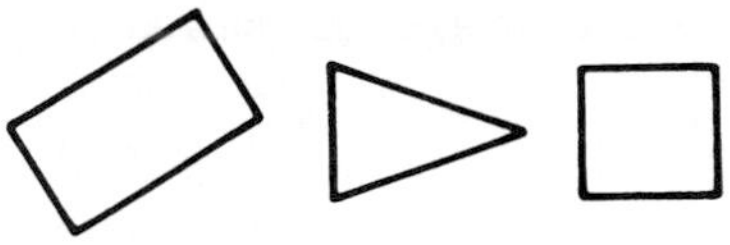

      Draw an X on the rectangle.

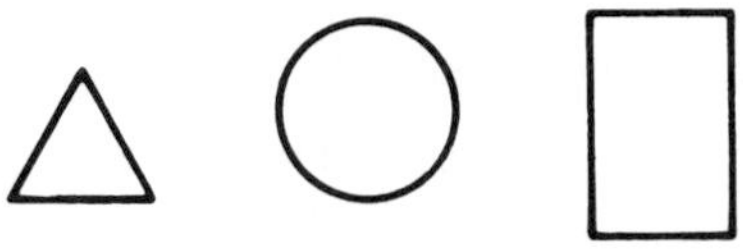

      Draw an X on the square.

      Mark the smaller rectangle.

      Mark the large triangle.

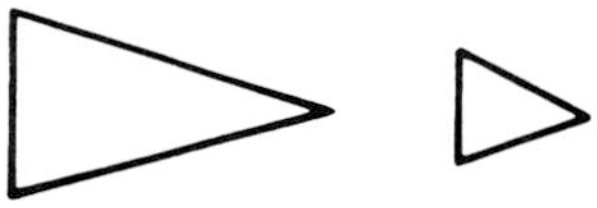

      Mark the squares that are the same size.

8. Place paper cutouts or drawings of various shapes on the chalk tray.

   Ask "How many sides does a rectangle (or triangle, and so on) have?" Have the child who answers correctly take the correct picture from the chalk tray.

9. Color the interiors of the triangles red, the rectangles green, the circles blue, and the pentagons brown.

10. Using yellow and red construction paper, make large cutouts of figures such as the following. For each figure you should have a yellow and red cutout that are exactly the same size and shape.

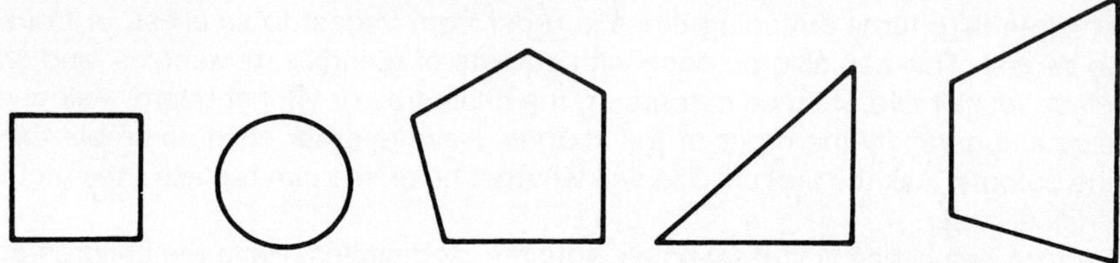

Shuffle the red cutouts and yellow cutouts and place them on a table. Let children take turns matching the figures that have the same size and shape.

11. Make available to the children paper, plastic, or wooden models of various space figures such as cubes, triangular prisms, and pyramids. Let the children handle and inspect these figures and have them sketch and identify the flat regions that form the faces of the figures.

12. Children should be encouraged to verbalize their intuitive understandings of space figures.

    a) Who is inside the playhouse? (Interior, exterior)
    b) What is the shape of the front of your book? (Shape)
    c) How many sides does a cube have? (Space perception)

13. Have the children use geoboards to construct simple shapes and open and closed curves.

14. Provide each child with a sheet of paper on which you have pasted or drawn a model of a geometric shape. Have each child look for similar shapes in magazines, cut them out, and paste them on the page. This can also be done with pictures of three-dimensional geometric shapes.

15. Cut geometric shapes out of cardboard. Make mobiles on clothes hangers and hang them from the ceiling. For example:

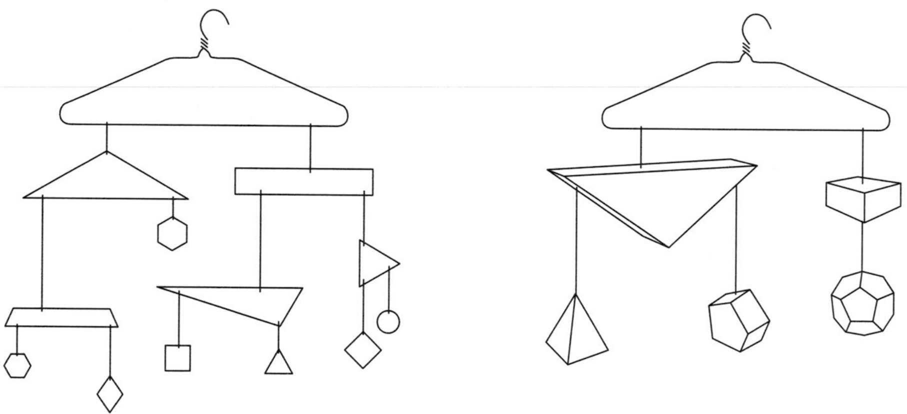

16. Use drinking straws and pipe cleaners or string to make geometric shapes and space figures. "Flexible" straws also work well for this activity.

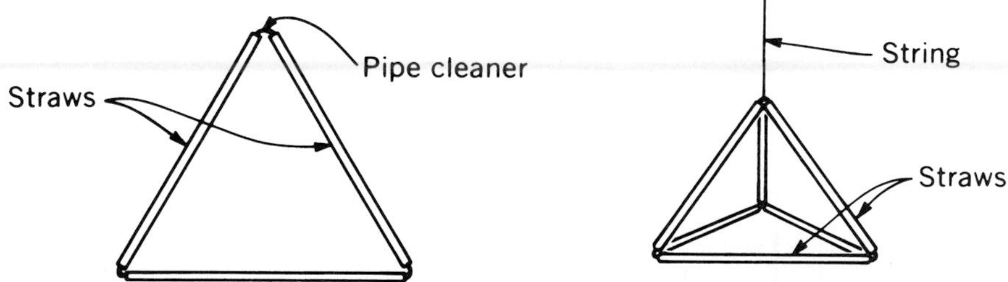

17. Using cubes of the same size, ask the children to see how many cubes will fit snugly in a cardboard box.

18. Draw pictures of the following figures on the chalkboard and have children answer the questions:

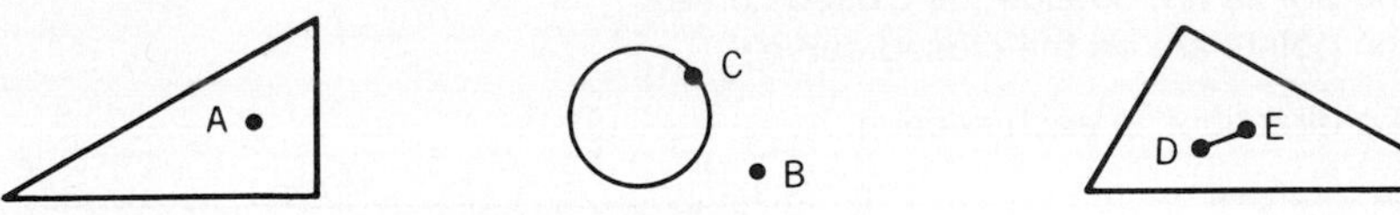

a) Is point A inside or outside the triangle?
b) Is point B inside or outside the circle?
c) Is point C inside or outside the circle?
d) Where is the line segment DE?

19. Use questions similar to the following in a class discussion to determine depth of understanding:

a) If you drop a rock from an upstairs window to the ground, will it follow a straight path down?
b) Does a space shuttle orbiting the earth follow a straight path or a curved path?
c) Would a bridge over a creek be straight or curved? (This, of course, will depend on the kind of bridge and the size of the creek. Let the children explain their answers.)
d) What are some things you see in the classroom that represent a straight path?
e) How many points are there on a path?

20. Follow the directions in each section.

<table>
<tr><td colspan="2">Draw a line segment from point A to point B.

A •   • B</td></tr>
<tr><td>A •

B •   • C

Draw line segment AB.
Draw line segment BC.
Draw line segment CA.</td><td>W•   • Z

X •   • Y

Draw line segment WX.
Draw line segment XY.
Draw line segment YZ.
Draw line segment ZW.</td></tr>
</table>

21. Look at the following diagram:

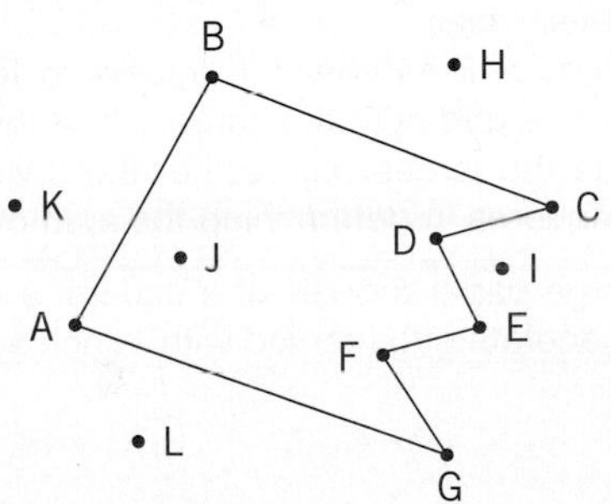

Answer these questions about the diagram.

a) Which points are inside the closed curve?
b) Which points are outside the closed curve?
c) Which points are on the closed curve?

22. Follow the directions in each section.

A • • D

B • • C

Connect points A and B.
Connect points B and C.
Connect points C and D.
Connect points D and A.
Connect points B and D.
Connect points A and C.
How many line segments did you draw?

B •
A • • C

E • • D

Connect points A, B, C, D, and E in every possible way. How many line segments did you draw?

A

Mark a point B on the boundary of the figure so that a line segment connecting A and B will be inside the figure. Can you mark a point C on the boundary of the figure so that you can draw line segment AC outside the figure?

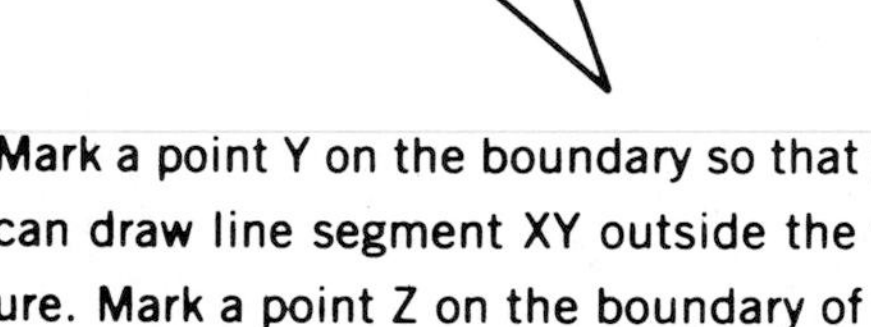

Mark a point Y on the boundary so that you can draw line segment XY outside the figure. Mark a point Z on the boundary of the figure so that you can draw line segment XZ inside the figure.

23. On the chalkboard draw a large square, a large rectangle, and a large triangle. These should be drawn so that their areas appear to be equal.

Ask "Which figure is smallest? Which is largest?" Ask for suggestions as to how we could actually determine if one of the figures covers more area than the others. Give children a chance to explain their ideas.

Draw horizontal and vertical lines over the figures to form equal squares, or use an overhead projector to project a grid onto the figure. Ask if this would give us a method that we could use to determine the largest figure. Let the children discuss how they would count only parts of some squares in determining the area of the triangle.

24. Give each child a set of large paper models of a square, a triangle, and a rectangle. Then provide each child with an acetate grid marked with 1-inch squares. Have children measure

the area of each shape and record the results in terms of the number of squares. Encourage them to compare their results.

25. Give the children many opportunities to practice tracing figures (not necessarily the common geometric figures). This will help to reinforce the idea that congruent figures are exactly alike in size and shape.

26. When children can add whole numbers on the calculator, then they can add the numbers to find the perimeter of a figure. Have the children sit on a carpet on the floor; then have one of the children walk along the edge of one side of the carpet, counting the steps. Use this procedure to find the number of steps on each side. Ask the children, "How could we find the number of steps needed to walk all around the edge of the carpet?" Use the calculator to add the number of steps. Have a child walk all around the carpet, following the edge as closely as possible. Check to be sure that the calculated answer is approximately equal to the actual number of steps taken. It is not necessary to use technical language (perimeter) at this point of development.

27. Use masking tape to mark off other figures on the classroom floor. Follow the same procedure as suggested in Activity 26 for calculating the perimeter of these figures. For example:

28. Mark off large figures on the playground blacktop with chalk. Children need many experiences actually seeing measurements such as 10 meters or 20 feet on the playground. Thus children will begin to develop a foundation for visualizing measurements in the real world. Seeing the actual 5 meters should mean much more than a short line segment drawn on a chalkboard to represent 5 meters.

29. Count and record the number of steps taken as children walk. On returning to the classroom, add the recorded numbers to find the total distance traveled in steps. Steps for the length of the hall or the distance to the cafeteria, restroom, and the office can be counted and recorded. Designate certain children to act as recorders.

30. Use geoboards to calculate perimeters of figures. At this stage of development, remember to use only figures with right angles on the geoboard. Young children cannot "calculate" the length of diagonals. They can, however, compare this length to other lengths on the geoboard by using a card marked with those distances.

31. Teachers who are proficient in programming graphics could have perimeter activities simulated on the video screen for children to calculate. Remember that, at this stage of development, the children must be ready for semiconcrete and semiabstract levels of functioning. Continue to use the Logo language (see Chapter 15) to draw geometric shapes on the video screen with the help of the children. Encourage children to experiment.

32. Which of the following are pictures of simple closed curves?

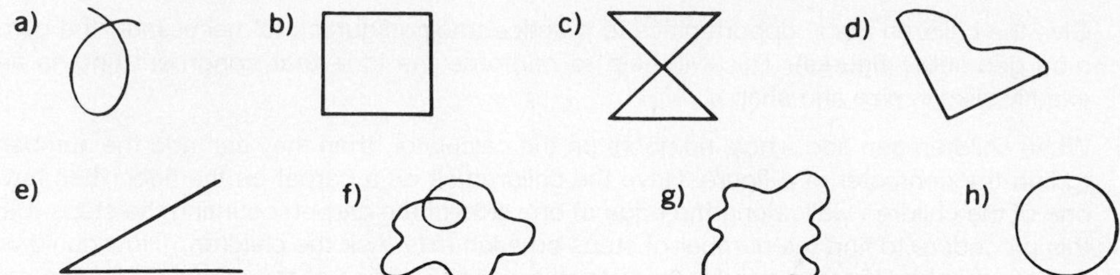

33. Draw a simple closed curve on your paper. Use a blue crayon to draw the curve and a red crayon to color the part of the plane inside the curve. Use a green crayon to color the part of the plane outside the curve.

34. Mark a point on your paper and label it C. Draw a circle with C as the center.

   a) Mark a point on your circle, and label it D.
   b) Draw $\overleftrightarrow{CD}$.
   c) $\overleftrightarrow{CD}$ is a __________ of the circle.
   d) Draw another radius of the circle.

35. Mark two points approximately 2 inches apart. Name the points A and B.

   a) Draw a circle having its center at point A.
   b) Draw a different circle having point A as its center.
   c) Draw a third circle having point B as its center.
   d) Draw a radius of each circle.

36. Use the calculator to find the perimeters of geometric figures by adding the lengths of the sides of the figure. Perimeters for regular geometric figures can be calculated using multiplication. Multiply the length of a rectangle by 2; then multiply the width by 2 and add the two products. When children record the measurement on paper, remember that units must be written with the numbers.

   Use many figures with different shapes, such as:

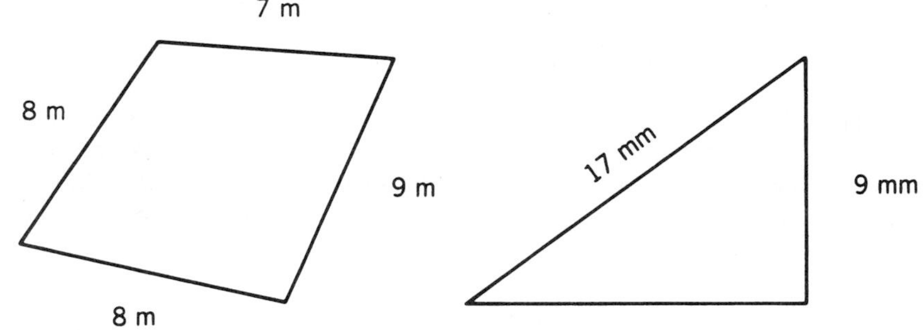

INSTRUCTIONAL AND ASSESSMENT ACTIVITIES FOR GRADES 5-8

1. Children at these levels are more adept at using the straightedge, and they should be given opportunities to draw and label a wider variety of polygons. Precision is not to be expected; only reasonable accuracy. At this level, children are capable of understanding quadrilaterals and should be able to use the term freely in their vocabulary.

2. Use a geoboard to model:

   a) geometric shapes
   b) an angle with the least number of degrees

c) an angle with the greatest number of degrees
d) a geometric shape with the greatest area
e) a geometric shape with the least amount of area

3. If you could walk around the sides of rectangle ABCD, about how many units of measure would represent the distance you would walk?

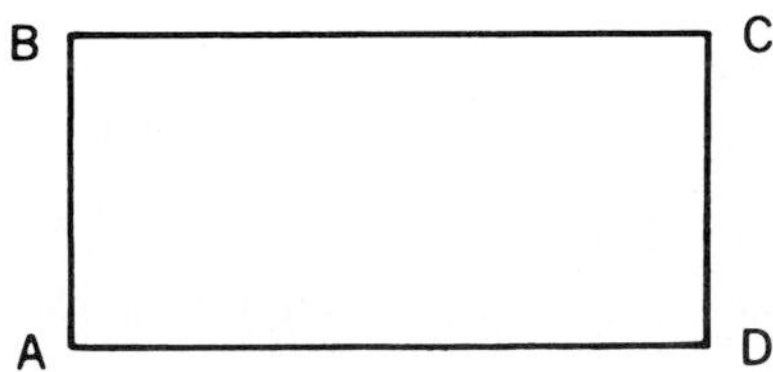

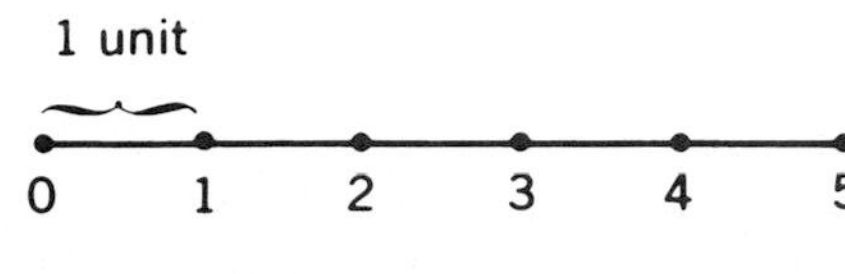

4. Use your ruler to find the perimeter of each polygon (to the nearest inch).

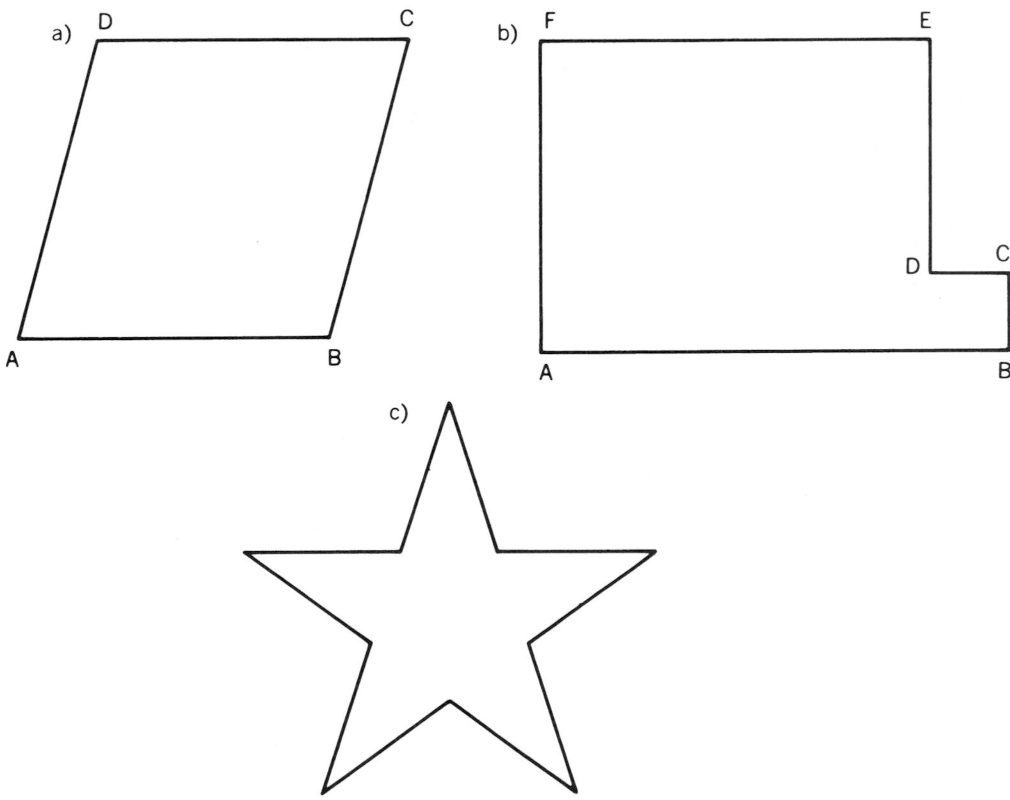

5. Have the children mark large geometric shapes on the school yard or other appropriate area with chalk, yarn, or twine. The children can then calculate the areas and perimeters of the shapes.

6. Mark two points R and S approximately 2 inches apart.
   a) Draw a circle having its center at point R and passing through point S.
   b) Draw a circle having its center at S and passing through point R.
   c) Is $\overleftrightarrow{RS}$ a radius of both circles?

7. a) Draw two different circles so that a radius of one has the same length as a radius of the other.
   b) Draw two different circles so that one has a radius of different length from the other.
   c) Draw two different circles with the same center.

8. Trace points A, B, and C on your paper.

A•

•C

•B

a) Draw $\overleftrightarrow{AB}$.
b) Draw a circle having its center at A and passing through B.
c) Draw a circle having its center at C and a radius equal in length to the length of $\overleftrightarrow{AB}$.
d) Draw a radius of the circle you have just made.
e) Is the length of this radius equal to the length of $\overleftrightarrow{AB}$?

9. Provide the children with the opportunity to experiment and discover ways to make paper models of cones and pyramids.

10. Which polygon of each following pair has the interior region with the greatest area? (You may make a paper model of one of these regions and cut it to see whether the pieces can be placed on the other region without overlapping.)

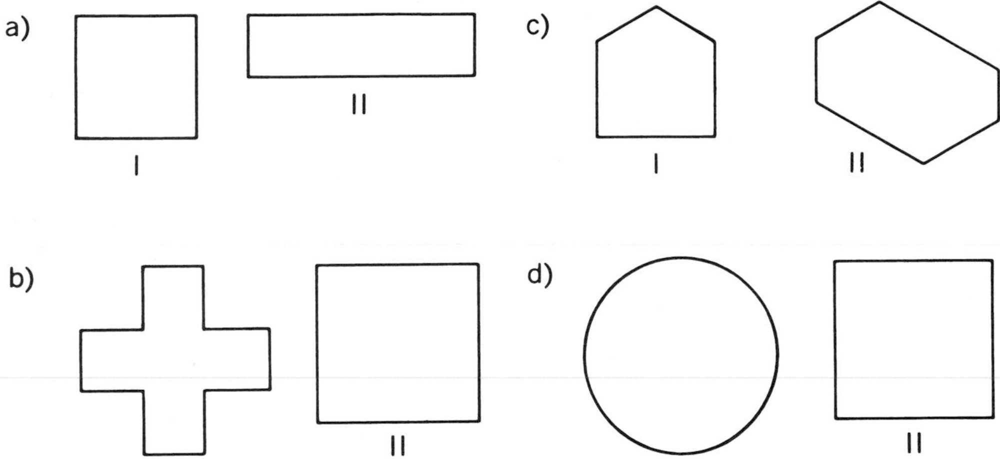

11. Study the diagram and answer the questions.

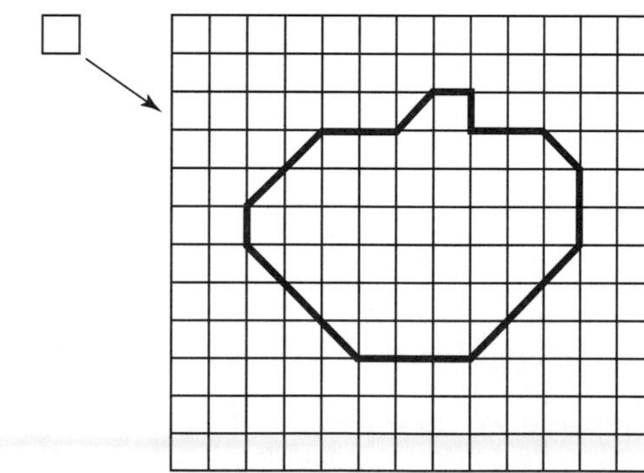

a) How many unit regions fit entirely within the polygonal region?
b) How many unit regions are necessary to cover the region?
c) The area of the polygonal region is exactly __________ units.

12. Draw a rectangle $4\frac{1}{2}$ inches long and $1\frac{1}{2}$ inches wide.

a) What unit can you use to measure the area of the enclosed region?
b) Find the area of the region.

13. Use the geoboard and rubber bands to help develop geometric concepts. For example, have students model two distinctly different figures, each with an area of five square units. Task cards are commercially available and can suggest many ideas that teachers can modify for their classroom needs.

14. Find the number of square units in each shaded region.

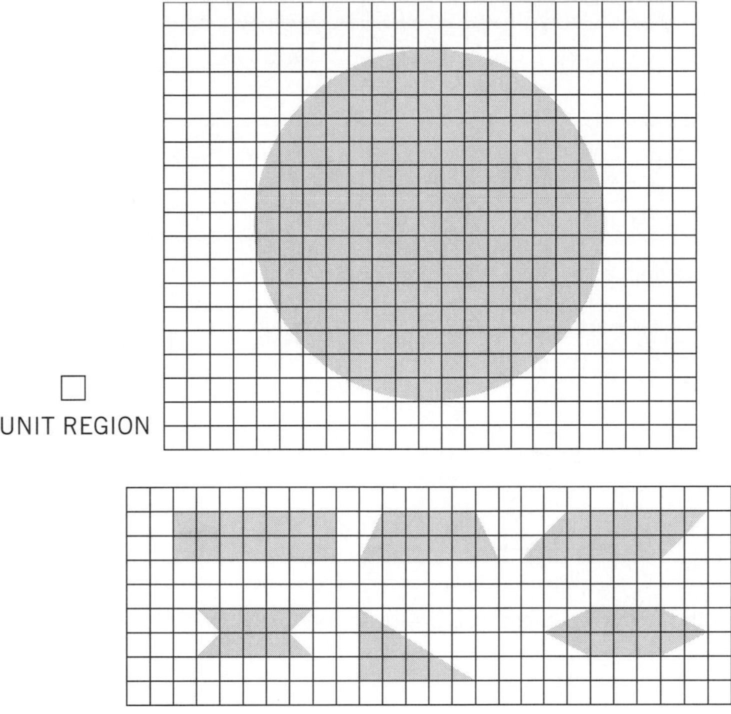

15. On 1-inch-squared paper, draw two different rectangular regions, each having a total area of 14 square inches. On the sides of each rectangle, write its measure in inches. On the interior of each rectangular region, write its measure in square inches.

16. For each of the following exercises, draw rectangles on squared paper; record the measures of the rectangular regions and the measures of their sides. Use paper marked off in either square inches or square centimeters.

    a) Draw three rectangles such that the measure of each rectangular region is 16 square inches.
    b) Draw three rectangles such that the measure of each rectangular region is 18 square inches.
    c) Draw four rectangles such that the measure of each rectangular region is 24 square inches.

17. Make a chart like the one shown. Use your drawings from Activity 16 for the information needed to fill in the chart.

Measures in Centimeters of Sides of Rectangle	Measure in Square Centimeters of Rectangular Region

What do you notice about the product of the measures of the sides in each case? What do you notice about the measure of the region in each case?

18. Classify each triangle according to both its angles and its sides.

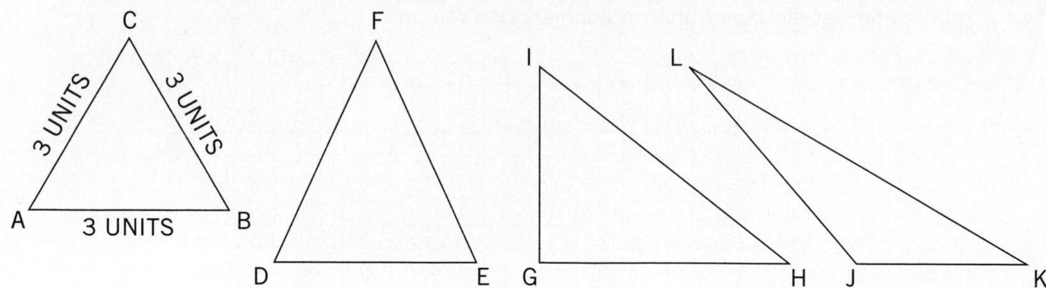

19. Classify each angle according to its measure.

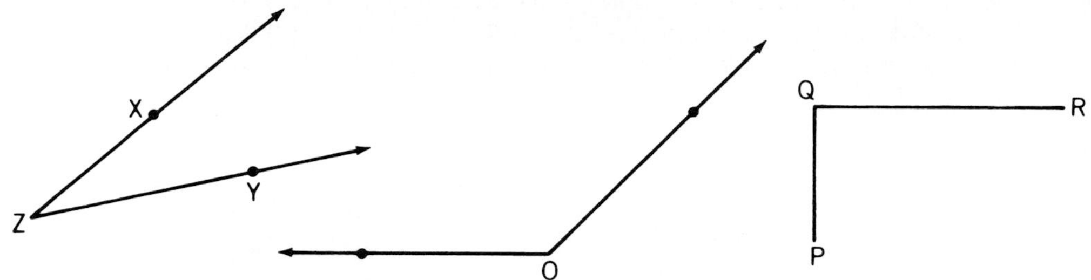

20. In each of the following exercises, the given triangle is a right triangle.

a.

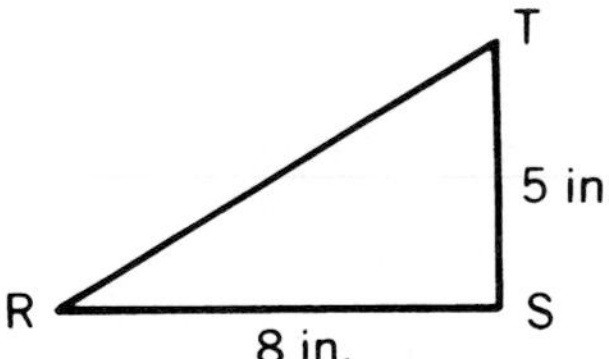

Area of triangular region RST is _____ square inches.

b.

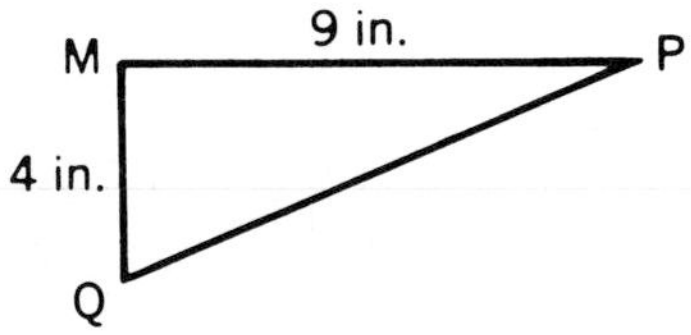

Area of triangular region MPQ is _____ square inches.

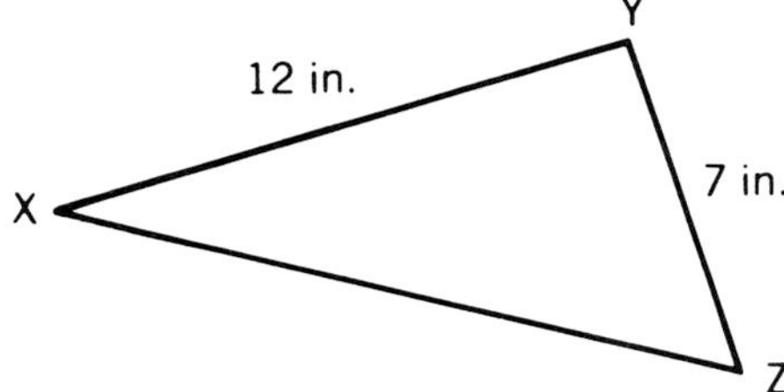

Area of triangular region XYZ is _____ square inches.

d.

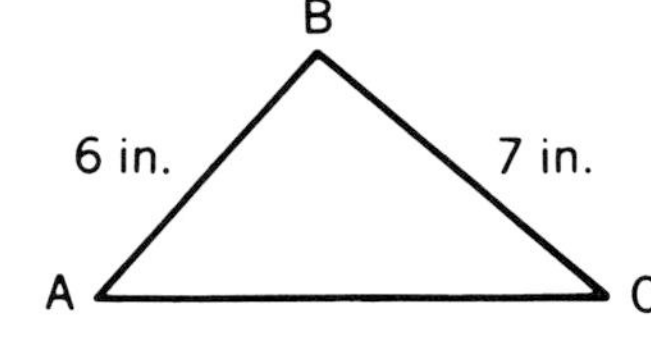

Area of triangular region ABC is _____ square inches.

21. The following picture is a diagram of a kitchen floor, with the lengths of the edges shown. Find the area of the floor.

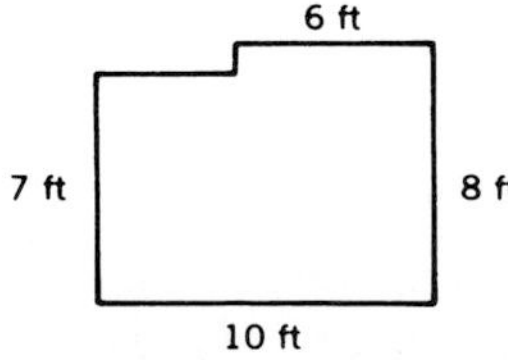

22. Have children measure the diameter and circumference of a circular object with a cloth tape measure. Using a calculator, have them calculate the ratio of circumference to diameter. Have them repeat this process with as many objects as time permits, each time keeping a record of the measurements. If the children make accurate measurements, they should obtain a reasonably good approximate value for pi (π).

23. Have cutout models of a circle, a rectangle, a square, and a triangle available. Then introduce models of a cube, a sphere, a cone, a cylinder, and a pyramid. Compare the two-dimensional and the three-dimensional models. Ask children to explain the ways in which the figures are alike and the ways in which they are different. (Children should be able to identify the three-dimensional shapes by name.) Ask one child to think of one of the three-dimensional shapes. Have another child try to identify the shape he or she is thinking of by asking a series of questions that can be answered only by yes or no. Continue the questions until the object is identified.

24. Spheres, cones, cylinders, and pyramids are easy to recognize, but distinguishing among different kinds of prisms and pyramids may be difficult for many children. Children should have the experience of cutting paper or cardboard prisms apart to see what patterns can be folded to form these prisms.

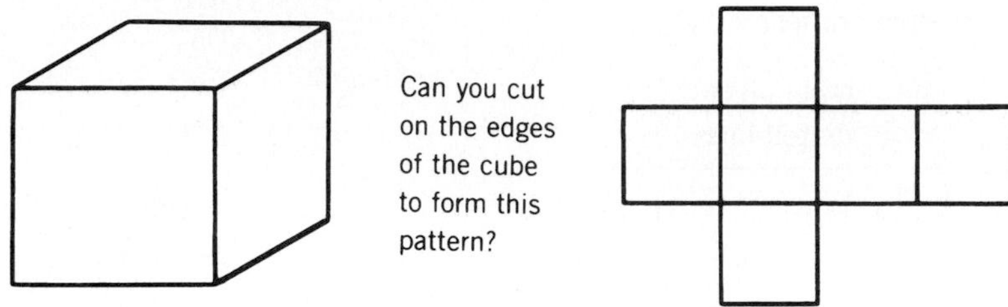

Can you cut
on the edges
of the cube
to form this
pattern?

Are there other ways you could cut the cube to form a pattern that can be folded into a cube? How many such patterns are there?

25. Have the children draw pictures using basic three-dimensional figures. For example:

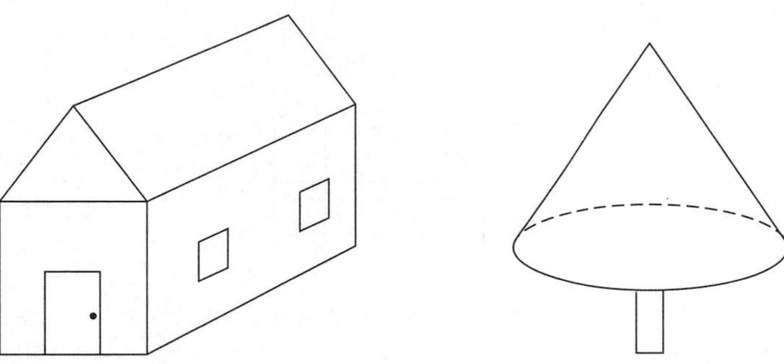

26. Ask the children to make patterns that can be folded into cylinders and cones. One way they can discover patterns for these figures is to wrap paper around wooden or plastic models and cut the paper to form the pattern. If the children have trouble with the cone pattern, have them cut ready-made paper cones along the seam.

27. Introduce regular polyhedra by showing the children models of a regular tetrahedron and a cube. Ask the children to make patterns for these figures. Also ask them to try making a pattern for a polyhedron with eight triangular faces.

28. Using real objects that have different shapes but the same volume, ask the children to see how many of each shape can be put into a box. Which would be a better shape for a unit of volume—a cube or a sphere?

29. Have the children cut shapes out of cardboard and fold them into space figures. Paste the shapes together. Hang them on wires and place them together to make mobiles. Hang the mobiles from the light fixtures in the classroom. An example is shown on the next page.

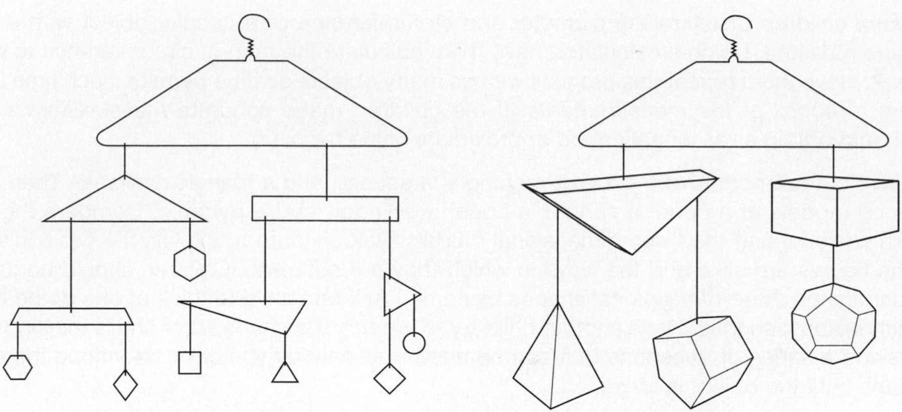

30. Give each child four or five sheets of paper the same size. The paper should be an even number of inches or centimeters in length or width. Let the children cut four squares out of the paper (one from each corner). Fold the sides up to make a five-sided box. Who can make a box that can hold the most cubes? What size square should be cut from each corner? Who can make a box that holds the least number of cubes? What size square should be cut from each corner?

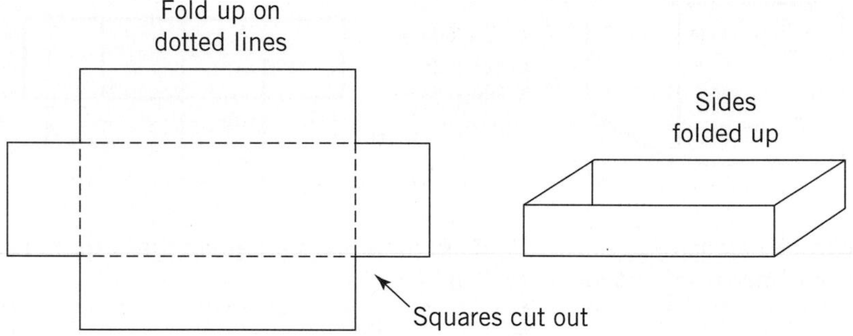

31. Children should be able to determine the volume of a box from a two-dimensional drawing such as the one shown.

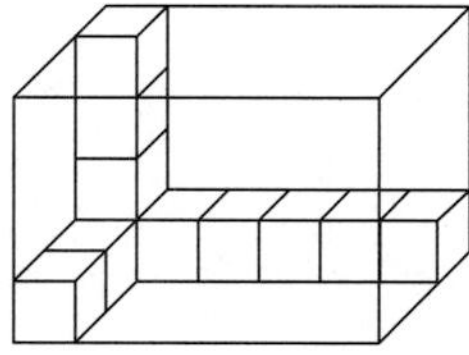

32. Use models of a prism and a pyramid that have equal heights and congruent bases. Ask children to predict which will hold more. If possible, encourage them to guess how much more. Have them experiment by filling the pyramid with sand, then pouring it into the prism. Have children repeat the experiment enough times to indicate the validity of the test. This same experiment can be done with a cone and a cylinder having equal bases and equal heights.

33. Provide the children with unit cubes (plastic or wooden), and encourage them to find how many cubes will fit into boxes of various sizes. At this stage, children will begin to discover how many cubes will fill the box by filling one layer and stacking cubes in a column to find how many layers there will be. Some will even do this:

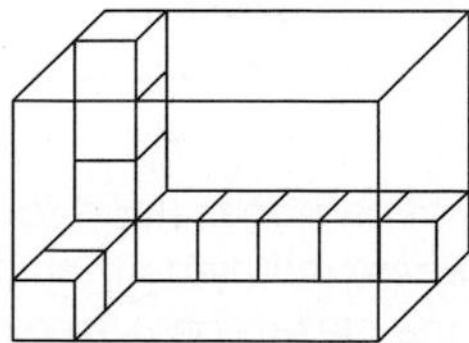

Children who use this method are only a step away from discovering the formula for the volume of a rectangular prism.

34. Measure the circumference and diameters of several cylinders. (This procedure is described in this chapter.) Divide the circumference of each cylinder by the diameter and record the displayed results. Discuss the results with the children.

35. Encourage children to create graphics on the microcomputer. Each computer and/or software package has its own unique techniques for producing graphics, so always have support information available for the children.

Suggested Readings

Battista, M. T., & Clements, D. H. (1991). Using spatial imagery in geometric reasoning. *The Arithmetic Teacher, 39*(3).

Beaumont, V., Curtis, R., & Smart, J. (1986). *How to teach perimeter, area, and volume.* Reston, VA: National Council of Teachers of Mathematics.

Bledsoe, G. (1987). Guessing geometric shapes. *The Mathematics Teacher, 80*(1).

Boykin, W. E. (1995). A middle school extension of Pick's theorem to areas of nonsimple closed polygonal regions. *School Science and Mathematics, 95.*

Bright, G., & Harvey, J. (1988). Learning and fun with geometry games. *The Arithmetic Teacher, 35*(8).

Burger, W. F. (1988). An active approach to geometry. *The Arithmetic Teacher, 36*(3).

Burger, W. F., & Shaughnessy, M. (1986). Characterizing the van Hiele levels of development in geometry. *Journal for Research in Mathematics Education, 17*(1).

Burns, M. (1994). What makes a square? *Instructor, 103*(6).

Campbell, P. F. (1983). Cardboard, rubber bands, and polyhedron models. *The Arithmetic Teacher, 31*(2).

Claus, A. (1992). Exploring geometry. *The Arithmetic Teacher, 40*(1).

Craig, B. (1986). Polygons, stars, circles, and logo. *The Arithmetic Teacher, 33*(9).

Craine, T. V., & Rubenstein, R. N. (1993). A quadrilateral hierarchy to facilitate learning in geometry. *The Mathematics Teacher, 86*(5).

Dunkels, A. (1990). Making and exploring tangrams. *The Arithmetic Teacher, 37*(6).

Hands-on, Inc. (1989). *Geometry: Kindergarten through grade nine.* Solvang, CA: Author.

Hersberger, J., & Talsma, G. (1991). Improving students' understanding of geometric definitions. *The Mathematics Teacher, 84*(7).

Hill, J. M. (Ed.). (1987). *Geometry for grades K-6.* Reston, VA: National Council of Teachers of Mathematics.

Jensen, R., & O'Neil, D. R. (1982). Informal geometry through geometric blocks. *The Arithmetic Teacher, 29*(9).

Juraschek, W. (1990). Getting in touch with shape. *The Arithmetic Teacher, 37*(8).

Kaiser, B. (1988). Explorations with tessellating polygons. *The Arithmetic Teacher, 36*(4).

Kleiman, G., & Zweig, K. (1995). *Designing spaces: Visualizing, planning, and building. Seeing and thinking mathematically in the middle grades.* Cambridge, MA: Education Development Center.

Kriegler, S. (1991). The tangram—More than an ancient puzzle. *The Arithmetic Teacher, 38*(9).

Larke, P. (1988). Geometric extravaganza: Spicing up geometry. *The Arithmetic Teacher, 36*(1).

Lappan, G., & Even, R. (1988). Research into practice: Similarity in the middle grades. *The Arithmetic Teacher, 35*(9).

Litwiller, B., & Duncan, D. (1991). Rhombus ratio activities. *The Arithmetic Teacher, 38*(7).

McDonald, J. L. (1989). Cognitive development and the structuring of geometric content. *Journal for Research in Mathematics Education, 20*(1).

McLaughlin, H. (1992). Determining area and calculating cost: A 'model' application. *The Mathematics Teacher, 85*(5).

Mansfield, H. (1985). Projective geometry in the elementary school. *The Arithmetic Teacher, 32*(7).

May, L. (1994). Shapes are everywhere. *Teaching PreK-8, 24*(6).

Miller, W. A., & Clason, R. G. (1994). Activities: Golden triangles, pentagons, and pentagrams. *The Mathematics Teacher, 87.*

Morrow, L. J. (1991). Geometry through the standards. *The Arithmetic Teacher, 38*(8).

Moses, B. (1990). Developing spatial thinking in the middle grades: Designing a space station. *The Arithmetic Teacher, 37*(6).

National Council of Teachers of Mathematics. (1987). *Learning and teaching geometry, K-12.* 1987 Yearbook. Reston, VA: National Council of Teachers of Mathematics.

National Council of Teachers of Mathematics. (1993). *Curriculum and evaluation standards for school mathematics addenda series grades K-4: Geometry and spatial sense.* Reston, VA: National Council of Teachers of Mathematics.

National Council of Teachers of Mathematics. (1992). *Curriculum and evaluation standards for school mathematics addenda series grades 5-8: Geometry in the middle grades.* Reston, VA: National Council of Teachers of Mathematics.

Norman, F. (1991). Figurate numbers in the classroom. *The Arithmetic Teacher, 38*(7).

Pappas, C. C., & Bush, S. (1989). Facilitating understandings of geometry. *The Arithmetic Teacher, 36*(8).

Periera-Mendoza, L. (1993). What is a quadrilateral? *The Arithmetic Teacher, 41*(4).

Poggi, J. (1985). An invitation to topology. *The Arithmetic Teacher, 33*(4).

Pohl, V. (1986). *How to enrich geometry using string designs.* Reston, VA: National Council of Teachers of Mathematics.

Prentice, G. (1989). Flexible straws. *The Arithmetic Teacher, 37*(3).

Renshaw, B. S. (1986). Symmetry the trademark way. *The Arithmetic Teacher, 34*(1).

Rowan, T. E. (1990). The geometry standards in K-8 mathematics. *The Arithmetic Teacher, 37*(6).

Sandefur, J. T. (1994). Using similarity to find length and area. *The Mathematics Teacher, 87.*

Shaw, J. M. (1983). Exploring perimeter and area using centimeter squared paper. *The Arithmetic Teacher, 31*(4).

Shaw, J. M. (1993). See it, change it, reason it out. *The Arithmetic Teacher, 40.*

Smith, L. R. (1993). Multiple solutions involving geoboard problems. *The Mathematics Teacher, 86.*

Szetela, W., & Owens, D. T. (1986). Finding the area of a circle: Use a cake pan and leave out the pi. *The Arithmetic Teacher, 33*(9).

Taylor, L. (1992). Exploring geometry with the *Geometer's Sketchpad. The Arithmetic Teacher, 40*(2).

Teppo, A. (1991). van Hiele levels of geometric thought revisited. *The Mathematics Teacher, 84*(7).

Thiessen, D., & Matthias, M. (1989). Selected children's books for geometry. *The Arithmetic Teacher, 37*(4).

Toumasis, C. (1992). The toothpick problem and beyond. *The Mathematics Teacher, 85*(2).

van Hiele, P. (1986). *Structure and insight: A theory of mathematics education.* New York, NY: Academic Press.

Wheatley, G. H. (1991). Enhancing mathematics learning through imagery. *The Arithmetic Teacher, 39*(1).

Wheatley, G. H., & Yackel, E. (1990). Promoting visual imagery for young pupils. *The Arithmetic Teacher, 37*(6).

Wilson, P. S. (1990). Understanding angles: Wedges to degrees. *The Mathematics Teacher, 90*(8).

Wilson, P., & Adams, V. (1992). A dynamic way to teach angle and angle measure. *The Arithmetic Teacher, 39*(5).

Winter, M. J., Lappan, G., Phillips, E., & Fitzgerald, W. (1986). *Spatial visualization* (middle grades mathematics project). Menlo Park, CA: Addison-Wesley.

Woodward, E., & Brown, R. (1994). Polydrons and three-dimensional geometry. *The Arithmetic Teacher, 41*(8).

Woodward, E., Gibbs, V., & Shoulders, M. (1992). A fifth-grade similarity unit. *The Arithmetic Teacher, 39*(8).

Chapter 17

A Look Back As You Move Ahead

Overview

In this text we have introduced you to mathematics found in contemporary elementary schools. Mathematics education is bringing together new learning theories and new materials for creative teachers to use in developing exciting classroom environments. The following discussion summarizes fundamental concepts and critical ideas for each grade level, K-8. Embedded in the discussion of each grade level is an outline of important ideas of eight content strands identified by the Ohio Department of Education and the Ohio Council of Teachers of Mathematics in their publication entitled *Model Competency-based Mathematics Program* (1990). These content strands are patterns, relations and functions; problem-solving strategies; number and number relations; geometry; algebra; measurement; estimation and mental computation; and data analysis and probability. The following brief descriptions of these content strands are reprinted from the *Model Competency-based Mathematics Program* (1990) with the permission of the Ohio Department of Education.

Patterns, Relations, and Functions

Students need to explore regularities and irregularities in their world. This leads to the building of models that reflect relationships and allow for predicting results. The special relationships described by functions are woven throughout the curriculum.

Problem-Solving Strategies

A purpose of mathematics is to solve problems. Students must have an opportunity to compare and contrast solutions developed by others.

Number and Number Relations

Every number activity should be in the context of situations real to the child or to the child's imagination. This includes the development of number sense, the understanding and the skill of computation with numbers of all kinds, and explorations of number theory. The objectives of this strand should be carefully correlated with other strands.

Geometry

Geometry is an important component of the mathematics curriculum at every level. Every geometry activity should involve exploring, describing, and understanding the world in which we live. Students should investigate, experiment, and explore with physical materials and drawings. Geometry must be more than the superficial study of terminology.

Algebra

Algebraic thinking serves to consolidate arithmetic skills and understandings and is a component of much of mathematics beyond the elementary school. Students should build basic algebraic ideas by making generalizations about numerical problem situations.

Measurement

Children learn to measure by measuring—not by working with pictures or memorizing relationships by rote. Activities should also include everyday situations that require only an estimated measure. Students should be encouraged to compare, but not convert, measurement systems.

Estimation and Mental Computation

Estimation is a useful skill for children as well as adults. Instruction should include when to estimate, ways of estimating, and reasonableness of an estimation. Mental computation, along with estimation, helps children become more flexible and better able to select a method most appropriate for a given situation.

Data Analysis and Probability

It is essential that students develop the ability to summarize and analyze data, to draw inferences, and to make accurate predictions and judgments. It is essential that students understand how statistics can be manipulated and recognize the potential uses and misuses of statistical information.

Now let us take a cursory look at mathematics content as it is sequenced by grade level in some programs.

SCOPE AND SEQUENCE IN GRADES K-8

Kindergarten

A contemporary mathematics program at the kindergarten level can be generally characterized as an opportunity for young children to explore and experiment with mathematical ideas in informal settings. The program should be designed for children to enlarge and develop their vocabulary through interacting with their environment. Teachers should provide many rich experiences that require exploration of materials with respect to color, number, size, shape, thickness, volume, weight, and other attributes. Observing, reconstructing, extending, and analyzing patterns from free exploration form a base for the structuring of mathematics.

Kindergarten children often delve informally into such topics as statistics, probability, and algebra concepts by describing relationships in words appropriate for their level of development. For example, such phrases as "almost," "maybe," and "if-then" often represent a child's interpretation of complex ideas.

Patterning is the underlying theme of mathematics. Piaget's theories and constructivist philosophies emphasize this concept very strongly. Recognizing and extending patterns is the very base on which problem-solving techniques should be developed. Consequently, children should be given many opportunities to experience patterns visually, aurally, and tactually.

The process of counting can be viewed from several different perspectives. Young children usually consider counting as the saying of arbitrary names in a special order. They must learn to associate a given quantity with a unique word. Only through convention do we know that the number name *five* comes immediately after the number name *four* when counting in increasing order. Just being able to say the number names in order does not mean that the child understands the counting process. Children sometimes say number names in proper order but are unable to use a one-to-one correspondence; that is, they are able to perform rote counting but not rational counting. They should be encouraged to subitize numberness (look at a group of objects and perceive the numerousness without having to count). Five-year-olds should be able to subitize groups of up to five objects. This aspect of number sense is the basis for the idea of *counting on.*

Do not rush young children into symbolic number activities in computation. The beginning skill steps in making comparisons and seeing relationships contribute an important stage to a child's growing mathematical understanding. Children must comprehend the concept of equal-sized groups before they can comprehend comparison fully.

Concrete graphing experiences form the beginning of an important problem-solving tool that helps children see and explore relationships. In this type of graph, children compare groups of real objects and then progress from the concrete to the abstract level.

Children must experience numbers from one to ten in a variety of ways using many different materials. Children are discovering and internalizing patterns and combinations encountered in number play. The understanding that a child gains in initially exploring numbers has a profound impact on later explorations. These experiences are the building blocks for later stages of the child's number sense development in mathematics. If this foundation is firmly established, dealing with abstract numberness will be simplified.

Kindergarten children also explore and extend their environment geometrically. They identify familiar two- and three-dimensional shapes and the ways in which these shapes make up their surroundings. Measurement, a topic closely tied to geometry, is also a focus of concrete exploration, with initial attention given to the process of linear measurement using physical examples of nonstandard units (erasers, crayons, etc.) followed by standard units such as the inch and centimeter. Other forms of measurement that are explored include basic time and money concepts.

Kindergarten—Patterns, Relations, and Functions

- recognize patterns of many kinds
- continue a pattern
- sort objects according to an attribute such as size, color, shape, number, etc.

Kindergarten—Problem-Solving Strategies

- act out problem situations
- use invented and conventional symbols to describe a problem

Kindergarten—Number and Number Relations

- compare the number of objects in two or more sets
- explore separating, joining, and ordering
- develop number-numeral relationships

Kindergarten—Geometry

- identify common solids in the environment
- identify common shapes in the environment

Kindergarten—Algebra

- use and understand the ideas of "if-then," "since," "because," etc.
- recognize the equivalence of a pattern described pictorially and auditorily

Kindergarten—Measurement

- compare and order objects of different lengths, weights, and capacities
- order events based on time

Kindergarten—Estimation and Mental Computation

- estimate the number of items in a set by comparing to a set where the number of items is known
- recognize situations for which an estimate is appropriate

Kindergarten—Data Analysis and Probability

- sort and describe objects according to attributes such as size, color, weight, etc.
- create floor and table graphs with actual objects

First Grade

In general, the first-grade program plays the crucial role of transition from informal readiness activities to the more structured experiences children will face in the primary and intermediate grades. The first-grade mathematics program should examine the relationships and number readiness developed in kindergarten. Vocabulary development should continue as it is related to rational counting. Pupils' number sense should be judged on the ability to rote count, to recognize number quantities, to match number symbols, and to demonstrate a one-to-one correspondence. Early experiences should involve children manipulating material on the concrete level, abstracting number concepts, and relating number names. As children become more experienced, they should be encouraged to move to more abstract level activities. Number activities associated with rational counting should be extended at least through 99, if not beyond, based on the level of individual development.

Counting activities should be extended to skip counting by twos and fives (remember that 1, 3, 5, 7, . . . is a valid way of counting by twos as well as 2, 4, 6, 8, . . .). Counting should also be extended into the development of ordinal numbers. The ordinal use of a number describes a position in a sequence. Ordinal number concepts from first through tenth should be developed. Ordinal numbers should be used in many classroom experiences, such as the order of children in a lunch line or the order in which children will take turns. Who is first? Who is second?

Using groups of objects, the concept of addition is developed from the concrete to the abstract level. Initially, couch addition within the context of a story rather than simply asking, "What is two plus three?" Avoid the premature introduction of abstract symbolization such as $2 + 3 = \square$. Instead, wait until the children have grasped the meaning underlying the addition concept. Two models are commonly used in developing addition understanding—groups of objects and the number line. If children have developed reversibility as defined by Piaget and have a good beginning on understanding addition, then subtraction can be introduced. The same two models are often used in developing subtraction understanding—groups of objects and the number line. There is only one form of addition to teach, but there are three forms of subtraction to teach—take-away, comparison, and add-on (although they should not be specifically identified as such for the children).

Basic addition and subtraction facts must be memorized. Many primary mathematics programs organize basic addition facts according to sums, such as all addition facts with sums less than five. This is only a teacher convenience and does not assist children in memorizing basic addition facts; often it does more harm. If children understand what addition is, have the facts organized according to logical structure, and have meaningful practice, then children will automatically memorize many of the basic addition facts. Additional memorization activities will be minimal. The same idea may be applied to memorization of the basic subtraction facts. Every step of addition and subtraction development must include development of problem-solving skills.

The basic addition and subtraction facts should be extended to adding tens with tens (for example, 4 tens and 3 tens, or 40 + 30). Next, the addition of two-place numbers and one-place numbers may be introduced. Regrouping (carrying) is usually postponed until later in the year. At this point, place value must be discussed. Now that a need for place value has been established, specific lessons must be taught developing place-value understanding. Place-value concepts can be extremely abstract and yet are very important concepts that must be well established through manipulations of concrete materials.

Children will need many experiences grouping counters in packages of ones and tens. A distinction must be made between ten groups of one and one group of ten. A place-value box can be very useful for this purpose. Children must realize that not more than nine counters may be left in the ones place. If more counters are placed in the ones place, they must be regrouped into a package of ten and placed in the tens place with the remainder of counters left ungrouped in the ones place.

Measurement study at the first grade level usually includes money, time, and linear measures. The major money objectives include recognition of all coins and the dollar bill, understanding that coins have different values, and matching equivalent values.

Time concepts are very abstract and difficult to develop. Children must have numberness and ability to read numbers through 60. Children usually learn to read a clock to the hour and half hour. Relating the reading of a clock to a number line is very beneficial. Avoid excessive terminology such as "half past" and "quarter after" at this level.

Linear measure is introduced in both U.S. customary and metric units, but the systems should not be related to each other through conversions. Units usually considered are inches, centimeters, and meters. Only rulers graduated with the units being taught should be introduced. Do not use rulers graduated in sixteenths of an inch when introducing inches. Children can easily make their own rulers from a standard ruler. The discussion of standard units of measure should be preceded by one about nonstandard units and the need for standardization.

The foundation for exploring geometry developed in the kindergarten is extended in the first grade. Characteristics of various two- and three-dimensional shapes are identified, terminology is refined, and problem-solving experiences utilizing geometric relations are considered.

Graphing is used as a method of analyzing data and representing statistical relationships collected through simple surveys. Bar graphs created with physical objects are often used to generate discussion and explore fundamental concepts in probability and statistics.

Grade One—Patterns, Relations, and Functions

- identify missing elements of patterns
- sort objects on multiple attributes

Grade One—Problem-Solving Strategies

- select appropriate notation and methods for symbolizing the problem statement and the solution process
- make tables to sort information

Grade One—Number and Number Relations

- count using ten frames
- skip count by two, five, and ten
- count backward
- symbolize addition and subtraction and relate them to joining and separating
- explore addition strategies such as "counting," "one more," "doubles," "doubles plus one," and "tenness"
- understand and use the terms halves, thirds, and fourths

Grade One—Geometry

- identify and compare two-dimensional shapes
- explore situations by manipulating shapes, measuring, and counting
- combine shapes to form a given shape

Grade One—Algebra

- use invented symbols to model problem situations
- use letters to describe addition situations

Grade One—Measurement

- measure lengths using nonstandard units, centimeters, and inches
- explore capacity using cups, pints, quarts, gallons, and liters
- explore weight using pounds and kilograms
- explore money and time as measures

Grade One—Estimation and Mental Computation

- estimate the value of a given collection of coins
- compare two sets of objects to determine whether there are about the same number of items in each set when the objects are arranged randomly or in a familiar pattern
- explore addition using strategies without reference to actual objects

Grade One—Data Analysis and Probability

- identify events that are sure to happen, events that are sure not to happen, and those we cannot be sure about
- expand sorting activities to more than one attribute at a time
- collect data and record using tallies

Second Grade

The second-grade mathematics program offers the opportunity to reinforce the learning experiences of kindergarten and first grade, and to extend those experiences into deeper understandings. Individual differences become more pronounced; close attention must be given to prerequisite knowledge and experiences; and students should be discouraged from using more immature mathematical methods such as finger counting and inappropriate numeral formations. Children must be encouraged to move from the concrete interpretation to the abstract interpretation of mathematics.

By means of a spiral curriculum approach, the early part of second grade concentrates on strengthening the skills and concepts already taught, and on the exploration of concepts that have not been effectively understood. Number development is usually extended to at least 999, and the writing of number words is usually extended to the hundreds. Counting by fives and tens is reinforced. Because of common references to the calendar, ordinal number development is also extended to "thirty-first" or beyond.

Place-value concepts are reviewed and extended through the hundreds and frequently to the thousands place. The importance of place-value understanding becomes more crucial as children progress in their mathematics development. Much work must be done to help the children bridge the gap from manipulative models to the abstract level of thought.

Addition and subtraction are reviewed and extended, with greater emphasis placed on regrouping (sometimes inappropriately referred to as "carrying"). The concept of an "unseen" number in column addition should be introduced as column addition skills are extended. The memorization of basic addition and subtraction facts is critical in second grade. This should be a goal prior to beginning the memorization of the basic multiplication facts.

Addition and subtraction should be extended to two- and three-place numbers. Place-value concepts must be integrated with addition concepts. Expanded notation and long algorithm forms will help children move toward development of standard short algorithm skills. Students should also be directed toward meaningful estimation and mental computation techniques to expand their power with mathematics.

Word problem development should be expanded as children begin to bring their reading skills and mathematics skills together. Every lesson should provide some opportunity to use word problem skills. In fact, word problem skills must be systematically developed and used at every level from kindergarten on.

Multiplication is introduced in second grade with the use of manipulative materials. Four models are commonly used on the concrete level—groups of objects, number lines, arrays, and successive addition. Do *not* have the children deliberately memorize basic multiplication facts at this level. Counting by groups other than one is readiness for multiplication. Children have counted by twos, fives, and tens. Now introduce counting by threes, fours, and so on. Second-grade work in multiplication is almost exclusively on the concrete level. State the ideas as three groups of four rather than symbolically as 3×4, or "three times four," to illustrate the meaning underlying the process.

Division is also introduced at this level. Relate subtraction with division, and follow similar procedures as those followed for multiplication. Remain strictly on the concrete level and do not worry about the abstract division algorithm or symbolism at this grade level.

Concepts of fractions are usually introduced at an informal level in second grade, if not sooner. Formal fraction work is reserved until the fourth-grade level. Concrete exploration is the basis for fraction development, with emphasis on the concept of equivalent parts. Denominators are usually limited to halves, thirds, and fourths. For the most part, unit fractions are considered (fractions with numerators of 1), but "simple" fractions with other numerators are considered. Do not have the children calculate with fractions.

Measurement is reviewed and expanded in second grade. Work is continued on the relative value of coins with the introduction of the idea of change. Time is reviewed and extended. Linear measure is extended and volume/capacity measures are explored.

The second-grade mathematics program includes such geometric concepts as comparing and contrasting geometric solids and plane figures. Students are asked to identify and name the shapes making up the faces of three-dimensional shapes. Attributes of geometric figures such as open/closed curves and convex/concave shapes are explored.

Statistics, at this grade level, involves the incorporation of "stem-and-leaf" displays to aid in presenting and analyzing data. Picture graphs are also commonly used to represent information and to serve as a means of transition from concrete graphs to bar graphs. Mean, median and mode can be explored visually and concretely. Probability is encountered as students conduct physical experiments to develop an intuitive understanding of likelihood.

Grade Two—Patterns, Relations, and Functions

- explore patterns in tables of number pairs as well as sequences of numbers
- identify missing elements in a pattern and justify their inclusion

Grade Two—Problem-Solving Strategies

- identify needed information to solve a problem
- look for patterns of numbers to find a solution

Grade Two—Number and Number Relations

- explore the concept of place value with models
- use concrete models of fractions and of equivalent fractions
- use a number line with whole numbers and fractions
- explore the concepts of multiplication and division

Grade Two—Geometry

- identify and compare three-dimensional shapes
- investigate congruence and symmetry
- investigate perimeter using concrete models

Grade Two—Algebra

- model problem situations using numbers and/or letters
- understand the use of letters in situations such as $a - b = 6$

Grade Two—Measurement

- explore length, capacity, and weight using both metric and U.S. customary units
- count and compare collections of coins
- tell time to the nearest 5 minute or minute intervals on both digital and dial timepieces

Grade Two—Estimation and Mental Computation

- make estimates in addition and subtraction using front-end digits
- determine whether a calculated solution is reasonable by using estimation
- use left-to-right addition to refine estimates obtained by front-end digits

Grade Two—Data Analysis and Probability

- create and interpret picture graphs and bar graphs and use them to predict
- sort based on multiple attributes
- identify information on a labeled picture map

Third Grade

Before the school year begins, the third-grade teacher might wish to study the second-year mathematics program, talk with the second-grade teacher, and study the children's cumulative folders. Then the teacher will have a reasonable idea as to where the third-grade mathematics program should begin and how it can build on the second-grade mathematics program and lead into the fourth-grade program.

Third-grade mathematics programs often begin with a check of addition and subtraction. Children's individual level of proficiency with fact memorization should be evaluated. Column addition and regrouping in addition must be reviewed and periodically reinforced during this grade.

Numbers up to 1 000 are studied—including counting, reading, writing, and using operations. Place value should be reviewed and extended using the place-value box and expanded notation. The Roman numerals that more commonly appear in everyday life (I, V, and X) are often introduced in third grade.

Much practice in group counting provides readiness for multiplication—this should include counting by twos, fives, tens, threes, and fours. Thus the idea of multiples of numbers may be developed. Multiplication is reintroduced using models—groups, the number line, arrays, and successive addition. The symbolization for multiplication is gradually introduced in both vertical and horizontal form. The students should have begun memorizing the basic multiplication facts. These basic facts are then extended with two- and three-place numbers multiplied by one-place numbers. Regrouping in multiplication is usually introduced at this level.

Division is reintroduced and is often kept parallel with the multiplication development. Groups, the number line, arrays, and successive subtraction are used as models for developing understanding of division. The division symbol $\left(\overline{)\quad}\right)$ is usually used. Do not introduce children to the ÷ symbol until later. Memorization of the basic division facts is started in third grade. Division with remainders is explored with concrete examples of such exercises as $3\overline{)16}$ or $5\overline{)22}$.

Fractions are reexamined using concrete materials such as rectangular and circular regions, groups, and the number line. The meanings of numerator and denominator are developed, but the words *numerator* and *denominator* are not necessarily used by children at this level.

In measurement, money is used up to one dollar, and the concept of change is developed. Simple addition and subtraction are used with respect to money. Time is developed to the minute and to the hour. The concepts of days, weeks, months, and years are reviewed. Linear measurement is extended to inches, feet, yards, meters, and centimeters. Measures of volume—pints, quarts, gallons, and liters—are introduced by actually using containers and pouring from one container into another. Mass is considered through physical interaction with objects measured in ounces, pounds, grams, and kilograms.

In geometry, students name such solids as cubes, cones, spheres, cylinders, pyramids, and rectangular prisms. Perspective is explored as students imagine solids from different views. Points, line segments, angles, lines, and planes are described through physical representations. Area is frequently introduced as both a geometric concept and as a form of measurement.

Probability and statistics involve the construction and interpretation of bar and picture graphs. Students use information taken from graphs to solve problems. Existing tables and charts are analyzed and students, through experimentation and/or given information, construct their own versions.

Grade Three—Patterns, Relations, and Functions

- recognize multiplication patterns
- make tables of values, then find and use the rule to generate additional pairs
- identify missing elements in a pattern and justify their inclusion

Grade Three—Problem-Solving Strategies

- extend the guess and check procedure by recording guesses and checks to help make better guesses until a solution is reached
- use more than one strategy to solve a given problem

Grade Three—Number and Number Relations

- nurture fluency in addition and subtraction
- explore strategies for multiplication and division
- incorporate symbols for fractions and develop the concept of tenths and hundredths as decimals

Grade Three—Geometry

- investigate area using concrete models
- investigate angles using concrete models
- describe three-dimensional objects from different perspectives

Grade Three—Algebra

- understand the use of letters in situations such as $ab = 12$
- explain, in words, thinking strategies for making computations

Grade Three—Measurement

- count and compare collections of coins and bills
- demonstrate the approximate size of units such as inch, centimeter, meter, and yard
- explore temperatures using both Fahrenheit and Celsius scales
- explore perimeter, area, and volume with string, tiles, and blocks

Grade Three—Estimation and Mental Computation

- add strings of numbers mentally by finding groups of tens
- explore multiplication using strategies without reference to actual objects

Grade Three—Data Analysis and Probability

- translate freely among pictographs, tables, charts, and bar graphs
- investigate and record all possible arrangements of a given set of objects

Fourth Grade

Fourth grade, not unlike other grades, might begin with a diagnostic instrument so that the teacher can evaluate the children's mathematics development and do any corrective teaching that is necessary. Teaching begins with the current level of the children's knowledge and not necessarily with what a grade-level textbook indicates. The memorization of the basic addition and subtraction facts should be evaluated and corrective teaching methods must be used regarding any facts not memorized.

Understanding of place value should be assessed and extended to more places. The number of places depends on previous teaching and the ability of the children, including their ability to generalize. Children should begin to realize that each place immediately to the left of a given place is ten times the value of the given place. A place-value box, counters, and place-value charts are valuable teaching aids. Children will accrue benefits from practice in reading and writing large numbers. Zero should be studied as a number and as a reference point. Roman numerals are sometimes extended to the symbols for 50, 100, and 1000 (L, C, and M).

A child's ability to add is evaluated, and a system of spaced practice is incorporated into the program. Attention should be given to strategies for mental computation and estimation techniques should be stressed. Likewise, subtraction of whole numbers should be evaluated and a review and practice program developed with emphasis on regrouping. Subtraction should be extended to more places and include practice with all three forms of subtraction: take-away, comparison, and add-on.

The main emphasis in fourth grade is on multiplication and division. Very often multiplication is reintroduced using the models of groups, the number line, arrays, and successive addition. After an understanding of multiplication is developed, students should concentrate on memorizing basic multiplication facts. The basic multiplication facts are then extended. Only one-place multipliers are emphasized in fourth grade; however, two-place multipliers are sometimes introduced. Children should be discouraged from writing the regrouped (carried) number above the next column. A multiplication algorithm should be established for placing products in proper place value.

The development of whole number division is kept parallel with whole number multiplication. Division, limited to one-place divisors, is redeveloped using groups, the number line, arrays, and successive subtraction. Measurement type of division is taught first, and partitive division is taught later. The phrase "goes into" should never be used with children to represent the division process. Division with remainders is reintroduced with the remainder concept taught as a "leftover" that is not large enough to form another full group. Division basic facts should be related to multiplication basic facts, with children beginning to memorize them.

Fractions become a major topic in fourth grade. Readiness was developed in second and third grades. Fractions should be introduced on the concrete level using regions (both rectangular and circular), number lines, and groups. Fraction boards may also be used. The concept of equivalent fractions is developed. Addition and subtraction of fractions are introduced and are usually limited to fractions with like denominators. Mixed numbers are also introduced at this level.

Measurement is reviewed and extended into halves and fourths of an inch. Metric linear measurement is continued. Liquid measure is continued using cups, tablespoons, pints, quarts, and gallons. Weight measures taught most frequently include ounces, pounds, tons, grams, and kilograms. Considerable attention is directed toward metric measure as well as U.S. customary units. U.S. customary and metric can be compared. However, do not *convert* from one system to the other.

Temperature measure is introduced using Fahrenheit degrees, including above and below zero. Time measures are emphasized—seconds, minutes, hours, days, weeks, months, and years. The study of money should be continued with emphasis on making change and using the operations with money.

Geometric concepts explored at the fourth-grade level include relationships such as parallel and perpendicular lines. Students name various types of angles, triangles, and quadrilaterals. Simple experiences with transformational geometry such as flips (reflections), slides (translations), and turns (rotations) are part of the "hands-on" geometric curriculum.

Interpreting simple tables, charts, and graphs is an important part of the fourth-grade curriculum. Students use an ordered-pair approach to identifying points on a map or grid. Probability continues to be considered through direct experimentation.

Grade Four—Patterns, Relations, and Functions

- find the rule in sequences of numbers and tables of values that include combinations of addition, subtraction, multiplication, and/or division
- explore patterns in other disciplines such as nature, art, and poetry

Grade Four—Problem-Solving Strategies

- make and use a table to record and sort information
- use a specific strategy to solve different kinds of problems

Grade Four—Number and Number Relations

- decompose numbers into factors
- use symbols for "greater than," "less than," "greater than or equal to," less than or equal to," as well as the terms "at most," and "at least"
- add and subtract fractions and decimals
- multiply and divide whole numbers fluently (not long division)

Grade Four—Geometry

- investigate reflections, rotations, and translations
- identify and illustrate intersecting, parallel, and perpendicular lines and right angles
- determine properties of two-dimensional figures

Grade Four—Algebra

- use variables in mathematical expressions to represent problems
- symbolize keying sequences on a calculator
- understand the use of letters in situations such as $a/b = 4$ or $c/2 = d$ and find the value of one letter when the other is given

Grade Four—Measurement

- choose appropriate units to measure lengths, capacities, and weights in both metric and U.S. customary units
- determine perimeters and areas of simple figures by measurement, not formulas
- use mental, paper-and-pencil, and physical strategies to determine time elapsed
- make change using coins and bills

Grade Four—Estimation and Mental Computation

- explore estimates of sums and differences and determine whether they are greater than or less than the exact sum or difference
- use compatible numbers to estimate in division
- use estimates to determine reasonableness of results in exact computations

Grade Four—Data Analysis and Probability

- expand on graphs to include time lines and diagrams
- find simple experimental probabilities (such as coin tossing, etc.)

Fifth Grade

The fifth-grade mathematics program is crucial because by the end of this grade the majority of the basic mathematical concepts of the elementary school, except decimals and percent, have been introduced and the memorization of basic operations facts should have been completed. Fifth grade provides a chance to reflect on all the mathematical concepts previously introduced, to practice the skills that have been previously taught, *and* to extend these mathematical concepts into new learnings.

The place-value system should be extended to billions, and place-value patterns should be generalized. Children should be able to read, write, and calculate with numbers up to nine places (with the greater numbers explored through the use of technology). The place-value system is extended to the right of the decimal point for at least two or three places.

Operations with whole numbers are thoroughly revised and extended to more places. Divisors are extended into two, but usually not three places because this is not a major priority for skill development. Three methods of interpreting remainders are taught (as a "leftover," as a fractional number part, and as a decimal number part). After a thorough understanding of the meaning of division has been developed, calculators can be used to show how time can be conserved and the workload simplified.

Concept development of fractions from concrete to abstract levels is continued, as are operations with fractions—including like denominators, unlike but related denominators, and unlike and unrelated denominators. Children need skill in calculating the least common multiple and the greatest common factor. Less emphasis is being devoted to the division of fractions because very few real-life examples are apparent. Fractions indicative of division are taught, as well as fractions indicative of ratios. Ratios are extended into proportions. Children also learn how to rewrite fractions in decimal form. Writing fractions in simplest form and simple calculations with mixed numbers are also developed.

Considerable instruction in understanding decimals and in operations with decimals is provided in the fifth grade. Decimals are very often related to the teaching of fractions. Rational numbers may be written in two different forms—fractions and decimals. Decimals represent special fractions in which the denominator is a power of ten. Children need to realize that much of what they know about whole numbers also applies to decimal numbers—numbers are written in proper place value, the operations are performed in the same manner, the "basic facts" are the same, and regrouping is handled in the same way. In this way, decimals provide an opportunity to review whole number concepts and operations.

The concept of rounding numbers is examined and related to place value. Children need to round both up and down. They need to explore several different methods of rounding that do not necessarily result in the same answer, and they need to justify why one method might be preferred to another in a given situation. They also need to learn how to use rounded numbers in estimating answers to examples and problems.

Linear measure is continually used, and children learn to convert within a given system. All measure taught thus far is reviewed—both U.S. customary and metric units. Measurement is related to simple geometric figures with the concepts of area and perimeter being continually developed. Cardboard cut into square inches and square centimeters is used to explore the concept of area. The formulas of area and perimeter are introduced through models. Scale drawing is included in some fifth-grade mathematics programs, often using proportional concepts.

Grade Five—Patterns, Relations, and Functions

- explore patterns in the decimal equivalents of common fractions
- explore patterns in the expanded form of numbers
- graph ordered pairs
- explore patterns in other disciplines such as music and science

Grade Five—Problem-Solving Strategies

- read a problem carefully and identify subgoals that need to be attained in order to solve a problem
- read a problem carefully and restate it without reference to the original

Grade Five—Number and Number Relations

- explore prime factorization
- examine long division with two-digit divisors only
- multiply and divide decimals
- identify and use the order of operations
- introduce the concept of ratio and relate it to fractions

Grade Five—Geometry

- compare and contrast angles in relation to right angles
- explore concepts of similarity by enlarging shapes
- explore patterns that result from a combination of reflections, rotations, and translations

Grade Five—Algebra

- symbolize keying sequences on calculators and know the difference between calculators with arithmetic and algebraic logic
- use variables to describe arithmetic processes

Grade Five—Measurement

- make reasonable estimates of lengths, weights, and capacities
- determine what to measure in order to find the perimeters, areas, and volumes of simple shapes and solids

Grade Five—Estimation and Mental Computation

- round fractions to 0, $\frac{1}{2}$, and 1 and use these values to estimate sums and differences of fractions
- halve and double factors to determine products
- use place value and trailing zeroes to mentally divide when the known numbers are multiples of powers of ten

Grade Five—Data Analysis and Probability

- explore the effects of changing the scale on bar graphs
- explore averages and calculate the arithmetic mean
- determine and make predictions based on experimental and theoretical probabilities

Sixth Grade

Because the children have presumably mastered the basic operations on whole numbers by the end of fourth grade, and because they have had contact with most of the major mathematical concepts of elementary school by the end of fifth grade, goals for sixth grade include, but are not limited to, the development of higher level understanding of the arithmetic operations that have been previously introduced, the introduction of some new operations (such as square root), and the continued emphasis on mathematics as a way of thinking, a way of communicating, and as a tool to help solve real problems.

The number system is reviewed and generalized into "any" number of places. Children should be able to read and write (in numbers and in words) "any" number. The number system is extended to more decimal places, at least to thousandths and possibly to millionths. Rounding of numbers—both whole numbers and decimals—is used in estimating answers.

Whole numbers and their operations are reviewed. Diagnostic assessments are commonly used to appraise each student's mathematical strengths and weaknesses. Individualized mathematics programs are developed to help each student with specific mathematical deficiencies. Students should be able to function effectively with many-place addition and subtraction, with and without a calculator. Multiplication should include up to three-place multipliers, and division should include two- and possibly three-place divisors. Both measurement and partitive division are studied.

Common fractions are reviewed, including addition and subtraction of fractions. The concept of the least common denominator is redeveloped and related to addition and subtraction of unlike but related fractions and to unlike but unrelated fractions. Much attention is given to addition and subtraction of mixed numbers, with emphasis on renaming fractions and mixed numbers. Multiplication and division using fractions are redeveloped from the concrete level to the abstract level. The study of fraction multiplication and division is extended into mixed numbers and culminates in the development of the algorithms. Problem-solving skills should be worked on during every step of the redevelopment.

Many sixth-grade mathematics programs redevelop decimals from the concrete level to the abstract level. Fractions and decimals are related, and one form is rewritten as the other form. Equivalence, place value, and operations are redeveloped. Addition and subtraction of decimals include at least three decimal places with and without regrouping. Multiplication of decimals is dependent on placing numbers in proper place value. Decimal points are placed in products by using place-value concepts.

Some programs introduce percentage in sixth grade. The understanding of percent should be based on concrete examples and related to fractions and decimals. Operations involving percent may also be introduced at this time.

All measurement units are reviewed and extended. Much attention is directed toward working with denominate numbers. Area and perimeter are related to geometric shapes and extended into space figures. The use of protractors as a measuring device is continued. Geometric compasses are used to perform simple constructions. Properties of various polygons are considered. These polygons include, among others, pentagons, hexagons, octagons, and decagons. Parts of circles, such as radius, diameter, center, chord, and arc, are named and defined.

Graphs, tables, scale drawings, and maps are studied. Students are asked to interpret data given in percents on a circle graph. Frequency tables are used to summarize raw data and box-and-whisker plots are constructed to show range, quartiles, and outliers. Experiments are conducted to identify possible outcomes and whether the outcomes are equally likely.

Grade Six—Patterns, Relations, and Functions

- build simple functions based on concrete models and express them mathematically
- explore patterns in other disciplines such as history and language arts

Grade Six—Problem-Solving Strategies

- identify needed and given information in a problem situation as well as irrelevant information
- extend specific solutions to more general problems

Grade Six—Number and Number Relations

- solidify computation with whole numbers, fractions, and decimals
- understand and describe in words the relationship between addition, subtraction, multiplication, and division
- build on ratio ideas to develop percent and proportion
- explore Roman numerals and other number systems and bases

Grade Six—Geometry

- measure angles and explore relationships between angle measure and other characteristics of figures
- identify and distinguish among similar, congruent, and symmetric figures
- visualize and demonstrate the results of a rotation, translation, reflection, or stretching
- explore, compare, and contrast properties of three-dimensional figures by building models

Grade Six—Algebra

- explore the use of parentheses on a calculator to change the result of a computation
- solve linear equations using concrete representations

Grade Six—Measurement

- convert, compare, and compute with common units of measure within the same measurement system
- explore and use formulas to compute areas and perimeters of common polygons and circles

Grade Six—Estimation and Mental Computation

- estimate the product or quotient of decimal numbers by rounding them to a single decimal place and then performing the operation
- look for compatibles in multiplication and division to help perform these operations mentally
- estimate the sum of several close addends by estimating an average and multiplying the average by the number of values
- use estimation to eliminate unreasonable answers

Grade Six—Data Analysis and Probability

- extend the exploration of graphs to circle graphs
- construct tree diagrams to represent sample spaces
- make predictions of outcomes of experiments based on theoretical probabilities and explain actual outcomes

Seventh Grade

The seventh-grade program was, at one point, considered solely as a time of transition between the elementary grades and the secondary level. Flanders, in a 1987 report, stated that 65 percent of the content of the typical seventh-grade mathematics textbook was a repetition of content explored at previous grade levels. As such, the seventh-grade curriculum frequently had no direction of its own, but tried, most often unsuccessfully, to serve both masters by attempting to resolve all the deficiencies of the earlier grades through review, leaving little time or options to explore significant new ideas. Fortunately, this view of the role of the middle grade/junior high program is no longer prevalent.

The seventh grade provides an excellent opportunity to refine the use of methods and techniques that underlie mathematical thought and reasoning. Teachers can still facilitate the systematic maintenance of skills and understandings by incorporating review in different contexts and new topics. Students should continue to experience the use of technology, cooperative work, open discussions, questioning, hypothesizing, justifying, and writing about mathematics. Integration of mathematical content, a common thread throughout the mathematics curriculum, can be extended further. Mathematical connections to other disciplines should be commonplace. By the time students reach the seventh grade they should have sufficient mathematics background to make significant connections within mathematics as well.

In numberness and operations, students explore perfect squares, squares, and square roots. Divisibility rules are used as a mental mathematics tool. Decimal and percent equivalents of fractions are determined by division. Scientific notation is studied as a convenient means of writing both extremely large and extremely small numbers. The connection between scientific notation and calculators is made clear.

Students are exposed to relationships between bar graphs, broken line graphs, pictographs, and circle graphs. Statistics such as range, mean, median, mode, and quartiles are determined from raw data and from frequency charts. Students determine the probability of an event through experimentation and theoretical models.

Geometry and measurement are related through the formulas for area and circumference of a circle. Surface areas of common solids such as cubes, rectangular prisms, pyramids, and cylinders are explored. Volumes of cylinders and prisms are determined through experimentation and formula. Perspective and proportional drawings are frequently included at this grade level as are geometric constructions using a straightedge and compass. Simple geometric proofs are verified through constructions and through "hands-on" transformational geometry. The distinction between congruence and similarity is made clear.

While algebra is sometimes considered only as a subject in secondary mathematics, nothing could be further from the truth. Students begin exposure to algebraic concepts as early as kindergarten through such activities as using one symbol to represent another or using simple "if-then" logic to explain consequence. Algebra is also embedded in such tasks as determining the value of $\square$ in the open sentence $3 + 4 = \square$. In the seventh grade, algebra does take on a more formal appearance. If not already explored in earlier grades, the number system is extended to include the set integers and operations on integers, including absolute value. The distinction between "positive" and "plus" as well as between "negative" and "minus" must be made (in each case, the former is used to name a signed number while the latter names an operation between two numbers). Students begin to explore linear relationships and the equations that represent these relationships.

Grade Seven—Patterns, Relations, and Functions

- describe and represent relations with tables, graphs, rules, and words
- generate ordered pairs with and without a calculator to graph linear equations
- extend the investigation of number patterns

Grade Seven—Problem-Solving Strategies

- use an open sentence (algebraic equation) to symbolize a problem situation and solve the equation to find a solution to the problem
- rephrase a problem as a simpler problem to find a method of solution

Grade Seven—Number and Number Relations

- explore percent through proportions and algebraic equations
- develop integer concepts
- compare, order, and determine the equivalence of whole numbers, fractions, decimals, percents, and integers
- work with bases other than ten
- examine scientific notation relative to calculators

Grade Seven—Geometry

- develop minimum sets of properties that describe a geometric figure and develop definitions of common figures
- validate fundamental geometric theorems using concrete representations and informal arguments
- build models of figures given top, side, and front views

Grade Seven—Algebra

- solve linear equations with one variable by working backward
- evaluate algebraic expressions (simple substitution)
- use ratios, proportions, and percents

Grade Seven—Measurement

- choose appropriate units to measure length, area, volume, weight, capacity, time, money, and temperature in both metric and U.S. customary units
- state and apply area formulas for circles, rectangles, parallelograms, trapezoids, and triangles
- compute surface areas for various solids

Grade Seven—Estimation and Mental Computation

- estimate with percents, using 1%, 10%, and 50%, and multiples of these numbers
- estimate the square root of a given number to the nearest whole number or range of whole numbers

Grade Seven—Data Analysis and Probability

- collect data and display information using an appropriate graph
- compute averages
- make logical inferences from statistical data

Eighth Grade

Eighth-grade mathematics may be characterized in a variety of ways. For some students, eighth grade is defined as an algebra course. For others it takes the form of pre-algebra. Still other students explore an integrated set of topics designed to emphasize the myriad of connections found within and outside of mathematics. Whatever the emphasis, the eighth-grade mathematics program has the potential to extend significantly the students' perspective of the ways in which mathematics will become a lifelong tool in work, home, and recreation.

Eighth-grade students evaluate expressions that involve sums, differences, products, and quotients of both positive and negative rational numbers. The student also learns to identify appropriate "tools" for specific computational situations—paper-and-pencil, the calculator, the computer, or mental mathematics. They explore the properties of number systems and, often with the use of calculators, the distinction between algebraic and arithmetic logic. Variable expressions, including those with exponential notation, are evaluated and simplified. Linear equations and inequalities based on real-world relationships should be graphed and/or solved by algebraic manipulation.

Students should be able to identify and construct the appropriate type of graph to best represent a given set of data (including the construction of circle graphs from appropriate raw data). They should also be able to find the mean, median and mode of a set of data.

Eighth-grade students determine various possible and impossible outcomes from situations that involve two or more variables. They learn to define sample spaces and count outcomes for a specific event. Students distinguish between and identify appropriate uses of permutations and combinations. Students recognize that in certain situations the probability of an event occurring can only be determined through experimentation and the collection of data. They explore the role of sampling and collecting raw data in formulating a statistical argument. The notion that statistics can be misinterpreted or misused must be explored. Students need to be able to analyze an argument based on statistics to determine any fallacies.

The eighth grade provides an opportunity to extend geometric concepts and reasoning from the seventh grade. This involves the analysis of three-dimensional solids including the study of surface area, volume, and the relationship between the number of faces, edges, and vertices. Geometric and algebraic topics such as the Pythagorean Theorem, Pascal's Triangle, the Golden Ratio, and the Fibonacci sequence are explored for their benefits in hypothesizing, generalizing, and justifying. Students explore the visual interpretation of geometric theorems dealing with such characteristics as corresponding, vertical, central, and inscribed angles.

Grade Eight—Patterns, Relations, and Functions

- use patterns and keys on the calculator to develop the concept of inverse operations
- explore the right triangle relations of sine, cosine, and tangent and their applications to indirect measurement
- explore simple and complex patterns in the environment

Grade Eight—Problem-Solving Strategies

- validate and generalize problem solutions
- select appropriate notation and methods for symbolizing the problem and the solution process

Grade Eight—Number and Number Relations

- explore operations with integers
- explore irrational numbers
- explore topics such as palindromes, Fibonacci numbers, etc.

Grade Eight—Geometry

- sketch three-dimensional figures from different perspectives
- calculate missing measurements of similar figures
- graph similar figures, reflections, translations, and rotations on a coordinate plane
- find surface areas and volumes of rectangular solids

Grade Eight—Algebra

- apply formulas to problem situations
- solve linear inequalities in one variable
- explore the concept of slope

Grade Eight—Measurement

- compute area for composite figures
- make appropriate measurements and compute volumes of solids such as prisms, cylinders, pyramids, and cones
- read a scale on a measurement device and interpolate where appropriate

Grade Eight—Estimation and Mental Computation

- use fractions, decimals, and percent equivalents interchangeably in making estimates
- extend mental computation to the solution of simple equations

Grade Eight—Data Analysis and Probability

- detect misuses of statistical information
- explore the role of sampling and collecting data in making a statistical argument
- calculate and explore relationships between the mean, median, mode, and range for a data set

Closure

This discussion has been designed to provide a quick overview of the elementary school mathematics program. One must keep in mind that elementary mathematics programs will vary, often considerably, among schools. Examination of courses of study, curriculum guides, text materials, and resource materials along with grade level, building level, and district level conversations can help you become familiar with the local scope and sequence.

Suggested Readings

Center of Excellence for the Enrichment of Science and Mathematics Education. (1990). *Mathematics activities manual for kindergarten.* Martin, TN: University of Tennessee at Martin.

Center of Excellence for the Enrichment of Science and Mathematics Education. (1990). *Mathematics activities manual for grade one.* Martin, TN: University of Tennessee at Martin.

Center of Excellence for the Enrichment of Science and Mathematics Education. (1990). *Mathematics activities manual for grade two.* Martin, TN: University of Tennessee at Martin.

Center of Excellence for the Enrichment of Science and Mathematics Education. (1990). *Mathematics activities manual for grade three.* Martin, TN: University of Tennessee at Martin.

Center of Excellence for the Enrichment of Science and Mathematics Education. (1990). *Mathematics activities manual for grade four.* Martin, TN: University of Tennessee at Martin.

Center of Excellence for the Enrichment of Science and Mathematics Education. (1990). *Mathematics activities manual for grade five.* Martin, TN: University of Tennessee at Martin.

Center of Excellence for the Enrichment of Science and Mathematics Education. (1990). *Mathematics activities manual for grade six.* Martin, TN: University of Tennessee at Martin.

Center of Excellence for the Enrichment of Science and Mathematics Education. (1990). *Mathematics activities manual for grade seven.* Martin, TN: University of Tennessee at Martin.

Center of Excellence for the Enrichment of Science and Mathematics Education. (1990). *Mathematics activities manual for grade eight.* Martin, TN: University of Tennessee at Martin.

Hands-on, Inc. (1990). *Patterns and functions: Kindergarten through grade nine.* Solvang, CA: Author.

Hands-on, Inc. (1989). *Logic: Kindergarten through grade nine.* Solvang, CA: Author.

Hands-on, Inc. (1992). *Number and operations: Kindergarten through grade nine.* Solvang, CA: Author.

Hands-on, Inc. (1989). *Geometry: Kindergarten through grade nine.* Solvang, CA: Author.

Hands-on, Inc. (1990). *Algebra: Kindergarten through grade nine.* Solvang, CA: Author.

Hands-on, Inc. (1991). *Measurement: Grades three through eight.* Solvang, CA: Author.

Hands-on, Inc. (1990). *Statistics, probability, and graphing: Kindergarten through grade nine.* Solvang, CA: Author.

National Council of Teachers of Mathematics. (1989). *Curriculum and evaluation standards for school mathematics.* Reston, VA: National Council of Teachers of Mathematics.

National Council of Teachers of Mathematics. (1993). *Implementing the K-8 curriculum and evaluation standards.* Reston, VA: National Council of Teachers of Mathematics.

National Council of Teachers of Mathematics. (1991). *Curriculum and evaluation standards for school mathematics addenda series: Kindergarten book.* Reston, VA: National Council of Teachers of Mathematics.

National Council of Teachers of Mathematics. (1991). *Curriculum and evaluation standards for school mathematics addenda series: First-grade book.* Reston, VA: National Council of Teachers of Mathematics.

National Council of Teachers of Mathematics. (1992). *Curriculum and evaluation standards for school mathematics addenda series: Second-grade book.* Reston, VA: National Council of Teachers of Mathematics.

National Council of Teachers of Mathematics. (1992). *Curriculum and evaluation standards for school mathematics addenda series: Third-grade book.* Reston, VA: National Council of Teachers of Mathematics.

National Council of Teachers of Mathematics. (1992). *Curriculum and evaluation standards for school mathematics addenda series: Fourth-grade book.* Reston, VA: National Council of Teachers of Mathematics.

National Council of Teachers of Mathematics. (1992). *Curriculum and evaluation standards for school mathematics addenda series: Fifth-grade book.* Reston, VA: National Council of Teachers of Mathematics.

National Council of Teachers of Mathematics. (1992). *Curriculum and evaluation standards for school mathematics addenda series: Sixth-grade book.* Reston,

VA: National Council of Teachers of Mathematics.

National Council of Teachers of Mathematics. (1992). *Curriculum and evaluation standards for school mathematics addenda series grades K-4: Making sense of data.* Reston, VA: National Council of Teachers of Mathematics.

National Council of Teachers of Mathematics. (1993). *Curriculum and evaluation standards for school mathematics addenda series grades K-4: Number sense and operations.* Reston, VA: National Council of Teachers of Mathematics.

National Council of Teachers of Mathematics. (1993). *Curriculum and evaluation standards for school mathematics addenda series grades K-4: Geometry and spatial sense.* Reston, VA: National Council of Teachers of Mathematics.

National Council of Teachers of Mathematics. (1993). *Curriculum and evaluation standards for school mathematics addenda series grades K-4: Patterns.* Reston, VA: National Council of Teachers of Mathematics.

National Council of Teachers of Mathematics. (1991). *Curriculum and evaluation standards for school mathematics addenda series grades 5-8: Dealing with data and chance.* Reston, VA: National Council of Teachers of Mathematics.

National Council of Teachers of Mathematics. (1991). *Curriculum and evaluation standards for school mathematics addenda series grades 5-8: Developing number sense.* Reston, VA: National Council of Teachers of Mathematics.

National Council of Teachers of Mathematics. (1992). *Curriculum and evaluation standards for school mathematics addenda series grades 5-8: Patterns and functions.* Reston, VA: National Council of Teachers of Mathematics.

National Council of Teachers of Mathematics. (1992). *Curriculum and evaluation standards for school mathematics addenda series grades 5-8: Geometry in the middle grades.* Reston, VA: National Council of Teachers of Mathematics.

CHECKLIST OF MATHEMATICAL CONCEPT CLUSTERS

Initially Developed and Compiled by the Mathematics Education Team, Department of Teacher Development and Curriculum Studies, Kent State University. 1997 Revision by William R. Speer.

This checklist is a summary of mathematical concepts organized under headings named "Concept Clusters." The items on the checklist have been sequenced in a logical order within each concept cluster; however, a student does not learn all the concepts in a given concept cluster before he or she begins to study another concept cluster. For example, the student does not have to learn place value before beginning to study addition and subtraction of whole numbers. Teachers have the responsibility of arranging concepts from different concept clusters into a program that meets the mathematical needs of children.

Since children do not learn mathematics in a linear fashion, concepts as listed on the checklist should be introduced, developed, and reinforced through a spiral curriculum. Mastery of basic skills should follow concept development. Understanding (concept development) and skill (mastery of basic facts and algorithms) constitute power with mathematics.

The checklist should be continuously updated. In the appropriate space at the right of each concept, record the date (month and year) in pencil.

A. Concept Cluster—Relationships
B. Concept Cluster—Readiness Activities for Operations with Counting Numbers and Whole Numbers
    1. Numberness
    2. Counting
    3. Place Value
C. Concept Cluster—Addition and Subtraction of Whole Numbers
D. Concept Cluster—Multiplication and Division of Whole Numbers
E. Concept Cluster—Integers
    1. Readiness Activities for Operations with Integers
    2. Addition and Subtraction of Integers
    3. Multiplication and Division of Integers
F. Concept Cluster—The Set of Rational Numbers
    1. Rational Numbers Expressed as Decimals
        a. Readiness Activities for Operations with Decimals
        b. Addition and Subtraction of Rational Numbers Expressed as Decimals
        c. Multiplication and Division of Rational Numbers Expressed as Decimals
    2. Rational Numbers Expressed as Fractions
        a. Readiness Activities for Operations with Fractions
        b. Addition and Subtraction of Rational Numbers Expressed as Fractions
        c. Multiplication and Division of Rational Numbers Expressed as Fractions

3. Interrelating the Decimal Symbol with the Fraction Symbol for Rational Numbers
4. Rational Numbers Expressed as Percents

G. Concept Cluster—Ratio and Proportion

H. Concept Cluster—Measurement
1. Money
2. Time
3. Length (Metric units and U.S. Customary units)
4. Volume or Capacity (Metric units and U.S. Customary units)
5. Weight or Mass (Metric units and U.S. Customary units)
6. Temperature (Metric units and U.S. Customary units)

I. Concept Cluster—Geometry

J. Concept Cluster—Exponential Notation

K. Concept Cluster—Scientific Notation

L. Concept Cluster—Probability

M. Concept Cluster—Statistics

N. Concept Cluster—Graphs (Nonalgebraic)

O. Concept Cluster—Rectangular Coordinate Graphs

A. CONCEPT CLUSTER—RELATIONSHIPS	**Introduction**	**In Process**	**Mastery**
1. Size and quantity (single object)			
a. big—little			
b. long—short			
c. tall—short			
d. large—small			
e. many—few			
f. high—low			
g. all—none			
h. heavy—light			
i. thick—thin			
2. Position			
a. under—over			
b. first—last			
c. middle			
d. high—low			
e. far—near			
f. bottom—top			
g. above—below			
h. in front of—behind—on top of			
i. beside—by—next to			
j. between			
k. around			
l. inside—outside			
m. right—left			
3. Comparison of two or more quantities			
a. younger(est)—older(est)			
b. fewer(est)			
c. more (most)—less (least): referring to sets			
d. greater than—less than: referring to sets			
e. larger(est)—smaller(est)			
f. longer(est)—shorter(est)			
g. straight—crooked			

	Introduction	**In Process**	**Mastery**
h. bigger(est)—littler(est)			
i. heavier(est)—lighter(est)			
j. taller(est)—shorter(est)			
k. thicker(est)—thinner(est)			
4. Measurement			
a. capacity			
(1) empty—full			
(2) pair			
(3) cupful			
(4) spoonful			
(5) pint			
(6) quart			
(7) liter			
(8) gallon			
b. linear			
(1) ruler			
(2) meter stick			
(3) yardstick			
c. temperature			
(1) hot—cold			
(2) thermometer			
(3) degree			
d. weight			
(1) metric units: gram, kilogram			
(2) customary units: ounce, pound			
e. time			
(1) early—late			
(2) yesterday—tomorrow			
(3) today			
(4) morning—afternoon			
(5) noon—midnight			
(6) night—day			
(7) evening			

	Introduction	In Process	Mastery
(8) minute			
(9) hour			
(10) week			
(11) month			
(12) year			
(13) fast—slow			
f. money			
(1) penny			
(2) nickel			
(3) dime			
(4) quarter			
(5) buy—sell			
(6) spend—save			
(7) pay			
(8) cost			
5. Geometric figures and shapes (sorting activities and recognition)			
a. square			
b. rectangle			
c. circle			
d. triangle			
e. cube			
f. sphere (globe or ball)			
6. Awareness of similarities and differences (sorting activities according to one or more of the following characteristics)			
a. categories: animals, boys, girls, and so on			
b. shape			
c. size			
d. color			
e. thickness			
7. Patterns (Begin with two objects; then increase the number of objects to three or more.)			
a. observing patterns			
b. orally describing patterns			
c. duplicating and then extending patterns			
d. completing patterns			
e. creating patterns			

B. CONCEPT CLUSTER—READINESS ACTIVITIES FOR OPERATIONS WITH COUNTING NUMBERS AND WHOLE NUMBERS

	Introduction	In Process	Mastery
1. Numberness			
a. recognizing a group as a collection of distinguishable objects			
b. viewing a model of a group and verbally stating its cardinality (0-9)			
c. matching a group model of cardinal numbers (0-9) with the appropriate numeral			
d. matching the appropriate numeral with a group model of cardinal numbers (0-9)			
e. recognizing one-to-one correspondence between the objects of two equal groups (0-9)			
f. demonstrating one-to-one correspondence between the objects of two equal groups (0-9)			
g. using one-to-one correspondence to determine whether two groups (0-9) are equal			
h. recognizing, by visual inspection, whether two groups (0-9) are equal			
i. constructing two or more disjoint sets that model the same cardinal number (0-9)			
j. constructing a disjoint group that contains one object more (or less) than a given group (0-9)			
k. ordering numbers (0-9) on a number line			
l. writing numerals (0-9)			
m. recognizing odd and even numbers (0-9)			
n. recognizing a written word name for a number (0-9)			
o. associating a written word name with the appropriate numeral (0-9)			
p. writing a word name for a number when shown a given numeral (0-9)			
q. writing numerals 10-20			
r. writing numerals 21-99			
s. associating a Roman numeral with a given number (1-100)			
t. writing a Roman numeral for a given number (1-100)			
2. Counting			
a. rational counting by ones to			
(1) 10			
(2) 20			
(3) 50			
(4) 100			
b. rational counting by twos to			

	Introduction	In Process	Mastery
(1) 20, beginning with 2			
(2) 19, beginning with 1			
(3) 50 or more, beginning with any one-place number			
c. rational counting by fives			
d. rational counting by tens			
e. identifying the number of objects in a group (0-9) by			
(1) counting each object			
(2) grouping the objects into subgroups			
(3) visual inspection (subitizing)			
f. identifying equalities and inequalities			
g. relating the words *greater than, less than,* and *equal to* to *part of*			
h. recognizing the symbols >, <, and =			
i. relating the words *greater than* to the symbol > when comparing two numbers			
j. relating the words *less than* to the symbol < when comparing two numbers			
k. relating the words *equal to* to the symbol = when comparing two numbers			
l. identifying greatest/ least, given three or more numbers			
m. recognizing ordinal numbers (first through tenth)			
n. modeling counting on the number line			
o. naming the number that is 1 greater than or 1 less than a given one- or two-place number			
p. supplying the missing numerals when several are missing in sequence (0-100)			
q. writing the word names for numbers (10-100)			
r. writing the numeral, given the word names for numbers (10-100)			
3. Place value			
a. recognizing another way of modeling ten "ones" as one "ten"			

	Introduction	In Process	Mastery
b. modeling any two-place number as ones and tens (expanded notation)			
c. interpreting the place-value model of any two-place number in standard notation			
d. rewriting a number in expanded notation relating the word name for place value with the numeral (for example, 34 = 3 tens 4 ones)			
e. extending (b), (c), and (d) through the hundreds place			
f. renaming numbers in several different ways (for example, 273 can be renamed as 273 ones, or 27 tens 3 ones, or 2 hundreds 7 tens 3 ones)			
g. renaming numbers with zeros as place holders in several different ways (for example, 300 can be renamed as 300 ones, or 30 tens 0 ones, or 3 hundreds 0 tens 0 ones)			
h. extending (b) through (g) to the thousands place and beyond			
i. rounding numbers to the			
(1) nearest ten			
(2) nearest hundred			
(3) nearest thousand			
(4) any place value greater than thousands place			
j. expressing place value in exponential form			
(1) positive integral exponents			
(2) zero as an exponent			
(3) negative integral exponents			

REMARK: At this time in the program, numeration systems without place value could be contrasted with numeration systems having place value.

C. CONCEPT CLUSTER—ADDITION AND SUBTRACTION OF WHOLE NUMBERS

	Introduction	In Process	Mastery
1. Recognizing the joining of two groups as a model for addition			
2. Modeling the joining of two disjoint groups			
3. Associating the + sign as the appropriate symbol for addition			

	Introduction	In Process	Mastery
4. Modeling addition of two one-place numbers, using manipulative materials			
5. Modeling the commutative property of addition			
6. Interpreting group models for addition as addition sentences			
7. Modeling an addition sentence, given a basic addition fact			
8. Modeling addition on a number line			
9. Recognizing the words addend and sum			
10. Organizing the 100 basic addition facts according to a given sum (0-18)			
11. Memorizing the basic addition facts with			
a. 0 as one of the addends and the commutative property			
b. 1 as one of the addends and the commutative property			
c. 2 as one of the addends and the commutative property			
d. "doubles" and "related doubles" and the commutative property			
e. facts related to tenness (by the associative property) and the commutative property			
f. the ten remaining facts that were not included in (a) through (e)			
12. Comparing the sums of two basic addition facts using the $>$, $<$, or $=$ symbols			
13. Extending and expanding the basic addition facts, for example, the fact $2 + 3$ extended to $20 + 30$			

REMARK: Throughout this portion of the checklist, the word regrouping is used in place of carrying and borrowing; the latter terms are not mathematically meaningful.

	Introduction	In Process	Mastery
14. Naming the sum of a two-place whole number and a one-place whole number (no regrouping)			
15. Naming the sum of a two-place whole number and a two-place whole number (no regrouping)			
16. Naming the sum of a three-place whole number and a two-place whole number (no regrouping)			
17. Naming the sum of a three-place whole number and a three-place whole number (no regrouping)			

	Introduction	In Process	Mastery
18. Naming the sum of a many-place whole number and a many-place whole number (no regrouping)			
19. Naming the sum of three or more one-place whole numbers in column addition (no regrouping)			
20. Naming the sum of three or more two-place whole numbers in column addition (no regrouping)			
21. Naming the sum of three or more one-place and many-place numbers (no regrouping)			
22. Generalizing the sum of two even numbers			
23. Generalizing the sum of an even number and an odd number (and vice versa)			
24. Generalizing the sum of two odd numbers			
25. Naming the sum of a two-place whole number and a one-place whole number with a single regrouping			
26. Naming the sum of a two-place whole number and a two-place whole number with regrouping (ones to tens)			
27. Naming the sum of a many-place whole number and a many-place whole number with regrouping (ones to tens or tens to hundreds)			
28. Naming the sum of a two-place whole number and a two-place whole number with two regroupings			
29. Naming the sum of a three-place whole number and a two-place whole number with two regroupings			
30. Naming the sum of a three-place whole number and a three-place whole number with two regroupings			
31. Naming the sum of a many-place whole number and a many-place whole number with several regroupings			
32. Estimating sums			
33. Solving problems that require addition of whole numbers			
34. Finding missing addends (readiness for subtraction)			
35. Understanding subtraction as the inverse of addition			

	Introduction	In Process	Mastery
36. Understanding the subtraction sign			
37. Using groups as a model for subtraction			
a. take-away			
b. comparison			
c. how many more are needed			
38. Expressing a related addition sentence in subtraction form, for example, (addend + [addend] = sum → ← sum − addend = [addend])			
39. Modeling subtraction on the number line			
40. Organizing and then memorizing the basic subtraction facts			
41. Extending and expanding the basic subtraction facts, for example, the fact 5 − 3 extended to 50 − 30			
42. Naming the difference between a two-place whole number and a one-place whole number (not a basic fact and no regrouping)			
43. Naming the difference between two, two-place whole numbers (no regrouping)			
44. Naming the difference between a three-place whole number and a two-place whole number (no regrouping)			
45. Naming the difference between two, three-place whole numbers (no regrouping)			
46. Naming the difference between two, many-place whole numbers (no regrouping)			
47. Naming the difference between a two-place whole number and a one-place whole number (not a basic fact) with regrouping			
48. Naming the difference between two, two-place whole numbers with regrouping from tens to ones			
49. Naming the difference between a three-place whole number and a two-place whole number with regrouping from tens to ones			
50. Naming the difference between a three-place whole number and a two-place whole number with regrouping from hundreds to tens			
51. Naming the difference between a three-place whole number and a two-place whole number with double regrouping			
52. Naming the difference between two, three-place whole numbers with a single regrouping			
53. Naming the difference between two, three-place whole numbers with double regrouping			
54. Naming the difference between two, many-place whole numbers with several regroupings			
55. Naming the difference when a zero appears in a single place of the minuend			
56. Naming the difference when zeros appear in the tens and ones place of the minuend			
57. Estimating differences			
58. Problem solving that requires subtraction of whole numbers			

REMARK: The words *minuend, subtrahend,* and *difference* should be meaningfully related to *sum, given addend,* and *missing addend,* respectively.

D. CONCEPT CLUSTER—MULTIPLICATION AND DIVISION OF WHOLE NUMBERS

	Introduction	In Process	Mastery
1. Using groups as a model for multiplication of whole numbers			
a. recognizing the number of groups			
b. recognizing the number of objects in each group			
2. Recognizing the × sign as an appropriate symbol for multiplication			
3. Interpreting group models as basic multiplication facts			
4. Verifying the commutative property for multiplication			
5. Using group models to illustrate several basic facts			
6. Using arrays as a model for multiplication			
7. Modeling multiplication of two, one-place whole numbers on the number line			
8. Using successive addition as a model for multiplication			
9. Recognizing the words factor and product			
10. Memorizing the basic multiplication facts, using			

	Introduction	In Process	Mastery
a. 0 as a factor			
b. 1 as a factor			
c. 2 as a factor			
d. 5 as a factor			
e. 9 as a factor			
f. 3 and 6 as factors			
g. 4 and 8 as factors			
h. 7 as a factor			

REMARK: Attention should be given to "1" as the identity element for multiplication. From this point on, consider writing 6 × 6 and 7 × 7 as 6^2 and 7^2 respectively, introducing the words *exponent* and *base of the exponent.*

	Introduction	In Process	Mastery
11. Naming the product if one factor is a multiple of 10, 100, and so on			
12. Expanding the basic multiplication facts, for example, the fact 2 × 3 extended to 2 × 30			
13. Modeling the distributive property of multiplication over addition (*Caution:* Begin with a one-place whole number times a two-place whole number.)			
14. Naming the product of a one-place whole number and two-place whole number by using the distributive property of multiplication over addition (two partial products)			
15. Naming the product of a one-place whole number and a three-place whole number by using the distributive property of multiplication over addition (three partial products)			
16. Naming the product of two, two-place whole numbers by using the distributive property of multiplication over addition (four partial products)			
17. Naming the product of a one-place whole number and a two-place whole number by using the standard algorithm			
18. Naming the product of a one-place whole number and a three-place whole number by using the standard algorithm			
19. Naming the product of two, two-place whole numbers by using the standard algorithm			
20. Naming the product of two, three-place whole numbers by using the standard algorithm			

	Introduction	In Process	Mastery
21. Naming the product of two, many-place whole numbers by using the standard algorithm			
22. Estimating products			
23. Solving problems that require multiplication of whole numbers			
24. Finding the missing factor			
25. Using objects to model division (measurement and partitive interpretations of division)			
26. Using symbols that indicate division ($2\overline{)6}$, 6 ÷ 2, $\frac{6}{2}$)			
27. Expressing a related multiplication sentence as a division sentence (product ÷ factor = factor)			
28. Using the number line to model division			
29. Using arrays as a model for division			
30. Using successive subtraction as a model for division			
31. Memorizing the basic division facts for whole numbers			
32. Understanding division by 1			
33. Understanding division of a nonzero number by itself			
34. Developing the terms *dividend, divisor,* and *quotient*			
35. Naming the quotient of a one-place or two-place dividend and a one-place divisor with a remainder other than 0			
36. Expanding basic division facts, for example, $2\overline{)8}$, $2\overline{)80}$, $2\overline{)800}$			
37. Naming the quotient of a two-place dividend and a one-place divisor (not a basic fact)			
38. Naming the quotient of a three-place dividend and a one-place divisor			
39. Introducing uneven division. For example, $2\overline{)7}$			
40. Naming the quotient of a many-place dividend and a one-place divisor			
41. Developing the standard division algorithm			
42. Naming the quotient of a three-place dividend and a two-place divisor (where the divisor is a multiple of 10)			
43. Naming the quotient when the divisor is 100, 1000, and so on			

	Introduction	In Process	Mastery
44. Naming the quotient of a three-place dividend and a two-place divisor (other than a multiple of 10)			
45. Estimating the dividend and divisor as an aid in establishing the quotient			
a. place value			
b. numerical value			
46. Naming the quotient of a many-place dividend and a many-place divisor			
47. Solving problems requiring division of whole numbers, with emphasis on meaningful interpretation of a remainder			
48. Understanding why division by 0 is undefined			
49. Examining the divisibility rules for 2, 3, 5, and 10			
50. Differentiating between division and factoring			
51. Factoring one-place or two-place products			
52. Defining prime numbers and composite numbers			
53. Naming the prime factors of any whole number greater than 1			

E. CONCEPT CLUSTER—INTEGERS

	Introduction	In Process	Mastery
1. Readiness activities for operations with integers			
a. eliciting situations in which pupils need numbers other than whole numbers to communicate some measure of distance, temperature, and time (Explore some everyday, familiar uses of directed numbers.)			
b. using a number line to model magnitude and direction from zero			
c. recognizing that the symbols + and – take on new meanings (When these symbols are written to the upper left of the numeral, the numeral names an integer other than zero.)			
d. recognizing that zero has no sign of direction even though zero is an integer			
e. using the number line (both horizontal and vertical positions) to model the set of integers			
f. listing the set of integers using set notation $\{. . . , {}^-3, {}^-2, {}^-1, 0, {}^+1, {}^+2, {}^+3, . . .\}$			
g. investigating the law of trichotomy			
h. using the number line to model positive and negative movement from integers other than zero			
i. guiding the discovery of "opposites"			
j. discussing the isomorphic relationship between the counting numbers and the positive integers			
k. defining integers			
2. Addition and subtraction of integers			
a. modeling, on the number line, the sum of two integers with the same signs of direction (two positive integers or two negative integers)			
b. naming the sum of two integers with the same signs of direction (two positive integers or two negative integers)			
c. modeling, on the number line, the sum of two integers with different signs of direction			
d. naming the sum of two integers with different signs of direction			
e. defining and using additive inverse elements			
f. naming the sum of one-, two-, and three-place integers (two addends with both like and unlike signs of direction)			
g. naming the sum of more than two integers			
h. summarizing the basic properties under the operation of addition of integers			
i. establishing generalizations for addition of integers			
j. finding the missing addend			

	Introduction	In Process	Mastery
k. understanding subtraction of integers as the inverse operation of addition			
l. modeling, on the number line, subtraction of integers as the difference between two integers			
m. naming the difference between two integers			
n. establishing a generalization for subtraction of integers			
o. solving problems that require addition or subtraction of integers			
3. Multiplication and division of integers			
a. modeling, on the number line, the product of two positive integers			
b. naming the product of two positive integers			
c. modeling, on the number line, the product of a positive integer and a negative integer			
d. modeling, on the number line, the product of a negative integer and a positive integer (use the commutative property)			
e. naming the product of two integers with unlike signs			
f. discovering the product of two negative integers using "properties" and "patterns" approaches			
g. naming the product of two negative integers			
h. naming the product of more than two integers			
i. summarizing the basic properties under the operation of multiplication			
j. establishing generalizations for multiplication of integers			
k. finding the missing factor			
l. understanding division of integers as the inverse operation of multiplication of integers			
m. naming the quotient of any two integers			
n. establishing generalizations for division of integers			
o. solving problems that require multiplication or division of integers			

F. CONCEPT CLUSTER—THE SET OF RATIONAL NUMBERS

REMARK: The pupil should demonstrate power with all four operations on the positive rational numbers and zero. Once these competencies are achieved, the four operations on all rational numbers (positive, negative, zero) should be investigated.

	Introduction	In Process	Mastery
1. Rational numbers expressed as decimals			
a. Readiness activities for operations with decimals			
(1) understanding tenths place value, using manipulative models and the number line			
(2) generalizing that ten tenths can be written as 1.0			
(3) writing the word name for a number in tenths place			
(4) writing a symbol given the word name for a number in tenths place			
(5) understanding hundredths place value, using manipulative models and the number line			
(6) generalizing that ten hundredths can be written as .10			
(7) writing the word name for a numeral in hundredths place			
(8) writing a symbol given the word name for a number in hundredths place			
(9) understanding thousandths place value			
(10) generalizing that ten thousandths can be written as .010			
(11) writing the word name for a number in thousandths place			
(12) writing a symbol given the word name for a number in thousandths place			
(13) extending place value beyond thousandths place			

	Introduction	In Process	Mastery
(14) using the law of trichotomy in comparing two or more decimals			
(15) modeling decimals on the number line			
(16) generating equivalent decimals by appending zeros			
(17) recognizing place-value symmetry with respect to the ones place			
b. Addition and subtraction of rational numbers expressed as decimals			
(1) naming the sum of two rational numbers expressed as decimals having the same place value			
(2) naming the sum of two rational numbers expressed as decimals having different place values			
(3) naming the sum of more than two rational numbers expressed as decimals having different place values			
(4) verifying the basic properties for addition of rational numbers expressed as decimals			
(5) solving problems requiring addition of rational numbers expressed as decimals			
(6) naming the difference between two rational numbers expressed as decimals having the same place value (with and without regrouping)			
(7) naming the difference between two rational numbers expressed as decimals having different place values (with and without regrouping)			
(8) solving problems requiring subtraction of rational numbers expressed as decimals			

	Introduction	In Process	Mastery
c. Multiplication and division of rational numbers expressed as decimals			
(1) generalizing the placement of the decimal point in the product			
(2) naming the product of two rational numbers expressed as decimals when it is necessary to append zeros to the left of a nonzero digit as decimal holders			
(3) naming the product of more than two rational numbers expressed as decimals			
(4) verifying the basic properties for multiplication of rational numbers expressed as decimals			
(5) solving word problems requiring multiplication of rational numbers expressed as decimals			
(6) naming the quotient of rational numbers expressed as decimals when the divisor is a whole number			
(7) generalizing the placement of the decimal point in the quotient of rational numbers expressed as decimals when the divisor is not a whole number (using the multiplication identity element)			
(8) naming the quotient of any two rational numbers expressed as decimals by using the division algorithm			
(9) solving problems requiring division of rational numbers expressed as decimals			
2. Rational numbers expressed as fractions			
a. Readiness activities for operations with fractions			
(1) separating regions into equivalent subregions (circular and rectangular)			

	Introduction	In Process	Mastery
(2) expressing "1" many different ways			
(3) developing the terms *fraction, fraction bar, denominator, numerator, equivalent fractions,* and so on			
(4) using the number line to model rational numbers			
(5) modeling equivalent fractions using the number line			
(6) generating sets of equivalent fractions when			
(a) the first element of a set is a proper fraction			
(b) the first element of a set is an improper fraction			
(c) the first element of a set is a mixed numeral			
(7) renaming fractions in simplest form			
(8) rewriting improper fractions as mixed numerals			
(9) rewriting mixed numerals as improper fractions			
(10) developing the concept of least common denominator by using the concept of least common multiple			
(11) comparing fractional numbers			
(12) determining the least common denominator by using the concept of greatest common factor			
b. Addition and subtraction of rational numbers expressed as fractions			
(1) modeling addition of rational numbers expressed as fractions with like denominators			
(2) naming the sum of two rational numbers expressed as fractions with like denominators			
(3) modeling addition of rational numbers expressed as fractions with unlike but related denominators			

	Introduction	In Process	Mastery
(4) naming the sum of two rational numbers expressed as fractions with unlike but related denominators			
(5) modeling addition of rational numbers expressed as fractions with unlike and unrelated denominators			
(6) naming the sum of two rational numbers expressed as fractions with unlike and unrelated denominators			
(7) naming the sum of more than two rational numbers expressed as fractions			
(8) solving word problems requiring addition of rational numbers expressed as fractions			
(9) verifying the basic properties for addition of rational numbers expressed as fractions			
(10) modeling subtraction of rational numbers expressed as fractions			
(11) naming the difference between two rational numbers expressed as fractions with like denominators (with and without regrouping)			
(12) naming the difference between two rational numbers expressed as fractions with unlike but related denominators (with and without regrouping)			
(13) naming the difference between two rational numbers expressed as fractions with unlike and unrelated denominators (with and without regrouping)			
(14) solving problems requiring subtraction of rational numbers expressed as fractions			

	Introduction	In Process	Mastery
c. Multiplication and division of rational numbers expressed as fractions			
(1) modeling multiplication of two rational numbers expressed as fractions, using superimposed regions			
(2) naming the product of two rational numbers expressed as proper or improper fractions (using examples where no internal simplification is possible)			
(3) simplifying the example by using the multiplicative identity before naming the product of two rational numbers expressed as proper or improper fractions			
(4) naming the product of two rational numbers expressed as mixed numerals (rewritten as improper fractions)			
(5) naming the product of more than two rational numbers expressed in various forms (stress the use of internal simplification)			
(6) verifying the basic properties of multiplication of rational numbers expressed as fractions			
(7) naming the product of two rational numbers expressed as mixed numerals (using the distributive property of multiplication over addition)			
(8) solving problems requiring multiplication of rational numbers expressed as fractions			
(9) modeling division of rational numbers expressed as fractions (when the quotient has a remainder of zero)			
(10) modeling division of rational numbers expressed as fractions (when the quotient has a remainder other than zero)			
(11) naming the quotient of two rational numbers expressed as fractions using the division frame			
(12) generalizing the algorithm for naming the quotient of two rational numbers expressed as fractions (using the complex fraction form)			
(13) naming the quotient of two rational numbers expressed as fractions (using the algorithm)			
3. Interrelating the decimal symbol with the fraction symbol for rational numbers			
a. defining rational numbers			
b. rewriting fractions as decimals			
c. generalizing the types of decimals that represent rational numbers			
d. rewriting terminating decimals and decimals that have a repeating pattern of digits as fractions			
4. Rational numbers expressed as percent			
a. interpreting the symbol for percent (%) as a fraction and as a decimal			
b. rewriting percents as decimals and fractions			
(1) percents less than 100%			
(2) percents equal to or greater than 100%			
c. rewriting fractions or decimals as percents			
d. solving problems requiring percents			

G. CONCEPT CLUSTER—RATIO AND PROPORTION

	Introduction	In Process	Mastery
1. Defining ratio			
2. Writing a ratio in two different forms			
3. Defining proportion			
4. Writing a proportion in two different forms			

Introduction | **In Process** | **Mastery**

5. Developing vocabulary, for example, *means* and *extremes*
6. Discovering the relationship between the product of the means and the product of the extremes
7. Naming the missing term in a proportion by using
   a. the concept of equivalent fractions
   b. the relationship between the product of the means and the product of the extremes (sometimes called the *means-extremes property*)
8. Solving problems requiring proportions

H. CONCEPT CLUSTER—MEASUREMENT

1. Money
   a. identifying the following coins:
      (1) penny
      (2) nickel
      (3) dime
      (4) quarter
      (5) half dollar
   b. recognizing relationships between and relative values of
      (1) penny
      (2) nickel
      (3) dime
      (4) quarter
      (5) half dollar
   c. recognizing various combinations of coins equivalent to the value of a
      (1) nickel
      (2) dime
      (3) quarter
      (4) half dollar
   d. making change for amounts up to one dollar
   e. recognizing and using money notation (¢, $)
   f. recognizing currency and making change for currency
   g. solving examples and word problems involving money
2. Time (reading a clock)
   a. relating the face of the clock with the number line through 12 for hours
   b. relating the face of the clock with the number line through 60 for minutes

Introduction | **In Process** | **Mastery**

   c. telling time by the hour
   d. telling time by the minute
   e. translating time from the clock face to a digital clock
   f. understanding the difference between A.M. and P.M.
   g. solving examples and word problems involving time
   h. extending time to the 24-hour clock
3. Length (Metric units and U.S. Customary units)
   a. recognizing metric units and their symbols and interrelating them to each other
      (1) meter (m)
      (2) decimeter (dm)
      (3) centimeter (cm)
      (4) millimeter (mm)
      (5) dekameter (dam)
      (6) hectometer (hm)
      (7) kilometer (km)
   b. changing one metric unit to another
   c. measuring lengths, using a metric ruler or trundle wheel
   d. solving problems involving metric measures of length
   e. recognizing U.S. Customary units and their abbreviations and interrelating them to each other
      (1) inch (in.)
      (2) foot (ft.)
      (3) yard (yd.)
      (4) mile (mi.)
   f. changing one U.S. Customary unit to another
   g. measuring lengths, using a foot ruler or a yardstick
   h. comparing centimeter to inch, meter to yard, and kilometer to mile
4. Volume or capacity (Metric units and U.S. Customary units)
   a. recognizing metric units and their symbols and interrelating them to each other
      (1) liter (L)
      (2) kiloliter (kL)
      (3) milliliter (mL)
   b. changing one metric unit to another
   c. measuring volume (capacity), using a liter container

	Introduction	In Process	Mastery
d. solving problems involving metric measures of volume (capacity)			
e. recognizing customary units and their abbreviations and interrelating them to each other			
(1) cup (c.)			
(2) pint (pt.)			
(3) quart (qt.)			
(4) gallon (gal.)			
f. changing one U.S. Customary unit to another			
g. measuring volume (capacity) using a cup, pint container, and so on			
h. comparing a liter to a quart, a liter to a gallon, and so on			
5. Weight or mass (metric units and U.S. Customary units)			
a. recognizing metric units and their symbols and interrelating them to each other			
(1) gram (g)			
(2) kilogram (kg)			
b. changing one metric unit to another			
c. measuring weight (mass) using gram and kilogram weights			
d. solving problems involving metric measures of weight (mass)			
e. recognizing U.S. Customary units and their abbreviations and interrelating them to each other			
(1) ounce (oz.)			
(2) pound (lb.)			
(3) ton (T.)			
f. changing one U.S. Customary unit to another			
g. measuring weight (mass) using ounces and pounds			
h. comparing kilograms to pounds			
6. Temperature (Metric units and U.S. Customary units)			
a. recognizing the metric unit for temperature, namely, Celsius			
b. measuring temperatures using a Celsius thermometer			
c. solving problems involving the metric measure of temperature			
d. recognizing the customary unit for temperature, namely, Fahrenheit			
e. measuring temperatures using a Fahrenheit thermometer			
f. comparing Celsius to Fahrenheit			

I. CONCEPT CLUSTER—GEOMETRY

	Introduction	In Process	Mastery
1. Basic notions			
a. distinguishing between the concept of and model for			
(1) point			
(2) line			
(3) plane			
b. recognizing the "betweenness" relationship of points			
2. Identifying shapes			
a. closed curves			
(1) simple polygons			
(2) circles and other elliptical shapes			
b. regions			
(1) polygonal			
(2) circular and other elliptical regions			
3. Modeling shapes			
a. closed curves			
(1) simple polygons			
(2) circles and other elliptical shapes			
b. regions			
(1) polygonal			
(2) circular and other elliptical shapes			
4. Concept of a definition			
a. recognizing the necessity of definitions			
b. recognizing the characteristics of a definition			
(1) reversibility			
(2) unique characterization			
c. recognizing the necessity of undefined terms			
5. Using definitions to identify a(n)			
a. line segment			
b. half-line			
c. ray			
d. angle			
(1) vertex			
(2) sides			
e. angle degree			
6. Modeling a(n)			
a. line segment			

	Introduction	In Process	Mastery
b. half-line			
c. ray			
d. angle			
7. Measuring angles with a protractor and classifying them as			
a. right angles			
b. acute angles			
c. obtuse angles			
8. Distinguishing between *equal measure* and *equal* pertaining to geometric figures			
9. Developing the meaning of congruence			
10. Classifying pairs of angles by			
a. measure			
(1) complementary			
(2) supplementary			
b. location			
(1) adjacent			
(2) nonadjacent			
(3) vertical			
11. Recognizing the concept of *parallel to* for			
a. lines			
b. segments			
c. rays			
d. planes			
12. Modeling parallel			
a. lines			
b. segments			
c. rays			
d. planes			
13. Using definitions to identify simple two-dimensional closed figures			
a. polygons			
(1) triangles			
(a) according to angle measure			
(b) according to side measure			
(2) quadrilaterals			
(a) trapezoid			
(b) parallelogram			
(c) rectangle			
(d) square			
(e) rhombus			
(f) rhomboid			
(g) trapezium			
b. circles			
14. Recognizing terms related to simple, two-dimensional			
a. polygons			
(1) side			
(2) altitude			

	Introduction	In Process	Mastery
(3) median			
(4) diagonal			
(5) vertex			
b. circles			
(1) center			
(2) radius			
(3) diameter			
(4) arc			
(5) chord			
(6) tangent			
(7) secant			
15. Recognizing the concept of symmetry with respect to a			
a. point			
b. line			
c. plane			
16. Distinguishing between exterior and interior with respect to a(n)			
a. angle			
b. simple closed curve			
17. Using a compass and straightedge for basic constructions			
a. copying a segment			
b. copying an angle			
c. bisecting a line segment			
d. constructing a perpendicular to a line from			
(1) a point on the line			
(2) a point not on the line			
e. bisecting an angle			
f. constructing a parallel to a line through a point			
g. constructing simple, two-dimensional closed figures			
18. Developing the concept of perimeter			
a. understanding the meaning of perimeter			
b. applying the meaning of perimeter to problems involving plane figures			
c. developing formulas for the perimeter of polygons			
19. Developing the concept of circumference			
a. understanding the meaning of circumference			
b. developing the formula for the circumference of a circle			
20. Developing the concept of area			
a. understanding the meaning of area			

	Introduction	In Process	Mastery
b. developing formulas for the area of simple, two-dimensional closed figures			
c. using formulas to compute the area of			
(1) triangles			
(2) quadrilaterals			
(3) circles			
21. Identifying space figures			
a. prisms			
(1) triangular			
(2) rectangular (including cubes)			
b. pyramid			
(1) triangular			
(2) rectangular			
c. cylinder			
d. cone			
e. sphere			
22. Developing the concept of volume			
a. understanding the meaning of volume			
b. developing formulas for space figures			
c. using formulas to compute the volume of			
(1) prisms			
(2) cylinders			
(3) pyramids			
(4) cones			
(5) spheres			

J. CONCEPT CLUSTER—EXPONENTIAL NOTATION

REMARK: Begin all work with positive integral exponents. When children achieve power with those concepts, introduce nonpositive integral exponents.

	Introduction	In Process	Mastery
1. Expressing repeated factors as numerals using exponential form			
2. Rewriting numbers expressed in exponential form as repeated factors			
3. Understanding the terms *exponent, base of an exponent, exponential form,* and *power*			
4. Representing counting numbers as numerals in exponential form			
5. Understanding that any nonzero number raised to the zero power is equal to 1			
6. Writing a number in expanded form using exponents			
7. Multiplying numbers written in exponential form and expressing the product in exponential form			
8. Dividing numbers written in exponential form and representing the quotient in exponential form			
9. Understanding that, for any nonzero number *a* and any positive number *x*, $a^{-x} = \frac{1}{a^x}$□ and □$a^x = \frac{1}{a^{-x}}$			
10. Multiplying numbers expressed in exponential form (using any integral exponent) and expressing the product in exponential form			
11. Dividing numbers expressed in exponential form (using any integral exponent) and expressing the quotient in exponential form			

K. CONCEPT CLUSTER—SCIENTIFIC NOTATION

	Introduction	In Process	Mastery
1. Defining the term *scientific notation*			
2. Understanding the purposes of expressing numbers in scientific notation			
3. Expressing numbers in scientific notation			
4. Writing numbers expressed in scientific notation as numbers written in standard form			
5. Determining the number of significant digits in a number expressed in scientific notation			
6. Naming products and quotients of numbers written in scientific notation			
7. Rewriting factors, dividends, and divisors in scientific notation as a means of approximating products and quotients			
8. Applying scientific notation to problem solving			

L. CONCEPT CLUSTER—PROBABILITY

	Introduction	In Process	Mastery
1. Discovering the meaning of probability			
2. Investigating the social and economic significance of probability			
3. Identifying a sample space (all possible outcomes)			
4. Establishing the meaning of theoretical probability			

Introduction | In Process | Mastery

5. Establishing the meaning of experimental probability (including such terms as randomness and trial)
6. Recognizing an event as a subset of a particular sample space
7. Stating a formal definition for the theoretical probability of an event as the ratio of the number of favorable outcomes to the total number of outcomes
8. Expressing theoretical probability as a fraction, decimal, or percent
9. Understanding that the theoretical probability of an event, $P(E)$, is greater than or equal to 0 and less than or equal to 1 ($0 \leq P(E) \leq 1$)
10. Determining a sample space for a particular experiment
11. Recognizing an event as a subset of a particular calculated sample space
12. Stating a formal definition for the experimental probability of an event as the ratio of the number of favorable outcomes to the total number of outcomes of the experience
13. Expressing experimental probability as a fraction, decimal, or percent
14. Recognizing the essential difference between theoretical and experimental probability
15. Computing the theoretical probability of events
16. Practicing the computation of experimental probability of events
17. Understanding that, as the number of trials increases, the experimental probability for an event approaches the theoretical probability

REMARK: Throughout the previous discussion, we have assumed the presence of equally likely simple events.

18. Investigating experimental probability
    a. recognizing that the total set of outcomes for successive trials, each of which has exactly two outcomes, is a sample space
    b. drawing tree diagrams to illustrate the arrangement of total outcomes when the results of successive trials, each having exactly two outcomes, are recorded
    c. determining the theoretical probability of an event resulting from successive trials, each with exactly two outcomes
    d. generating Pascal's Triangle
    e. comparing Pascal's Triangle to the set of total outcomes yielded by the tree diagrams for two successive trials, each of which has exactly two outcomes
    f. comparing Pascal's Triangle to the set of total outcomes yielded by the tree diagram for three successive trials
    g. generalizing that Pascal's Triangle can illustrate the number of ways that events can occur after a given number of trials

M. CONCEPT CLUSTER—STATISTICS

1. Collecting data
2. Organizing data
3. Finding the range
4. Finding the mode
5. Finding the mean
6. Finding the median
7. Picturing data by drawing graphs
8. Reading graphs
9. Interpreting information from graphs

N. CONCEPT CLUSTER—GRAPHS (NONALGEBRAIC)

1. Observing and collecting data
2. Recording data
    a. experiences involving recording by placing physical objects in appropriate rows or columns according to a particular trait
    b. experience with recording by making tallies
3. Constructing graphs from materials

	Introduction	In Process	Mastery
a. block charts: using unlined paper, then using paper ruled in squares			
b. pictographs			
4. Interpreting data from tallies			
5. Developing graphing skills			
a. choosing an appropriate type of graph			
b. choosing appropriate labels			
c. choosing appropriate scales			
d. converting a record or tally to a graph			
e. writing or verbalizing a summary of the graph			

REMARK: Provide opportunities for children to become aware of incomplete information on graphs.

	Introduction	In Process	Mastery
6. Interpreting different types of graphs			
a. number lines			
b. graphs using concrete objects			
c. block charts			
d. pictographs			
e. bar graphs			
f. line graphs			
g. histograms			
h. frequency polygons			
i. smooth curves			
j. circle graphs			
k. percentile curves			
7. Experiences in constructing different types of graphs (see item #6)			

O. CONCEPT CLUSTER—RECTANGULAR COORDINATE GRAPHS

	Introduction	In Process	Mastery
1. Understanding the need for "order" in an ordered pair			
2. Finding the position corresponding to a given position in a coordinate system			
3. Naming the ordered pair corresponding to a given position in a coordinate system			
4. Understanding the one-to-one correspondence between points on a rectangular graph and the ordered pairs associated with these points			
5. Naming points located on the horizontal or vertical axes: (–3, 0), (0, 6), (0, 0)			
6. Associating the first number of an ordered pair with the horizontal axis and the second number of the ordered pair with the vertical axis			
7. Finding solutions to open sentences with two variables, for example, $\triangle + \square = 8$ and $3\square + 2\triangle = 12$			
8. Plotting solutions to linear equations on a coordinate graph as in item #7			
9. Writing simple open sentences given several ordered pairs			
10. Finding solutions to inequalities of the form $\triangle + \square \leq 7$ and $2\triangle + \square > 8$			
11. Plotting solutions to inequalities of #10			

THEMATIC MATHEMATICS ACTIVITIES

The National Council of Teachers of Mathematics, in the *Curriculum and Evaluation Standards for School Mathematics,* described 5 goals for students in learning mathematics. Students must: (1) learn to *value* mathematics; (2) learn to *communicate* mathematically; (3) learn to *reason* mathematically; (4) become *confident* of their mathematical abilities; and (5) become *problem solvers.* Students who see the value of mathematics, who have the opportunity to view mathematics in use, and who have a chance to converse about mathematics will not only benefit from increased confidence but are more likely to become mathematically literate citizens.

Students need to engage mathematical concepts in a variety of ways. They need to explore, organize, represent, describe, compare, contrast, chart, graph, verify, justify, extend, etc. Thematic activities provide for all of these and offer an avenue for teachers and students to develop and nurture connections between the mathematics classroom and the real world. A thematic focus offers the exploration of mathematics concepts contextually embedded in situations with which children are familiar and so initiate, build, and sustain interest in mathematics.

The following brief descriptions have been designed to show ways in which selected NCTM curriculum standards can be addressed through a thematic approach. The activities included here are not intended to be "classroom-ready." Instead, these represent basic ideas that a teacher can use as a foundation for further exploration and extension. Many of these activities are easily adapted to either learning center and/or cooperative learning environments thereby providing children with opportunities to develop responsibility, reasoning skills (analyzing, decision-making), and communication skills (listening, verbalizing and writing). At the same time, these activities encourage creative approaches. In many cases there isn't a single answer to the stated activity—rather, these are intentionally open-ended so that discussion, debate, and alternative perceptions are encouraged. Consequently, these activities approach problem solving in ways that encourage the development of tools for lifelong critical thinking.

A Trip to the Zoo

Mathematics as Problem Solving

K-4

A. Your class is going on an educational field trip to the zoo! There are 26 students, the class teacher, and two parents going. Find the Admission Information at the zoo. How much money is admission for a child? How much money is it for an adult to get into the zoo? How much money will it cost for all 29 people to get into the zoo? Keep in mind three of these people are adults.

B. Before you left for the zoo, your mom gave you $10, and then your dad gave you $10. How much money do you have left over for lunch if you paid to get into the zoo and bought a Panda bear t-shirt for $9.50?

C. The students should count the number of seats on the bus along with the number of students and adults going on the field trip and determine how many buses will be needed for the trip to the zoo.

D. The students should compute the number of ounces of birdseed needed per exhibit per day.

5-8

A. Suppose you are taking your spouse, your 14-month-old son, your 11-year-old girls, and your 64-year-old father to the Toledo Zoo on Saturday to see the new dinosaur exhibition. Your budget allows you to spend no more than $75 at the zoo. Describe your expenditures at the zoo. Be sure to include exactly how much you spent on what and how much you returned home with. Don't forget admission, lunch, and souvenirs for your family. Special note: The dinosaur exhibit is $1 extra per person.

B. Look at a map of your local zoo. Suppose it was based on a 1 in. = 100 feet scale. What is the total distance of the shortest route from the entrance to the Ape House; from the Playground to the Picnic Area; from the Children's Zoo through the Hippoquarium to the front of the Mammal House? Use a ruler to find the answers. You can check if your answers were close by walking these paths at the zoo and counting your steps as you go.

C. Given the number of students going to the zoo and the cost per ticket, the students should mentally estimate the total cost of admission and then check their estimate with a paper-and-pencil computation or a calculator.

D. When the children return from their trip to the zoo, have them recall, as a class, as many animals as they can that are amphibians, mammals, or reptiles and classify them accordingly. Then have them write the proportion of each to the total and determine which animal classification was the largest.

Mathematics as Communication and Mathematics as Reasoning

K-4

A. Look at the map of your local zoo. Suppose it is based on a 1 cm = 100 feet scale. What is the total distance of the shortest route from the Cheetah Cage to the Lion House? Use a ruler to find the answer. You can check your answer to see how close it is by walking from the Cheetah cage to the Lion House and counting your steps as you go.

B. Find the Hippoquarium at the zoo. Look at the hippopotamuses. Compare their shape to the shapes of other large, heavy objects. How heavy do you think a hippopotamus is? How many cars do you think the weight of a full-grown hippo is equal to? How many 12-year-old children do you think the weight of a full-grown hippo is equal to? (8000 lbs., two cars, and eighty 12-year-old children.)

C. If one goat gets to occupy a 3 sq. ft. space, two goats get to occupy 6 sq. ft., and three goats get 12 sq. ft., how much space do four goats get to occupy at the zoo?

D. The children should find different shapes in the zoo: circles, rectangles, squares, and triangles. On the trip back, they should talk about what they found.

E. On the trip to the zoo, give the children shape bingo cards. They should cross off a shape when they see one. The object is to cross off the entire card, row, column, or diagonal (depending on how long the trip is).

5-8

A. Go to the Elephants/Giraffes section. Look for the information about giraffes. How many gallons of water does a giraffe drink per day? Compare this number to its size. Think of how much water you drink per day. Look for the information about elephants. How many gallons of water does an elephant drink per day? Compare this number to an elephant's size. Interpret these data. Is the intake of water correlated positively or negatively to size?

B. Go to the Bird House. Find the incubation periods of pigeons, chicken, jungle fowl, quail, and partridges. Create a chart using these incubation periods. Create a bar graph depicting the incubation periods of these birds.

C. At some zoos it is possible to buy feed and give it to certain animals. Suppose one deer can eat as much as three cups of feed at one meal and a baby deer half the size can eat one-half cup of feed at each meal. Find an equation for how many cups of feed a certain number of deer can eat at one meal. How many cups of feed can four full-sized deer and three baby deer eat at one meal?

D. Given six animals of varying sizes (e.g., elephants, dolphins, lions, snakes, birds, insects) have the children estimate which has the greatest and least amount of living space. At the zoo, the children should compare their estimates to the actual sizes. ("Greatest" and "least" can be defined as total available area or as area proportional to the animals' sizes.)

E. After the zoo trip, give the children popsicle sticks, clay, cardboard, construction paper, glue, and miscellaneous materials to construct models of their favorite area of the zoo.

Mathematical Connections

K-4

A. Hippopotamuses like an African climate. What do you know about the weather in Africa? Is it hot or cold, wet or dry? What do you think hippos like about African weather? What range of degrees do you think is suitable as a living environment for a hippo?

B. Find a baby animal, say, a polar bear. Read the information panel to find out when it was born. How old does that make the animal today? Some bears hibernate during the winter. How many times would this bear have gone into hibernation by now?

5-8

A. Snakes are fascinating creatures. Go to the Reptile House and look for a chart that gives you data about snakes. Use these data to answer the following questions. What fraction of snakes on the chart lives in water? What fraction of snakes on the chart is poisonous? List the snakes in order from shortest to longest. What fraction of snakes on the chart lives on continents mostly above the equator? Using a scale of 1 in. = 1 m, sketch a prairie rattler and a hog-nosed snake. Sketch a half-sized anaconda. Create a problem using the data on the chart to be presented in class.

B. Elephants are hunted and killed by poachers for their ivory and meat. Between 50,000 and 150,000 elephants are killed each year. If the demand for ivory and meat doubles every 10 years, what will be the range of elephants being killed 25 years from now? How will this affect the population of elephants and the market for their ivory and meat?

Estimation

K-4

A. Go to the Water Fowl Pools. Are there a large number of ducks in this pond? If you wanted a general idea of how many ducks there are, how would you find out? Would you count the ducks? Would you estimate the number of ducks? Estimate how many ducks are in the pond. Next, count approximately half of the ducks and then double this number. Are your two estimates close to each other?

B. How many feathers do you think birds are capable of having? Find the answer to this question at the Bird House. Compare it to your estimation. Were you close, too high, or too low? Why did you estimate as you did?

C. Before the trip to the zoo, have the class make a list of the various animals and estimate how many of them they will see. On the trip back, they should compare this estimate to the actual count of how many of each they did see.

D. Given a map of the zoo and total time for visiting, the children should decide which exhibits they would like to see and estimate the amount of time they will be able to spend at each.

5-8

A. Go to the Amphitheater. Estimate how many seats are in the Amphitheater by (1) guessing, (2) counting the number of seats in one section then multiplying by how many sections are in the whole Amphitheater, and (3) counting the number of rows then multiplying by the number of seats in each row. How do your three answers compare?

B. Find the Elephants/Giraffes section. Listen to the sounds the elephants make. When scared, excited, or in danger these sounds can be much louder. Think of how far away you are from the elephant you are listening to and how loud the sound is. How far do you think an angered elephant's sound can carry? Check your answer by looking for the information on elephants.

C. Given the weights of certain animals, how many times a day they eat, and the portion of food given per feeding, ask the children to estimate how much food the animals need per day. Given the cost of the food, ask them to estimate how much it costs to feed the animals per day.

D. Ask the children to estimate the total cost of the field trip including tickets, food, gifts, and transportation.

Number Sense, Numeration, and Number Relationships

K-4

A. Go to the Gift Shop. While you are browsing around list a few items that you can buy for $.01 $.50, $1, $3, $5, $8, and $10. What do you notice about these items as the prices increase?

B. Suppose there is one sea lion in tank #1, two sea lions in tank #2, and three sea lions in tank #3. Each sea lion gets two fish at each meal. How many fish should the feeder throw in (1) tank #I, (2) tank #2, and (3) tank #3? How many sea lions are there total? If each sea lion is fed one meal, how many fish are there total? What is the relationship between sea lions and fish? What is the ratio of sea lions to fish?
C. What are some different ways in which to spend money at the zoo? Which did you experience? How much money did you spend at the zoo and on what?
D. The children should identify one specific cage of animals. Count the animals and write the type of animal and total number in the cage on a piece of paper. Have them find a second cage that has one more animal than the first cage and write that animal's name and total number in the cage. Then have them find a third cage that has one less animal than the first cage and write that animal's name and total in the cage.
E. Ask the children to count and record the number of seats on the bus. When they return to class, they will use Cuisenaire rods to figure out how many groups of tens and ones can be made from this number.

5-8

A. At the Gift Shop, you bought one animal mug, one animal plate, and one animal magnet as souvenirs for your family. Seven percent sales tax was also charged. How much is the subtotal of the items? How much is the tax for the three items? How much is the total bill?
B. An adult-sized giraffe's tongue is 18 inches long! Predict how long the tongue is of a giraffe (1) one-half the size, (2) one-third the size, and (3) one-quarter the size.
C. Shows at the Aquarium start at 1:30 and 3:30. Shows at the Amphitheater start at 1:00, 2:00, and 4:00. You want to see one of each show and be back on the bus by 5:00. The Aquarium shows last one hour and the Amphitheater shows last one and one-half hours. Which shows at what times can you see at the Aquarium and the Amphitheater and still be back to the bus by 5:00?
D. The alligators are located in the African Savanna. Go to this area and find the alligator facts. Fill in the missing information on your chart. Looking at the alligators and using the chart, answer these questions. What is the ratio of an alligator head length to that of a body and tail? When does a baby alligator become about (1) one-tenth of adult length and (2) one-fifth of the adult length?
E. The children should pick any animal in the zoo to observe for ten minutes, sketch the cage on a piece of paper, and shade in the area which they observed that animal using. They should then write a fractional number to describe the shaded area.
F. Given that the zoo is "x" miles away (choose an appropriate number), ask the children to determine the time it will take to get there using three different speeds.

Concepts of Operations and Computation

K-4

A. Write and solve your own story problem about the zoo using information you gain on your trip to the zoo. Share your problem with the class. Try your friends' problems.
B. Have students draw a picture of their zoo trip and discuss all the math they find in their drawings.
C. Take pictures at the zoo. Make a "Math at the Zoo" book by having the children write math titles for each picture.

5-8

A. Tomorrow there is going to be a sale at the Gift Shop. There will be a 25% discount off all items. What will you buy? How much will you save?
B. When a class takes a field trip the school requires that there be a ratio of one adult to every 10 children for grades K-2, one adult to every 15 children for grades 3-5, and one adult for every 18 children for grades 6-8. Choose three different grades, one from each group, and three different class sizes. Then find out how many adults will be needed for the trip.
C. Find out how much the zoo trip is going to cost. Include admission prices, transportation costs, and food and/or souvenir money if the students will be able to buy lunch, snacks, or souvenirs.
D. If your family bought a Family Zoo membership for $25 a year, how many times would you have to go to the zoo to pay for your membership? Choose five different number of times your family might visit the zoo that year and calculate how much your family would actually be paying each time you visited.

Patterns and Relationships

K-4

A. Play pattern games. Children should create and recognize a variety of patterns using animal pictures, animal sounds, and animal movements.
B. The Himalayan baby black bear was born on December 1, 1994. He weighed 6 lb. 8 oz. How old is he now?
   When were you born?
   How much did you weigh?
   How old are you now?
   Make a chart comparing you and the bear.
C. Use animal crackers to make patterns and act out zoo story problems.

5-8

A. Make a bar graph comparing animals' birth weights to average adult animals' weights. Describe the relationships that exist.

B. Choose a situation that would be a part of your zoo trip in which different factors depend on each other. Write an equation showing how change in one quantity causes change in the other or others. Make a graph representing what happens when one quantity changes. For example, there are seven first-grade classes at your school. Four classes have 24 students, two have 23, and one has 22. When the teachers call to schedule their trip to the zoo they find out that three classes can go on Monday, April 23rd, and the other four classes can go on Tuesday, April 24th. Then they receive a call from the bus operator informing them that there will only be one bus available to go to the zoo on Monday, April 23rd. What choices do the first-grade teachers have now? How will the numbers change?

C. You visit the gift shop. You buy five items. One is for yourself and the other four are for four different people. Make a list of what you buy, whom you buy it for, and how much it costs. Describe any patterns and/or relationships you find. Why do you think they occurred?

Algebra

K-4

A. Act out story problems about your zoo trip using open sentences. For example, if each adult going to the zoo had a group of five children and Mrs. Jones had her twin sons, how many of her sons' classmates would she have in her group? 2 + __________ = 5.

B. Write equations to represent animals or things found on your zoo trip. For example, "G = 18 in. T" means a "giraffe has an 18-inch tongue," or "4W = B" means there are "four wheels on a bus."

C. Given photographs of two animals taken at the zoo, the children will determine how many times bigger the larger one is than the smaller one.

D. Ask the children to look for designs on animals, buildings, floors, etc., to determine if there is a pattern and, if so, describe the pattern they've found.

5-8

A. Write mathematical sentences using animal names to symbolize numbers by counting the letters in the name.
For example, hippo + elephant = baby polar bear:

(5) + (8) = (13)

B. Use a *Zoo Pal* packet to make a graph representing the number of different animals you can "adopt" in each category: birds, mammals, fish, and reptiles at the different price levels. Discuss the relationships that exist between and within the categories.

C. If your class or school decided to "adopt" an animal, which one would you choose? Why? How could you get the money to "adopt" the animal? Show as many different ways as you can using algebraic equations.

D. Given the rates that a snake slithers, a fish swims, and a cheetah runs, the children will compute and compare the distance each can travel in one minute.

E. Given variables of average daily ticket sales, donations, salaries, building utility costs, cost of feeding animals and the quantity of each animal, ask the children to write an equation that describes monthly profit or loss.

Statistics and Probability

K-4

A. Observe all the animals at the zoo. Look for the funniest, the sleepiest, the happiest, the angriest, the scariest, the cutest, and the ugliest. Share your choices. Make a graph of your class results.

B. Assign groups of children to count specific numbers of different animals found at the zoo. Discuss findings as a class. Why do you suppose there are a lot of some animals and only one or two of some kinds?

C. After the zoo trip, the children should collect data as to what their favorite animal was and then create a horizontal bar graph depicting this information.

D. After the zoo trip, have the class create a list of land animals, water animals, and land and water animals and make a Venn diagram illustrating this information.

5-8

A. Record the number of different animals during the zoo trip. Make an animal card probability game. Turn all the cards over. Choose a card. Record it. Return it to the pile. Do this many times. Find the probability of choosing an elephant, fish, mammal, etc., card. What happens as you increase the number of trials?

B. If you were to choose an animal at random from the set: (monkey, gorilla, hippo, bird, fish, snake, bear, tiger, sheep, cow)
   1. What is the probability that you will choose a fish?
   2. What is the probability that you will choose a mammal?
   3. What is the probability that you will choose an elephant?
   4. What is the probability that you will choose an animal?

C. Find out the life expectancies of many different animals. Find the mean, median, and mode in number of years.

D. Given monthly zoo attendance over a period of two years, the children should make a line graph showing these data. From the graph they will determine when the zoo was the busiest and speculate reasons for differences.
E. Have the children record basic weather conditions on a daily basis for the month prior to the field trip to the zoo. From this information they will predict what the weather might be like on the day of the field trip. Is there a reason why the weather might not follow this trend? Is there a reason why it might?

Geometry and Spatial Sense

K-4

A. Look for circles, triangles, squares, and rectangles during every part of your zoo trip. Record your findings. Make class and/or individual shape books.
B. Do an art activity to experiment with combining, subdividing, using, and changing shapes to represent different parts of your zoo trip.
C. Make your own map of a zoo. Use a variety of shapes, lines, and curves. Include a key and a measurement scale.

5-8

A. Make a map of the zoo by drawing different sizes of rectangles on graph paper. Measure and record the length of each side of the rectangles. Find the measure of the rectangular region in square units. What do you notice about the product of the measures of the sides in each case? What do you notice about the measure of the rectangular region in each case?
B. Use the map you made in the preceding activity. Choose two points on the map and draw many possible paths between the two points and create stories about how you or someone or something traveled from one point to the other. Which path was the shortest? Which path was the quickest? Which path was the best? Which path was the worst? Share your map and stories.

Measurement

K-4

A. With a partner find out how tall you are in feet, inches, meters, and centimeters. Compare your height to the height of an elephant who is $6\frac{1}{2}$ ft. and a giraffe who is $11\frac{1}{2}$ ft.
B. Count the number of steps you take as you walk from the Hippoquarium to Monkey Island. Estimate how many steps you will take from Monkey Island to the Bird House.
C. How long do you think an average adult giraffe's tongue is? Cut a piece of string to show how long you think it is. Measure its length in centimeters and in inches. Make a graph on the board using sticky notes to show everyone's guesses. Compare your string with the string that is the actual length of a giraffe's tongue—18 inches. How many centimeters long do you think the giraffe's tongue is? Check and see.
D. Given pictures of different animals taken at the zoo, the children will arrange them in order from smallest to largest (or from heaviest to lightest). What other sorting criteria could they use?
E. The children should weigh themselves and make a mental or paper-and-pencil note of their weight. Then give them pictures of different animals taken at the zoo with the animals' weights written on the back. They should find the animal closest to their weight and share the information with the class.

5-8

A. Visit the Aquarium. Find the long-nose gars, the alligator gar, and the channel catfish. Estimate the length of each nose. Share your estimates. Find the mean, median, and mode length.
B. Make a Measurement Book of your zoo trip. Include a variety of measuring units: miles, km, yards, m, feet, inches, cm, lbs., grams, quarts, liters, and degrees Fahrenheit or Celsius. For example: The distance from our school to the zoo is 12 miles.
C. Write story problems about the zoo incorporating different measurement units. Write it by drawing a picture and using phrases.
D. Given the measurements of a tiger's cage and a snake's cage, the children should find the area of each and compare.
E. The children should use the same measurements of the tiger's cage and snake's cage to find the perimeter of each and compare. Have the students discuss the results.

Mathematics at the Grocery Store

Mathematics as Problem Solving

K-4

A. The teacher shows a paper bag and a plastic bag to the class. The teacher lets the students examine each bag. After the whole class has examined the bag, the teacher asks:
    1. Would the plastic bag hold more groceries or would the paper bag hold more?
    2. Why do you feel your answer is correct in question 1?
    3. When carrying a full bag of groceries, which would be easier to carry?
    4. Why do you think your answer is correct in question 3? How would you test the answer to the question? What procedure or method would you use?
B. The teacher presents the following situation to the class: You have a sale on Turkey Tuna (1 oz. cans) for $.89. You run out of the tuna one day before the sale ends, and you need to decide what product you will substitute for it.

1. Will you use a can that weighs less than 1 oz., but is the same price as the sale item was? Why or why not?
2. Will you use a can that weighs more than 1 oz. and costs less ($.85) than the sale item? Why or why not?

5-8

A. The teacher presents the students with the following situation: You are given the recipe for "Chocolotso Chip" cookies. This is the recipe you are given for one batch: Serves 16

4 Cups chocolate chips	$\frac{1}{8}$ tsp. vanilla
$2\frac{1}{2}$ C. sugar	$\frac{1}{16}$ tsp. salt
2 C. flour	4 oz. milk

You are then asked to make a double batch of these cookies for a birthday party.
1. Write the new recipe for the cookies, and how many people it will serve.
2. If there are going to be five people at the birthday party, will everyone get the same amount of cookies? If not how many would each person get?

A friend hears that the cookies you made for the birthday party were a hit. He asks you to make enough cookies so that 32 people get two cookies each.
1. How many cookies do you need to bake in all?
2. How many batches will you have to make?
3. Write the new recipe for the batch of cookies needed.

B. The teacher presents the students with the following situation: You are a newly hired stock boy at the local grocery store. The manager has given you a very big and challenging job to do. You have three cans of soup that are labeled yellow, red, and blue. You have three shelves that are also yellow, red, and blue. Each can is labeled either A, B, or C. You are to figure out what color can and colored shelve corresponds with the correct letter by using the following clues to help you:
1. No colored can is on a shelf with the same color as the can.
2. No colored can goes with a letter that has the same first letter of the colored can.
3. Can B is not on a yellow shelf.
4. The can on the yellow shelf outsells can A. Have the students design a chart to record their result.

Mathematics as Communication and Mathematics as Reasoning

K-4

A. Tell the class that they manage a grocery store. They carry 100 Whatchamacallit candy bars and 50 Turtle candy bars. Ask them to discuss in their preassigned small groups which would have more effect on selling the candy bars: the name or the price. They are to write about which choice they made and why.

B. The teacher and students discuss the pros and cons of advertising a product in the grocery store. The student then picks out a product in the grocery store, for example, macaroni and cheese, and two different brand names. One of the names has to be generic (for example: staff). The student must then call their grocery store or visit it with mom or dad, and talk to the manager about their product. They are to record for a month which brand sells more and why. Is it because of the advertisement that is done or is it the price? What other factors might there be on why one brand sells better than the other? The student is to write up a report on findings and present them to the class.

5-8

A. The students are to make an advertisement that compares their stores' prices with another store down the road. (Price list is provided.) Then they are to make an ad that they think will attract more people to their store. Give students hints to make their prices and items look and sound more appealing.

B. Have the students view several commercials that other grocery stores have made in the past. Have prearranged groups discuss the pros and cons of the commercials. Then have each group make a videotape of their own commercial, mentioning their prices and values. (Video camera should be provided by school.)

Mathematical Connections

K-4

A. Give the students a chance to pack their own "fantasy" lunch. Given $3 and a list of foods in a grocery store and their prices, the students are to create their own lunch without spending more than $3 and having one thing from each of the four food groups. (Four food groups have been studied previously.)

B. The teacher has a simulated grocery store set up in the room. One student is assigned to be the cashier and two other students are customers. (This can be done in small groups or a learning center.) The cashier does not have a machine that can add up the prices of the items all together. The cashier must ring up one item at a time. For example, if the customer has five items, they must make five different payments instead of adding up all the prices and only making one payment.

5-8

A. The teacher has x number of 12-oz. pop cans and x number of 12-oz. boxes of Stove-Top Stuffing. There is also a box that is 2 feet × 3 feet × 1 foot.

The teacher tells a student that he or she is a stock person at a grocery store. Given the empty box, could the student fit more pop cans in it or more boxes of stuffing? Have the student first estimate what he or she thinks the outcome will be, and then test that theory by placing each item in the box and seeing which item they can fit more of into the box.

B. Have students go to the grocery store with their mom or dad. Have them look at the different products and how they are boxed or canned. Then have the students get in their preassigned groups and design a new box for their own product. (Products will be preassigned to the groups or you could have each group think of their own product.) The groups need to decide the size of the container (in ounces) and the size of the lettering, colors, etc. that they think will appeal to the customer.

Estimation

K-4

A. Students should choose one full page of grocery advertising from the newspaper and estimate how much all of the items on the page would cost when added together. Comparisons among students will help determine the reasonableness of their estimates. Then use calculators to compute actual costs. Comparisons of estimations and actual costs should be examined.

B. Students should discuss strategies for estimating the numbers of actual food items in advertised packages and containers. For example, the number of lifesavers in a roll or the "pieces" of cereal in a box could be used. More than one strategy should be encouraged. After the estimates have been made, actual counts should be taken and compared.

C. Present the students with the following problem: You are Wanda Workhorse, the local grocery store stock person. A display for apples can hold 200 pounds of apples. About how many crates of apples should you roll out if a crate holds around 30 pounds of apples? After estimating your answer, solve the problem to check how reasonable your estimate was compared to the solution.

D. Present the students with the following problem: You are the boss of Mario's Macaroni Heaven, a business that provides macaroni to the town's grocery store. You need to decide whether or not to sell your macaroni in a box or in a jar, knowing that regardless of which one you choose the grocery store will only let you sell your product for $.89. Estimate which container you think will hold less macaroni since this is the container you will want to sell your product in. (Can you explain why?) Using the box, jar, macaroni, and scoop provided by the District Macaroni Inspector (the teacher), figure out whether or not your estimation was correct.

5-8

A. Tell the students to pretend that they are cashiers in Elle's Estimation Emporium, a grocery store that does not use registers or calculators to find how much their customers owe. Tell the students that while figuring the customer's exact total using addition is okay, that because of long lines there will be no time for exact answers today. Therefore, the students must try to use their best estimation techniques. Once the students are ready to begin, present them with 10 to 15 "products" (pencils, apples, etc.) and give them the exact price. Go slow enough so that the students do not get frustrated or completely lost, but go quick enough so that they must estimate the total as opposed to figuring it out exactly. Once you complete your "transaction," write the students' estimates on the board and ask them how they kept track (mental math, etc.). Then reveal the correct total.

B. Tell the students that they are Sandy the Sandwich Man, the head worker at the grocery store deli. The grocery store likes to make sure that all of their three-item sandwiches are as much alike as possible, so they provided Sandy with proportions of how much of each ingredient should go on the sandwich in relation to the weight of the bread. Provide the students with the proportions for each ingredient (i.e., ham, cheese, and lettuce) and also varying weights of bread (in ounces). Have the students estimate and then figure out how much of each ingredient should go on the differing sandwiches.

C. Students should cut up the advertising section of the newspaper so that there is one item and price per cut-up piece. Place all slips of paper in a grocery shopping bag (recyclable if possible). Students take turns drawing out three slips of papers. While one student reads the cost of each item out loud, each student mentally estimates the total cost of the three items. After comparing estimates, calculators are used to determine actual costs in relation to the estimates.

D. Students should use the grocery store advertisement sections to plan a grocery list with a cost estimated at $100. Calculators are used to determine actual costs of lists. A "Blue Light Special" of 15% off all canned goods is then announced by the teacher. Students should estimate how much this will be per item and how it will affect their total bill. Calculators may be used to either derive or to check estimations.

Number Sense, Numeration, and Number Relationships

K-4

A. With a partner, ask the students to count the number of pieces in a package of M&M's and record their results. The same procedure is followed with a bag of Reese's Pieces. When both packages have been counted, the students are to determine which package had the most, the least, and why. Answers should be shared and recorded.

B. Ask the students to explore grocery store inventory by helping a grocery store manager count a given amount of canned goods. Number amounts should be recorded. The students could also group the canned goods by food type, color, or size. Amounts of each group could also be counted and recorded.

C. Have the students bring soup labels into the class. Have each student write down all the different ways numbers are used and represented on the soup labels. Once all the students have completed their lists, combine the different lists into a class list for a discussion of all the different uses of numbers in a grocery store.

D. Present the students with the following problem: Your name is Marla the Meat Inspector, and it is your duty to check all the meat for freshness before it can be sold in the grocery store. Today you have inspected 800 pounds of meat, and you have found 200 pounds of it to be spoiled and not suitable to sell. What fraction of the meat did you have to throw away? How much meat will your friend Sam the Butcher have left to sell?

5-8

A. Present the students with the following problem: Congratulations! You have been hired to serve as a bagger at Wild Bill's Grocery and Chemical Mart, and you have just worked your first day. You figure out that you worked 7.9 hours, and your hourly pay is $4.06. How much did you make? You also remember that you must pay 6% of your total amount for taxes. Now how much money do you have? Do you think the tax made a big difference in your pay? How much?

B. Present the students with the following problem: The 18-ounce cans of Barry's Baked Beans are on sale! You can buy four cans of Barry's Beans for only $3.00! The regular price for a can of Barry's Beans is $.90 a can. How much would you save by buying four cans? What do you feel would be the advantage of buying four cans instead of buying only three? Would you still buy four cans even if a recipe you had only needed three cans? Why or why not?

C. The students are to determine the best buy on hot-dog buns for a class picnic. With a calculator, the students should divide the price of the package by the number of buns per package. After results are shared and recorded, students should arrange the packages of buns (at least five different packages) from least expensive to most expensive.

D. Each student is given a register receipt for taxable grocery items with tax and total amounts cut off. With a 6% sales tax, students are asked to determine the total cost of the bill. Next, students are given discount coupons with which they will need to calculate new totals. With a given amount of money, ask the students to determine how much change they will receive after paying their new total cost.

Concepts of Operations and Computation

K-4

A. Using a grocery list, a box of priced products, and a $10 bill, the students should purchase as many groceries as possible without going over $10. Special recognition could be given to the student who comes closest to $10, the student who buys the most products, and the student who has the greatest variety of products.

B. Using a box of randomly chosen and priced products and a stack of corresponding coupons, ask the students to determine their savings per item as well as their total savings.

C. Have the students bring in grocery store cash register receipts from home. Clip off all the totals and hand out the receipts to the class. Encourage the students to use calculators to figure out the total from their receipt. Once all the students have found their independent total, have them write it on the chalkboard. Then have the students figure out the total of all the receipts (using a calculator) to find a classroom total. Ask the students if they thought using the calculator saved time figuring the totals and why.

D. During a field trip to a local grocery store, have the students spend two minutes looking for five items whose prices will come close to equaling $20. Encourage the use of estimation because time will not allow for adding the actual prices. After the two minutes have expired, have the students go back and figure out the actual cost of the five items. After they compare their estimation with the true cost, have them explain how they estimated their answer and how well they think they did.

5-8

A. Present the students with the following problem: You go to the grocery store to do some shopping for a class party. When you get to the tomato section, you are faced with the following information: "Tommy's Tasty Tomatoes—33% off, Teresa's Tomatoes Galore—$\frac{1}{4}$ off, Ted's Tomatoes O'Plenty —$.47 off." If all the cans are normally priced at $2 each, which sale offers you and the class the greatest savings? Discuss your answer with the class.

B. Present the students with the following problem: Your name is Juan and you are in charge of buying gum for Juanita's Grocery Store and Gum Emporium. You are in a tough position because you have lost the price list for Double Your Trouble Bubble Bombs, the new favorite gum among all the children at the local school. The only thing you can remember is that the last time you ordered the gum that you were able to buy 12 packs of Bubble Bombs for $10. Now your boss Juanita has given you $50 to buy the gum for the increased demand from the children. Assuming the individual cost per pack has not changed, how many packs of the gum can you buy? How would you go about finding out the individual price per pack?

C. Using containers of identical grocery items with different weights, ask the students to determine which container size is cheaper per unit and by how much the particular container is cheaper.

D. Ask students to determine the cost per weight of different name brands and generic brands of soft drinks. They should then determine which brand is the best value for the money (and why).

Patterns and Relationships

K-4

A. Using the layout for part of a grocery store aisle, the students should be able to determine the items that are not shown by observing the patterns and relations of shown objects.

B. Using items of various shapes and sizes, have the students form their own grocery store aisle and explain the patterns and relations used. Students then duplicate a partner's aisle pattern with different products of similar shape and size.

C. During a field trip to a local grocery store, have the students try to find different patterns that might exist in a grocery store. If you feel the students might need some help getting started, give them suggestions to see if they notice any color patterns, patterns by size of product or price, etc. Provide the students with sheets to record their patterns to share with the class.

D. After the field trip, have the students develop their own grocery store patterns by drawing and cutting the products in their patterns with construction paper. Have the students present their patterns to the class. Encourage the students to describe and extend the patterns developed by their classmates.

5-8

A. Have a few students serve as "sales managers" whose responsibility is to call or stop by a cooperating grocery store three times a week (Monday, Wednesday, and Friday) for a month and check on the daily sales for two comparable products (i.e., Coke and Pepsi, Snickers and Almond Joy, etc.). Have the students report their daily findings to the class and have each student develop their own "sales report" to record the data. At the end of the month have the students construct a chart of the sales managers' findings and analyze the chart through a written paper. Have the students explain what factors they think might have affected the sales (better advertising, lower cost, etc.) and what they might do to improve the sales of the less popular product.

B. Present the students with the following problem: Your name is Andrea and you are the sales chairperson for Poopsie Cola. You notice that at the local grocery store Coo-Coo Cola is outselling Poopsie even though both are priced at $6.99 a case. You decide to lower the price of a case of Poopsie to $3.99 a case. Answer the following questions:
   1. What do you think is going to happen to the sales of Poopsie Cola?
   2. What do you think is going to happen to the sales of Coo-Coo Cola?
   3. If Poopsie Cola's sales do increase, what do you think Coo-Coo Cola's sales chairperson will do?
   4. If Poopsie Cola's sales do increase and Coo-Coo Cola does not change their price, what advantage may Coo-Coo Cola still have?

   (To extend this activity further, invite a grocery store manager to the class to describe the relationships and patterns between lower price and sales, and lower price and profits.)

C. Given information pertaining to the number of items per shelf and the average cost per item (on at least five different shelves), the students should prepare a graph comparing total money values per individual shelves.

D. Students should examine a line graph displaying the growing number of shoppers a particular grocery store has served each month. With consistent continued trends, the students will determine how many shoppers will be served during the next two months. Can we expect consistent growth forever?

Algebra

K-4

A. Present the students with the following problem: You are buying eggs from Ely's Egg-O-Rama. You need to purchase 144 eggs. How many cartons would you need?

B. Present the students with the following problem: You are receiving a truckload of bananas for a big sale. You need to end up with 5000 lbs. for your sale. The truck holds 250 lbs. a load. How many loads will your driver have to make before you have your 5000 lbs.?

5-8

A. Present the students with the following problem: Coo-Coo Cola is on sale for $4.99 a case, and you can only purchase one case per customer per visit. You are having a party and are expecting 24 people.
   1. How many cases of pop will you need if each person drinks two cans?
   2. How many trips will you have to make to the store?
   3. How much money will you end up spending?

4. You have to spend a minimum of $10 for each case of pop on sale. Would you go ahead and spend the extra money or would you just buy it for the regular price of $6.59? Discuss it as a class.

B. Present the following problem to the students: Fifty-five people came into the grocery store through the electric doors. If 22 customers came in by themselves and you know that no more than two people came through the door at a time, then how many pairs of people came in the store? Write an equation and explain how you figured out the problem.

Statistics and Probability

K-4

A. Display an advertisement for chocolate, vanilla, and strawberry ice cream and then ask students to choose a corresponding brown, white, or pink magnetic circle to "stick on" a metallic surface. Color choice represents the students' favorite ice cream flavor. Students should count the number of circles to determine number of ice cream choices.

B. Put two cans of soup (two different kinds) in a large box and ask students take turns drawing cans out and replacing them. The teacher, or another student, should record the types of cans drawn. After 20 to 25 drawings, students should discuss the probability of drawing one specific type of two products.

C. During a field trip to a grocery store, have the students record the price of ten different brands of soda pop in 2-liter bottles. When they return to the classroom, have them organize their findings in tables showing relationships between the brands (lowest to highest price, alphabetical order, etc.). Have them discuss their findings with the rest of the class.

D. Present the following problem to the students: Grover's Grocery and Office Supply Warehouse is having its grand opening, and you have been invited to attend. When you arrive at the door, Grover offers you a chance to win a free bag of Picasso Potato Chips and a stapler if you can pick a blue chip (without looking!) out of a container that has nine white chips and the lucky blue one. If you were to stick your hand in the can and take out a chip, what are your chances it is the blue one? Explain your answer.

5-8

A. Have the students call or visit a local company that supplies a specific product to a grocery store. Have the students ask how much of that product has been supplied to the store for the last year. Ask the students to display their findings in a graph. Once they have completed their chart, have them trade it with other students and orally analyze each other's graphs (in terms of sales, demand, etc.).

B. Present the students with the following problem: Barry the Bagger has found that for every 50 customers he helps to carry their groceries, he generally receives 10 tips. Using this information, how many tips should Barry receive in a week? (He usually helps 300 people a week.)

C. Students should form a chart listing numbers of calories per serving of 10 different breakfast cereals. After forming and reading the chart, students should determine the range of the numbers and calculate the mean, median, and mode.

D. Have students look at consumer surveys done on various products. From the given information, students should be able to determine the most popular and least popular products. Students should also be able to determine the percentages of people choosing particular items.

Geometry and Spatial Sense

K-4

A. Ask students to collect a full-page grocery store advertisement. Have them redraw the ad on white paper of equal size, only eliminating the words and copying only geometric shapes. Each shape should be labeled by name and colored a consistent color throughout the advertisement.

B. Ask students to collect the packaging of a variety of grocery store items. Students should carefully take apart the package and lay the package out on a flat piece of white paper. With a black marker, outline the packaging itself. Shapes making up the packaging will be colored with markers. Students should be able to identify congruent shapes. As an extension, students can trace their favorite packaging and refold to form their own special package.

C. Provide the students with a check sheet that contains pictures of different shapes. On their field trip to the grocery store, have them record how many times they see each shape. Leave space on the sheet for the students to draw shapes they see that are not represented on the check sheet. Discuss with the class the most common shapes they noticed at the grocery store.

D. Provide the students with 30 soup cans. Have each student or group of students take turns seeing who can position the cans in a way that uses the least amount of area on the floor. Allow the students plenty of time to experiment with positioning the cans in different shapes (square, circle, triangle, etc.) or with stacking the cans.

5-8

A. Have the students visit both the meat department and the fruit department on their field trip to the grocery store. Have the students record which products in the section appear to have symmetry and which do not. Ask the students if they think symmetrical products appear more appealing to eat or if they even think symmetry makes a difference to a consumer at a grocery store.

B. Provide the students with a fish bowl and a square box that appear to be approximately the same size. Have the students predict which container they feel could hold more gum balls and have them explain why. Then provide gumballs to the students and have them see if their prediction was correct. After they find the correct answer, ask the students if the shapes of the containers had any bearing on their predictions. Have the students see what shapes of containers are used to store products (such as gumballs) at their local grocery store.

C. Students should choose several aisle displays of advertised products. Have them calculate the surface areas and volumes of each box or can of the product. Students then determine the number of total items needed to completely fill the display shelf. Students may also make comparisons of weight and volume by comparing items of equal weights.

D. Have students use mirrors to find examples of symmetry in grocery store advertisements, displays, and packages. Five of the best examples of symmetry will be sketched. Students should then design their own symmetrical advertisement and package.

Measurement

K-4

A. Ask students to line up a set of ten cereal boxes by height from shortest to tallest. Determine which box is the tallest and which box is the shortest and discuss relationships. Which do you think holds more cereal?

B. Students should examine items in a grocery store and make comparisons using their foot rulers. As students find three items that are exactly one foot on at least one side, these items should be listed or illustrated.

C. During a field trip to the grocery store, have the students compare the weights of items that are weighed on a digital scale to items that are weighed on a traditional scale. Ask students: Which is more accurate? How accurate is one compared to the other? Which is more convenient and easier to use? Why?

D. Remove all the labels from a variety of cans (different sizes, weights, and shapes). Have the students estimate the weight of each can, and by using both the digital scale and the traditional scale, weigh each to see if their estimations were reasonable.

5-8

A. Compare different kinds of potato chips. Have the students weigh the bags to see if they are accurate with the manufacturer's weight. Ask the students: Are you getting your money's worth? If the bag of chips was crushed, would it weigh more? Compare the weight with the size of the bag. Are they fooling you with a bigger bag than what is really needed?

B. During the field trip to the grocery store, have the students weigh 15 different oranges and record the results. Back in the classroom, have the students graph their findings. Have them determine what was the lightest, the heaviest, what was the average weight, what was the difference between the heaviest and the lightest orange. Ask the students: Which would you buy? How would you choose them if you did not have a scale available before checkout?

C. Play a question/answer game in which an item is held up as students raise their hand to name the most appropriate unit for measuring the amount of the item. Students with correct answers are responsible for holding up the next item. It may be necessary to actually measure the items in the units suggested.

D. Ask students to examine a container of Quaker Oats and estimate the volume of the container. After all estimations have been shared, students should form groups, be given their own container, and asked to measure its volume. Different problem-solving strategies should be accepted and shared with the entire class.

Health

Mathematics as Problem Solving

K-4

A. Show the students a chart of many foods from each of the four food groups and also some of junk foods. Under each picture, put an approximate price for the items. Using the chart, ask the students to create a well-balanced meal and to calculate the cost of their meal. Break the students into groups of four or five. Ask the students to discuss whose meal costs more or less. Did everyone in your group create the same meal? Share their discussions with the class.

B. Susie woke up at 1:00 A.M. feeling very hot. Her mother came in and decided to take Susie's temperature. Her temperature was 103°F. Susie's mother came back two hours later and took her temperature again; it had risen 2°F. One hour later, Susie's temperature dropped 3°F.

1. What was Susie's final temperature?
2. At what time was Susie's temperature the highest?
3. At what time was Susie's temperature 101°F?
4. Could Susie's temperature during the night ever have been 102°F? Between what times could this have occurred?

5-8

A. If a bottle of cough medicine costs $4.98 and you get 20 doses of two teaspoons each out of the bottle:
   1. How much does each dose cost?
   2. How much does each teaspoon cost?
   3. How much would 20 teaspoons cost?

B. Your mother sends you to the grocery store to purchase a bottle of aspirin. She gives you $10 and tells you to buy the size bottle that is most economical. When you get to the store this is what you find:

   24 tablets @ $2.42
   50 tablets @ $4.13
   100 tablets @ $6.29

   1. Which bottle size would be the most economical to purchase? Why?
   2. Assuming there is no tax, if you purchase the most economical bottle, how much change would your mother receive?

Mathematics as Communication and Mathematics as Reasoning

K-4

A. Show the class a picture of a hospital sign. Discuss the characteristics of the sign (e.g., shape, size, color, etc.).

B. When your mom goes to the store to buy medicine, what kinds of things does she look for on the box/label?

5-8

A. After completing a chapter on nutrition, present the class with two frozen entrees, one regular and one light. Have the students compare the nutritional information on the boxes of both items and calculate any differences. Is the light entree really nutritionally better for you as compared to the regular? (Discuss proof to support your answer.)

B. Discuss the number of advertisements on the television and in magazines dealing with health that are potentially "false" advertisements. Why might they be false?

Mathematical Connections

K-4

A. If Julie takes her medicine at 7:00 A.M. and the directions on the bottle say to take every four hours, at what times will Julie take each of her next three doses?

B. Take a tour through a hospital. Make a list of the different wards you travel through. How many rooms are in each ward? Do all wards have the same number of rooms? Why or why not?

5-8

A. Discuss what a nurse and doctor would have to know about mathematics. Why do they need to know these things?

B. Do you eat a nutritious breakfast? Assuming you eat cereal, use the nutritional information on the box to make a graph of the vitamin and mineral content of the cereal with and without milk.

Estimation

K-4

A. Show the students a jar of cotton balls similar to the jars often seen in a doctor's office. Ask the students to tell you the number of cotton balls they think are in the jar. Record all answers. Count cotton balls to see who made the best estimate. (This can be followed up using a jar of tongue depressors.)

B. The elevator in the hospital has a sign that reads, "Maximum load: 1500 lbs." Ask the students to estimate the number of students in their grade who could enter or ride in the elevator without going over the 1500-lb. load limit.
   1. Would your entire class be able to ride?
   2. If you fill two elevators to the maximum weight, which would have more people in it, an elevator with only adults or an elevator with only children?

5-8

A. Two patients enter the doctor's office. The first is Ms. Annie Aerobics who exercises everyday, eats well-balanced meals, and leads a fairly carefree life. The second is Steve "The Super Salesman" who is always working hard, eats junk food and fast food on a regular basis, and whose life revolves around meetings, deadlines, and sales quotas.
   1. Which would you estimate to have the better blood pressure?
   2. Can you think of any other people who may have high blood pressure?

B. You live 15 miles from the nearest hospital. Your dad has to rush your mom to the hospital because she is having a baby. If he drives 60 mph, about how long will it take them to get to the hospital? How long will it take if he drives 65 mph?

Number Sense, Numeration, and Number Relationships

K-4

A. Twelve people are admitted to the hospital. The hospital has only six vacant rooms. How many people would be put into each room if we want the same number of people in each room?

B. You are in charge of sorting out the bandages in the children's ward of the hospital. There is a big box that contains five different sizes. Sort the bandages according to size and make a list of your findings.

5-8

A. There are 200 patients in the hospital and the hospital has 340 beds.
   1. What percentage of the beds are filled?
   2. What is the proportion of occupied beds to unoccupied beds?
   3. If 25 patients are released, what fraction is left?

B. Compare the small size, regular size, and large size packages of Q-tips. What is the percentage of increase in number? Compare that to the percentage of price increase between the sizes.

Concepts of Operations and Computation

K-4

A. One night 25 people came into the hospital emergency room. Of those 25, 7 were treated and released and the remaining were admitted. The next night, 16 people came into the emergency room. Of those 16 people, 6 were admitted and the remaining were treated and released. During those two nights:
   1. What is the total number of patients that were treated and sent home?
   2. How many people were admitted into the hospital?

B. You are sick and need to go to the doctor. To see the doctor, the cost is $25. While at the office, he takes a throat culture costing $7 and blood work costing $12. He gives you two prescriptions; one costs $5.50 and the other costs $8.25. If you have to go back once more to see the doctor, how much will the total bill be to get you back into good health?

5-8

A. You have been sick and finally decide to go to the doctor. The doctor prescribes three prescriptions for you. Due to your parents' medical plan, each prescription costs you only $2. If the original costs of the medicine were $6.75, $10.46, and $9.59:
   1. How much did you pay for your prescriptions?
   2. How much would you have had to pay without the medical plan?
   3. How much money did you save due to your parents' medical plan?

B. The hospital averages 213 patients in one day. How many patients would it average in a week, a month, a year, and five years?

Patterns and Relationships

K-4

A. Take a walk through a hospital. Make a map and trace the different hallways that you walk through. What numbers have been assigned to each hallway?

B. Present the students with a pattern of people admitted into a hospital (boy, boy, girl, boy, girl, girl, . . .). Have the students continue the pattern. Have the students make up patterns of their own.

5-8

A. With the permission of the doctor and patient, look at a few patients' charts. What are some things that are familiar to all patients? What are some things that are different? Do you see any patterns? (*Hint:* Dietary, prognosis, medications, etc.)

B. Six people go to the doctor for their annual checkup. The results show that three of the people are in good health and the other three are in poor health. What are some patterns you may find in their daily lives that may lead to their prognosis of health?

Algebra

K-4

A. Tubby Templeton goes to the doctor for his annual checkup. After all examinations and tests are complete, the doctor informs Tubby that his cholesterol level and his blood pressure are too high. The doctor tells Tubby that if he could lose some weight his overall health would improve. Tubby weighs 253 lbs. If the ideal weight for a man of Tubby's size and age is 185 lbs., how many pounds does Tubby need to lose? Write an equation.

B. You have $10,000 in your savings account. You have just found out that you are terminally ill and will need to be admitted into the hospital. If it costs $300 per day to stay in the hospital, how many days can you stay in the hospital before you need other financial help?

5-8

A. You work in the Dietary Department in a hospital. At lunchtime you deliver 48 meals per floor. Each cart will hold only 15 meals.
   1. How many trips do you need to make back to the kitchen to serve one floor?
   2. If the hospital has eight floors, how many trips will you have to make to serve the entire hospital?

B. During visiting hours at the hospital, 12 people get on an elevator on the first floor. Two people get off on the second floor and four people get off on the third floor. When the elevator gets to the fifth floor, there are only two people left on the elevator. How many people got off the elevator on the fourth floor? Write an equation to represent this situation.

Statistics and Probability

K-4

A. You have 14 vitamins left in your bottle of Flintstones Vitamin C. Of those 14, 4 are Fred, 3 are

Wilma, 5 are Barney, and 2 are Betty. If you reach into the bottle without looking, how many vitamins must you take out before you are guaranteed to have two of the same character?

B. Using the measuring tape on the wall, each group will take turns measuring each member of their group. After they have written down all the heights, each group will make a graph of their findings. Each group will then share their findings with the class. Make a graph of the entire class and discuss these findings.

5-8

A. Henry and Harriet decide to have a child. Both carry genes for blood types A and B. The child will have blood type A if both parents pass on their A genes, type B if both parents pass on their B genes and type AB if one A and one B gene are passed.
   1. What is the probability that the child will have type A blood?
   2. What is the probability that the child will have type B blood?
   3. What is the probability that the child will have type AB blood?

B. There are 25 students in your class. Of these, 13 students have come down with the chicken pox. What percentage of the class is out sick? What is the likelihood that the other 12 students in the class will come down with the chicken pox?

Geometry and Spatial Sense

K-4

A. Take the students on a tour of a hospital. Discuss the different shapes that are seen in the hospital.

B. Bring in a variety of fruits and vegetables. Classify, compare, and discuss the different sizes and shapes of these fruits and vegetables. Discuss the rationale for placing certain objects into each group. (For example, size, color, taste, shape, etc.) Could some belong to more than one group?

5-8

A. A hospital has 650 rooms. One room size is 12 ft. × 14 ft. and the other is 14 ft. × 24 ft. If 40% of the rooms are 14 ft. × 24 ft. and 60% are 12ft. × 14ft.:
   1. What is the total area of all the rooms?
   2. What is the area of one 12 × 14 room? All 12 × 14 rooms together?
   3. What is the area of one 14 × 24 room? All 14 × 24 rooms together?

B. Given a specific area of land, draw a hospital complex complete with buildings, parking lots, outside eating facility, etc. Draw your map to a specific scale.

Measurement

K-4

A. Take the students to the school nurse to be measured and weighed. Discuss the different instruments used to do these measurements and discuss the results.

B. A doctor recommends to your mother that in order to get you into good health habits you should start walking or running $\frac{1}{2}$ mile per day. Take the students to the school track or some suitably large area and measure the distance. Have students run/walk the distance of $\frac{1}{2}$ mile. (You could have the students count their paces.)

5-8

A. If a bottle of castor oil contains 8 oz., how many teaspoons are there in the bottle? If the directions say to take 2 tsp., how many doses will there be in each bottle?

B. A certain patient in the hospital is only allowed 5 oz. of meat, 2 cups of vegetables, 1/2 pint of milk, and 4 oz. of potatoes.
   1. How could you accurately measure these?
   2. What measuring devices would you need?
   3. Convert all measurements to ounces.

Mathematics through Transportation

Mathematics as Problem Solving

K-4

A. Each student should talk to five different people, one of whom may be a travel agent, to find out the most common mode of transportation they know people use for traveling more than 200 miles. Show results visually using a bar graph.

B. You are going to visit the state capital. What different means of transportation could you use to travel there? Using other various locations in the United States, determine which mode of transportation could be used to get there. The students should take into consideration that there is always more than one possibility.

5-8

A. Have resource books available for students that give information on fuel efficiency for different modes of transportation. Then have students find the two most economical ways to travel and the two least economical ways to travel. Students should be able to give information as to why they came to the conclusion they did.

B. Divide the class into four groups. Assign each group a different mode of transportation and have them study different aspects of their given mode. As a class, the groups will then debate on why they feel their mode would be the best form of transportation.

Mathematics as Communication and Mathematics as Reasoning

K-4

A. Have students develop ways of classifying different modes of transportation. Provide students with pictures of modes of transportation so they can use their classification system. Discuss in groups the systems they chose. Example: If students decide to classify by land, water, and air, then they place the modes of transportation in their respective categories.

B. In small groups, brainstorm as many different modes of transportation as you can. Choose one and write as many mathematical things down as you know about it. Example: A car has four wheels, two or four doors, different models, colors, shapes, etc.

5-8

A. You are planning a class field trip. Gather and record information on different modes of transportation, finding the most economical, fastest, most expensive, etc., packaged deal for your class trip.

B. In groups of two, discuss advantages/disadvantages of the packaged deals researched. Choose the one you feel is the best and write a letter to the principal justifying why you feel it is the best.

Mathematical Connections

K-4

A. Have students research a mode of transportation of their choice focusing on historic events. They will then create a time line depicting the historical progress of their mode of transportation.

B. Write a paragraph or two describing the importance of numbers in transportation. Example: mile markers, speed limits, exit numbers, highway numbers, fares, school bus numbers, etc.

5-8

A. Have students research transportation focusing on what companies are doing about the pollution problems. Which are handling it better than others? Which form of transportation causes the least amount of pollution? Discuss your findings in small groups.

B. Your family is going on a trip abroad. Because you will not have your own car, you need to use public transit while there. Given the rates of exchange for the currency of the place you are going, determine whether transportation is more or less expensive than transportation in the United States. Suppose you go to a neighboring country. Determine currency exchange differences between countries and compare the two countries with the United States.

Estimation

K-4

A. Provide students with different places to walk such as the principal's office, library, cafeteria, etc. Have them estimate how many footsteps it will take them to get to each place. Have students actually walk the distances and check their estimates. Discuss why some students' results will be different from others. Example: smaller steps, larger steps, etc.

B. Have students estimate how many people could occupy different modes of transportation. When possible, have students physically test their estimates (such as on a school bus). Take into consideration whether the occupancy is for comfort or maximum fit. Example: a car may fit eight, but only four comfortably.

5-8

A. Give the students a variety of modes of transportation. Have them estimate what they think is a reasonable average distance often traveled by that mode. Example: Would a plane be more likely to go 2 miles or 2000 miles?

B. Have students plan their own trip. Estimate how much it will cost. Using brochures and travel agencies, find out how much it would really cost.

Number Sense, Numeration, and Number Relationships

K-4

A. Give students play money and set up a cab company. They should decide on how much it would cost to walk to certain places. For example, walking to the bathroom and back should cost a certain amount. Students should pay and make change for the fare.

B. Using a train with numbered cars, have the children count and practice one-to-one correspondence. For variation, count by twos using the train wheels, by fives, etc.

5-8

A. Have students discuss why cab fares take into consideration fractions of miles. Try to get students to see that if you went 1.2 miles but were only charged for a mile, the cab company would lose money. On the other hand, if you went 1.7 miles and were charged for 2 miles, you would be paying too much. What other areas of transportation is this applicable to?

B. Make a pie chart and a bar graph of the number of people that own unicycles, bicycles, and tricycles after collecting data from class. Let the students decide how they are going to represent their data. Compare the appearance of the graphs among the classroom.

Concepts of Operations and Computation

K-4

A. Use the hallway to experiment with different lengths such as foot and meter. Have students walk down the hall to a certain spot. Measure the distance and record the data. Have the students continue walking to another location and again measure the distance and record it. Use that data to find out different relationships between the numbers such as difference, sum, greater distance, etc.

B. You are going 12 miles across town in a taxi cab. The driver informs you that your total fare is $5.40. What is the fare per mile? Discuss how the cab company could attract more riders. Is the price per mile reasonable? What other means of transportation would be more economical?

5-8

A. Given information from the manufacturers about the size of the gas tank, have students collect data concerning price of gas per gallon. Using the information collected, develop a calculator-ready formula that would give the cost for a fill-up at various stations. For example, if a car has an eight gallon tank and the station charges $1.029 per gallon, how would you show the formula as well as the actual price for a fill-up? For variations, show price per fill-up for different types of gas or fuel.

B. Students should be given a list of bus fares to various locations. Students must figure out new price rates after a 17% discount has been issued. Various price rates and discounts can be given.

Patterns and Relationships

K-4

A. Using precut pictures of different modes of transportation, have the students create a pattern such as the number of wheels (unicycle, bicycle, tricycle, etc.), windows, colors, etc., and have them discuss or explain how they came about their individual patterns.

B. Have students relate the size of one mode of transportation to another. For example, bicycle to car, car to semitrailer truck, bicycle to semitrailer truck, etc. In cases where it is appropriate, arrange for students to physically measure these objects and examine how they relate to one another in size, length, or weight. If not physically able to measure with actual objects, have scale models or pictures to scale available for students.

5-8

A. Have students create their own "model scale" to produce either a map or a scale representation of transportation. For example, one inch = one foot, so seven inches would represent the length of a seven-foot car.

B. Have students discuss why scales are used to represent objects or distances. Then discuss their reasoning for choosing the scale they did for the preceding problem and the advantages and disadvantages to it.

Algebra

K-4

A. Gather information from various sources such as almanacs, travel bureaus, airline ticket sales, etc. Make a class bar graph of the most common day of the week to fly.

B. Discuss why a certain day is the most common for air travel. Some children may suggest a cheaper price for that day, people have that day off, certain restrictions by airlines, etc.

5-8

A. Given the rate of fuel consumption for an airplane, determine the most efficient ratio of fuel to cargo. For example, given a 20-mph head wind and a round-trip destination of 300 miles, how much gas would you need to make the round-trip flight? Keep in mind that the head wind will impede your flight progress.

B. Compare a graph shown in *US News & World Report* with a graph in *USA Today* dealing with some aspect of travel such as miles flown per year by the different airlines. Analyze the data and discuss similarities and differences with how the data were presented and what was said.

C. After analyzing the two graphs from the preceding activity, combine data and form your own original pie or pictograph.

Statistics and Probability

K-4

A. Use pictures or drawings of various modes of transportation and place them on 2" × 2" tiles. Place 10 assorted tiles in a brown paper bag allowing students to randomly pick one tile at a time. Have students collect, organize, and describe data. For example, include pictures of seven cars, two trains, and one boat. After several trials, ask students to predict or guess how many of each mode are in the bag.

B. Have the class collect data on walking versus taking the bus to school. Make a bar graph or pictograph of data. Have students predict the chances of whether a particular student is a walker or a rider. (If applicable, take into account the number of students whose parents drive them.)

5-8

A. Collect and organize data on miles per gallon for various car models. Find the mean, median, and mode for a particular line of car (Honda, Ford, etc.). The students can then create an advertisement using either the mean, median, or mode to compare gas mileage. Students would have to decide what type of measure of central tendency to use and why. For example, if the mode was greater, you might use the mode in the advertisement. How would you word the advertisement so that it wouldn't be misleading?

B. Compare a chart that shows the number of airplane accidents in a year with a chart showing the number of people killed in car accidents each year. From these findings, discuss what form of transportation would be safest, and why.

Geometry and Spatial Sense

K-4

A. Given pictures of different types of transportation, students should look at the pictures and record different geometric shapes found in each.

B. Provide students with a variety of geometric shapes and have them create their own mode of transportation from them. They may create real or imaginary forms of transportation.

5-8

A. The students can discuss why certain modes of transportation incorporate geometric shapes for some of its parts such as shape of tires, wings, shape of airplane, shape of cars, etc.

B. Students should write a physical description of a specific mode of transportation emphasizing geometric terms without stating the actual name of the object (car, plane, bus, etc.). Pair students and have them try to figure out what each of them was describing. As an extension, the students could try to describe some mode of transportation without using geometric terms.

Measurement

K-4

A. Call different bureaus of transportation to determine the amount of time needed to travel to given destinations. Compare bus, train, and airplane times. Take into account stopovers.

B. Discuss different means of walking, hopping, skipping, and running certain distances. Ask students which option they would choose if going a certain distance. For example, would you run a mile or walk? Discuss different distances.

5-8

A. Walk the perimeter of the school building and estimate how many feet that distance is. Walk it again using a trundle wheel with a circumference of one meter. Check your estimation. Make several replacement wheels for the trundle wheel, each with a different circumference. With this trundle wheel adjustable to different measures, estimate how many yards, meters, etc., and then measure.

B. Given a map of your state, find different routes to various locations and/or large cities. Find the shortest distance on main highways and on secondary roads.

Mathematics in Geography

Mathematics as Problem Solving

K-4

A. The earth rotates from west to east. As a result, the sun "rises" earlier at places that lie farther east. It is three hours earlier in the Pacific time zone than the Eastern time zone. Given a certain time in one time zone, the students will determine the time in the other time zone. (For example, if it is 5:00 here, what time is it in a city in another time zone, as specified by the teacher?)

B. The lines of latitude are numbered from 0 to 90 degrees. The equator is 0 degrees, the North Pole is 90 degrees north. The numbers of the latitude grow larger the farther you go from the equator. Example problem: Seattle, Washington, is at 47 degrees north latitude. Los Angeles is at 34 degrees north latitude. What is the difference in degrees between Seattle and Los Angeles?

5-8

A. Students time themselves for one minute. How many pieces of paper can you tear in one minute? At this rate, how many pieces could you tear in one hour? How long would it take you to tear a piece of paper for everyone in the United States (approximately 225,000,000 people)?

B. You drove from Norfolk to Los Angeles, which is 3,400 miles. During the trip you purchased 200 gallons of gas. You made ten stops and bought an equal amount of gas at each stop. How much gas did you buy at each stop? What was your mileage per gallon of gas?

Mathematics as Communication and Mathematics as Reasoning

K-4

A. Give the students a table that compares the average monthly temperatures in two cities during the months of January, April, July, and October. The students should use the table to discuss the following questions: Would you expect to see snow in January in either of these cities? Why? During which season are the temperatures most different? How does the temperature of the cities compare with the temperature in your city during these four seasons?

B. Looking at a map with various physical features (e.g., rivers, mountains, and plains), the students should determine the quickest route to travel a specified distance (given a scale).

5-8

A. Look in an encyclopedia and research your favorite place in the world. What kinds of food would you eat? What kinds of clothes would you wear? Is this a result of climate? Check the temperatures year-round. Compare this information to a more extreme climate type area. Interpret the data.
B. Look at the United States on a world agriculture map. Check what crops are grown in what areas. Is this determined by temperature? If so, what would happen if a drastic temperature change of either extremely cold/hot occurred? How would the crops be affected? What percentage of the crops might be saved?

Mathematical Connections

K-4

A. Some mountain peaks were smoothed by glaciers. Discuss the size of mountains. How big do you think the glaciers were? Compare to the size of the mountains and valleys.
B. The population of the United States is growing rapidly. By the year 2000, there might be 300 million Americans. Compare this to the population of today. What does this tell us about the size of our cities? The use of natural resources? What problems arise in cities?

5-8

A. Discuss what means of travel you would take if you were asked to go around the world. How long do you think it will take you? What problems might you encounter?
B. Discuss the location of the continents on the globe and what caused this kind of result. As a class, write down the causes. Record the number of times each cause occurs. Graph your results. What could make your results different from what they are on the chalkboard?

Estimation

K-4

A. Looking at an area of a map with a large number of islands, estimate the number of islands in the group. Compute the actual number of islands. Discuss possible reasons for accuracy or error (size of islands, distance between islands, etc.).
B. When walking past an old volcano you find 10 lava rocks for every foot that you walk. Estimate how many feet you would have to walk to find 50 rocks, 100, 200, etc.

5-8

A. Estimate how long it would take you to fly from Washington, D.C., to Tokyo, Japan. Graph the estimates as a class. Use a time chart to check how your guesses compared to the actual time.
B. What season would it be in Canberra, Australia, if it was winter in Chicago, Illinois? Graph students' estimates of temperature as a class. Use a season chart to check the results.

Number Sense, Numeration, and Number Relationships

K-4

A. The students are to answer questions by referring to a time line regarding important dates in geographic history. For example, what year did the southern part of the Louisiana Territory become the state of Louisiana?
B. Looking at a globe, determine where it could be cut in $\frac{1}{2}$. What is such an imaginary line called? What countries are located on the line you chose? Where is $\frac{1}{2}$ of the original $\frac{1}{2}$? More than one place? What fraction represents this part of the globe?

5-8

A. Look at a map. What happens to the degrees of longitude as you move east or west on the equator? Notice what happens to the degrees of latitude as you move north or south of the equator. Is there a pattern? If so, describe it. Does the pattern hold true for all directions?
B. Look at different population rates for the countries. What happens to the population rate if the amount of food is increased or decreased? Is there a pattern or relationship? If so, does this hold true for every country of the world? Change another factor such as education or war and notice the results. Same or different?

Concepts of Operations and Computation

K-4

A. Have students use calculators to determine the total number of miles it is from one city to another.
B. Ask the students to calculate the average temperature for a week in a given area, using both above and below zero degree temperatures.

5-8

A. Find out how much it would cost to travel across the United States by plane, train, and automobile. Include cost of gas, food, and spending money. Also consider the differences in the cost of living from one area to another. Compare expenses.

B. You are leaving New York at 8:00 P.M. and are to arrive in Los Angeles at 9:53 P.M. What is the amount of time spent flying per hour and minutes?

Patterns and Relationships

K-4

A. Ask the students to look at a map of the world and consider the size and shape of the continents, noting the relationships in the shapes and the possibility of the land "fitting together."
B. Pretend you are sailing down a newly discovered river and need to map it out for future travelers. Draw the river using all the curves and turns you encounter. Look at what you have drawn. Note the patterns you have created. State the reasons for certain patterns in the river flow (e.g., erosion, mountains, trees, etc.).

5-8

A. Look at a map of the world. Describe what patterns you see among the physical features. Compare it to a globe.
B. Study the different sizes of states and countries. Is there a specific pattern? Why do you suppose they are similar/different?

Algebra

K-4

A. The Great Lakes make up the largest chain of freshwater lakes in the world. They form the most important inland waterway in North America, covering a total of 94,510 square miles. The students will study a table of the size of the Great Lakes and use the information to make a bar graph of their relative sizes.
B. The students will use a chart of "Coal mined in the United States since 1900" to complete a line graph showing increases and decreases over the years.

5-8

A. Identify a relationship between the longitude and latitude of cities around the world that have similar temperature variations.
B. Using a world temperature chart, make a graph representing the number of different temperature regions of the world (hot, warm, mild, cold, and freezing). Discuss the relationships that exist between the location and how far the region is from the equator.

Statistics and Probability

K-4

A. Take a class poll of regions of the country where students have visited. Display the results using a pie graph and a bar graph.
B. Have the students draw pictures to represent certain data collected. In groups, the students should design pictographs to represent the data.

5-8

A. Spin a globe and place your finger on a particular country/state. What is the probability that your finger will land on the same country/state on another spin?
B. Place the pieces of a United States puzzle in a bag. Draw a state one at a time and record the region the state is in (West, Midwest, East, etc.). After 10 drawings, guess the combination of regions in the bag. Guess after 20 drawings and after 30 drawings.

Geometry and Spatial Sense

K-4

A. The students will develop spatial sense by looking at a globe and recognizing that there are 360 degrees in a complete circle. If they travel halfway around the earth from the prime meridian, in either direction, they will come to the 180 degree meridian (International Date Line).
B. Have the students take a walk outdoors noticing the environment. Back inside the students should draw a picture of what they saw, using only geometric figures.

5-8

A. Using a world map, determine how many different geometrical shapes it takes to "fill up" one continent. Compare this to another continent. Which shapes "fit" best?
B. Trace one continent from a world map. Use a ruler, compass, and/or protractor to get precise measurements. Describe what shape your continent looks like.
C. Make your own world. Use a variety of shapes, lines, and curves. Include a key and a measurement scale.

Measurement

K-4

A. The students should weigh various rocks from their environment and analyze the difference in size and shape. Record the data.
B. The students should create their own measurement scale and determine the distance of certain locations on a given map. Compare to the distance using the standard means of measurement in the map key.

5-8

A. Find the circumference and diameter of a globe using a tape measure.
B. Find the area and perimeter of each continent using a piece of string and a ruler.

PUTTING IT ALL TOGETHER:*

A Classroom Example that incorporates aspects of NCTM's vision of content, teaching, and assessment.

The conventional stereotypic picture of mathematics classrooms includes: students sitting at desks in neat rows, textbooks, and daily instruction that follows a five-step sequence with respect to a two-page spread in the text—the class reviews homework, the teacher works sample exercises, the students work on similar exercises, from the text or on a worksheet, the lesson is summarized by the teacher, and homework is assigned on similar exercises. Assessment involves checking to see whether the homework was done, a weekly quiz, and a chapter test.

The reform vision of what should go on in classrooms is quite different. The setting for the following story, which is a fictionalized account of a real instructional experience, is an eighth-grade, urban classroom. The teacher in this story, Shelly, and her colleagues have selected curriculum units in keeping with the important mathematics presented in the Curriculum Standards.

The content taught in this story is based on NCTM's Grades 5-8 Statistics Standard. The unit, *Windows Into Our World,* takes some six weeks to complete; has an underlying theme, "What are the data telling us?"; and is rooted in a project that groups of students are to complete, in which they are to systematically collect, organize, and describe data. Shelly attempts to conduct her classroom in a way that is in harmony with the Teaching Standards. She provides worthwhile mathematical tasks based on "sound and significant mathematics; knowledge of students' understandings, interests, and experiences; and the knowledge of the range of ways that diverse students learn mathematics" (NCTM, 1991, p. 25). Also, the tasks "engage students' intellect; develop students' mathematical understandings and skills; call for problem formulation, problem solving, and mathematical reasoning; and promote communication about mathematics" (NCTM, 1991, p. 25).

*Reprinted with permission from the working draft of the *Assessment Standards for School Mathematics,* copyright 1993 by the National Council of Teachers of Mathematics.

The College Jail Tale

(This is a unit on statistical inquiry developed at Stanford University. It is a product of the "Program for Complex Instruction" directed by Elizabeth Cohen. The principal authors of the unit are Ruth Cossey, Brenda Gentry Norton, and Ruth Tsu.)

Dear Jana,

It was good to get your letter. It's already November. I'm glad you suggested during the summer workshop that we write "remember when" notes to each other.

You asked what was up with my 8th graders. Phil, my buddy down the hall, recommended a unit on statistics: Windows Into Our World. *It's from a university research project about cooperative learning and equity.*

Phil's kids got the idea that working with statistics is like reading and telling stories. The first two days the students brainstorm and decide on a research topic. In class, they build a mental kit of investigative tools. The first tool section, for example, has activities which explore graphic representations of data—the questions they answer and the questions they make us want to ask. My job is to get students to always ask, What are the data telling us?

Assessment's built right into the unit. Although they work in groups and have to prepare group reports, every child also writes something every day—perhaps about statistics, or group dynamics, or percents and fractions, or simply about his or her self-reflections. Even a Problem of the Week is included. With so much individual accountability, I'll have lots of evidence of their learning.

It took Phil's class six weeks. It'll take mine until winter break. Except for language considerations, I've always made random group assignments and switched them every three weeks. But since they'll work together both inside and outside the school for such a long time, maybe I'll let them choose their own group—it's important they stay together for the entire unit.

I can't believe how I'm rattling on. Good luck with your origami/surface area and volume unit.

Best wishes,

Shelly

"I started Phil's unit today on statistics," Shelly said, with panic in her voice.

She maneuvered her short but sizable body back through the maze of tables, chairs, copying machine, rolls of butcher paper, and sofa in the math office. Waiting for her were Phil and the math Chair, Rachel Coston.

"I let them choose whom to work with," Shelly continued. "Well, 2nd period looks like seating at the UN. I've got a Spanish speaking group. The Vietnamese kids got together. Tracer and Kenny called out across the room, 'Yo! Black dudes over here!' There's a group of African-American girls that I would never put together on purpose—Tammy and Shanika are real talkers. What a kick-off to a unit!"

"If you don't want the groups segregated," Rachel said, "go in there tomorrow and tell them you changed your mind."

"But the whole unit is about choice for students," Shelly answered.

"I agree," Phil said, sliding his chair closer to his two colleagues. "She can't take back the authority she delegated to them or she'll undermine their trust in her. But, Shelly, just look at how they sit in the lunch room. The only time most of your students ever talk to someone with a different ethnic background is in your math class, because you insist that they sit in mixed groups."

"Philip Bringem, you could have warned me about more than that!" Shelly said. "Look at the topics the kids suggested we research." She started to read from an overhead transparency. "Homosexuals in the military, AIDS, literacy, sex on TV, racism at school, rock music, racism in the work place, hobbies, drugs, smoking, abortions . . ."

"Whoa, girl, what kind of brainstorming prompt did you give them?" Philip responded with mock shock.

"Birth control, homelessness, suicide . . ."

"We get the idea," Rachel said.

"Well, whether or not these reflect student realities, they sure were interested. Each group selects a topic tomorrow. Do either of you think I should restrict their choices? Will I have trouble assessing their work?"

Phil spoke quickly. "Go for it. Think what the list would be like if teachers generated it."

"But will you—me too—get in trouble with parents or the administration?" Rachel asked. "Researching sex on TV. For example? You think I could have a look at that unit and maybe the next time . . ."

The bell rang. Shelly gathered her papers and promised to show Rachel the unit, dashing out the door.

Dear Jana,

The origami mobiles look great. They will make great Christmas decorations, or Chanukah, or Kwanza, or whatever you and your students celebrate. I don't know if I could figure out one way to find the ratio of the volumes of your stellated icosahedron to your stellated octahedron. I'm impressed!

A week into this statistics unit, I felt the full gamut of teacher emotions. Sometimes I was pleased and encouraged. For example, they did well on graph interpretation.

When Erica and Jesse made a family composition graph for the students in the class to sign in on, I was worried it would discriminate against non-traditional families. But they left room for people with none to five parent types and from one to ten nonadults. They prepared a drawing that showed a small photo of a "typical" family with 2.3 adults and 3.2 children. Their newspaper caption read: Our household: About 5 folk.

But I was also anxious, especially about assessment. It's been up and down. Once the unit was set up, I thought the students might have wanted to modify the criteria, but they didn't. And even though the standards were on the wall, I still wasn't sure students understood how I was evaluating them. When I took class notes on the quality of their conversations while working in groups, I had to talk again about the categories I used. Then I discussed self-assessment. During this last week, I've been having conferences with groups to make sure they were on the right track with their survey instrument. After I finish this letter tonight, I have to write notes to the groups with my evaluation of their progress to date and give them hints for finishing up their projects by the end of next week.

Most of all, though, I was tired and discouraged. The group of African-American girls—Tammy, Shanika, Vicki, and Daniella—wanted to investigate racism in the school, but their work was sloppy and incomplete. They talked too much and didn't use their time wisely, but

I was worried they'd claim racism if I gave them low evaluations. And then, after I returned their reports one day, Daniella accused me of lumping them in a group and not paying enough attention to her individual work. She said she even explained how she got her answers! She wadded up the paper I gave back to her and threw it in the trash can.

I guess it was a good thing I wasn't trying portfolios this unit or I'd have to do something about that wad of paper, aye?

But today, Jana—today was a great day! Five days like this a year and I'd stay in the profession for another twenty years.

I told you the topics they brainstormed at the beginning of the unit. Well, their actual topics didn't cool down much. Tara's group investigated gang affiliations, Jimmy's team is looking at the tie between homelessness and tax structures, Lakshan and mates are comparing people's opinions about endangered species with their feelings about lost timber jobs. We've got one report on rape, and two on drugs.

It had taken all my management skill to have the listeners be quiet and polite to the first two presenting groups—I made a note to introduce response sheets next week. Then Tammy, Shanika, and Daniella gave the third report of the day.

Shanika began by shrieking, "Not me! I'm not about to do a report!" She walked to the back of the room.

I noticed colored note cards in Tammy's hand when she stood up. "Don't look at me," she shouted, "I'm not going to give a report!" Then Vicki and Daniella bounded up from their sheets and went to opposite corners of the room, until they had us surrounded.

Vicki, too, said, "You'll get no report from me."

The class and I were stunned. There was absolute silence as eyes went from me to Daniella. How would I handle this rebellion? Daniella was the only one who hadn't spoken.

"Daniella," I said, evenly, "what's the story here?"

"Exactly the right question!" she said. "The class needs to tell a story, a statistical story. The College and Jail Tale!"

Like a circus barker, she continued: "My friends and I have positioned ourselves at the four corners of the room. We are going to come around and place a question on your back. Do not look at that question! But get out of your seats, with a piece of paper for recording. Ask your friendly classmates—FIVE of them—to answer the question on your back. When you have five answers, take your seat, look at your question (it will be easier to do this if at that time you remove it from your back, buckaroos). And, finally, summarize the data. Take an average, if appropriate, or report a mode, if that makes more sense. After you've all done that, sit back and tell the story of College Jail Tales."

Eyes that had been riveted on Daniella now turned toward me for a reaction. Lamely, I nodded. I just hoped I'd get a card for my back. The cards had these neat questions about equity and prison and college. Here are some of the questions:

- *The drop-out rate from freshman year to a bachelor's degree four years later is 32% for all freshmen. What do you think it is for Hispanic students?*
- *You know a bunch of students drop out of school. If the current trend continues, what percent of Navajo children entering kindergarten next fall will fail to complete high school?*
- *Which country has the highest rate of incarceration for black men (that means, who puts the most in jail)—Japan, England, USA, or South Africa?*
- *How much do you think it will cost you to spend one year in college?*
- *How much do you think it costs the taxpayers to keep one person in jail for a year?*
- *There are 29 students in calculus over at Ruggers High School. How many of them are African-American?*
- *Four years ago, 135 black students started their freshman year at Ruggers. How many black seniors do you think there are now?*

After we answered the questions, they had us report our answers before they told us the real statistic. They had prepared overhead transparencies with the answers, some graph sketches, and extra information. Somehow they chose to get the answers in such a sequence that a powerful story indeed was told about how more resources are put into jailing young African-American men than in educating them. They used this as an introduction to report about the survey questions they used to see if racism was alive today. They asked people two things: their age and if they felt they had ever been discriminated against because of their race or ethnic group. They hope to show that people of all ages still feel that there is discrimination. They are still collecting data and don't know yet if their hypothesis will hold. Can you believe it, they even said these words: "We don't know if our hypothesis will hold."

There is nothing in my criteria for mathematical communication that can capture what those girls did. They were, as the kids say, "Way past Cool!" Mathematically, they showed an ability to formulate problems, organize information from different sources into a coherent whole, interpret and design graphs, make sense of scales, make sense of data using measures of central tendencies, and on and on. I am eager to see their final analysis and to be alert to ways I can assist them.

Have a great winter break! Let's get together at the NCTM Regional Conference at the end of January.

I can hardly wait until tomorrow.

Peace,

Shelly

Now that you have read the story, reflect on the assessment system Shelly has used. Each of the six steps toward the development of a new assessment model can be found in Shelly's tale. Furthermore, on judging her system with respect to the six Assessment Standards we find that it meets the criteria of the *Important Mathematics* Standard; is making progress toward *Enhancing Student Learning,* especially in providing written, oral, frequent, and thorough feedback to students; is approaching the standard for *Equity,* as she struggles to allow and honor student choices of personalized learning environments; meets the *Openness* Standard, since her criteria are public and mutually constructed with the class; is shaky on *Valid Inferences,* but working on it as she takes into account evidence from several sources; and is *Consistent,* since her system relates to both making instructional decisions and monitoring student progress. Shelly encounters the struggle most teachers are experiencing as they try new approaches to the teaching of mathematics to fit the reform vision. Her mathematics classroom is no longer as orderly and quiet as before. There are more surprises and frustrations because the job of teaching has changed. The five-step lesson no longer fits. But, her students are actively learning important mathematics; they see mathematics as important to their lives; they understand on what and how their performance and progress is assessed; and their continued progress is encouraged.

Finally, enactment of the vision NCTM has presented in its three Standards documents will look and feel different at different sites. By making her teaching of mathematics relevant to the particular students in her class, Shelly was able to tap the vibrancy of students as they pursue important mathematics within areas of interest to them. This combination will vary by mathematical topic, city, state, province, school, classroom, and individual students and teachers. Our students present us with a variety of interests, experiences, and skills with which we can enhance the learning possibilities of all of us. This is not just about mathematics but about the human condition. We apply at our peril traditional methods and narrow evaluations that ignore the gift of diversity to which our continent is heir. The efforts of NCTM to guide and encourage reform in the teaching and learning of mathematics can only be realized if the mathematics curriculum, instructional methods, and assessment systems are designed to implement the notion of mathematical power for all students.

Appendix A

Calculators in the Classroom

Calculators have for some time been the focus of considerable discussion among mathematics educators, parents, representatives of the workplace, and others. Of course, some extreme viewpoints have been represented along with the more frequent moderate opinions. Some have argued that the calculator should not be used in an elementary school classroom until the basic facts have been mastered. Others, citing research that shows the calculator does not pose a threat to skill mastery, suggest that there is no harm—in fact, a considerable amount of good—in introducing the calculator at any point in the curriculum.

The aggressiveness of this debate has subsided in recent years. Now, the most commonly accepted position is that, *when used appropriately,* the calculator can be *effective at all levels* of instruction, including the primary grades. The phrase "used appropriately" implies that the calculator should be used for more than simply checking answers to seatwork or homework papers. The calculator can be incorporated into instruction so that it serves as an aid to understanding concepts.

Consider this: How can we find the square root of a given number, and what does square root mean?

To develop an understanding of square root, do not use the square root key on the calculator. For example, let's locate an approximate square root value for 13. Since we understand what squaring a number means, let's use this concept as the starting point for exploring square root. What square numbers are "on each side" of 13? We know that $3 \times 3 = 9$ and $4 \times 4 = 16$: 13 is between 9 and 16. So the square root of 13 must be between 3 and 4. Now let's identify the number in the tenths place of the square root. The number 13 is closer to the number 16 than it is to 9. So we will select a number a little greater than 3.5. Try 3.6, and square it. Using the calculator, we find that $3.6 \times 3.6 = 12.96$. Now let's try $3.7 \times 3.7 = 13.69$. Since 12.96 is closer to 13 than 13.69, we should try a number a little greater than 3.6. Using the calculator to multiply 3.61×3.61, we find that the square is 13.0321. Continue this estimating process until the square root of 13 is estimated to the number of places needed. A student that *explores* square root in the fashion described here will have an intuitive base off of which to build. The chances are dramatically increased that this student will have a better understanding of the underlying concept.

The calculator can also be a feedback device, as illustrated in the addition example described here. Round the following numbers to the nearest hundred. After rounding each one, enter the result in the calculator, and press the [+] key. When you finish, the number in the display should match the following boxed number.

```
 6137
13490
 2856
 9720
26882
59100
```

In this example, the objective is to round numbers to the nearest hundred. The student, not the calculator, must satisfy this objective. That is, the calculator does not perform the task; it merely serves as a self-checking device. If the student does not get a result of 59100 at the end of this exercise, then an error must have occurred, and the student will be made aware of this.

Note, however, that the calculator does not provide information about where the error occurred. This is beneficial in this case; because the number of exercises is not large, the student who has not mastered the objective must now check each exercise, rather than simply go to the one "marked wrong."

Since the calculator has appeared on the market, it has enjoyed tremendous popularity. As the price of calculators continues to decline, many more children have access to them. Obviously, the calculator boom is a phenomenon that schools cannot afford to ignore. Calculators are not a passing fad. Education must accept this and provide for instruction in mathematics making full use of the potential of the calculator as a teaching tool.

The National Council of Teachers of Mathematics has prepared a position paper on the use of calculators in the mathematics classroom. The full text of that paper is reproduced here with the permission of NCTM.

*Calculators and the Education of Youth**

Calculators are widely used at home and in the workplace. Increased use of the calculators in school will ensure that students' experiences in mathematics will match the realities of everyday life, develop their reasoning skills, and promote the understanding and application of mathematics. The National Council of Teachers of Mathematics therefore recommends the integration of the calculator into the school mathematics program at all grade levels in classwork, homework, and evaluation.

Instruction with calculators will extend the understanding of mathematics and will allow all students access to rich, problem-solving experiences. This instruction must develop students' ability to know how and when to use a calculator. Skill in estimation and the ability to decide if the solution to a problem is reasonable are essential adjuncts to the effective use of the calculator.

Evaluation must be in alignment with normal, everyday use of calculators in the classroom. Testing instruments that measure students' understanding of mathematics and its applications must include calculator use. As the availability of calculators increases and the technology improves, testing instruments and evaluation practices must be continually upgraded to reflect these changes.

The National Council of Teachers of Mathematics recommends that all students use calculators to—

- *explore and experiment with mathematical ideas such as patterns, numerical and algebraic properties, and functions;*
- *develop and reinforce skills such as estimation, computation, graphing, and analyzing data;*
- *focus on problem-solving processes rather than the computations associated with problems;*
- *perform the tedious computations that often develop when working with real data in problem situations;*
- *gain access to mathematical ideas and experiences that go beyond those levels limited by traditional paper-and-pencil computation.*

The National Council of Teachers of Mathematics also recommends that every mathematics teacher at every level promote the use of calculators to enhance mathematics instruction by—

- *modeling the use of calculators in a variety of situations;*

*Reprinted with permission from *Calculators and the Education of Youth,* copyright 1991 by the National Council of Teachers of Mathematics.

- *using calculators in computation, problem solving, concept development, pattern recognition, data analysis, and graphing;*
- *incorporating the use of calculators in testing mathematical skills and concepts;*
- *keeping current with the state-of-the-art technology appropriate for the grade level being taught;*
- *exploring and developing new ways to use calculators to support instruction and assessment.*

The National Council of Teachers of Mathematics further recommends that—

- *school districts conduct staff development programs that enhance teachers' understanding of the use of appropriate state-of-the-art calculators in the classroom;*
- *teacher preparation institutions develop preservice and in-service programs that use a variety of calculators, including graphing calculators, at all levels of the curriculum;*
- *educators responsible for selecting curriculum materials make choices that reflect and support the use of calculators in the classroom;*
- *publishers, authors, and test and competition writers integrate the use of calculators at all levels of mathematics;*
- *mathematics educators inform students, parents, administrators, and school boards about the research that shows the advantages of including calculators as an everyday tool for the student of mathematics.*

Research and experience have clearly demonstrated the potential of calculators to enhance students' learning in mathematics. The cognitive gain in number sense, conceptual development, and visualization can empower and motivate students to engage in true mathematical problem solving at a level previously denied to all but the most talented. The calculator is an essential tool for all students of mathematics.

The effective use of calculators in the classroom depends largely on the skill, knowledge, and ingenuity of the classroom teacher. The calculator should be an integral part of the mathematics curriculum and not just an appendage for checking calculations already performed. The calculator is especially useful in *developing understanding* of place value, reversibility, relationships among numbers, operations, decimals, metric measure, prime factoring, composites, changing fractions to decimals, and in percentages, as well as for making mathematical estimates. Other uses become apparent as we develop a curriculum that encourages calculator use during instruction.

There are many different types of calculators available for classroom use. Unfortunately (or, perhaps, fortunately—when used for exploration and discovery) these various calculators do not all function in exactly the same manner. There are some important differences in available keys and the ways in which operations are handled that make it worthwhile for you to be familiar with the characteristics of the individual calculators being used by your students. Ideally, a classroom set of calculators will alleviate these concerns. For most elementary school use, the calculator used should be based on algebraic logic (see the exercises following this section). The calculator should be inexpensive, durable, and accessible to the children, and it should have multiple uses. The keyboard should be of reasonable size, preferably with spring-loaded keys that click when they are depressed (some sort of input auditory feedback is helpful for many children). The display should be bright, easily readable, and easily seen since several children may share the same calculator. There are two types of calculator displays: LED (light-emitting diode) or the more common LCD (liquid-crystal display). The LCD uses less energy and is easier to read in sunlight or from an angle. The most desirable power source will depend on the facilities available to the teacher. Solar-powered calculators are the most popular and are cheaper than many other models in the long run—in fact, it is a challenge today to find a calculator that is not solar-powered.

Children *must* learn correct procedures for using the calculator at the outset. Proper development of a good foundation will help to avoid confusion at later grade levels. (Proper classroom management of the calculators should also be established early.) Right from the beginning, help children develop appropriate techniques for using the calculator. Watch the display panel and assess the reasonableness of the values that appear on it. When batteries are weak or the calculator is broken (even solar-powered calculators use batteries as back-ups for memory), wrong answers can appear on the display panel. Practice operating the calculator with the opposite hand from the one you use to write. This will allow you to hold a pencil and record results calculations with one hand while using the calculator with the other. Begin each calculator example by pressing the **clear key** [C] twice. This will prevent extraneous numbers already entered from interfering with the results of the current operation.

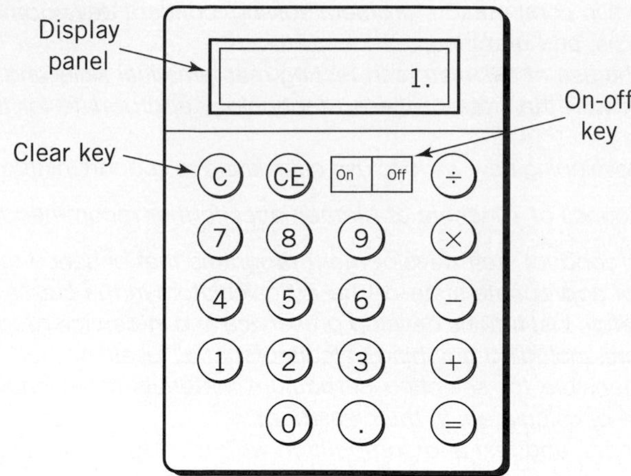

Encourage children to learn how to operate the calculator and understand when it would be beneficial and when it would not. The calculator will only do what it is told to do—students must learn to decide what kinds of situation require a calculator and how to use the calculator in those situations. Impress on the children that a calculator is only a supplemental tool. It is still important for the children to be able to solve "reasonable" mathematics problems and examples involving calculation without the benefit of a calculator (and to understand how to transfer their skill with these to using a calculator on the more "unreasonable" ones).

CALCULATOR ACTIVITIES FOR GRADES K-4

This text includes calculator activities in each of the relevant chapters for grades K-4. The following activities represent extensions that should be of interest to the reader. For further ideas, please consult the individual chapter instructional and assessment activities.

1. Have the children display a given number on the calculator screen:

   a) stated orally and simultaneously shown on a flash card
   b) shown only on a flash card
   c) stated orally only

2. Help the children set up the calculator so that it will count (by ones) to ten. Use [1] [+] [=] . . . .

3. Extend the preceding activity to numbers beyond ten.

4. Set up the calculator to count by twos; use this set-up: [0] [+] [2] [=] [=] . . . The children can use the "walk-on number line" and compare the numbers on the display screen with the number under the right (or left) foot. Compare this with walking up the stairs two at a time.

5. Set up the calculator to count by twos; start with the number 1.

6. Make the display read a given number, using *only* the [1] key and the operation keys (as many times as needed).

7. Using only the [1] and [2] keys, along with the operation keys, place a given number on the display screen using the least number of punches.

8. Count backward on the calculator, by pressing [1] [0] [−] [1] [=] [=] [=] . . . How will you handle the situation when the children press the equal key more than ten times?

9. Have students predict the final display to a key sequence such as $3 + 4 - 5 + 3 =$ or $4 \times 3 - 2 + 7 =$. Then ask students to predict the display for these key sequences prior to each key stroke.

10. Different calculators handle the display of remainders and/or decimals in different ways. Enter the key sequence "5 ÷ 3 =". Examine the display. Does it show 1.6666667? Why? Does it show 1.6666666? Why? Enter the key sequence "5 ÷ 3 × 3 =". Does the display show 4.9999999? Does it show 4.9999998? What *should* the answer be for "5 ÷ 3 × 3 ="? (*Note:* The TI Explorer can display the answer to "5 ÷ 3 =" as 1.6666667 or 1u 2/3 or 1 r 1.)

11. Calculators typically have one or more special function keys (e.g., a percent key, constant key, reciprocal key, exponent key etc.). Allow children opportunities to explore the use of these keys and the displays they yield. Some of these keys can even be used to explore patterns and relationships before the students have been exposed to the mathematical concepts the keys represent.

CALCULATOR ACTIVITIES FOR GRADES 5-8

This text includes calculator activities in each of the relevant chapters for grades 5-8. The following activities represent extensions that should be of interest to the reader. For further ideas, please consult the individual chapter instructional and assessment activities.

1. The phrase "order of operations" refers to the fact that a number expression involving operations and no parentheses should be evaluated by performing the multiplications and divisions first, from left to right, followed by performing the additions and subtractions. Some calculators, those with algebraic logic such as the TI Math Mate or Explorer, use the order of operations, others do not, such as the TI-108. Students can explore this characteristic on their calculator by entering $2 + 3 \times 5 =$. If the calculator uses algebraic logic then the display will show the correct answer of 17. If not, the calculator will display the incorrect answer of 30. Calculators having algebraic logic usually have parentheses keys in order to override this order. This allows the user to enter $(2 + 3) \times 5 =$ if the intention is to group the 2 and 3 before multiplying.

2. Children should be taught how to round numbers, since this is an important skill when working with calculators. The following examples are representative, but children will need many similar practice examples. Use the number line as a tool as children work through the following questions.

   a) Find the number 42 on the number line. What is the next smaller ten? What is the next greater ten? Which ten is closer to 42: 40 or 50? The number 42 would be rounded to 40.
   b) Use the same procedure with 27, 56, 63, and so on. Now try the number 45. Discuss with the children that, when a number ends in 5, the number is usually rounded up. Discuss other methods of dealing with numbers ending in 5.
   c) Using the number line and the same procedure, extend this idea to three-place numbers rounded to the nearest hundred, then round three-place numbers to the nearest ten. Use examples such as 127, 464, 812, 593, 453, 849, and 290.
   d) Round four-place numbers to the nearest thousand, hundred, and ten.

3. Round each addend to the nearest hundred and estimate a sum. Use the calculator to calculate the actual sum and compare the estimate with the actual total.

Example	Rounded Number
459	__________
208	__________
762	__________
+ 317	__________
Sum	__________

4. Round these numbers mentally to the nearest ten and estimate the sum. Check your estimated sum with the actual sum using the calculator.

$$\begin{array}{r} 47 \\ +34 \\ \hline \end{array} \quad \begin{array}{r} 52 \\ +48 \\ \hline \end{array} \quad \begin{array}{r} 83 \\ +26 \\ \hline \end{array} \quad \begin{array}{r} 78 \\ +41 \\ \hline \end{array}$$

5. Use the estimation techniques we have developed extended to the other operations. Check your estimated answers on the calculator.

6. State numbers; have the children enter the numbers into the calculator. Then write the numbers in words on the chalkboard, and have the children enter the numbers into their calculators.

7. Solve the following examples:

Add	Subtract
One hundred forty-three	Eight hundred sixty-three
Four hundred sixty-eight	Three hundred fifty-seven
One hundred seven	
Eight hundred twenty-nine	

8. Provide word problems for children to solve using their calculators. For example, if the escape velocity of a spacecraft going to the moon is 25,000 miles per hour, how fast is that per minute? Per second? Locate the distance to the moon, and calculate how long it would take for a spacecraft to go from the earth to the moon. (For the purposes of this exercise, assume that the spacecraft can follow a straight-line path.)
9. Using only the operation keys and digits 4, 5, and 6, place the number 23 on the display screen, using the least number of key punches.
10. Practice changing fractions to decimals by interpreting a fraction as division.
11. Study place value by multiplying and dividing by 10, 100, or 1000.
12. Factor numbers into prime number components.
13. Use the calculator to explore the concept of place value. Divide a given number by 10. Using 10 as a constant, divide many different examples. Children should generalize that every time the [=] key is pressed, the number is divided by 10 and this moves the decimal point one place to the right. Study many examples. (*Note:* this process does not work on all calculators.)
14. Gradually introduce the percent key to upper elementary and middle grade children. What is 38% of 128?

    Enter [C] [1] [2] [8] [×] [3] [8] [%]
15. We use 15,600 liters of water in our home each month. If 19% of the water is used in the bathroom, how many liters of water are used in the bathroom each day? (Use 30 days to equal one month.)
16. At the upper elementary and middle grade levels, children should learn how to use proportion. For example, John used 10.5 gallons of gas to drive 268 miles. How much gas will he need to drive 375 miles? The children can set up a proportion to solve the example:

$$\frac{268}{10.5} \times \frac{375}{x}$$

    Enter this in the calculator as follows:

    [C] [3] [7] [5] [×] [1] [0] [.] [5] [÷] [2] [6] [8] [=]
17. Children can use a calculator to compute the average of their mathematics grades. Discuss different ways of performing this computation.
18. Use the calculator to compute the batting averages of selected major league baseball players or other sporting percentage examples. Check these against reported results.
19. Use the calculator to prepare data for graphing. For example, find percentages to use in making circle graphs. Multiply the percent by 360° to find the number of degrees that each sector of the circle graph should have.
20. Using a constant or, if there is one, the constant key, to calculate the circumference of several circles.
21. Using a constant or, if there is one, the constant key, to find the area of several circles.
22. Use a sale advertisement from a newspaper to calculate the percent of savings for various sale items.

23. Have children study palindromic numbers; use the calculator to reverse the numbers and add them. Keep a record of how many times each number must be reversed and added before it again becomes a palindrome.

24. Explore the use of the memory keys available on most calculators. These keys are typically labeled MRC, M+, and M–. Common alternative labels are M, MEM, and STO. The MRC key is dual function—press it once and it *r*ecalls the number currently in the memory, press it twice and it *c*lears the memory. The M+ key and M– key add and subtract, respectively, from the number currently in the memory.

    Have students "open an automatic teller machine" in their calculator and deposit $20 in their account by pressing 20 M+. Suppose they buy 3 soft drinks for $.75 each and two hot dogs for $1.20 each. Have students enter 3 × .75 = M– and 2 × 1.2 M–. They should then check the money left in their account by pressing MRC once. The display should show 13.35. Then, suppose they get a birthday gift of $15. Have them enter 15 M+ and then press MRC. The display should now read 28.35. Continue using the memory function with similar transactions. Be careful of variations brought on through use of a calculator with nonalgebraic logic.

Appendix B

Computer Technology in the Classroom

The popularity of low-cost calculators and low-cost computers has raised serious questions concerning the teaching of mathematics. Obviously, technology has had a major impact outside the classroom. However, is the use of technology appropriate *inside* the classroom? Preparing children to function successfully in the real world is a primary goal of mathematics instruction. Since technology is an ever-growing part of the real world, school systems and teachers have an obligation to teach children how to use that technology to solve problems they face.

The responsibility for teaching children to understand and use computers rests almost entirely on the teachers and administrators in our school systems. Unfortunately, some elementary school teachers are unprepared to handle the planning and teaching of computer use and application to children. Some elementary school teachers have never touched a computer, let alone used the computer in their teaching. David Moursand, a well-known computer education expert, has stated that "We are asking computer-illiterate teachers to help students become computer literate at a functional level."

The growing placement of computers in classrooms is supported by school administrators, teachers, and parents. If we agree with the assumption that technology is a viable tool of mathematics instruction, then when should computers be introduced into the instructional program? Should technology be introduced in the primary grades, or should we wait until students have mastered basic mathematics concepts and skills? Should computers be an integral part of classroom instruction, or should they be reserved for special uses? The range of opinion concerning these and other related questions is indeed broad.

The National Council of Teachers of Mathematics has prepared a position paper on the role of computer technology in the mathematics classroom. The full text of that paper is reproduced here with the permission of NCTM.

The Use of Technology in the Learning and Teaching of Mathematics

Technology is changing the ways in which mathematics is used and is driving the creation of new fields of mathematical study. Consequently, the content of mathematics programs and the methods by which mathematics is taught and learning assessed are changing. The ability of teachers to use the tools of technology to develop, enhance, and expand students' understanding of mathematics is crucial. These tools include computers, appropriate calculators (scientific, programmable, etc.), videodisks, CD-Rom, telecommunications networks by which to access and share real-time data, and other emerging technologies. Exploration of the perspectives these tools provide on a wide variety of topics is required by teachers.

It is the position of the National Council of Teachers of Mathematics that the use of the tools of technology is integral to the learning and teaching of mathematics. Continual improvement is needed in mathematics curricula, instructional and assessment methods, access to hardware and software, and teacher education.

- *Although the nature of mathematics and societal needs are forces that drive the curriculum, the opportunities that technology presents must be reflected in the content of school mathematics. Curricular revisions allow for the de-emphasis of topics that are no longer important, the addition of topics that have acquired new importance, and the retention of topics that remain important. In the implementation of revised curricula, time and emphasis are to be allocated to the topics according to their importance in an age of increased access to technology. Instructional materials that capitalize on the power of technology must be given a high priority in their development and implementation. The thoughtful and creative use of technology can greatly improve both the quality of the curriculum and the quality of students' learning.*
- *Teachers should plan for students' use of technology in both learning and doing mathematics. A development of ideas is to be made with the transition from concrete experiences to abstract mathematical ideas, focusing on the exploration and discovery of new mathematical concepts and problem-solving processes. Students are to learn how to use technology as a tool for processing information, visualizing and solving problems, exploring and testing conjectures, accessing data, and verifying their solutions. Students' ability to recognize when and how to use technology effectively is dependent on their continued study of appropriate mathematics content. In a mathematics setting, technology must be an instructional tool that is integrated into daily teaching practices, including the assessment of what students know and are able to do. In a mathematics class, technology ought not be the object of instruction.*
- *Every student is to have access to a calculator appropriate to his or her level. Every classroom where mathematics is taught should have at least one computer for demonstrations, data acquisition, and other student use at all times. Every school mathematics program should provide additional computers and other types of technology for individual, small-group, and whole-class use. The involvement of teachers by school systems to develop a comprehensive plan for the ongoing acquisition, maintenance, and upgrading of computers and all other emerging technology for use at all grade levels is imperative. As new technology develops, school systems must be ready to adapt to the changes and constantly upgrade the hardware, software, and curriculum to ensure that the mathematics program remains relevant and current.*
- *All professional development programs for teachers of mathematics are to include opportunities for prospective and practicing teachers to learn mathematics in technology-rich environments and to study the use of current and emerging technologies. The preparation of teachers of mathematics requires the ability to design technology-integrated classroom and laboratory lessons that promote interaction among the students, technology, and the teacher. The selection, evaluation, and use of technology for a variety of activities such as simulation, the generation and analysis of data, problem-solving, graphical analysis, and geometric constructions depends on the teacher. Therefore, the availability of ongoing in-service programs is necessary to help teachers take full advantage of the unique power of technology as a tool for mathematics classrooms.*

*The National Council of Teachers of Mathematics recommends the appropriate use of technology to enhance mathematics programs at all levels. Keeping pace with the advances in technology is a necessity for the entire mathematics community, particularly teachers who are responsible for designing day-to-day instructional experiences for students.**

In 1981, only 18 percent of U.S. public schools had even a single computer for instructional uses. By 1995, 99 percent of U.S. schools had computers—a total of 5.8 million machines. The typical high school had one computer for every 6 students while middle schools had an average of one computer for every 12 students. The rapid growth in the number of computers in the schools has placed pressure on teachers to become knowledgeable about computers. Many teacher education programs require that all education majors have some structured experience with computers. Teachers must be afforded the time to become familiar with, and develop a degree of confidence with, computers and their use in the classroom before we can expect technology to be integrated with instruction.

*Reprinted with permission from *The Use of Technology in the Learning and Teaching of Mathematics,* copyright 1994, a position paper by the National Council of Teachers of Mathematics.

INSTRUCTIONAL SOFTWARE IN THE MATHEMATICS CLASSROOM

The focus of the debate over technology in the classroom has recently switched from the calculator to the computer. Many of the same arguments are presented although the opposition is considerably reduced. In fact, most schools are actively seeking ways to incorporate the computer into their curriculum in all subject areas. The remaining debate centers on the educational uses of the computer.

Teachers can begin using computers in the mathematics program by providing commercial software packages. A computer work area should become an important learning center in every elementary school classroom. Do not encourage games for their own sake. Use the classroom computer for educational purposes. Encourage children to become familiar with the immediate mode and to solve mathematics examples on the computer. Permit children the opportunity to complete mathematics assignments on the computer.

Develop a good filing system to allow easy access to programs needed for particular purposes. Individualizing mathematics will become easier as teachers learn how to change and create programs addressed to specific student needs. The computer can become a record-keeper for each child and free the teacher from the tedium of paperwork.

Various types of software programs have been developed and are available to teachers for classroom use. These include but are not limited to the following categories:

Drill and practice
Educational games
Simulations
Tutorial
Problem solving
Records management
Material generation

These uses are not mutually exclusive, but the majority of available computer programs focus mostly on one of the applications just listed. It is important for teachers to distinguish between these uses in order to judge the effectiveness and efficiency of a given program. For example, we might examine a program dealing with basic multiplication facts couched in an arcade-like setting and easily categorize this as an educational game. Actually, such a program would be better classified as drill and practice, since the concepts involved are to be memorized and subject to immediate recall.

Similarly, a program that involves estimating various lengths and angles (couched in a golf or artillery game) could be classified as drill and practice, although it should really be considered an educational game. In this instance, the game format is used not to drill knowledge-level material, but rather to assist the students in developing estimation skills not subject to immediate recall.

Commercial software that emphasizes the tutorial mode can be effectively used to provide instruction. The purpose of such software is to teach concepts, although such packages often include a drill and practice component to check on progress. Tutorial software is frequently used to introduce (or reintroduce) a topic. A student who is new to a school, or one who has been absent for several days, might make good use of a tutorial package to "catch up."

Simulation and problem-solving software packages may be the most valuable of all. These packages are designed to establish an environment for generating and testing hypotheses. Frequently, the setting is one that is not easily attained in the classroom without the use of a microcomputer. As an example, consider a software package that allows you to travel from one planet to the next collecting data about atmospheres, gravity, surface temperatures, and so on. The student is then free to make conjectures about life on those planets.

Teachers must become effective software evaluators. Software evaluation techniques and forms are available in the literature. Research the literature and locate available criteria for evaluating software. First isolate the purpose of the program. Then compare the purpose with the features of the program with respect to grade level, validity of content, correlation with curriculum, and instructional design features.

Drill and practice is too often the major use of computers in the classroom. The computer is sometimes used as a rather expensive electronic worksheet for children. However, more computer-assisted instruction (CAI) programs are becoming available for classroom use. CAI is an instructional situation between learner and computer that presents material in an interactive mode with systematic evaluation as an integral part of the program.

Teachers are also using computers for computer-managed instruction (CMI). CMI provides the classroom teacher with computer technology to keep records, store test information, and provide prescriptive information to meet individual student needs.

Each teacher needs to experiment with the computer and its use in the mathematics program in order to develop more effective and efficient techniques. The computer has great educational potential, but we must first learn to use the unique characteristics of the computer to increase the efficiency of mathematics teaching.

COMPUTER APPLICATION SOFTWARE IN THE MATHEMATICS CLASSROOM

Four of the most practical applications of the computer are to be found in programs that make use of word processing, databases, spreadsheets, and graphics. A *word processor,* through its editing features, helps students develop confidence in communication by providing a forum for recording ideas removed from the restrictions of linear and rigid thinking. A *database,* through its searching capabilities, gives students access to patterns and trends in large amounts of data. A *spreadsheet,* through its formula features, allows students to hypothesize and examine the effect of changing one variable in a multi-variable situation. A *graphics* program, through its drawing capabilities, gives students a vehicle for creative modeling of abstract concepts and geometric principles. All four programs assist students in formulating real-life situations, exploring problem-solving strategies, identifying and verifying hypotheses, and valuing sound decision-making processes.

The variety of application programs available and frequently used by teachers have individual distinctions that make a generic discussion of their operation difficult, at best. Instead of focusing on these idiosyncrasies, let's consider sample activities that make use of the power of these applications as tools for problem-solving and patterning.

Word processing programs offer more than the capabilities of a typewriter. Their flexible formatting allow you to move letters, words, phrases, sentences, and paragraphs around easily. Spell-checkers, find-and-replace, and automatic outliners make this a valuable tool for both students and teachers. Teachers, especially, can make excellent use of the "cut-and-paste" feature of a word processor in preparing lesson plans. The ability to save files for future modification and use is also a real "plus." Many word processing programs can incorporate enhancement options such as graphics and different fonts and styles.

Consider the following example of an activity that engages students in the use of a word processor. Have students create a story problem—not the common form of two sentences and a question, but a "real" story problem. Using a word processor, the students can refine and extend their creations. They can seek advice from other students to improve the story and motivate the need to help the characters solve their problem. Changes and different versions can easily be saved for later discussion. Printouts can form an informative bulletin board.

Database application programs have the advantage of storing a considerable amount of information in a form that makes searching, sorting, and retrieving data an easy process. Teachers can, of course, use a database to store relevant information about their students such as home address and phone numbers, important special notes about health or diet, or records of assignment completion. Students can make use of the sorting power to explore categories and attributes. For example, create a database file for each student that includes the number of pets owned, the type of pets, the names of pets, the color of pets, who feeds the pets, etc. Students can then search the files of all classmates to discover the most common pet type, pet name, etc. This information can then be translated to a graph.

A spreadsheet is often thought of as an electronic accounting pad. Indeed, their greatest power may well lie in calculation. While originally designed for business use as a standard ledger, they have become much more flexible and, consequently, more widely used in school programs. A teacher can, of course, incorporate the more traditional aspects of a spreadsheet by using it to record and average student grades, with, for example, weighted scores and/or percentage grades. One of the most valuable components to a spreadsheet program is the ability to change numbers or formulas quickly and easily to answer the question of "What if?" An interesting activity that demonstrates this feature is to set up a restaurant menu with columns for item names, how many of the item ordered, price per item, and the total price on the spreadsheet. Students can then change the number of items ordered and see the effect of different permutations on the bill.

A graphing or drawing program is often part of the word processing program, the database, and/or the spreadsheet. For example, many spreadsheet programs have automatic transfer of data to a graph with the push of a button. Stand-alone graphics programs can be used to create banners and signs for bulletin boards, greeting cards for special occasions, or enhancements to other documents. Students can use graphics programs to explore perspective, the two-dimensional/three-dimensional connection, and geometric properties of various shapes. Students can be asked to create a series of graphic images that illustrate a repetitive pattern such as images of a house, tree, tree, house, tree, ... Other students can be asked to determine the pattern and to continue it.

A SPECIAL APPLICATION PROGRAM FOR TEACHERS—*EXAM IN A CAN**

As teachers, you have the incredible task of managing your students' progress. But it doesn't end there. You must determine why students haven't mastered specific outcomes, the nature of their errors, re-teach specific concepts, organize students into similar learning groups, and create custom worksheets for each student. The *Exam in a Can* math (and science) assessment software packages represent the kinds of assistance teachers need and deserve by focusing on important objectives through easy-to-use classroom assessment and record-keeping systems. A fully-operational version of this outstanding applications software tool has been bundled with this edition of *Today's Mathematics.*

Exam in a Can uses algorithms to generate fresh, objective-specific test, quiz, or worksheet items with virtually unlimited variations. The program saves time by enabling teachers to quickly and easily print unlimited versions of individualized questions. *Exam in a Can* gives you unparalleled capabilities: textbook-quality illustrations, three dimensional graphs, and appropriate symbolic notation. Charts and graphs keyed to algorithms can vary to match the values used in individual test questions.

Exam in a Can—Today's Mathematics Version: It's as easy as . . .

1. CREATE a test or worksheet from the pre-written database of objectives. Selecting an objective more than once will generate different questions for that objective.
2. CHOOSE the exact iteration of the problems in either multiple choice or free response and preview them on the screen.
3. PRINT your test or worksheet and answer key complete with graphics, charts, diagrams, and perfect mathematics notation.

Exam in a Can is custom assessment software which can be aligned to your instructional goals and objectives. The strength of the software lies in its unique system of custom-designed algorithms which have revolutionized classroom testing. An algorithm works like a "test engine" to generate thousands of fresh questions.

In addition to printing practice tests, makeup tests, and worksheets, *Exam in a Can* provides a powerful authoring feature for users to add or edit questions. The *Exam in a Can* Editor gives content control to the teacher. With each *Exam in a Can* generated test or worksheet, *the teacher decides on the content*—the outcomes, the format (enhanced multiple choice, free response and conceptual), and the level of difficulty. *Exam in a Can* can be designed to accompany specific textbooks, or to meet school, district, or state testing requirements. The program's algorithm-based system also easily accommodates requirements for balanced representation of minorities and gender within test items. The *Exam in a Can* library contains thousands of model problems which can be adapted to your specific needs. *Exam in a Can* even facilitates the full scope of portfolio assessment.

Exam in a Can is also a natural for cooperative learning groups. Give each group member equivalent, but not identical, worksheets so that they may help each other with the method of problem-solving without sharing answers. If sample alternate forms of the test are made available, the students can use them for diagnosing their performance weaknesses and strengths in preparation for retesting. In addition, make-up exams are easy to give, since an equivalent test can be printed with just a few keystrokes. You can also improve test scores by creating targeted practice tests and worksheets.

**Exam in a Can* is available in all formats for IBM, Macintosh, and Apple II and is fully networkable. Further information can be obtained by writing to ips Publishing, Inc., 12606 NE 95th Street, Vancouver, Washington, 98682, or calling 800-933-8378. Visit their website at http://www.primenet.com/~examncan1.

Algorithm-based testing has the added benefit of effectively enhancing exam security by allowing a teacher to distribute multiple versions of a test to the class. Multiple foils on *Exam in a Can* questions are linked to common errors and scrambled to further discourage "creative guessing."

Exam in a Can algorithms are carefully developed to produce useful test items and practice worksheets. These items are crafted to reflect the NCTM Standards and to work with the most popular textbooks and state mandated standards. The *Today's Mathematics* version of *Exam in a Can* presents problems and exercises dealing with number theory, decimals, fractions, integers, ratio, percent, proportion, measurement, perimeter, area, volume, geometry, patterns and functions, equations and inequalities, graphing, and probability and statistics.

The following is a list of specific objectives found in the *Today's Mathematics* version. Each objective includes several multiple choice and free response problem types. Each of these uses an algorithm to produce many variations of the basic problem type. This allows you to generate worksheets of similar problems or tests in which each student receives a different version of the problem. You will never run out of fresh test questions.

Topic 1: Number Theory (36)

1. Find the factors of a number.
2. Find the multiples of a number.
3. Identify a number as prime or composite.
4. Write the prime factorization of a composite number.
5. Find the greatest common factor of two numbers.
6. Find the greatest common factor of three numbers.
7. Find the least common multiple of two numbers.
8. Find the least common multiple of three numbers.
9. Write fractions as decimals.
10. Write mixed numbers as decimals.
11. Write decimals as fractions.
12. Write decimals as mixed numbers.
13. Express mixed numbers as improper fractions.
14. Express improper fractions as mixed numbers.
15. Use divisibility rules.
16. Use the distributive property.
17. Express the area of a rectangle using the distributive property.
18. Write a repeated multiplication as a power.

Topic 2: Introduction to Decimals: Add and Subtract (34)

1. Explore decimals with models.
2. Identify place value in a decimal number.
3. Write decimals in words.
4. Write decimals in standard form.
5. Compare and order decimals.
6. Round decimals.
7. Estimate sums and differences of decimals.
8. Add a whole number to a decimal.
9. Add two decimals.
10. Subtract two decimals.
11. Subtract three decimals.
12. Solve problems by adding decimals.
13. Solve problems by subtracting decimals.
14. Add and subtract decimals in bank accounts.
15. Write numbers less than 1 in scientific notation.
16. Write numbers greater than 1 in scientific notation.
17. Convert a fraction to a repeating decimal.

Topic 3: Decimals: Multiply and Divide (22)

1. Estimate decimal quotients.
2. Estimate decimal products.
3. Multiply decimals.
4. Multiply a decimal by a power of ten.
5. Multiply a decimal by a whole number.
6. Divide a whole number by a decimal.
7. Divide two decimals.
8. Solve problems using multiplication of decimals.
9. Solve data base problems using multiplication of decimals.
10. Solve word problems using a division of decimals.
11. Use order of operations to simplify a decimal expression.

Topic 4: Introduction to Fractions: Add and Subtract (36)

1. Model fractions.
2. Compare and order fractions.
3. Estimate fractions.
4. Simplify fractions.
5. Find equivalent fractions.
6. Find the reciprocal of a number.
7. Classify a fraction as proper or improper.
8. Add fractions with like denominators.
9. Add fractions with unlike denominators.
10. Add mixed numbers with like denominators.
11. Add fractions and mixed numbers.
12. Subtract fractions with like denominators.
13. Subtract fractions with unlike denominators.
14. Subtract mixed numbers with unlike denominators.
15. Subtract mixed numbers, whole numbers, and fractions.
16. Subtract mixed numbers from whole numbers.
17. Solve problems by adding fractions.
18. Solve problems by subtracting fractions.

Topic 5: Fractions: Multiply and Divide (22)

1. Estimate fraction products.
2. Multiply fractions.
3. Multiply mixed numbers.
4. Estimate fraction quotients.
5. Divide fractions.
6. Divide mixed numbers.

7. Solve problems by multiplying fractions.
8. Solve problems by multiplying mixed numbers.
9. Solve problems by dividing fractions.
10. Solve problems by dividing mixed numbers.
11. Solve problems using combined fraction operations.

Topic 6: Integers (28)

1. Graph integers on the number line.
2. Compare and order integers.
3. Represent integers.
4. Add integers using models.
5. Add two integers.
6. Add three integers.
7. Subtract positive integers.
8. Subtract integers.
9. Multiply two integers.
10. Multiply three integers.
11. Divide integers.
12. Find the absolute value of an integer.
13. Find the opposite of an integer.
14. Raise integers to powers.

Topic 7: Ratio, Percent, Proportion (38)

1. Express ratios and rates as fractions.
2. Determine if a pair of ratios forms a proportion.
3. Solve proportions.
4. Solve problems using proportions.
5. Express percents as fractions.
6. Express decimals as percents.
7. Model percents.
8. Find equivalent ratios.
9. Find unit rates.
10. Estimate percent of a number.
11. Find the percent of a number.
12. Find what percent one number is of another.
13. Find a number when a percent is known.
14. Find actual length from a scale drawing.
15. Solve problems involving similar triangles.
16. Find percent increase.
17. Find percent decrease.
18. Solve problems involving discounts.
19. Solve problems involving simple interest.

Topic 8: Measurement (24)

1. Estimate length.
2. Change mixed units of length.
3. Perform arithmetic operations on units of measurement.
4. Solve problems involving units of measurement.
5. Change units of length.
6. Change units of weight.
7. Change units of capacity.
8. Work time passage problems.
9. Convert metric units of length.
10. Convert metric units of weight.
11. Convert metric units of capacity.
12. Convert metric units of area.

Topic 9: Perimeter, Area, Volume (32)

1. Estimate area.
2. Find the perimeter of a rectangle.
3. Find the area of a rectangle.
4. Find the area of a parallelogram.
5. Find the circumference of a circle.
6. Find the area of a circle.
7. Find the area of a triangle.
8. Find the area of a trapezoid.
9. Find the surface area of a rectangular prism.
10. Find the surface area of a cylinder.
11. Find the surface area of a triangular prism.
12. Find the volume of a rectangular prism.
13. Find the volume of a cylinder.
14. Find the volume of a triangular prism.
15. Find the volume of a cone.
16. Find the volume of a pyramid.

Topic 10: Geometry (20)

1. Classify angles.
2. Classify triangles by sides.
3. Classify triangles by angles.
4. Find the missing angle in a triangle.
5. Classify quadrilaterals.
6. Identify polygons.
7. Identify and work with congruent triangles.
8. Recognize and identify corresponding parts of similar triangles.
9. Identify three-dimensional figures.
10. Identify supplementary and complimentary angles.

Topic 11: Patterns and Functions (18)

1. Find the given term in a visual number pattern.
2. Write the first few terms of a described number pattern.
3. Solve investment problems using patterns.
4. Write a number pattern in words.
5. Identify and use function rules.
6. Complete a function table.
7. Evaluate an expression for a given value.
8. Write a word phrase given a variable expression.
9. Write a variable expression given a word phrase.

Topic 12: Equations and Inequalities (26)

1. Write simple algebraic expressions from word phrases.
2. Determine if a number is a solution of an equation.
3. Solve equations involving addition and subtraction.
4. Solve equations involving multiplication and division.
5. Solve two-step equations.
6. Combine like terms to solve equations.
7. Solve equations with variables on both sides.
8. Solve systems of equations in two variables.
9. Solve number problems using linear equations.
10. Solve age problems using linear equations.
11. Graph inequalities on a number line.
12. Solve one-step inequalities.
13. Solve two-step inequalities.

Topic 13: Graphing (24)

1. Plot an ordered pair on the coordinate plane.
2. Identify the coordinates of a point.
3. Identify new coordinates after translation.
4. Graph translations.
5. Identify new coordinates after reflection.
6. Graph reflections.
7. identify new coordinates after rotation.
8. Graph linear equations.
9. Graph linear inequalities.
10. Find the slope of a line passing through two given points.
11. Find x- and y-intercepts.
12. Solve systems of equations by graphing.

Topic 14: Probability and Statistics (40)

1. Use a tree diagram or the counting principle to count outcomes.
2. Determine number of permutations.
3. Determine number of combinations.
4. Find probability of independent and dependent events.
5. Find probability of a simple event.
6. Determine the number of arrangements of a group of items.
7. Find the odds of an event.
8. Find the probability of the complement of an event.
9. Find mean.
10. Find median.
11. Find mode.
12. Find the range of a set of data.
13. Use circle graphs.
14. Use bar graphs.
15. Use stem-and-leaf plots.
16. Use double line graphs.
17. Use frequency tables.
18. Use line plots.
19. Use histograms.
20. Use a scatter plot to determine the type of correlation.

If you wish to see samples of problems to create a test, you can easily print a test for each topic necessary. Then, keep printed topic tests on hand as a reference when creating tests in the future. To print all items for a given topic, follow the machine-specific directions below.

Printing All Items for a Topic—DOS Version

Before you print tests for the first time, you must tell *Exam in a Can* what type of printer is connected to your computer. Choose Printer . . . from the Options menu and select the printer type that best describes your printer.

It is easier to create topic tests if you first collapse the entire Library list, then expand the desired book to show all its topics. Click the icon next to the word Library at the top of the Library list, then click the icon to expand the Library, and click the icon next to the desired book to expand the book.

1. Press CTRLN to start a new test.
2. Click the name of the desired topic in the Library window. this selects the topic to be printed.
3. Press the + (plus) key. This adds all items in the selected topic to the Test list.
4. Press CTRLP. This opens the Print dialog box.
5. If you have not selected a printer, click the Printer button to tell *Exam in a Can* which type of printer is connected to your computer.
6. Click the Print button in the Print dialog box.

Printing All Items for a Topic—Macintosh Version

Before printing a test, make sure you are connected to a printer and it is selected in the Chooser desk accessory.

Double click the *Exam in a Can* icon and choose Open Library . . . from the Library menu. Choose the library which contains the topic you want to print.

1. Press ⌘ N to start a new test.
2. Select the topic to print by clicking the name of the desired topic in the Library window.
3. Click the << Add << button. This adds all items in the selected topic to the Test list.
4. Press ⌘ P. This opens the Print dialog box.
5. Click the Print button to print the test.

The Editor, the special word processor part of the *Exam in a Can* package, is an authoring tool complete with appropriate mathematical symbols that allows you to develop, store, and categorize customized test items. A special import function lets you load your favorite items into the item bank. Using the Editor, you can set your own teacher codes and level of difficulty on both existing and user-created test questions. You can easily create open-ended or multiple choice problems by editing existing items or adding new items to the *Exam in a Can* objective library. Write them once and save them in the system to be used year after year. The *Exam in a Can* Editor also gives you the added flexibility to create and phrase special questions to meet the challenges of the NCTM and regional mathematics standards. Here is your opportunity to include special items that measure concepts not adequately dealt with in other test sources.

Technology that helps teachers is part of the solution to doing better in the classroom. *Exam in a Can* is technology that makes dramatic sense. In short, *Exam in a Can* uses technology to do a critical part of a teachers' job in a better way . . . it saves teachers time and helps drive up test scores. Testing made easy, fast, and effective . . . so you can do a better job of what you do best: teach!

MULTIMEDIA IN THE MATHEMATICS CLASSROOM

Multimedia refers to the combination of visual and sonic information controlled by the computer. It can incorporate text, graphics, animation, photography, video, music, and sound. Both the potential of the medium and the applications are diverse. The power of multimedia is the visual image which goes beyond spoken or written words. One embodiment of multimedia is called *hypertext* or, sometimes, *hypermedia.* (Originally, hypertext was used to refer to text links while hypermedia suggested links to more visual forms of information.)

Historically, the most common organization for the preservation and presentation of information has been a linear mode. For example, books are typically read from cover to cover and TV programs are normally viewed from beginning to end. Information can be cross-referenced in a book, but the general layout is still linear and, therefore, confining. Hypertext provides an escape from linear presentation of information. Electronic links allow the user to quickly connect to other points of information by clicking on words or buttons, and provide a means of making information interactive. One reason compact disc players have, for the most part, replaced vinyl record albums and tape cassettes is this capability of immediately "jumping" to preferred sections of the music.

CD-ROM disks, similar to music CDs, store vast amounts of information in digital form which can be readily accessed by computer. A single CD-ROM holds about 600 megabytes of data (equivalent to more than 400 high-density floppy disks). Reference CD-ROM titles such as Grolier's *Multimedia Encyclopedia* or MicroSoft's *Encarta* offer photographs and video clips in addition to text information. The *3-D Atlas* CD-ROM provides outstanding visuals and vast amounts of statistical data on ecology, population, and economics, as well as many other categories. Education Development Center's *MathFINDER* offers a multitude of sample lessons taken from 30 curriculum programs indexed to the NCTM curriculum and evaluation standards. Any of these resources can be effectively used by both students and teachers as research materials in problem-solving and project-based inquiries or investigations.

A multimedia learning environment requires a teacher who is comfortable with technology and who is able to integrate that technology into the curriculum. Hypermedia tools can be used by teachers to create classroom applications, but they can also be used as student tools. Students involved in designing their own hypermedia projects or in using hypermedia programs designed by peers become actively involved in learning at many levels. A great deal of planning goes into organizing and linking information in meaningful ways. One of the key elements in asking students to develop hypermedia projects is to engage them in peer collaboration during the planning stages of the project.

HyperCard was one of the first programs for creating presentations, interactive stories, non-linear databases, and multimedia. It is basically a software construction kit designed for nonprofessional programmers. A HyperCard document, called a *stack,* is made up of a collection of *cards.* Each card contains a background, and "layers" of information can be added, including graphics, animation, and sound. *Buttons* are objects that allow user input. For example, clicking on a button may produce a sound, cause text to appear, or move the user to another card.

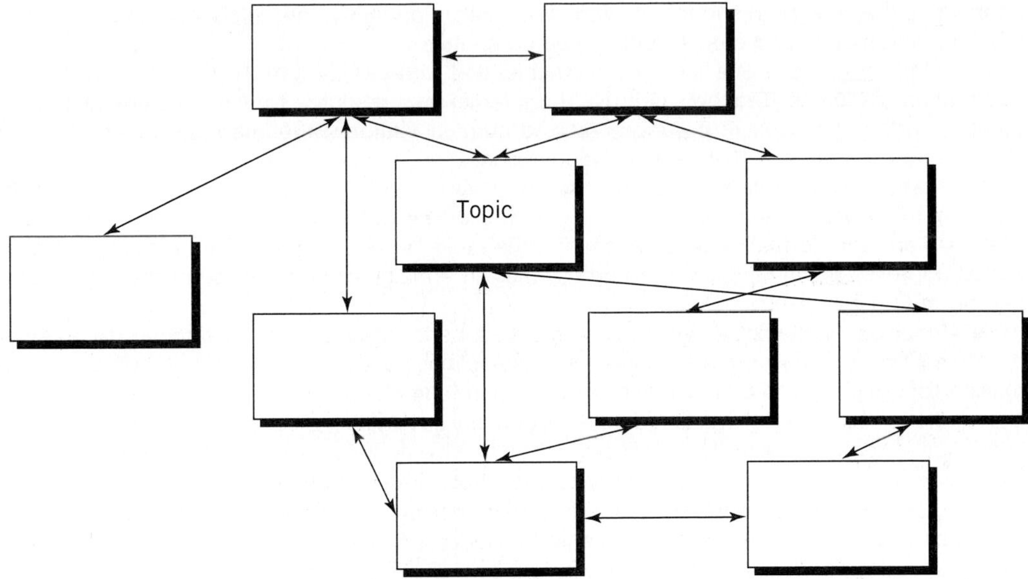

HyperStudio, another multimedia creation tool, allows for creation of stacks while providing a great deal of on-screen help. Pop-up windows guide the user through the steps of creating buttons and linking them to actions, animations, video, sound, or other cards.

In addition to curriculum-based topics, hypermedia tools can be used to develop electronic portfolios. This assessment strategy allows for much more information than the paper-based format. Student success can be documented with pictures, sound, video, and work samples. Ideally, the electronic portfolio should include student input when selections are made.

Commonly used hypermedia software:

HyperStudio (Macintosh or IBM)
Roger Wagner Publishing
1050 Pioneer Way, Suite P
El Cajon, CA 92020
800-497-3778

HyperCard (Macintosh)
Apple Computer Co.
20525 Mariani Ave.
Cupertino, CA 95014
800-776-2333

Digital Chisel (Macintosh)
Pierian Spring Software
5200 SW Macadam Ave., Suite 250
Portland, OR 97201
503-222-2044

Linkway Live (MS-DOS)
IBM, EduQuest
1000 NW 51st St.
Boca Raton, FL 33429-1234
408-372-8100

Educational software catalogs and computer stores offer several other titles.

TELECOMMUNICATIONS IN THE MATHEMATICS CLASSROOM

Imagine a giant web covering the globe, connecting thousands of networks of computers and allowing millions of users to access and share information! The *Internet* brings people and information together in a digital world unbound by time and space. Commonly referred to as the "network of networks," the Internet is comprised of thousands of computer networks interconnected around the globe, including many sites located at educational institutions. It began in the 1960s when the United States Department of Defense directed the Advanced Research Projects Agency (ARPA) to design a means of preserving communication in the event of a nuclear attack. If all communications were issued from a centralized location it could be destroyed, so a decentralized network of interconnected computers was designed. Researchers in various universities and laboratories found they could make use of the online communications as a means of sharing information and research findings. Gradually colleges, universities, and organizations began connecting their computers to the network, and most importantly, they allowed others to access research information and data stored in their computers.

Reasons for going online include communication with people (one-to-one or groups), and information resources. Teachers can use the Internet as a resource for lesson plans and information, and as a means of collaboration and communication. Students also benefit through learning how to gather and share information online.

Electronic mail (e-mail) is one of the most popular uses of the Internet. Communicating with a person in another country is as easy as communicating with a person in the same building—often easier! Using e-mail requires access to the Internet, an e-mail software program, and an e-mail address for the recipient of the message. An e-mail message can be addressed to one person or to a group of people.

An e-mail account also allows the user to subscribe to *listservs,* which are group discussions or interest groups. Classroom-to-classroom connections can be formed through subscribing to mailing lists designed to connect with people around the globe. International E-Mail Classroom Connections (ieec-request@stolaf.edu) is one of many such lists. To subscribe to an e-mail list, a subscription request is sent to the listserv administrative address, usually just, "subscribe LISTSERV NAME," with a similar message to unsubscribe. For example, to subscribe to the NCTM Listserv, send e-mail to: majordomo@forum.swarthmore.edu. In the body of your message type: subscribe nctm-l (*Note:* That last character is a lower case L, not the digit 1). Your e-mail address will be added to the NCTM Listserv and information will come to your e-mail account.

Collaboration ideas can be posted through special interest groups or *forums* such as the Teacher Information Network (TIN), a forum on the America Online commercial network. A project idea typically has a "Call for Collaboration" subject heading and a brief description. Existing online projects can be found in many locations through education forums.

As a research tool, the Internet offers databases of information in the form of encyclopedias, magazines, and museums. Unlike traditional materials in text form, digital information on the Internet can be updated at any time. In addition, many electronic references offer sound and video clips as well as text information.

The *World Wide Web,* commonly known as WWW, is a hypertext-based means of accessing and publishing information on the Internet. Web documents, referred to as *web pages,* can combine text, graphics, sound, and video, and often contain links to related resources. Links can be words in color text, underlined words, or icons (miniature pictures). Because the Web is composed of digital information, some parts of it are constantly evolving and changing.

Netscape, Lynx, and Mosaic are common *Web browsers,* software which allows you interactive access to Web pages. Through Netscape, for example, a user can point and click on links to move through information, and to explore. Clicking on Net Directory brings the user to a database listing of categories.

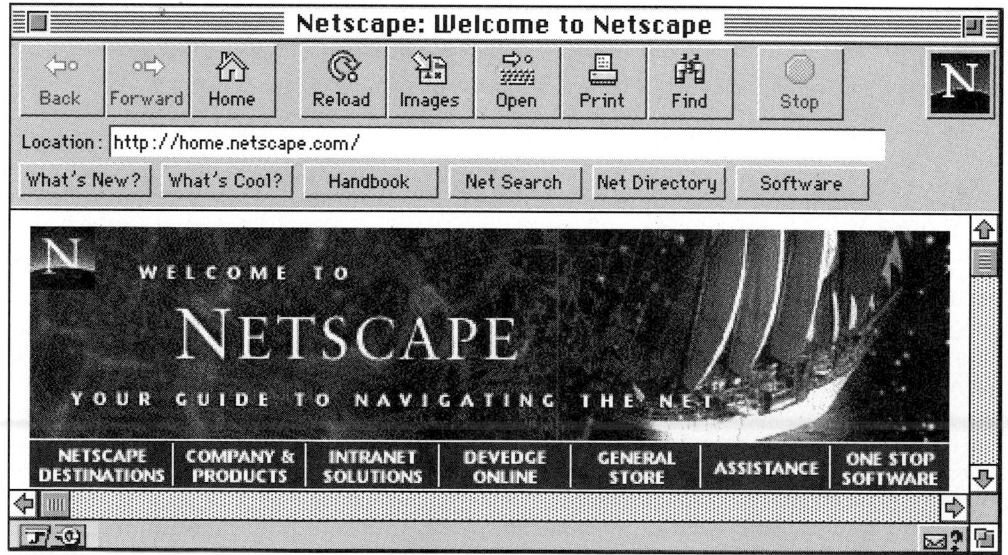

To access a particular Web page, the address or location of the page can be entered. A URL, "uniform resource locator" is the form of the address. For example, http://www.gsfc.nasa.gov/

nasa_online_education.html is the URL for NASA Online Educational Resources, and entering that URL brings their *home page* into view.

An invaluable resource for teachers, *AskERIC,* can be found by clicking on the following choices: Net Directory, Education, Databases, and AskERIC (Virtual Library). Key areas include ERIC's Lesson Plans, AskERIC's Collections, Search ERIC's Database, and AskERIC Toolbox. AskERIC can also be accessed by using the URL (http://ericir.syr.edu/). Another online document of interest to mathematics educators is the NCTM Standards. This can be located by selecting the following: Net Directory, Education, Mathematics and Science Education, Eisenhower National Clearinghouse, Online Documents.

Other valuable WWW sites include:

EdWeb (Online tutorial on education technology)
http://www.fws.gov/

Explorer Math & Science Education Initiative
http://unite.ukans.edu/

Geometry Center
http://www.geom.umn.edu

Geometry Forum
http://forum.swarthmore.edu/

Math and Science Gateway (Cornell Theory Center)
http://www.tc.cornell.edu/edu/mathscigateway/

Mathematics History Archive
http://www-groups.dcs.st-and.ac.uk:80/~history/

Mathematics Problems Internet Center
http://www.mathpro.com/math/mathCenter.html

Mathematics Virtual Library
http://euclid.math.fsu.edu/science/math.html

SAMI: Science and Math Initiatives
http://www.c3.lanl.gov/~jspeck/SAMI-home.html

Scholastic Central (Scholastic Network)
http://www.scholastic.com/

Science and Math Education Resources
http://www-hpcc.astro.washington.edu/scied/science.html

Technical Education Research Center (TERC: math./science ed.)
http://hub.terc.edu

U.S. Department of Education Online Library
http://www.ed.gov/

WebEd K-12 Curriculum Links
http://badger.state.wi.us/agencies/dpi/www/webed.html

Web 66 K-12 WWW
http://web66.coled.umn.edu/

Access to online databases provides entire libraries of information at the user's fingertips. Unfortunately, information does not equal knowledge. Finding ways to organize, use, and share information is vital. For example, students can use statistical data such as that found in the CIA *World Fact Book* (http://www.odci.gov/cia) to create graphs, make comparisons, and predict trends. Challenge problems and other related bits of mathematics history can be found in various locations such as the SAMI project (http://www.c3.lanl.gov/~jspeck/SAMI-home.html).

Several versions of grocery list comparisons, such as the Global Grocery List, have provided opportunities for collaboration and data analysis in a meaningful way for students. The "Let's Compare Prices" activity (http://gsn.org/gsn/roger.home.html) is repeated on a regular basis. A portion of this activity is shown below.

LET'S COMPARE PRICES

Roger Williams told us the amount he paid for some items when he shopped in Japan. In 1995, Roger sent these prices of things from Japan.

1.5 liter bottle of coke is $3.60
1 gallon diesel is $3.30
2 liters of oil for truck is $16.00
hotel room in Tokyo is $250 per night
Big Mac with medium coke and small fries is $7.00
Big Mac Value Meal only cost $9.00

Classes from around the world can investigate prices for similar products in their locale and report these through the Internet to other participants. Results can then be shared electronically. Classes can compare their information to others and, in the process, discover the variations in currency and economic influences.

Internet access is necessary to "surf the net." Colleges and universities frequently provide Internet accounts for students. Commercial online providers offer a wide range of services, some with limited access based on evaluation of material considered educationally sound, while others offer full Internet access. A few commercial providers of interest to educators are provided here. Some offer free hours to explore their services.

America Online, Inc.
8619 Westwood Center Drive
Vienna, VA 22812
800-827-6364, ext. 5670

Classroom Prodigy
445 Hamilton Ave.
White Plains, NY 10601
800-776-3449, ext. 176

CompuServe
5000 Arlington Centre Blvd.
P.O. Box 20212
Columbus, OH 43220
800-848-8199

eWorld
Apple Computer, Inc.
One Infinite Loop
Mailstop: 81-EAC
Cupertino, CA 95014
800-521-1515

GTE Educational Network Services
5525 MacArthur Blvd.
Suite 320
Irving, TX 75038
800-927-3000

Scholastic Network
555 Broadway
New York, NY 10012
800-246-2986

Benefits of telecommunications and multimedia to teaching and learning become obvious with use. The greatest impact of these technologies may well be the "knocking down of classroom walls," thereby enabling students and teachers to become part of the global community of learners.

COMPUTERS IN THE PROGRAM MODE: BASIC

We do not recommend an emphasis on programming in the elementary grades—in fact, many machines now in use do not readily allow users to enter a programming mode. This portion of the text is not intended to teach you how to program. Our purpose here is to expose you to a way that problem solving with computer programming might be integrated into a mathematics program. While we recommend that all elementary school mathematics teachers study computers and, to a degree, how they function, it is much more important that you learn what programming *is* than to learn how to program.

Let's examine a simple, short mathematics computer program that you may wish to write for children to use and, perhaps, modify. Again, the real benefit here is certainly not the act of programming, but providing children with an environment in which they can learn to hypothesize how a computer deals with data by making minor changes and observing the results.

```
10 REM**THIS PROGRAM WILL CALCULATE AVERAGES FOR YOU**
20 PRINT "HOW MANY NUMBERS DO YOU WANT TO AVERAGE"
30 INPUT N
40 PRINT "ENTER YOUR ";N;" NUMBERS."
50 FOR X = 1 TO N
60 INPUT Z
65 T = T + Z
70 NEXT X
80 A = T / N
90 PRINT "YOU HAVE ENTERED ";N;" NUMBERS."
100 PRINT "THE TOTAL IS ";T
110 PRINT "THE AVERAGE IS ";A
```

The process of interpreting the nuances in such a program can provide insight into aspects of robotics and how machines follow rules to make decisions. The goal is to help the student become a better problem solver by analytically examining a series of algorithmic steps. Again, don't "program for programming's sake"; instead, examine programs for problem-solving experience.

COMPUTERS IN THE PROGRAM MODE: LOGO

Logo, a computer language designed to promote problem-solving abilities using a computer, is finding favor in the elementary school curriculum. The graphics component of Logo is a particularly effective tool for exploring geometric concepts and principles. This aspect of Logo involves immediate reinforcement through the movement of a symbol, referred to as the turtle. Orders are given to the turtle through commands, called *primitives,* such as FD 50, RT 90, BK 30, and LT 45 in which the letters represent a directive to the turtle; the number refers to a quantity for that directive (for example, FD 50 moves the turtle forward 50 units).

To command the turtle to draw a square, you can use the following sequence of primitives:

```
FD 50 <RETURN> RT 90 <RETURN> FD 50 <RETURN> RT 90 <RETURN> FD 50 <RETURN>
   RT 90 <RETURN> FD 50 <RETURN> RT 90 <RETURN>
```

(Use CS to clear the screen and return the turtle to its home position before continuing. A list of some other Logo commands can be found at the end of this appendix.)

Many different versions of Logo are available. Each version is supported by its own set of primitives, but these differ only slightly in form and in use. Once one version of Logo is mastered, other versions are not difficult to learn.

By combining primitives students can create programs that demonstrate their abilities to observe patterns and make generalizations. *Procedures* are Logo programs that combine several primitives to accomplish a task. For example, the following procedure will yield a square:

```
TO SQUARE
   FD 50
   RT 90
   FD 50
   RT 90
   FD 50
   RT 90
   FD 50
   RT 90
END
```

At first glance this appears to be no less work than simply typing in the primitives. The difference is that we have defined a procedure that will produce a square whenever we type its title. That is, having defined this procedure, to form a square, just type SQUARE and the turtle will recall the necessary steps.

Procedures can be often shortened using "loops" that repeat a series of commands. For example, the square defined above could be written as:

```
TO SQUARE
   REPEAT 4 [FD 50 RT 90]
END
```

In this case, the bracketed primitives are carried out four times in succession.

It is also possible to write a procedure that makes use of previously defined procedures. For example, the following yields a drawing resembling a window:

```
TO WINDOW
   REPEAT 4 [SQUARE LT 90]
END
```

It is even possible to write a procedure that makes use of itself. This is called *recursion* and is illustrated by the following example that forms a flower:

```
TO FLOWER
   FD 50
   RT 81
   FLOWER
END
```

Even though this procedure has an END statement, it will continue to run because it calls itself internally. To stop this routine, you'll need to type <CTRL> G.

Logo is most generally known for its usefulness in drawing and problem solving, but it can also be used to print information on the screen. It is possible to define word and list procedures and to use word and list variables in procedures. A Logo *word* is a set of characters that begins with a quotation mark and ends with a blank space. For example, PRINT "Apple will cause the computer to output Apple. A Logo *list* is a collection of words or lists and must be enclosed in brackets to indicate to the computer that it is a list.

Whatever form and depth of Logo is explored, children will benefit from the exploration, hypothesis formation and testing, and freedom to discover. Encouraging students to experiment in the Logo environment will result in enthusiasm and interest.

SOME LOGO COMPUTER TERMS

The Logo computer language can provide a powerful motivational tool for exploring such elementary school mathematics topics as geometry, measurement, problem solving, and logical reasoning. With this language, children are encouraged to hypothesize, verify, and generalize.

FD The command to move the turtle forward is FD or FORWARD. It is used in conjunction with a quantity representing millimeters, such as FD 40.

BK The command to move the turtle backward is BK or BACK. It is used in conjunction with a quantity representing millimeters, such as BK 40.

RT The command that causes the turtle to turn right is RT or RIGHT. It is used in conjunction with a quantity representing degrees, such as RT 90.

LT The command that causes the turtle to turn to the left is LT or LEFT. It is used in conjunction with a quantity representing degrees, such as LT 90.

PD The command PD or PENDOWN causes the turtle to draw when it moves.

PU The command PU or PENUP allows the turtle to move without drawing.

PE The command PE or PENERASE erases lines that the turtle moves over.

CS The command CS or CLEARSCREEN erases the screen and returns the turtle to its home position.

CLEAN The command CLEAN clears the draw screen but does not move the turtle.

HOME The command HOME will return the turtle to its home position but does not clear the screen.

ST The command ST or SHOWTURTLE puts the computer in the draw mode and causes the turtle to appear on the screen.

HT The command HT or HIDETURTLE makes the turtle disappear.

<CTRL> L Holding down the CONTROL key and pressing L puts the entire screen in the graphics mode and covers up the typed commands. The same is accomplished by typing FULLSCREEN.

<CTRL> S Holding down the CONTROL key and pressing S returns the screen to the usual viewing mode that displays the turtle movement and the typing.

REPEAT The REPEAT command is used to have the turtle carry out a command or sequence of commands several times. It is used with a number and a bracketed set of commands such as REPEAT 4 [FD 40 RT 90].

TO The use of TO, along with a name such as TO SQUARE, tells the computer that you are about to define a procedure.

END The command END signifies the end of a procedure.

POTS The command POTS prints out the names of the procedures in the workspace.

ERALL The command ERALL erases all of the procedures in the workspace.

ER The command ER or ERASE, when used with a procedure name, erases the procedure from the workspace.

SAVE The command SAVE copies the workspace to a Logo file disk.

SETBG The command SETBG changes the color of the draw screen.

SETPC The command SETPC allows the user to change the color of the turtle's pen.

SETCURSOR The command SETCURSOR allows the user to move the cursor to any point on the text screen.

Appendix C

Computer Software to Support Mathematics Instruction

A number of companies offer the elementary school mathematics teacher a variety of computer software programs designed to (1) help anchor understandings sought in classroom lessons, (2) provide tutorial environments, and/or (3) present simulations and problem-solving opportunities. The following list of major suppliers should provide a base for your own collection to use as the need arises. The cost of a postcard or, when available, the use of a toll-free number can get you a copy of a current catalog that will help keep you apprised of what is available.

Broderbund Software, Inc.
17 Paul Drive
San Rafael, CA 94903
800-521-6263

Bingwa Software Company
544 Sayre Drive
Princeton, NJ 08540
800-404-MATH

Cambridge Development Laboratory, Inc.
214 Third Avenue
Waltham, MA 02154
800-637-0047

Gamco
P.O. Box 1911
Big Springs, TX 79721
800-351-1404

Great Wave
5353 Scotts Valley Drive
Scotts Valley, CA 95066
408-438-1990

Hartley Courseware
3001 Coolidge Road
East Lansing, MI 48823
800-247-1380

Heartsoft
3101 Hemlock Circle
Broken Arrow, OK 74012
918-251-1066

International Society for Technology
in Education
1787 Agate Street
Eugene, OR 97403
503-346-2403

Key Curriculum Press
2512 Martin Luther King Jr. Way
P.O. Box 2304
Berkeley, CA 94702
800-338-7638

LCSI—Logo Computer Systems, Inc.
P.O. Box 162
Highgate Springs, VT 05460
800-321-5646

Lawrence Productions
1800 S. 35th Street
Galesburg, MI 49053
800-421-4157

The Learning Company
6493 Kaiser Drive
Fremont, CA 94555
800-852-2255

MECC
6160 Summit Drive North
Minneapolis, MN 55430
800-685-6322

Micrograms
1404 N. Main Street
Rockford, IL 61103
800-338-4726

Mindplay
160 W. Ft. Lowell
Tucson, AZ 85705
800-221-7911

Nordic
P.O. Box 6007
6911 Vandorn
Lincoln, NE 68506
402-488-5086

Optimum Resources, Inc.
5 Hiltech Lane
Hilton Head, SC 29926
800-327-1473

Orange Cherry
P.O. Box 390
Pound Ridge, NY 10576
800-672-6002

Queue, Inc.
338 Commerce Drive
Fairfield, CT 06432
800-232-2224

Scholastic, Inc.
2931 East McCarty Street, Box 7502
Jefferson City, MO 65102
800-541-5513

Sunburst Communications
101 Castleton Street
Pleasantville, NY 10570
800-321-7511

Tom Snyder Productions
80 Coolidge Hill Road
Watertown, MA 02172
800-342-0236

Troll Associates
100 Corporate Way
Mahwah, NJ 07498
800-526-5289

Unicorn Software
Building 9, Suite A
6000 S. Eastern Avenue
Las Vegas, NV 89119
702-597-0818

Ventura Educational Systems
910 Ramona Avenue
Grover Beach, CA 93433
805-499-1407

The titles and descriptions that follow are representative of the types and variety of software resources available to the classroom teacher. This alphabetical list includes icons to help you quickly identify possible uses. The icon key is as follows:

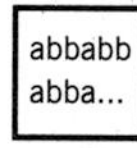

Patterns, Relations and Functions

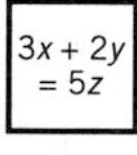

Algebra

Problem Solving Strategies

Measurement

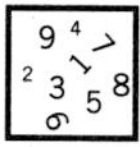

Number and Number Relations

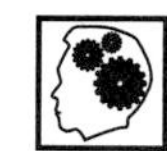
Estimation and Mental Computation

Geometry

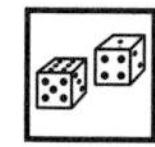
Data Analysis and Probability

Ace Detective 

Grades 3-up
Students use critical reading, organize information, and draw conclusions to solve mysteries before time runs out.
Mindplay

Addition and Subtraction Defenders 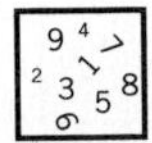 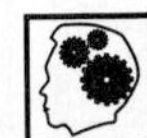

Grades 1-4
An arcade game involving addition and subtraction fact drill. Players protect a castle from fireballs by loading cannons with correct answers.
Gamco

Algebra Shop 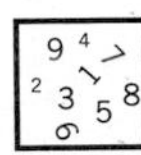 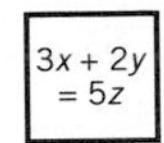

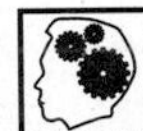

Grades 7-10
Students practice pre-algebra and algebra problem-solving skills involving factoring, squares/square roots, cubes/cube roots, positive and negative numbers, fractions, decimals, and number series. They also practice simultaneous equations, solving for one and two variables, using composite functions, reducing equations, and using functions with two variables.
Scholastic, Inc.

Algernon 

 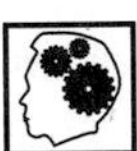

Grades 3-Adult
Algernon is a mouse that must be programmed to run through a maze to find the cheese. The level of difficulty increases as the students use logic, estimation, and spatial reasoning.
Sunburst Communications

Bake & Taste 

 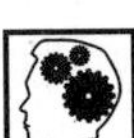

Grades 3-up
Teaches users to follow directions, builds math skills in a "real-life" setting.
Mindplay

Balancing Bear 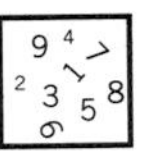 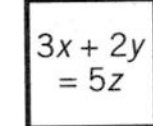

Grades K-4
Balancing Bear is a visual introduction to addition and inequalities. Four levels of difficulty are available.
Sunburst Communications

Blockers and Finders 

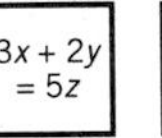

Grades 2-Adult
Students collect and organize data to make conjectures and formulate proofs.
Sunburst Communications

Bounce! 

Grades K-8
A sequence of balls bounces into the air. Students must predict which ball will be next by using pattern-recognition and information-gathering skills.
Sunburst Communications

Building Perspective 

Grades 4-Adult
Students work with perspective by viewing depictions of buildings from the side and then visualizing how the building would be depicted when viewed from above.
Sunburst Communications

Campaign Math

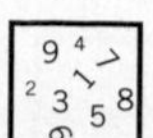
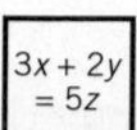
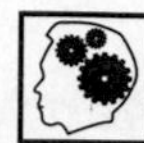

Grades 6-12

One to two players practice their fraction-decimal conversion and ratio skills while they research political science issues.

Mindplay

Categorizing: Detective Games

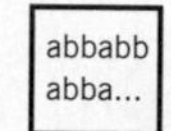

Grades 3-6

Students put categorizing skills and logical thinking skills to use. In doing so, they develop critical thinking skills and learn to draw conclusions.

Troll Associates

Clock

Grades 1-4

Graphics help students learn to convert between digital time and "clock" time. Multilevel lessons cover all aspects of telling time.

Hartley

Clock Shop

Grades K-6

Hands teach children to read and write digital and analog time.

Nordic

Clock Works

Grades 1-3

Students practice setting the hands of an analog clock. Students visit a "museum" of clock faces and explore the many ways of designing a clock.

MECC

Coin Changer

Grades PreK-4

Students learn to recognize each coin by both sight and value, then demonstrate their knowledge by adding coins.

Heartsoft

Coin Critters

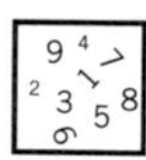

Grades K-6

Kids develop a real sense of money by learning the face value of coins, purchasing, matching and counting back change, and other applications.

Nordic

Counters

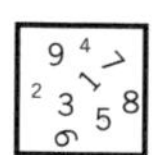

Grades PreK-1

This colorful, animated program helps students learn to count, add, and subtract single digit numbers.

Sunburst Communications

Counting and More Counting

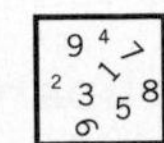

Grades 1-3
Counting shows coins being moved and counted on the screen. Teachers can control the number of problems presented. *More Counting* expands the concepts introduced in *Counting* to include coins and dollars.
Hartley

Data and Decisions

Grades 4-8
Students design real-world investigations, gather data, explore measurements, and construct graphs. This program includes the *Bar Grapher* software.
Sunburst Communications

Data Insights

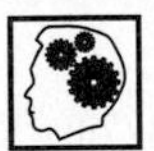
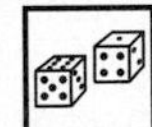

Grades 7-12
This program allows easy display of data with six different types of plotting techniques, including box plots. Students can also select the particular statistics that they want calculated from the data.
Sunburst Communications

Decimal & Fraction Maze

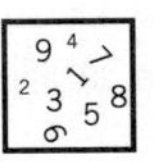
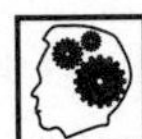

Grades 3-up
Covers 18 math skills including addition, subtraction, multiplication, division, comparing and rounding decimals, converting decimals to fractions, reducing and comparing fractions, improper fractions, and mixed numbers.
Great Wave

Discover Time

Grades 3-6
In this two-player game, player pirates advance toward treasure by correctly telling time. Questions focus on any one of four time intervals. The student management system holds up to 100 records for play.
Gamco

DynoPark Tycoon

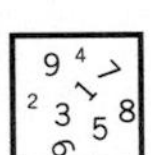

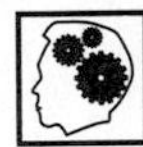

Grades 3-12
This simulation software provides opportunities to integrate mathematics, business, economics, and science. Students budget, analyze data, interpret profit and loss charts, and more, as they build dinosaur theme parks "from the ground up."
MECC

Easy Street

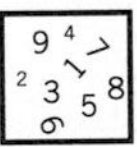

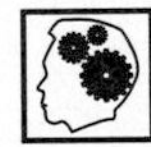

Grades PreK-2
Students stroll down Easy Street, a street filled with interesting and amusing stores. Each player has a list of items to buy.
Scholastic, Inc.

Elastic Lines: The Electronic Geoboard

Grades 2-8

This program puts students in an environment where they can create geometric shapes and patterns and study concepts such as area and perimeter. The program consists of a geoboard on which "electronic" bands can be stretched over pegs.

Sunburst Communications

The Electric Chalkboard

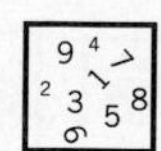

Grades K-4

The Electric Chalkboard draws electronic pictures as questions are correctly answered. Students select addition, subtraction, multiplication, or division questions.

Heartsoft

The Enchanted Forest

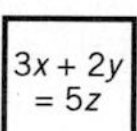

Grades 4-Adult

Students explore the logic concepts of conjunction, disjunction and negation.

Sunburst Communications

Expanded Notation

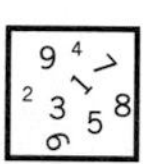

Grades 2-4

A numeral is presented in expanded form and the student must write the numeral.

Hartley

Exploring Tables and Graphs

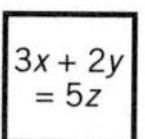

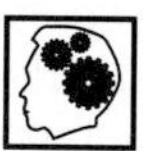

Grades 2-7

Children learn how to create and interpret tables, bar, picture and area graphs. Application and topics include animals, languages, and populations.

Stickybear Software

Exploring Tables and Graphs I and II

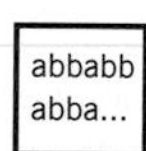

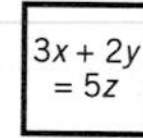

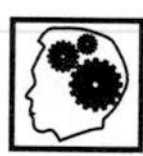

Grades 3-5

Students learn to use tables and bar, picture, and area graphs. Data can be shown in a picture graph. An area graph (also known as a pie graph) can be used to show the relationship of each part to the whole.

Scholastic, Inc.

The Factory

Grades 4-Adult

This three-level program challenges students to create geometric "products" on a simulated machine assembly line that they design.

Sunburst Communications

Fast-Track Fractions

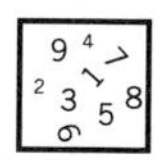
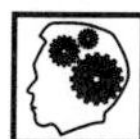

Grades 4-12

Games provide practice comparing, adding, subtracting, multiplying, and dividing fractions and mixed numbers.

Cambridge Development Laboratory, Inc.

Fraction Action

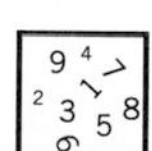
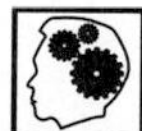

Grades 3-up

Add, subtract, multiply, or divide fractions in an arcade game format.

Unicorn

Fraction Bars Computer Program

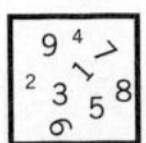
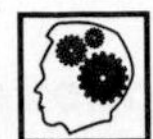

Grades 3-12
This seven-disk set reinforces the pictorial representations of fractions and provides practice at the abstract level.
Cambridge Development Laboratory, Inc.

Fraction Concepts, Inc.

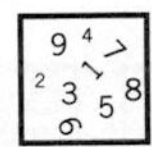
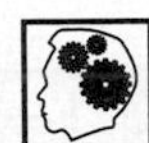

Grades 3-5
Students practice recognizing equivalent fractions, adding fractions, and using fraction terminology.
MECC

Fraction-oids

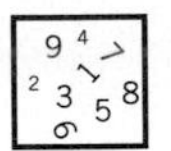
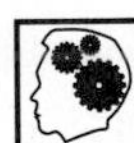
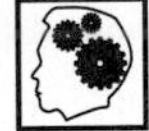

Grades 1-4
Enjoy adding, subtracting, and reducing fractions with the arcade excitement of controlling space ships on a rescue mission. Graphics help students visualize and solve fraction problems.
Mindplay

The Function Supposer

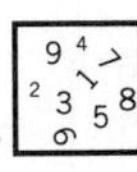
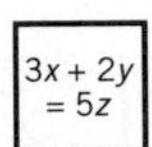

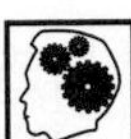

Grades 8-Adult
This program allows the exploration of relationships among functions. The student forms and tests conjectures about a function's behavior based on observations. The eight programs are geared for more advanced students of algebra, but they can be of some use in the early development of algebraic concepts in the middle ages.
Sunburst Communications

Gears

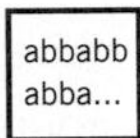

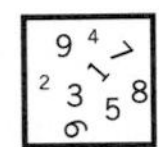
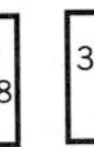
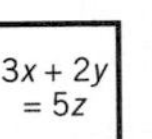

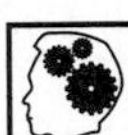

Grades 6-Adult
Students experiment with ratios and decimals as they use gears and build a gear factory to create mathematical formulas that can predict a desired outcome.
Sunburst Communications

Geoart

Grades 5-9
Includes *Shapes* Game for learning the names and characteristics of common geometrical figures. *Perimeter Drill, Area Drill,* and *Drawing Game* allow the user to draw a figure and then rotate the figure.
Ventura Educational Systems

Geometer's Sketchpad

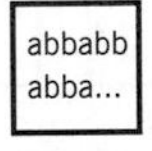

Grades 5-Adult
Construct geometric objects and transform them. Measure lengths, angles, and areas. Make hypotheses about geometric principles.
Key Curriculum Press

The Geometric preSupposer: Points and Lines

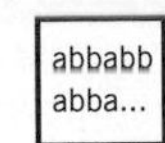

Grades 5-Adult
This program enables students to explore concepts such as congruence, similarity, and parallelism, and to investigate properties of shapes, in preparation for high-school geometry.
Sunburst Communications

The Geometric preSupposer: Problems and Projects

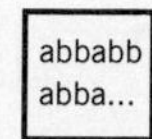

Grades 5-9

This program allows exploration of introductory concepts of geometry such as geometric relationships, definitions, properties of shapes, and making conjectures.

Sunburst Communications

Geometry Inventor

Grades 6-Adult

This program encourages inquiry and the exploration of geometric constructions and geometric terminology. Students can construct, measure, and perform calculations as they test conjectures they have formed.

Sunburst Communications

Geometry Toolkit

Grades K-8

This program offers interactive geometry environments to assist in the discovery of important geometric concepts.

Ventura Educational Systems

Gertrude's Puzzles

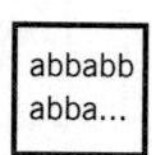

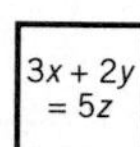

Grades 4-7

By ordering and sorting playing pieces by shape and color, students learn to recognize patterns and relationships.

The Learning Company

Gertrude's Secrets

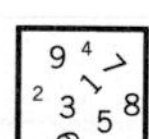

Grades K-3

Students manipulate colorful playing pieces as they learn classification, grouping, and sequencing skills.

The Learning Company

Graph Action

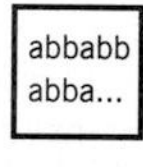

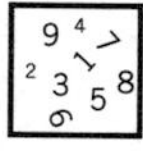

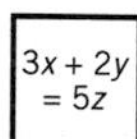

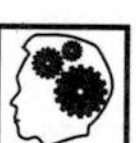
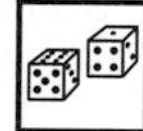

Grades 6-9

This manipulative platform provides a context for exploring patterns and functions. It helps students gather and organize data, create various types of graphs, and analyze and interpret trends.

Tom Snyder Productions

The Graph Club with Fizz & Martina

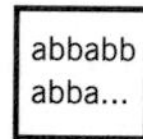

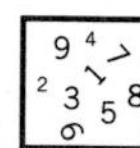
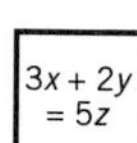

Grades K-4

A graphing tool that helps students learn to gather, sort, and classify information. The software assists students in constructing and analyzing circle, bar, table, and picture graphs.

Tom Snyder Productions

Graph Maker: Introduction to Graphs and Charts

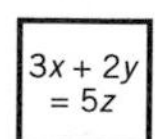

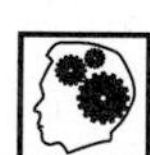

Grades 3-5

In *Graph Maker,* students learn how to use the information found in charts and graphs, as well as how to make their own charts and graphs.

Troll Associates

Graphers

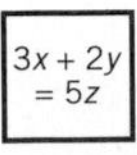

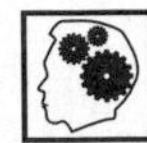

Grades K-6

Designed as a graphing tool for young children, this program encourages data collection by counting or by survey. Students then organize these data and construct, modify, and interpret graphs.

Sunburst Communications

GraphPower

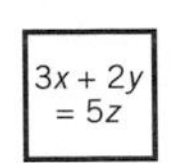

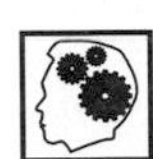
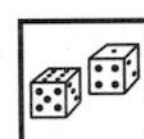

Grades K-8

GraphPower is a comprehensive tool for creating graphs and helping students learn how to analyze data.

Ventura

Green Globs and Graphing Equations

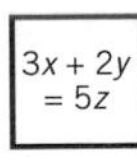

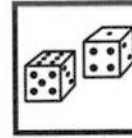

Grades 9-Adult

Students must enter equations to create graphs that will hit 13 green globs scattered randomly on a grid.

Sunburst Communications

Guestimation

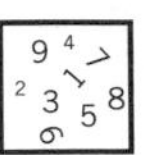

Grades 5-9

Students estimate the number that corresponds to the location of a marker on a line with only its end points numbered.

Cambridge Development Laboratory, Inc.

Hands-On Math Series

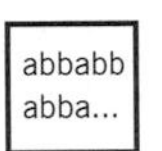

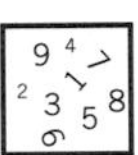
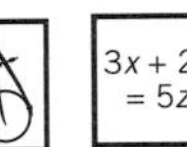

Grades K-8

This three-volume set explores the use of a variety of manipulative devices presented in a computer environment. Topics explored include problem-solving, number sense, geometry, estimation, measurement, probability, and patterns.

Ventura Educational Systems

How the West Was One + Three × Four

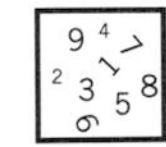

Grades 4-Adult

This program teaches the order of operations and the significance of parentheses in an arithmetic expression.

Sunburst Communications

James Discovers Math

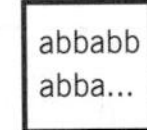

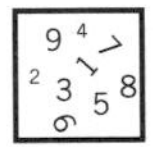

Grades PreK-2

Early learners are presented with 10 activity areas that offer challenges in counting, addition, subtraction, shapes, attributes, measurement, and problem solving.

Broderbund

Kids Math

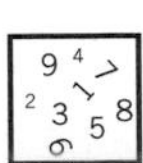

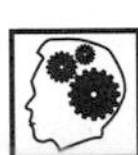
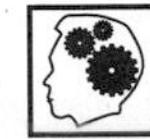

Grades PreK-3

Eight exciting math programs that help children learn math concepts, reinforce beginning math skills, learn to use a Macintosh, and develop positive attitudes toward learning math.

Great Wave

Kindercomp

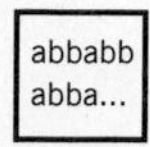

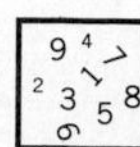

Grades PreK-3

A package of 8 programs for young children designed to offer practice with counting, number sequence, and simple addition.

Queue, Inc.

Kinder Koncepts: Math

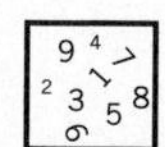

Grades PreK-2

This math skill program covers many important math skills such as counting, one-to-one correspondence, and simple addition and subtraction using picture groups of objects with numerals. It also teaches the concept of one-half by using shapes.

Cambridge Development Laboratory, Inc.

Label Land

Grades 4-8

This program challenges students to identify attributes, make inferences, and develop problem-solving strategies through activities based in mathematics, visual thinking, and geography.

Sunburst Communications

Learning Math Skills Package

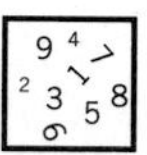

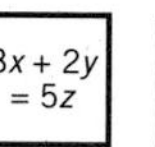

Grades 6-9

A series of interactive tutorials that deal individually with such topics as whole numbers, fractions, decimal numbers, ratio and proportion, percent, algebra, measurement, statistics and reading graphs, and geometry. Each program includes a diagnostic self-test and a variety of practice question types.

Queue, Inc.

Let's Learn About Money

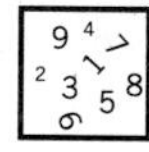

Grades 1-4

Learn about dollars and cents, how to count money, and how to make change. A special simulation enables youngsters to use their new skills by going on a "Silly Shopping Spree."

Troll Associates

The Logic Master

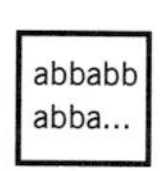

Grades 5-up

Develops critical high-level thinking skills through the introduction of analogies and number series activities.

Unicorn

Math Activities Using LogoWriter Series

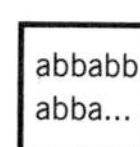

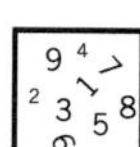

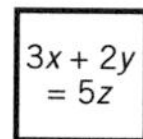

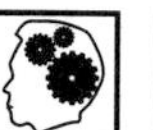

Grades 1-Adult

Presents *LogoWriter* activities for patterns, number and operations, basic number theory, and probability and statistics.

International Society for Technology in Education

MacKids Turbo Math Facts

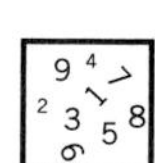
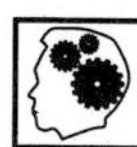

Grades K-6

Develop solid math skills in addition, subtraction, multiplication, and division. Correct answers earn dollars that can be used to purchase race cars and compete against "Turbo Tom."

Nordic

Maps and Navigation

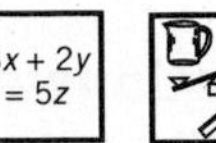

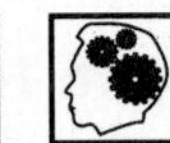

Grades 4-8
A simulation program that provides opportunities to plot points, triangulate locations, and determine headings and distance traveled on a map.
Sunburst Communications

Math Blaster

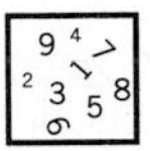
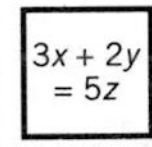

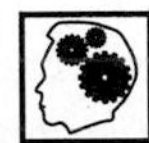

Grades 1-6
After students have practiced their math, they can demonstrate their skill at the circus. Math Blaster contains more than 600 problems.
Scholastic, Inc.

Math Blaster Mystery

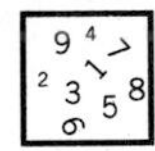
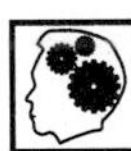

Grades 5-12
Four learning activities cover such skills as solving word problems and working with positive/negative numbers, fractions, decimals, and percents.
Scholastic, Inc.

Math Keys Series

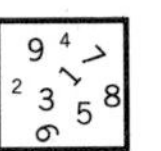
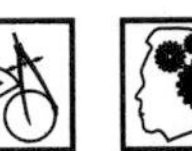
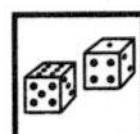

Grades K-6
Software that links manipulatives, symbolic notation, and writing tools. Individual programs deal with whole numbers, geometry, and probability.
MECC

Math Mystery Library

Grades 5-8
Math problem-solving experiences presented in motivating contexts. Individual programs help students improve their ability to set up problems, identify relevant data, and choose appropriate operations.
Tom Snyder Productions

Math Rabbit

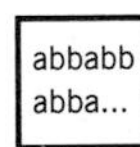

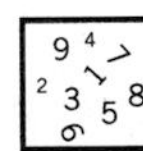

Grades K-2
Students explore basic number concepts and develop skills in counting, adding, subtracting, and recognizing number relationships and patterns.
The Learning Company

Math Shop

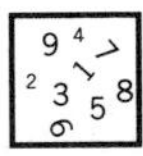
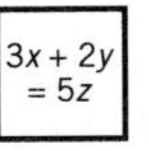

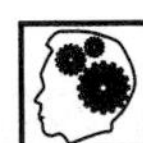

Grades 4-8
Students use problem-solving skills involving addition, subtraction, multiplication, division, fractions, decimals, percents, ratios, proportions, linear measures, coin values, base two, equations with two variables, and functions.
Scholastic, Inc.

Math Shop Jr.

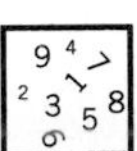

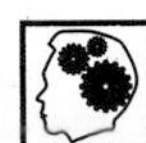

Grades 1-4
Students develop problem-solving skills involving addition, subtraction, multiplication, division, odd and even numbers, estimation, and identifying coins.
Scholastic, Inc.

Math Shop Spotlight: Fractions and Decimals I

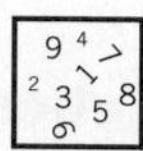
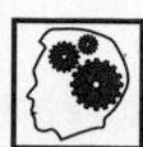

Grades 4-8
Students fill orders that involve fractions and decimal concepts, including adding and subtracting fractions, multiplying a fraction by a whole number, converting fractions to decimals, and identifying a fractional part of a number.
Scholastic, Inc.

Math Shop Spotlight: Weights and Measures

Grades 4-8
The program provides practice with such measurement concepts as pounds and ounces, feet and inches, cups, pints and quarts, days and weeks, money and time, and meters and centimeters.
Scholastic, Inc.

Math Wizard

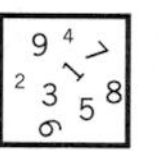
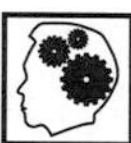

Grades K-8
Elves, trolls, and wizards help with addition, subtraction, multiplication, division, and word problems.
Unicorn

Mathematical Heritage Series 1 and 2

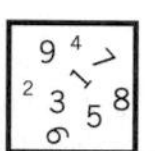

Grades 3-8
Improve math skills and enhance the awareness of the contributions of minorities in mathematics and science.
Bingwa Software Company

Mathematics Word Problems Series

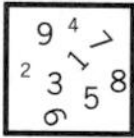

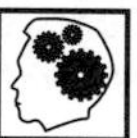

Grades 2-8
A series of disks by grade level that provide practice with word problems in the areas of computation, measurement, and geometry.
Queue, Inc.

Mathology: The Greek Legend Math Adventure

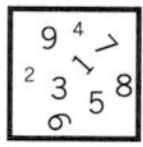

Grades 3-up
In the "Chamber of Numbers" you will solve math story problems dealing with units of weight and measure to earn weapons and strength that will help you fight your enemies.
Lawrence Productions

Mathology II: Fractions

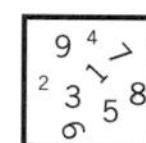

Grades 4-8
An arcade game that presents an exciting way to learn about fractions, decimals, ratios, proportions, and percents.
Lawrence Productions

Mathosaurus

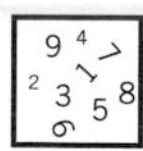

Grades PreK-4
From counting to computation, these programs build an understanding of primary math concepts at three levels.
Micrograms

Maya Math 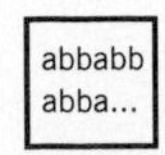

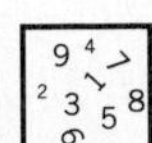 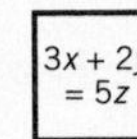

Grades 4-8
Students work with Mayan and other number systems to discover patterns and the importance of place value.
Sunburst Communications

Metric Skills 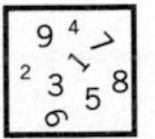 

Grades 3-6
A revised program in which metric terminology and relationships are introduced. Practice is provided in short, random drills.
Hartley

MicroWorlds Math Links 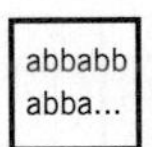   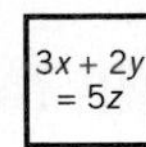  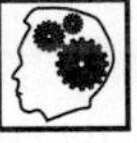

Grades 4-8
Students develop projects such as using polygons to create kaleidoscopic images and examining patterns in Indian blankets.
LCSI—Logo Computer Systems, Inc.

MicroWorlds Project Builder 

Grades 4-8
A Logo-based tool kit that can combine text, graphics, music, and animation. Students develop problem-solving strategies while creating school projects.
LCSI—Logo Computer Systems, Inc.

Midnight Rescue 

Grades 3-5
Students explore clues as well as collect and analyze facts to discover who is painting the school with disappearing paint. The intent is to emphasize reading skills, but the game does involve basic problem-solving techniques.
The Learning Company

Mind Castle 

Grades 4-8
This adventure game motivates students to develop their reasoning skills, critical reading, strategy, spatial orientation, and patience as they solve puzzles to reach the treasure stored in the tower of a Victorian castle.
Lawrence Productions

Money Challenge  

Grades 1-5
This tic-tac-toe game for two players uses realistic money to provide drills for improving money skills. You may set one of four difficulty levels in each of the four activities. The student management system holds up to 100 records.
Gamco

Money! Money! 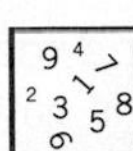  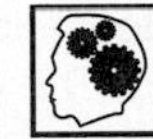

Grades 2-6
Students count coins and determine their value in cents. Then, given a set of coins and the cost of an item, they must answer the question "Do you have enough money?"
Scholastic, Inc.

Money Works

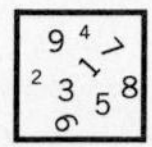

Grades 1-4

This program helps students determine the difference between coins and paper currency, recognize denominations, make purchases, count change, and design their own currency.

MECC

Muppet Math

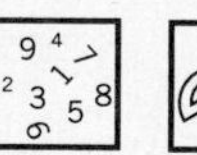

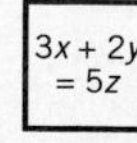

Grades K-6

Patterns, number sense, graphs, and geometry are encountered as students visit with various Muppets.

Sunburst Communications

My Travels with Gulliver

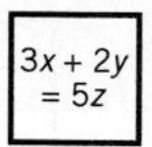

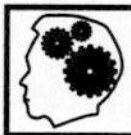

Grades 4-6

This program uses the children's classic to solve problems while exploring such topics as perimeter, area, estimation, scaling, and proportion.

Sunburst Communications

Number Facts Fire Zapper

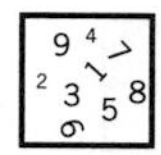
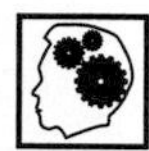

Grades 1-5

An arcade game involving basic number facts in addition, subtraction, multiplication, and division. Facts appear in flames and are doused by correct answers.

Gamco

Number Munchers

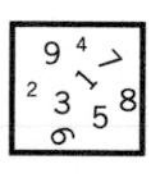
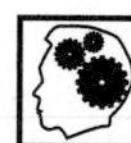

Grades 3-12

Students search for numbers that meet specified criteria. For example, they must "munch" numbers that are multiples of a number, equivalent fractions, or prime numbers.

MECC

On Target Multiply and Divide

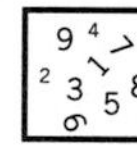

Grades 3-6

Players shoot at moving targets in a carnival gallery that have multiplication and division facts on them. Players have control of the speed and the duration of the program.

Gamco

Operation Neptune

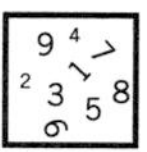

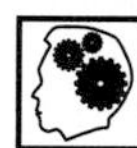

Grades 5-9

Students solve word problems involving decimals, fractions, percents, area, perimeters, volume, and estimation.

The Learning Company

OutNumbered

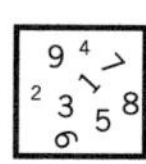
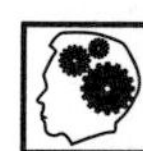

Grades 3-6

Students must solve word problems, match clues, and decipher a secret code to find the room in which the "Master of Mischief" is hiding. The emphasis is on basic facts and problem-solving and thinking skills.

The Learning Company

Parking Lot

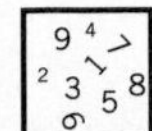

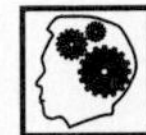

Grades 6-9
In this arcade game simulation, students are parking lot attendants. They calculate charges based on an hourly rate, using a clock that figures in-and-out time. They learn to subtract hours and minutes from elapsed time and to subtract dollars and cents when making change.
Scholastic, Inc.

Patterns

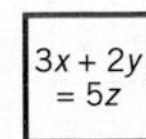

Grades K-3
These four programs let young students experience patterns visually and develop skills in recognizing and extending linear patterns.
MECC

Perimeter, Area and Volume

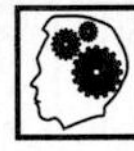

Grades 5-10
Students are given a run of randomly generated problems, including word problems.
Gamco

Piece of Cake Math

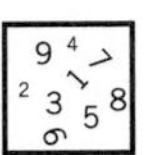

Grades 1-6
A bakery simulation in which children practice addition, subtraction, multiplication, and division. The program offers hints and explanations for incorrect answers.
Queue, Inc.

Place Value 1s, 10s, 100s

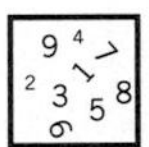

Grades 3-6
Students gain a better understanding of place value as they see 1-cubes, 10-sticks, and 100-blocks visually illustrated and matched with numerals.
Cambridge Development Laboratory, Inc.

Plane View

Grades 4-Adult
Students watch a block move around 24 different paths to discover the relationship between top and side views. Students can also view the block from the top, from the side, or from both directions simultaneously.
Sunburst Communications

The Pond

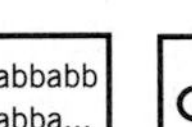

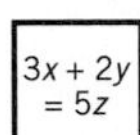

Grades 2-Adult
A small green frog helps students recognize and articulate patterns, generalize from raw data, and think logically.
Sunburst Communications

Pondering Problems

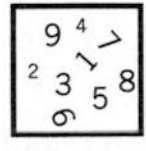
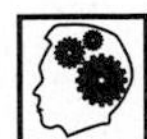

Grades 2-5
Provides students with hundreds of interesting math word problems to exercise valuable critical thinking skills.
Micrograms

Quations  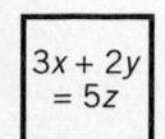 
Grades 1-8
Up to three students play against the computer. At each turn, they score points by using as many number and operations "tiles" as possible to build equations vertically and horizontally.
Scholastic, Inc.

Recycling Logic   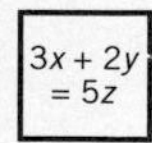
Grades 6-Adult
Students must solve logic puzzles in order to help their recycling club clean up the environment.
Sunburst Communications

The Right Turn 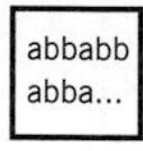  
Grades 4-Adult
Students use such concepts from transformational geometry as rotation as they play a game of patterns and shapes.
Sunburst Communications

Roman Numerals 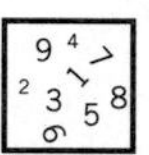
Grades 3-6
This introduction to Roman numerals presents the symbols used in the Roman system, along with devices for remembering their values. The students then build numerals according to the Roman rules.
Scholastic, Inc.

Safari Search  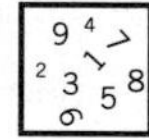
Grades 3-Adult
Safari Search is a fun and creative way to enhance math abilities and develop problem-solving strategies and logical thinking.
Sunburst Communications

Scholastic A.I.  
Grades 6-Adult
Students engage the computer in a game they have devised that the computer quickly "learns" how to play. The computer then challenges the students to learn a game it creates.
Scholastic, Inc.

SemCalc 
Grades 6-12
This program approaches the solution of word problems by focusing on the units used rather than the numbers.
Sunburst Communications

Sesame Street Crayon—Numbers Count 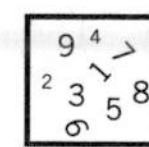
Grades K-1
The cast of Sesame Street helps present 30 pictures that involve the numbers 1 through 10.
Scholastic, Inc.

Sesame Street—Opposites Attract

abbabb
abba...

Grades K-1
Relationships that form opposites such as "up and down" or "push and pull" are presented by the Sesame Street characters.
Scholastic, Inc.

Shape Up!

Grades K-6
This program exposes students to the language of geometry and the development of spatial relationships in an informal manner. The students can use "tools" to select, manipulate, measure, and modify shapes.
Sunburst Communications

Sidewalk Sneakers

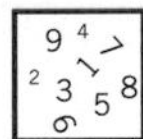

Grades K-5
This program provides a representative model to help children understand basic operations and number sense. The emphasis of the program is on counting skills
Sunburst Communications

Solve It!

Grades 4-12
This program uses a game format in which students play the role of a detective using a detective agency database search.
Sunburst Communications

Space Mission Problem Solving

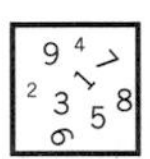

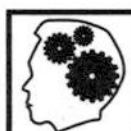

Grades 4-7
Weight, volume, rate, time, and distance are some of the types of math problems faced in the journey to the Moon or Mars.
Orange Cherry

Sphinx's Secret

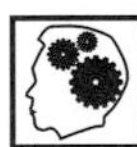

Grades 5-10
In this one- or two-player game, student archaeologists collect Egyptian artifacts by solving perimeter, area, and volume problems.
Gamco

Statistics Workshop

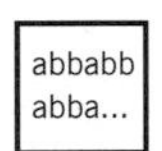

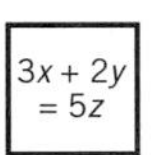

Grades 6-Adult
This data analysis program provides a tool for entering, manipulating, and displaying numerical or categorical information. Students can plot histograms, bar charts, box plots, or scatter plots.
Sunburst Communications

Stickybear Numbers

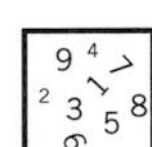

Grades K-1
Stickybear has a good time with the numbers 0 through 9. A different and delightful scene is presented with each number.
Optimum Resources, Inc.

Stickybear Shapes 
Grades K-2
Stickybear shows off circles, squares, triangles, and rectangles. Students pick a shape, and colorful animations demonstrating the shape are displayed. Students must name the shape and find it among other shapes.
Optimum Resources, Inc.

Stickybear Town Builder  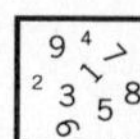
Grades K-2
Students must drive a car through a maze of streets to reach a particular destination. The program emphasizes map skills and decision making and includes the option of constructing their own town using symbols for buildings and trees.
Optimum Resources, Inc.

Stickybear Word Problems  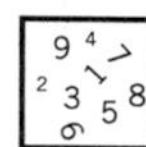
Grades 2-5
Choose from six levels of difficulty for addition, subtraction, or multiplication problems. Students can also create their own problems.
Optimum Resources, Inc.

The Super Factory   
Grades 6-Adult
Students are taught problem-solving strategies as they research and design products and challenge each other.
Sunburst Communications

Survival Math  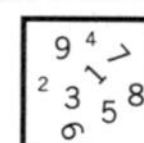
Grades 6-Adult
Four simulations—*Travel Agent Contest, Smart Shopper Marathon, Hot Dog Stand,* and *Foreman's Assistant*—help students apply math skills to everyday life.
Sunburst Communications

The Tabletop Jr. 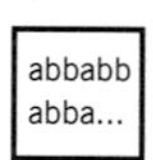  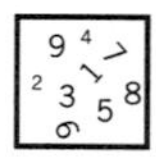  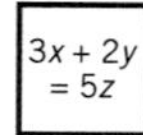
Grades K-3
Students explore attributes, Venn diagrams, graphs, and place value as they group objects and develop language skills.
Broderbund

The Tabletop Sr.   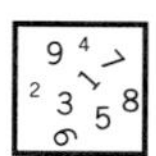  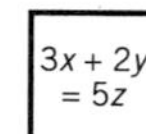
Grades 4-12
This program can be used to integrate mathematics, science, social studies, and any subject that makes use of data analysis. Students can work with existing databases or with databases they create themselves.
Broderbund

Taking Chances  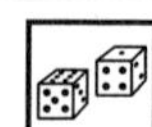
Grades 4-8
This program provides opportunities to work with simple examples of experimental probability, with and without replacement.
Sunburst Communications

Talking Addition and Subtraction 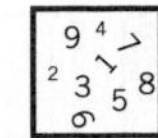

Grades PreK-3
Activities using sets and numbers, picture problems, a number line, and more help for kids with beginning addition and subtraction.
Orange Cherry

Talking Multiplication and Division 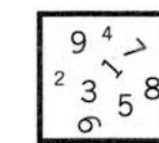

Grades 3-6
Children apply math facts and theory to a variety of practice exercises including word problems and math skills games.
Orange Cherry

Talking Numbers 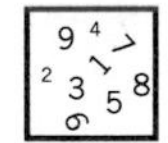

Grades PreK-2
A human voice teaches the numbers 1 through 10 and their values.
Orange Cherry

Talking Using Money and Making Change 

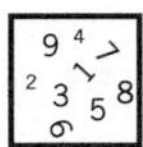  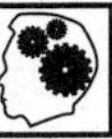

Grades 2-4
Kids learn the value of coins and bills. They also get hands-on experience with running their own cookie shop.
Orange Cherry

Teasers by Tobbs 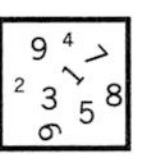 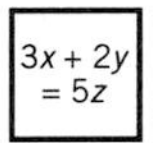

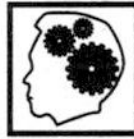 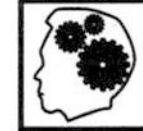

Grades 2-Adult
Using whole numbers or integers, Tobbs presents addition and multiplication problems with one or more missing numbers. Students must then decide which number can't be, might be, or must be the one that solves the problem.
Sunburst Communications

TesselMania 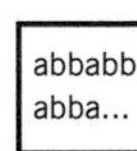

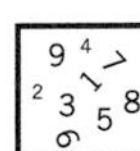 

Grades 3-12
Students interpret and create simple to complex geometric tesselations as they explore translations, reflections and rotations.
MECC

Thinkin' Things Collection 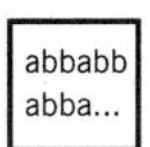

Grades PreK-6
A total of 11 engaging activities that help students think analytically, develop visual and auditory memory, spatial awareness, and creativity.
Sunburst Communications

TimeLiner 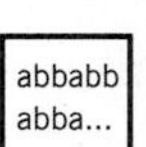

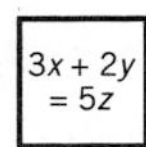

Grades K-12
This easy-to-use program allows students to create their own personal and historical time lines, up to 99 pages long, with whatever information they want.
Scholastic, Inc.

Tobbs Learns Algebra 

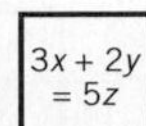

Grades 8-Adult

Tobbs Learns Algebra develops students' algebraic thinking, hypothesis-making and hypothesis testing abilities, and problem-solving skills.

Sunburst Communications

Tommy the Time Turtle 

Grades PreK-4

In each module, students learn a specific part of time telling and then test their knowledge by answering multiple choice questions.

Heartsoft

Touchdown Math Bundle 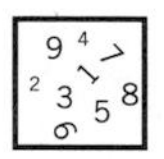 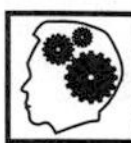

Grades 4-12

This series combines football action with whole number, decimal, fraction, percent, and rounding drills.

Gamco

Treasure MathStorm! 

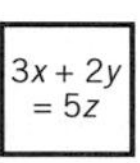

Grades 2-4

Students learn to read and set clocks, count money and make change, understand equalities and inequalities, and recognize number patterns.

The Learning Company

Treasure Mountain 

Grades 2-4

Students search for and collect hidden treasures by outwitting elves who ask challenging questions that require reading, mathematics, science, and general problem-solving skills.

The Learning Company

Turtle Math 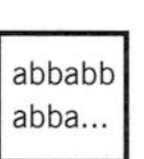

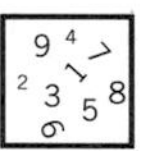  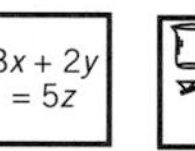

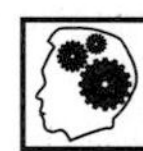 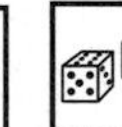 

Grades 3-6

Turtle Math comes with 36 investigations that make use of geometry and measurement to explore a variety of ideas including symmetry, probability, patterns, and computation.

LCSI—Logo Computer Systems, Inc.

What Do You Do with a Broken Calculator? 

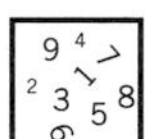 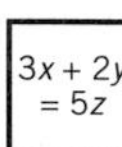

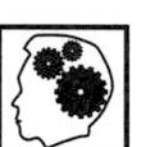

Grades 4-Adult

This program challenges students to find different ways to reach a mathematical solution to computation exercises.

Sunburst Communications

The Whatsit Corporation 

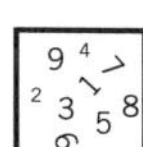  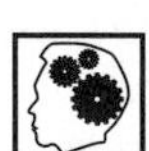 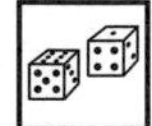

Grades 6-Adult

Students use mathematical skills in this simulation of running a business.

Sunburst Communications

What's Your Strategy?

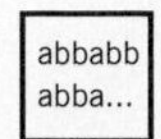

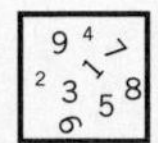

Grades 4-6

Students use coins, pattern blocks, and *The Factory* software to explore number patterns, shapes, and spatial relationships.

Sunburst Communications

Where in Time Is Carmen Sandiego?

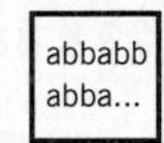

Grades 6-12

Students must travel through history, collecting and analyzing clues about the whereabouts of the infamous Sandiego. Problem-solving and reference skills are put to the test.

Broderbund Software, Inc.

Where in the USA Is Carmen Sandiego?

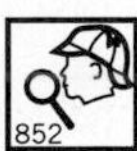

Grades 6-12

Students become experts in U.S. geography with this exciting game.

Broderbund Software, Inc.

Where in the World Is Carmen Sandiego?

Grades 6-12

Students search for the elusive criminal throughout the world by using logic and reference skills.

Broderbund Software, Inc.

Word Problem Square Off

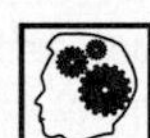

Grades 3-8

In the format of an exciting game, this program provides practice in solving math word problems. *Level A:* One-step problems with addition or subtraction of up to four digits; multiplying or dividing through 9×9. *Level B:* One-step and multi-step problems with whole numbers and decimals. *Level C:* One-step and multi-step problems with whole numbers and money in decimal form.

Gamco

Appendix D

Suppliers of Mathematics Instructional Resource Materials

A number of companies offer the elementary school mathematics teacher a variety of support materials such as resource books on specific topics or manipulative aids that help model concrete understandings sought in classroom lessons. The following list of major suppliers should provide a base for your own collection to use as the need arises. The cost of a postcard or, when available, the use of a toll-free number can get you a copy of a current catalog that will help keep you apprised of what is available.

Activity Resources Company, Inc.
P.O. Box 4875
Hayward, CA 94540
510-782-1300
FAX: 510-782-8172

AIMS Education Foundation
P.O. Box 8120
Fresno, CA 93747-8120
209-255-4094
FAX: 209-255-6396

American Guidance Service
Publishers' Building
P.O. Box 99
Circle Pines, MN 55014-1796
800-328-2560; in MN: 800-247-5053
FAX: 612-786-9077

Cabisco Mathematics
Carolina Biological Supply Company
2700 York Road
Burlington, NC 27215-3398
800-334-5551
FAX: 910-584-3399

Center for Innovation in Education, Inc.
20665 4th Street
Saratoga, CA 95070-5878
800-395-6088 (course offerings)
FAX: 408-867-0222

Creative Publications
5623 West 115th Street
Worth, IL 60482
800-624-0822
FAX: 800-624-0821

Cuisenaire Company of America, Inc.
10 Bank Street
White Plains, NY 10602
800-237-3142
FAX: 914-576-3480

Dale Seymour Publications
P.O. Box 10888
Palo Alto, CA 94303-0879
800-872-1100
FAX: 415-324-3424

Delta Education
P.O. Box 3000
Nashua, NH 03061-3000
800-442-5444
FAX: 800-282-9560

DIDAX Educational Resources, Inc.
One Centennial Drive
Peabody, MA 01960
800-458-0024
FAX: 508-532-9277

Educational Teaching Aids
620 Lakeview Parkway
Vernon Hills, IL 60061
800-445-5985
FAX: 800-ETA-9326

Gamco Educational Materials
P.O. Box 1911G2
Big Springs, TX 79721
800-351-1404
FAX: 915-267-7480

Good Apple
1204 Buchanan, Box 299
Carthage, IL 62321-0299
800-435-7234
FAX: 217-357-3987

Institute for Math Mania
P.O. Box 910
Montpelier, VT 05601
800-NUMERAL
FAX: 802-223-5871

Janson Publications, Inc.
P.O. Box 860
Dedham, MA 02027-0860
800-322-MATH
Fax: 617-326-5432

Midwest Publications
P.O. Box 448, Dept. 67
Pacific Grove, CA 93950
800-458-4849
FAX: 408-372-3230

Math Learning Center
P.O. Box 3226
Salem, OR 97302
503-370-8130
FAX: 503-370-7961

MPI, School and Instructional Supplies
1200 Keystone Avenue
P.O. Box 24155
Lansing, MI 48909-4155
800-444-1773
FAX: 517-393-8884

NASCO
901 Janesville Avenue
P.O. Box 901
Fort Atkinson, WI 53538-0901
800-558-9595
FAX: 414-563-8296

National Council of Teachers of Mathematics
1906 Association Drive
Reston, VA 22091-1593
703-620-9840
800-235-7566 (orders only)
FAX: 703-476-2970

Scott Resources, Inc.
1900 East Lincoln
Box 2121
Fort Collins, CO 80522

Spectrum Educational Supplies, Limited
125 Mary Street
Aurora, Ontario, CANADA
416-841-0600
FAX: 416-727-6265

Summit Learning
P.O. Box 493
Fort Collins, CO 80522
800-777-8817
FAX: 303-484-8067

The Teachers' Laboratory, Inc.
104 Canal Street
P.O. Box 6480
Brattleboro, VT 05302-6480
802-254-3457
FAX: 802-254-5233

Teaching Resource Center
P.O. Box 1509
San Leandro, CA 94577
800-833-3389
FAX: 800-972-7722

Tricon Publishing
Box 146
Mt. Pleasant, MI 48804
517-772-2811
FAX: 517-773-5894

Universal Education
320 South El Dorado
Mesa, AZ 85202
800-248-3764
FAX: 602-829-0599

J. Weston Walch
321 Valley Street
P.O. Box 658
Portland, ME 04104-0658
800-341-6094
FAX: 207-772-3105

Index